SOCCER AND SOCIETY IN DUBLIN

Soccer and Society in Dublin

A History of Association Football in Ireland's Capital

CONOR CURRAN

FOUR COURTS PRESS

Set in 10.5 pt on 12.5 pt for Ehrhardt MT
FOUR COURTS PRESS LTD
7 Malpas Street, Dublin 8, Ireland
www.fourcourtspress.ie
and in North America for
FOUR COURTS PRESS
c/o IPG, 814 N. Franklin St, Chicago, IL 60610

A catalogue record for this title is available
from the British Library.

ISBN 978-1-80151-039-4

SPECIAL ACKNOWLEDGMENT
This publication has been made possible with
financial assistance from Dublin City Council.

Comhairle Cathrach
Bhaile Átha Cliath
Dublin City Council

Printed in England by
CPI Antony Rowe, Chippenham, Wilts.

Contents

Abbreviations

AC	*Anglo-Celt*
AFC	Association Football Club
AN	*Athletic News*
AUL	Athletic Union League
BET	*Belfast Evening Telegraph*
BG	*Boston Globe*
BISP	British and Irish Steam Packet (Company)
BMN	*Belfast Morning News*
BN	*Belfast Newsletter*
BSU	Butchers' Social Union
BT	*Belfast Telegraph*
CBPPU	Christian Brothers' Past Pupils Union
CBS	Christian Brothers' School
CC	Catholic curate
CS	*Connacht Sentinel*
CT	*City Tribune*
CT	*Connacht Tribune*
CYMS	Catholic Young Men's Society
DAFC	Dublin Association Football Club
DC	*Drogheda Conservative*
DC	*Dundee Courier*
DD	*Donegal Democrat*
DDE	*Dublin Daily Express*
DDM	*Dublin Daily (Evening) Mail*
DDN	*Dublin Daily Nation*
DDSL	Dublin and District Schoolboys' League
DE	*Daily Express*
DEM	*Dublin Evening Mail*
DET	*Dublin Evening Telegraph*

DI	*Drogheda Independent*
DJ	*Derry Journal*
DN	*Daily News*
DN	*Donegal News*
DUD	*Dundalk Democrat*
DUTC	Dublin United Tramways Company
EE	*Evening Echo*
EH	*Evening Herald*
EP	*Evening Press*
FA	Football Association
FAI	Football Association of Ireland
FAIFS	Football Association of the Irish Free State
FAIS	Football Association of Irish Schoolboys
FÁS	Foras Áiseanna Saothair
FC	Football Club
FH	*Fermanagh Herald*
FI	*Fingal Independent*
FIFA	Fédération Internationale de Football Association
FJ	*Freeman's Journal*
FSW	*Football Sports Weekly*
FTCD	fellow of Trinity College Dublin
GAA	Gaelic Athletic Association
GNR	Great Northern Railway
GPO	General Post Office
GSWR	Great Southern and Western Railway
IAAA	Irish Amateur Athletic Association
IE	*Irish Examiner*
IFA	Irish Football Association
II	*Irish Independent*
INBMN	*Irish News and Belfast Morning News*
IPT	*Irish Post*
IP	*Irish Press*
IRA	Irish Republican Army
IRB	Irish Republican Brotherhood
IRFU	Irish Rugby Football Union

ISN	*Ireland's Saturday Night*
IT	*Irish Times*
ITGWU	Irish Transport and General Workers' Union
IUCFU	Irish Universities' and Colleges' Football Union
KP	*Kilkenny People*
LFA	Leinster Football Association
LFAI	Ladies' Football Association of Ireland
LFC	Liverpool Football Club
LJ	*Longford Journal*
LL	*Longford Leader*
LS	*Londonderry Sentinel*
ME	*Munster Express*
NASL	North American Soccer League
NCAA	National Collegiate Athletic Association
NIHE	National Institute for Higher Education
NUI	National University of Ireland
NW	*Northern Whig*
PFAI	Professional Footballers' Association of Ireland
PRO	public relations officer
PRONI	Public Record Office of Northern Ireland
QMS	quartermaster sergeant
QPR	Queen's Park Rangers
QUB	Queen's University Belfast
RAF	Royal Air Force
RDS	Royal Dublin Society
REAP	reinvention, education, appraisal and preparation
RMI	Railway Mechanics Institute
RUI	Royal University of Ireland
SARI	Sport Against Racism Ireland
SAT	Scholastic Aptitude Test
SC	*Sligo Champion*
SC	*Strabane Chronicle*
SDLP	Social Democratic and Labour Party
SI	*Sunday Independent*
ST	*Sunday Tribune*

STE	*Sunday Times*
TCD	Trinity College Dublin
TD	teachta dála
TDE	*The Daily Express*
TFTCGN	*The Field: The Country Gentleman's Newspaper*
TG	*The Guardian*
UCC	University College Cork
UCD	University College Dublin
UCG	University College Galway
UDA	Ulster Defence Association
UDR	Ulster Defence Regiment
UEFA	Union of European Football Associations
UFCN	*Ulster Football and Cycling News*
UPS	United Parcel Service
USSR	Union of Soviet Socialist Republics
UVF	Ulster Volunteer Force
YMCA	Young Men's Christian Society
YTS	youth training scheme

Illustrations

Acknowledgments

This book has its origins in a Euro 2020 Football History Legacy Project which was commissioned by Dublin City Council in 2019. While I was able to carry out the intended interviews with players and supporters, the onset of Covid-19 in the spring of 2020 meant that along with the proposed matches in Dublin, a number of the related activities planned for that summer's scheduled European Championship finals unfortunately had to be cancelled. This included an exhibition at Pearse Street Library and a number of related talks around the city's libraries. Despite this disappointment, Brendan Teeling and Aoife McSwiney of Dublin City Council showed great flexibility and understanding in allowing the project to continue as I switched my attention to writing a history of soccer in Ireland's capital. I am also thankful to Cormac Moore of Dublin City Council for encouraging me to undertake the project. Hopefully this book can go some way to repaying their faith and will stand as a written record of how the game developed in the city and its wider areas, particularly in the period from 1880 until the early twenty-first century.

I am especially grateful to my wife, Joanne, and our family, for their support throughout my academic career. Writing this book allowed me to get to know a number of local historians, including Gerry Farrell, who gave two fascinating talks on aspects of Dublin soccer, the first at Dalymount Park, followed by one at Drumcondra Library. Gerry was always willing to share his information on Dublin's rich soccer history and was very helpful. Michael Kielty of Dublin Business School also freely gave his time to offer his opinions on the game in Dublin, and both contributed articles to a special issue of *Soccer and Society* on Dublin soccer, published in December 2021, which I edited. Tom Hunt, Cormac Moore, Conor Heffernan, Joseph Taylor, Ken McCue, Julien Clenet and Aaron Ó Maonaigh also took the time to research and write articles for that collection, and I am thankful to them for their input. Aaron also gave an interesting talk on local soccer history at Ballyfermot Library early in 2020 as part of the initial project.

Prior to the outbreak of the Covid pandemic, I was able to carry out a number of interviews with players and supporters who have been closely involved in the game in Dublin. These mainly took place at a number of venues around Dublin ranging from Trinity College Dublin to the office of the Professional Footballers' Association of Ireland in Abbotstown, although some telephone calls were necessary as social restrictions were put in place from March 2020 onwards. I am

therefore grateful to the twenty-four players and five supporters whose insights
appear later in this book: Shane Supple, Mick Meagan, Seamus Kelly, Paddy
Mulligan, Turlough O'Connor, Chris Bennion, Stephen McGuinness, Dave
Henderson, Seán Prunty, Chris Deans, Brian O'Shea, Harry McCue, Gary Kelly,
John Coady, Alf Girvan, Frank O'Neill, Pat Fenlon, Paul Byrne, Liam Buckley,
Mick Lawlor, Susan Heapes, Chloe Darby, Olivia O'Toole and Jamie Finn (players) and supporters Gerry Farrell, Dermot Looney, Gavin White, Ryan Clarke
and Mark Keane. As Covid-19 restrictions ended, I was again able to return to
a number of archives in a physical capacity, having previously utilized the online
Irish Newspaper Archives and the British Newspaper Archives, which have been a
huge help to many researchers over the past decade. I am grateful to the staff of the
University College Dublin Archives, while those working in Drumcondra Library,
the Dublin Diocesan Archives at the Archbishop's Palace, Trinity College Dublin
Archives, the National Library of Ireland in Kildare Street, the National Archives
of Ireland in Bishop Street and the Public Record Office of Northern Ireland also
deserve thanks for their assistance. Similarly, I would like to thank Alex Jackson of
the National Football Archives in Preston for his assistance during an earlier visit.
I am also thankful to Anne Marie McInerney of Dublin City Council Photographic
Collection and to Clair Walton of Dublin City Council City Library and Archive
for granting me permission to publish a number of photographs from their collection. I am grateful to Berni Metcalfe of the National Library of Ireland for her
help and her colleague, Glenn Dunne, for granting me permission to publish a
number of pictures stored in the National Photographic Archive.

   Luke O'Riordan of Bohemians FC, who supplied me with the photograph of
the 1928 Bohemians on this book's cover, and Frank Connolly of Drumcondra also
deserve thanks for their interest in and support of my study. I am also thankful to
Taylor and Francis and in particular to Professor Boria Majumdar for allowing me
to publish extracts from two of my recent *Soccer and Society* articles, on League
of Ireland players and Dublin players' cross-border movement, and to Professor
David Mayall and Dr Erato Basea for granting me permission to publish parts of
my *Immigrants and Minorities* article on historic relations between soccer organizers in Liverpool and Dublin.[1] Finally I am very grateful to Martin Fanning and
Sam Tranum and the rest of the team at Four Courts Press for their support and
encouragement and for publishing this book.

1 Conor Curran, 'The playing and working conditions of League of Ireland footballers in a part-
time Euro 2021 host nation: the Republic of Ireland's League of Ireland' in 'The EURO Cup and
European football: some critical reflections', special edition of *Soccer and Society*, 22:4 (2021), pp
343–54; 'The cross-border movement of Republic of Ireland-born footballers to Northern Ireland
clubs, 1922–2000' in Conor Curran (ed.), 'The growth and development of soccer in Dublin', special
edition of *Soccer and Society*, 22:4 (2021), pp 858–72; '"Ireland's second capital?" Irish footballers'
migration to Liverpool, the growth of supporters' clubs and the organization of Liverpool Football
Club matches in Dublin: an historical assessment', *Immigrants and Minorities*, 36:3 (2018), pp 258–86.

Introduction

Following the disappointment of the city of Dublin losing the four Euro 2020 finals matches it had been selected by UEFA to host, due to the Covid-19 pandemic, early in 2022 it emerged that a joint bid to host the 2028 tournament was in the pipeline.[1] Along with cities in the United Kingdom, Dublin has again been pinpointed as a potential host venue for the European soccer championships.[2] Dublin has a rich soccer history and it would be a fitting venue for a major international soccer tournament. The Republic of Ireland's capital city, it was built on the rivers Liffey/Poddle on the east coast of Ireland, and its origins as a trading, transport and dwelling place stretch back to the ninth century.[3] Norse invaders, attracted by the treasures available in Irish monasteries such as Clondalkin and Dubh Linn, had begun to settle from 841 CE onwards.[4] Although the Norsemen were famously defeated in battle by Brian Bóruma in 1014 at Clontarf, the early foundations had been laid.[5] While its population lay at 64,500 in 1688, it grew steadily to 348,525 in 1881, despite having lost its parliament at College Green through the Act of Union of 1800.[6] English control over Ireland, which effectively became more pronounced from the late sixteenth century onwards, meant that the economic impact of Dublin grew significantly.[7] The number of Catholics in Dublin in 1881 had increased by approximately 13,000 since 1871, but Protestant strength within politics and trade remained.[8]

As D. George Boyce has stated, 'Ireland in the nineteenth century shared many of the characteristics of Victorian Britain: mass politics, mass literacy and mass sport'.[9] By the late 1800s, British governmental influence was being challenged through the Home Rule movement, with the Gaelic Revival seeing a number of important cultural developments such as the foundation of the Gaelic Athletic Association by Michael Cusack and Maurice Davin in 1884.[10] This was part of the codification of modern sport as well as being an attempt to develop Irish games for its native people.[11] As David Goldblatt has stated,

> [association] football's fate was to arrive in Ireland at the very moment that a broad-based opposition to British rule and the Anglo-Irish landlord

---

1 *IT*, 22 Feb. 2022. 2 Ibid. 3 David Dickson, *Dublin: the making of a capital city* (London, 2014), p. 4. 4 Ibid. 5 Ibid., p. 7. 6 *Thom's official directory … 1883* (Dublin, 1883), p. 1271. 7 Dickson, *Dublin*, p. xiv. 8 *FJ*, 24 Mar. 1882 and Dickson, *Dublin*, pp 391–401. 9 D. George Boyce, *Nineteenth century Ireland: the search for stability* (Dublin, 2005), p. 277. 10 *Sport*, 8 Nov. 1884; Conor Curran, *The development of sport in Donegal, 1880–1935* (Cork, 2015), p. 71. 11 Ibid.

ascendency was being mobilized; sport and politics would become insepa-
rable and the tenor of that politics would be a bitter struggle between the
forces of imperialism and nationalism.[12]

Other governing bodies for sport were already being forged by that time. A
national association for rugby – the Irish Rugby Football Union – was operational
since 1879.[13] Cycling had a national governing body, with the Irish Bicycling
Association becoming the Irish Cyclists' Association in 1884.[14] The Irish Amateur
Athletic Association was founded in 1885.[15] Governing bodies for soccer were
also being organized in Ireland in the late nineteenth century. In 1880, the Irish
Football Association was founded, but this was centred in Belfast and soccer was
much slower to take off in Dublin, with the Leinster Football Association meeting
in Dublin for the first time in the autumn of 1892.[16] While membership of clubs
and associations at times overlapped, soccer administrators faced stiff competition
from the GAA and IRFU as they attempted to attract interest.
    Along with benefiting from an increase in railway networks, the growth of codi-
fied sport in Ireland was assisted by the development of a dedicated sporting press,
while more general national and regional newspapers also spread news of clubs,
competitions, matches and related social developments. The numbers of those who
could read and write in Dublin grew from 61 per cent of inhabitants in 1871 to
66 per cent in 1881.[17] There was an adequate transport network, and the city was
compact enough to allow the movement of teams and players without any major
travelling issues.[18] As will be shown, Dublin's journey to becoming the centre of
soccer in Ireland was not always smooth, but its location, population, infrastructure and demography gave it a significant advantage over many other Irish urban
settings in this regard. What is surprising is that soccer took so long to get off the
ground there given the close ties with Britain, where the game was already growing
in popularity, with the FA Cup having been inaugurated in 1871.[19]
    The early development of sport in Ireland was in many ways part of the
wider sporting 'revolution' taking place in Britain in the late nineteenth century.
Dublin's population in 1881 was lower than those of London, Glasgow, Liverpool,
Manchester and Edinburgh, and was said to be 'about equal to Birmingham'.[20]
Soccer was already beginning to take hold in a number of these cities. Tony Collins
has written that 'Glasgow's football culture from the 1870s blossomed into the
most glorious summer to create the archetypal football city.'[21] While Glasgow had
more in common culturally and industrially with Belfast than with Dublin, it can

12 David Goldblatt, *The ball is round: a global history of football* (London, 2006), p. 101.   13 Ibid.,
p. 46.   14 Brian Griffin, *Cycling in Victorian Ireland* (Dublin, 2006), p. 34.   15 Curran, *The development of sport in Donegal*, p. 43.   16 Neal Garnham, *Association football and society in pre-partition
Ireland* (Belfast, 2004), p. 5 and *UFCN*, 28 Oct. 1892.   17 *FJ*, 24 Mar. 1882.   18 Garnham,
Association football and society, pp 8–12.   19 Tony Mason, *Association football and English society,
1863–1915* (Brighton, 1980), p. 16.   20 *FJ*, 24 Mar. 1882.   21 Tony Collins, *How football began: a
global history of how the world's football codes were born* (Abingdon, 2019), p. 47.

also act as important site of where soccer can be said to have succeeded in the late nineteenth century. Collins has also noted that 'Sheffield was the first city to develop something resembling a modern football culture, which within a generation was replicated in almost every town and city in Britain.'[22] He notes a number of key features of this, including 'regular competition between clubs representing their local communities, the crowds that matches attracted and the regular discussion of football matters in the press'.[23]

Despite this, it was not until late 1883 that Dublin's first two soccer clubs, the Dublin Association Football Club and Dublin University Association Football Club (Trinity College Dublin), were operational.[24] Rugby was initially the most popular football code in Dublin and some of its supporters were eager to keep it that way.[25]

Competition from other sports has also hindered soccer's development in Ireland. As a result of the GAA's strong parish and county identity in rural Ireland, its nationalist appeal, the 'Ban' on its members' participation in foreign games (which ran from 1901 until 1971) and the ability of its more efficient organizers to offer a regular calendar of fixtures for Gaelic football in many counties, since the early twentieth century, soccer has struggled to compete at a grassroots level in many areas.[26] However, soccer clubs and competitions have flourished in Dublin since the Leinster Football Association was established in 1892.[27]

Dublin attracted numerous migrants from the Irish countryside, and immigrants from Britain, and the diversity of the city allowed for a greater spread of clubs and more choice of those to join as members than in many country towns and villages. In 1881, almost 62 per cent of Dublin's population were reported to be 'natives', while 'the remainder were born either in other parts of Ireland or abroad'.[28] There were twelve towns and ten townships in Dublin with populations of over 500 people.[29] Military involvement was also significant, although this varied throughout Ireland and in Dublin it was less pronounced than in some towns. Around 5,000 of Dublin's inhabitants were registered as naval or military men by the early 1880s, but as will be seen, while initially providing opposition for occasional friendly matches, military teams did not come to the fore until the early twentieth century when the Leinster FA's first competitions had already been established.[30]

By the early 1900s soccer was beginning to take hold in Dublin, with these factors also noticeable in its development. By then, Dublin was the largest city on the island of Ireland, with a population of 375,135 which included suburban municipalities.[31] As Friedman and Bustad have stated, 'cities provided the concentrations of participants, audiences, media, and affluence that were all essential ingredients

22 Ibid., p. 28.   **23** Ibid.   **24** *IT*, 16 Oct. 1883; *Sport*, 24 Nov. 1883.   **25** *IT*, 15 Oct. 1883.   **26** See, for example, Curran, *The development of sport in Donegal*, p. 226.   **27** *Sport*, 5 Nov. 1892.   **28** *FJ*, 25 Mar. 1882.   **29** *Thom's official directory ... 1883*, p. 1669.   **30** *FJ*, 24 Mar. 1882.   **31** Conor Curran, *Irish soccer migrants: a social and cultural history* (Cork, 2017), p. 23.

for modern sport to evolve'.[32] Because of the high population of Dublin (in comparison to many parts of rural Ireland), and the perseverance of a number of men, soccer was eventually allowed the space to breathe and had enough organizers and players to be sustained, and became attractive to spectators.

Although most initial matches were poorly attended, in 1904 6,000 people attended the Leinster FA's Senior Cup final.[33] David Dickson has noted that Dublin clubs' performances in the Irish Senior Cup strengthened its appeal, with Shelbourne and Bohemians lifting the trophy in 1906 and 1908 respectively.[34] Tony Mason has stated in his major work on English soccer that in the late nineteenth century 'finding a ground on which to play was a serious problem for a football club'.[35] In Dublin, designated space was available in the Phoenix Park, while the development of clubs such as Bohemians saw the purchase or rental of grounds with the aim to maintain a fixed venue nearby to the club's own area.[36] These venues acted as focal points within communities and as meeting places for those with an interest in the game. Writing in 1908 after they had won the Irish Cup final on their home ground, Dalymount Park, against Shelbourne, one reporter was of the view that 'no club that ever was formed in Dublin did so much to popularize and improve the game in Leinster as Bohemians'.[37]

As will be seen, the role of migrants who had experienced the game elsewhere was crucial to the organization of Dublin's first matches. Matthew Taylor has stated that 'the game of [association] football travelled with the movement of people' and 'migration, both short and long term, was essential to its dissemination, with those in peripatetic occupations playing a key role'.[38] Dublin's industrial, economic and cultural progress meant that immigrants came to the city in search of work and they also assisted the development of soccer clubs through administration, management, coaching and, of course, as players. Trading and transport links with Britain, and Dublin's east-coast location and proximity to English cities such as Liverpool, also meant that connections between clubs could be developed through friendly matches.[39] By the early 1900s player movement from Dublin to English professional teams was beginning to take hold as aspiring footballers went in search of higher wages and a better standard of play.[40] The vast majority of these Irish soccer migrants were born in Dublin, illustrating the city's status as the powerhouse of Irish soccer, while the most successful clubs in the League of Ireland have also been located there.[41]

32 Michael T. Friedman & Jacob J. Bustad, 'Sport and urbanization' in Robert Edelman & Wayne Wilson (eds), *The Oxford handbook of sports history* (Oxford, 2017), pp 145–58, p. 154.   33 *Sport*, 17 Nov. 1883 and Garnham, *Association football and society*, p. 108.   34 Dickson, *Dublin*, pp 409–10.   35 Mason, *Association football and English society*, p. 27.   36 *Thom's official directory … 1883*, p. 1577; Mike Cronin & Roisin Higgins, *Places we play: Ireland's sporting heritage* (Cork, 2011), pp 103, 230.   37 *IT*, 4 Apr. 1908.   38 Matthew Taylor, 'The global spread of football' in R. Edelman & W. Wilson (eds), *The Oxford handbook of sports history* (Oxford, 2017), pp 183–95, p. 184.   39 See Curran, 'Ireland's second capital?', pp 258–86.   40 Curran, *Irish soccer migrants*, pp 26–7.   41 Ibid., pp 27–38.

While soccer struggled to make inroads in schools after the partition of Ireland in 1921 as a policy of 'Gaelicization' was aggressively pursued by various governments, the development of schoolboy clubs and competitions, which was mainly undertaken by voluntary organizers who simply had a love of the game and liked to socialize through it, meant that underage structures for soccer in Ireland's capital were not neglected.[42] Again, it was in Dublin where the best of these young players were nurtured, with clubs such as Home Farm, Cherry Orchard and Belvedere being among the strongest in the country by the late twentieth century.[43] While this has been well established, less has been written about the origins and development of the competitions in which they honed their skills.

THE HISTORIOGRAPHY OF DUBLIN SOCCER

Although there are numerous works relating to Dublin's rich social and cultural history, soccer does not feature heavily in these accounts.[44] Dickson focuses briefly on the background and geography of a number of professional clubs, stating that 'Dublin clubs were linked to large employers (Guinness, Jacob's) or drew support from particular districts (Shelbourne from around Ringsend; Shamrock Rovers, more broadly, the suburban south side; St Patrick's from Inchicore and Kilmainham; Home Farm from Drumcondra and Whitehall; and Bohemians drawing wide north-side support).'[45] While rugby has traditionally been associated with Dublin's south side, aside perhaps from a few northern Dublin areas such as Clontarf, soccer clubs can be found more commonly both north and south of the river Liffey. A trial match for the Leinster XI late in 1899 saw players divided into north and south Dublin selections, but teams can be found located around the city and its suburbs, although particular pockets of soccer-player production such as Ringsend, where thirty-eight Irish internationals had grown up by 1994, stand out, with a number of those capped referring to street football as being central to this figure.[46]

The general lack of engagement by 'mainstream' historians is somewhat surprising given the role the game has played in the lives of many Dublin residents since its introduction in the capital in the early 1880s, and the obvious popularity of local, national and international matches held there at various stages in the twentieth century. Some academics from other disciplines have offered assessments. Max Jack has examined the role of the Shamrock Rovers FC ultras, although this is vague on the history of soccer supporters in Dublin.[47] By the late twentieth century, the demography of Irish society was changing significantly, with the

---

42 Ibid., pp 81–92. 43 Ibid., p. 34. 44 See, for example, Dickson, *Dublin*, pp 409–10, p. 550, p. 551; Ruth McManus, *Dublin, 1910–1940: shaping the city and suburbs* (Dublin, 2006); and Ruth McManus & Lisa Marie Griffith (eds), *Leaders of the city: Dublin's first citizens, 1500–1950* (Dublin, 2013). 45 Dickson, *Dublin*, p. 550. 46 *FJ*, 1 Jan. 1900; *STE*, 3 July 1994 and 14 Nov. 1999. 47 Max Jack, 'On the terrace: ritual performance of identity and conflict by the Shamrock Rovers Football Club ultras in Dublin', *Ethnomusicology Review*, 18 (2013), pp 94–9.

Republic of Ireland's immigrant population growing substantially due to the economic growth associated with the Celtic Tiger era of the late 1990s/early 2000s.
Historian Thomas Bartlett has noted that 'foreign-born residents registered a 58
per cent increase to bring them to at least 14 per cent of the Irish population of
just over four million in 2006'.[48] However, studies of the impact of this on soccer in Dublin have been scarce. An exception is Max Mauro's sociological study
of two clubs: Insaka FC, an under-18 team based in Blanchardstown, founded
in 2009 by a Nigerian ex-professional footballer; and a youth club based in the
same area, Mountview FC, which was much older in its origins, established in
1980.[49] While the latter contained 'Irish (white) boys and boys of different African
backgrounds', the former team was made up of 'immigrant youth (of African and
Eastern European backgrounds)'.[50]

A few historical studies by 'mainstream' historians have also looked at key
issues in association football's general development, with R.V. Comerford's chapter on sport in his 2003 publication *Ireland: inventing the nation* highlighting
soccer's struggle for acceptance in post-partition Ireland.[51] Dermot Keogh has also
acknowledged the importance of the game to some extent, noting in 1994 that the
foundation of the Football Association of Ireland in 1921 'left two rival soccer capi-
tals, Belfast and Dublin', after a number of disputes between Dublin clubs and the
Belfast-based Irish Football Association.[52] These works and a few others aside, this
general absence from academic writing can be partially explained by the low number of full-time sports historians working in Ireland's universities, and the fact that
studies of the history of sport in Ireland have only recently become accepted as
worthy of investigation as post-graduate or doctoral theses. The opening decades
of the twenty-first century have seen a significant rise in the number of academic
publications relating to sport's historic role within Irish society (but not related
employment opportunities), reflecting a growing awareness within academia that
sport has its place within history.[53]

Neal Garnham's *Association football and society in pre-partition Ireland* (2004)
provides an important assessment of soccer's early development in Belfast and
Dublin, but, as the title suggests, his study finishes in the early 1920s.[54] In his
groundbreaking study, the first academic monograph to examine soccer's early
history in Ireland in detail, the focus is predominantly on the north-eastern city,
although Dublin is also discussed.[55] Garnham's seminal monograph is an important starting point for any study of soccer in Ireland, particularly because of his

48 Thomas Bartlett, *Ireland: a history* (Cambridge, 2010), p. 546.   49 Max Mauro, *Youth sport,
migration and culture: two football teams and the changing face of Ireland* (London & New York, 2018),
pp 3–4, 50.   50 Ibid., pp 3–4.   51 R.V. Comerford, *Ireland: inventing the nation* (London, 2003),
pp 226–30.   52 Dermot Keogh, *Twentieth-century Ireland: revolution and state building* (Dublin,
2005), p. 35.   53 See, in particular, James Kelly, *Sport in Ireland, 1600–1840* (Dublin, 2014) and Paul
Rouse, *Sport in Ireland: a history* (Oxford, 2015).   54 Garnham, *Association football in pre-partition
Ireland*.   55 Ibid., and see also Martin Moore, 'The origins of association football in Belfast: a reappraisal', *Sport in History*, 37:4 (2017), pp 505–28.

use of original archival research in his examination of the early years of clubs and competitions. He has also assessed a number of aspects of soccer's development in Dublin in a chapter on soccer in Ireland published in an international collection on soccer in the interwar years between 1918 and 1939.[56] Cormac Moore's *The Irish soccer split*, published in 2015, was the first full-length examination of the conflict between the Irish Football Association and the Football Association of Ireland, while in 2017 *Irish soccer migrants: a social and cultural history*, by Conor Curran, examined the movement of Irish-born soccer players to international leagues in the years from 1888 until 2010.[57] Soccer has also been a prominent part of county histories of sport such as Tom Hunt's *Sport and society in Victorian Ireland: the case of Westmeath* (2007) and this writer's *The development of sport in Donegal, 1880–1935* (2015).[58] David Toms' *Soccer in Munster: a social history, 1877–1937* (2015) is an important work, along with his jointly edited collection with this author, *New perspectives on association football in Irish society: going beyond the 'garrison game'* (2018).[59] Mark Tynan's doctoral thesis on soccer in the interwar period provides an important assessment of the game's development.[60]

One more recent collection edited by this author, a special edition of the journal *Soccer and Society* with a focus on the growth and development of the game in Dublin, was published late in 2021, and has also added to what we know about soccer's historical development there.[61] To date, soccer's presence in Derry, Kilkenny and Galway has not yet been fully examined. Although of course these cities lacked the industrial growth and rates of population expansion found in Belfast and Dublin in the late nineteenth century when Ireland's fledgling soccer clubs were being established, the game has had a presence there.[62] The growth of soccer in two other urban settlements, Athlone and Sligo, has received scholarly attention, through the work of Hunt and Gunning, respectively.[63] This is significant as these two towns, along with Belfast, Dublin, Cork, Waterford, Limerick and Dundalk, have traditionally been thought of as strongholds of the game within an Irish setting.[64] Original research on west and south Ulster has also been undertaken by this author in recent years and similarly can act as an important comparison for

56 Neal Garnham, 'Ein spiel in zwei nationen? fussball in Irland, 1918–1939' in Christian Koller & Fabian Brändle (eds), *Fussball zwischen den kriegen: Europa 1918–1939* (Zurich, 2010), pp 65–85. **57** Cormac Moore, *The Irish soccer split* (Cork, 2015); Curran, *Irish soccer migrants*. **58** Tom Hunt, *Sport and society in Victorian Ireland: the case of Westmeath* (Cork, 2007); Curran, *The development of sport in Donegal*. **59** David Toms, *Soccer in Munster: a social history* (Cork, 2015) and Conor Curran & David Toms, *New perspectives on association football in Irish history: going beyond the 'garrison game'* (Abingdon, 2018). **60** Mark Tynan, 'Association football and Irish society during the Inter-War period, 1918–1939' (PhD, NUI Maynooth, 2013). **61** Curran (ed.), 'The growth and development of soccer in Dublin'. This features related articles by Julien Clenet, Cormac Moore, Aaron Ó Maonaigh, Conor Heffernan and Joseph Taylor, Conor Curran, Gerard Farrell, Tom Hunt, Michael Kielty and Ken McCue. **62** Curran, *Irish soccer migrants*, pp 32–4, 42. **63** Hunt, *Sport and society in Victorian Ireland*, pp 170–89 and Paul Gunning, 'Association football in the Shamrock shire's Hy Brasil: the "socker" code in Connacht, 1879–1906' in Curran & Toms (eds), *New perspectives on association football in Irish history*, pp 10–32. **64** Keogh, *Twentieth-century Ireland*, p. 36.

studies of soccer elsewhere in Ireland.[65] Journalist Peter Byrne has also written an important account of the history of Irish soccer, albeit with a focus on international soccer and events in Belfast and Dublin, but as yet, the game lacks a full-length academic study of its history on a county-by-county basis.[66] Some notable club histories have also been published, including those of Bohemians, Home Farm, Shamrock Rovers and Shelbourne, but an overall examination of the history of soccer in Dublin from its early beginnings until the end of the twentieth century has not yet been undertaken until now.[67]

METHODOLOGY

Specialist collections were consulted for this book, including the Leinster Football Association and Football Association of Ireland Archives at University College Dublin and the Dublin Diocesan Archives (Catholic church) at the Archbishop's House in Drumcondra. However, club files proved more difficult to access, and some clubs were unfortunately reluctant to offer their assistance. Online records of Liverpool and Everton football clubs were consulted in order to identify matches between these clubs and those from Dublin. A few specialized soccer-based news-papers and journals, such as *Charles Buchan's Football Monthly*, *Football Sports Weekly*, *Irish Soccer* and *Soccer Reporter* were published at various stages in the twentieth century, and, along with match programmes, these provide an impor-tant insight into Dublin's soccer culture. While newspapers, directories and other works of reference such as census material naturally formed the core of this book, a significant part of this study involved player and supporter interviews to supple-ment this archival material. Supported by Dublin City Council between 2019 and 2020, these included twenty male players with experience of various levels of the game in Dublin, although the overwhelming focus was on those who had played for Dublin's League of Ireland and schoolboy clubs. Interviews took place with

65 See Conor Curran, *The development of sport in Donegal*; 'Networking structures and competitive association football in Ulster, 1880–1914', *Irish Economic and Social History*, 41 (2014), pp 74–92; 'The social background of Ireland's pre-World War I association football clubs, players and administrators: the case of South and West Ulster', *International Journal of the History of Sport*, 33:16 (2016), pp 1982–2005; '"It has almost been an underground movement": the development of grassroots foot-ball in regional Ireland: the case of county Donegal, 1971–1996' in Jürgen Mittag, Kristian Naglo & Dilwyn Porter (eds), 'Small worlds: football at the grassroots in Europe', Special issue of *Moving the Social: Journal of Social History and the History of Social Movements*, 61 (2019), pp 33–60; 'From Ardara Emeralds to Ardara FC: soccer in Ardara, 1891–1995', in Gary James (ed.), 'International football history: selected submissions from the 2017 & 2018 conferences', special edition of *Soccer and Society*, 21:4 (2020), pp 433–47. 66 Peter Byrne, *Green is the colour: the story of Irish football* (London, 2012). 67 See, for example, *Shelbourne Football Club golden jubilee, 1895–1945* (Dublin, 1945); Tony Reid, *Bohemian AFC official club history, 1890–1976* (1977); Brendan Menton, *Home Farm: the story of a Dublin football club 1928–1998* (1999); Eoghan Rice, *We are Rovers: an oral his-tory of Shamrock Rovers FC* (London, 2005); Paul Doolan & Robert Goggins, *The Hoops: a history of Shamrock Rovers* (Dublin, 1993); Christopher Sands, *Shels: a grand old team to know* (Dublin, 2016).

those who had been involved in Dublin soccer since the late 1950s, and more recent players were also included. Some of these players also had experience of league football in England (Frank O'Neill, Mick Meagan, Paddy Mulligan, Turlough O'Connor, Shane Supple, John Coady, Seamus Kelly and Paul Byrne) while a few (Dave Henderson, Liam Buckley, Harry McCue and Paddy Mulligan) had played in the North American Soccer League (NASL). Brian O'Shea, Harry McCue, Pat Fenlon and Paul Byrne had experience of the Irish League, with clubs in Northern Ireland, while John Coady had played in the League of Ireland with Derry City following his time at Shamrock Rovers and in England with Chelsea. Buckley is somewhat unique among Irish football migrants in that he did not appear for an English club but instead had spells at clubs in Belgium, Spain and Switzerland in the 1980s as well as a sojourn in Canada with Vancouver Whitecaps. Utilizing the views of these players of their experiences at Dublin clubs and those in Northern Ireland and abroad provides an important insight into transnational links between clubs, and players' experiences of the game in different environments.

While not all players interviewed appeared in English league football, most of those players who did not had trials with English clubs (Mick Lawlor, Brian O'Shea, Dave Henderson, Stephen McGuinness, Gary Kelly) or had contracts with clubs in England at some point in their careers (Seán Prunty, Chris Deans). Alf Girvan had experience of competitive soccer in Canada as well as the League of Ireland, while Chris Bennion, a Scot who moved to the League of Ireland via Middlesbrough and Scunthorpe United and played for a number of clubs in Dublin and elsewhere, was also interviewed. Another goalkeeper, Gary Kelly, played most of his career in the Leinster Senior League with clubs such as Ashtown Villa but also had spells at a number of League of Ireland clubs.

Professional football for ladies has been a much more recent development in England than the men's game, and female teams have only lately began to receive attention in the media. A number of female players with experience of the game at Dublin clubs were also interviewed, including Olivia O'Toole, Susan Heapes, Jamie Finn and Chloe Darby. Interviews were also conducted with a small number of supporters of Dublin clubs and this proved beneficial in illustrating the importance that the game has had, and continues to have, in the lives of many within Dublin.

This book has generally been written thematically and consists of eight chapters. The first six chapters focus on the development of the game's clubs and competitions in Dublin. The final two chapters focus mainly on players and their movements for professional football purposes. In its entirety, this book offers a fresh look at the development of soccer in Dublin and makes an important contribution to the historiography of sport in Ireland and to studies of social life within Irish cities.

The origins of association football in Dublin

PRE-CODIFIED FOOTBALL

Early forms of folk football, which were often chaotic and violent, were played in Ireland from at least the sixteenth century. Neal Garnham has stated that 'perhaps the earliest explicit mention of the game comes in 1518, when an ordinance of the Archbishop of Dublin decreed that in the diocese of Ossory "clerks playing football" should be fined and were to pay for any damage they caused to church property'.[1] Despite this, as Eoin Kinsella notes, forms of football were probably played long before this given that it was being played in Britain since the medieval era. The Galway Corporation's decision to allow 'football' to continue there in 1527 is also one of the earliest recorded examples in Ireland.[2] James Kelly has stated that pre-codified football 'took sufficiently firm root among the English (later Old English) communities of Galway, Cork and Dublin in the sixteenth century to merit specific mention in the decrees' issued by authorities in these urban areas.[3] The political decline of the Old English, with the resulting loss of their land and power, had an impact on its playing.[4] By the late seventeenth century, it had failed to gain much attention nationally outside of south Ulster and north Leinster, with one contemporary noting its presence as being largely focused in the Fingal area.[5] Protestant authorities' suspicions of the motives behind the organization of mass gatherings remained, despite the conclusion of the Williamite-Jacobite wars in 1691.[6]

Along with a form of hurling, football was banned on Sundays under the 1695 Irish Sunday Observance Act, but both continued to be played, and a game of football at Oxmanton Green in Dublin in 1720 was commemorated in a lengthy poem written by Matt Concannon.[7] This six-a-side match between players representing Swords and Lusk illustrates elements of the event such as the dress style of these men, the physicality of the play and the joy it brought to those present.[8] In general, however, throughout the eighteenth century, football continued to be deemed as socially unacceptable, as references to its playing in Dublin in 1730 and 1740 attest.[9]

---

1 Garnham, *Association football and society*, p. 2. 2 Eoin Kinsella, 'Football and hurling in early modern Ireland' in Mike Cronin, William Murphy & Paul Rouse (eds), *The Gaelic Athletic Association, 1884–2009* (Dublin, 2009), pp 15–31, pp 16–18. 3 Kelly, *Sport in Ireland, 1600–1840*, p. 273. 4 Ibid. 5 Ibid. 6 Ibid., p. 274. 7 Garnham, *Association football and society*, p. 2. 8 Liam P. Ó Caithnia, *Báirí cos in Éirinn (Roimh bhunú na ncumann eagraithe)* (Dublin, 1984), pp 30–42. 9 Kelly, *Sport in Ireland, 1600–1840*, p. 276.

1. Trinity College Dublin's College Park (1865). Courtesy of the National Library of
Ireland.

Damage to property, such as what occurred in fields near Baggot Street in 1754,
was frequently a concern of authorities.[10] By the middle of the following decade, it
had been driven outside the city to fields in areas such as Kilmainham, Dolphin's
Barn, Drumcondra, Phoenix Park, Eccles Street and Rathfarnham.[11] Violent incidents such as the accidental death of a baker's apprentice at a sports meeting in
fields beside Eccles Street in 1780 did nothing to help the cause of football.[12] As
Kelly states, the lack of support from the authorities for mass ball games in Ireland
was similar to that in England, and this was an attitude that remained into the
nineteenth century, so much so that by the 1830s hurling, football and commons
were generally in decline, although traditional forms of hurling continued in a
number of counties such as Donegal, even after the foundation of the GAA and
its codes.[13] Football-related violence continued in some areas into the nineteenth
century. In March 1850, one man was brought to court in County Roscommon
for stabbing another following an argument 'relative to a game of football'.[14] The
National Folklore Collection, gathered nationally in schools throughout Ireland in
the 1930s in a government-backed initiative, contains a number of references to
pre-codified football in areas in Dublin such as Mulhuddart and Swords, but there
is scant evidence of specific soccer matches or the formation of association football
teams there in this archive in the late nineteenth century.[15]

Trevor West has noted that pre-codified football was played in the 1780s in
the College Park at Trinity College Dublin, which was founded in 1592, although
it was not until 1854 that a rugby club was established there.[16] Matthew Taylor

10 Ibid., p. 277.   11 Ibid., p. 278.   12 Ibid., p. 279.   13 Ibid., p. 282. See Curran, *The development of sport in Donegal*, pp 33–41. Commons was a form of pre-codified hurling played along the
ground.   14 *FJ*, 2 Mar. 1850.   15 National Folklore Collection, 'School: Mulhuddart (roll number
16675)', Schools' Collection, vol. 0790, p. 102, duchas.ie/en/cbes/4498605/4385153, accessed 2 Aug.
2020; 'School: Swords (roll number 7339)', vol. 0788, p. 125, duchas.ie/en/cbes/4428186/4384680,
accessed 2 Aug. 2020.   16 Trevor West, *The bold collegians: the development of sport in Trinity College
Dublin* (Dublin, 1991), pp 5, 23–4.

has stated that association football's spread in Ireland was 'multifaceted' and it 'came to Dublin via students at Trinity College who had played at England's public schools but in the north the game arrived through the region's cultural and socio-economic connections with Scotland.'[17] Soccer in Ireland did not begin to take root until the mid-1870s and its early growth was based mainly in Belfast, with Martin Moore noting that matches took place there in this code in 1875 and in 1877. This was therefore before what had been generally accepted to be the first match, played at Ulster Cricket Club's ground in Belfast between two Scottish clubs in 1878.[18] In 1879 the first Irish association football club, Cliftonville, was established in north Belfast through members of the cricket club bearing the same name.[19] In November 1880 the Irish Football Association was founded at the Queen's Hotel in the city after a meeting organized by Cliftonville Football Club.[20]

Tony Collins has stated that the successful growth of soccer in the English city of Sheffield was partially because the city's economy in the early nineteenth century 'was based on small-scale, highly skilled metal manufacturing, which meant that the working classes had more leisure time and disposable income to watch and, albeit in a limited fashion at first, take part in sport'.[21] As Garnham has stated, Dublin was second to Belfast in terms of its industrial prowess within the island of Ireland, but by the early 1880s, 'less than a quarter of the city's male workforce was employed in any kind of manufacturing', which meant that they were 'far less likely to benefit from factory legislation' than those in the northern city.[22] It was in the latter city that the development of linen and shipbuilding industries boosted the economy greatly and through the Factory Act of 1874, there was more free time for employees in these sectors to engage in sport. He concludes that 'the Belfast working population, more than any other in Ireland, therefore seems to have had the necessary leisure time and financial resources to participate in some form of modern sporting pastime'.[23]

Like Nottingham, Sheffield had developed a strong culture of cricket and this assisted soccer's growth by providing an infrastructure, with crossover of players between cricket and soccer clubs common.[24] This was less evident in Dublin in the late nineteenth century, despite cricket's popularity in Ireland at that time. Soccer was slower to take root in Dublin, despite attempts by the Scottish Football Association to host exhibition matches on the grounds of a number of rugby teams there as well as those in Belfast during the 1876–7 season.[25] Moore has identified that three soccer matches took place in Dublin towards the end of 1878.[26] In October 1878, the rugby-playing Dublin University FC held 'an impromptu game

17 Taylor, 'The global spread of football', p. 184.   18 Moore, 'The origins of association football in Ireland', pp 509–10.   19 Garnham, *Association football and society*, pp 39, 45.   20 Ibid., pp 5–6.   21 Collins, *How football began*, p. 28.   22 Garnham, *Association football and society*, p. 11.   23 Ibid.   24 Collins, *How football began*, p. 29.   25 Moore, 'The origins of association football in Ireland', pp 510–11.   26 Martin Moore, 'Early association football in Ireland: embryonic diffusion outside Ulster, 1877–1882' in *Sport in History* 42:1 (2022), pp 24–48, pp 27, 31–2.

under association rules', while the following month, the Queen's Bays met the 7th
Hussars and also the 7th Dragoons Guards in separate matches at Phoenix Park.[27]

The 1878 Trinity College Dublin rugby club match took place when a team
known as 'Field' had insufficient numbers for a rugby match against 'Dissylables'.[28]
Apparently, 'a fair number picked up an association match, which was kept up for
about an hour'.[29] This ad hoc match took place the week before the exhibition
match in Belfast between Scottish clubs Queen's Park and Caledonians, which
was long thought to be the first soccer match held in Ireland. Recent research by
Moore highlighted an intra-club match played between members of the Ulster
Cricket Club in Belfast in December 1875 and subsequent other efforts in the
following years.[30] While it has now been clarified that the 1878 Belfast match was
not the first in Ireland, it did have an important role in leading to more matches
in that city, the foundation of clubs and the establishment of the IFA there in
1880, and it was at least the first between two established (Scottish) soccer clubs
to be held in Ireland. Although John McAlery claimed to have organized the 1878
match in Belfast himself, it is more likely help came from Windsor Rugby Football
Club, whose members had played a soccer match in Belfast in 1877.[31] One club
history has posited that McAlery was assisted by Caledonians secretary J.A. Allen
in arranging the 1878 match, although again its true origins are not entirely clear.[32]

At least one contemporary source has claimed that there was a rugby background to the 1878 Belfast match. Prior to the event, one newspaper reporter
speculated that it was organized 'under the auspices of the Ulster and Windsors
FCs', which were rugby clubs, with a view to improving rugby.[33] He added that

> There has long been a desire on the part of Windsor FC to introduce asso-
> ciation practice here, for the purpose of improving the rugby forward play,
> which will be greatly changed now since the alteration of Rule 18, which
> compels men to put down the ball the instance it is collared. The North of
> Ireland FC has held strictly aloof from this innovation, but the match must
> draw well.[34]

Rule 18 was introduced by the Rugby Football Union in 1878 and stipulated that
when the player running with the ball was tackled, they had to release the ball on
to the ground as soon as they could not make forward progress.[35] Before this was
amended, when a player in possession of the ball was tackled, play was stopped
and a scrum was formed around him, and then he would put the ball down and the

27 Ibid. and West, *The bold collegians*, p. 25.   28 *FJ*, 18 Oct. 1878.   29 Ibid.   30 See, for example,
Garnham, *Association football and society*, p. 4; Moore, 'The origins of association football in Ireland:
a reappraisal', p. 509.   31 Moore, 'The origins of association football in Ireland: a reappraisal', pp
512–15.   32 E.J. O'Mahony (ed.), *Bohemian Football Club golden jubilee souvenir* (Dublin, 1945), pp
3–4.   33 *FJ*, 18 Oct. 1878.   34 Ibid.   35 See Tony Collins, *A social history of English rugby union*
(Abingdon, 2009), pp 136–7. I am grateful to Tony for explaining this rule to me.

scrum would begin.[36] The new rule had a huge impact on rugby, because it reduced the number of scrums and made the game much faster and more attractive to spectators, who could now see the ball in play more often. This rule change came three years after teams were reduced from 20-a-side to 15-a-side, which also made the game faster and more open (before 1875 most rugby matches were just a succession of endless scrums).[37] The reporter is also alluding to the fact that dribbling the ball was a common skill for rugby forwards. In the 1870s, the aim of the forwards in a scrum was to kick the ball forward through their opponents in the scrum and dribble the ball downfield.[38] Playing soccer would have helped them develop these skills, which is perhaps why two rugby clubs may have organized an association game. The match, played at the Ulster Cricket Ground 'under Scottish association rules' on 24 October 1878, was won by Queen's Park by three goals to one.[39]

In the first of the two military matches in Dublin in 1878, played on a Saturday afternoon early in November of that year, the Queen's Bays and 7th Hussars teams, described as 'two distinguished cavalry regiments', were already well acquainted, 'having spent all their spare afternoons during last summer in trying their merits at cricket'.[40] The reporter had 'never seen a pleasanter or more friendly game' and stated that he hoped that 'more regiments' would 'take to football and association rules'.[41] He also noted that

> Spurred on by the memory of their defeats in the summer, the Bays charged their lighter opponents with great vigour, no result, however, was obtained by either side, though twice the goal of the Bays was in great jeopardy. Mr Tattersall led the Bays valiantly, well supported by Trumpet Major Whitehead, Trumpeter Bailey, and a Sergeant Major, conspicuous by a forage cap and waistcoat, garments not often seen at football. Mr Ridley, backed up by corporals Murray and Urquhart, was well to the front for the Hussars.[42]

A return match was fixed for Newbridge, County Kildare, for the following week with the Hussars, who were based in the barracks there and practised twice a week, noted as the home side for that match, which they won by three goals to nil.[43] The Queen's Bays also beat the 7th Dragoon Guards in Dublin by two goals to nil that month at Phoenix Park, but these matches did not lead to the formation of any clubs there at that time.[44] Certainly there was an awareness of association football within Dublin at that point, and along with newspaper reports from other areas, there was the opportunity for some to familiarize themselves with how the game was played through these intermittent matches, and also as John Lawrence was selling copies of the rules of rugby and association football in Grafton Street by that time.[45]

36 Ibid. 37 Ibid. 38 Ibid. 39 *FJ*, 25 Oct. 1878. 40 *DDE*, 5 Nov. 1878. 41 Ibid. 42 Ibid. 43 Ibid., and *FJ*, 16 Oct. and 21 Nov. 1878. 44 Moore, 'Early association football in Ireland', pp 27, 31–2 and *FJ*, 21 Nov. 1878. 45 *FJ*, 21 Oct. 1878.

Other rugby teams also toyed with soccer during their practice sessions. As Julien Clenet has shown, in December 1880, Lansdowne Football Club held 'a capital practice match' under association rules 'purely as a medium of improving the rugby game'. They attempted to do this through focusing on dribbling, which was 'a great success', but they reverted back to their primary code again in their next session.[46] Moore has also noted a match between Cusack's Academy 'association' and 'rugby' selections, which took place in September 1881.[47] This was held on the Nine Acres at Phoenix Park, with 'an unusually large number of association football students having turned up' that year.[48] It was noted that 'play, which extended over two thirties, was fast for warm weather, and necessarily loose, inasmuch as it was a compromise between "Association" and "Rugby"'. However, the scoring system in both halves involved tries and conversions.[49] It appears that soccer was not taken up by Cusack's Academy at this point. Three months later a school match was held at Terenure College under association rules, but the group involved were more focused on rugby, with the availability of school opponents for this code a factor in this.[50]

The idea that Scottish clubs would help develop the game in Dublin was at times circulated. In September 1880, John McAlery had expressed hopes through the Dublin press that there would be an exhibition match between 'two crack Scotch clubs', but these were not realized.[51] Calls in one Dublin newspaper from one local resident, John McFarlane, for the establishment of an association football club in the city at the beginning of 1882 went unheeded, despite his promise that 'fully half a dozen clubs from the North, and a few from Scotland, would gladly visit the Irish capital for the sake of starting the game'.[52] He had claimed that he had spoken to 'men prominent in the football field' and that an inter-city match between Belfast and Dublin could be arranged.[53]

Despite some rugby clubs' involvement in a number of Dublin's first Association football matches, discussed above, opposition to the introduction of the soccer code in the city came from within rugby circles, with the *Irish Times'* rugby correspondent fearful in October 1883 that an exhibition soccer match was to be played at Lansdowne Road, primarily a rugby venue.[54] To his relief it did not go ahead 'owing to one of the clubs being unable to attend'. He outlined the reasons for his fears when he wrote that:

> without wishing in any way to condemn the game, we must say that we would regret extremely to see Association play started in Dublin, for the simple reason that there is hardly room for it. It is difficult enough to maintain the rugby game, to keep the men together, organize matches and travelling

46 Julien Clenet, 'Association football in Dublin in the late nineteenth century: an overview' in Conor Curran (ed.), 'The growth and development of Soccer in Dublin', Special edition of *Soccer & Society*, 22:8 (2021), pp 805–19, p. 806; and *FJ*, 24 Dec. 1880.   47 Moore, 'Early association football in Ireland', pp 3, 7–8.   48 *FJ*, 28 Sept. 1881.   49 Ibid.   50 Clenet, 'Association football in Dublin', p. 806.   51 *FJ*, 22 Sept. 1880.   52 *Sport*, 7 Jan. 1882.   53 Ibid.   54 *IT*, 15 Oct. 1883.

teams. Any split in the ranks would only injure the rugby game without materially benefitting the Association. We question strongly are there many men who desire the dribbling pastime, and we trust that our rugby players will remain united, and as they have done fairly well in the past, there is no reason why they should not do better in the future.[55]

Similarly, one rugby advocate in *Sport*, alarmed by the possible visit of Welsh and Scottish soccer players for exhibition matches, commented that 'this means mischief'.[56]

THE EARLY YEARS OF SOCCER IN DUBLIN

Despite these concerns, the organization of association football matches, with their relatively simple rules and a lower number of players required than rugby, could not be prevented. Dublin's first soccer club was based fairly close to the centre of the city and by the middle of October 1883 was up and running.[57] On Friday 12 October 1883 the Dublin Association Football Club (DAFC) held a meeting at 7 Tyrone Place, Sackville Street, with a number of 'gentlemen' elected to key roles.[58] These included Frank T. Armatyge, who was named as captain, while J. Bell became vice captain. James Hood of 35 Great Charles Street, Mountjoy Square, was appointed secretary and treasurer. The committee consisted of three members, messrs Quinn, Quaid and W. Ledley. It was noted that those present 'pledged themselves to use every effort to introduce the "Association" game into this city'.[59] In addition, they resolved that 'all gentlemen knowing the game and desiring to become members, be requested to communicate, at their earliest convenience, with the secretary'. A meeting was also scheduled for the following Friday at the same venue.[60]

The fact that some of rugby's organizers did not want another rival football code in the city did not go unnoticed. At the next gathering, the captain 'made a short speech, in which he assured the Rugby men in Dublin that the DAFC had not the slightest wish to cause a split in their (Rugby) ranks, or even induce a single player of the handling code to join the club', and 'rules were passed and the committee enlarged'.[61] They also 'decided to procure a private ground' and noted that they would play 'their opening scratch match' on Saturday 27 October at the Nine Acres, Phoenix Park, with 'all Association men being invited to attend'.[62] The chairman told 'the gentlemen present that the club could now put one team of "Association" men upon the field, all of them knowing the game' while it was noted that 'taking into consideration the difficulties to be surmounted, the announcement as the result of one week's work was very encouraging'. Dublin Association FC also enrolled 'several new members' and a good luck letter from the IFA's

---

55 Ibid. 56 *Sport*, 27 Oct. 1883. 57 *Sport*, 5 Apr. 1884. 58 *IT*, 16 Oct. 1883. 59 Ibid. 60 Ibid.
61 *IT*, 22 Oct. 1883. 62 Ibid.

secretary in Belfast was acknowledged.[63] The club also placed an advertisement in the national press seeking new members.[64]

The Dublin Association Football Club's first practice match was an intra-club one. Apparently, 'for an inaugural attempt, [it] was attended with a large share of success'.[65] The players involved were not novices and some had experience of the game in England, Scotland or in Belfast. It was noted that 'over a score of players, all of whom were old "association men", took part in the game'. These included players from Old Carthusians, Pilgrims, Notts County, St Mark's College, Old Westminster, Glasgow City and Cliftonville, and 'play was up to a high standard'. The teams were selected by Messrs Armatyge and Grier, with the latter man's team winning by five goals to three 'after a game extending over two forties'.[66] Dublin Association FC's early committee also included two Trinity men, J. Collins and H.D. Hamilton, and players from Minerva and Doncaster.[67]

Dublin Association FC initially struggled to gain the attention of newspapers despite their enthusiasm. Writing much later in 1926, one journalist recalled that 'in those days it was difficult to get even a few lines into the Dublin newspapers about the club and its matches, although adverse criticism of the sport was frequent and free'.[68] He added that 'one Dublin newspaper stipulated for payment at advertisement rates for reports of the matches', illustrating the early struggle to promote the game in the capital.[69] On 30 October 1883 they held another meeting, with the secretary noting 'the suppression of fixtures, letters and reports concerning the club by some of the Metropolitan papers, and considered that the Dublin Association Football Club were as much entitled to recognition and space in the columns of those journals as rugby clubs of equal standing'.[70] The club agreed to hold another practice match the following Saturday, and to invite 'all gentlemen knowing the association game' as well as those who did not. This public display, it was hoped, would 'push the real game of football'.[71]

By November 1883 they had 'secured the ground in connection with the Hospital for Incurables, Morehampton Road, Donnybrook, and now being fairly established' were 'open to receive challenges from other association clubs throughout the country, home and away'.[72] Clubs were asked to contact the secretary, James Hood, and 'all prospective players' were invited to join in a practice match scheduled for 3 p.m. on Saturday 3 November 1883.[73] This 'practice match' went ahead in Donnybrook, 'and was well attended'.[74] Prior to the game, 'sides were picked by Messrs Armatyge and Knox, the latter of whom set the ball in motion'. In addition, 'the game covered a period of two forties, and after a close fight resulted in favour of Knox's team by two goals to one'. Those to impress for the winners included Powell, Lawson, Redding and Foley, and Pocock, Butler, Cleig and Collins on the opposing team. They then arranged to hold a meeting

63 Ibid. 64 *IT*, 23 Oct. 1883. 65 *FJ*, 29 Oct. 1883. 66 Ibid. 67 *FJ*, 13 Nov. 1883. 68 *FSW*, 23 Jan. 1926. 69 Ibid. 70 *FJ*, 31 Oct. 1883. 71 Ibid. 72 *Sport*, 3 Nov. 1883. 73 Ibid. 74 *IT*, 5 Nov. 1883.

on Wednesday 7 September in the Royal Arcade Hotel on College Green.[75] This went ahead, with T. Armatyge presiding.[76] It appears that Frank T. Armatyge of 35 Great Charles Street had by then taken over as secretary, and the club officers and a committee were again elected. Those present decided the club colours would be red and blue, with white shorts. Training was arranged for 'Wednesday and Thursday, alternately', at '5.15 pm sharp', illustrating that those with less flexible work schedules were less likely to become involved. Subscriptions were collected from two new members and a 'scratch match' was arranged for the forthcoming Friday.[77] The fact that regular training was being held, and that the club had a growing membership and intended to purchase a new kit is indicative of their intentions. This intra-club match went ahead as scheduled at Donnybrook. Messrs Moorhead and Brown selected the teams, with the match won by the team picked by the former, despite having two players less in a 'game extending over two thirties'.[78] At this point, the club had not met any external playing opposition, but these games served to develop their skills and were an important social function for those involved.

A few weeks later, a report appeared of the club's supposed first match, which was gathered by *Sport*'s rugby correspondent and was clearly penned with the intention to run down the newly initiated code. It was noted that the game, held on the grounds of the Incurables' Hospital in Donnybrook, began as a five-a-side until two more players arrived shortly after the kick-off.[79] The writer was not very impressed by what he saw, and noted that 'the goalkeepers on Friday were hardly men to impress the public (consisting of two gentlemen, well-known rugby men, two small boys, and our correspondent) with the enormous responsibility of their position'.[80] One of the goalkeepers was 'considerably over thirty years of age, with thick-set beard, silver looking watch-guard, in ordinary clothes, minus the coat'.[81] Apparently, he 'kicked violently with his left foot, and his only idea of the game seemed to be that he should kick the ball whenever it came his way'.[82] Evidently, the game was played at a rather slow pace, as 'for twenty minutes he stood with collar up round his neck smoking a briar pipe. The tobacco did not last long, but then, this new player assumed a second coat, and, with hand in pocket, carefully guarded the precincts of the goal.'[83] The report also included references to hacking and dribbling and the lack of playing kit, with the writer also noting that 'out of all the players' he 'could not find two jerseys alike'.[84]

Dublin's second soccer club was set up later that year at Trinity College Dublin.[85] On Monday 19 November 1883, 'a general meeting' was held in what were then the New Buildings at Trinity College Dublin.[86] Those present decided to start a soccer club and 'some thirty members were enrolled'.[87] The club was captained by Mr Eamers, while the treasurer was named as Mr Collins FTCD.[88] 'Gentlemen wishing to join' were asked to contact the honorary secretary, Mr F.W.

75 Ibid. 76 *IT*, 8 Nov. 1883. 77 Ibid. 78 *DDE*, 10 Nov. 1883. 79 *Sport*, 17 Nov. 1883. 80 Ibid. 81 Ibid. 82 Ibid. 83 Ibid. 84 Ibid. 85 *Sport*, 24 Nov. 1883. 86 Ibid. 87 Ibid. 88 Ibid.

Moorhead, who lived nearby at 39 Lower Mount Street.[89] The group's first practice match had been played on Friday 16 November 1883 in the College Park,
with another arranged for the following Monday.[90] It appears that the new soccer
club formally replaced the Dublin University Hurley Club, as the latter's membership total had dropped below thirty, the number required for affiliation to the
University Athletic Union.[91]

The first match between the two Dublin clubs took place at the end of November
1883 when Dublin University AFC met Dublin Association FC at College Park
(Trinity), with the away team winning by four goals to nil.[92] Dublin Association
FC's goals were scored by T.W. Butler, of Hill View, Chapelizod, who scored twice,
and H.J. Hamilton and C. Clegg, while 'WD Hamilton's passing was a fine exhibition of skill'.[93] A return match was also scheduled but does not appear to have taken
place at that time.[94]

Later that year Dublin Association FC were confident enough to meet a team
from Belfast. At the beginning of December 1883 they played Belfast Athletics
on the Wesley College rugby team's grounds, which they had hired for what was
only the Dublin soccer club's second match against a club.[95] It appears that maintaining their original playing-field arrangement was unsustainable. The visit of
the Belfast team seems to have been encouraged by the IFA at their meeting the
previous month.[96] Exhibition matches were also backed by the IFA in Coleraine,
Monaghan and Derry that year, but there is scarce evidence this was a regularly
occurrence, particularly outside Ulster.[97] Dublin Association FC were beaten by
three goals to two, having squandered a two-goal half-time lead before 'a large
crowd of spectators'.[98] However, given the Belfast club's reputation, one reporter
felt that 'the result of the match augurs well for the future of the Association game
in the metropolis' and noted the strong performances of H.L. Pocock and William
Drummond Hamilton, 'one of the finest wing players in Ireland', and his brother,
Willoughby James. Others to impress were Collins and Buller, 'who played mag-
nificently', while Lawton in goal was 'an able custodian'.[99] It was also noted that
with 'a little more combination in the front division ... few teams would lower the
colours of the Trinity College or Dublin Association teams'.[100]

Some teams from other parts of Leinster travelled to Dublin to challenge
the Dublin Association FC. Prior to Christmas 1883 the Dublin Association FC
defeated Tullamore AFC from Offaly by four goals to nil at Donnybrook.[101] The
fact that they faced Tullamore again a few months later is illustrative of the lack
of local opposition.[102] University commitments were also a hindrance at times. In
January 1884, a match between the two Dublin clubs was postponed 'owing to the

89 Ibid.   90 *IT*, 20 Nov. 1883 and *FJ*, 23 Nov. 1883.   91 West, *The bold collegians*, p. 55.   92 *IT*,
29 Nov. 1883.   93 Ibid.   94 Ibid.   95 *BN*, 3 Dec. 1883. See also *FSW*, 23 Jan. 1926. Apparently,
the Dublin Association FC played against Cliftonville around this time, but contemporary reports
suggest otherwise.   96 *BN*, 10 Nov. 1883.   97 Cash Book of the IFA 1880–97, 8 Dec. 1883, IFA
Archives D/4/196/5/1, PRONI.   98 *BN*, 3 Dec. 1883.   99 Ibid.   100 Ibid.   101 *Midland
Counties Advertiser*, 27 Dec. 1883.   102 *Sport*, 8 Mar. 1884.

term not having opened, the examinations being in progress'.[103] By the beginning
of April 1884, the Dublin Association FC had played a total of seven matches,
and rightly claimed to be 'the pioneers of the dribbling code in the Metropolis'.[104]
Along with defeating Tullamore, they also had victories against Dublin University
AFC, who they played twice, Terenure College, who they also met on two separate
occasions, and who appear to have been their only school opposition that season,
and a military team at the Curragh Camp in County Kildare.[105] Their only loss
came in the aforementioned match against Belfast Athletics 'on whose team were
no fewer than five internationals'.[106] By April, Dublin Association FC had 'some
forty members' and these also included representatives of Oxford University,
Old Carthusians, Glasgow, Old Harrovians, Minerva, Cliftonville, Westminster,
Ramblers (London) and Southsea.'[107] It would therefore appear that Dublin's
first soccer club was heavily influenced by migrants to the city who had previous
experience of the game. By the end of the season, they had played nine matches,
winning six, having also travelled to England on their Easter tour, where they lost
to Walsall and Small Heath Alliance.[108]

By the start of the 1884–5 season the Dublin Association FC had increased their
membership to fifty, having elected thirteen at their AGM at the Wicklow Hotel.[109]
The club's captain was A.O. Clegg, while the vice captain was L.J. Pocock.[110] Their
committee was made up of F. Kennedy, M.G. Foley, W.W. Hamilton, J. White, J.
Caldwell and E.G. Hogg. Honorary secretary Fred W. Butler was resident at Hill
View, Chapelizod.[111] That same month, the club held their first practice match
of the season at their third 'new ground' at the Strand Road, Sandymount, with
'about twenty gentlemen' taking part in the game, which lasted 'eighty minutes'.[112]
They also invited visitors to come and view their practice matches, and hoped
to draw interest by advertising that the tram went past the gate of their pitch.[113]
Shortly afterwards, one writer offered an outline of the game's progress in the city
and felt, rather prematurely, that it was 'firmly established' there.[114] The teams
from Terenure College and Trinity College Dublin were also noted, as it was stated
that there had been three clubs now playing in the city 'under the dribbling code'
and an additional two military teams were also acknowledged.[115] The Dublin soccer
scene was 'augmented by the appearance of the Hibernian FC, recently formed in
connection with the [Royal] Hibernian Military School, and another club composed of some of the 71st Highland Light Infantry, at present stationed at Beggars'
Bush'.[116] The Hibernian Military School was located in the Phoenix Park area,
which meant the team had the space to play.[117] It was also stated that Dublin clubs
could expect visits from 'Cliftonville, Wellington Park, Curragh, Tullamore, Rhyll
(North Wales), and possibly one or two English clubs, who last year expressed

103 *Sport*, 26 Jan. 1884.   104 *Sport*, 5 Apr. 1884.   105 Ibid.   106 Ibid., Dublin Association FC
scored a total of twenty-four goals and conceded nine in those matches.   107 Ibid.   108 *Sport*, 26
Apr. 1884 and *IT*, 2 Oct. 1884.   109 *Sport*, 4 Oct. 1884.   110 Ibid.   111 Ibid.   112 *Sport*, 11 Oct.
1884.   113 Ibid.   114 *Sport*, 18 Oct. 1884.   115 Ibid.   116 Ibid.   117 Dickson, *Dublin*, p. 380.

wishes for fixtures'.[118] At this point they were still relying on opposition from out-side Dublin to supplement matches against the small number of teams located there.

By the middle of November 1884, Dublin Association FC were capable of field-ing a second team, a feat said to be a first in their locality.[119] These early soccer matches offered the opportunity for socializing. After Dublin Association FC's Second XI had beaten Hibernian at Chapelizod that month, 'both teams adjourned to the Mullingar Hotel, and joined in a smoking concert'.[120] British opponents came to the city later that winter, as Dublin Association FC played Welsh team Rhyll at Sandymount the following month.[121] Some weeks later, Dublin Association FC defeated Wellington Park, a Belfast team that featured 'one or two internationals' and 'also men who have won honours in other walks of the athletic world'.[122] These included 'Dodds, the Irish 100 yards champion; Herd, a noted long-distance man, and Gibb, the winner of numerous prizes on the track'.[123] After the match, the teams retired to the Wicklow Hotel, which appears to have been a base for a num-ber of their off-field activities, and 'a pleasant time was spent' with songs sung and the clubs, umpires and the press toasted, indicating that they were finally winning favour in some newspapers.[124]

The club at Trinity, Dublin University AFC, were also set 'to field a junior team' and it was felt by 'Goalpost' that 'with the schools taking to the game, there is every indication of a rapid increase in the popularity of Association football' in the city.[125] He also had hopes that a Leinster branch of the Irish Football Association would soon be formed, with a meeting scheduled to be held at the Wicklow Hotel to discuss a Leinster versus Ulster fixture.[126] At that point, it appears that Dublin Association FC and Dublin University AFC were the only Dublin clubs affiliated to the IFA.[127] Despite the sentiments about schools' soccer, noted above, there is little to suggest that the game was any challenge to rugby. By 1887 the Leinster Schools' Cup (for rugby) had been organized, but it was not until the early 1900s that a competition was established in Dublin for schools wishing to play soccer.[128]

Dublin's two main soccer clubs also attempted to branch out nationally given the scarcity of local opponents and looked to the IFA in Belfast. Both Dublin Association FC and Dublin University AFC were in the draw for the IFA Cup, along with seventy-nine other clubs, mostly from the north of Ireland, in November 1884, with the match between these two Dublin clubs the following month ending in a 1–1 draw at Sandymount before 'an enthusiastic crowd of spectators', which included 'several ladies'.[129] By May 1885, Dublin Association FC's fortunes on the field had declined. Over the 1884–5 season, they had played seven matches, losing

118 *Sport*, 18 Oct. 1884.   119 *Sport*, 15 Nov. 1884.   120 *Sport*, 22 Nov. 1884.   121 *Sport*, 13 Dec. 1884 and *IT*, 20 Dec. 1884.   122 *Sport*, 3 Jan. 1885 and *IT*, 26 Dec. 1884.   123 *Sport*, 3 Jan. 1885. 124 Ibid.   125 Ibid.   126 Ibid.   127 Cash Book of the IFA, 1880–97, 28 Oct. and 5 Nov. 1884, IFA Archives D/4/196/5/1, PRONI.   128 Seán P. Farragher & Annraoi Wyer, *Blackrock College, 1860–1995* (Dublin, 1995), p. 80 and *SI*, 24 Mar. 1907.   129 *Sport*, 29 Nov. 1884 and 3 Jan. 1885.

five, drawing one and winning only one.[130] It was reported that 'their ill success may be accounted for by their playing very first-class clubs and by the fact that they were, in the majority of cases, unable to put their best team into the field'.[131] The club had drawn 1–1 with Dublin University AFC in the aforementioned IFA Cup tie, but had not fulfilled the requirement to play the replay and were removed from the competition.[132] Their second team had enjoyed more success, winning four out of six matches against the Royal Hibernian Military School, Dublin University Second XI and the Highland Light Infantry Second XI.[133]

The 1885–6 season was not much more encouraging for Dublin Association FC or the Trinity club than their previous three. In October 1885 Dublin Association FC played their first practice match of the season, an intra-club game.[134] The news that a club was being formed in Wicklow was said to be helpful for them, indicating that they still struggled to find opponents.[135] That same month, the IFA were said to be willing to cover 'in large part' the expenses of any club who would visit Dublin for a match, but this seems a fanciful notion given their overall attitude to spreading interest in the game outside of Belfast.[136] Dublin Association FC were drawn against Belfast Athletics in the IFA Cup first round, while Dublin University AFC were pitted away against Albert FC, with no other Dublin clubs in the draw, which featured thirty-five clubs in total.[137]

The coming and going of players was a problem, particularly for the Trinity club. In January 1885, one reporter noted that 'football according to Association rules seems to have been under a cloud in this district for the past week or two'.[138] This was because 'the long vacations at Trinity and the Royal Hibernian School have sent the players at those seats of learning east, west, north and south, anywhere but on the fields of play'.[139] Rugby remained the most popular football code at Trinity College. A December 1886 soccer match between Dublin Association FC and Dublin University AFC was said to have attracted 'a large number of spectators', mainly because a rugby fixture was also being played there that day.[140]

Connections with a new club in the Midlands were nurtured earlier that year in an attempt to provide more fixtures. In January 1886 Dublin Association FC travelled to Athlone to meet 'the local club', which was 'only a short time started'.[141] In the 1886–7 season Dublin Association FC continued to look outside of Dublin for matches due to the scarcity of soccer clubs in the locality. They travelled to Athlone for a match on St Patrick's Day 1887 against a club 'only two months in existence', and were beaten 2–1.[142] Tom Hunt has noted that soccer in Westmeath in the late nineteenth century was 'informal, devoid of structure and formal competition, and restricted to a narrow Athlone-based social group', and that 'in this

130 Ibid., 2 May 1885. 131 Ibid. 132 Ibid. and *Sport*, 24 Jan. 1885 and 2 May 1885. They had also beaten the same club 6–1, but had also lost 0–2 to them, in friendly matches. In addition, they suffered defeats against the 71st Highland Light Infantry (0–3), Old Park (1–3), Ulster (2–6) and Cliftonville (0–1). 133 Ibid., 2 May 1885. 134 Ibid., 10 Oct. 1885. 135 Ibid. 136 Ibid., 7 Nov. 1885. 137 Ibid., 24 Oct. 1885. 138 Ibid., 3 Jan. 1885. 139 Ibid. 140 Ibid., 11 Dec. 1886. 141 Ibid., 23 Jan. 1886. 142 Ibid., 12 and 19 Mar. 1887.

phase of development friendly matches were organized through personal contact within a socially restricted network'.[143] On New Year's Eve 1887, at Ranelagh
School grounds in Westmeath, the Athlone club defeated a Dublin Association FC
team that had only eight players present, and had to be supplemented by 'a couple
of subs'.[144] The Westmeath team featured six students from Ranelagh School and
two military men as well as landowner Orlando Coote.[145]

By the end of 1887 three new teams had appeared on the fledgling Dublin
soccer scene – Montpelier, Britannia and Bell's Academy – with a man who
had experience of the game at a number of other clubs one of Britannia's key
players.[146] Britannia were captained by J. Connor, formerly of Glentoran and
Cliftonville.[147] Britannia had been founded in 1887 and was the club of the
Central Model School.[148] Bell's Academy, located at 46 North Great George's
Street, was an institute where classes were held for 'excise, clerkships and Civil
Service appointments', with Hamilton Bell as principal.[149] The more working-
class Montpelier club were formed in 1887 from a cricket club in Stoneybatter,
and Clenet has stated that they were nationalist in outlook as they also appeared
at local GAA athletic meetings.[150]

Despite their presence, by the end of 1888, the situation had not greatly
improved as the Dublin Association FC and Dublin University AFC were the only
two Dublin clubs in the IFA's list of registered senior clubs.[151] Dublin Association
FC's leading administrator at that time was William St George Perrott, who resided
at St Mary's Lodge, Simmonscourt Road, while L.V. Bennett of Ellerslie, Temple
Road, Rathmines was listed in the press as Dublin University AFC's contact.[152] In
October 1888 Dublin Association FC were defeated 4–0 at home by Glentoran in
the first round of the IFA Cup but received praise for their 'gentlemanly play'.[153]
Dublin University AFC forfeited their match against Whiteabbey in the same
round as they could not field a team until term began in November.[154] Early in
December, Dublin University AFC met the Dublin Association FC at London
Bridge Road ground in 'an important match', which would 'entitle the winning
club to the position of premier', illustrating the continued rivalry between the two
in the capital and the scarcity of other local challengers.[155] While festive football
fixtures would later become an important tradition in British leagues, at Christmas
1888 soccer in Dublin was said to 'have been very quiet' as Trinity and Hibernians
were 'away'.[156] Dublin Association FC met a Gloucestershire military team that
month but could field only seven players, and 'as usual, started very late' and were
defeated.[157] On 21 December 1888 the Dublin Association FC held a general meeting in the Wicklow Hotel 'to consider the advisability of winding up the club on

143 Hunt, *Sport and society in Victorian Ireland*, p. 173. 144 *Sport*, 7 Jan. 1888. 145 Hunt,
Sport and society in Victorian Ireland, p. 172. 146 *Sport*, 10 Dec. 1887. 147 Ibid. 148 Clenet,
'Association football in Dublin', p. 807. 149 *FJ*, 4 Mar. 1889. 150 Clenet, 'Association football in Dublin', p. 807 and Garnham, *Association football and society*, p. 17. 151 *UFCN*, 7 Dec.
1888. 152 Ibid. 153 Ibid., 26 Oct. 1888 and *Sport*, 27 Oct. 1888. 154 *UFCN*, 12 Oct.
1888. 155 Ibid., 7 Dec. 1888. 156 *Sport*, 29 Dec. 1888. 157 Ibid.

account of the apathy of the members'.[158] However, 'it was decided to keep on the club. A new committee was formed, and a new secretary elected'.[159]

The two Dublin clubs affiliated to the IFA contrasted with fifteen Dublin-based rugby clubs registered with the Irish Rugby Football Union for the 1887–8 season.[160] By the end of 1888, the number of IRFU-registered rugby clubs had risen to twenty-one.[161] Along with competition from rugby, by the late 1880s Dublin's soccer clubs also faced competition from Gaelic football, with a Dublin championship operational in addition to clubs' challenge matches by 1887.[162] Wren, De Burca and Gorry have estimated that in 1888 there were 'close on 120 Gaelic football clubs' in Dublin, 114 of which were registered with the GAA, and around 6,000 Gaelic footballers.[163] Although the overall number of affiliated clubs dropped to fifty-two in 1890 with the Parnell Split, these figures are indicative of the early interest in Gaelic football there, and the challenge these GAA clubs provided to soccer in terms of public interest levels and the allegiances of players, administrators, patrons and supporters.[164]

By March 1889, there were two military teams in Dublin, 'all owing to the Army Cup', which was in its first year having been promoted by the FA's president, Major Marindin.[165] The Irish Army Football Association had established this cup and was affiliated to the IFA by the late 1880s.[166] Progress in the growth of Dublin soccer clubs remained slow in 1889, and the city's two main clubs were relatively content to keep to themselves when it came to local representative selection. In March 1889, delegates from Dublin University AFC and Dublin Association FC met and selected a team composed of their own players to represent Leinster against Ulster in 'the annual interprovincial match' in Belfast the following month, which Ulster won by three goals to two.[167] However, Dublin did not host its first of these fixtures until the teams met at Sandymount in December 1894.[168]

In April 1889 one of *Ulster Football and Cycling News'* reporters noted a further glimmer of hope that the game might take off.[169] He stated that

> It may be interesting to record the growth of Association football in Dublin. On last Saturday evening, in the fifteen-acres ground, Phoenix Park, a well-contested game, between a young club named Montpelier FC and a team composed of players from the teachers of the Hibernian School and the Bell's Academy Clubs, resulted in a scoreless draw, neither side being able to score. It may be mentioned that two of the Montpelier players formerly belonged to the late Beechmount FC of Belfast. Good old Beechmount, a few more of your players are wanted in Dublin to spread the game. For the

158 Ibid. 159 Ibid. 160 Ibid. 161 Ibid. 162 Jim Wren, Marcus de Búrca & David Gorry, *The Gaelic Athletic Association in Dublin*, i: *1884–1959*, ed. William Nolan (Dublin, 2005), p. 13. 163 Ibid., pp 17–19. 164 Ibid., p. 26. 165 *UFCN*, 15 Mar. 1889. 166 Garnham, *Association football and society*, p. 19 and *IT*, 30 Mar. 1899. 167 *Sport*, 30 Mar. 1889; *DE*, 4 Apr. 1889. 168 *II*, 10 Dec. 1894; *EH*, 28 Jan. 1899. 169 *UFCN*, 12 Apr. 1889.

Montpelier, as a young club, they all played a good game, while Blaney, the
two Sheehans, and Wilgar played best for the scholars.[170]

However, the decline of the Bell's Academy club, with a scarcity of opposition
evident, was imminent. Members attempted to resurrect it by renaming the club
Richfield, with A.P. Magill becoming honorary secretary and Hamilton Bell named
as honorary treasurer at a meeting in October 1889.[171] Both men would later take
up governmental positions and the fledgling club developed ties with a much more
successful one, Bohemians.[172]

Dublin Association FC and Dublin University AFC were, by late 1889, still
meeting annually in the IFA Cup first round, given they were the only Dublin
clubs to register with the national soccer governing body. Unlike the previous year,
Dublin University AFC were allowed to push the game back until their students
returned in early November, and both sides were reported to be 'greatly strengthened' that season, but it was the Dublin Association club who progressed.[173] By the
end of November 1889, Dublin Association FC had been drawn against Limavady
in the fourth round of the IFA Cup having received a bye in the previous round.[174]
The match was played at Sandymount, with the home team winning 'a splendid
game' with the help of a number of soldiers from the 93rd Highlanders on their
team, against whom Limavady later protested.[175] The protest was dismissed and
Dublin Association FC were drawn to face Cliftonville on 25 January 1890 in the
semi-final.[176]

As 1889 drew to a close there was some indication of further promise. A County
Dublin selection that met a team representing Derry in Belfast a few days after
Christmas 1889 was said to be made up of 'Trinity, Dublin Association and the
doughty champions of the Army Cup from the Curragh'.[177] These 'county con-
tests' were noted as being 'a new feature of the Christmas soccer programme that
year with a match against County Antrim arranged the following day.[178] The Dublin
selection won both matches, illustrating further that the potential was certainly
there, particularly when military assistance was given.[179] They were strengthened
by the inclusion of Neill of Notts County and Carson of Cambridge University,
while they also fielded four military players and Irish international Manliffe Francis
Goodbody.[180]

Dublin Association FC's IFA Cup semi-final match in January 1890 took place
in Belfast against Cliftonville and was a close contest with the local side winning
3–2.[181] Both teams had overcome influenza in the week before the match, with nine
players from the Dublin Association FC affected.[182] The fixture was replayed after
a protest by the Dublin club that one of the umpires was not from a neutral club,

170 Ibid.   171 O'Mahony (ed.), *Bohemian Football Club golden jubilee souvenir*, p. 9.   172 Ibid.
173 *UFCN*, 20 Sept., 8 Nov. 1889.   174 *Sport*, 30 Nov. 1889.   175 *Sport*, 14 Dec. 1889; *UCFN*,
22 Nov. 1889.   176 *Sport*, 14 Dec. 1889.   177 *UFCN*, 20 Dec. 1889.   178 Ibid. and 27 Dec.
1889.   179 Ibid., 3 Jan. 1890.   180 Ibid.   181 Ibid., 31 Jan. 1890.   182 Ibid., 17 and 24 Jan.
1890.

with Cliftonville again winning a tough encounter, this time by four goals to two, against a team that contained four members of the Argyle Highlanders, the Army Cup holders.[183] Garnham has stated that the Dublin Association Football Club disbanded following a disagreement with the IFA over the result of this match. However, a few of the club's members later helped to form the Leinster Nomads club.[184]

By the autumn of 1890 association football was, according to one *Ulster Football and Cycling News* reporter, 'flourishing in the North' but 'rapidly dying out in the South', with both the Dublin Association FC and Dublin University AFC having 'ceased to exist'.[185] He felt that 'the poor success of the Association game in the capital may be attributed to the fact that the Rugby code is intensely popular there', although he remained hopeful that 'if the game but advances as rapidly in public favour as it has done in the last decade, it will not be long before we will have more clubs in the Association than we will know how to deal with'.[186]

Dublin Association FC did not appear in the IFA Cup first round draw for the 1890–1 season, although their closest city rivals remained, as Dublin University AFC faced the Gordons (Highlanders) in their opening match.[187] The insecure nature of association football was not unique to Dublin, with one correspondent representative of Queenstown AFC of Cork, established in February 1889 by 'a few followers of the association game', noting in *Sport* that 'at the beginning of 1889 scratch teams were all that could be relied upon'.[188] However, by the start of 1890 this had improved and they had played sixteen matches, having been formally established at the start of the 1889–90 season.[189] As David Toms has shown, by 1900, while the majority of teams there were based in military barracks, there was also 'a fine mix of educational, residential and associational clubs' located within Cork city.[190]

The early 1890s saw the emergence of Bohemians FC, with the club apparently founded at the Gate Lodge, at Phoenix Park's North Circular Road entrance, in the opening year of the decade.[191] One history of the club published in 1945 also states that its initial meeting consisted of Richfield players, Dublin medical students and some junior masters from the Hibernian Military School.[192] Writing in 1940, William P. Murphy stated that Bohemians were formed through an amalgamation of Montpelier FC and Hibernian FC and that their initial ground was the Fifteen Acres at Phoenix Park, with goalposts carried from the gate lodge at the entrance for matches.[193] Contemporary newspaper evidence of the club's actual foundation date is scarce. In September 1891 Bohemians held their AGM, having apparently been established two years prior to this, which raises some doubts about whether the club was actually founded in 1890.[194]

183 *FJ*, 27 Jan. 1890; *UFCN*, 31 Jan. and 14 Feb. 1890; *Sport*, 8 and 15 Feb. 1890.   184 Garnham, *Association football and society*, p. 6.   185 *UFCN*, 19 Sept. 1890.   186 Ibid.   187 Ibid., 26 Sept. 1890.   188 *Sport*, 1 Feb. 1890.   189 Ibid.   190 Toms, *Soccer in Munster*, p. 15.   191 O'Mahony (ed.), *Bohemian Football Club golden jubilee souvenir*, p. 1.   192 Ibid.   193 *SI*, 15 Dec. 1940. 194 *Sport*, 19 Sept. 1891.

The membership of the early Bohemians club had a strong medical connection at playing and administrative levels, with six men who later became doctors taking up organizational roles; other key members included Hamilton Bell, who became treasurer, while civil servant Dudley Hussey chaired the club's first meeting.[195] Following a vote, the name Bohemians was chosen in reference to the club's search for a ground.[196] Garnham has noted the role of Alexander Blaney as chairman of the early Bohemians club, while there were three Sheehan brothers – William, James and George – in attendance at the club's first meeting. These men all had experience of school soccer in Belfast; the Sheehans had played for Belfast Mercantile College while Blaney had played for St Malachy's College, as well as Cliftonville.[197] By 1892, Blaney had been 'elected a Fellow of the RUI [Royal University of Ireland] in consideration of his distinguished knowledge', with this award said to be 'one of the University's highest honours'.[198]

Bohemians' early matches were non-competitive. In February 1891 they played Geneva Cross AFC at the Esplanade, Royal Barracks, which later became Collins Barracks.[199] While the passing was said to be good, it was noted that 'both teams suffered from want of practice'.[200] The following month Bohemians defeated a team from Cecilia Street School of Medicine by 7–0 in what was described as a 'rough-and-tumble' game. The Cecelia Street School team were organized by a Mr Cassidy and it was noted that 'a few of the best Bohemians hail from that school'.[201]

In 1890, the Emerald Football Club was established by workers of the General Post Office, which had been located since 1818 in what was then Sackville Street (now O'Connell Street).[202] Members of the Emerald club, which had first and second teams, apparently had flexible work hours as they were requested to meet at 11 a.m. 'for general practice' on Thursdays at the Nine Acres in Phoenix Park.[203] Despite earlier fears, there is scarce evidence that soccer clubs led to the demise of rugby selections in Dublin at this time. In November 1889, Wanderers' captain F.O. Stoker played for Dublin Association FC against Lancashire Regiment.[204] As will be seen in this book, numerous other players also switched codes, and changed to other sporting clubs, but the direct transferral of full clubs, as occurred elsewhere, was not a common occurrence in Dublin in the 1880s. A soccer club was founded at the Mater Misercordiae Hospital (opened in 1861), in November 1891 by Frank Whitaker, 'an enthusiastic lover of the dribbling code'.[205] He had 'received a shilling subscription from some and downright opposition from others', who were more interested in maintaining the 'moribund rugby club' which had been in existence there.[206] The rugby club was revived, but Whitaker was supported by some northern players, and although 'some intolerant rugbyites obstructed the

195 O'Mahony (ed.), *Bohemian Football Club golden jubilee souvenir*, p. 9. 196 Ibid. 197 Garnham, *Association football and society*, p. 17; *UFCN*, 20 Oct. 1893. 198 *UFCN*, 29 Jan. 1892. 199 *Sport*, 21 Feb. 1891. 200 Ibid. 201 Ibid., 21 Mar. 1891. 202 Garnham, *Association football and society*, p. 49; *FJ*, 31 Mar. 1818. 203 *EH*, 7 Dec. 1892; *IDI*, 12 Jan. 1893. 204 *Sport*, 16 Nov. 1889. 205 *IE*, 25 Sept. 1861; *Sport*, 5 Nov. 1892. 206 *Sport*, 5 Nov. 1892.

little band of pioneers in every possible way', they eventually established cordial relations and 'the two clubs worked together in the greatest concord'.[207]

THE FOUNDATION OF THE LEINSTER FOOTBALL ASSOCIATION

Given the lack of surviving club files from that era, it is unclear how much communication there was between the Dublin Association FC and Dublin University AFC in regard to promoting the game, other than in their irregular friendly and IFA Cup matches and in selecting the Leinster team to face Ulster.[208] However, between them, they were unable to organize a soccer league or cup competition in the 1880s. By the latter part of that decade, county associations were present in Antrim and Derry and by January 1890 Down had its own association, while a Mid-Ulster Association was established by the spring of 1888.[209] It was posited in some sections of the sporting press that Dublin soccer was being ignored by the IFA. One reporter stated that

> There are flattering accounts in from a good many country districts, notably Cookstown, East Antrim, Lurgan and Armagh. The committee have decided to play an exhibition match at Strabane. In time, perhaps the association committee may remember that there is such a place as Dublin in Ireland.[210]

Some representative teams from the north had in fact visited Dublin for friendly matches, with a County Antrim team playing a County Dublin selection in late March 1890 as well as an army team in the Curragh, County Kildare.[211] A few clubs also visited for matches following encouragement from the IFA, including, as mentioned, Belfast Athletics in 1883.[212]

Some Dublin clubs did appeal to the IFA for financial assistance, but appear to have had little success. Dublin Association FC called off a trip north to play Ballynafeigh in January 1889 as the IFA refused to give them £3 for expenses.[213] In November 1890, a proposal for funding by an unnamed Dublin club was adjourned at an IFA committee meeting, along with that to bring the Shamrock club of Lisburn to the city for an exhibition match.[214] There is no evidence of a subsequent visit from the Lisburn team. The following month, the IFA's committee decided to send a representative to Dublin to investigate further after a proposal from Clonliffe FC for a 'grant to rig them out with ground and all the other accessories', but again, there is no evidence that this resulted in anything concrete.[215]

In November 1891 one journalist noted 'a revival of the Association game in Dublin' and stated that 'a few teams have taken it up as well', with Bohemians due to face Cliftonville Olympic in Belfast on Boxing Day.[216] The aforementioned Mater

207 Ibid. 208 Ibid., 30 Mar. 1889. 209 Cash Book of the IFA 1880–97, 3 Oct. 1887, 12 May 1888, 30 Aug. 1888 and 8 Jan. 1890, IFA Archives D/4/196/5/1, PRONI. 210 Ibid., 10 Oct. 1891. 211 *UFCN*, 4 Apr. 1890. 212 *BN*, 3 Dec. 1883. 213 *UFCN*, 11 Jan. 1889. 214 Ibid., 14 Nov. 1890. 215 Ibid., 5 Dec. 1890. 216 Ibid., 20 Nov. 1891.

Hospital team, whose honorary secretary, Frank Whitaker, was 'indefatigable in his endeavours to give the game a hold', were noted as being 'the only Dublin hospital team' at that point, and defeated a Trinity selection on the hospital grounds by three goals to nil that same month.[217] Bohemians travelled to the Curragh in late November 1891 and beat 'the premier team of the camp', the Engineers, by three goals to one.[218] The following month, Bohemians were reported to be the first junior soccer club from Dublin to visit Belfast, and their team included 'old Belfasters' William Sheehan (Belfast Mercantile Academy), James Sheehan (Richmond) and Alexander Blaney (St Malachy's College).[219]

By the middle of January 1892 soccer was said to be 'gaining ground in Dublin, there being quite a large number of junior clubs in the Metropolis playing the dribbling code', although this was clearly an exaggeration[220] The Leinster Nomads continued in the vein of their predecessors, mainly playing irregularly held friendly matches. The club's fixture list that month included matches against Bohemians and Britannia, while they also took on three military teams.[221] In February the Leinster Nomads played Cliftonville at Sandymount, with both teams playing with ten men as Leinster Nomads did not have a full team and had to borrow a Cliftonville player, Martin, to keep goal.[222] The IFA's committee granted £6 to Cliftonville to play this exhibition match following the success of Bohemians' trip north at Christmas.[223] Cliftonville won by four goals to two, but interest in the game itself apparently remained low in the city.[224] One northern reporter stated that having arrived in a snowy Amiens Street on the train from Belfast, the travelling party went to Atkin's Hotel. He and his acquaintances were taken by a local jarvey to Lansdowne Road rather than the soccer venue, and saw this as an indication of how little the general public in Dublin knew about soccer.[225] The Nomads team contained a number of 'good' players but showed 'a total lack of combination'.[226] The match was followed by 'dinner in the Tavistock' where 'a high old time was spent' by both teams.[227] In October 1892, they were the only Dublin team listed in the draw for the IFA Cup, and had evidently improved by then, beating Moyola Park of Castledawson away by four goals to one the following month in the second round.[228]

Briggs and Dodd have noted the importance of members of the Leinster Nomads in raising attention to the game's plight in Dublin, as the representative of the former Dublin Association club had called for more to be done in the Leinster area at the IFA's AGM in 1890.[229] The Leinster Nomads' IFA Cup run in the 1892–3 season, when they reached the quarter-final (losing to Distillery in December 1892), was noteworthy, but despite this, there is little evidence that the

217 Ibid. and 25 Dec. 1891.   218 Ibid., 4 Dec. 1891.   219 Ibid., 25 Dec. 1890.   220 Ibid., 15 Jan. 1892.   221 *FJ*, 20 and 23 Jan. 1892.   222 Ibid., 22 Feb. 1892.   223 Ibid.   224 Ibid.   225 *UFC N*, 26 Feb. 1892.   226 Ibid.   227 Ibid.   228 Ibid., 21 Oct. and 11 Nov. 1892.   229 George Briggs & Joe Dodd, *100 years of the LFA Leinster Football Association: centenary yearbook, 1892–1992* (Dublin, 1993), p. 22.

national governing body for the game were willing to take direct action to set up a Dublin Football Association.[230] Although some reporters circulated the idea of the benefits of having a football association in Ireland's capital city, Dublin clubs did not get their first local governing body until late autumn in 1892, and this came through the efforts of local clubs.[231] The Leinster Football Association was founded on 26 October 1892 at the Wicklow Hotel (before Leinster Nomads' cup run had ended), with representatives of the clubs of Bohemians, Montpelier, Leinster Nomads, St Helen's School and Dublin University in attendance. The Reverend Canon Morley of St Helen's School (Pembroke Road) was in the chair at the inaugural meeting and 'the association was duly formed on the proposition of Mr A. Blaney, seconded by Mr Sheehan', both of whom had experience of administrative duties at Bohemians.[232] At the Leinster FA's inaugural meeting, a sub-committee made up of one delegate per club was instructed to draw up the rules, a challenge cup was to be procured for registered clubs, and Bohemians representative Dudley Hussey was appointed as honorary secretary.[233]

The role of the Boys' Brigade in promoting soccer was recognized in that they were given an honorary affiliation to the Leinster Football Association.[234] One reporter noted in November 1892 that their companies were starting soccer in Dublin at that time, and the following month the 7th Dublin Company beat the 9th Company at Tokay Park.[235] The first Boys' Brigade company in Dublin had been founded through St Matthias's Church in 1891 and in 1894 a soccer league for Boys' Brigade teams was operational there.[236] The first match between Dublin and Belfast selections took place in 1895.[237]

There were also clubs present in Dublin under the names of Chapelizod, the Mater Hospital, Emeralds, the GPO, Ordnance Survey and Phoenix in the winter of 1892.[238] School teams included Catholic University School, Blackrock College, Terenure College and Kingstown Grammar School, while army selections included the Scots Guards, the Royal Hussars, Royal Irish Rifles, Gordon Highlanders and the Sussex Regiment.[239] These generally remained too strong for the local civilian teams, most of which were still in their infancy. 'Critic' noted the defeat of Leinster Nomads, Trinity and Bohemians by military teams on the same weekend in November 1892, and advised the Leinster FA to 'consider well before allowing army teams to compete for the Leinster Cup'.[240] At the Leinster FA's Executive meeting at the Central Hotel in Dublin at the end of November, which was chaired by Mr Perrott and attended by delegates from Leinster Nomads, Bohemians and Dublin University AFC, it was agreed that military teams indeed would be

230 Ibid. and *UFCN*, 16 Dec. 1892; and *Sport*, 24 Dec. 1892.   **231** See, for example, *UFCN*, 14 Mar. 1890.   **232** *IT*, 27 Oct. 1892.   **233** Ibid.   **234** Garnham, *Association football and society*, p. 17.   **235** *UFCN*, 11 Nov. and 16 Dec. 1892.   **236** Brendan Power, 'The functions of association football in the Boys' Brigade in Ireland, 1888–1914' in Leann Lane & William Murphy (eds), *Leisure and the Irish in the nineteenth century* (Liverpool, 2016), pp 41–58, pp 41, 55.   **237** Garnham, *Association football and society*, p. 17   **238** Briggs & Dodd, *100 years of the LFA*, p. 26.   **239** Ibid.   **240** *UFCN*, 25 Nov. 1892.

excluded from the competition.[241] Newspaper reports also allude to the continued
presence of Britannia around this time.[242] Other Leinster-based clubs included
military teams in Athlone, Dundalk and Kilkenny.[243] There were also civilian teams
in Mullingar and Wicklow and further south, there was also a team in Kilkenny.[244]
One reporter, noting the formation of a Leinster Association for the game, wrote
in November 1892 that 'there is no doubt that Dublin is a fine field for Association
football, and once properly started it should catch on'.[245] Although similar sentiments had previously been expressed in the press, with the foundation of a local
administrative structure for the game, this comment offered greater promise.

CONCLUSION

While some rugby enthusiasts had initially been concerned about soccer taking
over their sporting space, there is little to suggest any major conflict between these
codes in that decade, but tensions were clear, including at the Mater Hospital.
Similarly, the GAA in Dublin did not suffer from any huge loss of players to soccer in the 1880s. However, the presence of two alternative football codes by the
mid-1880s undoubtedly hindered soccer's growth in Dublin. Despite this, by the
autumn of 1892, there were at least twenty-two soccer teams in Dublin. Many of
these clubs grew out of existing institutions or were formed through those with
previous experience of the game. However, this growth had only taken place in
earnest at the start of the decade, and Dublin's first two clubs, Dublin Association
FC and Dublin University AFC, struggled to find regular opponents throughout
the 1880s, with their only competitive matches coming in the IFA Cup against each
other and teams in the north of Ireland. At times both struggled to field teams and
while they also occasionally met clubs from other counties, there was also a dearth
of clubs in nearby counties such as Louth and Meath, which meant that Dublin's
civilian clubs looked to the Curragh military base for opposition, and to military
teams stationed in Dublin itself. Meath's first match in the association code did not
take place until January 1891 when a Ladyrath selection travelled from Monaghan
to play a Slane team.[246] The presence of military teams was therefore crucial to
keeping the game alive in the capital, but the lack of a regular calendar of league
and cup matches hindered the game's spread there in the 1880s. Not every military selection was well organized, however, with 'a team of the Lincoln Regiment',
which met the Dublin Association FC in November 1887 at London Bridge Road
fielding fifteen players, 'which created confusion amongst themselves and seemed
to disorganize the Dublin men'.[247] In any case, most soccer clubs sprung up in
Dublin and throughout Ireland without the assistance of the military, with, for
example, a club established in the County Donegal village of Kerrykeel in the early

241 Ibid., 2 Dec. 1892. 242 *Sport*, 5 Nov. 1892; *EH*, 14 Nov. 1892. 243 Joe Dodd, *100 years: a
history: Leinster Senior League centenary, 1896/7–1996/7* (Dublin, 1997), pp 33–58. 244 *Sport*, 5
Nov. 1892. 245 Ibid. 246 Ibid., 24 Jan. 1891. 247 Ibid., 12 Nov. 1887.

1880s by local man P.G. Green, who had brought back a football after seeing it on sale in a shop window in Derry city, and was subsequently heavily involved in the foundation and early administration of the County Donegal FA.[248] The ways in which the game spread not just in Ireland but globally varied, and as Taylor has stated, soccer, 'along with other British sports, was highly fashionable' and associated with 'modernity' in the late nineteenth century.[249]

As noted, by 1890 Dublin Association FC had strengthened sufficiently to reach the IFA Cup semi-final, with a number of military players said to have assisted the team in this.[250] The foundation of the Leinster FA in October 1892 was in many ways inevitable, as governing bodies for sport grew substantially in the late nineteenth century and soccer initially grew in popularity in many cities around the world. However, the early figure for registered Dublin clubs was quite low with only five represented. When the County Donegal FA was founded in 1894, for example, there were eight clubs present at the inaugural meeting.[251] Without the input of key individuals such as Alexander Blaney and the Reverend Canon Morley soccer in Dublin may have been further delayed. Competitive structures were not, however, as slow to emerge as in Cork, where the Munster FA was not founded until 1901.[252] Chapter two looks at Dublin's early competitions and clubs and how the game took off in the late 1890s.

248 *UFCN*, 8 Nov. 1895. See also Curran, *The development of sport in Donegal*, pp 163–98 and 'The role of the provincial press in the development of association football in pre-First World War Ulster' in Kenneally & O'Donnell (eds), *The Irish regional press, 1892–2018*, pp 53–64. **249** Taylor, 'The global spread of football', p. 186. **250** *Sport*, 14 Dec. 1889 and *UFCN*, 22 Nov. 1889. **251** Conor Curran, *Sport in Donegal: a history* (Dublin, 2010), p. 53. **252** Garnham, *Association football and society*, p. 6.

2

The development of competitions and clubs,
1893–1921

THE EARLY DAYS OF THE LEINSTER FA SENIOR CUP

Despite the establishment of the Leinster FA in October 1892, monetary assistance from the IFA in Belfast was not immediately forthcoming, although they did
express their approval of the new regional body and supplied a copy of their rules.[1]
In January 1893, the secretary of the Leinster FA, Dudley Hussey, was asked by
that body to write to the IFA to seek funding and a cup to help with the spread of
the game in the new organization's opening season.[2] They also hoped to organize
an inter-provincial match 'to be played in Dublin as an exhibition game', but the
IFA noted at their own meeting that month that this 'could not be entertained'.[3]
Similarly, the IFA turned down an application from Linfield FC for a grant to visit
Dublin for a match at the end of January.[4] One reporter at that time noted that 'the
IFA are a peculiar body, and although anxious to foster provincial football won't
spend any money this season to do so'.[5] This was also the case in Donegal, whereby
clubs in the County Donegal FA had affiliated to the IFA by the middle of the decade, but received scarce financial support or administrative visits and the fledgling
organization there relied heavily on individuals.[6]

Subsequent reports continued to highlight the IFA's reluctance to financially
aid the game's growth in the capital. At the Leinster FA's meeting in February
1893, it was stated that the IFA had refused to give them a grant for that year.[7] One
journalist remarked that this policy had produced 'a very bad effect in Dublin',
and he also stated sarcastically that 'the game (thanks to a few enthusiasts of the
old school) is going ahead well, notwithstanding the IFA's *generosity* in the matter'.[8]
Eventually, despite their initial refusal, the IFA did agree to have the interprovincial match in April, but Leinster could not field a team and it had to be postponed.[9]
The IFA's hesitation in financing the game in Dublin in the Leinster FA's first
season appears to have been because the Dublin organization had not initially affiliated to the national body, with one journalist hopeful that, as they had done this
by April, there would be more interaction between the two governing bodies in the

---

1 *ISN*, 4 Feb. 1899. 2 *UFCN*, 20 Jan. 1893. 3 Ibid. 4 Ibid. 5 Ibid., 27 Jan. 1893. 6 Curran,
The development of sport in Donegal, pp 165–71. 7 *IDI*, 16 Feb. 1893. 8 *UFCN*, 17 Mar.
1893. 9 Ibid. and 7 Apr. 1893.

coming seasons.[10] It is also apparent that the IFA were eager to see how the first season would develop before stepping in to help financially. At the IFA's general meeting the following month, it was agreed that their new committee would 'look into the question' given that 'the first practical step' had been taken by those in Dublin in establishing an organization.[11]

Despite the IFA's reluctance to assist, the Leinster FA had pushed on with its own competitions in its first season. In February 1893 the Leinster FA's Challenge Cup first round draw was made, with just four teams represented in what effectively were semi-finals.[12] All matches were scheduled for Leinster Nomads' ground at Sandymount, with the home team facing Montpelier while Dublin University took on Bohemians, who had already played five drawn 'private' matches against the Trinity club.[13] There was no involvement of military teams, although the game in Dublin remained popular with soldiers. While general admission for these matches was 6*d.*, soldiers gained entry at a reduced rate of 3*d.* and ladies were charged nothing.[14] Schoolboys were given entry to cup matches at half-price, in an attempt to increase interest in the game.[15]

Having drawn their initial match, Leinster Nomads beat Montpelier 4–0 at Sandymount in the replay on 4 March 1893.[16] In the second semi-final, Bohemians, wearing scarlet and white, faced Dublin University, who wore light blue and black, on Saturday 18 February at Sandymount.[17] 'Several hundred spectators' attended the match, which Dublin University won 6–0, with the ground 'in splendid condition'.[18] It was noted that 'the game was keenly but fairly contested throughout, but the hooting and remarks of some of the spectators was simply disgraceful'.[19] After a protest by Bohemians was thrown out, the final was advertised in the press, and publicity was also sought through 'two handcarts and three sandwich men promenading the streets the week previous to the tie'.[20] It was played at Sandymount on 11 March 1893, with 'nearly a thousand' spectators watching the Leinster Nomads, playing on their home pitch, defeat Dublin University AFC 2–0.[21] Apparently 'the play was extremely good' and the cup and gold medals were presented to the winners afterwards.[22]

Sandymount was an important location for Dublin's early matches, with the nearby tram line easing transport difficulties by the late nineteenth century.[23] By 1940 the Leinster Nomads' ground on the road leading to Sandymount Green had been built over, but 1890s team member James H. Webb described it as once being 'splendid' and 'as level as a billiard table'. He also noted that 'the sandy soil gave it that grand springy surface such as one sees at Portmarnock Golf Club'.[24] Webb recalled of the 1893 Leinster Cup final that

> In those days ... groundsmen were not readily available to mark the pitch in nice white lines, and a more permanent form of marking was provided

10 Ibid., 7 Apr. 1893. 11 Ibid., 12 May 1893. 12 *IDI*, 11 Feb. 1893. 13 Ibid. and 17 Feb. 1893. 14 Ibid., 11 Feb. 1893. 15 Ibid., 16 Feb. 1893. 16 *EH*, 4 Mar. 1893. 17 Ibid., 18 Feb. 1893 and *UFCN*, 24 Feb. 1893. 18 *IDI*, 20 Feb. 1893. 19 Ibid. 20 *ISN*, 4 Feb. 1899. 21 *IDI*, 13 Mar. 1893. 22 *IDI*, 11 and 18 Mar. 1893. 23 *FJ*, 27 Oct. 1891. 24 *SI*, 22 Dec. 1940.

by a small groove cut all around the pitch to term a touchline. Our captain
and full-back, Claude Bennett, received a shoulder charge over at the side
of the field, and turned his ankle in this groove so badly that he was almost
crippled.[25]

Bennett went into goal and the regular goalkeeper took his place outfield for the
remainder of the match as they held on to win.[26] Webb later became more interested in hockey, and noted that 'the Leinster Nomads did not last for many years
as a club, and that their remaining members became associated afterwards with
the famous Buccaneers'.[27] While the Leinster Nomads had disbanded by the
mid-1890s, by the middle of the opening decade of the twentieth century, the
Buccaneers Hockey Club was operational, with this Dublin team, which contained
a number of internationals, active in Christmastime matches as part of an 'annual
northern tour' against opposition such as an Ulster League selection and Malone.[28]
This illustrates that the Leinster Nomads were mainly middle class, and also hints
at their ability to develop similar networks in the Belfast conurbation.

One English traveller from Sunderland, R.S. Litchfell, who observed the inaugural Leinster FA Cup final, later claimed, in a letter to the *Irish Daily Independent*,
that the Trinity team's style of play reflected their smaller home pitch and was
impeded by this.[29] He was told by other spectators present that, although their
ground was 'the minimum limit, and nearly always a sea of mud', the college club
were happy not to look for another ground due to 'the convenience of the pavilion, the situation in the park, [and] the short distance from the men's rooms'.[30]
The writer of the letter followed up by stating that he would be happy 'though
not a rich man, to contribute towards the expense' if the club decided to find a
new ground.[31] One unnamed member of the Dublin University team also wrote to
the same newspaper to suggest that a sub-committee be formed to look for a new
ground for Trinity, such was his dissatisfaction with the muddy Trinity pitch. He
called on past and present Trinity players to fund the proposed venture, and stated
that 'the Leinster Nomads found no difficulty in getting a magnificent ground',
which was being rented at 'about £12'.[32] It appears that the Trinity soccer team
shared their pitch with the college's rugby team.[33] As will be shown later, Trinity's
ground issues continued into the 1950s.

THE DEVELOPMENT OF STRUCTURES ASSISTING SOCCER'S
GROWTH IN DUBLIN

The Leinster Junior Cup had also been put in place by the Leinster FA by the
beginning of their second season in the autumn of 1893. One reporter felt that 'the

---

25 Ibid.   26 Ibid.   27 Ibid.   28 *IDI*, 23 Dec. 1904; *BN*, 23 Dec. 1905, 21 and 27 Dec. 1906; *II*,
20 Dec. 1906, 24 Dec. 1907 and 23 Dec. 1908.   29 *IDI*, 14 Mar. 1893.   30 Ibid.   31 Ibid., 15 Mar.
1893.   32 Ibid.   33 *FJ*, 20 Nov. 1893.

institution of a Junior Cup may bring some otherwise buried talent to the front; but, above this, it will have a much better effect in encouraging several good teams and second elevens who have had a pretty hard struggle to live for some time back'.[34] At a meeting of the Leinster FA at St Helen's in November 1893, with Canon Morley in the chair, the draw for the first round of the senior and junior cups was made.[35] In the Senior Cup, Dublin University AFC, having gained 'several good men, who had learned the game in the best football counties in England', through fresh student enrolment, were drawn against Montpelier, while Bohemians were drawn against Leinster Nomads.[36] In the Junior Cup, Britannia were drawn against Royal Hibernian Military School, while Dublin University 2nd XI were to face Montpelier 2nd XI. The GPO were drawn at home to Athlone, while Bohemians Reserves faced St Helen's School; Leinster Nomads 2nd XI drew Wellington and Phoenix drew Celtic. While the clubs in the senior cup remained the same as the previous season, it was noted that as there were twelve entries for the junior competition, the game was 'making rapid headway in the province'.[37] However, soccer in Leinster was mainly centred in Dublin at this time. Other soccer clubs formed by the winter of 1893 included one established through the Dublin Young Men's Christian Association and a team known as Rangers who were based at Dolphin's Barn, although they did not enter the Leinster FA's competitions.[38] By that point, the Medical Staff Corps were also fielding a team.[39] Athlone AFC, the only entrant from outside of Dublin, won the 1893–4 Leinster Junior Cup, defeating the GPO, Leinster Nomads 2nd XI, St Helen's and Britannia along the way.[40] Bohemians won the 1894 Leinster Senior Cup, beating Dublin University AFC by three goals to nil in a replay after a two-all draw, with both games taking place on the Leinster Nomads' ground at Sandymount.[41]

Inter-provincial fixtures assisted the development of relations between the Leinster FA and the IFA in the aftermath of the former's foundation, but, as will be shown later, tensions remained. In December 1893 a Leinster team made up of players from Bohemians, Trinity, Leinster Nomads and Montpelier was chosen to play Ulster at the Ulsterville Grounds, Belfast, on 9 December, with the home team winning 4–3.[42] It was noted that 'the splendid play of the Leinster team was not only a delight to northern lovers of the game present, but a positive surprise, their dribbling, passing and speed being equal if not superior to that displayed by the most ardent and best-practised of the Ulster players'.[43] In May 1894, Thomas Kirkwood Hackett of Leinster Nomads secured a seat on the IFA's committee.[44] While he welcomed the professionalization of the game in Belfast, he did not advocate a similar development within his own club at that time, who remained amateurs.[45] Kirkwood Hackett had gained interest in the game at a boarding school in Dorset and was a founding member of the Leinster FA.[46]

34 *UFCN*, 6 Oct. 1893. 35 *IDI*, 24 Nov. 1893. 36 Ibid., and *UFCN*, 28 Sept. 1893. 37 *IDI*, 24 Nov. 1893. 38 *EH*, 10 Nov. 1893; *UFCN*, 17 Nov. and 15 Dec. 1893. 39 *Sport*, 11 Nov. 1893. 40 Hunt, *Sport and society in Victorian Ireland*, p. 179. 41 *II*, 12 Mar. 1894 and *BN*, 19 Mar. 1894. 42 *IDI*, 6 and 11 Dec. 1893. 43 *IDI*, 11 Dec. 1893. 44 *UFCN*, 11 May 1894. 45 Ibid. 46 Garnham, *Association football and society*, p. 21.

Leinster's victory over Ulster by four goals to two in December 1894 was said to have drawn gate receipts of 'over £10, a record for Dublin in the Association code', with IFA officials noting 'the enthusiasm of the people in Dublin just now over the Association game'.[47] These matches were to become an annual fixture in the Irish soccer calendar.[48] Leinster selections also occasionally played the IFA's divisional associations, with a Leinster XI meeting a County Antrim selection in the 1894–5 season at Belfast, while in March 1899 a North-west FA representative team played the Leinster Senior League's XI on the grounds of the Catholic University at Sandymount.[49]

At times, travelling teams received invitations to take part in non-footballing activities. The Leinster team that played Ulster in Belfast in December 1893 stayed at the Shaftsbury Hotel in College Square North and were invited by Robinson and Cleaver to visit their warehouse.[50] At that point, relations between Dublin and northern clubs were relatively cordial. After Distillery had beaten Bohemians in the IFA Cup at Phoenix Park in December 1895, the visitors were treated to dinner and 'impromptu concert' afterwards, with the northern team seen off on the train trip home by a number of the Bohemians party.[51]

By the autumn of 1894 new IFA-affiliated associations had been set up in Donegal and South Derry, with other local governing bodies present in Antrim, Down, the North-west (Derry City) and in Dublin.[52] The Mid-Ulster Association was said to have fallen into 'a moribund condition', illustrating the difficulties in maintaining competitions in some rural areas at that time.[53] By that point, soccer was growing in popularity in Dublin and this meant that there was an increased eagerness among clubs for more competitive matches. A new feature of the 1894–5 season was the organization of a Leinster Senior League.[54] Along with Montpelier, it contained Bohemians, Leinster Nomads, Phoenix, Dublin University and Britannia, following their election at a meeting of the Leinster FA.[55]

Administrative duties were shared among club officials and some players also took up roles. The Leinster FA was chaired at the start of the season by James Sheehan of Bohemians, while James Gough of Phoenix FC was honorary treasurer and Patrick McManus of Montpelier was honorary secretary.[56] Sheehan, formerly of Belfast teams Mercantile College and Chichester Park, was described by one reporter at that time as 'the life and soul of Dublin football'.[57] However, he had resigned from his position as chairman by the end of September 1894; it is not clear why, as he remained involved in the game.[58] He was replaced by A.W. Pim, a BA graduate who was also a player for Dublin University.[59] It appears that Sheehan went on to found a club in Grangegorman in 1895, illustrating further how those with experience of soccer were helpful in encouraging its spread elsewhere.[60]

47 *UFCN*, 14 Dec. 1894. 48 Ibid., 4 Dec. 1896. 49 *EH*, 28 Jan. 1899; *IT*, 30 Mar. 1899. 50 *UFCN*, 8 Dec. 1893. 51 Ibid., 6 Dec. 1895. 52 Ibid., 7 Sept. 1894. 53 Ibid. 54 Ibid., 14 Sept. 1894. 55 Ibid. 56 Ibid. 57 Ibid. 58 Ibid., 21 Sept. 1894. 59 *IDI*, 7 Nov. 1894. 60 Reid, *Bohemian AFC official club history, 1890–1976*, p. 29.

At the start of the 1894–5 season there were twenty-five junior teams in Dublin, while clubs were also noted in Athlone and Dundalk, and at least ten military teams were operational.[61] Not all junior clubs in the area entered competitions. The draw for the 1894–5 Leinster Junior Cup, completed in November 1894, included GPO, Trinity Reserves, St Helen's, YMCA, Ramblers, Britannia, Nomads Reserves, Bohemians Reserves, Phoenix, St Matthias and Athlone.[62] Athlone retained the Leinster Junior Cup the following season and they met Bohemians in the 1896 Leinster Senior Cup final, with the Dublin team defeating the midlanders by three goals to one.[63]

By the autumn of 1896 the Leinster Junior League was operational, with twelve teams involved in the First Division.[64] The Junior League's secretaries were drawn from a range of social backgrounds and ten of these men's occupations were positively identified, with the majority of these positions unsurprisingly related primarily to written work. Dublin-born George Morton of Wellington FC was based at the Ordnance Survey office and was employed as a civil servant.[65] Fellow Dubliner William Sheffield of Phoenix FC was also employed by the Ordnance Survey, at Phoenix Park as a draughtsman.[66] He was a friend of Leinster FA honorary treasurer James Gough and by 1901 they were sharing lodgings, as Gough was a draughtsman at the Ordnance Survey and Sheffield was a boarder in the Gough home.[67] Sheffield would later go on to become the Leinster FA's first paid secretary and according to Peter Byrne, he was 'central to the development of the game in the greater Dublin area'.[68] Another Dublin man, James Bullock of Tritonville, was a commercial clerk in a biscuit factory, possibly Jacob's.[69] Thistle FC's secretary, J.A. Dawson, was a bookbinder who was born in Dublin, as was Irenes FC's R.J. Barr, a stationer, but not all were Irishmen.[70] Botanic FC's John Francis Bridgman was a clerk who had been born in Scotland.[71] Two were migrants from the north of Ireland. County Tyrone-born Henry Fisher of the General Post Office club was a

61 *UFCN*, 14 Sept. 1894. 62 *IDI*, 7 Nov. 1894. 63 *FSW*, 9 Oct. 1926. 64 *DDE*, 3 Nov. 1896 and *II* 23 Nov. 1896. 65 *IDI*, 26 Aug. 1896 and 'Residents of a house 1 in Harcourt Lane (Fitzwilliam, Dublin)', census.nationalarchives.ie/pages/1901/Dublin/Fitzwilliam/Harcourt_Lane/1306492, accessed 17 Mar. 2022. 66 *IDI*, 26 Aug. 1896 and 'Residents of a house 2 in Valleymount (Ushers Quay, Dublin)', census.nationalarchives.ie/pages/1901/Dublin/Ushers_Quay/Valleymount/1303479, accessed 17 Mar. 2022. 67 *IDI*, 26 Aug. 1896 and 'Residents of a house 2 in Valleymount (Ushers Quay, Dublin)'. 68 Byrne, *Green is the colour*, p. 25 and pp 37–8. 69 *IDI*, 26 Aug. 1896 and 'Residents of a house 176.2 in New Grove Avenue (Pembroke East & Donnybrook, Dublin)', census.nationalarchives.ie/pages/1901/Dublin/Pembroke_East__Donnybrook/New_Grove_Avenue/1285532, accessed 17 Mar. 2022. 70 *IDI*, 26 Aug. 1896; 'Residents of a house 37.4 in Lr. Gloucester St. (Mountjoy, Dublin)', census.nationalarchives.ie/pages/1901/Dublin/Mountjoy/Lr__Gloucester_St_/1327595/, accessed 17 Mar. 2022; and 'Residents of a house 74 in Seville Place (North Dock, Dublin)', census.nationalarchives.ie/pages/1901/Dublin/North_Dock/Seville_Place/1277239/, accessed 17 Mar. 2022. 71 *IDI*, 26 Aug. 1896 and 'Residents of a house 44 in Carlingford Rd. (40 to End.) (Glasnevin, Dublin)' Retrieved from census.national-archives.ie/pages/1901/Dublin/Glasnevin/Carlingford_Rd__40_to_End__/1273851, accessed 17 Mar. 2022.

telegraphist.[72] Belfast-born Robert Ward of Abbey FC was a printer-compositor.[73] An exception in terms of employment was Dubliner James Rowan of Shelbourne, who was a general labourer.[74] Similarly, Benjamin Moir of Pembroke FC was a glass-bottle maker who had migrated from Scotland.[75] The birthplaces of Moir, Bridgman, Ward and Fisher are indicative of the migratory nature of Dublin city as a hub for industry and commerce, and role of migrants in some of Dublin's early soccer clubs.

The Leinster Junior League's Second Division, which was inaugurated following a meeting in September 1896, also initially contained twelve teams, including some reserve selections.[76] The Dublin Junior Alliance, established in November 1896 through Brighton Wanderers and Tritonville, was for 'those clubs not entered in any other league'.[77] By the middle of March 1897 it was said to have been 'an unqualified success, its weekly fixtures coming off most punctually'.[78] This league initially contained ten teams.[79]

With the organization of the Leinster FA and its senior and junior leagues and cups, the number of Dublin clubs involved in competitive matches grew, while they also gradually began to enter the IFA's competitions in greater numbers. Bohemians had outlined their ambitions relatively soon after the founding of the Leinster FA. In October 1893 the club held their AGM at Wynn's Hotel, with Dr Alex Blaney in the chair.[80] It was reported that 'new grounds had been secured at Jones's Road', while the club was said to be 'in a highly satisfactory position from the points of view of finance and membership'. In addition, 'a large number of new members were enrolled' and officers were elected and the club's colours were changed to red and black. They also announced they would enter for the IFA Cup and Leinster Senior Cup and that the reserves would play in the IFA Junior Cup.[81] In November 1893, Bohemians, Leinster Nomads, Dublin University and Montpelier were in the draw for the first round of the IFA Cup, although only one

72 *IDI*, 26 Aug. 1896 and 'Residents of a house 51 in Arranmore Terrace (Inns Quay, Dublin)', census.nationalarchives.ie/pages/1901/Dublin/Inns_Quay/Arranmore_Terrace/1323855, accessed 17 Mar. 2022.   73 *IDI*, 26 Aug. 1896 and 'Residents of a house 87 in Innisfallen Parade (Inns Quay, Dublin)', census.nationalarchives.ie/pages/1901/Dublin/Inns_Quay/Innisfallen_Parade/1324659, accessed 17 Mar. 2022. The employment positions of Britannia 2nd XI's H. McCallum and Richmond Rovers' J. Brady could not be established.   74 *IDI*, 26 Aug. 1896 and 'Residents of a house 13.1 in Bath Avenue Place (Pembroke West, Dublin)', census.nationalarchives.ie/pages/1901/Dublin/Pembroke_West/Bath_Avenue_Place/1286776, accessed 17 Mar. 2022.   75 *IDI*, 26 Aug. 1896 and 'Residents of a house 239 in Pembroke Cottages Ringsend (Pembroke East & Donnybrook, Dublin)', census.nationalarchives.ie/pages/1901/Dublin/Pembroke_East___Donnybrook/Pembroke_Cottages_Ringsend/1285685, accessed 17 Mar. 2022.   76 *II*, 3 Sept. 1896 and *DET*, 23 Sept. 1896 and *II*, 23 Nov. 1896. This division included Albion, Irene Reserves, Brighton Wanderers, Normans, Phoenix Reserves, Usher Celtics, Rangers, Belgrave, St Teresa's, Richmond Rovers Reserves, Ashby and Pembroke. Tritonville 3rd, Lilly, Blackrock Reserves, Clontarf appear to have joined later that season.   77 *DDE*, 2 Nov. 1896.   78 Ibid., 15 Mar. 1897.   79 *II*, 7 Jan. 1897. These included Tritonville Reserves, Lilys, Dalymount, Myras, Sandymount, Brighton Wanderers Reserves, Victorias, Emorville Rovers, Osmonds and Merton.   80 *FJ*, 13 Oct. 1893 and Garnham, *Association football and society*, p. 17.   81 *FJ*, 13 Oct. 1893.

tie was played in Dublin as Trinity scratched to Montpelier and Bohemians beat Leinster Nomads by one–nil.[82] Dublin clubs also entered the IFA's Junior Cup and in December 1893 Athlone beat the GPO in that competition.[83] However, it appears that they did not enter the following year due to 'slackness' on the Leinster FA's part.[84] With the exception of Phoenix, all Leinster Senior League clubs entered the 1894–5 IFA Senior Cup along with St Helen's, the GPO and Athlone.[85]

In 1895, Bohemians became the first Dublin club to reach the Irish Senior Cup final. However, they were defeated by ten goals to one by Linfield in Belfast in March of that year.[86] One Belfast-based reporter called the one-sided match 'the fiasco of fiascos' and noted that the Dublin club had refused to travel the day before the match unless their full expenses of £10 were paid.[87] The absence of George Sheehan and McCann from the Bohemians team was noticeable and the impact of John Blaney, despite scoring the opening goal, was said to have 'sadly deteriorated'.[88] Despite this, it was reported that 'Dublin football has improved, and is improving, though it is still a year or two behind the best Northern form'.[89]

As noted above, the club initially moved between grounds in search of a permanent venue. In October 1892, Bohemians invited visitors to their practice match at the polo grounds at Phoenix Park.[90] However, they also temporarily played in Whitehall, on a pitch located near Glasnevin Cemetery, according to William Sanderson.[91] As shown earlier, they moved to Jones's Road in 1893, before returning to their Whitehall location in 1895.[92] Sanderson had been involved in the founding of the YMCA and Tritonville clubs before becoming involved with Bohemians later in the 1890s.[93] By the end of 1893, other teams were also playing at Jones's Road, as Richmond Rovers played Suburban Rangers there in December.[94] Ruth McManus has noted that 'in the 1890s Maurice Butterly rented ground in the vicinity of Jones's Road for use as the "city and suburban racecourse"', with cycling and other pastimes also held there.[95] In 1908, the land was bought by Frank Dineen, who had acted as GAA secretary from 1898 to 1901, and was later president from 1906 until 1909; he sold it to the association in 1913 and it is now known as Croke Park, the headquarters of the GAA.[96]

Sanderson stated in a 1940 interview that the Whitehall venue used by Bohemians was 'too inconvenient for the public since the horse-tram only brought them to Doyle's Corner' in Phibsboro.[97] Although there is scarce reference in the club's 1945 history publication to his involvement, he claimed to have 'found' the field from which Dalymount Park later developed, in 1901, stating that he 'walked right out the back gate of a friend's house near the Tramway sheds and there she was, with a couple of old nags grazing at one end and a disused cabbage

82 *Sport*, 11 Nov. 1893. 83 Ibid., 9 Dec. 1893. 84 *UFCN*, 12 Oct. 1894. 85 Ibid., 28 Sept. 1894. 86 Ibid., 29 Mar. 1895. 87 Ibid. 88 Ibid. 89 Ibid. 90 Ibid., 1 Oct. 1892. 91 *SI*, 15 Dec. 1940. 92 O'Mahony (ed.), *Bohemian Football Club golden jubilee souvenir*, p. 13. 93 *SI*, 15 Dec. 1940. 94 *IDI*, 28 and 29 Dec. 1893. 95 McManus, *Dublin, 1910–1940*, p. 311 and *Shelbourne Football Club golden jubilee*, p. 17. 96 McManus, *Dublin, 1910–1940*, p. 311 and Michael Foley, *The bloodied field: Croke Park, Sunday 21 November 1921* (Dublin, 2014), p. 98. 97 *SI*, 15 Dec. 1940.

plot at the other'.[98] Sanderson apparently persuaded the owner of the field, the Reverend Henry Taylor, who was a chaplain of a local female orphanage, to let the field to the club rather than build 'two streets of houses' on the cabbage plot as he had intended.[99] Taylor decided to lease the ground for £48 a year with three months' notice to be given if he wanted to end the agreement.[100] Following the enclosure of the ground, the building of a small stand and the flattening of the pitch with the Corporation steamroller, Bohemians' first match at their new venue took place against Shelbourne in September 1901.[101] The lord mayor of Dublin, Tim Harrington, a nationalist MP, opened Dalymount Park before the game, which Bohemians won 2–1.[102]

The growth of transport networks in Dublin was beneficial in allowing clubs to travel around Dublin to compete in Leinster FA competitions and friendly matches. The foundation of the Dublin United Tramways Company in 1880 'resulted in the near-total integration of horse-tram services across greater Dublin into a thirty-two mile network', while the decision taken by DUTC co-founder William Martin Murphy to switch from horse power to electricity and to take over the last independent tram company increased the system to around fifty-five miles by the late 1890s.[103] In November 1893 the General Post Office team travelled from Nelson's Pillar by 1 p.m. tram to play the Royal Munster Fusiliers at Dolphin's Barn.[104] That same month, the Leinster Nomads took the train from Kingsbridge (now Heuston) to meet the Lancashire Fusiliers at the Curragh.[105]

The acquiring of venues was important for teams, but, as shown by Mason, it could be difficult, particularly for teams made up of working-class men.[106] By the late nineteenth century a number of Dublin clubs had regular grounds for their matches, including Richmond Rovers (Clonturk), Freebooters (Simmonscourt) and Inchicore (South Circular Road).[107] For military selections playing in Dublin, London Bridge Road was a venue that could be used for matches.[108]

Phoenix Park became an important venue for soccer and other games in the late nineteenth century, with clubs such as Aughrim (Polo Ground) and Ashburn Rovers (Fifteen Acres) utilizing the area.[109] As shown above, it was there that many clubs had their first taste of this code, often beginning with intra-club matches, then friendlies, before moving on to competitive games. Soccer's development in Dublin was helped by the Commission of Public Works' laying out of a number of pitches in Phoenix Park in 1901.[110] As Dickson has stated, at that point,

> the park itself had become a popular amenity, what with the success of the zoo and of the nearby Promenade grounds (later the People's Gardens), the proliferation of middle-class sporting grounds (with the first of several

98 Ibid. 99 Ibid. 100 Ibid. 101 Ibid. 102 Ibid. 103 Dickson, *Dublin*, p. 386. 104 *FJ*, 9 Nov. 1893. 105 *IDI*, 18 Nov. 1893. 106 Mason, *Association football and English society*, p. 27. 107 *DDN*, 21 Jan. 1899. 108 Ibid. 109 Ibid. 110 Garnham, *Association football and society*, p. 12.

cricket pitches in 1838, a polo ground in 1873, and briefly a golf club in the 1880s), and its choice as a venue for large protest meetings.[111]

Garnham has noted that the secretary of the Leinster FA had complained in 1898 and 1900 that facilities for the game were inadequate.[112] This public complaint on the Leinster FA's part was also an attempt to prevent further accidents in the erection of goalposts.[113] Meanwhile, the Commission of Public Works were concerned that damage was being done to cricket pitches and flower beds there.

In 1902 there were nearly one thousand applications to use the pitches, and by 1905 there were over three thousand. In early 1906 there were twenty-nine soccer pitches located there, and in 1907 dressing rooms were provided.[114] Diarmaid Ferriter has stated that at that point only three pitches out of thirty-two were used for Gaelic games and 'soccer was the most popular sport in Dublin' by the beginning of the second decade of the twentieth century.[115] Despite this, getting to the Phoenix Park venue was awkward for some soccer teams, with one reporter noting the benefits of Trojans acquiring of 'a private ground', Belgrove Park, at Chapelizod in 1906.[116] He commented that 'the Dublin and Lucan Tram passes close beside it' and although it was 'further from the city than the Fifteen Acres' it was still more accessible 'by means of the tram'.[117] At times, some Dublin matches had to be postponed due to difficulties in procuring pitches, with Seaview having to call off their home County Dublin League match against Belleville AFC in September 1906 as a result of 'being unable to secure a ground'.[118]

Despite difficulties with playing fields, by the late 1890s the Leinster FA's administrative structures had also improved, with a Referees Association, which had governing rules, 'similar to those of the Lancashire Referees' Association with a few amendments', active by 1898.[119] The Dublin-based body was formed 'for the purpose of banding together the referees of Leinster, and appointing competent referees for the various matches in and around Dublin and district'.[120] By 1905, referees were required by the Leinster FA to pass examinations and a system of grading them became operational, as certification to officiate in matches involving affiliated clubs was deemed necessary.[121] The involvement of army men, who had experience of the game, as referees was also important in establishing standards of officiating. By the latter part of that decade the Leinster FA were sanctioning the appointment of military men based at the Curragh to act in that capacity.[122]

Military teams' involvement in competitions had grown in the latter part of the 1890s as the Leinster FA became more open to their involvement in its

111 Dickson, *Dublin*, p. 381. 112 Garnham, *Association football and society*, p. 12. 113 Ibid. 114 Ibid., p. 12. 115 Diarmaid Ferriter, 'Social life and the GAA in a time of upheaval in Ireland: a retrospect' in Gearóid Ó Tuathaigh (ed.), *The GAA & Revolution in Ireland, 1913–1923* (Cork, 2015), pp 251–60, p. 258. 116 *DDE*, 2 Oct. 1906. 117 Ibid. 118 Ibid., 22 Sept. 1906 119 *II*, 12 Aug. 1898. 120 Ibid. 121 Senior League Council Minutes, Council Meeting, 1 June 1905, Leinster Football Association Archives, P239/23. 122 Senior League Council Minutes, Council Meeting, 10 Nov. 1909, Leinster Football Association Archives, P239/24.

competitions. In October 1897, after the first round of matches for the season, there were three military teams, the West Kent Regiment, Durham Light Infantry and the Yorkshire Regiment, at the top of the Leinster Senior League, in which seven teams in total took part.[123] The other clubs competing for the Elvery's Cup included Shelbourne, Phoenix, Hibernians and Bohemians.[124] With the strong presence of the military throughout Ireland, and particularly in Dublin, soccer remained an important pastime for soldiers in the army.

Relations between civilian and military clubs were not always cordial, particularly in regard to army teams entering competitions, but in many cases they were positive. In February 1893 Bohemians played the Royal Engineers at Phoenix Park, with Bohemians fielding 'a rather weak team' while the Engineers, 'who travelled from the Curragh', lined out with 'a good one'.[125] The match ended in a three-all draw, and afterwards, 'a very pleasant evening was spent in the City Arms Hotel, where a capital dinner was served for thirty guests'.[126] Entertainment was provided by Corporal Wilson, who 'created roars of laughter with his inimitable songs and recitations, and most of his comrades ably contributed to the harmony'.[127] During their Leinster League match in November 1897 at the Esplanade, both Bohemians and West Kent gave 'a splendid exhibition of the game to the crowd', which was divided between the military on one side and civilians on the other, 'and this arrangement caused a considerable amount of good-humoured banter and counter-cheering in the course of the game'.[128]

THE FURTHER GROWTH OF DUBLIN'S CLUBS

There was a diverse mix of backgrounds within soccer clubs, and closely related to their origins, in the late nineteenth and early twentieth centuries. Julien Clenet has noted that while places of employment, the military and schools were important sources of clubs in Dublin, as in other areas, 'by and large, however, community, neighbourhood and friendship ties were primordial in the creation of clubs'.[129] He states that while there was an even balance of twelve military teams and twelve civilian teams (six neighbourhood, five school and one workplace) in 1883–92, during the years 1892–7 there were seventy-three neighbourhood teams in existence out of a civilian total of ninety-one, and between 1897 and 1902, 201 neighbourhood teams were identifiable out of 245 non-military selections.[130] In the latter period, twenty-one school teams were present, while twenty-three workplace teams were operational. The existence of military teams was inconsistent as only seven were 'present for three seasons or more'.[131] Evidence from regional Ulster also suggests that the role of the military in the spread of soccer was much less influential than that of local organizers, particularly in Donegal, Fermanagh and Cavan.[132] However,

123 *Sport*, 23 Oct. 1897.   124 Ibid. and *II*, 16 Feb. 1898.   125 *Sport*, 28 Feb. 1893.   126 Ibid.
127 Ibid.   128 *FJ*, 22 Nov. 1897.   129 Clenet, 'Association football in Dublin', p. 813.   130 Ibid.,
pp 808–15   131 Ibid., pp 813–14.   132 Curran, 'The role of the provincial press in the development of association football', pp 53–64.

fixtures between military teams did allow locals the opportunity to view the game (at least outside their own barracks), and civilian clubs attempted to match their prowess in challenge matches, despite the reluctance of some competition organizers to allow them to enter.[133]

Some new clubs grew out of those already in existence that had catered for other sporting codes. In the autumn of 1893, one reporter noted that 'a number of Gaelic and Rugby clubs have taken on greatly with the Association code, and may be seen practicing at all times at the game'.[134] By the winter of 1893 there was 'a striking apathy' in the organization of GAA branches, according to P.J. Graham, the honorary secretary of Dunleary Independents GAA club.[135] Following the Parnell Split, and clerical opposition to involvement of the Irish Republican Brotherhood in GAA clubs, some teams certainly switched from Gaelic football, including Ireland's Own and Benburb, who met in a soccer match at Phoenix Park in January of that year.[136] In some cases, this transferral may only have been temporary, and movement of players between codes could be fluid, as in November 1893 the 'resuscitated' Benburb met the Feagh McHughs of Blackrock in a 'friendly' Gaelic football match at the end of a tournament.[137] However, the GAA did undoubtedly experience a direct loss of players to some soccer teams, including at least three clubs in Derry city and two in Donegal in the late 1880s and early 1890s.[138] Dublin's early soccer clubs lacked the political naming policies shown by many GAA clubs there, who generally did not use 'the actual name of their district' as 'most club names commemorated either individuals or incidents in Irish history'.[139]

Garnham has noted that player movement between differing codes was relatively common.[140] Emerald, the soccer team of the General Post Office, which had previously 'always affected the Rugby code', had a line-up in September 1893 that was said to consist of 'some good men from England and Scotland, several past masters in the Gaelic code', and some rugby players were also set to join.[141] By October 1893 the dual GPO club was said to have eighty members.[142] Naturally, this cross-over of players was not always well received by those in other codes where clubs lost players, or where they were attempting to play a variety of football codes. In November 1893, J. Fitzgerald, the honorary secretary of the Dolphin's Barn-based Rapparee hurling club, expressed his discontent with the Dublin GAA county committee, as an unnamed club 'prominently represented on the present provisional committee' had entered a team in the [Leinster] Junior Cup competition, being held under soccer rules, while they were also fielding a team 'under Gaelic rules'.[143] The following month, he claimed that he was not getting enough

133 Ibid., pp 55–9 and Clenet, 'Association football in Dublin, p. 814. 134 *UFCN*, 18 Aug. and 20 Oct. 1893. 135 *IDI*, 5 Dec. 1893. 136 *Sport*, 21 Jan. 1893. 137 *IDI*, 9 and 16 Nov. 1893. 138 Curran, *The development of sport in Donegal*, pp 74–5 and p. 91. 139 Wren, de Búrca & Gorry, *The Gaelic Athletic Association in Dublin*, i: *1884–1959*, p. 22. 140 Garnham, *Association football and society*, pp 66–7. 141 *UFCN*, 28 Sept. 1893. 142 Ibid., 20 Oct. 1893. 143 *IDI*, 11 and 24 Nov. 1893 and *EH*, 12 Dec. 1893. It is unclear which of the twelve entrants in the Leinster Junior Cup this was.

support in regard to GAA members participating in soccer, and called for greater measures to be put in place to prevent this.[144] A revival took place in many areas later in the decade, with the GAA and its secretary, Richard Blake, bringing in a number of administrative changes at Central Council level as they sought to distance the organization from the IRB.[145] He was also keen to improve the rules of Gaelic football, which he believed were 'inadequate' and too vague in comparison with those of soccer and rugby.[146] In 1901, the GAA introduced a 'ban' on its members taking part in 'foreign' games such as cricket, rugby, hockey and soccer. Initially 'it was introduced on a voluntary basis, leaving it to the discretion of the county boards to enforce it'.[147] However, in 1902 this rule was made compulsory, only to be removed in 1903 with county boards given the power to implement it or not, but in 1905 it was again made mandatory by the GAA, and remained in place until 1971.[148]

Other soccer clubs also gained former Gaelic football players in the 1890s, as well as recruits from Britain who were working in Dublin and some of those who had established reputations in other sports were also sought after on account of their athleticism. At the start of the 1894–5 season, Montpelier had been strengthened by Sweeny from East Stirlingshire, who played on the right wing, J.J. Mullen, 'the mile champion', and 'a couple of recruits from the Gaelic ranks' who were reported to be in 'first-rate' shape.[149] Crossover of players remained common in many team sports in Dublin and elsewhere. In September 1894, those wishing to become members of a new soccer team were asked to attend a meeting at the Warrington Athletic Club in Ringsend, illustrating how sports clubs could develop offshoots in other codes.[150]

Some soccer clubs also lost players when they faced difficulties, and new clubs at times grew from their remains. By the start of the 1895–6 season, Leinster Nomads had disbanded, having failed to secure their Sandymount ground with the result that their members 'drifted into other clubs'.[151] Montpelier players apparently combined with other soccer enthusiasts to start a new club called Hibernian. In August 1895, a meeting was held to form a senior soccer team in connection with the Hibernian Football and Athletic Club in the Workman's Club, 41 York Street Dublin, 'a few well-known Dublin footballers being the organizers'.[152] The club enrolled 'over sixty members' at the meeting, which was said to be 'a very healthy augury' and it was noted that the committee had gathered together 'a very good team in the pick of the defunct Montpelier, a couple of the Leinster Nomads, and two Liverpool League players'.[153]

Some clubs were founded through religious institutions. In November 1893 the Dublin Young Men's Christian Association (YMCA) established a soccer

144 *EH*, 15 Dec. 1893. 145 Curran, *The development of sport in Donegal*, pp 95–6. 146 *Sport*, 28 Jan. 1893. 147 Cormac Moore, *The GAA v Douglas Hyde: the removal of Ireland's first president as GAA patron* (Cork, 2012), pp 34–5. 148 Ibid., p. 35. 149 *UFCN*, 28 Sept. 1894. 150 *II*, 20 Sept. 1894. 151 *EH*, 16 Nov. 1895. 152 *UFCN*, 23 Aug. 1895. 153 Ibid.

club, and invited visitors to a practice match near the Polo Ground shortly after-wards.[154] The Dublin YMCA was founded in 1849 and its headquarters were at the Metropolitan Christian Buildings, Lower Abbey Street.[155] Along with 'a well-selected library' and reading room, the organization's facilities in the early 1880s also included a gymnasium, with this amenity becoming more prominent in Ireland's cities by the late nineteenth century.[156] It appears they refrained from playing on Sundays.[157] Garnham has noted that 'a number of junior clubs existed in Dublin by 1902 which bore the names of the city's Church of Ireland par-ishes', and 'even one of the city's synagogues boasted its own football team'.[158] Clubs bearing religious names included St Mark's, St Patrick's, St George's and St Werburgh's. The Father Mathew organization, which was heavily linked to the temperance movement, had a team in operation in the early 1900s.[159] By 1906 Christ Church Cathedral, which was associated with the Church of Ireland, was fielding a team.[160] St Mark's, which was later renamed St Mark's Athletic Club, was composed of former 2nd Company Boys' Brigade members and began play-ing at a field off Baggot Street owned by the Carry family.[161] While Dublin clubs were not as explicitly divided on religious lines as was the case in Belfast and Glasgow, some did highlight their allegiances in their naming policies, including Balbriggan Celtic.[162] Clenet has noted that two clubs, Molyneaux and Richmond Athletic, 'were exclusively composed of Protestants' but religion was not 'the sole decisive factor in granting membership' as 'other forms of social bonding' were more significant.[163] Almost three-quarters of the Dublin-born players in his sam-ple of players from 1896 to 1902 were Catholics.[164]

In November 1893, Phoenix FC, said to be only 'a week in existence', defeated Bohemians Reserves at Phoenix Park by a goal to nil.[165] The Phoenix club were made up of employees of the Ordnance Survey office at Phoenix Park.[166] Some other clubs developed through industrial paternalism, such as Jacob's, a biscuit producer, and St James's Gate, which had its links with the brewing company Guinness.[167] By the beginning of the twentieth century, Jacob's, which was then based in Bishop Street, had more than 2,000 workers, and its brand had become internationally recognized.[168] The soccer team was first organized in 1907 and having played in the Factory League (which was unaffiliated to the Leinster FA) for one season, they then joined the provincial governing body.[169] St James's Gate were affiliated to the Leinster Junior League in 1906.[170] The soccer club had been

154 *IDI*, 10 Nov. 1893. **155** *Thom's official directory … 1883*, p. 845. **156** Ibid., and Conor Curran, *Physical education in Irish schools, 1900–2000: a history* (Oxford, 2022), pp 63–5. Established in 1860, the Church of Ireland Young Men's Christian Association, based at Dawson Street, was also operational in the late nineteenth century. **157** *Soccer Reporter* (May 1978), p. 13. **158** Garnham, *Association football and society*, p. 45. **159** *EH*, 2 Oct. 1903. **160** *DDE*, 22 Sept. 1906. **161** *Soccer Reporter* (Jan. 1976), p. 11. **162** *FJ*, 16 Dec. 1905. **163** Clenet, 'Association football in Dublin', p. 812. **164** Ibid. **165** *EH*, 14 Nov. 1892. **166** *II*, 13 Sept. 1895. **167** Garnham, *Association football and society*, p. 48. **168** Dickson, *Dublin*, pp 393, 533. Jacob's moved to Tallaght in 1975. **169** *Sport*, 29 Sept. 1917. **170** *DET*, 28 Aug. 1906.

founded in 1902 by John Lumsden, who was a medical officer at the brewery.[171] They initially played their home games at Bellevue Lodge in Inchicore.[172]

Garnham has noted that by the late 1890s, 'in Dublin the Pembroke club was formed by bottle blowers from the Ringsend area of the city, all of whom chose to start work thirty minutes early each day, at 5.30 am, in order to finish at lunchtime on Saturdays and thus be able to play football in the afternoon'.[173] Some other clubs were made up of industrial workers, and an announcement in the local or national press that a newly formed club was open to challenge matches was a common way of establishing initial networks in the game. In October 1893 Aldborough House AFC announced in the press they were open to meet 'weak medium clubs' for matches.[174] Later that month they played 'a practice match', the sides being 'Bakers and Butchers v Junior Clerks'.[175] Located on the North Circular Road, Aldborough House was one of a small number of townhouses formerly run by aristocratic families near the city. By the mid-nineteenth century, it was being used as an army barracks, and it later became a post office branch.[176] Some clubs emerged from transport establishments, with the Irish Railway Clearing House setting up a team in September 1899 and procuring a ground at West Park, Kenilworth Square.[177] Teams made up of skilled workers also developed. In November 1896, Artisan Wanderers announced they were open to receive challenges from juvenile clubs.[178]

A few early clubs were established through charities. Glasnevin FC were said to have been founded in 1908 through the St Vincent de Paul orphanage and initially were known as Vintans before 'broadening the basis of its membership' and being given the nickname 'the diggers'.[179] In September 1899, the New Harmonic Club, based in Camden Street, announced their intentions to form an association football club, although it appears that music remained their primary interest.[180] Along with Dublin University AFC, by the late nineteenth century other college teams were operational, including Catholic University, 'the lineal antecedent' of University College Dublin.[181] The Freebooters, who faced Dublin University AFC in a Leinster Senior Cup match at Simmonscourt in the spring of 1899, 'being largely recruited from Trinity, had to be content to see some of their own men playing against them for the "Varsity"'.[182] As students, they also had time for other sports, with Scroope and the O'Reilly brothers playing tennis to keep fit over the course of that summer; the Meldons played cricket, while other team members 'kept up their fitness at various games'.[183]

Some teams appeared only occasionally and were more interested in the game simply for recreational purposes. In March 1893 Leinster Nomads beat Mr F.R.

171 'Our History', stjamesgatefc.com/club-history, accessed 3 Jan. 2022 and Cronin & Higgins, *Places we play*, p. 66.   172 'Our History', stjamesgatefc.com/club-history, accessed 3 Jan. 2022. 173 Garnham, *Association football and society*, p. 49.   174 *FJ*, 14 Oct. 1893.   175 Ibid., 21 Oct. 1893.   176 Dickson, *Dublin*, p. 278 and *IT*, 26 May 2018.   177 *FJ*, 28 Sept. 1899.   178 *IDI*, 13 Nov. 1896.   179 *Sport*, 22 Sept. 1917.   180 *II*, 6 Sept. 1899.   181 *DDE*, 3 Nov. 1896; *II*, 23 Nov. 1896; *IT*, 30 Mar. 1899; Richard Killeen, *Historical atlas of Dublin* (Dublin, 2009), p. 132. 182 *DDE*, 27 Feb. 1899.   183 *Sport*, 30 Sept. 1899.

Benson's Company, who were appearing at the Gaiety Theatre, at Sandymount.[184] The return match was a closer game, and 'it was necessary to play ten minutes extra' before the home team won 3–2.[185] As well as playing rugby in Dublin, the Benson's team also played a roller polo match against the Elite Rink at Earlsfort Terrace.[186] Place-names also indicate the growing presence of clubs outside the city. Suburban AFC, founded in September 1895, hoped to establish their club by initially playing friendly matches against junior teams.[187]

The public house was a common venue for the formation of early soccer clubs, although at times clubs such as the Pioneers, founded in 1908 and based in Mountjoy Square, were drawn from those who chose to abstain from drinking.[188] Shelbourne were formed in a pub, possibly Nolan's of Beggar's Bush, near Ringsend, in 1895.[189] Along with a number of other men who frequented the venue, the aforementioned James Rowan was a key man in their foundation and an early success as a player and administrator.[190] An employee of Dublin Corporation Cleaning Department, he was also a player and acted as club treasurer, living in Bath Avenue Place, where they initially held their meetings.[191] Shelbourne was said to be 'an offspring of the old Tritonville club'.[192] Naturally, clubs were often simply named after the locality in which they were based; they took their name from the local Shelbourne Road.[193] With the formation of Shelbourne, and their subsequent success, Ringsend grew in importance as a location for the game's development. Like many clubs at that time, Shelbourne initially rented their pitch, which was formed on 'waste ground in the Havelock Square vicinity'.[194]

Initially, the club turned out in chocolate and sky-blue shirts, for a year, rather than red, following a mistake in the kit delivery from the branch of sports outfitter Gamage's, located in Grafton Street.[195] It was not until 1896–7 that they took part in competitive soccer, winning the Leinster Junior League and Cup while playing their home matches at Bath Avenue.[196] That season, the club lost only one of twenty-eight matches and promptly joined the Leinster Senior League, finishing runners-up in both that competition and the Leinster Senior Cup final in their initial season.[197] The Tritonville club, based at London Bridge Road, did not die away and by 1900 had a membership card structure in operation.[198] Development from other clubs continued to be one method of a soccer club's growth into the twentieth century. Bendigo, who took on that name in 1909, grew out of Ormond Athletic of Chancery Street, initially formed for 'boxing and amusement', which had amalgamated with the nearby struggling St Michan's FC.[199] At times, some

184 *IDI*, 8 Mar. 1893. 185 *IDI*, 14 Mar. 1893. 186 *IDI*, 15 Mar. 1893. 187 *EH*, 30 Sept. 1895. 188 Mason, *Association football and English society*, pp 26–8; *Soccer Reporter* (Apr. 1983), p. 11. 189 Garnham, *Association football and society*, p. 46; Sands, *Shels*, p. 1. 190 *SI*, 9 Sept. 1956. 191 Sands, *Shels*, p. 3. 192 *Sport*, 17 Nov. 1917. 193 Brian Kennedy, *Just follow the floodlights! The complete guide to League of Ireland football* (Dublin, 2011), p. 214; *SI*, 9 Sept. 1956. 194 *Shelbourne Football Club golden jubilee, 1895–1945*, p. 11. 195 Ibid., pp 13–14. 196 *SI*, 9 Sept. 1956. 197 Ibid. 198 *FJ*, 26 Sept. 1900. 199 *FSW*, 3 Apr. and 10 July 1926.

clubs were severely weakened by the lure of playing for those of a higher standing. In September 1904, Pembroke, who had won the County Dublin League Cup that year, were 'dissolved' owing to the loss of seven of their players to the reserve teams of Tritonville (four) and Shelbourne (three).[200]

There is some dispute about the origins of Shamrock Rovers, arguably Ireland's most famous soccer club. Some club historians have stated that it was 1901 rather than 1899 in which they were established, as this is when they registered with the Leinster FA. By the early 1900s, having grown out of Shamrock Avenue, they were playing at Ringsend Park on a pitch referred to locally as 'the Clinkers'.[201] However, contemporary newspaper evidence suggests a team bearing the club's name was in existence by the last year of the nineteenth century. In April 1899 a team known as Shamrock Rovers met Rosemount, with the match ending in a draw.[202] By the autumn of the following year, the former club was fielding two teams.[203] Eoghan Rice has noted the origins of their rivalry with Shelbourne, who 'played their football on the northside of the river Dodder, which runs through Ringsend, while Rovers played on the southside' of the river.[204]

THE GROWING STRENGTH OF DUBLIN SOCCER AT THE TURN OF THE CENTURY

By the last years of the nineteenth century, interest in soccer in Dublin had grown substantially. The Bohemians versus West Kent match in November 1897, played at the Esplanade, was also the cause of 'a very large buzz of excitement round the touchlines, fringed by some 4,000 spectators', with one reporter predicting that 'the extraordinarily large crowd which assembled at the above match, following up the increasing attendances at soccer matches elsewhere in the Metropolis, leave no doubt that the Association game has a big future before it in Dublin'.[205] Writing in 1898, 'Ralph the Rover' stated that he was 'really glad to see that the Association game has caught on in Dublin'.[206] He noted that a recent match there had attracted 12,000 supporters and felt that 'Dublin should get one of the international matches, and if a suitable ground could be found we are quite sure they would'.[207] Managing crowds initially could prove difficult at some Dublin soccer venues, particularly when the visitors came from Belfast and were of a unionist background. In 1899, Richmond Rovers reached the IFA Intermediate Cup final against Linfield Swifts, with the venue set as the Catholic University School's ground in Sandymount. The match, which drew a crowd of five thousand, had to be stopped 'owing to interference from spectators', with the Belfast side winning by three goals to one with five minutes remaining.[208] Linfield Swifts were awarded the trophy later that month.[209] It appears that some of the crowd had

200 *EH*, 2 Sept. 1904. 201 Doolan & Goggins, *The Hoops*, pp 1–3, 11; Rice, *We are Rovers*, p. 31. 202 *EH*, 10 Apr. 1899. 203 *IDI*, 15 and 28 Sept. 1900. See also *IDI*, 8 Dec. 1908. 204 Rice, *We are Rovers*, p. 32. 205 *FJ*, 22 Nov. 1897. 206 *BET*, 12 Dec. 1898. 207 Ibid. 208 *DDN*, 13 Mar. 1899; *INBMN*, 15 Mar. 1899. 209 *BT*, 22 Mar. 1899.

thrown stones at the referee, while a number of the Swifts players were attacked by spectators.[210]

The following year 'Ralph the Rover' noted that 'one of the leading Dublin clubs' had offered a top Linfield player 'terms of the most satisfactory character' to act as their trainer.[211] The columnist felt that 'this only shows how anxious the Metropolitans are to be recognized in the first flight. Dublin has come to stay, and Dublin must be considered [by the IFA] in the future'.[212] In March 1900, the international fixture between Ireland and England was finally held in Dublin.[213] The match was patronized by the lord lieutenant and the duke of Connaught, with admission costing one shilling.[214] Seats could be reserved at Cook's in Grafton Street for an additional sum.[215] The match 'aroused considerable local interest' and attracted approximately five thousand spectators, with many of these said to have come on 'a big excursion train' run by the Great Northern Railway Company, from Belfast.[216] Excursion tickets were also issued for stops from Limerick Junction to Dublin.[217] A smoker was organized by Bohemians FC for the evening before the match in the Rotunda, with players from both teams present, and tickets were available at the cost of two shillings.[218]

The match, which took place at Lansdowne Road, primarily a rugby ground, as there was no other Dublin venue suitable to host such a fixture, was the nineteenth between the teams, and was won by the visitors, by two goals to nil. The Irish team was made up of 'eight Belfast players, two Anglo-Celts (Goodall and Reilly) and one Dublin [respresentative] (Sheehan)'.[219] At that point, Archie Goodall was based at Derby County while Matt Reilly was at Portsmouth, and the rest were playing with teams in Ireland.[220] Bohemians' George Sheehan was the sole Dublin-based representative, reflecting the power wielded by the IFA's Belfast selectors, and the strength of the game in the northern city.[221] While the game was growing in stature in Dublin, friction remained between the IFA and the LFA, with a number of those in Dublin unhappy with international selection policies, the allocating of venues for international matches and the failure of the Belfast-body to sanction Sunday matches.[222]

By the early 1900s the diversity of Dublin clubs was reflected in the presence of a Richmond Asylum team in the Leinster Junior League, while the existence of the Railway and Steampacket Companies Irish Athletic and Social Union AFC, initially based at the organization's headquarters at Park Avenue, was another example of how the growth of soccer since the 1880s in Dublin had become more widespread.[223] By 1901 there were sixty-five clubs from the Leinster FA affiliated with the IFA in Belfast, which had 259 clubs in total.[224] To cater for the growth in Dublin

210 *Scottish Referee*, 17 Mar. 1899. 211 *BET*, 13 Apr. 1899. 212 Ibid. 213 *NW*, 19 Mar. 1900. 214 *II*, 15 Mar. 1900. 215 Ibid. 216 *NW*, 19 Mar. 1900. 217 *DDN*, 12 Mar. 1900. 218 *II*, 15 Mar. 1900. 219 Ibid. 220 Ibid. 221 Ibid. 222 Garnham, *Association football and society*, pp 164–7; Moore, *The Irish soccer split*, pp 231–5. 223 *EH*, 2 Oct. 1903; *FJ*, 21 Oct. 1904; *Soccer Reporter* (Apr. 1979), p. 10. See also *FSW*, 29 Jan. 1927. The Richmond club, based at Grangegorman, went into decline but were revived by the early 1920s. 224 Minute Book of the IFA 1898–1902, Annual Report 1901, p. 303, IFA Archives, D/4196/A1, PRONI.

clubs, by July 1903, a new Leinster Junior Football Association had been formed.[225]
By October 1903, there was a much more extensive soccer calendar in Dublin than
had been the case a decade earlier, with Leinster Senior, Intermediate and Junior
leagues in existence, while a Leinster Junior Combination League, a County Dublin
League (sponsored by the *Evening Mail* and won by Shamrock Rovers in 1904) and
a Dublin Junior Alliance League were all operational.[226] By the end of 1904, the
Athletic Union League was established.[227] The Sunday Junior League was formed in
the 1905–6 season, with Liffey Wanderers initially its most successful club, winning,
for three years running, the Empire Cup, which was donated by Empire Theatre
manager G.H. Marsh.[228] According to some secondary sources, they were founded
by dockers in the Ringsend area in 1885, but contemporary newspaper evidence for
this is difficult to find, and it was not until the early 1900s that they were recorded
as competing in the Annaville Cup and the Leinster Junior Combination League.[229]

By 1901 there were 21,000 soldiers and officers, almost 4,000 militiamen and
yeomantry and more than 2,000 Royal Navy and Royal Marines members in
Ireland.[230] Military teams had by then a more organized structure for their matches
in Dublin. By the end of 1903, a Dublin Garrison League was in place, and by the
end of the following year eight teams were involved.[231] The Royal Ulster Rifles
Regimental Depot 2nd Battalion team won the league in 1904–5 and again in
1905–6.[232] Military teams also maintained a strong position in the mainly civilian
Leinster League, with the Cameron Highlanders winning the First Division in
1906.[233] Leagues that catered specifically for work groups were also established by
the early 1900s. By January 1907, the Leinster Workshops and Factories' League
was operational and included ten teams.[234] By 1909, there were 107 clubs registered with the Leinster FA, a rise of 19 from the previous year.[235] However, this
figure is not fully reflective of other clubs in Dublin and the rest of Leinster who
took part in other local leagues at that time.[236]

More cup competitions also became established in that decade. The
Metropolitan Cup, donated by James McCann MP, for competition between the
Leinster League's top four clubs, was operational in 1902.[237] In September 1905,
the *Evening Herald* donated a trophy, which became known as the Hospitals' Cup,
and a set of gold medals, for an annual match to raise money for Dublin hospitals.[238]

225 *DDM*, 8 July 1903. 226 *EH*, 3 Oct. 1903 and Doolan & Goggins, *The Hoops*, p. 4. 227 *EH*,
3 Dec. 1904. 228 *SI*, 15 May 1910 and 'Liffey Wanderers FC: a history – centenary year, 1885–
1985, part 2', *New Link*, 93 (2011), p. 17 229 See Vincent Caprani (ed.), *Liffey Wanderers centenary
year, 1885–1995* (Dublin, 1985); Aileen O'Carroll & Don Bennett, *The Dublin docker: working lives
of Dublin's deep sea port* (Newbridge, 2017), p. 200; 'Liffey Wanderers FC', p. 17 and *FJ*, 11 Dec.
1902. See also *EH*, 23 Oct. 1903. 230 David Fitzpatrick, 'Militarism in Ireland, 1900–1922' in
Thomas Bartlett & Keith Jeffery (eds), *A military history of Ireland* (Cambridge, 1996), pp 379–406,
p. 381. 231 *DEM*, 6 Nov. 1903; *IT*, 6 Dec. 1904. 232 *BT*, 3 Feb. 1906; *Ballymena Observer*,
1 Mar. 1957. 233 *DDE*, 2 May 1906. 234 *EH*, 5 Jan. 1907. 235 Briggs & Dodd, *100 years of the
LFA*, p. 37. 236 Ibid. 237 *Sport*, 19 Apr. 1902; *DDE*, 28 Apr. 1908. 238 Senior League Council
Minutes, Council Meeting, 27 Sept. 1905, Leinster Football Association Archives. P239/23. This
competition was renamed as the President's Cup in 1930.

This was a match between representative teams, with a Leinster League selection initially meeting a combined Bohemians and Shelbourne team in February 1906 at Dalymount Park.[239] As well as the aforementioned Empire Cup, for the Sunday Junior League, the Kelly Cup was run for that organization's cup matches.[240] One early indoor soccer competition of less significance (won by Shelbourne) was the Circus Cup, a five-a-side event held in the Round Room of the Rotunda in the 1903–4 season.[241]

Some Dublin clubs still travelled outside the county for friendly matches. At Easter 1903 Tritonville visited Longford Wanderers on the local park grounds, while later that month Longford Swifts travelled to Phoenix Park to play a return match against Egerton.[242] At Christmas 1904 Tritonville and Inchicore both travelled to Navan to play the local team there 'on the first soccer ground in the district'.[243] Richmond Rovers travelled to the Brigade Grounds, Drogheda, to play a team known as the Centaurs on St Stephen's Day 1904.[244] Fermanagh's Enniskillen Celtic, who were also keen to invite clubs from more distant areas for friendly matches, organized a trip for their opponents, Tritonville, the Leinster Senior League champions, to the *Cinderella* given by the Irish National Foresters' Dancing Class on St Stephen's Night 1905.[245] Reginald agreed to travel to face Sligo Athletic in a friendly match in March 1907 after they had got 'a large amount guaranteed', illustrating that some clubs necessitated payment to play exhibition and friendly matches regionally.[246]

THE SUCCESS OF BOHEMIANS AND SHELBOURNE AND THE FAILURE OF FREEBOOTERS AND REGINALD

The first Dublin club to win the IFA's Irish Junior Cup was Reginald. They were from Reginald Street in the Coombe/Meath Street area of Dublin and initially held their meetings at their rooms in Fishamble Street before moving to Bridge Street, where they had 'a well-equipped clubroom' for their '50 odd members'.[247] They were captained by Michael Balfe, a local man who worked in a brewery as a labourer.[248] Without a nearby space for a ground, they had their home venue initially in Dolphin's Barn and then at Crampton Lodge in Rialto, and defeated Stanley from Belfast at Dalymount Park to win the competition in 1904.[249] Described as 'the best junior combination in Leinster' in 1905, having also won the Leinster Junior league the previous year, they were defeated in the Irish Intermediate Cup final by Woodvale at the Oval in Belfast at the end of the 1904–5 season.[250] By the 1905–6 season, they were fielding teams in the Leinster First Division and Second Division,

239 *II*, 13 Feb. 1906. See also *Irish Times*, 18 Apr. 1908. **240** *SI*, 15 May 1910. **241** *Shelbourne Football Club golden jubilee, 1895–1945*, pp 41, 45. **242** *LJ*, 18 Apr. 1905. **243** *DC*, 31 Dec. 1904. **244** Ibid. **245** *Fermanagh Mail*, 23 Dec. 1905. **246** *SC*, 16 Mar. 1907. **247** *FJ*, 27 Jan. 1904; *EH*, 30 Nov. 1905; Briggs & Dodd, *100 years of the LFA*, pp 31, 86. **248** Clenet, 'Association football in Dublin', p. 808. **249** *LS*, 12 Mar. 1904; *EH*, 30 Nov. 1905; *DDE*, 21 Dec. 1906. **250** *TM*, 5 Nov. 1904; *BT*, 6 Apr. 1905.

and they won the Second Division title, the Johnson Cup, in 1905 and 1906.[251] They also reached the Irish Cup semi-final at the first attempt, and lost the Leinster Senior Cup final to Bohemians in 1907 in a replay.[252] Prior to their visit to Sligo in March 1907 for the Sligo Athletic friendly match, they were referred to as 'a club which had made its name famous, not alone in Leinster, but throughout Ireland'.[253] Despite their potential, by the latter years of that decade they appear to have disbanded, as an attempt by their honorary secretary to raise the subscription necessary to re-affiliate to the Leinster League proved unsuccessful in March 1908.[254]

Another club that showed potential nationally were Trojans, who were administered from Meath Place and had their home ground at Chapelizod.[255] They had won the 1907 Irish Junior Cup final initially, but were then defeated following two replays after a protest over a Royal Irish Constabulary man who had also played senior matches for Tritonville.[256] They won the Leinster Junior Cup in 1910 and also reached the 1914 Irish Intermediate Cup final.[257] However, the club were 'reluctantly compelled to resign' from the Leinster FA at the beginning of 1917, 'owing to shortage of players'.[258]

Instead, it was the national achievements of Shelbourne and Bohemians that stood out in the pre-war period and helped them grow and to develop long-term success. Bohemians joined the Irish League in the 1901–2 season and were followed by Shelbourne two years later, which helped the game as an attraction in the city by assuring more regular visits of northern teams for competitive matches.[259] In March 1905, the Leinster FA decided to legalize professionalism.[260] While Shelbourne adopted this shortly afterwards, Bohemians did not; Shelbourne's first professional player is thought to have been James Wall, who was paid a half penny per week.[261] Sands has also noted that this decision was a result of the labourers and general workers in their team having to take time off work for matches, and 'it would have been difficult to be available to travel often as might be necessary'.[262] As Sands also states, this can be contrasted with Bohemians, who remained amateur 'as many of those were in educationally qualified professions, often with their own or family businesses or practices' and 'they would likely have had more flexible work arrangements, and better financial support'.[263]

National success also helped to strengthen the popularity of soccer in Dublin and to boost the game's profile. Shelbourne and Bohemians dominated the Leinster FA Senior Cup following Leinster Nomads' success in 1893, and between themselves, they retained a hold on the trophy until Olympia won it in 1918.[264]

251 *DDE*, 2 May 1906. 252 *SC*, 16 Mar. 1907; *DEM*, 8 Apr. 1907. 253 *SC*, 16 Mar. 1907. 254 Senior League Council Minutes, Council Meeting, 11 Mar. 1908, Leinster Football Association Archives, P239/24. 255 *DE*, 2 Oct. 1906; *EH*, 19 Aug. 1913. 256 *EH*, 9 Feb. 1907; *INBMN*, 21 Feb. 1907 and 4 Mar. 1907; *FJ*, 1 Apr. 1907. 257 *DDE*, 26 Mar. 1910 and 27 Nov. 1915; *BN*, 18 Mar. 1914. 258 *II*, 12 Jan. 1917. 259 Briggs & Dodd, *100 years of the LFA*, p. 30 and O'Mahony (ed.), *Bohemian Football Club golden jubilee souvenir*, p. 15. 260 *LS*, 23 Mar. 1905. 261 Sands, *Shels*, p. 2. 262 Ibid., pp 12–13. 263 Ibid. 264 Briggs & Dodd, *100 years of the LFA*, p. 40 and *Sport*, 24 Aug. 1918.

Apparently the Shelbourne club had bought the Olympia team a set of medals as a memento prior to the match, as only the winners received medals at the time, only to be defeated one–nil by the junior team.[265] Bohemians and Shelbourne also experienced success in the IFA's competitions after a number of failures at the final hurdle. Following Bohemians' defeat in the 1895 Irish Cup final they did not return to that stage until 1900, when they lost to Cliftonville by two goals to one.[266] They again reached the final in 1903, losing 3–1 to Distillery of Belfast.[267] In 1905, Shelbourne lost the Irish Cup final to Distillery by four goals to nil.[268] However, Shelbourne again reached the final the following season and were victorious against Belfast Celtic before a crowd of 7,000 on 28 April 1906 at Dalymount Park as they won 2–0.[269] Excursion trains were laid on for the match, while the Dublin United Tramways also provided cars. Jimmy Owens scored both goals with Val Harris' performance central to the victory.[270] Sands has written that through Shelbourne's 1906 Irish Cup final win, they had 'quickly become the team favoured by almost all of south-side Dublin, plus many inner-city areas on the north side, especially those inhabited by dock workers, plus carters and labourers. This gave rise to the club being sometimes called 'the Dockers team'.[271] Triumph and exposure on a national stage meant they could recruit better players. Billy Lacey joined Shelbourne for the 1906–7 season and the club also recruited Carthy from Stockport County and Cardiff City goalkeeper House.[272] Shelbourne again reached the Irish Senior Cup final in 1907, but lost to Cliftonville.[273]

Other senior Dublin clubs also showed they could compete on a national stage. In March 1901, the amateur Freebooters reached the Irish Cup final but were defeated the following month by Cliftonville, who were also non-professional at that point.[274] The Freebooters had defeated Linfield in the semi-final at Jones' Road, Drumcondra, by two goals to one 'before a large and enthusiastic crowd of spectators'.[275] The Dublin club, which featured three Irish internationals, were forced to travel to Grosvenor Park in Belfast without three of their best players, who had withdrawn at the last moment and they lost another through injury early in the match, which Cliftonville won one–nil, despite a resilient performance by Irish cap and goalkeeper Nolan.[276] Following the match, the Dublin club were 'entertained to dinner' by the Belfast side in the local Grand Central Hotel.[277] They had also reached the Leinster Senior Cup final in 1900, losing 1–0 to Shelbourne at Jones's Road.[278]

This early promise was not fulfilled, however. A lack of enthusiasm was reported to be the reason why the Freebooters, 'the Irish Corinthians', were in decline by early 1906.[279] They were beaten 10–1 by Bohemians in the Leinster Intermediate Cup in January of that year and their tactics were reported to have deteriorated greatly since their earlier progress in the IFA and Leinster FA cups.[280] Chris Bolsmann and

265 *Soccer Reporter* (Oct. 1983), p. 14. **266** *BN*, 23 Mar. 1908. **267** Ibid. **268** Ibid. **269** Ibid.; *SI*, 9 Sept. 1956. **270** Ibid. **271** Sands, *Shels*, pp 14–15. **272** *SI*, 9 Sept. 1956. **273** *BN*, 23 Mar. 1908. **274** Ibid., 15 Apr. 1901. **275** *INBMN*, 18 Mar. 1901. **276** *BN*, 15 Apr. 1901. **277** *INBME*, 15 Apr. 1901. **278** *DDN*, 28 and 30 Apr. 1900. **279** *NW*, 5 Mar. 1906. **280** *DEM*, 22 Jan. 1906.

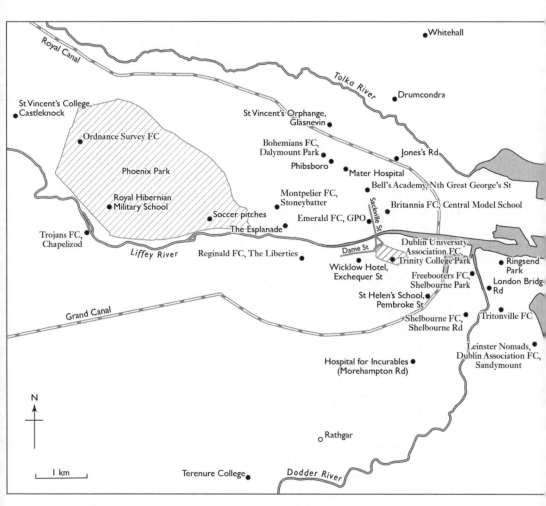

2. Late nineteenth- and early twentieth-century areas of soccer's development in Dublin. Courtesy of Matthew Stout.

Dilwyn Porter have noted that 'social exclusivity was a defining characteristic' of the English Corinthians club, which indicates that the Freebooters may also have been less open to recruiting those whom they deemed to be their social inferiors, and appear to have contained a number of those who were university-educated.[281] At least one of the Freebooters players, 1901 Irish Cup final goalkeeper Jim Nolan-Whelan, who had changed his name by deed poll, played for the Corinthians against the Army at Queen's Club in London in January 1903.[282] He also attended Oxford University, where he studied law and played in the 1902–3 Varsity match versus Cambridge.[283] According to one source, he had initially joined Freebooters because of a scarcity of clubs in his local area, Monkstown, at that time, although it is more likely that he was seen by the Freebooters club as being of a similar social background.[284] In the 1906–7 season, Shelbourne availed of the 'splendid' Sandymount Road ground previously used by the Freebooters, who had disbanded earlier in 1906, with the venue subsequently becoming known as Shelbourne Park.[285]

The first Dublin derby in the Irish Senior Cup final took place in 1908, when Bohemians met Shelbourne at the former team's home venue of Dalymount Park.[286] The match ended in a one-all draw and 'a feature of the play was the brilliant goalkeeping of [J.C.] Hehir, the home custodian, who saved two penalties and otherwise kept a magnificent goal'.[287] He naturally remained in goal for the replay, and his absence elsewhere was felt as Bective Rangers, his rugby team, were beaten by Dublin University at Lansdowne Road in the Leinster Senior Cup semi-final.[288] In the replay, Bohemians won 3–1, with one reporter noting that their teamwork and levels of physical fitness were significant factors, along with the play of R.M. Hooper, their centre forward.[289] Following Bohemians' win, there was 'a remarkable scene of enthusiasm' as 'the team were mobbed on their way to the pavilion, the crowd insisting on "chairing" the members of the victorious team, a "service" which was likewise rendered to Harris and members of the losing side'.[290] That night, the Bohemians club celebrated at the Empire.[291] At the end of April 1908, 'about 120 members' were present for the club's dinner in the Dolphin Hotel, Essex Street, when the Irish Cup was formally presented to club captain, J. Balfe, by the chairman of the IFA, Alexander Thompson.[292]

In May 1908 Shelbourne gained a measure of revenge when they beat Bohemians 2–1 in the Metropolitan Cup final before around 3,000 spectators at Dalymount Park.[293] They retained it the following year and also won the Belfast City Cup,

281 Chris Bolsmann & Dilwyn Porter, *English gentlemen and world soccer: Corinthians, amateurism and the global game* (Abingdon, 2018), p. 3; *DDE*, 27 Feb. 1889. **282** 'NIFG-Jim Nolan-Whelan', nifootball.blogspot.com/2007/12/jim-nolan-whelan.html, accessed 11 Aug. 2021; *The Sportsman*, 2 Feb. 1903. I am grateful to Dilwyn Porter for drawing my attention to this appearance. **283** 'NIFG-Jim Nolan-Whelan' and Colin Weir, *The history of Oxford University Association Football Club, 1872–1998* (Harefield, 1998), p. 28. **284** Joe Dodd, *Soccer in the Boro' year book* (Blackrock, 1990), p. 16. **285** *II*, 5 Mar. 1906; *NW*, 5 Mar. 1906; *SI*, 9 Sept. 1956. **286** *BN*, 23 Mar. 1908. **287** Ibid. **288** *IT*, 4 Apr. 1908. **289** Ibid. **290** Ibid. **291** *INBMN*, 30 Mar. 1908. **292** *IWT*, 2 May 1908. **293** *DDE*, 4 May 1908.

the Leinster Senior Cup and the Leinster League Cup that season.[294] National success also came to St James's Gate, who won the Irish Intermediate Cup in 1910, defeating Mountpottinger 1–0 in the final at Grosvenor Park, with 800 of their supporters travelling north to the match.[295] That same season, they had won the Leinster League First Division.[296] They also reached the Irish Intermediate Cup final in 1913, but were defeated 3–0 by Glentoran's 2nd XI.[297] The growing strength of Dublin's two most successful clubs in the pre-war years, Shelbourne and Bohemians, was illustrated as they met again in the 1911 Irish Senior Cup final at Dalymount Park, when Shelbourne won by two goals to one in front of around 10,000 spectators in a replay after a goalless draw.[298] However, in 1912, following a dispute over finances and power, the majority of Irish League clubs quit the IFA, leaving only Bohemians and Linfield, but an attempt to arrange a breakaway organization lasted only briefly, as, following negotiations in the summer of that year, the discontented clubs were given increased rights.[299]

National triumph also came at junior level, with Chapelizod winning the Irish Junior Cup in March 1911, when they defeated South End Rangers of Ballymena by a goal to nil.[300] At the end of the 1910–11 season there were 122 clubs affiliated with the Leinster FA, a slight increase on the figure of 119 the previous season.[301] Following instruction from the IFA Ltd, who decided to take over the control and management of referees, a new Referees' Committee was also founded within the Leinster FA.[302]

Some clubs' development was impeded by difficulties in securing their own ground, including Clarence, who had won the Leinster Junior League Championship and Leinster Junior Cup by 1911 'and would have been in senior ranks but for this'.[303] Tritonville, who had no issues with this, took part in the Irish League in the 1912–13 season, returning to the game after a notable absence and having been resurrected for this purpose.[304] Despite having 'a splendidly equipped ground, conveniently situated', they lost their place along with Derry Celtic as both clubs finished bottom.[305] Tritonville's members then took the decision to disband, while Derry Celtic switched to Gaelic football.[306] In October of that year, the lord mayor of Dublin, Lorcan Sherlock, having been elected the previous May, turned down the Leinster FA's offer of the position of president.[307] It appears that the GAA had decided that the lord mayor would not to be permitted to attend their matches as he had initially accepted the position of Leinster FA president, and this may have influenced his decision not to take up the offer.[308] However, by early 1917, Lord Mayor Laurence O'Neill announced his intention to attend

294 *SI*, 9 Sept. 1956. 295 *Sport*, 27 Oct. 1917. 296 Ibid. 297 *NW*, 17 Mar. 1913; *BN*, 18 Mar. 1913. 298 *BT*, 18 Apr. 1911. 299 Moore, *The Irish soccer split*, pp 35–44. 300 *TDE*, 13 Mar. 1911. 301 19th Annual Report, May 1911, Leinster Football Association Archives, P239/24. 302 Ibid. 303 *FSW*, 5 Feb. 1927. 304 *Sport*, 6 Apr. 1912. 305 *FJ*, 9 Sept. 1912; *EH*, 24 and 29 May 1913. 306 *EH*, 15 Aug. 1913; Moore, *The Irish soccer split*, p. 43. 307 *FJ*, 5 May 1913; *EH*, 11 Sept. 1913. 308 Central Council Minute Books, 1899–1981, GAA Archives Croke Park, GAA/CC/01/02 1911–25, p. 19.

soccer matches in Dublin, illustrating the divergent views on the subject that prevailed within society.[309]

THE 1913 LOCKOUT AND THE FIRST WORLD WAR, 1914–18

As Dickson has noted, Jacob's Biscuit Factory, 'one of the largest sources of employment in the inter-war period', was 'in the eye of the storm during both the 1913 Lockout and the Easter Rising'.[310] The soccer club did not participate in competitions in the 1913–14 season 'owing to the Labour troubles' but returned to the Junior League in the 1914–15 season.[311] Bohemians and Shelbourne also gained attention during the Lockout, which saw around 400 employers, 'headed by the redoubtable William Martin Murphy, former nationalist Member of Parliament and owner of the *Irish Catholic* and *Irish Independent* newspapers, engage in a full-scale lock out in Dublin' in order to put down Jim Larkin's Irish Transport and General Workers' Union (ITGWU).[312] Garnham has noted that at the end of August 1913, during the industrial disputes, the ITGWU's official newspaper, the *Irish Worker*, alleged that Bohemians' Jack Millar and Shelbourne's Jack Lowry were 'scabs' or strike-breakers.[313] The subsequent meeting of the two clubs to officially open Shelbourne's ground at Sandymount saw trams and supporters being stoned as trade union leaders had encouraged their members not to attend the game. He adds that the violence was only halted when a tram passenger fired a revolver. 'It was apparently this incident … that catalysed two days of sporadic rioting across the city, during which two men died.'[314] Around 6,000 supporters had attended the match.[315] Gerry Farrell has stated that Millar was not actually a Bohemians first-team player, and all of the Bohemians footballers 'who played that fateful day in Shelbourne Park were in another form of employment, mainly as clerks and civil servants with a couple of soldiers and students thrown in'.[316] In addition, 'none were in any role or profession that could lead them to being accused of scabbing'.[317] Shelbourne FC later took to the press to state that the club were not to blame for any 'blacklegging', although they did not deny any involvement of players as 'scabs'.[318] Despite the establishment of the Citizen Army by James Connolly in November 1913, the workers had no option but to accept the poor working conditions and return to employment in January 1914.[319]

Following victories over England and Wales and a draw with Scotland, the Irish international team, which featured Dublin-born players Val Harris and Patrick O'Connell, won the home championship for the first time, although only one player at a Dublin club, W.G. McConnell of Bohemians, was in the team,

309 *EH*, 15 Mar. 1917.   **310** Dickson, *Dublin*, p. 488.   **311** *Sport*, 29 Sept. 1917.   **312** Bartlett, *Ireland*, p. 369.   **313** Garnham, *Association football and society*, p. 150.   **314** Ibid.   **315** Padraig Yeates, *Lockout: Dublin 1913* [paperback edition] (Dublin, 2013), p. 48.   **316** Gerry Farrell, 'Who you calling scab? Bohs, Shels and the 1913 Lockout', abohemiansportinglife.wordpress. com/2020/10/04/who-you-calling-scab-bohs-shels-and-the-1913-lockout, accessed 11 Aug. 2021. **317** Ibid.   **318** Ibid.   **319** Bartlett, *Ireland: a history*, p. 369.

the rest being Britain-based.[320] However, the outbreak of the First World War
later that year prevented any further development of the international team at that
time. Some 24,644 men enlisted in Dublin during the war, which began in the
autumn of 1914, although overall recruitment lessened on a yearly basis throughout the war 'as the pool of prospective recruits was drained and the fate of former
recruits became known'.[321] A notable absence from the Leinster Senior Cup first
round matches at the start of the 1914–15 season were military teams, with none
involved in the six matches listed.[322] The previous season, seven military teams
had been among the sixteen in the first-round draw.[323] The outbreak of war also
had a detrimental effect on many civilian teams, including Bendigo, Bohemians
and St James's Gate. Bendigo had become 'very much disorganized' at the beginning of the war in September 1914, as at that time 'about seventy-five per cent
of the members were in the British Army Reserve, all of whom were called to
the front'.[324] By the end of 1914, forty Bohemians players had joined the military, while St James's Gate had lost eight of their players by that time.[325] As will
be shown in more detail in chapter seven, numerous soccer players from other
Dublin clubs also fought in the war.

Despite Leinster FA membership being halved, competitions continued and
Dublin's two Irish League clubs, Shelbourne and Bohemians, joined the Leinster
Senior League in 1915 as the Irish League was suspended, and, later re-suspended,
as it turned out, until the end of 1919.[326] A Belfast and District league was formed
for clubs in that area. Garnham has stated that 'a practical partition of the game
was already taking place'.[327] He has also highlighted a decline of crowds in Belfast
with additional Saturday shift work in war-related industries while enlistment also
impacted on the numbers present to attend matches by early 1915.[328] In Derry city,
the number of clubs affiliated with the North-West FA dropped from thirty-seven
to eleven by the end of the 1914–15 season, due to 'the flocking of players in large
numbers to the colours'.[329] The organization's honorary secretary 'had to resort to
selling such scrap as old footballs and jerseys in order to successfully carry out' his
'book keeping operation'.[330] He also noted that 'in county Derry, there were only
three clubs where there were formerly twenty, and from Tyrone just one as against
a round dozen'.[331]

Certainly the loss of Irish League matches impacted on Shelbourne's professional footballers, who had won the Irish Gold Cup for the 1914–15 season, with
a benefit match held for them in May 1915 at Ringsend against 'a team of Dublin

320 *IE*, 16 Mar. 1914.   321 Padraig Yeates, *A city in wartime: Dublin, 1914–18* (Dublin, 2011), p. 75
and Fitzpatrick, 'Militarism in Ireland, 1900–1922', p. 388.   322 Senior League Council Minutes, 13
Jan. 1915, Leinster Football Association Archives, P239/24.   323 Senior League Council Minutes,
10 Dec. 1913, Leinster Football Association Archives, P239/24.   324 *FSW*, 3 Apr. and 10 July
1926.   325 *Sport*, 27 Oct. 1917; Garnham, *Association football and society*, p. 171. See, in particular, Gerry Farrell, 'Bohemians of World War I', abohemiansportinglife.wordpress.com/2016/06/29/
bohemians-of-world-war-i, accessed 29 July 2021.   326 Garnham, *Association football and society*, p.
168.   327 Ibid.   328 Ibid., p. 169.   329 *DJ*, 2 June 1915.   330 Ibid.   331 Ibid.

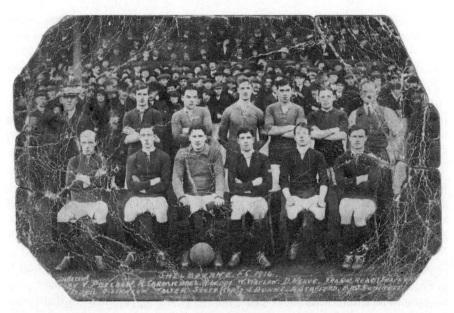

3. Shelbourne FC (1914). Courtesy of Dublin City Library and Archives.

Amateurs' before 'a large crowd'.[332] Some other clubs and representative selections took part in fundraising matches during the war. In December 1914, the Leinster FA donated the gate receipts from a Shelbourne versus Leinster selection match at Dalymount Park to the National Relief Fund at the Mansion House.[333] A Linfield and Belfast Celtic team met a 'Rest of League' selection at Belfast in May 1915 'for the Wounded Soldiers' and Sailors' Fund'.[334] In December 1915, a selection of Linfield, Belfast Celtic and Dublin players took on a team representing 'the rest of the league' in a fundraising match in aid of the Irish Football League at Grosvenor Park in Belfast.[335] A Linfield team featuring Elisha Scott played Glentoran at the Oval in order to raise funds for the Women's Gift Fund 'for the comforts of the East Belfast men' in May 1916.[336] In November 1916, players representing north and south Dublin met in a benefit match for the Leinster League.[337] Shelbourne and Bohemians selections met at Dalymount Park in May 1918 with the receipts of the match going to a fund set up for dependents of submarine victims.[338] Dublin clubs also supported St Vincent de Paul Day at that time.[339]

By November 1915 Shelbourne and Bohemians had therefore joined Strandville, Ulster, St James's Gate, Frankfort, Chapelizod, Shamrock Rovers, University College and Orwell in the Leinster Senior League.[340] Shamrock Rovers were apparently revived in 1914 following a decline in 1906 when they struggled

332 *II*, 17 May 1915; *Shelbourne Football Club golden jubilee*, p. 22.   333 *DDE*, 19 Dec. 1914.   334 *II*, 17 May 1915.   335 *BN*, 28 Dec. 1915.   336 *NW*, 13 and 15 May 1916.   337 *DDE*, 27 Nov. 1916.   338 *FJ*, 11 May 1918.   339 *Sport*, 24 Nov. 1917 and 26 Oct. 1918.   340 *II*, 1 Nov. 1915.

to find enough players for their Leinster Senior and Junior League teams, while they also had issues with their home ground in Ringsend.[341] In 1915, they won the Irish Junior Cup, beating Derry Swifts at Ulster Park. They again had problems with their home venue in 1916, which meant another decline in activity, as they dropped out of the Leinster Senior League before again being revived in 1921.[342] Some Shamrock Rovers members had maintained their connections during these years by playing exhibition matches, while a few players also lined out for a club named St Patrick's, which played in the Sunday League, during the 1916–21 period.[343]

There is evidence that the number of matches being played in Dublin declined during the war, with applications for the use of public pitches in Phoenix Park dropping by a third in the 1914–15 season.[344] One reporter noted in February 1915 that 'the daily lists of the fortunes and favours of sportsmen at the front afford ample evidence of the serious drain made on clubs of every description including football, hockey, cricket, swimming, polo, etc.'.[345] Elsewhere, it was stated in September 1915 that 'the year of war we have passed through since the beginning of last season has told upon the game as well as the country, and such football as we have must conform to the altered conditions'.[346] One reporter noted that 'the Irish League and the English League have disappeared, and instead we have local combinations'.[347] Some other Dublin clubs did enjoy success in the IFA's competitions in 1915, with University College Dublin winning the Irish Intermediate Cup.[348] In 1917, Strandville won the Irish Intermediate Cup to become the third Dublin club to do so, illustrating further the mixed nature of the effects of war on Dublin's clubs.[349]

According to Peter Byrne, in the weeks following the Easter Rising of 1916, which took place from Easter Monday, 24 April to 29 April, 'many events had to be postponed for a short period', with the result that the Dublin soccer season was extended until 10 June, but 'it had only a minimum effect on sport in the capital'.[350] A force of around 1,200 members of the Irish Volunteers and the Irish Citizen Army seized control at a number of points mainly around the city and its outskirts, and at least 300 people were killed and 2,600 injured.[351] Around 3,500 prisoners were taken by the British forces, with ninety later court martialled and fifteen executed.[352] One match of note that reportedly took place on that Easter Monday in Dublin was between Shelbourne and a Junior Metropolitan League XI at Shelbourne Park, although details are scarce.[353] Travel was certainly disrupted. The Bohemians first team were returning from a friendly match against Athlone by train that day when the violence broke out, and as a result their journey back to

341 Doolan & Goggins, *The Hoops*, pp 7–8.   342 Ibid., pp 7–9 and Rice, *We are Rovers*, p. 33; Gerard Farrell, 'Rovers of the Sea', abohemiansportinglife.wordpress.com/2018/01, accessed 30 July 2021.   343 Doolan & Goggins, *The Hoops*, pp 8–11.   344 Garnham, *Association football and society*, p. 171.   345 *II*, 24 Feb. 1915.   346 *Sport*, 25 Sept. 1915.   347 Ibid.   348 Briggs & Dodds, *100 years of the LFA*, p. 40.   349 *II*, 19 Mar. 1917.   350 Byrne, *Green is the colour*, p. 54.   351 Dickson, *Dublin*, pp 449, 455.   352 Ibid., p. 455.   353 *EH*, 20 Apr. 1916; *Sport*, 13 Oct. 1917.

Dublin was delayed.[354] Under martial law, Phoenix Park was temporarily closed and only those with passes could enter.[355] The Leinster FA held a special meeting on 13 May to make arrangements for the rescheduling of postponed matches for the rest of the season.[356] Matches in Dublin resumed on Saturday 20 May, although there was still a scarcity of pitches.[357] Almost a month after the Rising began, the Junior Shield final replay between Glasnevin and Olympia went ahead at Shelbourne Park that day, with Glasnevin victorious.[358] The two sides had initially drawn on Good Friday, three days prior to the outbreak of violence.[359] The Leinster Junior Cup final between CYMS and GSWR also went ahead at Shelbourne Park after that replay.[360] By the end of May most of the Leinster FA's competitions had concluded, with Bohemians winning the Leinster Senior Cup and Shelbourne winning the Leinster Senior League.[361]

The return of some football migrants, such as Val Harris, by early 1916, with the suspension of the regular season and the threat of conscription in England, led some other players to also come to Ireland, and this was said to have improved the standard of the game.[362] Billy Lacey's inclusion in the Shelbourne team in 1916 drew protest from Shamrock Rovers, but this was dismissed by the Leinster FA, whose chairman noted that Liverpool's secretary had given Lacey permission to play as an amateur, as 'all professionals were reinstated amateur [*sic*] by the FA'.[363] However, the disbandment of clubs was notable, with Richmond Rovers, Pembroke, Reginald and Tritonville all said to have gone 'into oblivion for lack of support' by the start of the 1917–18 season.[364] There were also concerns that Shelbourne were about to do this, as none of their players from the previous season had again signed up.[365] Despite this, in September 1917, it was reported that 'the prospects for a successful season are much rosier than they were twelve months ago, as all the Dublin leagues have filled well'.[366] Shelbourne continued, 'but on a different footing from that which obtained since the establishment of the Shelbourne Sports Company' in 1912.[367] This had been founded 'for the purpose of establishing on the south side of Dublin a suitable recreation ground for the carrying on of all classes of sports', but with a particular focus on soccer, cycling, athletics and trotting.[368] This was not a success and was discontinued in 1923, but the soccer club persevered.[369]

Despite the decline of some clubs, including the aforementioned Trojans in 1917, which saw two of their players transferred to Bohemians, structures of the game do not appear to have been too badly affected in Dublin during the war.[370] By autumn 1918 Jacob's had improved their 'splendid enclosure' at their Rutland

354 Gerry Farrell & Brian Trench, 'Bohemians during Easter 1916', abohemiansportinglife.wordpress. com/2016/03, accessed 29 July 2021. 355 *II*, 6 May 1916. 356 *SI*, 14 May 1916. 357 *DDE*, 20 May 1916. 358 *Sport*, 22 Sept. 1917. 359 *EH*, 18 May 1916. 360 Ibid. 361 *SI*, 28 May 1916. 362 Garnham, *Association football and society*, p. 171. 363 Emergency Committee Meeting Minutes, 15 Mar. 1916, Leinster Football Association Archives, P239/36. 364 *EH*, 18 Aug. 1917. 365 Ibid. 366 *FJ*, 1 Sept. 1917. 367 Ibid.; *II*, 2 Nov. 1912. 368 *II*, 2 Nov. 1912. 369 Byrne, *Green is the colour*, p. 18. 370 *EH*, 12 Jan. 1917.

Avenue ground and were said to have had 'comparatively inexhaustible' resources and had 'done a great deal to popularize the game on the south-west side of the city'.[371] At the start of the 1918–19 season the Leinster Senior League Division One contained Bohemians, Shelbourne, St James's Gate, Frankfort, Jacob's, University College, Dublin Military, Ulster and Olympia, while junior soccer was also said to be in a 'healthy' state in Dublin.[372] There were eight teams in Division Two of the Leinster Senior League at the start of the 1918–19 season, while the Athletic Union League had two divisions.[373] There was also a Metropolitan League, the Minor League and a Central League, as well as junior leagues.[374]

Some clubs, such as Ormeau and Brooklyn, were actually said to have flourished during the war in terms of the winning records they set in local competitions.[375] Ormeau were founded in 1914 by their captain, Albert Cowzer, who gathered together 'some of the best players from unsuccessful teams in the junior leagues'.[376] They were evidently a close-knit club and by 1917 their membership was made up of only eleven players and a secretary, and while they ran the club through paying for costs themselves, they also had 'two staunch friends in Rev. Father Union, Ringsend, and Mr W.J. Tunney, chairman of the Shelbourne Sports Company'.[377] While the role of the clergy in the growth of sport in Ireland has not yet been fully assessed, some soccer clubs (as well GAA clubs) clearly benefited from their assistance, with Rev. Father Neary acting as club patron of Brooklyn FC of Vernon Avenue (Clontarf), who changed their name to Leinster in 1917.[378] The former Brooklyn club, which began in 1914–15 in the Central League, drew their players from the Merchant's Quay area in the city, with Joe Kendrick later emerging as one of the stars of Dublin soccer, having also gained experience of the game at Wasps before joining Shelbourne.[379] As the war neared its conclusion, some reporters tried to paint a positive picture of events within Dublin football circles. Writing in *Sport* in August 1918, 'Viator' claimed that

> the war has absolutely nothing to do with Dublin football. That is to say, it is not responsible for any serious leakage of players or any big falling away of support. It hit Bohemians and Shelbourne severely, and they have experienced a bitter time since the Irish League was confined to Belfast clubs. Still these clubs have succeeded in keeping things tolerably lively within the past four seasons, and there is no doubt they will succeed in maintaining their best traditions during the coming season.[380]

However, as will be shown in more detail later, while many clubs continued, the loss of individual players to military involvement was notable.

371 *Sport*, 31 Aug. 1918. 372 Ibid., 24 Aug. and 26 Oct. 1918. 373 Ibid., 26 Oct. 1918. 374 Ibid. 375 Ibid., 6 Oct. 1917. 376 Ibid., 13 Oct. 1917. 377 Ibid. 378 Ibid., 6 Oct. 1917. 379 Ibid.; Tom Hunt, 'Ireland's footballers at the 1924 and 1948 Olympic Games: compromised by the politics of sport' in Curran (ed.), 'The growth and development of soccer in Dublin', Special issue of *Soccer and Society*, pp 887–900, p. 890; *Sport*, 5 Sept. 1925. 380 *Sport*, 24 Aug. 1918.

Despite the difficulties within the Irish League, noted above, John McAlery, writing in *Sport* in December 1918, stated that in Belfast, 'war did not seriously interfere with football, even from the first day, although a few regulations in connection proved irksome'.[381] He added that 'the war brought many good players to Belfast from across Channel and all helped to create interest and competition'.[382] While cricket and rugby were said to have suffered there, boxing apparently enjoyed 'a wonderful revival' and 'no sport held its ground better than whippet racing'.[383]

There is no question that a drop in the number of clubs was experienced. Malcolm Brodie has noted that the number of clubs affiliated to the IFA fell from 221 to 140 during the war.[384] At the Leinster FA's AGM in May 1919, it was stated that the number of affiliated clubs had dropped from 77 in the 1917–18 season to 73 in the 1918–19 season, but the outgoing council were confident this would increase again and that there would be 'a revival of some of the leagues which were suspended owing to the war'.[385] Other reports illustrated a different story regarding how clubs fared during the war. The IFA's commission, which was set up to investigate the state of the game around its affiliated divisional associations, revealed in June 1919 that 'since the war some very prominent clubs went out of existence through no fault of their own, and the number of clubs affiliated has fallen by half'.[386] There was also recognition given by the Leinster FA that they had to compete with other football codes as it was stated that they 'at present suffer opposition from other quarters, which has to be worn down'.[387] The IFA agreed to give additional funding to a number of areas, with the Leinster FA receiving £200, while £150 was given to the Mid-Ulster FA and £75 to the Derry-based North-West FA.[388]

Attendances in Dublin dropped during the War of Independence (1919–21), and subsequent Civil War (1922–3), with some clubs losing players to those in England and Scotland.[389] The involvement of clubs and players in these conflicts will also be discussed in detail in chapter seven. In October 1919, a benefit match took place between Ulster and Leinster selections in Dublin to raise funds for the Leinster Football Association and to heighten the game's profile in Dublin.[390] The Ulster team, which was essentially a County Antrim selection, won five–nil, but a number of their players were assaulted near the end of the game by supporters who came on to the Dalymount Park pitch.[391] In November 1919, a Leinster League selection met 'the pick of the Garrison League' at Dalymount Park in a match to raise money for the Irish National War Memorial Fund.[392]

St James's Gate won the Irish Intermediate Cup again in 1920, defeating Dunmurry at Dalymount Park.[393] They also won the Leinster Senior Cup

381 Ibid., 28 Dec. 1918.	382 Ibid.	383 Ibid.	384 Malcolm Brodie, *100 years of Irish football* (Belfast, 1908), p. 12.	385 *FJ*, 2 June 1919.	386 Minute book of the IFA, 1909–28, Report of Commission, 20 June 1919, p. 269, IFA Archives, D/4196.	387 Ibid.	388 Ibid.	389 Curran, *Irish soccer migrants*, p. 110.	390 Garnham, *Association football and society*, p. 176.	391 *Freeman's Journal*, 27 Oct. 1919; 28th Annual Report, May 1920, Leinster Football Association Archives, P239/25.	392 *DET*, 18 Nov. 1919.	393 Briggs & Dodd, *100 years of the LFA*, p. 42.

for the first time that year (defeating Bohemians two goals to one in a second replay), the Leinster Senior League and the Metropolitan Cup.[394] The replay of the Leinster Senior Cup final had been postponed for ten days in April 1920 'in view of the prevailing conditions in Dublin'.[395] IFA Cup finalists Shelbourne were awarded that trophy after the already suspended Belfast Celtic's protest against Glentoran, who had beaten them at the semi-final stage, was upheld.[396] By that stage, Shelbourne's ground had been closed following crowd trouble in their semi-final win against Glenavon. As Byrne has stated of the highest levels of the domestic game, 'Irish football was in a shambolic state and, in the opinion of many, headed for even more squalls.'[397] Despite these issues, the number of registered clubs did begin to pick up in the Leinster area. At the end of the 1919–20 season, the Leinster FA reported that the number of clubs registered had risen to 120 from 73 the previous season.[398] By the end of 1920, along with Leinster Senior and Intermediate leagues, there were also teams competing in the Junior League, the Athletic Union League, a Combination League, which had two divisions, an Alliance League, a Metropolitan League, a Central League and a Leinster Junior Alliance League.[399]

The failure of the IFA to arrange the 1921 Irish Cup semi-final replay in Dublin, rather than Belfast, where the drawn match between a weakened Shelbourne team and Glenavon had taken place, was perceived by many within Dublin soccer as another example of the national governing body's failure to show 'understanding for the interests of southern clubs'.[400] Shelbourne's refusal to travel back to Belfast for the replay, citing travel risks, meant that the match was not played, and 'their action precipitated the "Split" and hastened the birth of a new regime, the Football Association of Ireland, with headquarters in Dublin'.[401] Cormac Moore has stated that 'the split was not nurtured by national politics; it was nurtured by power. Both bodies vied for the right to govern soccer in Ireland'.[402] In June 1921 the Leinster FA voted to remove their affiliation to the IFA and the Dublin body's secretary, J.A. Ryder, informed the Belfast organization of this in a brief letter. The League of Ireland met initially at the beginning of the month and the FAI held its first meeting on 1 September.[403] This became the national governing body for soccer in the Irish Free State, while the Leinster FA continued as a provincial body, although naturally there was to be some overlap between members of the FAI, the Leinster FA and the Football League of Ireland.[404]

Competitive structures under the FAI were similar to those of the IFA with the development of senior, intermediate and junior sections, while the former

394 28th Annual Report, May 1920, Leinster Football Association Archives, P239/25; 'Our History', stjamesgatefc.com/club-history, accessed 3 Jan. 2022.   395 Emergency Committee Minutes, 13 and 16 Apr. 1920, Leinster Football Association Archives, P239/ 36.   396 Byrne, *Green is the colour*, p. 61.   397 Ibid.   398 28th Annual Report, May 1920, Leinster Football Association Archives, P239/25.   399 *FJ*, 4 Dec. 1920.   400 *Shelbourne Football Club golden jubilee*, p. 23.   401 Ibid.   402 Moore, *The Irish soccer split*, p. 234.   403 Garnham, *Association football and society*, pp 177–8.   404 Ibid., p. 179.

administrative body's national league and cup were arranged for the best teams.[405] The new Free State League was established by the autumn of 1921 with eight teams as members, these being Bohemians, Dublin United, Frankfort, Jacob's, St James's Gate, Olympia, Shelbourne and YMCA.[406] The cup and shield were inaugurated shortly afterwards.[407] St James's Gate were the winners of the league in the opening season, which lasted for only three months from September until December 1921 and was aided through significant promotion in the Dublin newspapers.[408] Sunday matches were also a major boost to the game's development at that level.[409] The first FAI Cup final was decided after a replay when St James's Gate, which played their home matches at St James's Park in Dolphin's Barn between 1921 and 1928, beat Shamrock Rovers in a replay at April 1922 following a draw the previous month.[410] That same month, they added the Leinster Senior Cup to their list of silverware for that season, defeating Jacob's.[411] By that point, it was becoming evident that senior soccer in Dublin could retain public interest following the break from administration in Belfast, and had made considerable progress since the fragile days of the 1880s and early 1890s.

CONCLUSION

Following the foundation of the Leinster FA in 1892, its competitions grew in the remainder of the decade, as did the number of soccer clubs in Dublin. By the early 1900s, Shelbourne and Bohemians were the two strongest clubs in Dublin, and both joined the Irish League in the opening years of the new century. Other clubs, such as Reginald and Freebooters, showed promise in the IFA's competitions, but faded away without sufficient support and commitment. The development of Dalymount Park as a venue was an important step in progress, and as well as the hosting of a number of cup finals, further recognition from the IFA that Dublin had an adequate venue for international soccer was notable in the staging of a match against Scotland there in 1904.[412] More improvements were made to the ground later in that decade, including the widening and draining of the pitch, the building of wooden stands behind the goals and provision of a telephone box for the *Evening Mail*.[413] The administrative efforts of Leinster FA secretary William Sheffield, and, after 1907, J.A. Ryder, in the same role, were significant in the game's growth in early twentieth century Dublin.[414] Ryder later became the FAI's first paid secretary

405 Garnham, 'Ein spiel in zwei nationen? Fussball in Irland, 1918–1939', p. 79. 406 *SI*, 8 Aug. 1956. 407 Ibid. 408 Phil Soar, Martin Tyler & Richard Widdows, *The Hamlyn encyclopaedia of football* (London, 1980), p. 163; Conor Heffernan & Joseph Taylor, 'A league is born: the League of Ireland's inaugural season, 1921–1922' in Curran (ed.), 'The growth and development of soccer in Dublin', Special issue of *Soccer and Society*, pp 845–57, pp 851–3. 409 Curran, *Irish soccer migrants*, p. 24. 410 *II*, 18 Mar. and 10 Apr. 1922; *SI*, 21 Oct. 1956; 'Our history', stjamesgatefc.com/club-history, accessed 3 Jan. 2022. 411 *II*, 18 Apr. 1922. 412 O'Mahony, *Bohemian Football Club Golden jubilee souvenir*, p. 20. 413 Ibid., p. 20. 414 Byrne, *Green is the colour*, pp 25–6, 37–8.

and was important in securing the new national organization's international status as a member of FIFA in 1926.[415]

Soccer was not immune to the tensions within Dublin society on the eve of the First World War, and while the game itself survived, some of the related effects of the global conflict were evident, including a loss of players, which will be discussed more fully later. Similarly, at a more local level, the events of the Irish Revolution of 1913–23 affected sport in Ireland, but despite the notion held by many nationalists that soccer was a 'foreign' game, support for it remained throughout the War of Independence and subsequent Civil War, particularly in Dublin. As shown above, soccer in Dublin had made great strides in terms of its ability to compete with other codes by the opening year of the Irish Free State, as the FAI's initial season came to a close. The 1922 FAI Cup final replay at Dalymount Park drew 8,000 spectators 'despite the counter-attraction' of an international rugby match at Lansdowne Road that same Saturday.[416] The Leinster Senior Cup final drew a similar figure of onlookers the following week.[417] Chapter three examines the growth of soccer in Dublin up to and including the Emergency, as the game continued to increase in popularity within the area.

415 Ibid., pp 25–6.   416 *EH*, 10 Apr. 1922; *II*, 10 Apr. 1922.   417 *II*, 18 Apr. 1922.

3

Soccer in post-partition Dublin, 1922–45

THE DEVELOPMENT OF THE FREE STATE LEAGUE AND OTHER COMPETITIONS IN THE 1920s

After the setback of losing the 1921–2 FAI Cup final, Shamrock Rovers began to raise standards, and won the Free State League, which by then included twelve clubs, and the Leinster Senior Cup in 1923.[1] In the 1924–5 season, with a panel of fourteen players, they did not lose a match in the league, cup or shield.[2] The inclusion of the 'Four Fs' – John 'Kruger' Fagan, Billy 'Juicy' Farrell, Bob Fullam and John Joe Flood – along with William 'Sacky' Glen and Dinny Doyle, was fundamental to their success.[3] The club won the FAIFS Cup, as it became known in the 1923–4 season when the FAI was renamed Football Association of the Irish Free State, five years running, from 1929 until 1933 inclusive.[4] The take-over by Joseph Cunningham, who ran a bookmaker's business at Irishtown, in the late 1920s, when the club was struggling financially, was a major help, along with the acquisition of a new ground at Milltown in 1926.[5] As Toms has stated, the introduction of the Betting Act in 1926 by the Cumann na nGaedheal government 'brought with it the licensed betting shop, which would have a profound effect on how sport was enjoyed in Ireland'.[6] The opening of Glenmalure Park (named after the area in Wicklow where the Cunninghams were originally from), on a site owned by the Jesuits at Milltown, in September of that year, further strengthened Shamrock Rovers' position, while they also took on their green and white hooped jerseys late in that decade.[7] Although the Jesuits retained ownership and the venue was rented, it gave the club a more secure base at the time.[8]

From 1921 until 1923, they had mainly played on a field owned by a farmer named Bernard Rogan at Windy Arbour but alternated between other venues, before temporarily playing on a pitch beside Glenmalure Park.[9] Doolan and Goggins have noted that prior to Cunningham taking on a central role, financial support had also come from local families in the Ringsend area.[10] Rice has written that 'growing from a local Ringsend club, Rovers quickly gained support from

1 Briggs & Dodd, *100 Years of the LFA*, p. 46; Thomas P. Walsh, *Twenty years of Irish soccer: under the auspices of the Football Association of Ireland, 1921–1941* (Dublin, 1941), pp 13, 44. 2 *SI*, 21 Oct. 1956. 3 Rice, *We are Rovers*, p. 35. 4 Ibid.; Walsh, *Twenty years of Irish soccer*, p. 13; *SI*, 21 Oct. 1956. 5 *FSW*, 11 Dec. 1926; *SI*, 21 Oct. 1956. See also Doolan & Goggins, *The Hoops*, p. 14. 6 Toms, *Soccer in Munster*, p. 67. 7 Rice, *We are Rovers*, p. 36. 8 Doolan & Goggins, *The Hoops*, p. 14. 9 Ibid., pp 3, 13–14. 10 Ibid., pp 14–15.

all areas of the city'.[11] Between 1922 and 1949 the club won forty-four trophies, establishing themselves as the Republic of Ireland's most successful club in that period.[12] The recruitment of Billy Lord, as trainer, in 1938 was significant.[13] He had studied physical culture at Liverpool University and was later given responsibility for the treatment of the international rugby and soccer teams.[14]

As well as patrons, soccer in Dublin in the 1920s was aided by a number of dedicated administrators. Among these was J.S. Murphy, 'a whole-hearted enthusiast and highly-capable legislator', who by 1925 was chairman of the Free State League and the Athletic Union League.[15] He was also vice chairman of the Leinster FA Council and was involved in 'various committees' as well as Athlone Town FC and Pioneers FC, a team developed from former Annally and Leinster FC players.[16] By the middle of the decade, the success of the Free State League was being fostered by its secretary, Basil W. Mainey, who had experience of secretarial duties at Shelbourne.[17] Bill Sheeran became secretary of the Leinster FA in the early 1920s, a position he held until his death in 1954.[18] William C. Foster, a representative of Fordsons of Cork, was 'one of the most useful and active officials in Free State football', and an important figure in securing 'reduced fares for teams travelling to and from the Metropolis'.[19] Joseph Macken was by the end of 1926 'one of the best-known and most essential personages in Leinster Junior Associational football' and 'also a useful helper in several of the senior circles'.[20] He had begun with 'the original St Vincent's club' and was said to have 'helped to keep things going very satisfactorily every Saturday and Sunday on the Fifteen Acres' at Phoenix Park while 'morning, noon and night' he was 'always at the services of the footballers, the Associations, the Leagues and the clubs'.[21]

Dublin clubs dominated the Free State League and Cup competitions in the years between 1921 and 1939, with one reporter asserting in 1936 that the league was 'Dublincentric'.[22] It was not until 1933 that a club from outside Dublin, Dundalk, won the league, and although Cork United also did so in 1937, St James's Gate, Bohemians, Shelbourne and Shamrock Rovers and Dolphin were all successful in this competition.[23] In the same period, Dublin clubs were to the forefront of the FAI Cup, with only Alton United (1923), Fordsons (1926), Cork (1934) and Waterford (1937) taking the trophy away from Dublin as St James's Gate, Shamrock Rovers, Drumcondra, Bohemians and Shelbourne all enjoyed success in finals.[24]

Lower league soccer also thrived in Dublin by the second half of the 1920s, with the Leinster FA's Senior League and Challenge Cup still operational, along with the Leinster Junior Shield, Athletic Union League, Junior Alliance League,

11 Rice, *We are Rovers*, p. 36.   12 Ibid.   13 *II*, 21 Oct. 1956.   14 Ibid.   15 *FSW*, 12 Sept. 1925.   16 Ibid.; *Sport*, 24 Aug. 1918.   17 *FSW*, 7 Nov. 1925.   18 Briggs & Dodds, *100 years of the LFA*, p. 74.   19 *FSW*, 17 Oct. 1925.   20 *FSW*, 4 Dec. 1926.   21 Ibid.   22 Garnham, 'Ein spiel in zwei nationen?', p. 80.   23 Soar, Tyler & Widdows, *The Hamlyn encyclopaedia of football*, p. 163.   24 Ibid.; Garnham, 'Ein spiel in zwei nationen?', p. 80.

Junior Metropolitan League, Minor League, Intermediate League, Central League and Junior League, held on Saturdays.[25] The Sunday Alliance League had a First Division and a Second Division, along with three sections in its Third Division and another division catered for juveniles. A Wednesday League was also run, with two divisions in place, the second catering 'more or less for the juniors'.[26] By November 1926 teams playing in an Hotels and Cinemas' League were also active.[27]

Newly formed teams continued to blossom into the 1920s. In 1925–6, the Leinster FA reported that their affiliation figures had risen to 300, with 250 of these junior clubs.[28] One of these new clubs was Vickers FC, who had begun participating in the Dublin Dockyard Company's works league.[29] The players were 'as far as possible, dockyard workers who had played previously for other clubs such as Strandville, Tritonville and Bohemians, while a number of their committee members had experience of administration at Tritonville and St Barnabas FC.[30] The Maguire and Paterson match company, which had been established in the late nineteenth century, also had a soccer team by the mid-1920s.[31] In October 1926 Findlaters, the wine and grocery business, had a team up and running, and by November 1926 a team 'attached to the well-known oil company' British Petroleum had just come into existence.[32] Other work teams to be formed included one catering for employees of the Irish Glass Bottle Company in Ringsend, which was set up in 1927 and also doubled up as a social club, like many others.[33] More notable was the rise of Inchicore's Brideville, who defeated Bohemians in the Free State League in September 1925.[34] They had begun only in the 1919–20 season, 'when they entered the lowest of leagues playing in the Phoenix Park, namely, the Central League'.[35] With a number of high finishes in their early years, they strengthened significantly to also win the Free State Junior Cup in 1923–4 and the Leinster Junior Cup and the Leinster Senior Second Division championship. They also reached the Leinster Senior Cup final, losing narrowly to Shelbourne by 2–1 before winning it the following season against Glasnevin. By 1925–6 they had been accepted into the Free State League, having proved their capabilities within Dublin soccer.[36]

THE GEOGRAPHICAL DISTRIBUTION OF DUBLIN CLUBS, THE HOSTING OF MATCHES AND PLAYER WELFARE

At the beginning of the 1925–6 season the vast majority of teams in the Leinster Senior League First Division were based in Dublin, with Dundalk of Louth the only exception in the sixteen-club Leinster League First Division.[37] There was a mix of city and suburban teams at this level, with Free State League clubs Shamrock Rovers, Bohemians, Shelbourne and St James's Gate all fielding 'B'

25 *FSW*, 2 Jan. 1926. 26 Ibid. 27 Ibid., 20 Nov. 1926. 28 Ibid., 21 Aug. 1926. 29 Ibid., 12 Sept. 1925. 30 Ibid. 31 Ibid., 25 Dec. 1926. 32 *EH*, 8 Oct. 1926; *FSW*, 20 Nov. 1926; *IT*, 7 June 2019. 33 *FSW*, 29 Jan. 1927. 34 Ibid., 19 Sept. 1925 and 14 Aug. 1926. 35 Ibid., 19 Sept. 1925. 36 Ibid. 37 Ibid., 29 Aug. 1925.

sides; Midland Athletic were at home at Dolphin's Barn; Glasnevin's ground was on the Ballymun Road; Drumcondra played at home at Richmond Road; St Paul's ground was at Ashtown; Strandville Park, where Strandville played their home matches, was located on Richmond Road, although the club had their roots in the North Strand area.[38] They had initially been known as 'the Tigers', with James Burke, one of their founders, said to have 'assisted in bringing the club to the high standard' they attained in Dublin soccer circles.[39] The 1925 Leinster Senior League Second Division winners, Lindon, had their home ground at Tudor Park in Clontarf; University College Dublin's home matches were played at Terenure; CYMS's ground was also in Terenure; Edenville were based at Longford Lodge in Dunleary (Dún Laoghaire); Bendigo played at the Thatch; Chapelizod played at Belgrove Park, the former home of Trojans; and Dundalk's pitch was located at the Grammar School Athletic grounds in that town.[40] At times, the supply of public transport was inadequate for matches. One reporter lamented the lack of transport available for spectators at the Thatch, Richmond Road and Shelbourne Park in April 1926.[41] The following year, the poor transport laid on for Shamrock Rovers' match against Barnsley at Glenmalure Park was also criticized in the press.[42] Another correspondent questioned the lack of development at Shelbourne Park in 1926, stating that it was 'the finest playing pitch, without exception, in Ireland, but the worst equipped ground imaginable for spectators. This ground, if provided with stands all around the pitch, could be made to accommodate over 50,000 people.'[43]

In the Leinster Senior League Second Division, which also had sixteen teams, some Free State League clubs fielded second teams (Brideville, Drumcondra, Jacob's and Bray Unknowns of Wicklow). Bohemians fielded their third team; Strandvilla of North Strand played at Church Road; 1924–5 Free State Junior Cup winners St Mary's United were at home at Monkstown Farm; Richmond, composed of employees of the Mental Hospital, played their home matches at Grangegorman; the Civil Service first team were located at Elm Grove in Cabra for home fixtures, and also fielded a team in the Athletic Union League.[44] Some clubs shared grounds with those in the First Division, including Richmond United (Strandville Park) and Vickers (Tudor Park, Clontarf); Distillery played their home matches at Parnell Park on the Malahide Road (which has since become a GAA ground); Portrane were based at Donabate; Blackrock Hospital played at home at Carysford Avenue and Talbot United played at Church Road. Along with Bray Unknowns, the only non-Dublin club in that division was Mullingar Town of County Westmeath, who played at the Showgrounds in that urban setting.[45] This geographical spread is further indication of the strength of soccer in Dublin within Leinster itself, and is illustrative of the fact that the game, while highly popular in

38 Ibid.   39 Ibid., 21 Aug. 1926.   40 Ibid., 29 Jan. 1927.   41 Ibid., 10 Apr. 1926. The Thatch was at Whitehall.   42 Ibid., 7 May 1927.   43 Ibid., 6 Feb. 1926.   44 Ibid., 29 Aug. and 5 Sept. 1925.   45 Ibid., 29 Aug. 1925.

inner-city areas, also had a notable presence in some suburban villages outside the city, including Clontarf, Monkstown, Terenure and Blackrock, which have since become more commonly associated with rugby.

Wren, De Burca and Gorry have stated that the establishment of the Irish Free State in 1922 'radically altered the political and social background against which the GAA operated' as 'overnight, the association, so to speak, became part of the new social and political establishment'.[46] Numerous lower-league clubs continued to line out in the main venue for Dublin soccer at those levels, Phoenix Park, despite the loss of eight pitches to Gaelic games through the instigation of J.J. Walsh, a pro-GAA Cumann na nGaedheal representative, in 1923.[47] By the middle of 1925, the number of soccer grounds at that venue was said to be 'totally inadequate' despite the park's authorities increasing this the previous year.[48] One reporter noted that 'unless at least eight or ten more are marked out and equipped with posts, hundreds of the city youths, who have organized themselves into football clubs, will be compelled either to disband or join the growing crowd of onlookers'.[49] At that time, clubs were requested to fill in official cards to request grounds, and some teams, such as Haroldville and Camac Rovers of the Intermediate League, found themselves with none available to play their matches.[50] Despite this, it emerged later that year that the Department of Public Works would not provide any more pitches, although one reporter noted that 'there is room, and to spare, for scores more grounds'.[51] By the early months of 1926, there was reported to be a 'dearth of grounds' in Dublin.[52] The following year, Lansdowne Road was the venue for the Free State team's first home international match, which they lost 2–1 to Italy before 28,000 spectators in April, with the match also said to have improved relations between the IRFU and the FAIFS.[53] A few years prior to this, Dalymount Park had been the stage for a number of trial matches for the Irish Olympic XI and in the aftermath of the Paris Olympic Games in June 1924, the venue hosted the visit of the United States Olympic team for a match against the Irish team as the FAI sought to further cement its independence through international team selections.[54] However, developing a new venue fit for international matches was not a major concern of theirs for most of the twentieth century, as they lacked the financial ability to organize this.

A lack of enclosed pitches in some areas meant that less affluent clubs had to contend with members of the public who were not particularly interested in their games being run smoothly. At Herbert Park in Ballsbridge, it was reported in 1925 that 'encroachment' by spectators was spoiling matches, while 'some of the people there' had a tendency to 'wander across the field, ignoring the footballers' as it was a public park.[55] There were also issues at the Phoenix Park with interference

46 Wren, de Búrca & Gorry, *The Gaelic Athletic Association in Dublin*, i: *1884–1959*, p. 217.   47 Tynan, 'Association football and Irish society during the inter-war period, 1918–1939', p. 215.   48 *FSW*, 12 Sept. 1925.   49 Ibid.   50 Ibid., 12 and 19 Sept. 1925.   51 Ibid., 31 Oct. 1925.   52 Ibid., 13 Feb. 1926.   53 *BN*, 25 Apr. 1927; *II*, 16 July 1927 and 11 Apr. 1989.   54 Hunt, 'Ireland's footballers at the 1924 and 1948 Olympics', pp 892–4.   55 *FSW*, 3 Oct. 1925.

from some onlookers, whose behaviour while matches were ongoing was described as 'so notoriously infamous', with the Fifteen Acres noted by one former Trojans footballer in the autumn of 1925 as being 'unsafe' for players.[56] The previous year, a player had been kicked to death there. The venue was also a public park and matches had scarce security as it was 'not properly policed'.[57] The lack of marking of park grounds was said to be a concern, illustrating the difficulties players faced.[58]

While a private room was available for referees at the pavilion in the Fifteen Acres, players had less security and theft of their property was an issue by the late 1920s.[59] Rivalry between teams also added to difficulties, with Bray Wanderers' players apparently having to endure 'a very unpleasant time in the Junior Shield competition' when they faced Pearse United 'B' at Phoenix Park in 1926.[60] They had 'a long list of serious complaints about the treatment they received in the Phoenix Park' and had 'great difficulty in getting away after the match, some players having to run away without part of their clothes'.[61]

The conduct of some supporters was not always satisfactory, even at the more developed Dublin clubs. Mark Tynan has written that in the interwar years, hooliganism was an issue at some soccer matches in Ireland as attendances at Free State league and cup matches rose. In particular, he has noted that it 'was in many ways a reflection of wider society'.[62] He states that while hooliganism in Dublin in 1919 and 1920 'was primarily borne of the strong anti-northern outlook that prevailed in the city', it 'was considered far less serious than that which occurred in Belfast'.[63] While the partition of the governance of soccer in Ireland in 1921 'eliminated the threat of anti-northern violence at soccer matches hooliganism was not eradicated from the sport in the south of the country'.[64] He also states that hooliganism in the Irish Free State in the 1920s and 1930s 'can be attributed to growing partisanship around the sport, as well as issues [of] class, community and local identity'.[65] In addition, 'unemployment, poverty, social disaffection and alcohol consumption' were also factors in this disorder.[66] In particular, Tynan has noted that the supporters of Shamrock Rovers, Bray Unknowns and Dundalk GNR (Great Northern Railway) were the most notorious in the 1920s, while in the latter part of the following decade a section of Waterford followers became infamous for poor behaviour at matches.[67]

Clubs who did not have their own venues continued to have to make do with public playing fields. In order to aid teams arriving at the Magazine Fort in Phoenix Park, in 1926 *Football Sports Weekly* published a map of the park, which teams were advised to cut out and bring to the venue, where twenty-eight soccer pitches were located at that point.[68] One reporter also lamented that the Board of Works had

56 Ibid., 26 Sept. 1925. 57 Ibid. 58 Ibid., 10 Oct. 1925. 59 Ibid. and 15 Oct. 1927. 60 Ibid., 26 Feb. 1926. 61 Ibid. 62 Mark Tynan, '"Inciting the roughs of the crowd": soccer hooliganism in the south of Ireland during the inter-war period, 1919–1939' in Conor Curran & David Toms (eds), *New perspectives on association football in Irish history: going beyond the 'garrison game'* (Abingdon, 2018), pp 50–64, p. 61. 63 Ibid. 64 Ibid. 65 Ibid. 66 Ibid. 67 Ibid., pp 56–9. 68 *FSW*, 21 Aug. 1926.

not carried out any repairs to the pitches over the summer, 'so that the holes and bad spots remain and will be as evident as usual when the wet weather comes'.[69] In addition, the Lucan tram line was said to be inefficient for players as it did not fully reach the venue.[70] At their annual general meeting in 1929, the Leinster FA agreed that the pitches at the Phoenix Park were still unsatisfactory, and the organization's president, Osmond Grattan Esmonde TD, stated that he would contact 'the proper authorities with a view to improving the existing conditions'.[71]

The poor state of some other pitches was at times voiced, with Glasnevin FC critical of Strandville FC's ground in 1925 as a result of injuries received by their players there.[72] Playing through injuries was not uncommon. Val Harris was said to have played 'almost on one leg for about fifteen years' following a knee injury he sustained for Everton against Tottenham Hotspur in 1910, and by the end of his career in England was walking with a limp, but later continued to play for Shelbourne, having returned to Dublin during the First World War.[73] One reporter noted of a cup match between Drumcondra and Athlone in 1926 that 'McCabe defended the Athlone posts contrary to his doctor's orders. The man was a cripple with sciatica. His play in the circumstances was little short of heroic.'[74] In January 1928, it was noted in the press that Joe Leonard of Shamrock Rovers was 'all right again for the present, but may have to undergo an operation at the end of the season for his injuries'.[75]

By the middle of the 1920s a first-aid hut was operational at the Fifteen Acres in Phoenix Park.[76] Clubs using the Phoenix Park for matches had to pay a penny a week to pay off the cost of building a railing around the ambulance hut there, which one reporter felt was 'ridiculous' given that it would take years for them to pay off when it might have been paid in full sooner.[77] The availability of emergency treatment varied. Following a collision in which a player broke his leg during a match between St Kevin's and Grange at Sallynoggin in April 1926, 'the game was stopped immediately and all available first-aid appliances used until the ambulance arrived and brought him to Monkstown Hospital'.[78] However, receiving treatment outside of the club remained an issue, with one reporter noting how an unnamed hospital had refused to send an ambulance to assist a player who had broken his leg at a junior match in Blanchardstown in February 1927.[79]

While some players undoubtedly enjoyed lengthy spells playing in Dublin – one Jacob's player, Scott, was reported to have been in his twenty-seventh year of soccer in 1922 and made his first appearance in a final that year – keeping physically well enough to play was certainly a challenge.[80] Players were advised in the press to 'use Rexall Embrocation freely and often' in the mid-1920s 'to keep fit', with the product available in at least one Dublin chemist.[81] Charlie O'Hagan, a

69 Ibid.   70 Ibid.   71 Annual General Meeting, 15 Aug. 1929, Leinster Football Association Archives, P239/31.   72 *FSW*, 14 Nov. 1925.   73 *Shelbourne Football Club golden jubilee, 1895–1945*, pp 37–9.   74 *FSW*, 6 Feb. 1926.   75 Ibid., 28 Jan. 1928.   76 Ibid., 23 Jan. 1926.   77 Ibid., 13 Feb. 1926.   78 Ibid., 10 Apr. 1926.   79 Ibid., 26 Feb. 1927.   80 *II*, 18 Apr. 1922.   81 *FSW*, 16 Jan. 1926.

Donegal-born football migrant who temporarily became editor of *Football Sports Weekly* in that decade, also published his own tips on training and preparation, which included taking a cold bath in the morning after his own personal training routine, which included skipping and shadow boxing.[82] He said little about dealing with injuries, however. Some clubs did utilize machinery to treat injuries and at least one player saw the business opportunities that came with the treatment of injured players. In September 1926, Bohemians full-back C.P. Reddy was said to be 'busy installing new electric massage appliances in clubs' which were reported to be 'a great asset for training purposes'.[83] The following year, Dr Willie Hooper offered general tips in *Football Sports Weekly* in a front-page article entitled 'How to Play the Game'. He advised players to keep themselves fit, avoid alcohol, go to bed early and to rest up before matches.[84]

The St John's Ambulance Brigade was an important asset to Dublin's leading soccer clubs at the time. In May 1927, the Free State League title decider between Shamrock Rovers and Drumcondra at Milltown was also said to be 'a "benefit" for the St John Ambulance Brigade in Ireland, whose aid has always been unsparingly given, not only to soccer, but to every branch of sport'.[85] Elsewhere, by the end of the 1926–7 season, the organization was said to have 'rendered invaluable service' to soccer in Dublin.[86] Given the physical demands of match preparation, even some trainers suffered. In July 1927, Bohemians trainer Charlie Harris was said to be 'troubled with a strained muscle in his left arm' and attended Dr Burke at the Richmond Hospital for treatment.[87]

Players also received benefit matches, particularly when they had received serious injuries on the pitch that meant retirement or time off work.[88] Leaving the country to take up a position abroad could also be a cause for a benefit match, although poor weather conditions at times lessened the attendance and the finance gathered.[89] In December 1927, Dalton, a Shamrock Rovers' reserves player, was said to be on the injured list and 'in the trainer's hands at Milltown'.[90] Subscriptions were taken at that time in *Football Sports Weekly* for injured players who were 'not receiving any benefit'.[91]

Match preparation at Leinster League level was not always adequate. The slowness in setting up a playing pitch inside some grounds was an issue, with one reporter noting how teams visiting Ringsend Park 'very often' had to 'wait fifteen minutes "till the home team is selecting the pick of the area"'.[92] Naturally, clubs also faced issues with paying rent for grounds they did not own. One journalist noted in 1925, in calling for a Playing Fields' Movement similar to that in England, that 'we know a landlord of a ground two miles from Nelson's Pillar who has increased the rent of a wretched bit of land to a junior club each year for the past four years, and he now receives five times the original rent'.[93] The following year,

82 Curran, *Irish soccer migrants*, pp 166–7.   83 *FSW*, 25 Sept. 1926.   84 *FSW*, 2 July 1927.   85 *II*, 21 May 1927.   86 *FSW*, 21 May 1927.   87 *FSW*, 16 July 1927.   88 See, for example, *FSW*, 15 May 1926.   89 Ibid.   90 *FSW*, 24 Dec. 1927.   91 *FSW*, 10 July 1926.   92 *FSW*, 12 Dec. 1925.   93 *FSW*, 10 Oct. 1925.

one newspaper noted how a number of clubs had protested against the 'exorbitant rents demanded' by some grounds owners.[94] Some teams shared their ground with those from other (non-GAA) codes, particularly if it was a general organization behind the club in question. The revived YMCA club, who were elected to the Athletic Union League in 1926, shared their ground with their hockey and rugby teams, with a view to them finding a new one, although this was said to be difficult at the time as many Dublin clubs were having issues with securing playing fields.[95] Dublin was not alone in this regard, with similar issues in the provision of playing fields in other cities such as Belfast and Paris at various stages during the twentieth century.[96]

Clubs naturally tried to raise money through social events away from match days. Some of the more prominent clubs held smokers in their own clubrooms, with Bendigo's own venue, which in 1926 was 'situated behind Messrs. O'Hara's, grocers, Chancery Street', at the rear of the old Four Courts, said to be 'a credit to any club'.[97] This clubroom was 'well furnished and electrically lighted, with a good stage platform as you enter'.[98] These events allowed other footballers to socialize with their opponents away from matches. Players from other clubs attended their smoker in April 1926, including Bob Fullam and 'Doc' Malone of Shamrock Rovers, as well as McElroy, Kerr and the Tucker brothers of Bohemians.[99]

Following Shamrock Rovers' successful season in 1924–5, the club were honoured by the Free State League with '"a do" on the grand scale in Jury's Hotel, where a convivial evening was spent and finished by a visit to the theatre'.[100] At Bohemians' 1926 dinner and smoker, which took place after the Leinster Senior Cup final on Easter Monday that year, the club's committee and members 'heartily enjoyed a sumptuous dinner and a delightful musical programme on that night at Jury's Hotel'.[101] Later that year, three hundred people attended a dance organized by Bohemians for the visit of Scottish Cup holders St Mirren, whom they defeated.[102] These dances proved popular with many clubs. In February 1928, over 300 people, including managing director J.H. Cooper, attended the Maguire and Paterson's FC annual dance in Rathmines Town Hall.[103] Fundraising events also took other forms. In August 1926, Bohemians hosted an 'at-home', which included croquet, tennis and other sports.[104] The club also ran a tennis team at that time, which included former Aston Villa player Norman MacKay.[105] St James's bazaar and fete, held in early June 1928, included a five-a-side competition featuring Shelbourne, Great Southern Railways, St James's Gate, St James's Gate United, BSU 'A', Richmond Rovers' 'A' and 'B' teams and Drumcondra, with trams 23 and 24 and 'several buses' passing the home club's ground, easing transport difficulties

94 *FSW*, 6 Feb. 1926. 95 *FSW*, 21 Aug. 1926. 96 Curran, *Physical education in Irish schools*, p. 273; Keith Rathbone, *Sport and physical culture in occupied France: authoritarianism, agency and everyday life* (Manchester, 2022), p. 42. 97 *FSW*, 3 Apr. 1926. A smoker was a type of concert popular at the time. 98 Ibid. 99 Ibid. 100 *FSW*, 1 Jan. 1927. 101 *FSW*, 10 Apr. 1926. 102 *FSW*, 8 May 1926. 103 *FSW*, 11 Feb. 1928. 104 *FSW*, 7 Aug. 1926. 105 Ibid. and 24 July 1926.

for patrons.[106] St James's Gate had moved to the Iveagh Grounds in Crumlin that year, with the venue opened by the earl of Iveagh in a special ceremony in April.[107]

THE EMERGENCE OF DRUMCONDRA, DOLPHIN AND ST PATRICK'S ATHLETIC

Some clubs such as Bendigo (in 1922) and YMCA of Claremont Road and Richmond Rovers (both in 1926) had been reorganized in that decade.[108] In 1927 Freebooters were noted as being revived, but lacked any real impact.[109] How much their administrative set-up and players reflected the spirit of the team with the same name of the early 1900s is not recorded, but it is doubtful there were any strong connections. The mid-1920s saw the emergence of Drumcondra FC as a major strength within Dublin soccer. Tracing the club's exact origins is difficult, but according to one newspaper report, they lay in a nearby club named Botanic, with 'a group of young Dublin men' meeting on the banks of the river Tolka on an unspecified date in the late nineteenth century, with Larry Sheridan said to have made a significant contribution to these early clubs.[110] One correspondent, writing in *Football Sports Weekly* in 1927, felt that the Drumcondra club was begun by 'messrs. Coleman and Scully', but these founding details remain vague.[111] In 1899 Drumcondra lost a Leinster Junior Cup semi-final 2–0 to Bohemians Reserves 'before about 1,000 spectators' at Sandymount.[112] In November 1902 Drumcondra were participating in the Leinster Senior League, but did not begin to challenge Shelbourne and Bohemians for national honours until after partition.[113]

It was in the 1920s that the club took off. By September 1924 Drumcondra were competing in Division One of the Leinster Senior League.[114] Based at Richmond Road, they had adopted their famous blue and gold colours by the middle of the decade.[115] In August 1925 they were described in the national press as 'another of the more progressive clubs'.[116] In December 1926, *Football Sports Weekly* reported that due to the 'energy of the club officials', Drumcondra FC now had 'an enclosure that bears favourable comparison with the best in the city, and is much superior to many grounds'.[117] The newspaper later described the new setting in detail:

> It is perfectly laid out in every detail as far as the club have permission to make structural alterations. The playing pitch is perfectly laid with a splendid sod. One side of the ground is well banked. There are dressing rooms with all sorts of accommodations for players and visitors. The playing pitch

---

106 *II*, 1 June 1928. **107** 'Our history', stjamesgatefc.com/club-history, accessed 3 Jan. 2022 and Walsh, *Twenty years of Irish soccer*, p. 118. **108** *FSW*, 5 June, 10 July and 21 Aug. 1926. **109** *FSW*, 26 Mar. 1927. **110** *SI*, 26 Aug. 1956. **111** *FSW*, 23 Apr. 1927. **112** *FJ*, 12 Apr. 1899. **113** *IDI*, 3 Nov. 1902. **114** *FJ*, 20 Sept. 1924; *II*, 8 Nov. 1924. **115** *FSW*, 29 Aug. 1925. **116** Ibid. **117** *FSW*, 18 Dec. 1926.

is surrounded by a substantial railing, and the ground well fenced where it touches the public road. The ground is a credit to the enterprise of the club, and they are to be heartily congratulated on their great work.[118]

Drumcondra's initial matches in the Free State Cup in 1926 were against Bendigo, and they overcame them in a replay 1–0 after a nil–nil draw in December 1926. The matches drew great attention locally, with the first game at the Thatch receiving a vivid description in the press:

> Never before was the Bendigo ground compelled to 'house' such a mighty gathering. The ground was packed inside and outside the railings enclosing it. On the wall, and far from the playing pitch, hundreds were standing, getting a view from the wider range. On the trees surrounding the venue, young men and boys were perched just like the birds in the air, who rest themselves.[119]

Drumcondra became the first Leinster Senior League team to win the Free State Qualifying Cup (later known as the FAI Intermediate Cup) and the FAIFS Cup, in 1927, although they did not win the League of Ireland until 1948, having been elected to it in June 1928 along with Bray Unknowns.[120]

Some 25,000 people were present for the 1927 FAIFS Cup final between Drumcondra and Brideville at Dalymount Park on 17 March, which ended in a 1–1 draw with McCarney scoring for Drumcondra and McCarthy finding the net for Brideville. The match drew 'gate' receipts of £1,500 and the crowd was also strikingly described in *Football Sports Weekly*:

> The huge crowd present were of the best sporting element that any city might be proud of. It was a tribute to the Dublin football enthusiasts and supporters. Men, women and children were bedecked with the colours of the teams they were interested in. Berets, paper hats, and even a busbie [*sic*] were worn. Rosettes, small and large flags, were in evidence everywhere in the ground. They were an exceedingly happy throng, and their presence added considerably to the game.[121]

The replay, held at Shelbourne Park before a crowd of 10,000, was said to be 'a disappointing affair from many aspects', with the expensive prices leaving many seats unoccupied in the reserve enclosure. The poor weather was also a factor, 'it being cold and wet', but it did not deter Drumcondra as they became the first Leinster Senior League team to win the FAIFS Cup. Johnnie Murray scored the

118 *FSW*, 25 Dec. 1926.   119 Ibid.   120 *II*, 11 Apr. and 5 May 1927; 26 and 27 June 1928; *FSW*, 16 Apr. 1927; Soar, Tyler & Widdows, *The Hamlyn encyclopaedia of football*, p. 163.   121 *FSW*, 26 Mar. 1927.

4. Bohemians FC (1928). Courtesy of Luke O'Riordan.

winner at the end of the first period of extra-time after 'a lucky opening'.[122] They
had again reached the FAIFS Cup final in 1928, but lost to the all-conquering
Bohemians team, who also won the Free State League and Shield that year.[123] The
match was played before a crowd of approximately 25,000 at Dalymount Park, but
Drumcondra failed to retain the trophy, losing by two goals to one.[124]

Accommodating young supporters was not always straightforward. Writing in
1925, one journalist called for the restoration of a 'boys' gate' at Dalymount Park as
it would 'nip the growth of cadging in the bud, which frequently pains many people
passing through the approaches to the ground'.[125] He added that 'quite respect-
able looking lads follow people begging to be brought in in quite the professional
mendicant style. It is very distressing from many points of view.'[126] Drumcondra's
success on the pitch naturally led to a rise in support. Those intending to view
their FAI Cup second round replay against Bray Unknowns in February 1928 were
advised in the press to 'come early and avoid the crush'.[127] Almost 12,000 attended
the match, with 'the headquarters of the local club … packed to overcrowding, and
many witnessed the match under difficulty as a consequence'.[128] By the late 1920s
the threat of crushing at Tolka Park, which had a 'less commodious enclosure'

122 *II*, 11 Apr. 1927; *FSW*, 16 Apr. 1927.   123 36th Annual Report, May 1928, Leinster Football
Association Archives, P239/27.   124 *II*, 19 Mar. 1928; *FSW*, 24 Mar. 1928.   125 *FSW*, 12 Sept.
1925. This was a specific area for schoolboys to watch the match.   126 Ibid.   127 *FSW*, 28 Jan.
1928.   128 *FSW*, 4 Feb. 1928.

than Dalymount Park, was also a public concern and was said to have kept some supporters away from the Free State Cup semi-final there in February 1929, along with a dispute between the FAIFS and Bohemians and Shelbourne regarding rental terms at grounds.[129]

Travel to away matches was also an important part of being a supporter. Drumcondra, captained by Joe Grace, completed a rare double in May 1927 when they defeated Cobh Ramblers in the final of the Free State Qualifying Cup by 2–0 in Cork, with Swan scoring two goals. Approximately 800 Drumcondra fans had travelled down on the excursion train, the match having been switched to Cork from Dublin to facilitate the Free State Council in the above FAIFS Senior Cup final replay.[130] The following year Drumcondra FC advertised a special excursion train for their trip to Cork to meet Fordsons, with departure and 9.30 a.m. from Kingsbridge (Heuston) followed after the match by the return at 7.30 p.m.[131] Children were offered tickets at half price of the adult 10s. fare.[132] The match at the Mardyke grounds, which the Dublin club won 3–0, drew a crowd of 18,000 with gate receipts of £460 said to be 'a record for Cork'.[133]

By the end of the decade, Drumcondra FC were also able to secure a significant venue for their most important off-the-pitch event on one of the busiest social nights of the year, having grown in stature. On New Year's Eve 1929 they held their 'annual reunion dance' in Clery's Imperial Ballroom, and this proved to be 'one of the jolliest dances of the old year'.[134] More than 200 people, including many old members and supporters, were present. It was reported that 'carnival novelties of all kinds were introduced, whilst the addition to the programme of the old waltz and barn dance added much to the night's entertainment'.[135] Music was provided by George Hornsly's band.[136]

In 1930 Dolphin joined the Free State League when the number of clubs was raised to twelve, after the club had 'a very successful run in junior and senior football'.[137] They had been formed by members of the Butchers' Social Union, which had its headquarters at Gardiner Hall in Gardiner Street.[138] There is some indication the club initially contained 'converts from the Gaelic code'.[139] After a spell at the Iveagh Grounds, in 1934 they returned to their home ground, Dolphin Park in Crumlin, which had suffered fire damage in their initial year in the league.[140] The club took the step of advertising for players with 'Free State League and Leinster League experience' in 1932, although they were also happy to invite 'good juniors'.[141] They reached the FAI Cup final in both 1932 and 1933 before winning the Free State league and the Dublin City Cup in 1935.[142] However, in 1937 they resigned from the Free State League and were replaced by Limerick.[143] This was

129 *II*, 4 Feb. 1929.   **130** *II*, 9 May 1927.   **131** *FSW*, 18 Feb. 1928.   **132** Ibid.   **133** *FSW*, 25 Feb. 1928.   **134** *II*, 1 Jan. 1930.   **135** Ibid.   **136** Ibid.   **137** *EE*, 8 Jan. 1937.   **138** *FSW*, 21 Aug. 1926; Seán Ryan, *The official book of the FAI Cup* (Dublin, 2011), p. 51.   **139** *FSW*, 26 Nov. 1927.   **140** *EH*, 25 Nov. 1930; *II*, 8 Jan. 1931; *IP*, 11 May 1934.   **141** *EH*, 9 July 1932.   **142** *EE*, 8 Jan. 1937; Kennedy, *Just follow the floodlights!*, p. 302.   **143** Kennedy, *Just follow the floodlights!*, p. 302; Walsh, *Twenty years of Irish soccer*, p. 39.

because a 'portion of their ground' was 'acquired by the Dublin Corporation, and alternative quarters could not be secured in time' to allow them to compete in the 1937–8 season.[144]

The late 1920s also saw the establishment of St Patrick's Athletic. Founded by a number of Inchicore men in 1929 as St Patrick's FC, and having failed to join the Institute club of the Great Southern Railway League, St Patrick's Athletic instead joined the Dublin Intermediate Novice League.[145] They featured in the Leinster Senior League, and later were accepted as a League of Ireland club prior to the 1951–2 season.[146] Interest in the game was slower to take hold in some areas than others, with Malahide Town playing what one reporter thought to be the first match there in fourteen years in the winter of 1925.[147]

WOMEN'S SOCCER IN DUBLIN IN THE 1920s

As in many other areas, including Belfast, where a few exhibition matches were played in 1895, 1921 and 1925, women's soccer was slow to attract interest and to gain support in Dublin, despite some efforts.[148] In May 1896, an Ireland and Scotland selection met England on two consecutive evenings at the City and Suburban Grounds, Jones's Road, Drumcondra, under the auspices of the British Ladies' Football Club.[149] A few weeks later, posters advertising additional ladies' matches in Drogheda drew a protest on religious grounds from one correspondent in a local newspaper.[150] The Belfast matches mainly involved touring teams and as Tony Collins has written of the early British Ladies' team, its organizers 'did little to encourage other women to take it up and left behind no legacy' as their matches were 'primarily a money-making exercise that sought to capitalize on the novelty of watching women playing football'.[151] In May 1927, Scottish team Rutherglen, managed by a Mr and Mrs Kelly, visited Dublin and played an exhibition game between themselves.[152] They also played a Dublin ladies' team trained over six weeks by Shamrock Rovers' captain Bob Fullam.[153] The Dublin women's team were reportedly the first in the capital and their picture was carried on the front page of the *Saturday Herald*.[154] A dance and buffet was organized by Mrs Margaret Cunningham, the wife of club owner Joseph, with proceeds given to the National Maternity Hospital in Holles Street. It had 'one of Dublin's finest dance orchestras', the Selma Follies, providing music.[155] The party of twenty-eight players and officials visited Guinness's brewery and La Scala Theatre and attended matches between Free State men's clubs at Milltown and at Shelbourne Park as

144 *IE*, 25 May 1937. See also *IE*, 24 Jan. 1936. Dolphin registered Tolka Park as their ground for the remainder of the 1935–6 season. 145 Kennedy, *Just follow the floodlights!*, pp 246–7; *II*, 26 Nov. 1947. 146 Kennedy, *Just follow the floodlights!*, pp 246–7; *II*, 15 Aug. 1951. 147 *FSW*, 12 Dec. 1925. 148 *BN*, 17 and 22 June 1895, 21 May 1921, 18 and 25 May 1925; *Northern Whig and Belfast Post*, 30 May 1921. 149 *IDI*, 18 May 1896. 150 *DI*, 30 May 1896. 151 Collins, *How football began*, p. 67. 152 *FSW*, 28 May 1927. 153 *FSW*, 21 May 1927. 154 *ESH*, 21 May 1921. 155 *FSW*, 21 May 1927.

well as greyhound racing at the latter. They later travelled north to play in Windsor Park and Derry.[156]

The first ladies' match at Milltown, between Rutherglen and Edinburgh selections, drew receipts of £130, while the second, between Rutherglen and the Dublin Ladies, saw £400 gathered.[157] The latter turned out to be 'a disappointing game' due to the gulf between the Scottish team, who were six years in existence, and the less experienced Dublin selection.[158] In June 1927, a Miss Smith, who had played in Dublin against Edinburgh and the Dublin Ladies at Milltown, was reported to have signed for Linfield, but the idea that a female player could be accommodated in a male team did not take hold.[159] That same month, the Rutherglen team who had beaten the Dublin Ladies 'by such a large margin', which was not disclosed, were said to be returning to Dublin for a match against Belfast.[160] Apparently, 'many objectors raised their voices' against the Dublin match, but 'a certain city goalkeeper' had been giving another group of Dublin ladies 'severe training' in the Phoenix Park and was hoping to develop a team.[161]

Despite proposals by one writer in *Football Sports Weekly* for a Dublin ladies' league to be started, this did not develop.[162] By July 1927, plans were underway for the Rutherglen team to play 'an Anglo-Irish XI' at Shelbourne Park, but this did not lead to any long-term structures for women's soccer in Dublin at this time.[163] Proposals in the press in 1937 similarly did not lead to anything concrete, despite the promise of S. Smith, manager of P.T. Selbitt's Company, who were based at the Gaiety Theatre, to field a team to meet any challengers.[164] While letters of support for ladies' matches were published in the press, there was also correspondence received from those who opposed them. One Dollymount writer felt that the idea was 'ridiculous' and that the game was 'too robust' for females.[165] He added that 'on some occasions male players are bad, so it is not hard to imagine the deplorable performance that would be provided by two ladies' teams'.[166] Despite calls from 'Upright' for a league for working teams to be started, and for 'some prominent citizen' to present a cup, with medals also to be supplied and ladies trained as referees, no further action was taken.[167]

Given the close links between Dublin and English soccer circles, the FA's decision to ban women's football from their grounds in December 1921 was unhelpful, and this ban was not relaxed until the late 1960s, with the first women's FA Cup final not played until 1971.[168] Although some other British ladies' teams did travel abroad, such as Nomads and Manchester Corinthians, the lack of a permanent structure for the game in England for such a long period had far-reaching consequences for its wider development.[169]

156 Ibid. 157 *FSW*, 2 July 1927. 158 *FSW*, 28 May 1928. 159 *FSW*, 11 June 1927. 160 *FSW*, 18 June 1927. 161 *FSW*, 25 June 1927. 162 Ibid. 163 *FSW*, 2 July 1927. 164 *EH*, 11 Dec. 1937. 165 *FSW*, 11 Dec. 1937. 166 Ibid. 167 *FSW*, 20 Dec. 1937. 168 *TT*, 4 Dec. 2021. 169 Ibid.

SOCCER IN DUBLIN AND THE GAELIC ATHLETIC ASSOCIATION

Since the early 1900s, members of the GAA had been prohibited from participating in 'foreign games' such as rugby, soccer, hockey and cricket under the
organization's Rule 27, with those caught given suspensions of varying lengths,
although in January 1905 it was noted that this should be for the duration of two
years.[170] The GAA had voiced its opposition to the formation of the FAI in 1921,
with a motion passed that the new Free State national soccer governing body
was, like the IFA in Belfast, 'antagonistic to the national ideals of the GAA' and
that FAI members were not permitted to take part in Gaelic football, hurling or
athletics under GAA rules.[171] While the GAA had established vigilance committees to monitor members' participation in 'foreign games' in 1924, the Ban
was not always strictly adhered to and the indiscretions of players were often
ignored.[172] This was particularly the case in Dublin in 1925, when one writer to
the *Gaelic Athlete* stated that these committees were not doing the job they were
supposed to do.[173] Some improvements were made as, early in 1932, three Dublin
GAA players were suspended, having been identified by the local vigilance committee as having breached the rule.[174] Wren, De Burca and Gorry have stated that
'although Dublin favoured the removal of the "Ban", it was pointless bringing
the question before Congress when the majority opinion was definitely for its
retention'.[175]

By the mid-1920s, Val Harris was said to be 'one of the few footballers holding an All-Ireland Gaelic championship medal as well as an Irish Cup medal'
as well as a number of other soccer trophies.[176] He had played Gaelic football
for Sarsfields before taking up soccer more seriously after being banned by the
GAA for playing it.[177] Harris was not the only Shelbourne player who achieved
success in the latter code, with Pat Kelly and Harry Collins also prominent in
All-Ireland competitions in the early 1900s.[178] Pat Kelly won an All-Ireland medal
with Dublin in 1901 while Harry Collins was a member of the Dundalk Young
Irelands in 1903.[179] Other Shelbourne players to represent Dublin in the early
twentieth century included Joe Ledwidge and Jack Heslin, while Wicklow-born
Jack Kirwin of Chelsea, Tottenham Hotspur and Ireland also played Gaelic football.[180] Ledwidge was an All-Ireland Gaelic football winner, and was also capped
by Ireland. He was a noted cricketer with Clontarf and also won All-Ireland
Gaelic football championships with Geraldines in 1898 and 1899 as well as the
Irish Cup with Shelbourne in 1906, but did not move abroad.[181] As well as playing rugby, hockey and soccer, Bohemians goalkeeper J.C. Hehir won two Dublin

170 Curran, *The development of sport in Donegal*, pp 199–200. 171 Central Council Minute Books,
1899–1981, GAA Archives Croke Park, GAA/CC/01/02, 1911–25, p. 19. 172 Curran, *The development of sport in Donegal*, pp 217–21. 173 Ibid., p. 219. 174 Wren, de Búrca & Gorry, *The
Gaelic Athletic Association in Dublin*, i: *1884–1959*, p. 236. 175 Ibid., p. 291. 176 *Sport*, 7 Nov.
1925. 177 Ibid. 178 Sands, *Shels*, p. 10. 179 Ibid. 180 Ibid. 181 'NIFG-Joe Ledwidge',
nifootball.blogspot.com/2007/04/joe-ledwidge.html, accessed 6 Aug. 2021.

championship medals with Keatings and a Leinster championship medal, and narrowly missed out on an appearance in the All-Ireland final when he had to withdraw at the last minute.[182]

After the First World War, Bohemians goalkeeper Commandant Harry Cannon had experience of hurling at Fontenoy's and of Gaelic football with McCracken's before joining the Dalymount club, and as well as going on to play an administrative role at Bohemians, he was appointed to the International Boxing Federation.[183] A contemporary player of his era, Paddy O'Kane, also played hurling and Gaelic football with Faughs and Eoghan Ruadh.[184] Late 1920s Bohemian players to delve into other sports included Fred Horlacher, who won a water-polo Irish Cup medal as well as representing Ireland at that pastime.[185] Cross-over to cricket remained common after partition with M. Lynam, F. Collins, J. Cross and P. Scott of Jacob's involved in the game in the summer of 1925.[186] By June 1927, Louis Bookman was playing for Leinster, while another soccer player named Blackford was playing for Richmond CC.[187] Stephen Boyne of Jacob's, Reilly of CYMS, Morton of Bohemians and R. Meade of Richmond also took up the game during the summer.[188]

It is clear that there were many soccer players in Dublin who took part in Gaelic games at some stage. In September 1925 one journalist writing in *Football Sports Weekly* questioned why Bohemians' Joe Stynes' was being 'described as "the ex-Gaelic player"'.[189] He added that 'if we were to name all the ex-Gaelic players at present playing [association] football we could fill this paper'.[190] Frank Brady had apparently 'matriculated as a footballer under the Gaelic code' before playing soccer, while Vickers FC were strengthened in 1925 by Charlie McDonald, 'a convert from Gaelic' who 'at one time played for Dublin in the All-Ireland championships'.[191] Some Gaelic footballers played soccer under false names, with one newspaper noting in 1926 that 'another Gaelic [player] has taken up soccer' and his identity was 'hidden under the name "Burns." He is some sprinter.'[192] Cross-over of players continued later in the decade. In February 1928, Strandvilla, who were formed earlier in the decade, were said to have previously played football under GAA rules and apparently 'won all there was to be won at that game' within their own level.[193]

There is some evidence of players' motives for changing codes. Dublin Gaelic footballer Joe Stynes recalled that he had first played soccer having been 'arrested and interned in Tintown Camp for nine months' in June 1923 for his role on the anti-Treaty side in the Civil War.[194] He added that 'the football field allotted to us in the Camp was so small that the only game possible for us to play was soccer'.[195] There, he played along with Jimmy Dunne and noted that 'the many games

---

182 Reid, *Bohemian AFC official club history, 1890–1976*, p. 34.   183 Ibid., p. 35.   184 Ibid., p. 37.   185 Ibid.   186 *FSW*, 12 Sept. 1925.   187 *FSW*, 18 June 1927.   188 Ibid., and 29 Jan. 1927. Others to enjoy playing the game included Jim Shirley, Cecil and Bonnie Pemberton and Frank Connell of the Richmond Asylum club.   189 *FSW*, 5 Sept. 1925.   190 Ibid.   191 *FSW*, 12 Sept. and 7 Nov. 1925.   192 *FSW*, 6 Feb. 1926.   193 *FSW*, 21 Feb. 1928.   194 *FSW*, 30 Jan. 1926.   195 Ibid.

played there fascinated me so much that I determined, when released, to give the game a trial'.[196] As Aaron Ó Maonaigh has shown, along with the lack of space, defiance against their pro–Free State jailors was another reason soccer, as opposed to Gaelic games, was played by some anti-Treaty internees, particularly those from Dublin.[197] Stynes returned to playing Gaelic football for Dublin, but, having been approached by a member of the Shelbourne committee after the 1925 Gaelic football Leinster championship replay versus Wexford, he signed for the then Ringsend club. The following season, he joined Bohemians where he felt his progress was helped greatly by Dr Willie Hooper and trainer Charlie Harris.[198] By September 1926 Stynes was said to have settled in the USA, and was playing both soccer and Gaelic football.[199] Rivalry with Gaelic football in America affected the sustainability of some soccer clubs there, with William J. O'Brien, the manager of Boston Celtic, writing to *Sport* in the winter of 1925, noting that the club had availed of the services of a number of Irish League and Free State players, but that their 'only trouble' was 'the fact that we cannot find enough good Irish players to sign up … as most of the Irish lads coming over are Gaelic players'.[200] Many GAA members were covert soccer fans in any case, and some had no issue attending matches in Dublin. One reporter noted after the decision to again retain the Ban in 1926 that '"the powers that be" will have some job to enforce their ruling, as we noticed a very prominent Gaelic official and several All-Ireland men among the crowd at Shelbourne Park on Easter Monday for the Hospitals' charity match'.[201]

In addition to the GAA's 'Ban', some soccer clubs took action against their players for taking part in Gaelic games. Con Coyle, 'one of the best half-backs in the country', was suspended by Drumcondra in March 1929 for playing in a Gaelic football match on the same day as a Free State Shield match involving his soccer club.[202] Coyle had joined Newry Town by October of that year.[203] Some Gaelic football players felt that they could get away with infringing the Ban rules because of their playing quality, with Kerry-born Jimmy Joy, who won an All-Ireland Gaelic football final with Dublin in the 1940s, of the view that the GAA would not suspend a player if he was good enough.[204] Joy had played for and captained the Blackrock Rugby Club during the same period, and having been initially reported for playing rugby, his suspension was lifted by the GAA in 1942 apparently because the person who informed on him was not officially part of a vigilance committee.[205] However, numerous players were suspended from GAA activity as a result of their involvement in other codes, including Con Martin, who had played Gaelic football for St Mary's of Saggart and Dublin, and was suspended by the GAA for playing soccer for Drumcondra, helping Dublin win the Leinster Gaelic football final in 1942.[206]

196 Ibid.   **197** Aaron Ó Maonaigh, '"In the Ráth Camp, rugby or soccer would not have been tolerated by the prisoners": Irish Civil War attitudes to sport, 1922–3' in Curran (ed.), 'The growth and development of soccer in Dublin', Special edition of *Soccer and Society*, pp 834–44, pp 838–9.   **198** *FSW*, 30 Jan. 1926.   **199** *Sport*, 18 Sept. 1926.   **200** *Sport*, 14 Nov. 1925.   **201** *FSW*, 10 Apr. 1926.   **202** *II*, 13 Mar. 1929.   **203** *II*, 14 Oct. 1929.   **204** *CT*, 24 May 1996.   **205** Ibid.; See also *SI*, 18 July 2010.   **206** *II*, 19 Dec. 1999.

The Leinster FA made efforts to spread interest in soccer in some regional areas where Gaelic games were the dominant codes.[207] By the end of the 1927–8 season soccer was apparently 'firmly established' in 'almost every county of the province'.[208] The Association stated that 'quite a good deal of credit is due to the clubs in the metropolis' who were 'playing a prominent part in the work of propaganda'. It was also noted that 'not only are their frequent visits to the outlying districts, where hitherto soccer was practically unknown, having a beneficent effect', they were also helping to popularise the game throughout the Free State.[209] One area targeted was Wexford, following an invite from the Wexford and District League.[210] In March 1928 the Leinster FA selected a team to travel for an exhibition match there, with *Football Sports Weekly* noting the difficulties faced in that area:

> The visit to Wexford was a huge success notwithstanding the efforts of the GAA to enforce a boycott on the game. After their efforts to stop the landlord from giving the park for the game had failed, they tried their utmost to get the local clergy to stop the band from attending. A big counter attraction was staged at Enniscorthy, but this also failed in its objects, as there was a fine attendance at the match, the gate receipts being close on £100.[211]

This method of organizing Gaelic football matches to clash with soccer exhibition matches was also common in Donegal at that time.[212] In Wexford, a league had been formed with eight clubs, with five of these, 'composed of mostly Gaelic players', operational earlier that year, which helps explain the concerns of the GAA there.[213] Assistance also came from Shamrock Rovers, who gave a set of goal nets to the Wexford clubs.[214] As Mark Tynan has shown, some Dublin-based individuals such as Leinster FA and FAIFS administrator J.S. Smurthwaite also attempted to encourage the development of soccer in regional areas, with the Jacob's factory welfare manager assisting in attempts to form a league in Galway early in that decade.[215] In June 1926, the Galway FA, which contained five clubs, completed its first season.[216] Progress was slow in many areas, however, with one reporter noting the first serious attempt to establish soccer in Carlow in the 1926–7 season, which 'in face of much opposition', had 'been a great success, when everything is considered'.[217]

FURTHER DEVELOPMENTS IN THE PRE-EMERGENCY YEARS

In 1930 the Leinster FA gained a more permanent home when they moved from their rented headquarters in Mary Street to Parnell Square, with a new

---

207 *FSW*, 24 Mar. 1928. 208 36th Annual Report, May 1928, Leinster Football Association Archives, P239/27. 209 Ibid. 210 Ibid. 211 *FSW*, 31 Mar. 1928. 212 See Curran, *The development of sport in Donegal, 1880–1935*, pp 214–17. 213 *FSW*, 25 Feb. 1928. 214 Ibid., 27 Feb. 1926. 215 Tynan, 'Association football and Irish society during the inter-war period, 1918–1939', pp 124–5. 216 *FSW*, 19 June 1926. 217 *FSW*, 16 July 1927. See also Norman & Douglas McMillan (eds), *A history of soccer in county Carlow* (Dublin, 1984), p. 33.

competition inaugurated to cover the costs of the purchase of this new building.[218] By the end of the 1929–30 season, the President's Cup, donated by Leinster FA president Osmond Grattan Esmonde TD, was operational with this in mind. The competition was initially open to all Leinster senior clubs, although this rule was later amended on a number of occasions.[219] The Leinster FA reported at the end of the 1930–1 season that they had 392 affiliated clubs, which was an increase of 45 from the previous season.[220] A Leinster Junior Sunday Cup was also initiated to cater for the growing number of Sunday football junior clubs, with Westland Rovers initially winning it.[221] Another politician who was involved in promoting the game in that decade was Alasdair McCabe, a former footballer who apparently was 'the first to move on the question of the Entertainment Tax' and was 'instrumental in getting the status of the F[ree] S[tate] A[ssociation] internationally recognized'.[222] One newspaper claimed that 'no man did more while a member of the Dáil to forward the interests of the game' in the early days of the Irish Free State.[223] Under the 1927 Finance Act, introduced in May that year, the GAA had been deemed exempt from paying income tax on its profits, although no other sporting body was shown this leniency by the Cumann na nGaedheal government.[224] In June 1927, *Football Sports Weekly* had noted the election of 'three able representatives' who would ensure that 'the popular game will not be wanting for a voice in the new government, if needed'.[225] These were Oscar Traynor, Dr Myles Keogh and Alfie Byrne.[226] Despite this, in May 1932 the minister for finance under the new Fianna Fáil government, Seán McEntee, after meeting with a delegation of soccer officials, including Traynor, who wanted to see the entertainment tax removed, refused to allow any concessions.[227] This came despite the GAA still being deemed exempt from the tax. In particular, M.J. Kenny of Bohemians, who was vice president of the Free State League and chairman of the Leinster FA, noted that 'country clubs were already in a bad state' as a result of economic conditions, 'and to harass these clubs further may possibly precipitate a crisis which would mean the end for some'.[228] In addition, he noted the impact it would potentially have on clubs' attendances and 'on the poor working man, whose only entertainment for the week is his hour-and-a-half's football at the week-end'.[229] He also highlighted 'the unfair discrimination between one body and another in football'.[230] The matter was raised, albeit to no avail, in the Dáil in July 1932, with J.J. Byrne, a Cumann na nGaedheal deputy representing Dublin North, noting that there were 'some 60,000 people who go to witness Soccer football matches every week and that they come from the masses of the people, the ordinary every-day working people who manage to scrape up 6*d.* each with the necessary few extra pence to pay their bus or tram

218 Briggs & Dodd, *100 years of the LFA*, p. 47.   219 Ibid., p. 84 and p. 98; *EH*, 2 May 1930. 220 39th Annual Report, May 1931, Leinster Football Association Archives, P239/27.   221 Briggs & Dodd, *100 years of the LFA*, p. 47.   222 *FSW*, 29 Aug. 1925.   223 Ibid.   224 Moore, *The GAA v Douglas Hyde*, p. 67.   225 *FSW*, 18 June 1927.   226 Ibid.   227 *II*, 31 May 1932.   228 Ibid. 229 Ibid.   230 Ibid.

fares to get to a football match'.[231] He highlighted the possible impact it would have on clubs if it was not removed:

> You have two very fine provincial clubs – Dundalk and Cork. Both of these are in an extremely precarious condition financially. We have three clubs in Dublin in a similar position – Dolphin, Drumcondra and Jacob's. The gates that these clubs are getting under existing circumstances are not sufficient to pay working expenses. How will these gates be affected if the tax is imposed? I want to say that in my opinion there can be no possibility or hope of carrying on Soccer football if the tax is imposed. I do not see why there should be discrimination against one form of outdoor sport in preference to another.[232]

Despite the poor state of the economy in the 1930s, and the entertainment tax, interest in soccer continued. Garnham has noted that one measure of the popularity of soccer in Dublin on the eve of the Emergency can be seen in the rise in attendance levels at the annual FAI Cup finals, as these grew from 8,000 in 1922 to 30,651 in 1939.[233] The number of clubs continued to grow early in the decade and in 1932 the Leinster FA had 420 of these affiliated.[234] However, these figures often disguised the poor state of some clubs, particularly in more rural areas.[235] He has also noted that it was a struggle to maintain professionalism and the best players in the Irish Free State generally continued to move to England and Scotland.[236] While Linfield and Belfast Celtic dominated the IFA's competitions, similarly it was Shamrock Rovers and Bohemians who were the most successful teams in the Irish Free State in the interwar years. Bohemians' development of Dalymount Park was notable in this period, but the club remained amateur despite spending £20,000 to modernize their ground between 1927 and 1938.[237] Prior to the Leinster League's match against the Scottish Alliance at Dalymount Park in October 1927, it was noted in the press that 'community singing with band and choir, the effects of which will be enhanced by Marconi amplifier installation, is a strong added attraction'. The reporter also felt that 'the wet weather should not deter spectators, as there is ample covered accommodation at the Bohemian enclosure'.[238]

Cronin and Higgins have noted that 'in line with developments at other sporting venues across the country the facilities in Dalymount Park were significantly improved in the 1920s and 1930s'.[239] In 1927, £2,520 was spent on boundary walls, turnstiles and stands, designed by Donnelly, Moore and Keating, were built to replace the corrugated iron perimeter.[240] In 1931, renowned stadium architect Archibald Leitch designed an extension to the grandstand as well as amendments to the terrace.[241] Much of the financing of this came from individual members.[242] In

231 Dáil Éireann Debate, Thursday 7 July 1932, vol. 43, no. 3, 'Finance Bill 1932 – Committee (Resumed)', oireachtas.ie/en/debates/debate/dail/1932-07-07/11, accessed 8 Apr. 2022. 232 Ibid. 233 Garnham, 'Ein spiel in zwei nationen?', p. 81. 234 Ibid., p. 80. 235 Ibid. 236 Ibid., pp 80–2. 237 Ibid., p. 82. 238 *II*, 22 Oct. 1927. 239 Cronin & Higgins, *Places we play*, p. 105. 240 Ibid. 241 Ibid. 242 Ibid.

July 1934, Bohemians became 'a company limited by guarantee', whereby there were no shareholders but in the event of the threat of winding-up, each member promised to contribute at least £10.[243] By the middle of the following decade, they remained the only major Dublin soccer club to have invested significantly in improving their ground, though the IRFU and the GAA had also done this to their central venues at Lansdowne Road and Croke Park, respectively, in line with increased attendances.[244] International soccer matches were generally held at Dalymount Park at that time, with the attendance of the president, Douglas Hyde, at the friendly against Poland in November 1938 leading to his removal as GAA patron under the organization's 'Ban', for attending a 'foreign' code.[245] It was not until 1945, under pressure from Taoiseach Eamon de Valera, that the GAA conceded that the Irish president should be entitled to attend 'foreign' games, but Rule 27 remained in place.[246]

Some attempts were made by the Leinster FA to form connections with administrative soccer bodies in the west of Ireland. The 1931 inter-provincial match between Leinster and Connacht at Westport, County Mayo, was the first meeting between the teams.[247] The election of Connacht club Sligo Rovers to the Leinster League was also ratified by the Leinster FA early in the decade.[248] This meant that Dublin clubs of a non-Free State League level began to branch out more regularly for competitive league matches. Travelling longer distances was not always easy, given the state of Ireland's roads in more peripheral areas. In January 1934, Brideville FC's secretary, Timothy Finn, was killed when their team bus crashed on a greasy road on their way to a fixture in Sligo, but the other passengers, including the players, escaped unharmed.[249] Financial difficulties in the early part of the decade, and a change of committee, meant that they were unable to pay service fees of £12 to An Garda Síochána to assist with the crowds on match days.[250] An enquiry in April 1934 highlighted that although a committee of four and a treasurer and secretary were active, they owned no playing grounds, had no registered office, funds or assets and were in debt to the tune of £360.[251] They were not the only club who struggled to pay for this assistance, as Cork Bohemians were also unable to pay the Gardaí and Dolphin were slow to pay a debt of £18 for policing services later in the decade.[252] Despite these troubles, Brideville persevered, while Dolphin went into decline, and by the early 1940s Brideville's home ground, Harold's Cross Park, was reportedly 'one of the biggest and most suitably equipped in the country'.[253]

243 O'Mahony (ed.), *Bohemian Football Club golden jubilee souvenir*, p. 23. 244 Ibid. 245 Moore, *The GAA v Douglas Hyde*, pp 86–7, 104. 246 Ibid., p. 213. 247 39th Annual Report, May 1931, Leinster Football Association Archives, P239/27. 248 Dodd, *100 years: a history*, p. 45. 249 *SC*, 6 Jan. 1934. 250 An Garda Síochána claim against Brideville Association Club for services rendered (1934–5), Department of Justice, 90/5/42, NAI. 251 Ibid., Letter from the deputy commissioner of An Garda Síochána to the secretary of the Department of Justice, 6 Apr. 1934. 252 Ibid., Minute Sheet, 235/134, 18 Dec. 1934; An Garda Síochána: Gardaí services requisitioned. Dolphin AFC Limited (1937), Non-payment of accounts for £18 by Dolphin (Association) Football Club Ltd, 25 Nov. 1937, Department of Justice, 90/5/45, NAI. 253 Walsh, *Twenty years of Irish soccer*, p. 114.

Even the stronger clubs could have their administrative issues. Shamrock Rovers had a social club in operation by the mid-1930s with billiards, cards, croquet and tennis taking place at Glenmalure Park, but when they applied for a sports club licence for running a bar there, the Pioneer Total Abstinence Association objected.[254] Shelbourne temporarily left the Free State League after falling out with the FAIFS in 1934 and attempted to join the Irish League.[255] They were fined £500 and banned for twelve months, during which time a number of their personnel joined Reds United, who were in the Leinster Senior League and also based in the Ringsend area.[256] They won the league and were elected to the Free State League, but having failed to secure a new ground or to amalgamate with Shelbourne, they resigned their position.[257] Having played in the Athletic Union League, in the 1936–7 season Shelbourne's ban was lifted by the FAI, which had reverted back to its early title that season, and they returned to the Free State League following support for this from Shamrock Rovers' representatives.[258] As they struggled to deal with the cost of moving to a permanent headquarters, the Leinster FA reported a loss of over £186 at the end of the 1938–9 season, with the Leinster Senior Cup semi-finals and final not attracting the support they had anticipated.[259] However, the visits of Motherwell and, in particular, Glasgow Celtic that season had significantly helped their finances.[260] As will be shown in more detail in chapter five, these cross-Channel visits by clubs were an additional source of income for many of the bigger clubs, but they did not come free of charge. As Tynan has noted, most Free State League clubs failed to properly reinvest the money taken in at the turnstiles, which ultimately hindered their overall development.[261] Some work-based clubs were able to develop from their own resources and compete successfully at a lower level, with the British and Irish Associated Shipping Company winning the Free State Junior Cup, the Leinster Junior Cup, the Leinster Senior League Second Division and the Edmund Johnson Cup in the 1933–4 season, further illustrating that a sound financial struc-ture was a major help to any club.[262]

THE SECOND WORLD WAR (1939–45)

Soccer in Dublin was not seriously affected by the Second World War, which began in September 1939.[263] Former goalkeeper Oscar Traynor was parliamentary secre-tary to the minister for defence in the Fianna Fáil government, which advocated a policy of neutrality, although assistance was covertly given to the Allied forces.[264] As

254 Doolan & Goggins, *The Hoops*, p. 16.   255 Sands, *Shels*, pp 54–5.   256 Ibid.; Gerry Farrell, 'The lost clubs: Reds United', abohemiansportinglife.wordpress.com/2020/03/25/the-lost-clubs-reds-united, accessed 14 Oct. 2021.   257 Farrell, 'The lost clubs: Reds United'.   258 Ibid. 259 Report and Statement of Accounts, Season 1938–9, 7 June 1939, Leinster Football Association Archives, P239/30; Briggs & Dodd, *100 years of the LFA*, pp 48–50.   260 Ibid.   261 Tynan, 'Association football and Irish society during the inter-war period, 1918–1939', pp 136–7.   262 *IP*, 17 May 1934; *Soccer Reporter* (Nov. 1982), p. 12.   263 *II*, 7 Nov. 1939.   264 Garnham, *Association football and society*, p. 85.

Ó Maonaigh has stated, Traynor was crucial in asserting the right of National Army soldiers to play whatever sport they chose following his appointment in 1939, as soccer had been banned within the Irish Army since the early 1920s.[265] Dublin suffered significant damage when the North Strand area was bombed by the Luftwaffe in May 1941, with one source estimating that forty-five people were killed although as Kevin C. Kearns has stated, the final death toll 'will never be known for certain'.[266] Alf Girvan, who was born in Blessington Street in 1934 and grew up in Fleming Street, recalled visiting relatives in North Strand the day after the bombings.[267] He stated that during the war, conditions 'were tough, there were all sorts of restrictions'.[268] Mick Meagan, who was born in Churchtown the same year, recounted his fear as a child of hearing aeroplanes flying overhead, and how he was able to buy his first pair of football boots for £1 in Camden Street, having worked on a government-backed turf-cutting scheme.[269] Like in the First World War, clubs were affected, and membership figures dropped, but soccer competitions continued to be played. The Leinster FA noted in their annual report at the end of the 1940–1 season the 'adverse effect' that 'the world wide conditions' had had on its progress, with 'a falling off in membership of some 50 teams'.[270] However, while stating it was 'unfortunate', it was 'not serious enough to cause any grave concern' as they felt it would 'be only temporary' and the drop in membership could be 'readily explained by the fact that a good many' of their 'young players' had 'joined the various defence forces, thereby causing the suspension of activity of some' of their teams.[271] Some adaptions were made to competitions as the number of registered clubs decreased to 228, with the Leinster Council taking the decision to merge the Saturday and Sunday of the Junior Cup and Junior Shield sections into Saturday sections in 1941, with the Sunday section matches not returning until 1947.[272]

One club to enjoy success during the war was Leinster Senior League club Distillery, who played their home matches at Rutland Avenue in Dolphin's Barn before losing their ground to the Crumlin-Kimmage housing scheme and moving to Seafield Road in Clontarf.[273] They won the FAI Intermediate Cup for the fourth year running in 1941, and they also won the Leinster Senior Cup in 1942, but disbanded in 1944.[274] They had again been refused entry to the League of Ireland the previous year, and initially withdrew from all soccer, only to re-enter other competitions for another season, but in August 1944 they pulled out of a Leinster Senior Cup tie against Grangegorman, and did not return.[275] It appears they had sought entry to the highest level of Irish soccer since 1938 but were unsuccessful.[276] Internal league politics also hindered the progress of St James's Gate, who won the League of Ireland in 1940 but, having finished last in 1944, failed to be

265 Ó Maonaigh, 'In the Ráth Camp', p. 837. 266 Kevin C. Kearns, *The bombing of Dublin's North Strand: the untold story* (Dublin, 2010), p. 345. 267 Interview with Alf Girvan, 27 Jan. 2020. 268 Ibid. 269 Interview with Mick Meagan, 30 Sept. 2019. 270 49th Annual Report, 1940–1, May 1941, Leinster Football Association Archives, P239/30. 271 Ibid. 272 Briggs & Dodd, *100 years of the LFA*, p. 51 and p. 53. 273 Ibid., p. 103. 274 Ibid., pp 51, 53. 275 *IP*, 31 Aug. 1944. 276 *IP*, 23 May 1940.

5. St James's Gate with the Leinster Senior Cup in 1935. Courtesy of Dublin City Library and Archives.

elected again.[277] Apparently some rival clubs were unhappy that they did not have full control of their finances, as their profits went to the Guinness Athletic Union, while its members did not have to pay into their home matches, which impacted on the amount that away clubs received for fixtures there.[278]

Another work-based club to achieve some success during the war was Bradmola from Blackrock Hosiery Factory, who won four trophies in the 1942–3 season.[279] Factory owner Mr Bradbury was a sports enthusiast, a director of Leicester City FC and also donated the Bradmola Cup for local competition.[280] Those organizing charity matches also received trophies from benefactors. In March 1942, P. Masterson, the chairman of Shelbourne Sports Club, presented a silver cup and replicas for a match between Shelbourne and Shamrock Rovers at Dalymount Park in aid of the St Andrew's Church Westland Row Reconstruction Fund.[281]

Attendances were naturally affected in some competitions, with one reporter noting in 1950 that 'gates' had decreased during the war as 'football was generally

277 'Our history', stjamesgatefc.com/club-history, accessed 3 Jan. 2022. 278 Ibid. 279 Briggs & Dodd, *100 years of the LFA*, pp 51, 53. These trophies were the Athletic Union League First Division, the Leinster Junior Cup (Saturday) and the Leinster Senior League Second Division and the Johnson Cup (Sunday). 280 Dodd, *100 years: a history*, p. 47. 281 *II*, 1 Apr. 1942.

at a low ebb'.[282] The gate for the 1942 Leinster Senior Cup final 'was the worst on record, and not at all in keeping with the importance of the competition'.[283] Some junior competitions were not finished by the middle of May that year, with clubs apparently struggling to complete fixtures.[284] However, the game remained in a stable condition in Dublin. At the end of the 1943–4 season, the Leinster FA reported that 'despite the adverse circumstances, including difficulties in transport and the many other causes arising out of the World War conflict', their position was 'fairly well maintained'.[285] The association's membership compared 'very favourably' with the previous season, with 'just an unappreciable decrease of ten clubs, 183 as against 193'.[286] It was also noted that provincially, 'notwithstanding all the transport difficulties, teams in the outlying areas' were 'making a brave effort to carry on'.[287]

Some fixtures between clubs north and south of the border took place during the war. Byrne has noted the significance of the Inter-city Cup in being 'the best of the north-south competitions in the post-split era', although it declined in 1949 with 'the total breakdown in relations between the FAI and the IFA'.[288] According to Seán Ryan, the competition can be seen as 'the unofficial All-Ireland' and Bohemians were victorious in the 1945 final, defeating Belfast Celtic.[289] Some Dublin clubs took part in charity matches during the war to alleviate war-related distress in Belfast. Following the Belfast Blitz in 1941, St James's Gate took part in a benefit match at the Oval in Belfast against Glentoran.[290] The Dublin club paid their own expenses and requested that their share of the attendance receipts should go to the lord mayor's fund for the relief of distress caused by the air raids.[291] The match drew receipts of almost £85, while nearly £40 in related subscriptions were gathered from that game.[292] Following assistance from Dublin fire services during the Belfast Blitz in April 1941, the annual match between Dublin and Belfast firemen began in Belfast in 1942 and continued during and after the war, but was discontinued after 1971 on account of the Troubles.[293]

Other matches featuring teams related to the war effort also took place in Dublin. In July 1943, teams representing the civil defence forces of Northern Ireland and Dublin air raid precautions played a friendly match at Tolka Park.[294] In November 1945, Bohemians beat a RAF XI from Belfast at Dalymount Park.[295] Footballers were not untouched by these attacks close to home. At least one player, Glenavon outside-left John McCunnie, was killed in the Belfast air raids.[296] The previous year, Wexford Gaelic footballer 'Lallie' Murphy had been killed in London during the Blitz there.[297]

282 *SI*, 11 June 1950.   283 Report and Statement of Accounts Season 1941–2, May 1942, Leinster Football Association Archives, P239/30.   284 Ibid.   285 51st Annual Report, 31 May 1944, Leinster Football Association Archives, P239/31.   286 Ibid.   287 Ibid.   288 Byrne, *Green is the colour*, pp 170–1.   289 Ryan, *The official book of the FAI Cup*, p. 109.   290 Byrne, *Green is the colour*, pp 168–9; *BN*, 23 Apr. 1941.   291 *BN*, 23 Apr. 1941.   292 *NW*, 29 July 1941. A match between 'past internationals and future internationals' at Windsor Park raised £38.   293 Kearns, *The bombing of Dublin's North Strand, 1941*, pp 339, 343–4.   294 *BT*, 16 and 22 July 1943.   295 *EH*, 28 Nov. 1945.   296 *II*, 10 May 1941.   297 Ibid., 31 Oct. 1940.

Soccer was reported to be making 'commendable progress' in the army and civil defence forces by the end of the war, with 'several army units' participating 'in the various leagues' and 'doing very well'.[298] In 1941, Rathfarnham Sports Club, which had a military background, was established, with the club later merging with local schoolboy club St Joseph's in 1949, the year they won the FAI Junior Cup.[299] An army selection, which included Con Martin, were also involved in matches against the Irish international team at Dalymount Park during the war, with these fixtures drawing capacity crowds.[300] Efforts to revive the Leinster versus Ulster interprovincial fixture had to be abandoned, due to the circumstances and 'the difficulty of securing suitable dates'.[301]

The 1945 FAI Cup final, in which Shamrock Rovers beat Bohemians one-nil at Dalymount Park, was described by one reporter as 'an anticlimax', because 'those in attendance could have found much better entertainment pottering around the back garden, for instance, or walking around the gardens in the Phoenix Park'.[302] The match had been sold out and drew a record attendance of 37,348. Frank O'Neill, who was 5 years old when he attended, recalled that he became a Shamrock Rovers supporter afterwards.[303]

At the end of the 1944–5 season, the Leinster FA reported 'a substantial increase in membership', with 261 clubs registered as opposed to 183 the previous season' and 'not for years' had the provincial association 'been in such a sound financial position'.[304] However, they noted cautiously that 'though hostilities have ceased [in Europe], it is rather too soon to expect an immediate return to normal conditions'.[305] The Leinster FA again identified transport as the 'principal difficulty' for teams outside Dublin, but were optimistic that friendly matches with Dublin clubs would again commence.[306] A few years later, they reflected that 'one of the principal causes' in the decline in membership had been because 'a lot of the younger junior players had gone away'.[307]

Soccer in Dublin had come through the Second World War in a reasonable condition, and at the end of the 1945 season the Leinster FA looked forward 'with confidence' and expressed hope that supporters could soon enjoy the game 'in perfect comfort'.[308]

CONCLUSION

While soccer has traditionally been associated with inner-city areas in Dublin, this is not to say that the game did not develop in areas which are more commonly

298 52nd Annual Report, May 1945, Leinster Football Association Archives, P239/31. 299 *Irish Soccer*, 1:9 (1955), p. 18. St Joseph's were founded in 1943. 300 Briggs & Dodds, *100 years of the LFA*, p. 55. 301 52nd Annual Report, May 1945, Leinster Football Association Archives, P239/31. 302 *IE*, 23 Apr. 1945. 303 Ibid., and interview with Frank O'Neill, 30 Jan. 2020. 304 52nd Annual Report, May 1945, Leinster Football Association Archives, P239/31. 305 Ibid. 306 Ibid. 307 54th Annual Report, June 1947, Leinster Football Association Archives, P239/ 32. 308 52nd Annual Report, May 1945, Leinster Football Association Archives, P239/31.

thought of as being rugby strongholds, including Blackrock and Monkstown, albeit to a much lesser extent. This was notable by the middle of the 1920s with a number of clubs from suburban areas capable of challenging those which might have had a longer history and growing tradition of involvement. As Dublin soccer administrators gained increased independence from the Belfast-leaning IFA following the 'split', the number of competitions centred in the city and its immediate surroundings continued to grow in stature. The semi-professional nature of the game remained detrimental, however, particularly in terms of player welfare. Care of injured players remained rudimentary within some League of Ireland grounds, with one Drumcondra player carried off the pitch on a tactical billboard, having broken his leg in a cup match against Shamrock Rovers in 1940, as the stretcher normally used at Tolka Park had not been returned from the hospital.[309]

Financial difficulties were evident, particularly for League of Ireland clubs in the 1930s with the global depression following the 1929 Wall Street crash. While independent Ireland remained officially neutral during the Second World War, the game in Dublin was affected through a decline in membership and matches against provincial Leinster clubs became less common due to travel restrictions. Many clubs relied on volunteers and supporters to keep their day-to-day activities operational. By the middle of the 1940s, both Bohemians and Shelbourne each had a 'ways and means committee' in operation, with these members responsible for fundraising, organizing the club's social events and functions, as well as taking care of match-day programmes, and naturally this type of work was a social outlet in itself for them.[310] Despite administrative issues, the Leinster FA were able to maintain the majority of their competitions notwithstanding the withdrawal of some players who were serving in the British forces, and the organization could look forward to the aftermath of the global conflict with much enthusiasm despite the social conditions that prevailed. In chapter four, the state of Dublin soccer in the immediate years after the Emergency and the second half of the twentieth century are assessed.

---

309 Ryan, *The official book of the FAI Cup*, p. 86. Tactical billboards were normally used prior to matches to indicate formations within teams in the dressing room. 310 *Shelbourne Football Club golden jubilee, 1895–1945*, p. 35; O'Mahony (ed.), *Bohemian Football Club golden jubilee souvenir*, p. 27.

4

Clubs and competitions, 1946–2000

THE POST-WAR YEARS

The Leinster FA reported at their AGM in May 1946 that the previous season had been 'very successful ... financially and otherwise' and that 'things were gradually returning to normal'.[1] Membership was said to compare 'very favourably' with the previous year as there were 270 clubs enrolled, and as 'travelling difficulties' were 'gradually being overcome', the game was 'making commendable progress' in other areas of Leinster.[2] Clubs were certainly affected by travel restrictions brought on by the Emergency, particularly those in outlying areas of Leinster who took part in Dublin-centred competitions, with Longford reportedly going into decline until they returned to face St Patrick's Athletic in the 1946–7 season with a team made up of Sligo and Athlone players.[3] Regional teams were again able to enter the Leinster Junior Cup and by the end of the decade over 500 clubs were affiliated to the Leinster FA.[4] Some League of Ireland teams continued to field 'guest' players in the years immediately after the war, with Peter Doherty giving 'a superb display' for Drumcondra in their opening President's Cup match against Shamrock Rovers in August 1946.[5] The visit of the England international team in late September 1946 was a welcome financial boost for soccer in Dublin, given that this was the first time the English team had played the FAI's national XI.[6] Almost 32,000 were in attendance at the match at Dalymount Park, including President Seán T. O' Kelly, but Ireland failed to breach Frank Swift's goal and lost one–nil to a strike from Tom Finney. The English team were received by Taoiseach Eamon de Valera at the Dáil during their stay.[7]

In the winter of 1946–7, local matches were postponed for six weeks due to the adverse weather conditions.[8] Despite this having temporarily 'severely handicapped the junior competitions', the Leinster FA reported at the end of the season that most programmes had been completed through 'strenuous efforts'.[9] In June 1948, the FAI noted that 551 clubs had registered the previous season (1947–8), which was a new record for them, and an increase of 126 from 1946–7.[10] The FAI Cup final, in which Shamrock Rovers beat Drumcondra by two goals to one, had

---

1 53nd Annual Report, May 1946, Leinster Football Association Archives, P239/31. 2 Ibid. 3 *SI*, 1 Feb. 1953. 4 Briggs & Dodd, *100 years of the LFA*, p. 56. 5 *II*, 12 Aug. 1946. 6 *IE*, 1 Oct. 1946. 7 Ibid. 8 Ryan, *The official book of the FAI Cup*, p. 121. 9 54th Annual Report, June 1947, Leinster Football Association Archives, P232/32. 10 *IP*, 16 June 1948.

drawn record gate receipts of £3,634.[11] Oscar Traynor TD was appointed president of the association, a position that had been vacant since the death of Dr Willie Hooper.[12] It was also agreed to adopt a resolution that would see the transfer of junior players to senior clubs becoming regularized.[13] New clubs continued to be formed towards the end of the decade, including Belgrove, founded by a priest in 1947, and in 1949, Glebe North, who had begun as a street league team, and the same year, Earl Celtic, who grew from South Earl Street in the Liberties area.[14] Another club located close to the city centre, Broadstone United, was founded in 1947 'as a result of lads playing with a "bouncer" (a small rubber ball), on the roadway adjoining Broadstone Bus and Railway Stations where a bridge spanned the Phibsborough Road'.[15] The United Churches League was also established in the latter years of the 1940s, with the aforementioned St Mark's Athletic a founder member.[16]

Despite this progress, international success was scarce. The Irish Olympic team were knocked out of the London Olympic Games in July 1948 before the opening ceremony had even taken place.[17] Another notable international development at the end of the 1940s was the Irish team's 2–0 defeat of England before 51,000 spectators at Goodison Park in 1949, in a friendly, the first time the home side had been beaten by a non-British nation.[18] While nine of the Irish team that day were members of English clubs, two of the team were playing for Shamrock Rovers, forward Tommy O'Connor and Tommy Godwin, who put in a top class performance in goal, and subsequently joined Leicester City.[19] However, by that point the Irish team had failed to qualify from their World Cup group, which included Finland and Sweden.[20]

THE 1950s AND DUBLIN DERBIES

The 1940s had ended with Drumcondra as League of Ireland champions, and throughout the following decade they were to continue, albeit intermittently, to challenge for domestic honours.[21] By the early 1950s there were over 700 clubs registered with the Leinster FA, and although not all the initial Free State League teams had grown in strength, a revived Jacob's enjoyed success in the Leinster Senior League, having found their home there in the early 1930s, and won the 1950 FAI Intermediate Cup.[22] It was the more senior clubs that attracted the most public interest. The Leinster Senior Cup final, played on St Stephen's Day, had become an important Christmas tradition in Dublin at that point, with the 1955 match between Shamrock Rovers and St Patrick's Athletic raising a record gate of £1,610.[23]

11 Ibid. 12 Ibid. 13 Ibid. 14 *Soccer Reporter* (Dec. 1975), p. 1; *Soccer Reporter* (Apr. 1976), p. 11; *Soccer Reporter* (Summer 1976), p. 9; *Soccer Reporter* (Sept. 1976), p. 9. 15 Eddie O'Neill, *Broadstone United FC, 1947–1997* (Dublin, 1997), p. 11. 16 *EH*, 6 Aug. 1949. 17 Hunt, 'Ireland's footballers at the 1924 and 1948 Olympics', p. 897. 18 *II*, 14 Sept. 1949; *IP*, 30 Dec. 1949. 19 *II*, 22 Sept. 1949. 20 *IP*, 30 Dec. 1949. 21 Ibid. 22 Briggs & Dodds, *100 years of the LFA*, p. 57; *IP*, 16 July 1932, 25 May 1950; *EH*, 1 June 1953. 23 Briggs & Dodds, *100 years of the LFA*, p. 57 and *IP*, 3 Jan. 1956.

6. Jacob's FC with one of their trophies won in the 1950s. Courtesy of Dublin City Council Photographic Collection, Dublin City Library and Archives.

However, it was the League of Ireland and FAI Cup that provided the highest quality of regular matches over the season. This is often recalled as a great period for Dublin soccer and the 1950s has been described as 'the golden era' of the competitive domestic game in Ireland.[24] There is much to validate those claims. Shamrock Rovers were strengthened considerably by the recruitment of schoolboy players by player-manager Paddy Coad, a Waterford man who had played for the club since 1942.[25] By the latter years of the 1950s he was assisted by coach Frank Radford, a Donnybrook-based bus-garage worker, who rejoined the club after spells at Leinster League club Distillery, Shelbourne and Transport. He had also coached Drumcondra.[26] Commonly known as 'Coad's Colts', Shamrock Rovers won three League of Ireland titles and two FAI cups in that decade. The club was still backed financially by the Cunninghams, and the players benefited from a professional outlook within the club in terms of coaching, fitness, transport, meals, playing kit (this was given to the club by Glasgow Celtic) and the encouragement of a smart dress style on match days.[27] Their fast style of play was attractive to supporters, and matches were generally well attended as strong rivalries developed with other clubs, including Cork Athletic, St Patrick's Athletic, Shelbourne and Drumcondra.[28] The maximum wage discouraged some players such as Ronnie Nolan and Gerry Mackey from moving to English football, although signing-on fees in England remained an incentive for some players.[29] Cunningham himself noted in 1956 that

24 Rice, *We are Rovers*, p. 59. 25 Ibid., p. 53. 26 *IP*, 5 July 1955, 2 Mar. 1956 and 22 June 1965. 27 Rice, *We are Rovers*, pp 57–9. 28 Ibid., pp 55, 59. 29 Ibid., p. 60.

> Good management has contributed to the success of Shamrock Rovers. Our club is run on business-like lines, but we are concerned, above all, with the welfare and contentment of the players. We try to foster a strong team spirit, realizing that the best way to do that is to provide everything possible for the development, the self-respect, and even the social happiness of our players. We are proud of our team – our whole team – those on the field and those behind the scenes.[30]

This made a strong impression on many young aspiring players in Dublin. Eamon Dunphy has written of Glenmalure Park in the 1950s that

> The atmosphere inside the ground was wonderful. Milltown was special. Almost invincible during the game, Rovers looked the part as well. The green and white hooped shirts, the neat body-hugging white shorts, a contrast to the baggy drawers favoured by other teams. Coad's Colts would dash onto the pitch like well-groomed movie stars. They looked fitter, moved more gracefully than any other team. They had presence, an aura about them that radiated confidence. In this theatre of dreams, Rovers were the leading men.[31]

'Football Specials' from Burgh Quay were put on for big matches within Dublin, while clubs organized excursion trains to fixtures outside the capital.[32] With a scarcity of non-sporting entertainment in Ireland at that time, and a lack of televised sport from abroad, domestic soccer provided a compulsive outlet for many Dubliners who decided to stay in the capital. High levels of unemployment led to mass emigration in that decade, particularly from the countryside, but also from the capital.[33] Dickson has written that 'there was certainly a downbeat character to the city in the 1950s' as 'the literary and cultural world was small, male, and more than ever, centred on a few pubs and clubs'.[34] For many of those who remained, the Sunday afternoon match was an eagerly awaited occasion. Dunphy, a Drumcondra fan at that time, has also written that

> The northside/southside contests between Drums and Rovers in fifties Dublin are part of the city's folklore. We crossed town more in hope than expectation ... the bus to College Green. And then the special match buses bound for Milltown, which were lined along the walls of Trinity College. Long queues stretched back down Pearse Street, full of fans anxious to make kick-off.[35]

30 *SI*, 21 Oct. 1956.   31 Eamon Dunphy, *The rocky road* (Dublin, 2013), pp 47–8.   32 Ibid., p. 63.   33 Enda Delaney, *Irish emigration since 1921* (Dundalk, 2002), p. 18.   34 Dickson, *Dublin*, p. 516.   35 Dunphy, *The rocky road*, p. 47.

This is not to say that every game was a classic. In the middle of the decade some reporters were critical of the standard on offer and the progress of the game, with some competitions noted as being treated much less seriously than the FAI Cup and League of Ireland championship, and too much repetition of fixtures between the same clubs.[36] Even the FAI's showpiece did not always satisfy those in search of entertainment. The 1955 FAI Cup final between Shamrock Rovers and Drumcondra, which drew 33,000 spectators to Dalymount Park, was described by one reporter as 'a waste of ninety valuable minutes of a fine weekend', with the teams giving 'the impression that they were merely fulfilling an "end of season" League fixture' until late in the game.[37] He noted that the match, which Shamrock Rovers won by a goal to nil through a Liam Tuohy header, was 'the worst final' that he could recall, with some members of 'the crowd, tiring of slow hand-clapping', deciding 'to confiscate the ball after it had been ballooned over the wire fence'.[38] The *Irish Independent*'s W.P. Murphy felt that the loss of Rovers' player-manager, Paddy Coad, who was unable to play that day due to a septic ankle, was one reason for the poor game, as 'his shrewd generalship' was missing on the pitch.[39] Coad himself was of the view afterwards that the dull affair was due to the nervousness of some players.[40] The veteran Drumcondra team's use of the offside trap against the younger Shamrock Rovers team may have contributed to the lack of excitement.[41] One reporter noted at the start of the 1954–5 season that 'inter-league matches have shown that Irish football falls far below the cross-Channel standard – and recent events in the international sphere have proved that British soccer is not the best in the world'.[42] While this was a clear reference to recent England defeats against Hungary earlier in the decade, he added that 'our soccer public is simply not big enough to beget serious modern professionalism', and training methods and facilities were said to be underdeveloped.[43]

Not every club were as well looked after as Shamrock Rovers, whose players remained semi-professional. St Patrick's Athletic of Inchicore were apparently on £500 a man to win the FAI Cup in 1954, having 'placed a substantial bet at generous odds before the first round'.[44] However, they received only £5 each when they lost the final to Drumcondra.[45] Drumcondra had improved in the early 1950s when Sam Prole took over the club at the end of the 1952–3 season.[46] In March 1953, St Mirren of the Scottish League came to Dublin for a floodlit match against Drumcondra at Tolka Park.[47] The new lighting was the initiative of Drumcondra director Prole, and had 'given Dublin soccer followers their first taste of a practical innovation'.[48] The match, which the home side won by two goals to nil, with Benny Henderson and Shay Noonan scoring, was described by one reporter as 'a fine performance and a great spectacle'.[49] In a review of Irish soccer in 1955, one reporter noted that 'an

36 *Irish Soccer*, 1:10 (1955), p. 7. **37** *IP*, 25 Apr. 1955. **38** Ibid. **39** *II*, 25 Apr. 1955. **40** *IP*, 25 Apr. 1955. **41** *II*, 23 Apr. 1955. **42** *SI*, 15 Aug. 1954. **43** Ibid. **44** Ryan, *The official book of the FAI Cup*, pp 146–7. **45** Ibid. **46** Dunphy, *The rocky road*, p. 44; *IP*, 29 Dec. 1953. **47** *DUD*, 28 Mar. 1953. **48** *IP*, 31 Mar. 1953. **49** Ibid.

7. Flooding at Tolka Park, Drumcondra FC (1954). Courtesy of the National Library of Ireland.

important development was the growing popularity of floodlit games at Tolka Park, which has been considerably improved'.[50] By the middle of the 1950s, the proximity of the venue to the river Tolka meant that it remained prone to flooding.[51] Despite the attraction of soccer under floodlights, accessing the ground on match days was still difficult, with one reporter noting that

> The soccer public will be glad to know that they will be able to get into Tolka Park twice as fast as last season for the entrance at the Ballybough end has been widened, and though the banking is rough at this end of the ground, it is expected to hold up to ten thousand when completed in a year or so.[52]

At that point, Shelbourne had moved 'home' to a new stadium at Irishtown, and hoped to have a new stand erected before the end of the 1955–6 season, their Diamond Jubilee.[53] Previously, the club had been lodgers at Milltown, Dalymount Park and Tolka Park, while their new venue was said to be capable of accommodating

50 Ibid., 3 Jan. 1956.   51 *EH*, 13 Dec. 1954.   52 *II*, 12 Aug. 1955.   53 Ibid.

25,000 spectators on terracing, with 'cover on the seaside and a stand on the opposite side'. Their supporters' club had assisted in developing these features.[54] In September 1955 Shelbourne Stadium held its first match, with the club returning to their 'homeland', and although the ground lacked a roof, it 'had comfortable accommodation for 25,000 spectators on concrete terracing'.[55]

Crowd safety at sporting events in Ireland remained a concern by the late 1950s, and although there had been no major disasters in Dublin like that at Burnden Park in Bolton in 1946, which saw thirty-three spectators killed and hundreds injured, there had been scares.[56] The chief superintendent of An Garda Síochána later expressed the view that Croke Park was dangerously overcrowded during the 1944 All-Ireland Gaelic football final and that no more than 50,000, rather than the estimated 80,000 attendance, should have been allowed entry.[57] There were two separate incidents at Glenmalure Park within the space of just over a month, as twelve supporters were hospitalized on 3 February 1946 and fifteen also needed hospital treatment on 10 March 1946, which led to the ground being temporarily closed and structural repairs being completed.[58] However, a Garda Síochána investigation into safety at Tolka Park, Dalymount Park, Croke Park, Glenmalure Park and Lansdowne Road late in the following decade concluded that safety standards were adequate at these venues, with Minister for Justice Oscar Traynor satisfied that there was no need to attempt to bring in proposed legislation in 1958.[59]

The latter years of the decade were marked by the Republic of Ireland's failure to close out a decisive World Cup qualifier against England at Dalymount Park in May 1957, which they had led by a goal to nil until England equalised in injury time. The match was played before 47,600 spectators, which was slightly higher than the ground's 'holding capacity'.[60] Interest also remained high in Dublin derbies, despite the aforementioned sentiments of some sections of the contemporary press. Drumcondra and Shamrock Rovers' meeting at Tolka Park in January 1958 in the first ever all-ticket League of Ireland match, which had

---

54 Ibid.   55 *II*, 3 Sept 1955.   56 Statement of Mr John Fagan, Kim Grove House, Milltown, Secretary of Shamrock Rovers Association Football Club, 11 Mar. 1946, Suggestion that legislation should be introduced providing for public safety precautions, Football and sports fields, and Report by Sergeant Neil J. Gribben, Garda Síochána, City Division, Accident at Glenmalure Park, Milltown, on 10 Mar. 1946, 15 Mar. 1946, NAI, Department of Justice, 90/71/16.   57 Suggestion that legislation should be introduced providing for public safety precautions, Chief superintendent of the Garda Síochána, Football and hurling matches at Croke Park, 3 Oct. 1944, ibid.   58 Letter from Assistant Commissioner of the Garda Síochána to the Secretary of the Department of Justice, Apr. 1946, Suggestion that legislation should be introduced providing for public safety precautions, ibid.   59 Letter from Minister for Justice, Oscar Traynor to Minister for Local Government, Neil Blayney, 4 Mar. 1958, An Garda Síochána Metropolitan Division, Safety of spectators at Football Matches, G. Murray, Deputy Commissioner, 3 June 1958 and Letter from Minister for Justice, Oscar Traynor to Minister for Local Government, Neil Blaney, 4 July 1958, ibid.   60 *IP*, 20 May 1957; and Suggestion that legislation should be introduced providing for public safety precautions, An Garda Síochána, Safety of spectators at Football Matches, Superintendent R.C. Kingston, 14 May 1958, Football and sports fields, NAI, Department of Justice, 90/71/16. Superintendent Kingston stated that Dalymount's 'holding capacity' was 47,500.

a restriction of 20,000, had to be abandoned after sixty-five minutes, with the crowd overflowing onto the pitch and disrupting play.[61] Other sports also experienced issues into the next decade, with Gaelic football supporters forcing gates open at the Railway Cup final at Croke Park on St Patrick's Day 1961, which led to some minor injuries.[62]

The death of Liam Whelan in the Munich Air Disaster in February 1958 was a huge blow to Irish soccer. Following Whelan's death, 'virtually the entire five-mile route was lined with sympathizers' as his remains were taken from Dublin Airport to Christ the King Church in Cabra, located near his home at St Attracta Road.[63] Alf Girvan recalled that the death of his former Home Farm teammate was a 'massive' shock in Dublin at that time.[64] Paddy Mulligan also noted the popularity of Whelan and Manchester United in Dublin in the late 1950s:

> By all accounts, a lovely fella, I never had the privilege of meeting him, but he played with Home Farm, and when his remains came back to Dublin Airport, every player and committee person in Home Farm lined the Swords Road in honour of his homecoming, after the Munich Disaster. It was a very, very sad and poignant night. I'll never forget that night, it was a few weeks after the Munich Disaster at the time.[65]

THE CATHOLIC CHURCH AND SOCCER IN DUBLIN

Whelan's funeral Mass was celebrated by his friend the Rev. C. Mulholland, an RAF chaplain from Weston-Super-Mare, who had been scheduled to officiate at the player's wedding to Ruby McCullough later that year.[66] However, the archbishop of Dublin, Dr John Charles McQuaid, does not appear to have been in attendance.[67] Soccer in Dublin had began attracting more interest from the leading authorities of the Catholic church by the late 1950s. Following the postponement of an international friendly fixture between the Republic of Ireland and Yugoslavia in 1952 after pressure from Archbishop McQuaid, who drew attention to the persecution of the Catholic cleric Cardinal Stepinac by the Communist Yugoslav government, the FAI took the decision to play the same nation at Dalymount Park again in 1955.[68] This was confirmed at a special meeting of the soccer governing body in October of that year despite representations from the Department of Justice, and a representative of Archbishop McQuaid.[69] Dermot Keogh has written that allied to this religious disapproval, the 'implicit government support given to the boycotting

61 Daire Whelan, *Who stole our game?: the fall and fall of Irish soccer* (Dublin, 2006), p. 18; *IE*, 27 Jan. 1958; *II*, 31 Jan. 1958. Shamrock Rovers were later awarded the points.   62 Report of superintendent T. O'Brien re: Forcing of gates and persons injured at Croke Park on Friday, 17 Mar. 1961, Suggestion that legislation should be introduced providing for public safety precautions, Football and sports fields, NAI, Department of Justice, 90/71/16.   63 *IE*, 12 Feb. 1958; *II*, 13 Feb. 1958.   64 Interview with Alf Girvan, 27 Jan. 2020.   65 Interview with Paddy Mulligan, 4 Oct. 2019.   66 *II*, 13 Feb. 1958.   67 Ibid.   68 *DJ*, 17 Oct. 1955.   69 *DJ*, 17 Oct. 1955.

of the match' also highlighted how soccer was not fully accepted by many of those in power in Ireland.[70] The Department of Justice, did, however agree to supply visas to enable the Yugoslav team to enter Ireland 'after making some demur', and 22,000 people rejected appeals in the build up to the game, including handbills publicly distributed, and protests from a number of Catholic groups to stay away, and attended the friendly match at Dalymount Park.[71] Excursion trains from areas such as Drogheda and Sligo brought regionally-based supporters to the capital for the match.[72] The attendance was 'well up to that of normal mid-week representative games' and the match passed without any major interference; Yugoslavia won 4–1.[73] The teams were greeted on the field by FAI president Oscar Traynor, and the visitors received a banquet at the Gresham Hotel after the match, with Traynor stating that 'as a sporting organization we have nothing to do with anything outside sport'.[74] He added that 'we have nothing to defend. Our actions have been above board, and will continue so', as he toasted the Yugoslavs.[75] Yugoslavian FA president Rato Dugovic stated that 'our feelings after the wonderful reception we got at today's match are different from when we arrived and read your newspapers', many of which featured letters opposing their visit.[76]

There were some notable absentees from the match, including the Number 1 Army Band.[77] The Irish team trainer, the Garda boxer Dick Hearns, cried off and was replaced by Billy Lord of Shamrock Rovers.[78] Taoiseach Seán T. O'Kelly, did not attend, and Radio Éireann broadcaster Philip Greene refused to commentate on the match, which was in any case not broadcast on that channel.[79] The 1950 FAI Cup winners, Transport FC, withdrew their support for the event, but many clubs, including Shelbourne, in an editorial in a programme for a match against Sligo Rovers, and Bohemians, in providing the match venue, openly gave their approval.[80] Shelbourne manager David Jack stated in his newspaper column that he had met the Yugoslav team and 'found them a friendly, well behaved bunch of sportsmen' who could not understand why they were being 'embarrassed and pilloried'.[81] Some Irish players, including Con Martin, had been stopped in the street and asked not to play, while Peter Farrell stated that 'it's the finest thing possible to play these people. We must not isolate ourselves.'[82]

Some individual priests took to condemning those who attended the Yugoslavia match from the altar, with Fr O'Sullivan of Holy Child Parish, Larkhill, branding them as 'traitors' to their faith.[83] Inability to stop the 1955 match led to internal

70 Keogh, *Twentieth-century Ireland*, p. 235. 71 *DJ*, 17 and 19 Oct. 1955; *NW*, 20 Oct. 1955; *BT*, 3 Nov. 1955; and Untitled newspaper clipping, Oct. 1955, Trade Unions XXII/48/2, Archbishop McQuaid Papers, Dublin Diocesan Archives. 72 *DI*, 15 Oct. 1955; *SC*, 15 Oct. 1955. 73 *NW*, 20 Oct. 1955. 74 *IP*, 20 Oct. 1955. 75 Ibid. 76 Ibid. See also Visit of Yugoslavia soccer team to Ireland, Oct. 1955, NAI, DFA/5/305/298. 77 *DJ*, 17 Oct. 1955. 78 Ibid., 19 Oct. 1955. 79 Ibid., 17 Oct. 1955. 80 Untitled newspaper clipping, Oct. 1955 and *Shelbourne v. Sligo Rovers Official Programme* (Dublin, 1955), 9 Oct. 1955, Trade Unions XXII/48/2, Archbishop McQuaid Papers, Dublin Diocesan Archives. 81 *Empire News*, 23 Oct. 1955. 82 Ibid. 83 Letter from J. Wickham to His Excellency, Most Reverend Albert Devane, Apostolic Nuncio, 4 Nov. 1955, Trade Unions XXII 48/9/1, Archbishop McQuaid Papers, Dublin Diocesan Archives.

Catholic church concerns that more needed to be done by them to influence the FAI in the future, but without the soccer organization's knowledge of any hidden agenda.[84] Having noted that he would speak to Fr O'Sullivan 'quietly about the matter', Archbishop McQuaid took the decision to establish a committee of priests interested in soccer with a view to them gaining influence with the national soccer governing body.[85] A committee was duly formed early the following year, with Reverend G. Finnegan of Corpus Christi Church in Drumcondra as chairman.[86]

Like the GAA, the Catholic church utilized vigilance committees; however, the latter organization also sought to monitor socialist groups' meetings while nightclubs and cinema timetables were also scanned for anything that might be deemed inappropriate.[87] The five-man soccer committee met at the Archbishop's House in February 1956, with the purpose 'to consider the means of apostolate among the association football followers'.[88] It was there that they identified the difficulties facing them, noting that:

> It would prove difficult, especially in the beginning, to influence directly the central committee of the FAI. However, it should prove possible to exercise an influence directly through club representatives on the Central Committee. At present some priests are presidents or vice presidents of Junior clubs. There is room for expansion here. Perhaps priests could take up similar honorary positions on senior clubs. Even if that were not feasible in the beginning, priests could develop the contacts they had with club members, could attend social functions, etc.[89]

They also noted that in some parishes, priests had organized leagues for altar boys, as well as street leagues, and that as soccer was the game played in the seminary at Holy Cross College, Clonliffe, students with an interest in the game might be encouraged to keep playing on the priests' team there after they had been ordained, and also to explore 'the possibilities of apostolic work in this field'.[90]

84 Handwritten note related to the Yugoslav football match, 21 Feb. 1956, Trade Unions XXII 48/12/1, Archbishop McQuaid Papers, Dublin Diocesan Archives. 85 Letter from Archbishop John Charles McQuaid to His Excellency, Most Reverend Albert Devane, Apostolic Nuncio, 9 Nov. 1955, Trade Unions XXII 48/9/2 and Letter from Archbishop John Charles McQuaid to Reverend G. Finnegan, 21 Feb. 1956, Trade Unions XXII/48/13, Archbishop McQuaid Papers, Dublin Diocesan Archives. 86 Letter from Archbishop John Charles McQuaid to Reverend G. Finnegan, 21 Feb. 1956, Trade Unions XXII 48/13, Archbishop McQuaid Papers, Dublin Diocesan Archives. 87 See, for example, Minutes of 'V' Committee Meeting, 23 Mar. 1959, Communists XXIII, Archbishop McQuaid Papers, Dublin Diocesan Archives. 88 Letter from Fr G. Finnegan to Archbishop John Charles McQuaid, 26 Feb. 1956, Trade Unions XXII 48/14/(2) and Meeting of the committee of priests to consider the means of apostolate among the association football followers, 28 Feb. 1956, XXII 48/15, Archbishop McQuaid Papers, Dublin Diocesan Archives. 89 Meeting of the committee of priests to consider the means of apostolate among the association football followers, 28 Feb. 1956, Trade Unions XXII 48/15, Archbishop McQuaid Papers, Dublin Diocesan Archives. 90 Ibid.

8. An aerial view of the Fifteen Acres playing fields at Phoenix Park (1956). Courtesy of the
National Library of Ireland.

The following year, the committee noted that the playing of soccer by some
boys in the Phoenix Park on Sunday mornings was an issue as it clashed with Mass
times, and the idea of a Mass for the FAI was considered, but rejected 'as it would
attract publicity'.[91] Later in 1957, a 'B' international match against Romania caused
concerns, with the Reverend Finnegan complaining that the FAI had learned
nothing from the Yugoslavia match.[92] The idea that 'a small presidium of brothers
interested in soccer' would assist in ensuring that the boys in Phoenix Park went
to Mass was also discussed, which seems to have been an ongoing issue, as was the
idea of organizing retreats for priests who favoured the game.[93] By the time of the
Romania match in the autumn, Oscar Traynor had become minister for justice,
and his influence in the fixture going ahead can be seen in that he stated that if the
visas were not granted to the visitors, he would see that they were permitted into
the country without them.[94]

91 Confidential note regarding the football group written by James A. MacMahon, 1 Feb. 1957,
Trade Unions XXII 48/18, Archbishop McQuaid Papers, Dublin Diocesan Archives.   92 Notes on
interview with Fr Finnegan, 13 Oct. 1957, Trade Unions XXII 48/21, Archbishop McQuaid Papers,
Dublin Diocesan Archives.   93 Ibid.   94 Visit of Romanian football team to Ireland. Oct. 1957,
Untitled Memo, Department of the Taoiseach, 17 Oct. 1957, NAI, Department of Foreign Affairs,
5/305/345.

By 1958 the diocesan soccer committee had failed to infiltrate the FAI. One report compiled in September of that year highlighted that 'the necessity for the Committee's remaining anonymous made it difficult to approach' the soccer community, 'and some projects had to be abandoned because of that fact'.[95] It was noted that although one of the committee's priests had managed to obtain a position on the Leinster League's Council, he had to give this up 'owing to diocesan changes'.[96] The clerical soccer committee then decided it might be better to identify the soccer bodies organizing the game in Dublin, and having made 'a discreet approach' to 'a prominent Catholic official of the Football Association of Ireland in order to get the Association's viewpoint on international games', a number of points were noted.[97] These included the fact that the FAI had to accept arrangements made by FIFA in regard to internationals; that they saw matches against 'communist-held Catholic countries as useful means of advertisement' and that these fixtures constituted 'the few remaining contacts we have with oppressed Catholic populations'.[98] Finally, it was established that the FAI held that 'continental Catholic countries follow a policy of fraternization in sport'.[99] In 1959, one clerical vigilance committee responsible for monitoring communist activities discussed the idea that newspaper articles might be the best way of reaching the Irish public in regard to fixtures against communist-governed nations in light of a forthcoming match against Czechoslovakia, but it appears that the Catholic church's soccer committee failed in their aims.[100] The European Championship preliminary first-leg match went ahead in April at Dalymount Park, with Ireland winning 2–0 before 37,500 spectators.[101] This is not to say that religious involvement in soccer was not genuine for some priests or was simply driven by the perceived evils of matches against 'communist' nations. Many priests were involved in soccer through youth clubs in areas including Ballyfermot and Sallynoggin and this will be discussed further in chapter six.[102]

As Dublin expanded, new clubs were also established, including Nutgrove Celtic, who were founded in 1955 in line with a housing scheme in the Rathfarnham area at the foot of the Dublin mountains, and Ballyfermot United, established in 1961 in the an area beyond Kilmainham in the west, which had been developed along with Finglas (north-west), Walkinstown (south-west) and Artane, Coolock/ Raheny (north-east).[103] Along with the 'massive extensions' to Cabra and Crumlin in the early years of the 1950s, the shape of Dublin was changed.[104] Some clubs

95 Diocesan Soccer Committee's General Report, Sept. 1958, Trade Unions XXII 48/22/2, Archbishop McQuaid Papers, Dublin Diocesan Archives. 96 Ibid. 97 Ibid. 98 Ibid. 99 Ibid. 100 Minutes of 'V' Committee Meeting, 23 Mar. 1959, Communists, XXIII, Archbishop McQuaid Papers, Dublin Diocesan Archives. 101 Soar, Tyler & Widdows, *The Hamlyn encyclopaedia of football*, p. 50. 102 Individual Youth Clubs, Ballyfermot, 18 Apr. 1961 to 29 July 1963, XXVIII 1426 and Sallynoggin-St Joseph's Youth Centre, 7 July 1958 to 8 July 1970, XXVIII 1464, Archbishop McQuaid Papers, Youth Affairs, XXVIII, Dublin Diocesan Archives; and Curran, *Irish soccer migrants*, p. 235. 103 *Soccer Reporter* (Summer 1976), p. 9 and *Soccer Reporter* (Feb. 1977), p. 6 and Dickson, *Dublin*, p. 514. 104 Dickson, *Dublin*, p. 514.

continued to be founded through groups of friends who enjoyed a kickaround, including Dalkey United, who were established in 1953.[105] Workplace teams continued to leave their mark on Dublin soccer too, with Virginians, a club founded by employees of Players' Cigarette Factory on the Botanic Road, Glasnevin, winning the FAI Junior Cup in 1958.[106] East Wall was another area of Dublin that had become closely linked to soccer by the middle of the twentieth century. Mick Lawlor, a son of Kit Lawlor, was born in 1949, and recalled the importance of the game in his locality, and the sense of occasion he felt around the FAI Junior Cup finals in his youth:

> I grew up in East Wall, which was a hotbed of football really. It was quite similar to the areas in Dublin like Finglas and Cabra, Ringsend. Some very good footballers came out of East Wall, but football was a huge part of a lot of people's lives in my time growing up in East Wall and, for instance, I had a brother who played for East Wall, for twenty-four years unbroken service, Willie. And you know, going out even to watch his games was inspiring. It was great, I remember walking behind a band, it was a couple of FAI Junior Cup finals, played in Dalymount, but they organized a little band to lead supporters over the Spencer Dock bridge and up the Five Lamps and all the way up to Dalymount.[107]

THE 1960s

In January 1960, Manchester United manager Matt Busby visited Dublin to watch Shelbourne and Shamrock Rovers' league match at Tolka Park, with the Scot reported to be interested in Ronnie Nolan and a few of the Shamrock Rovers players.[108] The match attracted 15,000 spectators, while that same day 13,000 fans attended the clash between Cork Celtic and Cork Hibernians at the Mardyke.[109] One journalist noted that these attendances were larger than those at three FA Cup matches in England the previous Saturday.[110] At this point, League of Ireland soccer remained in a relatively healthy state. However, professional soccer in Ireland remained underdeveloped by the early 1960s. In February 1961, when the newly organized Professional Footballers' Association of Ireland (PFAI) met with League of Ireland officials at Merrion Square, opinions on the necessity of a trade union for soccer in Ireland varied. FAI secretary Joe Wickham noted at the time that 'the official attitude' was that professional players in Ireland 'were only part-timers' and 'not on the same par as cross-Channel players, who are all on a full-time basis'. He added that the FAI were not responsible for players' contracts, and that the football governing body could only attempt to see they were 'carried

---

105 Barney Kavanagh, 'All these years ago' in Pauline Seymour (ed.), *Dalkey United AFC Golden Jubilee 1953–2003* (Dublin, 2003), pp 17–19. 106 *EH*, 27 May 1958; *Soccer Reporter* (Oct. 1979), p. 10. 107 Interview with Mick Lawlor, 29 Feb. 2020. 108 *IP*, 12 Jan. 1960. 109 Ibid. 110 Ibid.

out in a proper fashion'.[111] PFAI chairman Shay Keogh of Shamrock Rovers stated that they wanted to resolve issues surrounding 'players' contracts and the retention system'.[112] Bohemians coach George Lax was in favour of the introduction of 'a basic minimum wage', as although the players were only part-time, they 'should get proper wages'. Brian McMahon, Bohemians' goalkeeper, also wanted to see this, along with an improvement in facilities, although he noted that those at Dalymount Park were the best.[113] However, Bohemians did not sign their first professional player until March 1969, when Tony O'Connell joined the club.[114] Bohemians' amateur status meant that at times they struggled to retain their best players at the end of each season.[115] Club administrators Gerry Devlin and Liam Rapple were instrumental in pushing for this change in status.[116] Turlough O'Connor, who signed for Bohemians in 1965 before moving to Fulham the following year, recalled the training set-up at the Dublin club in the mid-1960s:

> We trained three times a week, and we played then our matches at weekends. So it was completely amateur. But we had a very good amateur team. Sean Thomas was the manager and we'd a lot of good players: Kevin Murray; Larry Gilmore; Willie Brown, who was actually an international at that time, even though he was an amateur, he played for Bohs at the time; and Billy Young himself, he later became manager in Dalymount, he was actually there as a player too. So it was very enjoyable and we did exceptionally well, we won the President's Cup, and we finished I think it was fourth in the league, against all the semi-professional clubs it was a very successful team, at that particular time.[117]

The success of Shelbourne, in winning the FAI Cup in 1960 and 1963, and the league in 1962 under manager Gerry Doyle, was said to have been assisted by the recruitment of a number of players including Eric Barber and Jackie Hennessy, from 1959 FAI Minor Cup winners St Finbarr's.[118] The FAI Cup-winning achievements of Shamrock Rovers in the 1960s were more remarkable, however. In 1959, Paddy Coad returned to Waterford, and the Shamrock Rovers team he had put together broke up.[119] His replacement, Albie Murphy, lasted only one season and was replaced by Sean Thomas, and in 1964 Shamrock Rovers won all the domestic honours available to them, with the exception of the Top Four Competition.[120] However, Thomas was unhappy with interference from the Cunninghams in team selection and left, with Liam Tuohy taking over. Tuohy, who had been at Newcastle United in the early 1960s, became player-manager. In the period from 1964 until 1969, the club won a record six FAI Cups in a row.[121]

111 *IP*, 15 Feb. 1961. 112 Ibid. 113 Ibid. 114 Ryan, *The official book of the FAI Cup*, pp 212–13. 115 Reid, *Bohemian AFC official club history, 1890–1976*, p. 29. 116 Ibid., p. 30. 117 Interview with Turlough O'Connor, 10 Oct. 2019. 118 Seán Fitzpatrick, *Shelbourne cult heroes: from Bulawayo to Ballybough* (Dublin, 2009), p. 54. 119 Rice, *We are Rovers*, p. 69. 120 Ibid., pp 69–71. 121 Ibid., pp 72–3.

By the late 1960s, Shamrock Rovers and Waterford had developed as the two best domestic teams of the decade, as Mick Lawlor recalled of the 1968 FAI Cup final:

> We played Waterford in the March in Milltown, they beat us 1–0, went on to win the league, but then the following month we played them in the cup final in Dalymount, and we beat them 3–0, so that was the way it was. But, [it was] a great occasion, the cup final, with that many people at it, but you just took it as the norm, like when I say to people now there was 39,128 people there, they say, 'What?' You know, it's incredulous really, but that's the way it was, and that's the way football was in those days. Like when Waterford beat us 1–0 in the league the month before the cup final, the official attendance in Milltown was 22,000. Now how people weren't injured and hurt, I just ... when I reflect back on it now, but that was the type of following that League of Ireland had at that time.[122]

Shamrock Rovers' players' celebrations of their cup final victories were generally low-key, with the team going for 'a few drinks' after the 1964 final, while in 1965 the Cunninghams brought them to the then Inter-Continental Hotel for food.[123] Paddy Mulligan also recalled getting dinner at the Metropole Hotel after the 1969 final, then going for a game of snooker with a work colleague at Milltown, and noted that it 'never even dawned on us about six-in-a-row, we just wanted to go and play games and win games. And I suppose the most important thing – we wanted to play ... there were no wild celebrations.'[124]

Internationally, the Republic of Ireland were left to rue a 1–0 defeat to Spain in Paris in a World Cup qualifying play-off in 1965, with the FAI accepting a pay-off from their counterparts in Spain to ensure the match would take place in the French city rather than at Wembley Stadium, where Irish support would have been more notable.[125] Ironically, as most of the team were based in England, the FAI would have had to pay less in terms of travel, but saw the finance offered as more important.[126] Dubliner Mick Meagan recalled that it was,

> you could sort of say, a bit frightening ... there was talk earlier about they were going to toss to play in London. But little did we know. So when we arrived, you had a look out onto the pitch, there was a big tunnel going up to the pitch, I think it was the Parc de Princes, but the place was packed. Next thing, 'There's only one Irish flag out there' – a fella in the corner, waving the tricolour – there's only one – [it was like] 'Where are all our sup-porters?' Little did we know ... that Parc de Princes was like Ireland playing in Liverpool – It was a home game for Spain – so anyway, we got on with

122 Interview with Mick Lawlor, 29 Feb. 2020. 123 Interview with Paddy Mulligan, 4 Oct. 2019. 124 Ibid. 125 *EH*, 11 Nov. 1976. 126 Interview with Frank O'Neill, 30 Jan. 2020.

it. But that was a great experience – you know, we were beaten one–nil, but
we'd no chance of winning it – it was backs to the wall all night.[127]

One of his team-mates that night, Frank O'Neill, expressed similar sentiments
about the team's chances in Paris against Spain.[128] Meagan reluctantly became the
Republic of Ireland's first manager in 1969, with O'Neill and John Giles encouraging him to name his own panel, rather than let the selectors continue to do this.[129]
This was an important step in the management of the team, but it would not be
until the later twentieth century that they would regularly seriously challenge some
of European football's top teams.

THE 1970s

By the early 1970s, the attraction of Dublin soccer had lessened for many supporters. While the 1972 FAI Cup final between Cork Hibernians and Waterford
attracted 22,500 spectators, by the mid-1980s the figures for those attending this
annual match had dropped significantly, with only 8,000 at the 1984 final between
UCD and Shamrock Rovers and 6,000 at the replay and 7,000 noted at the 1985
final between Sligo Rovers and Galway United.[130] Interest in FAI cup finals ebbed
and flowed, and by the late 1980s this had increased substantially, with 21,000 present at Dundalk's 1–0 victory over Derry City in 1988, while the presence of the
Derry club again boosted receipts at the 1989 final against Cork City, which drew
a crowd of 20,100, although the replay drew only 10,800 spectators.[131] Much of the
initial loss of interest from the early 1970s onwards can be put down to the counter-attraction of English soccer on television.[132] As will be shown in some detail
in the next chapter, increased access from Irish ports on the east coast to matches
in Britain through ferry lines also meant that League of Ireland crowds deteriorated substantially in that decade.[133] The results of a questionnaire undertaken by
one reporter in 1973 highlighted that supporters were of the view that League of
Ireland matches had no atmosphere, poor facilities and the standard was not high
enough, while one fan felt that it was 'rubbish'.[134] A government-backed commission established to examine the state of soccer in Ireland in 1972 failed to have any
significant impact in reversing issues with attendance and coaching standards in
regional areas.[135] An inability to build on the success of Dublin soccer in the 1950s
and a failure to compete with the GAA in terms of marketing and organization of
a national infrastructure, allied to a growth in support for the All-Ireland-winning
Dublin Gaelic football team in the 1970s, was also detrimental to League of Ireland
soccer's development in the latter decades of the twentieth century.[136] Despite this,

127 Interview with Mick Meagan, 30 Sept. 2019. 128 Interview with Frank O'Neill, 30 Jan.
2020. 129 Interview with Mick Meagan, 30 Sept. 2019. 130 Ryan, *The official book of the
FAI Cup*, pp 225, 281, 282, 287. 131 Ibid., pp 304, 310. 132 Curran, *Irish soccer migrants*, p.
38. 133 Ibid. 134 *SI*, 9 Dec. 1973. 135 Curran, *Irish soccer migrants*, pp 94–5. 136 Whelan,
Who stole our game?, pp 51–72.

the game continued to retain its importance for many players at grassroots level in Dublin, with 'about 150 teams' availing of the twenty-nine soccer pitches at the Phoenix Park by May 1974.[137]

Eoghan Rice has written that Bohemians were 'the only power in Dublin football' by the early 1970s.[138] They won the FAI Cup in 1970 and again in 1976, along with the League of Ireland, the League Cup, the President's Cup and the Leinster Senior Cup in 1975.[139] The appointment of Billy Young as manager in 1973, along with Mick Byrne as trainer, allied to the decision to turn professional, was fundamental to their progress in the mid-1970s.[140] In 1972, Home Farm became a member of the League of Ireland, having purchased Tolka Park from Drumcondra, who retired from that competition at that time, and although initially it appeared that the club was to carry the name Home Farm-Drumcondra, the name Drumcondra was removed after one season.[141]

Drumcondra's great rivals from the 1950s, Shamrock Rovers, also went into decline in the 1970s as the Cunninghams sold the club to the Kilcoynes, who were not as willing to invest in the club, while some of the best players were sold and not adequately replaced.[142] In 1977, John Giles returned to Dublin from England to manage Shamrock Rovers.[143] A brother-in-law of the Kilcoynes, he attempted to give the club a more professional structure as other returning players such as Paddy Mulligan, Eamon Dunphy and Ray Treacy were brought in, with players given full-time contracts.[144] An apprentice system was set up at Pearse College in Crumlin, with the idea that the best young players would remain in Ireland rather than go to Britain to play football.[145] Despite winning the FAI Cup in 1978, the club failed to win the league under Giles, who was at times also balancing the position of manager of Vancouver Whitecaps in Canada and also that of the Republic of Ireland team manager.[146] He resigned from Shamrock Rovers in February 1983, with some fans claiming the style of football was too defensive, particularly in away matches, where pitches were often not of the quality of Glenmalure Park.[147] Giles has written that he made the mistake of bringing in young players too quickly, but felt that the press displayed an attitude that was at odds with his efforts to modernize Irish soccer.[148] Internationally, the Republic of Ireland had showed some promise in his managerial term, which ran from 1974 until 1980, most notably in defeating the USSR at Dalymount Park in 1974, but while there was also a significant win over France in 1977 at Lansdowne Road, qualification for a major international tournament eluded the team.[149]

137 Dáil Éireann Debate, Tuesday 7 May 1974, vol. 272, no. 6, 'Ceisteanna – Questions. Oral Answers. – Phoenix Park Amenities', oireachtas.ie/en/debates/debate/dail/1974-05-07/36, accessed 8 Apr. 2022. 138 Rice, *We are Rovers*, p. 88. 139 Reid, *Bohemian AFC official club history, 1890–1976*, p. 31. 140 Ibid., p. 30. 141 Menton, *Home Farm*, pp 37–8; Whelan, *Who stole our game?*, pp 82–3. 142 Rice, *We are Rovers*, p. 90. 143 Ibid., pp 93–4. 144 Ibid., pp 95–6. 145 Ibid., p. 97. 146 Ibid., p. 102. 147 Ibid., pp 98–103. 148 John Giles, *A football man: the autobiography* (Dublin, 2010), p. 298. 149 *BN*, 31 Oct. 1974; *II*, 31 Mar. 1977.

THE 1980s

The narrow failure of the Republic of Ireland international senior team, managed by Eoin Hand, to qualify for the 1982 World Cup in Spain (on goal difference), following debateable refereeing decisions away to Belgium and France, meant that the development of soccer in Ireland was denied what might have been a major boost early in that decade.[150] One Irish reporter stated that two Irish goals in the home games against Holland and Belgium were also marginal decisions, which is perhaps more indicative of a tendency of international match officials to favour the home teams in the late twentieth century in tight decisions.[151] Attempts to qualify for the 1984 European Championship also ended disappointingly, as Spain finished top of the Republic of Ireland's group. The Irish team had squandered a two-goal lead in their match against Holland at Dalymount Park, which saw the emergence of Ruud Gullit and Marco Van Basten, and they appeared to have worsened after the despair of 1981.[152] Despite a 1–0 victory over the USSR at Lansdowne Road in their opening World Cup qualifying match in 1984, the team also failed to qualify for Mexico '86, with Denmark and the Soviets emerging from the group, which the Republic ended with a 4–1 home defeat against the Danes.[153]

It was Shamrock Rovers who dominated the domestic game in that decade, which was another tough one financially for many clubs, including Shelbourne, who were said to be in their 'death throes' in the spring of 1981, with the state of the Irish economy not helping matters.[154] Following John Giles' resignation from Shamrock Rovers in the 1982–3 season, Noel Campbell temporarily took over, but the club then turned to Jim McLaughlin, who had been successful at Dundalk.[155] Shamrock Rovers were strengthened considerably through the signing of players with funds acquired through the transfer of Jim Beglin to Liverpool in 1983. These included Jody Byrne and Noel King from Dundalk, Drogheda's Mick Neville, Bohemians' Terry Eviston, Kevin Brady and Liam O'Brien, while they also brought in Anto Whelan from Manchester United and Thurles' Neville Steedman.[156] Despite getting rid of some fan favourites such as Alan O'Neill, McLaughlin led the club to two FAI cups and three leagues between 1983 and 1986, with the club losing the 1984 FAI Cup final to UCD in a shock result after a replay.[157] John Coady, who joined the club in 1982, recalled that, as a Shamrock Rovers supporter who became a vital part of the team,

> it was incredible, it was an absolutely amazing experience, breaking records left, right and centre, four league titles, three doubles in a row, extraordinary times, extraordinary ... it was a very, very special time in my life anyway and I'm sure the rest of the lads were the same.[158]

150 Eoin Hand, *First hand: my life and Irish football* (Cork, 2017), pp 80–90. 151 *Soccer Reporter* (Jan. 1982), p. 7. 152 Hand, *First hand*, pp 129–32. 153 Ibid., pp 138–60. 154 *Soccer Reporter* (Mar. 1981), p. 1; *Soccer Reporter* (Jan. 1982), p. 1. 155 Rice, *We are Rovers*, p. 125. 156 Ibid., pp 126–7. 157 Ibid., pp 132–4. 158 Interview with John Coady, 22 Jan. 2020.

With key figures such as Pat Byrne and Dermot Keely (who took over as manager in 1986 with the club again winning the league and cup in the 1986–7 season) to the fore in their success, the club fostered a professional image, but nationally the league attracted scarce interest, due to a lack of strong competition from other clubs (along with continuous competition from the GAA and English soccer), and attendances were rarely above 3,000 at Milltown.[159] As a result of a lack of revenue,

9. Shamrock Rovers with Dublin Lord Mayor James Tunney, Mansion House (1986). Courtesy of Dublin City Council Photographic Collection, Dublin City Library and Archives.

10. An exterior view of Shamrock Rovers' ground, Milltown, in the late twentieth century. Courtesy of the National Library of Ireland.

159 Rice, *We are Rovers*, pp 138, 190.

11. Dalymount Park (1977). Courtesy of Dublin City Council Photographic Collection, Dublin City Library and Archives.

12. Lansdowne Road (1977). Courtesy of Dublin City Council Photographic Collection, Dublin City Library and Archives.

club owner Louis Kilcoyne took the decision to sell Glenmalure Park in 1987, which stunned many fans.[160] The ground had been leased from the Jesuits from 1926 to 1985, when Kilcoyne had bought it; after he sold it, it was later turned into a housing estate.[161] The club temporarily moved to Tolka Park, many of their fans who felt they had lost their spiritual home boycotted the move, and the 'four-in-a-row' team gradually broke up.[162] Shamrock Rovers supporters later erected a monument at the former Glenmalure Park site.[163]

The most significant development in the late twentieth century within Dublin soccer was the success of the national senior men's team, who went on an unbeaten home run in competitive matches that stretched for almost seven years. In qualifying for two World Cups and one European championship, the 'boys in green' did not lose a competitive home qualifying match at Lansdowne Road, under manager Jack Charlton, who took over in 1986, until the visit of Spain for a World Cup qualifier in the autumn of 1993.[164] While improvements to terracing had been made to Dalymount Park in 1953 and floodlights were installed there in 1962, by the mid-1980s it was clear that the stadium was no longer fit to host senior international matches, with the visit of Italy in 1985 and the resulting overcrowding of spectators firm evidence of this, although some friendly matches continued to be played there.[165]

Qualification for Euro '88 was ultimately a surprise, given that Bulgaria only needed a point from their last two games, which they failed to obtain, and the Republic of Ireland's victory over them at Lansdowne Road in the first of these in October 1987 drew only 26,000 spectators.[166] Interest in the national team grew further with the team's performance in the European Championship finals in West Germany, as they recorded their first ever competitive victory over England before drawing with the USSR and losing narrowly to Holland later that same week. The team received a civic reception in Parnell Square on arrival back in Dublin, which was celebrating its Millennium, with 250,000 fans greeting them.[167]

In the aftermath of this success, interest in and support at international matches had taken on a different dimension as qualification for Italia '90 was secured in November 1989 with an away win in Malta.[168] Home qualifying matches, which were by then usually sold out at the 50,000-capacity Lansdowne Road, generally began in the afternoon due to the absence of floodlights at the south Dublin venue.[169] Players became less accessible than they had previously been to supporters in the aftermath of matches as the team's profile and security increased, while related radio and television sponsorship commercials featuring members of the team became commonplace. The FAI continued to rent the Ballsbridge facility from

---

160 Ibid., p. 140.   161 Ibid., pp 153, 161.   162 Ibid., pp 148–9, 152.   163 Ibid., p. 155.   164 *SI*, 17 Oct. 1993.   165 Reid, *Bohemian AFC official club history, 1890–1976*, p. 43; Hand, *First hand*, pp 145–6.   166 *IP*, 15 Oct. and 12 Nov. 1987.   167 *II*, 20 June 1988.   168 *II*, 11 Dec. 1989.   169 *II*, 25 Apr. 1989.

13. The Republic of Ireland senior men's team's homecoming in O'Connell Street after Euro '88. Courtesy of Dublin City Library and Archives.

the IRFU, having lacked the will and finance to carry out a major redevelopment of the 'traditional' home of Dublin soccer, Dalymount Park.[170] Qualification for the World Cup meant increased sponsorship opportunities for the FAI, although, as shown elsewhere, the benefits of this success did not filter down significantly enough to the domestic game.[171]

Following friendly matches against Wales, the USSR and Finland at Lansdowne Road, in the opening half of 1990, the Republic of Ireland travelled to Italy for their first ever World Cup finals.[172] In reaching the quarter finals, the team's achievements were the cause for much joy for Irish fans everywhere. Dublin Airport was again the scene of another memorable homecoming, with 500,000 estimated to have packed Dublin city centre to greet the team on arrival at College Green, 'the biggest welcome' since Pope John Paul II's visit in 1979.[173] While the team narrowly failed to qualify for Euro '92, qualification for the USA '94 World Cup was later secured, although the homecoming, this time staged at Phoenix Park, received less public attention given their second-round exit to Holland, following a successful group stage that included victory over Italy in New Jersey.[174] The visit of England to Lansdowne Road in February 1995 ended with the match abandoned following

170 See, for example, Council Minutes, 7 Sept. 1979, FAI Archives, P137/24.　171 Curran, *Irish soccer migrants*, pp 95–9.　172 *II*, 29 Mar., 26 Apr. and 17 May 1990.　173 *EP*, 2 July 1990; *II*, 7 July 1990.　174 *II*, 8 July 1994.

hooliganism by away supporters after David Kelly had given the home team the lead.[175] Charlton's departure in December 1995 following defeat to Holland in a European championship qualifying play-off at Anfield marked the end of an era for Irish soccer.[176] It was not until 2001 that the Republic of Ireland team qualified for another major tournament, the Japan/South Korea 2002 World Cup, with Mick McCarthy as manager.[177] The Irish team's shock victory over Holland in a decisive group qualifying match at Lansdowne Road before 49,000 supporters was key to this, as the reputation of the Dublin 4 venue as a fortress of Irish support still lingered from the Charlton days, along with the influence of Roy Keane on the pitch.[178]

DOMESTIC SOCCER IN THE LATE TWENTIETH CENTURY

Domestically, the 1990s had begun with inner-city club St Francis FC reaching the FAI Cup final, losing to Bray Wanderers before an estimated 29,000 at Lansdowne Road, with the attendance mainly 'composed of family units from all over Wicklow and the Liberties'.[179] However, financial issues were a recurring issue for a number of Dublin clubs in that decade. In the 1990–1 season, St James's Gate replaced Newcastlewest in the League of Ireland First Division.[180] Prior to the beginning of the 1996–7 season the Dublin club pulled out due to financial issues, and were replaced by St Francis's FC, who had won the Leinster Senior League by fifteen points.[181] Despite a section of the St Francis club amalgamating with St Patrick's Athletic in 2001, and playing under the name 'the Dublin Saints', many within the Liberties club were unhappy with the move and the 'real saints' (who remained) retreated to the more familiar surroundings of the Leinster Senior League.[182]

By 1985, there were 1,432 teams affiliated with the Leinster FA.[183] However, by the later twentieth century, issues with playing fields remained, particularly with matches being called off at the last minute on mildly wet mornings, and even at times being stopped with the teams in action by overzealous park rangers.[184] Some clubs lost their grounds, including Kinvara Boys, whose pitch by the Navan Road was acquired by a property developer in the winter of 1981.[185] Gaining independence from local authorities in terms of the decision to play or postpone matches was certainly difficult, but by the early 1990s the Leinster FA had a 'Public Parks

175 Mike Cronin, 'The Lansdowne Road riot of 1995: Ireland, the English far right and the media' in Neil O'Boyle & Marcus Free (eds), *Sport, the media and Ireland: interdisciplinary perspectives* (Cork, 2020), pp 75–92. 176 *II*, 28 Dec. 1995. 177 *IE*, 17 Nov. 2001. 178 *TG*, 2 Sept. 2001. 179 *II*, 14 May 1990. 180 'Our History', stjamesgatefc.com/club-history, accessed 3 Jan. 2022. 181 Ibid.; *ST*, 22 Sept. 1996. 182 *IE* and *II*, 4 July 2001; *EH*, 6 July 2001. 183 Minute Book of the Senior Council, FAI Annual Report 1984–5, June 1985, FAI Archives. P137/24. 184 Senior Council Minutes, 28 Nov. 1990, Leinster Football Association Archives, P239/35. 185 Senior Council Meeting Minutes, 26 Nov. 1981, Leinster Football Association Archives, P239/34.

Co-ordinating Committee' in operation.[186] The Leinster FA's competitions were hugely significant in the development of soccer in Dublin, and despite the afore-mentioned issues, these matches remained hugely popular with players of all levels. Some clubs such as Ashtown Villa of the Athletic Union League were able to grow and temporarily compete with those in the League of Ireland in cup competitions, and others also challenged the traditional forces of Bohemians, Shamrock Rovers, Shelbourne and St Patrick's Athletic at various times.[187]

A proposal to have then Premier League club Wimbledon FC relocate to west Dublin in the late 1990s failed to materialize, with the FAI and League of Ireland clubs, and many sports followers in the city, such as Taoiseach Bertie Ahern, opposed to the move, while some other members of the Dáil were in favour of it for economic reasons.[188] For Shamrock Rovers, the final decade of the twentieth century was a disappointing one, as the club remained without a permanent ground, spending spells at Dalymount Park, the RDS (a showjumping arena owned by the Royal Dublin Society) in Ballsbridge, Tolka Park (Drumcondra), Morton Stadium (Santry) and Richmond Park (Inchicore).[189] Although Shamrock Rovers won the league again in 1994 under manager Ray Treacy and owner John McNamara, both men resigned the following season because they lost the goodwill of supporters as some of the best players were let go as the pair started a rebuilding process with younger players, who were less expensive, being brought in.[190] It was not until 2009 that Shamrock Rovers finally acquired their own ground, Tallaght Stadium, after years of planning, objections (including that from a local GAA club) and financial difficulties.[191] It is currently 'owned and operated by South Dublin Council'.[192] Despite this, Dublin's League of Ireland clubs continue to retain support, with family connections and a sense of locality important for some of these fans such as Bohemians supporter Gerry Farrell.[193] Farrell's father played for Bohemians in the 1950s, while St Patrick's Athletic supporter Dermot Looney's father played for the Inchicore side in the same decade, thereby strengthening the connections with their preferred clubs.[194] Similarly, fellow Bohemians fans Mark Keane and Ryan Clarke also noted the sense of community in supporting their local club, while Gavin White, a Shelbourne fan, stated that 'the family link is big, but there's multiple elements to it, the tragedy, the romance, the eternal joys, the ups and

---

186 Emergency Committee Minutes, 20 Aug. 1984, Leinster Football Association Archives, P239/41; and Amalgamated Minutes, Public Parks Co-ordinating Committee Meeting, 3 Dec. 1993, Leinster Football Association Archives, P239/62.   187 *II*, 8 Apr. 1991.   188 Select Committee on Enterprise and Economic Strategy, 'Debate – Tuesday, 17 December 1996', oireachtas.ie/en/debates/debate/select_committee_on_enterprise_and_economic_strategy/1996–12–17/2, accessed 8 Apr. 2022, and Dáil Éireann Debate, Wednesday 25 Oct. 2000, vol. 524, no. 6, 'Ceisteanna – Questions. – Departmental Correspondence', oireachtas.ie/en/debates/debate/dail/2000-10-25/5, accessed 8 Apr. 2022.   189 Rice, *We are Rovers*, pp 165–78.   190 Ibid., pp 170–5.   191 Ibid., p. 190 and 'Tallaght Stadium – About Us', tallaghtstadium.ie, accessed 4 Aug. 2021.   192 'Tallaght Stadium – About Us'.   193 Interview with Gerry Farrell, 3 Apr. 2020.   194 Ibid., and interview with Dermot Looney, 31 July 2020.

downs, everything that goes with it, it seems to be uniquely Shelbourne as opposed to other clubs in Dublin'.[195]

WOMEN'S SOCCER IN DUBLIN IN THE LATTER DECADES OF THE TWENTIETH CENTURY

Opposition to the playing of association football by women continued into the late twentieth century. The Catholic church could exert their influence at a parish level when soccer was not wanted by locals in some areas. Attempts to hold women's soccer matches in Bray, County Wicklow, in July 1954 were stopped by one priest, who deemed the match 'vulgar' and 'nearly indecent'.[196] This view of the ladies' game was not the only reason it struggled to gain traction, but it was unhelpful. In England, the Women's Football Association was established in 1969, and in 1971 the FA rescinded their ban on women's teams affiliating, with the first women's FA Cup final also held that year.[197] Taylor notes how the late 1960s has been identified as a 'new age of women's football' in Britain with England's 1966 World Cup win and 'the rise of the women's movement' central to this view.[198] However, as he also notes, despite a rise in participation figures in the following decade, 'female participation remained constrained by a host of administrative, ideological and legal barriers'.[199] One FIFA survey undertaken in 1970 to ascertain the views of 139 affiliated nations on women's soccer highlighted that only twelve out of the ninety who replied (the other forty-nine did not answer) were in favour of its development.[200]

It was around this time that the game also began to develop in earnest in Ireland. Ladies' soccer in Dublin was slow to take off in comparison with activity in some other areas of the country where leagues were operational by the late 1960s. Patronage and encouragement were needed to run competitions, with Munster FA official Charlie Duggan presenting a set of medals for a match between Cork teams Blackrock and Ringmahon Rangers in June 1962, the proceeds of which went to the Blackrock Church Building Fund.[201] Helena Byrne has shown that the Abbey Ballroom Indoor Soccer League, which ran from 1966 to 1967, was set up by locals with the help of the venue's manager, Ben Gordon. However, damage to the property and a later fire there in 1969 meant that the league was not sustained.[202] In May 1967, Derry and Dundalk selections met in a 'novelty' match before two

195 Interview with Gavin White, 5 May 2020; interview with Ryan Clarke, 6 May 2020; and interview with Mark Keane, 9 May 2020. 196 Letter from Fr John Fitzpatrick to Archbishop John Charles McQuaid, 21 July 1954, Parishes LIV 28/16a, Archbishop McQuaid Papers, Dublin Diocesan Papers. 197 Matthew Taylor, *The association game: a history of British football* (Harlow, 2008), p. 263 and 'The History of Women's Football in England', thefa.com/womens-girls-football/ history, accessed 23 Jan. 2021. 198 Taylor, *The association game*, p. 262. 199 Ibid. 200 Pierre Lanfranchi, Christiane Eisenberg, Tony Mason, Tony & Alfred Wahl, *100 years of football: the FIFA centennial book* (London, 2004), p. 188. 201 *IE*, 16 June 1962. 202 Helena Byrne, 'How it all began: the story of women's soccer in sixties Drogheda' in Conor Curran & David Toms (ed.), *New perspectives on association football in Irish history: going beyond the 'garrison game'* (Abingdon, 2018), pp 110–31, pp 130–1.

men's teams made up of former Irish internationals and inter-league players met in a friendly at Oriel Park in Dundalk.[203]

In May 1968, return matches were played between 'the South Dublin "Red Garters" and the Finglas "Debs"' at Bushy Park in Terenure.[204] In July 1968, a Waterford selection defeated the 'Hooped Dollies', a team composed of members of the Shamrock Rovers' supporters' club, by ten goals to nil at Tycor Park in Waterford.[205] Some work teams also played occasional matches, including Roche's Stores and Lever Brothers at Fairview that same month.[206] This was relatively slow progress in comparison with that in nearby Louth, where the Dundalk and District Ladies' League, consisting of five teams, was completed the previous month.[207] In October 1968, a ladies' match was held before the St Patrick's Athletic versus Dundalk Shield match, with one reporter noting that 'these matches have been played with success in provincial centres and St Patrick's hope the idea will catch on in Dublin'.[208]

By the start of June 1969 the ladies' game in Dublin still lacked a coherent structure, with Sinners United, a team based in Ballyfermot who had played some teams in Waterford and Kilkenny in friendly matches, appealing for local opponents through the press.[209] A ladies' soccer match was also played at a men's seven-a-side tournament in Ballyfermot the following month.[210] Although reports are patchy, five teams were said to have competed in the first Dublin Ladies' Soccer League in 1969.[211] In 1970, the Dublin Ladies' League was won by the Avengers, who were unbeaten in ten games.[212] The number of teams involved had more than doubled since the previous year, with the Avengers' success said to be the result of their playing of friendly matches before the competition began, according to their captain Betty Duffy. With a panel of thirteen players, they were coached by Tony Grant, a Civil Defence Officer with Ballymun Warden Service. League and Cup matches were played on the Gaelic pitches at Phoenix Park.[213] Runners-up in the league were the Department of Lands team, while finalists in the cup were Anco.[214] In September 1970, Jeyes United defeated Urney United to win the Executive Training Service trophy.[215] Friendly matches also continued, with Liam Tuohy taking charge, as referee, of the meeting of a HB Ices team and Urney's at Nutgrove, Rathfarnham, in June 1970.[216]

It appears that Waterford city was the stronghold of ladies' soccer in the Republic of Ireland by August 1970, with teams from 'industrial and commercial enterprises in and about the city' taking part in a local league. Waterford AFC men's team, who were League of Ireland champions, had taken 'pride of place as the glamour team of Irish soccer', with one reporter noting how the ladies' game had been encouraged by administrators of their supporters' club.[217] In Kilkenny, a ladies' league had developed in 1968 with the help of some local male soccer

203 *II*, 18 May 1967. 204 *EH*, 29 May 1968. 205 *ME*, 12 July 1968. 206 *IP*, 18 July 1968. 207 *DD*, 22 June 1968. 208 *SI*, 13 Oct. 1968. 209 *EH*, 4 June 1969. 210 *EH*, 26 July 1969. 211 *EH*, 21 Oct. 1970. 212 Ibid. 213 Ibid. 214 Ibid. 215 *EH*, 26 Sept. 1970. 216 *IP*, 19 June 1970. 217 *EH*, 8 Aug. 1970.

organizers, but in 1970 the women broke away and established their own organization, retaining only one man, local referee, Tom Hogan, who was named as their
chairman.[218]

A Civil Service League was up and running in Dublin in 1970, with more than
forty teams involved in three leagues.[219] Two of the best of these met in a charity
match in November that year. Local Government, who had developed out of the
Department of Local Government's Ladies' Sports Club, and Civil Defence selections met at Tolka Park with the latter winning by five goals to one in a 'thrilling'
encounter.[220] The Civil Defence team were reportedly 'members of voluntary Civil
Defence units during winter and summer'.[221] One team member, teenager Catherine
Rafferty, had learned the game playing it with boys in her native Finglas, while her
father also took her to men's matches, although she preferred playing to watching.[222] The match raised a gate of £135, which was donated to the Irish Wheelchair
Association, while in January 1971 the Civil Service team met Jeyes United at the
same venue with the proceeds given to St John of God Institution for children
with physical disabilities.[223] The following month, ladies' soccer was reported to be
'fast becoming one of the most popular women's sports', with a Local Government
team meeting the Department of Social Welfare in the final of the Irish Wheelchair
Association Challenge Cup at Tolka Park.[224] Local Government were said to have
'lost only two of the eighty or more games' they had played in the last year, which
included a victory over Portadown, the Belfast ladies' league champions.[225] The
match was again held in aid of the Irish Wheelchair Association, with League of
Ireland referee John Carpenter officiating.[226]

Competitive structures for Dublin ladies' soccer were strengthened later that
year, with forty-six teams reportedly involved in 'the Dublin ladies' outdoor soccer league' and sponsorship undertaken by Jeyes Ltd.[227] In April 1971, Dublin
Ladies' Football League secretary Tony Grant announced that matches were to
be organized for Wednesday evenings, with the Dublin City Cup to be played for
at weekends in the summer.[228] Grant also noted that an all-Ireland competition
was scheduled for June, with clubs from Cork, Donegal, Dublin, Kilkenny, Sligo
and Waterford set to participate. It was also intended to run the Drumcondra
Cup, donated by Sam Prole, the chairman of Drumcondra FC, between sixteen
of Dublin's best clubs under floodlights on Monday nights.[229] It appears that this
league operated independently of that of the Civil Service, which was more government work-team focused.

Some teams began simply by meeting in local halls on a weekly basis.[230] While
work teams were among those who lined out in the Leinster Ladies' Cup at Phoenix
Park in May 1971, including the Central Bank, Fry-Cadbury and Clery's, others
took on nicknames such as Hotspurs and Hell's Raisers.[231] A Leinster League was

218 *EH*, 21 Nov. 1970. **219** *EH*, 10 Nov. 1970. **220** Ibid., and 25 Jan. 1971; *II*, 30 Nov. 1970 and
1 Dec. 1970. **221** *II*, 3 Dec. 1970. **222** Ibid. **223** *EH*, 25 Jan. 1971. **224** *IP*, 12 Feb. 1971.
225 Ibid. **226** Ibid. **227** *II*, 25 Mar. 1971. **228** *EH*, 12 Apr. 1971. **229** Ibid. **230** *EE*, 6 Apr.
1971. **231** *II*, 22 May 1971.

apparently also operational at that stage, with ten teams playing in Division One, although it is not clear if that was simply another name given to the Dublin Ladies' League.[232] In June 1971, a hat-trick by 15-year-old Inchicore native Anne O'Brien helped Vards win the Drumcondra Cup when they defeated Drimnagh Bosco by three goals to two at Tolka Park.[233]

Despite this, ladies' football remained on the periphery of the Dublin soccer scene, with the Ladies' Challenge Cup final between the Departments of Lands and Local Government in June 1971 scheduled for 9.30 p.m. on a Friday night at Dalymount Park after four charity and novelty men's matches.[234] By July 1972, there were two ladies' leagues in Dublin: the Leinster League and the Civil Service League.[235] It appears that the Dublin League had expanded to take in more provincial teams, and been renamed. Greater recognition was officially given to ladies' soccer in Ireland the following year. The Ladies' Football Association of Ireland was founded through the FAI in 1973.[236] This followed the foundation of the Women's Football Association in England in 1969 and the Scottish governing body in 1971.[237] The Northern Ireland Women's Football Association was founded in the Post Office Youth Club in College Square North in Belfast in November 1976.[238]

By the spring of 1977, a street league was operational in the Crumlin/ Kimmage area.[239] In May 1977, Dalymount Park was the venue for the Irish Wheelchair Association Cup final between Castle United and Welsox, with a friendly between Dublin Castle and the Central Statistics Office taking place beforehand.[240] Developing the game in regional areas was at times difficult, and some Dublin clubs attempted to help with this. In September 1977, a ladies' team from St Michael's Estate, Inchicore, travelled to Wexford to play a local selection in an attempt to revive the game there.[241] In April 1978, the Ladies' Soccer League of Ireland season began, with Pat McCaffrey of Dublin acting as chairman at the annual meeting.[242] Delegates present decided to appoint John A. Aherne of Cork as PRO following 'a long discussion' on the lack of publicity at both international and domestic level.[243] Representatives of provincial clubs Cork Celtic, Limerick and Waterford expressed their dissatisfaction with the state of pitches in Dublin, and it was decided that the Dublin clubs would take action to improve this state of affairs. Dublin club Suffragettes were unbeaten in the previous season's league and cup, while other Dublin teams included AIB and Avengers.[244]

Like some men's teams, a few ladies' teams placed advertisements in newspapers seeking aspiring players, including the Civil Defence team in 1971, and the 'Avengers' ladies team, who were based in the north side of Dublin, in August 1969 and again in January 1978.[245] In April 1978 Brighton Celtic of Cornelscourt

232 *IP*, 6 May 1971. 233 *II*, 4 June 1971. 234 *II*, 2 June 1971. 235 *EH*, 8 July 1972. 236 *IE*, 2 Nov. 1979. 237 Taylor, *The association game*, p. 262. 238 'Northern Ireland Women's Football Association', irishfa.com/ifa-domestic/leagues/northern-ireland-womens-football-association, accessed 9 Jan. 2022. 239 *Soccer Reporter* (Mar. 1977), p. 6. 240 *II*, 28 Apr. and 4 May 1977. 241 *New Ross Standard*, 9 Sept. 1977. 242 *IE*, 1 Apr. 1978. 243 Ibid. 244 Ibid. 245 *EH*, 11 Aug. 1969, 20 July 1971 and 24 Jan. 1978.

indicated they were entering the Leinster Ladies' League for the third year and hoped to recruit new players.[246] Similarly, Tallaght team Kilnamanagh Rockets sought opponents having announced their formation in the press in September 1978.[247] For some teams, the loss of players to other codes was at times a problem, with some Cork Celtic players also taking part in hockey in 1978.[248]

By September 1979, the Civil Service Amateur Football League had two sections, with section 'A' consisting of ten clubs while section 'B' had thirteen clubs.[249] Despite this, attracting interest nationally remained difficult. In November 1979, the Ladies' Football Association of Ireland launched a nationwide campaign 'to attract women into the game', with a focus on Dublin, Cork and Limerick and other major urban centres.[250] At that stage, Dublin was reportedly the centre of ladies' soccer in the Republic of Ireland, with three main leagues in operation there. These were the Civil Service Ladies' Amateur Football League, which had thirty-four teams, the Leinster Ladies' League, which had seventeen clubs, and the Greenhills League, which had fourteen teams registered.[251] An inter-league competition, the Bracken trophy, was also held annually, with nineteen teams present in the Limerick Ladies' League, while the Cork Ladies' League had six affiliated clubs.[252] The LFAI was hoping to organize underage competitions in order to raise awareness of the game nationally and sought volunteers to assist in this.[253] By August of the following year, the strength of the Republic of Ireland ladies' senior team lay in the Dublin Suffragettes club, who supplied half of the sixteen women panel, while a quarter of the team were from Limerick clubs.[254]

At the Ladies' Football Association of Ireland AGM in January 1981, secretary Breeda Finnerty expressed concerns that they were not receiving the recognition they deserved in the media.[255] The FAI also noted this later that year in their annual report, stating that 'some newspapers were cynical both in their reports and in their pictures' of Ireland's 1–0 victory over Belgium at Dalymount Park in October 1980.[256] They expressed their gratitude to Edwina Dooley for her coverage in *Soccer Reporter*, despite her criticism of the national governing body.[257] One general issue identified by Breeda Finnerty of the LFAI was the lack of facilities, with one team, St Brendan's, having to change in a player's house before home matches.[258] Finnerty stated that Dublin Corporation and Dublin Council closed down their pitches in June, which meant that the players had to change in cars over the summer as the season ran from April onwards.[259] In February 1982, the Leinster FA agreed to the hosting of Ladies' Civil Service League matches on Monday and Thursday nights at Phoenix Park from the end of March onwards, which gave the latter association an extra night there, having secured the use of pitches there on Mondays in February 1980.[260] However, they were not initially prepared to allow

246 *EP*, 11 Apr. 1978. 247 *EP*, 5 Sept. 1978. 248 *IE*, 1 Apr. 1978. 249 *EH*, 9 Aug. 1979. 250 *IE*, 2 Nov. 1979. 251 Ibid. 252 Ibid. 253 Ibid. 254 *LL*, 27 Aug. 1980. 255 *EP*, 4 Jan. 1981. 256 Annual Report 1980–1, June 1981, FAI Archives, P137/24. 257 Ibid. 258 *IP*, 11 Mar. 1981. 259 Ibid. 260 Emergency Committee Meeting, 4 Feb. 1980 and 1 Feb. 1982, Leinster Football Association Archives. P239/41.

the Ladies' FAI to organize an international match on a Sunday in May 1981, noting that this was a day that was 'traditionally allocated to juniors'.[261]

Another issue was the scarcity of qualified referees as most male referees were said to be either on their break over the summer or else involved in outstanding schoolboy or junior games.[262] Finnerty also noted that most female teams 'were either based in local areas or spring from firms, such as banks and manufacturers'.[263] At that stage, twenty-six teams were involved in the Leinster Ladies' Soccer League, with the majority based on Dublin's north side. One club from Naas, County Kildare, travelled into Dublin for their away matches, while a club from Kells, County Meath, applied to join the league that year.[264] On a positive note, it was also highlighted that more men's soccer clubs were taking on female members with a view to forming ladies' teams.[265] Internationally, progress was inconsistent, with Ireland beaten by five goals to nil by England at Dalymount Park in May 1981, having seemingly been granted the permission to play on a Sunday, with the visitors 'displaying a greater degree of teamwork and stamina'.[266] The FAI expressed regret that the winners of the LFAI Cup, Suffragettes, did not receive the trophy on the day of the final 'due to unavoidable circumstances', something that was highly unlikely to happen with the men's FAI Cup final.[267] The match was played at the VEC grounds in Terenure, again illustrating the perceived gap in significance between the male and female competitions.[268]

Progress continued in the Civil Service Ladies' Amateur Football League, with five divisions in operation by June 1981.[269] Among the six clubs in the Premier Division were Dublin Castle, Castle United, Green Angels, Welsox, Abbotstown and ESB.[270] The First, Second and Third Divisions had eight teams each, while the Fourth Division had fourteen teams, which meant that there were forty-four teams registered with this league in total.[271] By October of that year, it was estimated that there were 130 ladies' teams in the Republic of Ireland.[272] Some regional leagues were not always consistently run, with the Waterford League making a 'return to affiliated soccer' after three years in 1982.[273] The LFAI was at times critical of its own affiliated clubs, and warned that year that they would make it difficult for teams who were more interested in travelling abroad for tournaments to obtain permission to do so if they continued to neglect their own domestic fixtures.[274] They also expressed their annoyance about the FAI's delay in accepting invitations from UEFA to participate in their tournament for women (and how instead they had to seek information through the English Women's FA), but noted that some FAI members had reacted positively to their efforts to promote the game.[275]

In April 1983, 'two of the strongest ladies' soccer teams in Ireland', Glade Celtic, winners of the Leinster Ladies' League, and Dublin Castle, the winners

261 Senior Council Meeting Minutes, 1 Apr. 1981, Leinster Football Association Archives, P239/34. 262 *IP*, 11 Mar. 1981. 263 Ibid. 264 Ibid. 265 Ibid. 266 *II*, 4 May 1981. 267 Annual Report 1980–1, June 1981, FAI Archives, P137/24. 268 Ibid. 269 *EP*, 23 June 1981. 270 Ibid. 271 Ibid. 272 *EP*, 16 Oct. 1981. 273 *IE*, 8 Sept. 1982. 274 *Soccer Reporter* (Feb. 1982), p. 13. 275 Ibid.

of the Civil Service League, met in the final of the FAI President's trophy at St Patrick's College Drumcondra.[276] Dublin Castle were noted as being 'one of the most experienced sides in Irish ladies' soccer', while Glade Celtic contained a number of Irish internationals.[277] The FAI President's trophy had been inaugurated the previous year and included teams from the Dublin Colleges League, the Galway League, Cork and the Dublin City League.[278] At the end of the 1982–3 season, the LFAI noted in their annual report to the FAI that although national and underage competitions were a success and relationships had improved with their 'parent body', financially, they were not getting the support they needed and had to undertake fundraising activities themselves in order to compete internationally.[279] By the summer of that year, the LFAI had 147 clubs, a growth of 26 from the previous year, with 'the continued rise of the Civil Service League in Dublin', along with 'the return of the Limerick League' and 'the entry of the Laois League' instrumental in this growth.[280] By June 1984, the Leinster Ladies' League had five divisions and the Civil Service League had six.[281]

The idea that ladies' matches were something of a novelty persisted, and at times these were simply pencilled in as a warm-up to men's fixtures. This had been the case in 1976 when the Republic of Ireland met Scotland prior to the Bass League Cup final at Dalymount Park.[282] The 1982 Leinster Ladies' Cup final between Glade Celtic and Suffragettes was scheduled before the Shelbourne versus Shamrock Rovers men's League of Ireland match at Harold's Cross in October of that year.[283] A few years later, the pre-season friendly between Manchester United and Shamrock Rovers at Tolka Park in July 1984 was preceded by a ladies game, with the performance of Anne Beirne the highlight as she was named 'player of the match'.[284] That same month, the Puma Cup, a ladies' competition involving local and foreign players and organized by the Dublin Castle club, took place at Belfield, but press coverage remained limited in comparison with that given to men's and schoolboy soccer.[285] At the end of the 1983–4 season, the FAI, in their annual report, regretted that the LFAI were having 'internal problems', which saw the resignation of both their honorary secretary and honorary treasurer, and also wished the association 'continued success in their efforts for ladies football throughout the Republic of Ireland'.[286] This illustrates that they saw the LFAI as a body that needed to take care of its own issues rather than offering them immediate assistance.

Anne Beirne was an important part of the Belvedere team, which won the Civil Service Cup in 1985, beating (on penalties) Dublin Castle, who won the Premier Division, and included Helena Stapleton, sister of Irish men's international captain Frank.[287] By the summer of 1985 a Leinster Schoolgirls' league was also up and running, with two under-15 and an under-17 league operational too.[288] There

276 *II*, 29 Apr. 1983. 277 Ibid. 278 Ibid. 279 Annual Report 1982–3, June 1983, FAI Archives, P137/24. 280 *EH*, 3 June 1983. 281 *EP*, 14 June 1984. 282 *Soccer Reporter* (Apr. 1976), p. 3. 283 *II*, 14 Oct. 1982. 284 *II*, 25 July 1984; *EH*, 14 Aug. 1985. 285 *II*, 7 July 1984; *EP*, 12 and 19 July 1985. 286 Annual Report 1983–4, June 1984, FAI Archives, P137/24. 287 *EP*, 2 Aug. 1985. 288 Ibid.

were 164 teams registered with the LFAI in the 1984–5 season, with eleven leagues, including the Leinster League, the Civil Service League and the Dublin Colleges' League.[289] Dublin Castle won the LFAI Senior Cup, which had a record entry of thirty-two clubs that season.[290]

The following year, the Leinster Ladies' League was reported to have 'enjoyed its best ever season' as Rathfarnham United won the LFAI Cup and a number of juvenile teams also winning national trophies, although the selection process for the Bracken Cup was stated to be in need of improvement.[291] The securing of sponsorship for the LFAI Cup, the President's trophy and the Bracken Cup was 'a major boost', while the LFAI Cup final and the President's trophy final were both played under floodlights at Dalymount Park for the first time, with the sponsors also providing videos of these matches.[292] Disappointingly, the FAI only afforded the LFAI 'observer status at Junior Council' level with the LFAI calling for 'proper representation and voting power'.[293] They also urged the FAI to 'eliminate sexual discrimination for once and for all'.[294] Financially, the LFAI largely depended on grants from the FAI and the National Finance Committee, with affiliation fees remaining the same as they were in 1981 and often being put back into council members' travelling expenses.[295] The visit of the Denmark national team attracted 1,500 spectators, while media coverage was said to have improved by the mid-1980s.[296] By the end of the 1987–8 season, the LFAI had 157 affiliated teams and ten divisions, while a new intermediate competition was initiated for teams not involved in premier division soccer.[297]

Taylor has noted that in Britain 'the 1990s was in many respects a decade of progress for women in football' and 'participation rates increased significantly' with the FA and the Women's Football Association taking greater control of the game early in that decade.[298] However, some of the more independent clubs, such as Doncaster Belles, suffered as rivals including Arsenal and Croydon, who had been assimilated into men's clubs, benefited from increased financial support and better facilities.[299] Progress was also evident within the ladies' game in Dublin in that decade. In May 1994, the Civil Service League amalgamated with the Leinster Ladies' League to form the Dublin and District Ladies' Soccer League.[300] Over 120 clubs were noted as being involved, with three premier divisions and six intermediate divisions at senior level, along with under-14, under-16 and under-18 leagues.[301] Some clubs were well established at that point, while some more recently founded ones grew out of men's clubs. LFAI Senior Cup finalists that year, Welsox, had been founded in 1970 while their opponents, Verona of Blanchardstown, had been founded much later, in 1992.[302] At times, the naming policies of some Dublin teams

289 Annual Report 1984–5, June 1985, FAI Archives P137/24. 290 Ibid. 291 *IP*, 17 Jan. 1986. 292 Annual Report 1985–6, June 1986, pp 7–9, FAI Archives P137/24. 293 Ibid. 294 Ibid. 295 Ibid. 296 Ibid. 297 Annual Report 1987–8, June 1988, p. 7, FAI Archives, P137/24. 298 Taylor, *The association game*, p. 384. 299 Ibid. 300 *Bray People*, 6 May 1994. 301 Ibid. 302 *EH*, 20 Sept. 1994.

did little to strengthen the notion that ladies' soccer was something to be taken seriously, with a few early 1990s Civil Service League clubs using names such as O'Connell's Chicks and Blue Angels.[303] However, at that point, these were becoming quite rare.

The finalists in the 1996 LFAI Senior Cup were also Dublin clubs.[304] O'Connell's were founded in 1985 and had begun in Division V of the Civil Service Ladies' Football League. In 1994 they entered the 'newly formed' Dublin Women's Soccer League's Premier Division.[305] While O'Connell's beat Shelbourne in the semi-final, their final opponents, Castle Rovers, defeated the cup holders, Rathfarnham, in the other match.[306] Castle Rovers were formed in 1983 and had similarly begun in the bottom division of the Civil Service Ladies' League and worked their way up to the top level. They had won the LFAI Intermediate Cup in 1991 and 1993 and also entered the Dublin Women's Soccer League in 1994 and finished in second place.[307] Both O'Connell's and Castle Rovers teams included internationals, with Emma Byrne part of the O'Connell's team while Olivia O'Toole was a member of the Castle Rovers side.[308]

Progress at international level was slow, however, with Belgium beating the Republic of Ireland 5–1 in Ghent in May 1996 to qualify for the European Championship finals.[309] When interviewed for this book, O'Toole recalled that she had spent much of her teenage years playing with Sheriff Street Boys in the 1980s, before moving to Drumcondra Ladies when she was 19.[310] She noted the lack of choice in relation to joining teams at that time, and after Drumcondra Ladies folded, she travelled to Blacklion of Cornellscourt because 'she just wanted to play football'.[311] Despite much personal success in soccer – she was the record goal scorer for the Republic of Ireland ladies' team and won numerous leagues and cups – she noted the poor treatment of the international team by the FAI, particularly in terms of travelling and eating arrangements, and recalled that 'we were playing in Minsk. And when we landed we were on a bus for nine hours straight, and that bus didn't turn left or right for nine hours.'[312] However, she felt that 'you loved playing for your country so you'd travel anywhere'.[313]

On the eve of the twenty-first century, much progress had been made in ladies' soccer in Dublin and elsewhere since the early 1970s. However, late in 1997, Irish ladies' captain Yvonne Lyons called for greater action to be taken to expand the game outside of Dublin, and stressed the need to develop it within schools.[314] She also wanted to see the expansion of coaching courses, and, in comparing the Republic of Ireland with the USA, highlighted that players were starting as young as five there.[315] She noted that she had not started playing until she was nineteen, and that in Ireland most female players began at the age of 14 or 15.[316] In many ways, the slow nature of regional development in ladies' soccer was reflective of

303 *EH*, 16 July 1992. 304 *IE*, 20 Aug. 1996. 305 Ibid. 306 Ibid. 307 Ibid. 308 Ibid. 309 *SI*, 5 May 1996. 310 Interview with Olivia O'Toole, 16 Apr. 2020. 311 Ibid. 312 Ibid. 313 Ibid. 314 *II*, 22 Dec. 1997. 315 Ibid. 316 Ibid.

the weak infrastructures for men's and underage soccer in many rural areas, some of which did not see county leagues established until after the Ban was removed in 1971, while numerous villages in Ireland still do not have schoolboy and schoolgirl soccer teams, or indeed soccer clubs of any kind.[317] Permanence was difficult to sustain at many levels, with a Women's National League run in 2003, but only for a short period. Olivia O'Toole recalled that 'it wasn't really a national league, it was just a name basically' as most clubs were located in Dublin.[318] However, in 2011, another attempt was made, and this Women's National League has been more successful, celebrating its first decade in 2021.[319]

THE EMERGENCE OF ETHNIC MINORITY CLUBS IN DUBLIN

While a Jewish club known as Maccabi FC, run by Louis Verby, was operational by the mid-1950s, there is less indication that soccer teams made up of ethnic minority players existed in Dublin until much later.[320] Maccabi were one of the founder members of the Amateur League in 1954, and by the late 1980s had six other sports teams based at their sports complex in Kimmage Road.[321] By then, the soccer team were run by manager Alan Ellison, chairman Alan Berber and treasurer Harold Solomon.[322] By the late twentieth century, the demography of Irish society was changing, as Ireland became a more multi-cultural society through the economic growth of the Celtic Tiger and its related immigration. As Thomas Bartlett has written, 'the Irish were initially not well equipped mentally, legislatively or educationally to meet the challenges posed by scores of thousands of immigrants who had different skin colours, different religions, different languages and different *mores*'.[323] During the years from 1996 to 2002, on average, over 25,000 immigrants were moving to Ireland annually.[324] While there were laws against racial discrimination, with the later economic decline, disproportionate numbers of unemployed immigrants meant that racism against foreigners 'was never far from the surface of Irish public life'.[325] The lack of clarity on immigration from coalition governments from 1995 to 2005 led to confusion on matters relating to the assimilation of immigrants into Irish society, and triggered resentment over social welfare benefits and jobs.[326]

Gerry Farrell has identified Ray Keogh, who was born in Dublin in the late 1930s, as being the first mixed-race player to appear in the League of Ireland.[327] He played for a number of clubs including Home Farm, Shamrock Rovers and

317 Curran, *Irish soccer migrants*, pp 53–60 318 Interview with Olivia O'Toole, 16 Apr. 2020. 319 Helena Byrne, 'Women's soccer in the Republic of Ireland', PowerPoint presentation, 2021. I am grateful to Helena for sharing this information with me. 320 *Irish Soccer*, 1:4 (1955), p. 8. 321 *EH*, 10 Jan. 1989. 322 Ibid. 323 Bartlett, *Ireland: a history*, p. 547. 324 Terence Browne, *Ireland: a social and cultural history 1922–2002* (London, 2004), pp 385–6. 325 Bartlett, *Ireland: a history*, p. 547. 326 Brown, *Ireland: a social and cultural history*, p. 386. 327 'A tribute to Ray Keogh-by Gerry Farrell', sseairtricityleague.ie/news/a-true-trailblazer-for-the-irish-game-tribute-to-ray-keogh/id-2967, accessed 1 Sept. 2021.

Drumcondra from the late 1950s until the end of the following decade.[328] Some players have suffered racist abuse while playing in Dublin, with Paul McGrath stating that he had walked off before he was sent off while playing for Dalkey United after he retaliated in a Leinster League match at the start of the 1980–1 season against Fatima following 'a familiar comment' about the colour of his skin.[329] To the credit of his club, they refused to pay the £3 fine sanctioned by a Leinster League disciplinary hearing, a figure that is apparently still outstanding.[330] More research needs to be undertaken on the experiences of later black players at Dublin clubs, including Mark Rutherford, Joey Ndo and Henry McKop.[331]

As Max Mauro has shown through his examination of two Blanchardstown teams, Mountview, a youth club founded in 1980, and Insaka FC, established in 2009 by an ex-Nigerian professional player, racism has remained within Irish soccer.[332] While Mountview contained 'Irish (white) boys and boys of different African backgrounds', Insaka was made up of 'immigrant youth (of African and Eastern European backgrounds)'.[333] In particular, Mauro has illustrated that adult club officials failed to deal with reporting incidents of racist abuse, despite the presence of FAI's Intercultural Plan, which outlines guidelines for officials and referees to deal with discrimination and racism.[334] More recently, Ken McCue has noted the work of Soccer Against Racism Ireland (SARI), which was founded in Dublin in 1997, in counteracting racism within sport in Ireland.[335]

Immigration also saw the emergence of grassroots soccer teams in Dublin in the early twenty-first century, which were made up of non-nationals. TC Ted EX, a club made up of Polish players (although other nationalities were also welcome to join) were based at St Anne's Park in Raheny.[336] They played in Division Two of the Athletic Union League.[337] Another Polish-run club is PFC White Eagles FC, founded in 2008, who play their home matches at the AUL Complex in Clonshaugh.[338] Similarly, Real Transilvania, another Athletic Union League club, but one with a Romanian background and founded in 2012, played their matches at Verona Grounds in Coolmine.[339] Dynamo Dublin, a team made up of players mainly from the former Soviet Union, were founded in 2002 and affiliated to the Leinster Football League with a home venue at the Phoenix Park.[340] Clubs consisting of immigrants have also taken part in local seven-a-side leagues, including Baltic United, a Lithuanian club founded in 2014, which is based in Artane.[341]

328 Ibid. 329 Paul McGrath, *Back from the brink* (London, 2006), p. 91. 330 Ibid. 331 Fitzpatrick, *Shelbourne cult heroes*, p. 154. 332 Mauro, *Youth sport, migration and culture*, pp 3–4, 82–3. 333 Ibid., pp 3–4. 334 Ibid., p. 85. 335 Ken McCue, 'Who's SARI now: social enterprise and the use of the medium of sport to further human rights in society' in Curran (ed.), 'The growth and development of soccer in Dublin', Special issue of *Soccer and Society*, pp 919–33. Soccer Against Racism Ireland is now known as Sport Against Racism Ireland. 336 'FC Ted EX', soccer-ireland.com/dublin-football-clubs/fc-tedex.htm, accessed 3 Aug. 2021. 337 Ibid. 338 'PFC White Eagles FC', soccer-ireland.com/dublin-football-clubs/pfc-white-eagles.htm, accessed 3 Aug. 2021. 339 'Real Transilvania FC', facebook.com/RealTransilvania, accessed 3 Aug. 2021. 340 'Dynamo Dublin FC', soccer-ireland.com/dublin-football-clubs/dynamo-dublin.htm, accessed 3 Feb. 2021. 341 'Baltic United FC', facebook.com/balticunitedfc, accessed 3 Aug. 2021. See also FC International.

CONCLUSION

As shown above, there was a marked decline in support for League of Ireland soccer in Dublin after the high interest levels of the 1950s and 1960s. By the summer of 1977, the FAI had 2,980 affiliated clubs, with the Leinster FA containing 1,070 clubs.[342] By the end of the decade, the Garda Metropolitan League was also active.[343] In the autumn of 1983 there were an estimated 200,000 soccer players in Ireland.[344] However, for many clubs, facilities and support remained an issue. Competition with Gaelic games affected loyalty, although many players had grown up with a variety of codes in Dublin, and, as will be shown later, some continued to play these when it suited them, despite restrictions. While individual clergy were important in the organization and running of some adult clubs, overall, the Catholic church's hierarchy were reluctant to embrace soccer in the way they had become involved in Gaelic games, even if, as Gillespie and Hegarty have stated, 'no single coherent attitude towards the GAA was adopted by Catholic Church' and this support was often only through patronage, ceremonial attendance at finals and the presentation of trophies.[345] Some individual priests did initiate soccer competitions for adults, including Fr Tom Hanlon, who organized an inter-seminary league for the Carmelite fathers in Donnybrook in 1980.[346] As will be shown later, clerical involvement in schoolboy clubs and competitions was more significant in the game's development at that level.

The strength of soccer in Dublin also assisted the growth of some clubs in nearby counties Louth and Wicklow, although soccer administrators in the latter county were at times unhappy with the loss of local clubs to Dublin leagues.[347] In other closely located counties, such as Meath and Kildare, the emergence of clubs of the strength of Bray Wanderers or Dundalk was less noticeable, with Gaelic football more prominent. Workplace teams continued to grow at lower levels of the game. Foreign investment in Dublin saw the establishment of some work teams, including Technicon, a club founded by the US company of the same name who set it up for their employees at their factory in Swords in 1967, with rugby and table tennis teams also established.[348]

By the late twentieth century, ladies' soccer in Dublin had made much progress in terms of the organization of adult structures, but as late as 1992, ladies' international matches were still playing second fiddle to those of the men's League of Ireland, with one European Championship match in March of that year taking place on the morning of a Bohemians versus Athlone Town fixture at Dalymount

---

342 Minute Book of the Senior Council, Annual Report 1976–7, June 1977, FAI Archives, P137/24.   343 *Soccer Reporter* (Sept. 1979), p. 6.   344 *Soccer Reporter* (Aug. 1983), p. 12.   345 Simon Gillespie & Roddy Hegarty, 'Caman and crozier: the Catholic church and the GAA' in Dónal McAnallen, David Hassan & Roddy Hegarty (eds), *The evolution of the GAA: Ulaidh, Éire agus eile* (Armagh, 2009), pp 112–22.   346 Emergency Committee Meeting Minutes, 30 Oct. 1980, Leinster Football Association Archives, P239/41.   347 Emergency Committee Meeting Minutes, 18 Sept. 1980, Leinster Football Association Archives, P239/41.   348 *EH*, 10 Jan. 1989.

Park.[349] This was despite the fact that Ireland had beaten Spain through an Olivia O'Toole goal earlier in that campaign, and still harboured hopes of qualification for the tournament.[350] Allied to these perceptions, the lack of school structures, along with those at a parish level, hindered the growth of women's soccer throughout Ireland. Competition with Gaelic football has also impacted on its appeal, particularly in rural areas. Despite these issues, women's soccer in Dublin, and throughout Ireland, is now on a much more solid footing than it had been in the twentieth century, and organizational structures appear more finely poised to continue to improve. In chapter five, relations between soccer clubs in Dublin and a number of those abroad are addressed.

349 Ibid., 19 Mar. 1992. The international match was scheduled for 12 noon and the League of Ireland fixture at 4 p.m. 350 Ibid.

5

Relations with clubs in Britain, Europe and further afield

EARLY CROSS-CHANNEL CONNECTIONS

Links with English and Scottish clubs were developed earliest in the north-east of Ireland, where the game was strongest. These connections were important in spreading interest in soccer. Irish teams were beginning to visit Scotland for matches by the early 1880s, with a trial match between Down and Antrim taking place on 26 December 1882 in order to select a team to travel to Kilmarnock to play Ayrshire in May 1883. A Belfast selection had been beaten 7–1 by Ayrshire on New Year's Day 1883 at Kilmarnock.[1] Cliftonville, winners of the IFA Challenge Cup in 1883, also welcomed the visit of English clubs, with Bootle, the holders of the Liverpool Challenge Cup, drawing nil–nil against the Belfast side in January 1884.[2] Dublin-based clubs do not appear to have engaged in friendly matches against English and Scottish clubs with the same frequency as those from Belfast in the late nineteenth century. However, at Easter 1884 the Dublin Association FC travelled to South Wales via boat and played two matches against the English clubs Walsall and Small Heath Alliance.[3] By the early 1880s, there were regular public shipping services run by a number of companies between Dublin (from North Wall and Kingstown) and a number of British ports, including Holyhead, Liverpool, Bristol, London and Glasgow.[4]

With the relatively short distance between Dublin and Britain, British teams also visited Dublin for matches. In what appears to be the first visit of a British club to the city, as noted earlier, the Dublin Association FC met Rhyll, who featured a number of Welsh internationals, in a friendly match at Sandymount prior to Christmas 1884.[5] In December 1887, Dublin University AFC defeated Liverpool Ramblers, the first English club to play in the College Park, by six goals to four, the away team having endured 'a terribly rough passage' via Holyhead.[6] The following March, Dublin University travelled to Liverpool, where they played out a three–all draw against the same opposition.[7] The Dublin University team's final match in 1888 was against the same opposition, who featured a number of 'well known English amateurs'.[8] One reporter expressed the hope that 'their efforts

---

1 *BN*, 2 Jan. 1883. 2 *BN*, 7 Jan. 1884. 3 *Sport*, 26 Apr. 1884. 4 *Thom's official directory ... 1883*, p. 1289. 5 *Sport*, 13 Dec. 1884; *IT*, 20 Dec. 1884. 6 *Sport*, 12 Nov. 1887; *Liverpool Daily Post*, 19 Dec. 1887. 7 *Lancashire Evening Post*, 17 Mar. 1888. 8 *Sport*, 15 Dec. 1888.

to make the Association game popular in Dublin will be rewarded' as they had 'been put to considerable expense in getting the Ramblers over'.[9] The Ramblers also played Dublin Association FC during their stay.[10] The Lansdowne versus Cambridge rugby match was said to be the top football attraction the day they faced Dublin University, however, illustrating how soccer remained in rugby's shadow in Dublin by the end of that decade.[11] In March 1889, Dublin University again travelled to Liverpool for the return match, which was played at Crosby Cricket ground, and afterwards were 'the Ramblers' guests at dinner, and a festive evening followed'.[12] The Ramblers team was made up of players from Trinity Cambridge, Corpus Cambridge, Malvern, Charterhouse, Repton and Magdalene Oxford, illustrating their social background.[13] This appears to have been the last time the clubs met.

In December 1892 the Leinster Nomads took part in a number of matches in Bristol.[14] On 29 December they beat St George's 5–0 before a crowd of 1,500 and they drew 1–1 with Gloucestershire County at the County Ground Bristol before 3,000 spectators the following day, with W.G. Grace noted in the press as refereeing both matches.[15] They returned again the following winter. In December 1893 the Leinster Nomads travelled to Bristol to play six matches over the Christmas period.[16] The aforementioned James H. Webb, who took part in this tour, later recalled that they had lost all their matches, and that they 'were inclined to blame it upon the lavish hospitality' of their hosts.[17] He added that 'Dr Henry Grace, brother of the famous W.G. Grace, gave some magnificent dinner parties' and a dance was also held in honour of the Leinster Nomads.[18]

At Christmas 1894, the Leinster Nomads again travelled to England on tour.[19] However, with their decline in 1895, their cross-Channel trips came to an end.[20] Writing in the *Athletic News* in a summary of festive football in Gloucestershire in December 1895, 'Cliftonian' lamented the loss of the Leinster Nomads as he felt that 'they used to furnish fairly reliable evidence as to the strength of our leading organizations' and 'were greatly missed in consequence'.[21] At the end of the decade, Leinster FA selections also met English opposition, with London Wanderers beaten in Sandymount in March 1899 before 3,000 spectators while the Leinster representative team also travelled to London and drew with Millwall on Easter Monday that year.[22] In the winter of that year, the Leinster FA's Senior Council noted applications to have the visits of Aston Villa, Bolton Wanderers, Manchester City and Queen's Park sanctioned, illustrating the increase in interest in matches against professional clubs in England at this point.[23]

9 Ibid.   10 *FJ*, 18 Dec. 1888.   11 *Sport*, 15 Dec. 1888.   12 *TFTCGN*, 16 Mar. 1889.   13 Ibid. 14 Briggs & Dodd, *100 years of the LFA*, p. 22.   15 *EH*, 29 and 30 Dec. 1892.   16 *FJ*, 22 Dec. 1893; *Beckshire Chronicle*, 30 Dec. 1893. These matches were against Bristol St George's, Reading, Warmby, Bedminster, Staple Hill and Trowbridge.   17 *SI*, 22 Dec. 1940.   18 Ibid.   19 *The Sporting Life*, 28 Dec. 1894; *II*, 26 Dec. 1894.   20 *EH*, 16 Nov. 1895.   21 *AN*, 30 Dec. 1895.   22 *Sport*, 25 Mar. 1899; Briggs & Dodd, *100 years of the LFA*, pp 26–7.   23 Senior League Council Minutes, Council Meeting, 16 Nov. 1899, Leinster Football Association Archives, P239/21.

By the early twentieth century the game was on a more solid footing in the Irish capital and this helped further encourage the visit of more English football league teams, and some senior clubs had by then developed the finance and facilities to attract them. Following the opening of Dalymount Park in 1901, Bohemians were able to host a number of British clubs.[24] Bohemians' second match at Dalymount after playing Shelbourne was against Bolton Wanderers, which, while costing the club £40 to attract the English club, resulted in a gate of £55 and ended in a 4–1 defeat for the Dublin side.[25] They then built 'a "standing" stand' that could hold 1,500 people. It was tested out by 'twenty big policemen' from Mountjoy before the visit of Preston North End.[26] Bohemians drew 4–4 against a Preston North End team featuring goalkeeper William 'Fatty' Foulke, who weighed in at twenty-two stone. Dr Willie Hooper, who later became FAI president, won a bet that he had made before the match with a Bohemians colleague for 'a gold mounted cigarette holder' that he would knock the goalkeeper over, having caught him off balance.[27] They also had visits from Wolverhampton Wanderers and Aston Villa that season, with the latter game held during the week and £150 obtained from 'takings'.[28] On St Stephen's Day 1901, Glasgow Celtic played Bohemians at Dalymount Park, with the Scottish team winning by two goals to nil.[29]

In April 1903 Liverpool FC visited Dublin and defeated Bohemians 5–2 as part of two fixtures along with Sheffield United, who also played a match against Distillery.[30] They returned twelve months later to play the Dublin club with poor weather contributing to 'the smallness of the crowd', who watched a 4–1 victory for the Merseysiders at Dalymount Park.[31] Attempts to arrange a match for Liverpool in Dublin in the 1925 close season were apparently prohibited by the English FA, although, as will be shown, other English teams did come to play there in the 1920s.[32] It appears there were no further fixtures of this nature between the club and those in Dublin until the 1960s, as Liverpool FC looked to other areas such as Scandinavia for non-competitive matches in the earlier part of the twentieth century.[33]

As shown earlier, Dublin did not host its first international fixture until 1900, when England arrived to play Ireland on St Patrick's Day, with the Belfast-based Irish Football Association reluctant to host these matches outside Belfast.[34] The first Irish League match against the Scottish League took place in 1893, while Irish League matches against the English League had taken place since 1894.[35] Trips abroad also provided the opportunity for socializing and at times work networks were utilized. The Great Southern and Western Railway team, based at Inchicore, travelled to Horwich for their annual tour at Easter 1907, and following a victory

24 *SI*, 15 Dec. 1940. 25 Ibid. 26 Ibid. 27 Ibid. 28 Ibid. 29 *II*, 21 Dec. 1901; *Daily News*, 27 Dec. 1901. 30 *DUD*, 18 Apr. 1903; 'Games for the 1903–1904 season', lfchistory.net/SeasonArchive/Games/88, accessed 29 Dec. 2017. 31 *FJ*, 11 Apr. 1904. 32 *FSW*, 5 Sept. 1925. 33 'Games for the 1903–1904 season', lfchistory.net/SeasonArchive/Games/89, accessed 29 Dec. 2017; and 'Games for the 1910–1911 season', lfchistory.net/SeasonArchive/Games/80, accessed 29 Dec. 2017. 34 Moore, *The Irish soccer split*, p. 63. 35 *Sport*, 27 Sept. and 25 Oct. 1924.

over 'their English Railway Rival Horwich RMI ... there was great enjoyment and festivities'.[36] This was said to have 'very probably' been the reason they failed to win any further matches in Lancashire.[37]

In 1912, during a number of senior clubs' dispute with the IFA, in which the Leinster FA had supported their parent Belfast governing body, some cross-Channel clubs such as Blackpool came to play against Bohemians, while Linfield also received visits from Scottish and English teams.[38] While relations between the English Football League and the Irish League had been frosty in the early 1900s, with the poaching of Irish players by British clubs central to this, in 1914 an Anglo–Irish Football League Board was established.[39] This was supposed to ensure player movement would be legitimate, but difficulties remained, despite the adoption of the 'retain and transfer' system in Ireland that year and the formation of the Scottish and Irish Football League Board in 1915.[40] Following the foundation of the Football Association of Ireland in 1921, British international selections refused to play the Free State team and England did not visit Dublin until 1946.[41] Despite this lack of international recognition, and a failed Irish Republican Army attempt to burn Old Trafford in March 1921, in the post-independence years, English clubs continued to come to Dublin.[42] Shelbourne beat a West Ham selection 2–1 in January 1922.[43] The performance of visiting teams from Britain was not always of the high standard expected, with one reporter complaining in April 1924 that 'never has a cross-channel team served up such a poor dish as that provided by Third Lanark in their game with Shelbourne at Ringsend'.[44] These trips often came along with a match against a Belfast team for the non-Irish club. In May 1924 Bohemians beat Blackburn Rovers 3–2 at Dalymount Park with the English team also losing to Linfield on that trip.[45] In April 1928, both Aberdeen and Glasgow Celtic came to Dublin to face Shamrock Rovers and Bohemians, respectively, as leading Scottish teams were also an attractive draw for Dublin football fans.[46]

Some Dublin teams also continued to travel to Britain on tour, with Bohemians visiting London for matches in August 1926, while one of their opposing teams, London Caledonians, the London Senior Amateur Cup holders, travelled to Dublin the following year for a friendly match at Dalymount Park against the home team.[47] The London club were treated to a dinner and dance afterwards in the Metropole, and the following day both teams enjoyed an excursion through County Wicklow.[48] The following season, Shamrock Rovers owner Joseph Cunningham arranged the visit of English Second Division team Barnsley to Glenmalure Park, which drew 'a big Sunday crowd' and made the venture a financial success, 'as the gate receipts reached close on £250', despite the aforementioned transport issues.[49]

36 *DEM*, 8 Apr. 1907.   37 Ibid.   38 Moore, *The Irish soccer split*, p. 40; *FJ*, 1 Apr. 1912; *EH*, 20 Apr. 1912.   39 Curran, *Irish soccer migrants*, p. 104.   40 Ibid.   41 Byrne, *Green is the colour*, pp 177–8.   42 *The Nationalist*, 20 July 1921; *IT*, 3 Feb. 2021.   43 *Sport*, 28 Jan. 1922.   44 *II*, 28 Apr. 1924.   45 *Sport*, 10 May 1924.   46 *FSW*, 21 Apr. 1928.   47 *FSW*, 21 Aug. 1926 and 16 Apr. 1927.   48 *FSW*, 23 Apr. 1923.   49 *FSW*, 7 May 1927.

The presence of local talent in an English team could strengthen interest in British clubs' visits to Dublin. In April 1933, a Sheffield United team met Shamrock Rovers at Dalymount Park, with Jimmy Dunne's presence in the English team said to have increased public interest in the match.[50] He had played in a benefit match at Dalymount Park the previous season and his appearance was apparently enough to have filled the ground.[51] By the middle of the decade the Leinster FA was struggling financially, and it was hoped that two friendly matches against Motherwell, played in 1936 and 1937 against the Leinster FA's selection, would help pay for their new headquarters at Parnell Square.[52] They also arranged home fixtures against Motherwell and Blackpool in 1938 and Motherwell again in April 1939, but it was the visit of Glasgow Celtic to Dublin later that month which drew most public attention and was the most financially successful for the Leinster FA.[53] Less prestigious sides also continued to visit for friendly matches. In May 1938, St Patrick's of Manchester met 'a strong' Hospitals' Trust team in a friendly at Tolka Park the same day as Blackpool met Shelbourne at Shelbourne Park.[54]

COACHES, MANAGERS, TRAINERS AND REFEREES

Irish clubs also benefitted from the input of non-Irish-born coaches such as Scottish player John Divers, who was recruited by Bohemians in this role in 1904.[55] Neil Carter has written that 'initially, there were limited ideas on what comprised training for footballers and the first generation of football trainers was largely made up of ex-professional athletes and athletic and rowing trainers'.[56] A number of Irish clubs kept on men who had retired from playing within their teams as trainers and managers, such as Shelbourne's Irish Cup-winning goalkeeper 'Bill' Rowe, who was their trainer by 1917, and Jack Feenan of Newry, who initially joined the Dublin club as a player from Sunderland in 1941.[57] However, some Dublin clubs continued to appoint British-born men as managers and coaches throughout the twentieth century. Bohemians, who relied on a selection committee until their appointment of Seán Thomas in 1964, had brought in former Everton centre-forward Bobby Parker in 1926 as coach and fellow Englishman George Lax in the same capacity in 1938.[58] In December 1950 Jock McCosh was noted in the national press as 'the Scot who built up Drumcondra into one of our leading clubs' and he also had spells with Dundalk and Limerick.[59] As well as appointing some former Irish players in managerial roles, such as Val Harris, British men with experience

50 *IP*, 28 Apr. 1933. 51 Ibid. 52 Briggs & Dodd, *100 years of the LFA*, p. 48. 53 Ibid., p. 50. 54 *II*, 7 May 1938. 55 Garnham, *Association football and society*, p. 93. 56 Neil Carter, *Medicine, sport and the body: a historical perspective* (London, 2012), p. 131. 57 *Sport*, 17 Nov. 1917; *Shelbourne Football Club golden jubilee, 1895–1945*, p. 32. Feenan also had a short spell at Bray Unknowns before returning to Shelbourne as trainer. 58 *FSW*, 8 May 1926; Gerry Farrell, 'Taking a lax attitude: George and the magic magnetic board', abohemiansportinglife.wordpress.com/2017/12, accessed 30 July 2021. 59 *II*, 2 Dec. 1950; *DALJ*, 18 Aug. 1951.

of English football leagues were often favoured by Dublin clubs.[60] In 1953, former England international David Jack took charge of Shelbourne while former Arsenal and Reading player Leslie Henley was coaching Bohemians.[61] By October 1954, Drumcondra were being coached by former Colchester United manager Ron Meades, who was also an accomplished organist.[62] This type of recruitment was no guarantee of success and Jack was later replaced by former Shelbourne player Eddie Gannon, but it was not until after Gerry Doyle had taken over at the end of the 1956–7 season that the club became successful again.[63] Some clubs benefitted from those who had done football training courses in England, with Royden Prole, the son of club chairman Sam, training the Drumcondra team at the start of the 1955–6 season, while Frank Radford assisted with tactics.[64] One reporter noted that Prole did not 'ask the players to do anything he cannot do himself, but with lapping, skipping, physical jerks and ball play it is hard work for all concerned'.[65]

Naturally, those with experience of Dublin clubs were also sought after in regional areas, including Seán Thomas, who moved to Sligo Rovers in August 1959 having previously coached Home Farm.[66] Admittedly, some non-Irish managers were more successful than others. Dave Bacuzzi was manager of Home Farm from 1974 until 1984, during which period the club remained amateur and struggled to retain its best players.[67] He had been appointed player-manager at Cork Hibernians in 1970, having played for Arsenal, Manchester City and Reading.[68] Following FAI Cup success with the Cork club in 1972 and 1973, he managed Home Farm to victory in 1975, having retired from playing, as they became the first amateur team to win the trophy in forty years.[69] In the semi-final, they defeated another club with an English manager, St Patrick's Athletic, who were led by Jack Burkett, an FA Cup winner with West Ham United in 1964, illustrating how Dublin soccer remained an alternative outlet for British players with an interest in managing and coaching.[70]

Those with specialized training in fitness were also recruited throughout the twentieth century. New York-born Thomas Monk, who trained Shelbourne's Irish Cup-winning team in 1906, was a professional 'athletic trainer' who lived in Gardiner Street.[71] Shelbourne's other trainers in the pre-First World War years included William Quinn, 'an expert in preparing participants in all forms of sport', who later moved to Scotland.[72] Davie Christopher, 'a great sprinter' and 'a fine footballer' who had a spell at Hibernians in Edinburgh, later took up the position of

60 Sands, *Shels*, pp 58–9. Harris was manager when Shelbourne won the FAI Cup in 1939. 61 *II*, 5 and 15 Aug. 1953; *IP*, 15 Mar. 1955. 62 *SI*, 3 Oct. 1954; *II*, 22 Apr. 1955. 63 Sands, *Shels*, p. 87. 64 *II*, 12 Aug. 1955. 65 Ibid. 66 *IP*, 5 Aug. 1959. 67 Brendan Menton, *Home Farm: the story of a Dublin football club, 1928–1998* (Dublin, 1999), p. 236; *Soccer Reporter* (Apr. 1984), p. 1. 68 Ryan, *The official book of the FAI Cup*, pp 222–3. 69 Ibid., p. 236. 70 Ibid., p. 237. 71 *Shelbourne Football Club golden jubilee*, p. 24; 'Residents of a house 7.7 in Gardiner Street, Lower (Mountjoy, Dublin)'. Retrieved from census.nationalarchives.ie/pages/1911/Dublin/Mountjoy/Gardiner_Street_Lower/24590, accessed 2 Jan. 2022. 72 *Shelbourne Football Club golden jubilee*, p. 22.

trainer with Shelbourne and helped them win the 1939 FAI Cup.[73] John Dundon, who had trained Shamrock Rovers in the 1920s, also gave instruction to cyclists B.J. and N.J. Donnelly, and 'the famous middle-distance runner' Tom Travers, who also played rugby for Lansdowne.[74] Recruitment of British personnel continued into the late twentieth century, with, for example, Shelbourne appointing Colin Murphy as manager in 1994.[75] Although he moved back to England within a few years, he later assisted in developing a youth programme between Hull City and the Dublin club.[76] The need for expertise in specialized positions has increased into the early twenty-first century. Scottish-born goalkeeper Chris Bennion had spells at Celtic, Hearts and Middlesbrough prior to coming to Ireland after being contacted by Pat Fenlon.[77] He initially joined Shelbourne on loan in 2002 before going to Scunthorpe and coming back to Ireland and later played for a number of clubs including Shelbourne, Dundalk, Athlone, St Patrick's Athletic, Monaghan United and Longford Town, having settled down with his family in Dublin. He became Bohemians goalkeeping coach after finishing playing.[78]

These appointments illustrate the close connections between Dublin clubs and those in Britain and how British soccer networks were closely linked to and often overlapped with those across the Irish Sea. Assistance was also given in refereeing, which could also be an additional source of payment for those willing to travel to Ireland to officiate at matches in the early 1900s.[79] Some Dublin clubs, including Shelbourne (in 1903 and again in 1916), actually sought cross-Channel referees to ensure greater neutrality.[80] The practice of appointing cross-Channel referees was common within Belfast soccer, with R.T. Murray of Stenhousemuir chosen for the 1905 Irish Intermediate Cup final between Dublin's Reginald and Woodvale of Belfast.[81] In the mid-1920s, the appointment of British referees continued at the highest levels of what had become Free State soccer, particularly for FAIFS Cup matches, with 1920 FA Cup final referee J.T. Howcroft from Bolton refereeing the FAIFS Cup final in 1925.[82] He had previous experience of the game in Dublin having been chosen for the 1916 Leinster Senior Cup final between Bohemians and Shelbourne.[83] Early in 1926, English referee Isaac Baker of Crewe noted that he had made his forty-second visit to referee a match, having had his first in 1914, and stated the game in Dublin was 'coming along by leaps and bounds'.[84] He added that 'as regards the crowds, they are as good sports as I have met'.[85] He later refereed the 1926 FA Cup final between Manchester City and Bolton Wanderers, and his son also took part in matches in Ireland as a referee.[86] Most others were also well-received, including Preston referee W.F. Bunnell, who was noted as 'an amiable

73 Sands, *Shels*, p. 5; *Waterford Standard*, 29 Aug. 1936; *DJ*, 19 July 1939. 74 *FSW*, 7 Nov. 1925. 75 Fitzpatrick, *Shelbourne cult heroes*, p. 140. 76 Ibid., p. 141. 77 Interview with Chris Bennion, 21 Oct. 2019. 78 Ibid. 79 See, for example, *INBMN*, 7 Nov. 1906. 80 Senior League Council Minutes, Council Meetings, 22 Apr. 1903 and 1 Mar. 1916, Leinster Football Association Archives, P239/22 and P239/25. 81 *BET*, 9 Mar. 1905. 82 *FSW*, 26 Dec. 1925 and Ryan, *The official book of the FAI Cup*, p. 24. 83 Senior League Council Minutes, Council Meeting, 1 Mar. 1916, Leinster Football Association Archives, P239/25. 84 *FSW*, 6 Feb. 1926. 85 Ibid. 86 *FSW*, 1 May 1926.

sort of chap who seems to gain popularity wherever he roams'.[87] This involvement did not always please all supporters, as Dilwyn Porter has shown. Percy Harper of Stourbridge, who later refereed the 1932 FA Cup final, received hate mail from one irate Cork supporter after a controversial decision in their 3–2 defeat against Dolphin in an FAIFS Cup tie that year.[88] Despite these issues, this practice of appointment continued, with, for example, Yorkshire man Mr Seymour refereeing the 1951 FAI Cup final.[89] The last English referee to officiate at the FAI Cup final was D.A. Corbett of Wolverhampton in 1964, after which the FAI appointed Irish referees for these finals for the rest of the century.[90]

SCOUTING NETWORKS AND THE GROWTH OF CONNECTIONS

By the opening decades of the twentieth century, Dublin clubs were also forging links with those in Britain through the sale of players, with Leeds City and Shelbourne developing these connections through transfers from Dublin between 1909 and 1911.[91] Inter-league matches offered Ireland-based players the opportunity to gain the attention of British scouts, as *Sport*'s reporter noted after the game between the Free State League and the Welsh League in November 1925:

> After the match at Swansea there were substantial bids for the services of [John Joe] Flood and [Frank] Brady by representatives of several big cross-channel clubs. Amounts running far into four figures were offered there and then, but no business was done. The offers may, however, be followed up in the form of correspondence.[92]

Friendly matches between British and Dublin clubs also afforded the opportunity to approach players, with St Mirren eager to sign Bohemians' Jimmie Bermingham following their match at Dalymount Park in May 1926.[93] At times, English club managers visited Dublin simply to sign players. In July 1933, Bradford City manager J.G. Peart approached St James's Gate player Ebbs, who was taken on a trial, while a second unnamed player, 'for business reasons, did not desire a change'.[94] Major Buckley of Wolverhampton Wanderers visited Dublin and Waterford in April 1937 and was reportedly 'only interested in extremely young players' as recruits.[95] At Christmas 1945, a representative of Huddersfield came to Dublin 'armed with the necessary cheque to complete the transfer of Hill, Shelbourne's outside right', while he also viewed two Drumcondra players on his trip.[96]

87 *FSW*, 14 Jan. 1928. 88 Dilwyn Porter, 'Whistling his way to Wembley: Percy Harper of Stourbridge, cup final referee', *Sport in History*, 35:2 (2015), pp 217–40, pp 227–8. 89 Sands, *Shels*, p. 73. 90 Ryan, *The official history of the FAI Cup*, p. 190. 91 Gary Edwards, *Every cloud: the story of how Leeds City became Leeds United* (Chichester, 2019), pp 112–13. 92 *Sport*, 14 Nov. 1925. 93 *FSW*, 8 May 1926. 94 *EH*, 25 July 1933. 95 *EE*, 27 Apr. 1937. 96 *EH*, 29 Dec. 1945.

One issue was that the clubs affiliated to the British associations did not recognize League of Ireland clubs' 'retained list' and so could sign a player, effectively for free, from a League of Ireland club, once they were out of contract and did not require the cooperation of the League of Ireland in transferring a player's registration. This was not ended until a meeting of the British associations with the Football Association of Ireland at a conference in the Central Hotel in Glasgow in November 1946.[97] It was at this meeting that it was agreed that each association would respect retained lists for players and registration and that transfer fees would be due.[98] The Irish League ratified this at a meeting in Belfast on 20 December 1946.[99] England and Scotland's return to FIFA assisted this development and it became necessary for British associations to provide the FAI with a clearance certificate when a player moved to a League of Ireland club.[100]

One reporter felt at that time that with this change in regulations, 'the period of really big signings' had 'passed' in regard to Irish clubs' recruiting of British players, but in the post-war years Dublin continued to be an important recruiting area for English clubs.[101] In May 1947, the scouts of Newcastle United, Hull City and West Ham United all visited the city on a single weekend to view players.[102] In turn, some Irish club representatives travelled to England to look for players, with Shelbourne manager Charlie Turner visiting Leeds in search of 'a couple of players' that same week.[103] Inter-league matches also assisted the development of links between those involved in soccer in England and Ireland through social events. The English League team that visited Dublin in April 1947 for a match against the League of Ireland at Dalymount Park stayed in Portmarnock, while their officials stayed in the Gresham Hotel, with the party also attending a League of Ireland dinner at Mills Hall.[104]

Gradually English clubs developed their own scouts in Ireland, with Arsenal nurturing strong links with Dublin by the latter half of the twentieth century. This move followed earlier connections that were not particularly prominent but existed nonetheless. In 1902 and 1903 Wexford-born Irish international Tommy Shanks had played for Woolwich Arsenal but at that point the club did not specifically target Irish players.[105] Among the first Dublin-born players to feature for Arsenal were Jimmy Dunne (1934–6), Dr Kevin O'Flanagan (1945–7) and Joe Haverty (1954–61).[106] Another player to move to Highbury was Frank O'Neill, who joined Arsenal in 1959 from Home Farm, having been signed by manager George Swindin.[107]

Although Arsenal had apparently not played in Dublin before the Second World War, by 1964 they had played four times at Dalymount Park.[108] The first of these meetings appears to have been an exhibition match involving the 1947–8 English league champions and a Bohemians selection in October 1948, which the

97 *EH*, 27 Nov. and 11 Dec. 1946. I am grateful to Gerry Farrell for drawing my attention to this. 98 *IE*, 21 Dec. 1946. 99 *BN*, 21 Dec. 1946. 100 *II*, 5 Nov. 1946. 101 Ibid. 102 *II*, 12 May 1947. 103 Ibid. 104 *EH*, 29 Apr. 1947. 105 Michael Joyce, *Football League players' records, 1888 to 1939* (Nottingham, 2012), p. 260. 106 *EH*, 6 Nov. 1975. 107 Interview with Frank O'Neill, 30 Jan. 2020. 108 *II*, 4 Feb. 1948 and 22 Apr. 1964.

away team won 6–0.[109] At that point, Bohemians were able to secure the visit of the best English sides, with FA Cup winners Manchester United (1948), Wolves (1949) and Arsenal (1950) visiting in consecutive seasons.[110] Benefit matches also brought English teams to Dublin. In June of 1947, Drumcondra FC hosted Stoke City at Dalymount Park in a benefit match for centre-half Kevin Clarke, who had spent five years at the Dublin club.[111] In May 1959, Norwich City visited Dublin to play Shamrock Rovers in a joint benefit match for Paddy Ambrose and Gerry Mackey.[112]

The appointment of scouts with special knowledge of the game in Ireland, and particularly its Dublin players, became more common in the late twentieth century. By the early 1970s warehouse manager Bill Darby was established as Arsenal's Dublin scout.[113] Darby had previously managed Longford Town and coached Drogheda United and had been given a six-month scouting trial by Arsenal manager Bertie Mee while on his summer holidays in London in 1967.[114] He had convinced Arsenal chief scout Gordon Clarke that they needed a scout in Dublin to counteract the work of Manchester United's Billy Behan in recruiting players there and initially approached St Kevin's Boys' player Liam Brady with senior scout Malwyn Roberts and invited him for a trial at Arsenal in 1969.[115] Brady's older brothers Ray and Pat had played for QPR and Millwall, respectively, and Ray also played for the Republic of Ireland.[116] His great-uncle, Frank Senior, had played for Belfast Celtic and Glentoran in the Irish League, captained Fordsons, appeared for the Irish Free State team in the 1920s and also had spells in Wales and England.[117]

By November 1975, Arsenal had nine Irish players, including five first-team regulars. One reporter noted that the borough of Islington, where Highbury is located, was known as 'Little Dublin', with almost 30 per cent of its population registered as Irish.[118] The migration of Irish skilled workers to London after the Second World War, and to that area in particular, was noted as a factor in the latter figure. One of the borough's three MPs was a County Clare man, Michael O'Halloran, who attracted local support.[119] Along with Liam Brady, Frank Stapleton, John Devine and David O'Leary (born in Stoke Newingham, where his parents were working at the time before returning to Dublin to Bluebell), other Dublin recruits on their books at the time included Philip Fitzgerald from Kilmacud and Bobby Duffy, who, like Brady, was from the north-side area of Whitehall.[120] Future rugby international John Murphy, from Bray, was also at Highbury.[121] Not all of these

109 *EH*, 15 Oct. 1948 and *II*, 18 Oct. 1948. The selection was made up of north Dublin players although attempts had been made to procure a number of guest players including those from Racing Club de France.   **110** *II*, 2 May 1950.   **111** *II*, 3 June 1947.   **112** *EH*, 17 Apr. 1959.   **113** *II*, 2 Mar. 1973; *EH*, 6 Nov. 1975.   **114** *IP*, 10 May 1967.   **115** Liam Brady, *So far so good: a decade in football* (London, 1980), p. 16 and 'Brady pays tribute to Bill Darby', arsenal.com/news/brady-pays-tribute-bill-darby, accessed 13 May 2021.   **116** Brady, *So far so good*, p. 14.   **117** Ibid., and *FSW*, 7 Nov. 1925.   **118** *EH*, 6 Nov. 1975.   **119** Ibid.   **120** Ibid. and *ST*, 31 Jan. 1998.   **121** *STE*, 31 Jan. 1998.

players broke into the first team and Stapleton, who played his schoolboy soccer with Bolton Athletic of Ringsend, later wrote that he had 'lots of ups and downs' in his first season at Highbury although he felt the apprentice system was good as it made players 'appreciate their position all the more'.[122] Stapleton grew up in Artane and Devine in the city centre in Jervis Street.[123] Following the departure of Stapleton and Brady in the early 1980s, O'Leary continued to play for the club, making 523 league appearances between 1975 and 1992 and 722 in total, a club record.[124] Fellow Dubliners Niall Quinn and Paul Gorman, both of whom were reared in Crumlin, did manage to break into the first team in the 1980s, but made less impact at the club, although Quinn later became an integral part of Republic of Ireland teams under Jack Charlton and Mick McCarthy.[125] Arsenal maintained a scout in Ireland into the early twenty-first century, with former player Joe Haverty taking up the role after Bill Darby.[126]

THE DEVELOPMENT OF SUPPORT IN DUBLIN FOR BRITISH CLUBS

Supporters' clubs had been present in Dublin earlier in the twentieth century, with Shelbourne supplying badges for their members early in 1928.[127] However, it was not until the second half of the 1900s that supporters' clubs for British teams became more common in Dublin, including Everton (1954), Glasgow Celtic (1966), Manchester United (1966), Liverpool (1970), Chelsea (1973) and Leeds United (1973).[128] Arsenal fans were meeting in the Theatre Bar on Monday evenings by the summer of 1973.[129] Despite this interest in a range of clubs, by the end of the twentieth century, support for Manchester United and Liverpool dwarfed that for other English clubs in Dublin. Affection for Glasgow Celtic also remained strong in Dublin, with 23,000 present for the visit of the 1967 European Cup winners in March 1968 for a friendly against Shamrock Rovers at Dalymount Park which ended in a two-all draw.[130]

The growth of support for Everton, then Manchester United and finally Liverpool within Dublin was also heavily linked to their success and fielding of Irish players. While Ireland-based supporters were eager to avail of the opportunity to see British and Irish players in the flesh when they visited Dublin, interest in some clubs naturally grew in line with Irish players' involvement in them. In contrasting Dublin with London and Liverpool, Liam Brady has written that Dublin is more comparable with the latter in that 'the people have a craving for

122 Frank Stapleton, *Frankly speaking* (Dublin, 1991), pp 8–9; *IP*, 25 May 1972.   123 *EH*, 6 Nov. 1975.   124 Barry J. Hugman (ed.), *The PFA Premier and Football League players' records, 1946–2005* (Harpenden, 2005), pp 76, 468, 583; 'David O'Leary', arsenal.com/historic/players/david-oleary, accessed 5 May 2021.   125 Hugman (ed.), *The PFA Premier and Football League players' records, 1946–2005*, pp 242, 507; *II*, 13 Nov. 1993; Niall Quinn, *The autobiography* (London, 2003), p. 17.   126 *TG*, 24 Feb. 2009.   127 *FSW*, 4 Feb. 1928.   128 *IP*, 4 Aug. 1954; *IE*, 3 June 1966; *EH*, 19 Dec. 1968, 22 July 1970, 6 Mar. 1973 and 12 Mar. 1973.   129 *EH*, 22 June 1973.   130 *II*, 19 Mar. 1968.

the game, a real need to be involved in it, to play it, discuss it, read about it, dream about it'.[131] Links between Irish cities and those in Britain had strengthened over a number of centuries through emigration and trade. In 1997, Liverpool and Dublin were twinned, illustrating the strong trading and cultural links between the two cities.[132] Despite the pull of North America in the nineteenth century, it was in Liverpool that many Irish migrants settled, whether consciously as a final destination or because it was simply where they ended up as they did not have the means to go any further.[133]

Surprisingly, however, despite the Irish presence in Liverpool, it was not until the latter half of the twentieth century that the popularity of Liverpool's two most famous soccer clubs, Everton and Liverpool, grew notably in the Republic of Ireland's capital. One Irish reporter commented in 1951 that Everton were 'the most interesting team in cross-Channel football as far as the home follower is concerned' as a result of seven Irish players appearing at various levels within the club.[134] Liverpool was beginning to lose its prominence as a destination for Irish migrants by the mid-twentieth century, with Enda Delaney noting that 'many of the new arrivals in the 1940s and 1950s went south'.[135] By the latter half of the 1900s, 'only London of the four nineteenth-century cities of Irish settlement (Glasgow, Manchester, Liverpool and London) retained its importance as a destination'.[136] However, with the success of both Liverpool and Everton in the late twentieth century, support was assured.

As Dublin's soccer culture grew, links between teams from the city and Liverpool were strengthened at senior, junior and underage level, with the fixture between the Liverpool Shipping League Champions and Concannon Cup holders Liverpool BISP and the Dublin team of the same company said to have been an annual one by May 1927.[137] Junior club Strandvilla's trip to Liverpool in April 1928 included matches against St Silvester's and St Peter's, while 'visits to big games in the afternoons, theatres in the evenings, gymnastics displays, concerts and a visit to Port Sunlight (to Lever Brothers) all helped to make the visit one to be remembered by all who participated'.[138] Before leaving for home, the Dublin club presented Mr Cullerton of St Silvester's 'with a handsome dressing case as a memento of their visit and as a recognition of all the work done by him on their behalf'.[139] As they left Lime Street Station, 'several hundred assembled ... to wish the Villa God Speed'.[140] In April 1935 three Dublin teams visited England for matches at Easter weekend, with Queen's Park playing against Miranda, while the Liverpool Boys' Brigade took on the Dublin Battalion and Inchicore United played Wallasey Combination champions Ash Villa.[141] In March 1952, Everton agreed to pay the hotel charges for Dublin club Castlevilla, who were undertaking a short Easter tour to Liverpool. They also decided to arrange a game between the club

131 Brady, *So far so good*, p. 19. 132 *IT*, 14 Feb. 1997. 133 Ibid. 134 *EH*, 12 Dec. 1951. 135 Enda Delaney, *The Irish in post-war Britain* (Oxford, 2013), pp 95–6. 136 Ibid., p. 95. 137 *FSW*, 21 May 1927. 138 *FSW*, 18 Feb. and 21 Apr. 1928. 139 *FSW* 21 Apr. 1928. 140 Ibid. 141 *IP*, 23 Apr. 1935.

and Everton's junior team for Easter Monday at Goodison Park.[142] In the 1950s, home and away matches between the Liverpool County FA youth team and the FAI's youth selection were regularly staged, with the fixtures introduced in 1948 and run annually until 1961.[143]

Jon Murden has written that the domestic success of Liverpool and Everton in the 1960s boosted the city's image and both clubs' performances 'provided a source of tremendous pride to the city during the 1970s and 1980s – a time when it seemed that little else was going Liverpool's way'.[144] While Everton built on earlier success and won further First Division championships and FA Cups in the 1960s and 1980s, it was in the 1970s and 1980s that Liverpool came to dominate European football, winning four European Cups and two UEFA Cups along with eleven First Division championships, three FA Cups and four League Cups in these two decades.[145] In turn, by the early twenty-first century, support for Liverpool within Dublin completely outweighed that for Everton. In particular, in August 2017, following Liverpool's friendly with Athletic Bilbao at the Aviva Stadium in Dublin, Liverpool manager Jurgen Klopp stated that 'it was really special today, I have heard about it – that Dublin is quite an LFC city – but it is completely different to feel it'.[146] Klopp was referring to the level of support for his club at the match, with Liverpool's status as the 'home' club reflected in the match programme and the singing of 'You'll Never Walk Alone' by the majority of a near sell-out crowd directly before kick-off. The following year they returned and defeated Napoli 5–0 before another largely partisan crowd.[147]

David Kennedy has noted that Everton were the first English team to have a supporters' club in Ireland.[148] Despite this, Everton appear to have initially been reluctant to travel to Dublin for friendly matches. At a meeting of directors held at Goodison Park in April 1910, an application to send a team to Dublin on 25 April was turned down.[149] Two years later they also turned down an invitation to send a team to Ireland for a benefit match for Shelbourne.[150] In 1913, the directors declined an application for a collection to be taken at Goodison Park 'in aid of the sufferers through the Dublin strike'.[151] They also turned down an offer from Bohemians for a match in February 1919 and, in November 1925, an application

142 Everton Football Club Minute Book, 17 Oct. 1950–19 Oct. 1953, Meeting held in Exchange Hotel Liverpool, 4 Mar. 1952, p. 149, evertoncollection.org.uk, accessed 11 May 2018. 143 *EH*, 13 May 1948; *IP*, 15 May 1954; *IE*, 22 May 1961. 144 Jon Murden, 'City of change and challenge: Liverpool since 1945' in John Belchem (ed.), *Liverpool 800: culture, character and history* (Liverpool, 2006), pp 393–45, p. 462. 145 John Williams, *Reds: Liverpool Football Club: the biography* (Edinburgh, 2010), pp 342–80. 146 *II*, 6 Aug. 2017. 147 *II*, 6 Aug. 2018. 148 David Kennedy, 'Red and blue and orange and green', *Soccer and Society*, 12:4 (2011), pp 552–64, p. 558. 149 Everton Football Club Minute Book, 14 Dec. 1909–28 Mar. 1911, Meeting of directors held at Goodison Park on 10 Apr. 1910, p. 91, evertoncollection.org.uk, accessed 11 May 2018. 150 Everton Football Club Minute Book, 4 Apr. 1911–26 Nov. 1912, Meeting of directors held at Goodison Park, 13 Feb. 1912, p. 162, evertoncollection.org.uk, accessed 11 May 2018. 151 Everton Football Club Minute Book, 29 Nov. 1912–4 May 1914, Meeting of the directors held at Goodison Park, 15 Oct. 1913, pp 173–4, evertoncollection.org.uk, accessed 11 May 2018.

from the Football Association of the Irish Free State to play a match in Dublin that season was refused.[152] However, in March 1928 they agreed to play a Leinster League selection on Easter Monday 'for a guarantee of £300 and half-gate over £600', but this did not become a regular occurrence at this time, with a similar request turned down two years later.[153] The match, held in April 1928, saw 1927–8 First Division champions Everton win by three goals to two with William Ralph '"Dixie" Dean the cynosure of all eyes' while home goalkeeper Harry Cannon was 'at the top of his form and enhanced his already fine reputation'.[154] Afterwards, Mr Gibbons of Everton presented Michael Hayden, the captain of St Joseph's (Cabra) Deaf Mutes FC, with an autographed football.[155] The Leinster FA entertained the Everton team and officials to dinner and musical entertainment, while there was also some political involvement through the presence of Osmond Grattan Esmonde, who presided at the event, and Alfie Byrne.[156]

It was not until the post-Second World War years that Everton showed more interest in playing friendly matches against Dublin opposition. In September 1947, they easily defeated Bohemians at home, with the Dublin-based players said to be 'tired by night travel' and a 'day of sightseeing'.[157] By May 1948, some English teams were appearing more regularly in Ireland to play friendly matches, with the Merseyside club, Manchester United, Newcastle United, Charlton Athletic and Luton Town arriving for fixtures against League of Ireland teams.[158] Shelbourne's friendly versus Notts County was reportedly part of a deal in which Eddie Gannon signed for the English club, a practice in the organization of these matches which at times strengthened links between British and Irish clubs.[159] Charlton Athletic's match versus Drumcondra was a benefit for the home side's half-back, Billy Mulville.[160] Mick Meagan recalled the attraction of these friendly matches:

> They were matches that we always looked forward to. You always got the best of the English sides coming over or maybe an English selection, with Irish lads thrown in on top of it, and we always, always made our way to Dalymount, once the matches were on. Now you got Matthews, Finney and

---

152 Everton Football Club Minute Book, 4 Feb. 1919–15 Feb. 1921, Meeting of directors held at the Bradford Hotel, Liverpool, on 25 Feb. 1919, p. 9, evertoncollection.org.uk, accessed 11 May 2018 and Everton Football Club Minute Book, 11 Dec. 1924–11 Jan. 1927, Meeting of directors held at Exchange Station Hotel on Tuesday 10 Nov. 1925, p. 137, evertoncollection.org.uk, accessed 11 May 2018. **153** Everton Football Club Minute Book, 25 Jan. 1927–15 Mar. 1929, Meeting of directors held at Exchange Station Hotel on Tuesday 13 Mar. 1928, p. 80, evertoncollection.org.uk, accessed 11 May 2018, and Everton Football Club Minute Book, 19 Mar. 1929–7 Apr. 1931, Meeting of directors held at Exchange Station Hotel, Tuesday 30 Sept. 1930, p. 231, evertoncollection.org.uk, accessed 11 May 2018. **154** *FSW*, 7 Apr. 1928. **155** *FSW*, 21 Apr. 1928. **156** *FSW*, 14 Apr. 1928. See also *IP*, 16 Jan. 1934. Bohemians attempted to bring Everton to Dublin that year but it appears they could not fulfil the fixture. **157** *II*, 9 Sept. 1947. **158** *II*, 16 Apr. 1948; *IP*, 15 May 1948. **159** Sands, *Shels*, p. 65. See also Fitzpatrick, *Shelbourne cult heroes*, p. 124. Manchester United's friendly against Shelbourne in 1974 'was part of the transfer deal' that brought Paddy Roche and Ray O'Brien to Old Trafford. **160** *II*, 16 Apr. 1948.

all these fellas coming over in those years, Billy Wright, all great, and of course, you had to go and see them.[161]

At times, English players guested for Irish teams, including Sam Bartram of Charlton Athletic, who appeared for a Shelbourne selection against Manchester United at Dalymount Park in May 1948.[162] Guest players often appeared for the home team, although Shelbourne chose to field their full team in a benefit match for Peter Keely against Everton in 1948.[163] The visit of Stanley Matthews to Dublin to appear as a guest player on a Bohemians selection in a friendly against Chelsea, shortly after he had won the FA Cup with Blackpool in early May 1953, was said to ensure that a crowd of 20,000 would be at Dalymount Park.[164] W.P. Murphy of the *Irish Independent* noted the esteem in which the England international was held:

> Last week a man turned up at Dalymount Park to buy two stand tickets. He had never been to a soccer game in his life but his wife wanted to see Stanley Matthews. That is the spirit, which, I reckon, will swell the throngs at Dalymount Park tonight, when Matthews will play in a Bohemian jersey. Incidentally, Bohemians have a new set of togs for this occasion, with white shirts and blue pants against the blue shirts and white pants of the Chelsea side.[165]

Matthews had also appeared for a Drumcondra selection against Distillery at Dalymount Park in a benefit match for Paddy Daly in 1947 and had turned 'a drab and uninteresting affair' into 'a near classic' through his skill.[166] In 1949, a Home Farm selection featuring a number of English internationals, including Ted Ditchburn and Nat Lofthouse, who was man of the match, played Glasgow Celtic in an exhibition match to raise funds for the Dublin club.[167] Naturally, Dublin clubs also continued to visit Britain for friendly matches, with Shelbourne taking part in the Festival of Britain tournament at the end of the 1950–1 season.[168] This was held to commemorate the Battle of Britain, with the Dublin team meeting Darlington, Crewe Alexandra, Chester and Bangor. Apparently some of the Shelbourne players brought their own food as they were concerned about post-war rationing in Britain, while the fears of some Irish players that they would be imprisoned for failing to complete military service having previously been registered with the British forces did not come to pass.[169] Manchester United's Tommy Hamilton returned to Dublin in 1953 having been conscripted and later stated that 'as an Irishman, I didn't like this idea and every effort was made to get me off military service – without success'.[170]

161 Interview with Mick Meagan, 30 Sept. 2019. 162 *IP*, 17 May 1948. 163 Sands, *Shels*, p. 65. 164 *II*, 8 May 1953. 165 Ibid. 166 *IP*, 15 Apr. 1947. 167 Menton, *Home Farm*, pp 36–7. 168 Sands, *Shels*, pp 73–4. 169 Ibid. 170 *Charles Buchan's Football Monthly*, 115 (Mar. 1961), p. 43.

By the late 1940s Everton had begun to include Irish players in their first team in greater numbers and travelled to Ireland to play in Dublin, Dundalk, Limerick and Waterford in 1948 with a squad including Irish internationals Peter Farrell, Alex Stevenson and Tommy Eglington.[171] Eglington and Farrell had joined Everton from Shamrock Rovers in 1946 in a move costing £7,000 spread over three years.[172] In the summer of 1949 Everton played a number of matches in Dundalk, Dublin, Cork and Sligo as part of another tour and in May 1953 they beat then junior club Home Farm 4–1 in an exhibition match watched by 20,000 spectators at Dalymount Park.[173] Everton noted 'the playing and social success' of the 1949 tour at a meeting of the board in May of that year.[174] Naturally, these types of fixtures were also organized to benefit the club as a business, with accommodation fees, expenses and part of the gate provided, and in 1954, the club visited Dublin, Waterford and Limerick for matches, although it appears they fielded their reserves.[175]

The ability to attract British opposition at times came through Irish connections living in Britain, with Dr Kevin O'Flanagan playing a significant part in this for Home Farm, who were only a junior and schoolboy club in the post-war years.[176] In the 1950s and 1960s the Dublin club were able to put on fundraising matches against clubs such as Aberdeen, Glasgow Celtic, Everton, Leicester and Manchester United.[177] Despite this, supporters in Dublin who wanted to see a more competitive level of soccer involving an English team generally had to travel abroad. In April 1954 the Dublin public had 'the unusual experience of seeing two English clubs in opposition' there, with a Luton Town selection that included Irish internationals Dunne, Aherne and Cummins taking on Blackburn Rovers, who were managed by Johnny Carey.[178] This Irish involvement was said to have given the teams 'a real Irish flavour' and took place in aid of rehabilitation of tuberculosis patients. Both teams, then in the Second Division, were welcomed at the Mansion House by the lord mayor of Dublin, Alderman Bernard Butler.[179] However, the visit of British teams was generally only an annual or seasonal occurrence and was not enough to sustain those who were beginning to favour watching English clubs.

At this point, Everton supporters in Ireland were also travelling to England for matches. In January 1954, one reporter claimed that 'nearly 2,000 Everton-minded Irishmen from Dublin, Dundalk, Drogheda and Waterford made the pilgrimage' to Goodison Park to see Everton beat Swansea.[180] Prior to the 1954 World Cup

---

171 *IE*, 6 May 1948; *IP*, 15 May 1948.   172 *Soccer Reporter* (Mar. 1981), p. 15.   173 *IP*, 9 May 1949; *EH*, 23 and 24 May 1949; *II*, 24 May 1949 and 6 and 7 May 1953.   174 Everton Football Club Minute Book, 1 Apr. 1947–11 Oct. 1950, Meeting held at Exchange Hotel, Liverpool, 26 May 1949, evertoncollection.org.uk, accessed 13 May 2018.   175 See, for example, Everton Football Club Minute Book, 17 Oct. 1950–19 Oct. 1953, Meeting held at Exchange Hotel, 28 Apr. 1953, p. 257, evertoncollection.org.uk, accessed 11 May 2018; Everton Football Club Minute Book, 27 Oct. 1953–30 Oct. 1956, Meeting held at Exchange Hotel, 4 May 1954, p. 55, evertoncollection.org.uk, accessed 11 May 2018; and *Irish Press*, 15 May 1954.   176 Menton, *Home Farm*, p. 36.   177 Ibid., pp 36–7.   178 *II*, 30 Apr. 1954.   179 Ibid.   180 *SI*, 31 Jan. 1954.

in Switzerland, the Everton Supporters' Federation was advertising trips to the tournament in Irish newspapers.[181] In August of that year, a Dublin branch of this organization was established after a visit from two officials of the Federation, with the 'many Irish stars' on Everton's books, such as Farrell, Eglington and Jimmy O'Neill, noted.[182]A few months later, it was reported that 'hundreds' of the Dublin branch saw Everton beat Sunderland at Goodison Park with 'Liverpool Irishman' Tony McNamara (who was born there) scoring the winner.[183] Everton director Dick Cyril had connections in Dublin and in total, nine Irish-born players broke into their first team between 1945 and 1955.[184]

Throughout 1956, the Dublin branch of the Everton Supporters' Federation, which had its headquarters at 22 Henry Street, made regular excursions to Goodison Park for matches.[185] One reporter claimed that year that 'the Liverpool Irish' were among the club's 'most enthusiastic supporters', with their home ground, Goodison Park, where Ireland had beaten England in 1949, apparently also having a special connection with the Irish on account of this victory.[186] In 1957, Everton defeated Drumcondra 7–1 in a friendly at Tolka Park, but by then Mick Meagan was the only Irish-born player who appeared in the team.[187] He had been spotted playing in an Irish Youths' match against a Liverpool selection by scout Howard Pickering and joined Everton in 1952.[188] He recalled when interviewed that trips home for matches were a lot easier as the pressure was less intense. In 1957, the players stayed at the Gresham Hotel and enjoyed a trip to a horse riding school at Stepaside while in Dublin for the Drumcondra match.[189] While Meagan did win the First Division Championship in 1963, the club were less successful in Europe and did not win a European trophy until 1985.[190] They did return to play in Dublin sporadically, but not with the regularity of the 1950s. In addition, a failure of Irish-born players to emerge in the team as they had done in that decade appears to have later afforded room for more support for Manchester United and Liverpool to develop within Dublin.

The work of Gavin Mellor has illustrated how Manchester United's popularity grew with the club's European Cup victory in 1968 and that this was more significant in the club's evolution into a 'super-club', along with British social, cultural and economic changes, than the Munich Disaster of 1958.[191] However, due to the club's Irish links, with the signing of players such as Liam Whelan and Joe Carolan in the 1950s, the club was highly popular in Dublin before their first European Cup final win.[192]

In October 1959 a Manchester United youth team featuring Johnny Giles were hosted by Home Farm at Tolka Park.[193] It was noted that 'Home Farm and the

181 *II*, 12 Mar. 1954.   182 *IP*, 4 Aug. 1954.   183 *SI*, 17 Oct. 1954.   184 Curran, *Irish soccer migrants*, p. 142.   185 See, for example, *SI*, 9 Dec. 1956.   186 *IP*, 29 Feb. 1956.   187 *II*, 11 Aug. 1958.   188 Interview with Mick Meagan, 30 Sept. 2019.   189 Ibid.   190 'Honours', evertonfc.com/honours, accessed 3 Jan. 2017.   191 Gavin Mellor, 'The genesis of Manchester United as a national and international "super-club", 1958–68', *Soccer and Society*, 1:2 (2000), pp 151–66, p. 151.   192 *IE*, 22 Nov. 1958.   193 *II*, 19 Oct. 1959.

spectators are assured of seeing stars, for among them, the Manchester team have gained an impressive collection of English, Scottish, Welsh and Irish youth and schoolboy international honours'.[194] Home Farm had recently beaten a German youths' selection by 4–3 at Tolka Park in a match that reportedly 'provided all the glorious football and excitement that one could wish for'.[195] By the middle of the 1960s, Manchester United had four Irish-born players in their squad, these being Pat Dunne, Tony Dunne, Eamon Dunphy and Noel Cantwell, while Manchester-born Shay Brennan was a future Irish international who was also on their books at that time.[196] The club also had an Irish scout who had been there as a player, former Shamrock Rovers and Shelbourne goalkeeper Billy Behan, who later became a manager and referee.[197] He had played one league game for the Old Trafford club, then in the Second Division, in the early 1930s and was able to establish a significant enough connection to later become the club's scout in Ireland, having tipped them off about Johnny Carey later in that decade.[198] Behan later helped recruit players such as Liam Whelan, John Giles and Paul McGrath but turned down the offer to join the club's permanent Old Trafford staff as his Manchester-born wife wanted to remain in Dublin.[199] In June 1966, a Manchester United Supporters' Club 'affiliated to the London and District branch' was established in Dublin.[200] Naturally, the Dublin and national press also contributed to the growth in interest in clubs such as Manchester United, with the *Evening Herald* publishing a series of interviews with Behan about the club's history in the months following their 1968 European Cup final win.[201]

THE IMPACT OF TELEVISED ENGLISH MATCHES AND IRISH PLAYERS' SUCCESS

As journalist Keith Falkiner has noted, the presence of Dublin-born Steve Heighway in the Liverpool team in the 1970s, Liverpool's European success and the advent of live televised matches in the previous decade all brought added interest in Liverpool FC in the Republic of Ireland.[202] In 1968, Liverpool FC supporters' club received the John White Cup, named after a Tottenham Hotspur player killed when he was struck by lightning while playing golf. This award followed voting by a panel headed by Alan Hardaker, the English Football League's secretary, with the *Irish Press* noting that there was 'a high number of Irish in their Spion Kop "choir"'.[203] While it is difficult to establish exactly how many Irish fans were travelling to England specifically as supporters of cross-Channel teams on a decade-by-decade basis, some assertions can be made about the 1970s. The decline of support in the League of Ireland in the late 1960s and early 1970s can be linked

---

194 Ibid.   195 Ibid.   196 *II*, 12 Jan. 1965.   197 Ibid.; *EH*, 16 July 1968.   198 *Soccer Reporter* (Oct. 1982), p. 3; Joyce, *Football League players' records*, p. 22.   199 *Soccer Reporter* (Oct. 1982), p. 3; *SI*, 27 Sept. 1998.   200 *IE*, 3 June 1966.   201 *EH*, 16 July 1968.   202 Keith Falkiner, *Emerald Anfield: the Irish and Liverpool FC* (Dublin, 2010), pp 69–108, 187–92.   203 *IP*, 6 Dec. 1968.

to the advent of televised English league matches, with the Football Association of Ireland's commission reporting in 1973 that attendances at League of Ireland matches had reduced by 60 per cent over the previous four years.[204]

Live coverage of English matches, in turn, added to more interest in English football in Ireland and this exposure saw some shipping lines offering special excursion prices for English matches. The Republic of Ireland's national television broadcaster, Teilifís Éireann, came on air in 1961 and showed the 1965 FA Cup final between Liverpool and Leeds United while the match was also available in Dublin and some other regions as part of BBC's *Grandstand* coverage.[205] Irish newspaper readers were alerted to the fact that John Giles would be playing for Leeds United, thereby increasing the attraction of English football, with 'Irish interest in the FA Cup final' said to be 'high' as a result of this national linkage.[206] By the latter part of that decade, viewers in the east and border areas could avail of fifty minutes of 'a top soccer league match' on *Match of the Day*, broadcast on the BBC on Saturday nights, while highlights of international fixtures on UTV were also becoming more regular.[207] In 1967, around 80 per cent of homes in urban areas had television sets although in some parts of rural Ireland the rate was only 25 per cent. However, by 1980 'there were few parts of the country where television was not a part of a majority of the people's daily lives'.[208]

Dave Russell has written that in Britain from the 1960s to the 1980s, 'more people experienced the game through television, and indeed the media in general, than through attendance at live matches'.[209] In addition, 'this shaped perceptions, loyalties and attitudes in a number of crucial ways' as 'the game's leading sides gained an increasingly glamorous image and a growing band of adherents'.[210] However, he also notes how 'images of a sport blighted by hooliganism lowered the game's status and standing' by the mid-1980s.[211]

By the early 1960s, there was much comment about people in England deserting their local teams for the glamour of big-city teams, particularly around Manchester and Liverpool. One writer in the *Economist* stated at the end of 1960 that

> professional football is no longer a sport, it is an entertainment … the day of the cloth-capped, faithful supporter of the local professional team has passed. Now he can afford to travel to the nearest city to see a really good game – or to watch one on television (screening of star matches for a fat fee should be part of the League's reforms) – the old-fashioned fan has not so much died as been transported to a higher sphere.[212]

With the improvement in prosperity in the Republic of Ireland in the 1960s, consumerism and upward mobility may have influenced the decision of spectators to

204 *IE*, 29 Dec. 1979. 205 *IP*, 1 May 1965. 206 Ibid. 207 Curran, *Irish soccer migrants*, p. 54. 208 Brown, *Ireland: a social and cultural history*, p. 249. 209 Dave Russell, *Football and the English* (Preston, 1997), p. 181. 210 Ibid. 211 Ibid. 212 *The Economist*, 31 Dec. 1960. I am grateful to Professor Dilwyn Porter for this information and reference.

seek a higher level of soccer elsewhere. Terence Brown has written that 'ostentatious consumption in a society enjoying a rapid rise in its standard of living marked the late 1960s and '70s in Ireland'.[213] Although excursion trips from Dublin to matches in England had been available much earlier, with day trips and longer excursions, via Holyhead, advertised in the Dublin press for the FA Cup final at Wembley in the late 1920s, it was not until much later that more regular trips really took off.[214] Some clubs had also organized prize draws for tickets for big matches in Britain, including Shamrock Rovers, who arranged a trip for two people to the FA Cup final at Wembley as part of a fundraiser for a new stand in 1928.[215] By the late 1950s, FA Cup final tickets remained difficult to obtain for those living in Ireland as they were distributed through clubs and not available on general sale, despite one Ballsbridge resident enquiring about their availability through the Irish embassy in London, although obviously relatives and other connections living in England may have been able to help some supporters.[216] It was later in the twentieth century that travel companies began arranging excursions to matches in England regularly. In 1971, journalist Seán Ryan noted how the B&I ferry company was benefitting from 'the tremendous interest Irish fans have in cross-channel soccer' by providing a 'football excursion' service from Dublin to Liverpool every Friday night, with the return trip on Sunday mornings.[217] B&I Press Officer Frank Nealis stated that during the 1969–70 season 10,000 Irish fans had made the journey, with most of them attending the matches of the Liverpool and Manchester clubs. He also noted that 'many of the men bring their wives, who go shopping while the men are at the match'.[218]

Nealis felt that the effect an Irish player at a club could have on attracting fans from Ireland was 'vitally important', with some fans enquiring if they could do a day trip to London after Paddy Mulligan joined Chelsea in 1969. However, Nealis stated that they generally waited 'until the London club visits either Liverpool or Manchester to see their favourite in action'.[219] Ryan noted that 'the top draw' in 1971 was Manchester United, followed by Liverpool, Manchester City and then Everton. More significantly, it was stated by Nealis that 'there was a traditional Irish support for Everton, but in latter years there's been a swing towards Liverpool, and Steve Heighway is going to become one of those draws'.[220] Indeed, by 1980 Heighway was being described as 'one of the biggest names in Irish and Liverpool soccer during the seventies'.[221] He had moved to England as a 10-year-old and apparently 'didn't kick a football until he was twelve years of age'. While completing a BA in economics and politics at Warwick University he played regularly for Skelmersdale United who, in the late 1960s, were 'not only the top amateur outfit on Merseyside but among the top amateur teams in Britain'. He signed for

213 Brown, *Ireland: a social and cultural history, 1922–2002*, p. 248. **214** *FSW*, 24 Apr. 1926, 9 Apr. 1927 and 21 Apr. 1928. **215** Ibid., 7 Jan. and 14 Apr. 1928. **216** Enquiry re tickets for football cup final at Wembley (1957). Letter from T. Woods, secretary to the Minister for External Affairs, to Patrick Ryan, 16 Apr. 1957, NAI, Department of Foreign Affairs. 6/410/260. **217** *II*, 26 Jan. 1971. **218** Ibid. **219** Ibid. **220** Ibid. **221** *IP*, 14 Mar. 1980.

Liverpool in February 1970 and quickly became a member of the first team, going on to achieve European and domestic success.[222]

In December 1973, one reporter estimated that more than 500 Irish fans, many of whom were from Dublin and Belfast, had travelled on the B&I Ferry from Dublin to Liverpool, for the Liverpool-Everton derby and Manchester United's home match at Old Trafford that same weekend, and noted that the average fan made six of these weekend trips per season.[223] By the middle of that decade, B&I Ferries were offering 'Football Specials' from Dublin to Liverpool for matches involving Manchester United, Liverpool, Everton, Birmingham City, Leeds United and Manchester City while they also provided day and weekend excursions from Cork to Swansea for Bristol City and Bristol Rovers.[224] It is difficult to define when exactly Irish supporters began to travel to matches in England in vast numbers and on a regular basis, but supporters' clubs were key to organizing trips. In addition, many of those travelling would have had family and friends in England, given the scale of Irish migration there.[225] This meant having someone to go to the match with and somewhere to stay.

A Liverpool supporters' club was operational in Dublin by the summer of 1970.[226] In April 1976 they held a dinner dance in the city and with the growing success of the club in the late 1970s, travel to England for matches became more popular.[227] In 1978 the *Irish Press* estimated that around 450 supporters left Dublin for the European Cup final between Liverpool and Bruges at Wembley. This was said to exceed the numbers who travelled the week before for the FA Cup final, in which a (then) record seven Irish players were involved in the Ipswich Town and Arsenal teams.[228] By 1987, the Liverpool FC Dublin supporters' club was said to have more than 150 members, with monthly meetings taking place and trips to Anfield organized 'on a regular basis'.[229] In addition, a branch had been set up in Waterford in 1972 'by a group of ardent supporters who used to travel regularly to Anfield' with a view to organizing transport and tickets. They were said to be making six trips per season to Anfield by the late 1980s and held monthly meetings along with hosting 'highly successful quiz nights'.[230] In Cork, a branch was established in 1983, with around 130 members having enrolled by 1987. Their main activity were said to be 'the regular trips to Anfield which are very well supported, with in excess of 40 travelling each time', while they also held monthly meetings and quizzes. These three branches were structured administratively with a secretary, treasurer and chairman, while the Dublin and Cork branches also had committees.[231]

While Irish clubs had been involved in European competitions since the late 1950s, by the late twentieth century Irish soccer supporters could look forward

222 Ibid. 223 *SI*, 9 Dec. 1973. 224 *II*, 24 Sept. 1976. 225 *II*, 16 Mar. 1974. 226 *EH*, 22 July 1970. 227 *EH*, 14 Apr. 1976. 228 *IP*, 10 May 1978. 229 'Liverpool Clubs in the Republic' in *Ireland Olympic XI versus Liverpool official programme*, 19 Aug. 1987 (Dublin, 1987), p. 22. 230 Ibid. 231 Ibid.

to visits from Liverpool FC for friendlies held in the summer or later in the new season in the days before Premier League clubs began to branch out to the USA, Asia and Australia for the marketing-orientated tours. Liverpool had played competitively in the Republic of Ireland by the end of 1960s, with Dundalk defeated four–nil in the second leg of a European Fairs Cup tie in 1969.[232] They played a Bohemians selection in a friendly in May 1962 at Dalymount Park and Limerick a few days later at Markets Field.[233] Liverpool also met Drumcondra in a friendly at Tolka Park in February 1963 during the 'Big Freeze' and they also took on a League of Ireland selection at Dalymount Park in the summer of 1970 in a friendly.[234] While the 1963 match had been poorly attended as it was rescheduled after being called off for twenty-four hours due to heavy snow, the 1970 match was notable as one reporter recorded that the

> hardest thing to understand was the Dublin crowd's insistence on clamouring 'Liverpool, Liverpool'. Even when the Liverpudlians were being made to look much less than great, by a League of Ireland team, which showed penetration in attack and maturity in defence, the Irish team's efforts went unlauded.[235]

It was not until the late 1970s that their visits became more frequent. With the onset of the Troubles, Dublin was a safer and more congenial place to play a friendly than in Belfast. A few weeks after winning the European Cup in 1978 the club announced that they would be visiting Dublin to take on a League of Ireland selection as part of a four-game European tour, with club secretary Peter Robinson stating that they had 'tremendous support' in Ireland and 'with the transfer market as it is at present, they were now anxious to foster associations with Ireland with a view to young players'.[236] He also felt that as Ireland was 'now potentially the best market for young players in the future they would be keeping a close eye on League of Ireland football'.[237] While it is unclear why it took them so long to realize the potential of League of Ireland players, it is not unreasonable to suggest that the club had one eye on the recruitment policies of Arsenal and Manchester United in their selection of Irish players in that decade.

Earlier that year, they had bought three players from Dundalk – Synan Braddish, Derek Carroll and Brian Duff – for a total of £55,000, although none of them managed to break into the first team.[238] While there is some indication that these three players were bought 'as corporation tax write-offs' by then manager Bob Paisley, it is evident that Liverpool were beginning to give first-team league football to more Irish-born players by the early 1980s.[239] It appears that there was a change in Liverpool's recruitment policy towards the end of the 1970s, with

232 *IP*, 1 Oct. 1969. 233 'Games for the 1962–1963 season', lfchistory.net/SeasonArchive/ Games/4, accessed 29 Dec. 2017. 234 *II*, 7 Feb. 1963; *IP*, 31 July 1970. 235 *IP*, 1 Aug. 1970. 236 *II*, 22 July 1978. 237 Ibid. 238 *EH*, 24 Apr. 1978. 239 Ian Herbert, *Quiet genius: Bob Paisley, British football's greatest manager* (London, 2018), pp 160–1.

Ronnie Whelan signed from Home Farm in 1979 to join three former Dundalk players at the club, while in 1983 Brian Mooney and Ken DeMange were also signed from Home Farm.[240] League of Ireland president Donie O'Halloran said the 1978 friendly was 'potentially the biggest money spinner ever organized by the League and they hoped to attract at least 25,000 fans to Lansdowne Road'.[241] The *Irish Press* stated that the match, a 3–1 victory for the Anfield side, was like a home game for Liverpool with the majority of supporters dressed in red and white, the reporter noting that Liverpool was Ireland's 'second capital'.[242]

Although other clubs such as Leeds United also attracted support in Dublin – they visited the city as part of Shelbourne's 75th anniversary celebrations in the 1970–1 season and at that point John Giles had become well-established in their team – Liverpool's European Cup and domestic success later in that decade strengthened their appeal greatly.[243] It would appear from the above evidence that Liverpool's success in domestic and European football in the 1970s had a strong impact on the club's support in Dublin and, in particular, the welcome they received in the 1978 friendly is illustrative of this, and afterwards visits to Dublin became more regular. In the period from 1978 until 2000, Liverpool visited the Republic of Ireland on an almost annual basis to play friendlies against League of Ireland clubs and international selections. In 1979 they played a League of Ireland selection at Dalymount Park, while two years later they played an Irish international selection at Tolka Park.[244] They also played Dundalk in 1980 at Lansdowne Road and appeared twice at Tolka Park the following year, playing Home Farm in the summer and later that year an Irish XI.[245] Despite the playing surface being damaged the night before the Home Farm game as part of the ongoing protest against conditions for Republican prisoners in the Maze prison in Northern Ireland, the match went ahead, with Ronnie Whelan scoring Liverpool's first goal.[246] In 1982 they played Shamrock Rovers at Glenmalure Park.[247] Liverpool also played Home Farm in 1984 and, despite being banned from European competitions along with other English clubs after the Heysel Stadium Disaster of 1985 in which thirty-nine Italian fans died, returned to the Republic of Ireland to take on an Ireland XI in Cork in 1986 and an Irish Olympic selection at Lansdowne Road in August 1987 in friendly matches.[248] Friendly matches abroad involving English teams had also been banned by FIFA in 1985, but this was rescinded shortly afterwards.[249] Stephen McGuinness recalled the 1984 game as a memorable part of his childhood:

240 *IE*, 24 Sept. 1979; *EH*, 10 Aug. 1983.   241 *II*, 22 July 1978.   242 *IP*, 3 Aug. 1978.   243 Sands, *Shels*, pp 113–14.   244 Seán Creedon, 'Previous meetings' in *Ireland Olympic XI versus Liverpool official programme*, p. 14; 'Games for the 1980–1981 season', lfchistory.net/SeasonArchive/Games/22, accessed 29 Dec. 2017; 'Games for the 1981–1982 season', lfchistory.net/SeasonArchive/Games/24, accessed 29 Dec. 2017.   245 Creedon, 'Previous meetings', p. 14.   246 Kevin Brannigan, 'Ronnie Whelan's homecoming during the tumultuous summer of 1981', the42.ie/ronnie-whelan-liverpool–1981–ireland–5292252-Dec2020, accessed 25 Aug. 2021.   247 'Games for the 1982–1983 season', lfchistory.net/SeasonArchive/Games/23, accessed 29 Dec. 2017.   248 Ibid.; *IE*, 21 Aug. 1984.   249 *TG*, 2 June 2020.

I was very, very lucky to go to them Dublin games, and my first image or first time of seeing football at a decent level was then. We queued in Finglas village to get tickets to go and see Liverpool. They'd just won the European Cup and they played Home Farm. We wouldn't have had a huge amount of money at the time and I remember we couldn't afford a taxi. We had to walk from our house to Tolka, which is quite a walk from Finglas, and walk home. And I still remember the walk there and the one thing that still strikes me is when I walked up into Tolka Park and when you came up, I just couldn't believe how big the pitch was, the place was packed. And then seeing the European Cup – the one thing I do vividly remember is the gold on the inside of the cup when they brought it out, you could see the gold inside it, and that was the thing that just struck me. But I was in awe of the stadium, I was in awe of the noise, I was in awe of everything. And that was my first experience of seeing it and luckily – Home Farm had got Liverpool involved a couple of times, and I think there'd been a couple of players that transferred across from Home Farm and it became – it wasn't every year – but it was a bit of a ritual where Liverpool would come and play Home Farm.[250]

The Hillsborough Disaster of 15 April 1989, in which ninety-seven Liverpool supporters lost their lives at the FA Cup semi-final against Nottingham Forest, was marked later that month by some supporters' clubs in Ireland. In Cork, a Mass was organized by the local branch of the Liverpool supporters' club and took place at St Francis's Church in Liberty Street.[251] A special Mass was held at the Pro-Cathedral in Dublin, at which 'red scarves also bedecked the altar', with 'thousands' reported to have attended.[252] It was also noted that

> The air was heavy with incense and sorrow as the people bowed their heads in the huge cathedral. The chief celebrant of the Mass was the Archbishop of Dublin, Most Rev Desmond Connell, who said there was no other diocese so closely linked with that of Liverpool.[253]

An RTÉ news report claimed that due to a scarcity of tickets that only around 100 supporters from Ireland had travelled to the match.[254] In 2016, an oak tree was planted in Phoenix Park at a special memorial service which was organized by Paddy Browne of the Dublin 15 Liverpool supporters' club and Cherry Orchard resident Lisa Maher.[255]

Matches between Liverpool and top Irish clubs were also fairly regular in the 1990s, with Liverpool playing Dundalk at Oriel Park in 1991 and Shelbourne at

250 Interview with Stephen McGuinness, 22 Oct. 2019.   251 *IE*, 24 Apr. 1989.   252 Ibid.   25 3 Ibid.   254 'Irish Football Fans at Hillsborough 1989', rte.ie/archives/2019/0403/1040446–irish-liverpool-fans-return-from-hillsborough, accessed 19 Jan. 2022.   255 'Relatives of Hillsborough Disaster victims at emotional park ceremony', echo.ie/relatives-of-hillsborough-disaster-victims-at-emotional-park-ceremony, accessed 19 Dec. 2021.

Tolka Park and also a League of Ireland selection at Lansdowne Road in 1993. The following year they again played Shelbourne in a friendly along with Dundalk, and in 1995 met University College Dublin as well as Shelbourne.[256] Seamus Kelly, who played for UCD in the Liverpool match, recalled that

> it was like, James, Thomas, Babb, Harkness, Matteo, Kennedy, McManaman, Redknapp, Clough, Walters, Fowler. And they brought over a full cohort. I played against Liverpool, Arsenal, and a lot of the other teams in pre-season friendlies, but a lot of the time they wouldn't bring the big names. I was surprised, I don't know how The Doc did it. But Robbie Fowler, we met him in the hotel afterwards like, he came over to us, bought us drinks, an absolute gentleman. He was like, 'You're in college?', really genuine. Yeah it was great, that was a great game.[257]

In 1997 Liverpool again met Dundalk at Oriel Park and a Shelbourne/UCD selection at Tolka Park.[258] Liverpool played in Dublin as part of a pre-season tournament along with Leeds United, St Patrick's Athletic and Inter Milan in August 1998 while two years later they played a League of Ireland selection in a testimonial.[259] However, by the early 2000s these matches had become less common, with destinations such as Hong Kong chosen instead for marketing reasons.[260] Interest in British clubs remained high in Dublin, and in other areas where there were supporters' clubs, such as Enniskillen, where a local branch travelled to see a revived Leeds United, then managed by David O'Leary and featuring fellow Dubliner Robbie Keane, in a match against a Dublin City FC selection at Tolka Park in August 2001.[261] With Northern Ireland-born Brendan Rodgers in charge, Liverpool returned to Dublin and their friendly against Celtic in 2013 was a sellout, and in 2014 they played Shamrock Rovers at the same venue.[262] The August 2017 match against Athletic Bilbao attracted 51,000 supporters while a similar number attended the 2018 match against Napoli at the same venue.[263]

256 'Games for the 1991–1992 season', lfchistory.net/SeasonArchive/Games/34; 'Games for the 1992–1993 season', lfchistory.net/SeasonArchive/Games/33; 'Games for the 1993–1994 season', lfchistory.net/SeasonArchive/Games/35; 'Games for the 1994–1995 season', lfchistory.net/SeasonArchive/Games/36; 'Games for the 1995–1996 season', lfchistory.net/SeasonArchive/Games/37, all accessed 29 Dec. 2017.   257 Interview with Seamus Kelly, 2 Oct. 2019.   258 'Games for the 1996–1997 season', lfchistory.net/SeasonArchive/Games/39; 'Games for the 1997–1998 season', lfchistory.net/SeasonArchive/Games/40, both accessed 29 Dec. 2017.   259 'Games for the 1998–1999 season', lfchistory.net/SeasonArchive/Games/41; 'Games for the 1999–2000 season', lfchistory.net/SeasonArchive/Games/43, both accessed 29 Dec. 2017.   260 See, for example, 'Games for the 2001–2002 season', lfchistory.net/SeasonArchive/Games/44, accessed 29 Dec. 2017.   261 *FH*, 22 Oct. 2001.   262 *This is Anfield: official matchday programme: Liverpool FC v Athletic Club Bilbao* (Liverpool, 2017), p. 10.   263 Ben Blake, 'Liverpool make light work of Athletic Bilbao in front of a full house at the Aviva Stadium', the42.ie/liverpool-athletic-bilbao-aviva-stadium-dublin-3532091–Aug2017, accessed 29 Dec. 2017; Shane O'Brien, 'Liverpool stroll to Napoli win in Dublin', rte.ie/sport/soccer/2018/0804/983172-liverpool-stroll-to-napoli-win-in-dublin, accessed 12 June 2020.

14. The Aviva Stadium, Liverpool versus Napoli in August 2018. Author's own collection.

An Everton supporters' club continued to have a presence in Dublin in the 1980s, meeting regularly in the Auld Dubliner in Fleet Street.[264] In 1984 they marked the visit of the club to face UCD at Belfield in the European Cup Winners' Cup by presenting their player of the year award to Everton goalkeeper Neville Southall.[265] Despite the formation of a new supporters' club for all Everton fans in Ireland in 1992, based in Dublin, and sponsorship links with Home Farm in the mid-1990s, Everton's support in the city had declined by then with only 3,000 attending a friendly between Home Farm and Everton in November 1995.[266] Regional branches were also set up, but by then, Liverpool were generally seen as one of the three main clubs with a big Irish following along with Manchester United and Glasgow Celtic.[267]

TOURS AND TRIPS ABROAD

By the 1960s a number of Dublin clubs were taking part in more extensive tours abroad, with Shamrock Rovers participating in a New York tournament in 1961.[268] Frank O'Neill recalled that for the trip, which lasted for five weeks, they

> were stationed in New York and we played in St Louis, Missouri, but we played in New York most of the time, and we played up in Montreal. Most of the games were in New York, against the likes of Red Star Belgrade,

264 *SI*, 1 Dec. 1985. **265** *II*, 18 Sept. 1984. **266** 'The Irish Toffees', irish-toffees.com/about-us. html, accessed 13 May 2018; *IE*, 10 Nov. 1995. **267** *Limerick Chronicle*, 4 Apr. 1995. **268** Curran, *Irish soccer migrants*, p. 259.

Dukla Prague, they were the top – they were a Czech team, so to speak.
They had about six or seven internationals in their side. Espanyol of Spain,
Monaco, teams like that ... we played about six or seven matches. We played
against Petah Tikva, they were from Israel. The Montreal team consisted of
Canadians and English players. But Dukla Prague and Red Star were the
big ones in Europe at that time. [Manchester] United had played Red Star
Belgrade before the crash. We had a great day against Red Star. They must
have been at a party the night before – we beat them 5–1![269]

Shamrock Rovers also travelled to Boston in 1967, this time for a seven-week stay,
to compete in the USA League with eleven other non-American teams, which took
on local names.[270] The Dublin club took on the name of Boston Rovers and were
based at the Manning Bowl in Lynn, Massachusetts, for their home matches and
were managed by Liam Tuohy. They were hampered by injuries while their semi-
professional status meant that they finished last in their group.[271] Dublin clubs
provided the opportunity for young players to undertake trips overseas and they
continued to travel to America for friendly matches in the late twentieth century.
Home Farm, who were sponsored by Budweiser in the early 1980s, travelled to St
Louis, where the Budweiser plant was located, and played six matches against local
teams.[272] Goalkeeper Gary Kelly recalled it as being 'a great experience'.[273] Some
clubs also visited Australia, with Shelbourne travelling there in the early 1990s.[274]

   Dublin clubs' trips to Europe were initially less common than those to Britain
in the early twentieth century, but there were some exceptions, with Freebooters
FC travelling to Belgium in the spring of 1903.[275] This was said to be 'a new departure as far as Ireland is concerned', with the Dublin team winning all their matches
'easily' and apparently establishing 'an entente cordiale', which *Sport*'s reporter
thought would 'be difficult to shake'.[276] However, these matches did not take off
at that time. As Gerry Farrell has shown, Bohemians FC took part in a number of
international tournaments in the interwar years. They played in Liege in 1929, Paris
in 1932 and Amsterdam in 1934, winning the first two of these competitions.[277]
Matches involving travelling European teams and Irish clubs were generally not
common, although even before the onset of regular, continent-wide European
competitions in the 1950s they did take place. In 1923, the Cercle Athlétique de
Paris 'Gallia' visited Dublin to play an FAI selection and the Bohemians team,

269 Interview with Frank O'Neill, 30 Jan. 2020. 270 Curran, *Irish soccer migrants*, p. 260. These
included Northern Ireland's Glentoran (Detroit Cougars); English clubs Stoke City (Cleveland Stokers),
Wolverhampton Wanderers (Los Angeles Wolves) and Sunderland (Vancouver Royal Canadians); Scottish
teams Dundee United (Dallas Tornado), Aberdeen Dons (Washington Whips), Hibernians (Toronto
City); Italian team Cagliari Calcio (Chicago Mustangs); Dutch club ADO Den Haag (San Francisco
Gales); Brazilian club Bangu (Houston Stars); and Uruguayan side CA Cerro (New York Skyliners).
271 Ibid., pp 260–1. 272 Interview with Gary Kelly, 12 Dec. 2019. 273 Ibid. 274 Sands, *Shels*,
p. 124. 275 *Sport*, 14 Mar. 1903. 276 Ibid. 277 Gerry Farrell, 'Bohs in Europe', abohemiansport-
inglife.wordpress.com/2020/09/08/bohs-in-europe, accessed 3 Mar. 2021.

with a short snippet of the match recorded by British Pathé still available today.[278] This visit was reported to be largely due to the efforts of R.F. Murphy and helped to promote the new FAI as an organization independent of the IFA and the other British football associations.[279] Peter Byrne has stated that 'it was the first formal acknowledgement by FIFA of the new organization in Dublin'.[280]

The following year, the South African national team played Bohemians at Dalymount Park while on a tour of Britain and Ireland, with a small highlights reel of the Dublin match, including the captains meeting and the teams posing for the camera, again recorded by British Pathé.[281] In May 1926, Cercle Athlétique de Paris were defeated 2–1 by a Leinster FA selection at Dalymount Park, with the St James's Brass and Reed Band in attendance.[282] The visit of a team of German players, working on the Shannon industrial scheme, to meet a Richmond Rovers selection including 'a number of prominent Free State players' in October 1927, 'attracted a large crowd' to Richmond Road, but matches against foreign industrial workers were generally uncommon given Ireland was for the most part of the twentieth century a nation that people left to seek work rather than one which attracted immigrants.[283] Visits by Continental clubs were not frequent but did occur in the following decade. In September 1933, a team made up of Peruvian and Chilean players travelled from Liverpool to Dublin to play Bohemians.[284] The match was organized by Reginald Gubbins, a candidate for the presidency of Peru at that time, who was a brother of their manager, Jack; their father was born in Limerick. The team was received by Taoiseach Eamon de Valera at Leinster House, while the Lord Mayor of Dublin, Alfie Byrne, also greeted them.[285] The game ended in a one-all draw, with some spectators viewing the match from the roof of the stand as the ground was packed.[286] The following year, a selection representing Sports Club Saaz of Vienna visited Dalymount Park to play Bohemians, with the home team winning by a goal to nil before 25,000 spectators.[287] Their arrival at Dún Laoghaire came at a time when one reporter noted that Continental soccer had 'reached such a high pitch of perfection' that the match was 'certain to stir the imagination of the Dublin public'.[288] Despite this, Bohemians' honorary secretary Joe Wickham's invitation to members of the government to attend was not taken up, with the secretary of the Department of External Affairs, Seán Murphy, citing 'prior engagements' in his reply.[289] Stand tickets were available for

278 Ibid.; 'French Footballers 1923', britishpathe.com/video/french-footballers/query/bohemians, accessed 2 Jan. 2022. 279 *DET*, 23 July 1923. 280 Byrne, *Green is the colour*, pp 81–2. 281 Farrell, 'Bohs in Europe'; see also 'Football-Dalymount', britishpathe.com/video/football–dallymount/query/bohemians, accessed 2 Jan. 2022. 282 *EH*, 18 May 1926; *Football Sports Weekly*, 21 Aug. 1926. 283 *II*, 3 Oct. 1927. The Richmond Rovers selection won 4–3. 284 *EH*, 29 Sept. 1933. 285 Ibid. 286 'One Goal Each', britishpathe.com/video/one-goal-each/query/bohemians, accessed 2 Jan. 2022. 287 *DEM*, 19 Jan. 1934; *IE*, 22 Jan. 1934. 288 *IP*, 18 Jan. 1934. 289 Invitation to football match between Bohemians and continental team, Sports Club Saaz (1934), Letter from Joseph Wickham to Seán Murphy, 18 Jan. 1934 and letter from Seán Murphy to Joseph Wickham, 20 Jan. 1934, NAI, DFA/2/35/123.

the match at Elvery's, Kapp and Peterson's, Sheridan's and through the club, while the Great Northern Railway offered reduced fares from Dundalk and Drogheda.[290] Afterwards, Bohemians held a dinner for their opponents in the Central Hotel, Exchequer Street.[291] The Austrians later travelled north to face Linfield, drawing two-all at Windsor Park, and later became involved in a dispute over payment conditions, arguing that they had been guaranteed £150 to play the match.[292]

Central European teams did occasionally play against each other in Dublin in the post-war years. On St Patrick's Day 1951 two selections representing Frankfurt FSV and Offenbach Kickers of the South German First Division came to play an exhibition match having been invited to do so by the League of Ireland, who were anxious 'to provide a top-class soccer attraction in Dublin' that day.[293] In November 1953 Austrian side Wacker came to Tolka Park and in April 1954 the GAK Graz club came to play Drumcondra.[294] The League of Ireland invited the German Hessian League to send a team to Dublin to play a League of Ireland selection that summer.[295] This meant that an additional inter-league match would be held, along with those against British league selections.[296] Drumcondra, fielding Liverpool star Billy Liddell, played Austrian club Simmeringer, in November 1954 and in January 1956 they welcomed another Austrian side, Sturm Graz, to Tolka Park.[297]

Dublin clubs' tours abroad continued in the following decades, with Bohemians travelling to Spain for an eleven-day tour in 1967.[298] Much later, in January 1985, Shelbourne travelled to Gran Canaria to take part in a tournament with a number of European clubs.[299] UCD also undertook trips abroad, to areas such as the USA, Australia, the Middle East and the Far East through the organization of Dr Tony O'Neill.[300] In September 1976, they became the first European club to play in China, while they also played in Thailand, Hong Kong and Macau on that tour.[301] In 1978 UCD finished third in the Far West Classic tournament in La Mirada, California.[302] The club continued their international trips in the following decade, travelling to Australia and to the Middle East in the 1982–3 season.[303]

THE ADVENT OF MAJOR EUROPEAN CLUB COMPETITIONS

The introduction of regular European competitions in the 1950s had meant that Irish clubs could also challenge those outside Britain on an annual basis in a structured setting via home and away matches. As Philippe Vonnard has written, the Union of European Football Associations (UEFA) was founded in Bern in June

290 *EH*, 19 Jan. 1934.   291 *IP*, 22 Jan. 1934.   292 *BN*, 23 Jan. 1934; *IP*, 24 Jan. 1934.   293 *IP*, 9 Mar. 1951.   294 *II*, 13 Apr. 1954.   295 *II*, 22 Jan. 1954.   296 Ibid.   297 Ibid., and *IP*, 24 Jan. 1956.   298 Curran, *Irish soccer migrants*, p. 259.   299 Sands, *Shels*, p. 120.   300 Ryan, *The official book of the FAI Cup*, p. 278.   301 Minute Book of the Senior Council, FAI Annual Report 1976–7, June 1977, FAI Archives. P137/24.   302 Minute Book of the Senior Council, FAI Annual Report 1977–8, June 1978, ibid.   303 Minute Book of the Senior Council, FAI Annual Report 1982–3, June 1983, ibid.

1954 following an initial meeting of European soccer officials in Paris in April of that year.[304] The French newspaper *L'Equipe* was the driving force behind the establishment of what was known as the European Champion Clubs' Cup until the UEFA Champions League was established in 1992.[305] As Vonnard states, the newspaper had 'an extensive network of foreign correspondents, the financial capacity to undertake the project and the desire of journalists to contribute to the development of the game', while 'favourable circumstances' were also important in the development of the European Cup in the 1950s.[306]

While the first European Cup, as it was more commonly known, was held in the 1955–6 season, with Real Madrid defeating Stade de Reims 4–3 in the final in Paris, it was not until the 1957–8 season that Irish clubs participated.[307] As League of Ireland champions, Shamrock Rovers represented the Republic of Ireland and were drawn at home to Manchester United in the preliminary round. They were defeated 6–0 at home, but put up a better show at Old Trafford, where they lost 3–2.[308]

League of Ireland teams were generally no match for clubs in Europe that had professional structures and top-class international players. Alf Girvan recalled his experiences of playing for Drumcondra against Atletico Madrid in the European Cup preliminary round in the 1958–9 season:

> Well, we were hammered over there, eight–nil I think it was. And it was embarrassing. But over here, my memory is, I think we took the lead, we may have gone 1–0 up, and then they got five goals. But in those days, they were one of the top teams in the world, they were full-time professionals, we were part-time. There was a huge gap between the two of us. It was a great pleasure to play against them, to be able to say, 'I played against Atletico Madrid, one of the best teams in the world.' And they were, and they were so much fitter and better. We had no chance, but it was a great experience … because there was really big crowds there as well, you know, because it was a big competition, and it wasn't too long going I think as well, so the crowds were big, the atmosphere was great, and it was just lovely to be playing against guys of that talent.[309]

Drumcondra lost the home leg by 5–1 to go out 13–1 on aggregate, while their opponents went on to reach the semi-final but were defeated by eventual winners and local rivals Real Madrid.[310] The following season, Shamrock Rovers were defeated by OCG Nice in France by 3–2 but drew one–all in Dublin.[311] Drumcondra returned to the European Cup in the 1961–2 season after Limerick had won the league in 1960.

304 Philippe Vonnard, 'A competition that shook European football: the origins of the European Champion Clubs' Cup, 1954–1955', *Sport in History*, 34:4 (2014), pp 595–619, p. 599.   **305** Ibid. **306** Ibid.   **307** Soar, Tyler & Widdows, *The Hamlyn encyclopaedia of football*, pp 60–1.   **308** Ibid., p. 61.   **309** Interview with Alf Girvan, 27 Jan. 2020.   **310** Soar, Tyler & Widdows, *The Hamlyn encyclopaedia of football*, p. 62; *IP*, 19 Nov. 1964.   **311** Soar, Tyler & Widdows, *The Hamlyn encyclopaedia of football*, p. 63.

The Dublin club, who began training earlier than the other League of Ireland clubs in preparation for that season, were drawn away to 1FC Nuremburg of Germany but lost 9–1 on aggregate, and the following season Shelbourne were defeated 7–1 on aggregate versus Sporting Lisbon, with their Portuguese hosts laying on a drinks reception for the Dublin team in the city hall.[312] Shamrock Rovers were the League of Ireland's representatives in the 1964–5 season, but were defeated 5–0 on aggregate against Rapid Vienna, and the following year Drumcondra were defeated 3–1 on aggregate against ASK Vorwaerts of East Germany.[313]

With the failure of Dublin clubs to win the league championship between 1965 and 1975, they did not return to the European Cup for a decade, until Bohemians were drawn against Glasgow Rangers, against whom they lost 5–2 on aggregate.[314] In the 1979–80 season Bohemians became the first Dublin club to win a first-round European Cup match when they went through on away goals after a 2–2 draw against Omonia Nicosia of Cyprus.[315] Despite drawing nil–nil at home against East German side Dynamo Dresden in the second round, they lost 6–0 away.[316]

As league champions from 1984 until 1987, Shamrock Rovers were the League of Ireland's representatives in the European Cup for four seasons in a row, but they failed to get past the first-round on each occasion. In the 1984–5 season, they met Linfield in the first round of the European Cup, but went out on away goals nil–nil in Belfast and 1–1 at home.[317] John Coady recalled that Windsor Park was 'a nasty, nasty place' for a club visiting from Dublin at that time and that

> it was very intimidating, hugely intimidating. But we managed it well, played well, they had a man sent off early enough and we dominated the whole game, and we had Paul McGee playing up front for us, Ski McGee. He played for teams like QPR and Sligo Rovers, but missed a couple of chances. Mick Byrne also missed a couple of chances, and if we had brought a goal back to Milltown I'm sure we would have beaten them but – at nil–all – we still thought we'd do the job and I think that was part of the problem.[318]

The club's poor record in Europe continued in the latter half of the decade. In the 1985–6 season they were eliminated by Honved of Hungary on away goals on an aggregate scoreline of 3–3. In the 1986–7 season they met Glasgow Celtic in the first round, losing 3–0 on aggregate. In the 1987–8 season they lost 1–0 to Omonia Nicosia on aggregate.[319]

312 Ibid., pp 64–5; *II*, 22 Aug. 1961; Football match in Lisbon between Shelbourne and Lisbon Sporting Club (1962), Letter from minister plenipontiary charge d'affaires, Irish Embassy Lisbon, to Secretary of the Irish Department of External Affairs, 27 Sept. 1962, NAI, Department of Foreign Affairs, 2001/43/366.   313 Soar, Tyler & Widdows, *The Hamlyn encyclopaedia of football*, p. 66.   314 Ibid., p. 75.   315 Ibid., p. 79.   316 Ibid.   317 'Linfield 0 Shamrock Rovers 0', uefa. com/uefachampionsleague/match/63894--linfield-vs-shamrock-rovers/events, accessed 5 Apr. 2021.   318 Interview with John Coady, 22 Jan. 2020.   319 Julian Canny & Fergus Desmond, 'Irish clubs in European Cups', rsssf.com/tablesi/ier-ec.html, accessed 5 Apr. 2021.

In the 1990s, Dublin clubs also failed to have any major impact on the competition, which, as stated above, became known as the European Champions League in the 1992–3 season.[320] In 1990, St Patrick's Athletic were defeated by Dinamo Bucharest by 5–1 on aggregate. Having drawn the home match, they travelled to Romania, but lost 4–0, as Pat Fenlon recalled:

> It was different, it was very different! There wasn't a lot there at the time and we brought our own chef with us, so Brian [Kerr] was well ahead of his time, and brought some food as well. But they were a good side. We played over there, and they absolutely pulverized us. They were very, very good. But we gave them a really good game in Dublin, played really well on the night. To be honest, great for me as a young boy, playing in the European Cup as it was, and then to score was obviously fantastic.[321]

Shelbourne, as league champions in 1992, met Tavrira Simferopol of Ukraine in the preliminary round but lost 2–1 on aggregate. In the 1994–5 season Shamrock Rovers were hammered 8–0 on aggregate against Gornik Zabrze of Poland in the preliminary round.[322] St Patrick's Athletic, in winning the League of Ireland Premier Division in 1996, 1998 and 1999, were the final Dublin club to compete in the European Champions League in the twentieth century, but lost in the preliminary round to Slovan Bratislava (3–5 on aggregate), Glasgow Celtic (0–2 over the two legs) and Zimbru Chisinau (0–10 on aggregate) respectively in those years.[323]

DUBLIN CLUBS AND THE EUROPEAN CUP WINNERS' CUP

Similarly, success was hard to come by in Europe's second club competition, which was held for national cup winners. The European Cup Winners' Cup was inaugurated in the 1960–1 season with Fiorentina beating Glasgow Rangers 4–1 over two legs in the first final.[324] In the 1961–2 season, St Patrick's Athletic, Dublin's first representatives in the competition, were defeated 8–1 on aggregate by Scottish club Dunfermline Athletic.[325] In 1962–3 Shamrock Rovers received a bye in the first round but were defeated 5–0 on aggregate by Botev Plovdid of Bulgaria.[326] Shelbourne met Barcelona in the first round of the 1963–4 European Cup Winners' Cup but lost 5–1 on aggregate.[327]

In the 1966–7 first round, Shamrock Rovers became the first Dublin team to win a match at this stage of the competition when they beat Spora Luxembourg 8–2 on aggregate.[328] In the second round, they lost 4–3 on aggregate to eventual winners Bayern Munich.[329] Having drawn the home leg 1–1, they lost 3–2 in Munich.[330]

320 '1992/93 season: French first in augural Champions League Season', uefa.com/uefachampionsleague/history/seasons/1992, accessed 5 Apr. 2021. 321 Interview with Pat Fenlon, 7 Feb. 2020. 322 Canny & Desmond, 'Irish clubs in European cups'. 323 Ibid. 324 Soar, Tyler & Widdows, *The Hamlyn encyclopaedia of football*, p. 90. 325 Ibid. 326 Ibid., p. 91. 327 Ibid. 328 Ibid., p. 93. 329 Ibid. 330 Ibid.

Frank O'Neill recalled that 'we came so close, particularly against Bayern Munich [in November 1966]. Ten minutes away from reaching the quarter finals of the European Cup Winners' Cup. They were great memories.'[331] Paddy Mulligan recalled that as players travelling around Europe, they were fully focused on the match:

> You see nothing. You see the hotel. You see a restaurant in the hotel. You see your room. You see the training ground. That's it. Because you're there to play football, not as a tourist. You can't be walking around, because that's going to drain you.[332]

In 1967, 1968 and 1969 they failed to make it past the first round of the competition, losing to Welsh, Danish and German opposition in each of those years respectively.[333]

In the 1970–1 preliminary round, Bohemians were defeated 4–3 on aggregate against T.J. Gottwaldov of what was then Czechoslovakia.[334] In the 1975–6 season, Home Farm were defeated 6–0 away to R.C. Lens after a 1–1 draw in Dublin in their only European fixture.[335] The following year, Bohemians defeated B.K. Esbjerg of Denmark by 3–1 on aggregate in the first round but were then defeated 4–0 on aggregate against Śląsk Wrocław of Poland.[336] In the 1978–9 season, Shamrock Rovers defeated Apoel Nicosia by 3–0 on aggregate in the first round but then lost 6–1 on aggregate to Banik Ostrava.[337] In the 1984–5 season, UCD, after winning their first FAI Cup, welcomed eventual competition winners Everton to Belfield, drawing nil–nil before losing one–nil at Goodison Park.[338]

Despite Shamrock Rovers winning the FAI Cup in 1985, 1986 and 1987, Dublin clubs were not again represented in the European Cup Winners' Cup until the 1992–3 season, as the Milltown club, as noted above, took their place in the European Cup in those three years. In 1992, Bohemians lost 4–0 on aggregate to Steaua Bucharest.[339] In 1993, 1996 and 1997, Shelbourne were the League of Ireland's representatives in the competition, but failed to make it past their initial fixture on each occasion.[340]

DUBLIN CLUBS IN THE FAIRS CUP/UEFA CUP

The Fairs Cup was initially based on the idea of a competition between teams representing cities and normal clubs and the first competition was held between 1955 and 1958 with Barcelona defeating a London combination 6–2 on aggregate.[341] In October 1962 Drumcondra took on Danish side Odense BK 09 in the first round of the Fairs Cup. It was reported that 'not much interest was taken in the Fairs Cup in the Republic until Mr S.R. Prole's bold decision to enter the Fairs Cup this year'.[342] Odense, who were said to be an amalgamation of four Danish clubs,

---

331 Interview with Frank O'Neill, 30 Jan. 2020.   332 Interview with Paddy Mulligan, 4 Oct. 2019.   333 Canny & Desmond, 'Irish clubs in European cups'.   334 Soar, Tyler & Widdows, *The Hamlyn encyclopaedia of football*, p. 96.   335 Ibid., p. 100.   336 Ibid.   337 Ibid., p. 102.   338 Canny & Desmond, 'Irish clubs in European cups'.   339 Ibid.   340 Ibid.   341 Soar, Tyler and Widdows, *The Hamlyn encyclopaedia of football*, p. 108.   342 *II*, 2 Oct. 1962.

had five internationals in their team.[343] Having made the trip by 'train, plane and boat', Drumcondra lost 4–2 but beat Odense 6–5 on aggregate having won the home leg 4–1.[344] However, they were hammered 6–0 in West Germany by Bayern Munich before winning the home leg 1–0.[345] Girvan recalled that the opposition were 'much better ... they seemed to be stronger and faster'.[346] He also recalled that:

> We never felt that we were not welcome there, you know. But the support was obviously for the home team. There wouldn't have been too many Drumcondra supporters flying to Germany to support us, but we never bothered about the crowd. If there was 100,000 cheering for Munich, we wouldn't give two hoots.[347]

Some members of the Drumcondra club also suffered the frustration of being overcharged for drinks in a Munich nightclub, a matter which was later brought to the attention of the Irish Department of Foreign Affairs, although no further action was taken despite reports that their passports had been temporarily seized by the German police.[348] Overall results continued to be poor as the decade progressed, despite some victories. In the 1963–4 first round, Shamrock Rovers were defeated 3–2 on aggregate against Valencia.[349] In the 1964–5 season, Shelbourne progressed past Belenenses after three matches by an aggregate scoreline of 3–2.[350] However, they then lost 2–0 on aggregate against Atletico Madrid, who sent their coach, Sabino Barinaga, to Dublin, to watch Shelbourne against Sligo Rovers prior to the first leg of the second round.[351] With forty-eight teams having entered in the 1965–6 season, a number of clubs including Shamrock Rovers received byes in the first round.[352] However, they lost 3–2 on aggregate to Real Zaragoza in the second round.[353] In the 1966–7 season, Drumcondra were defeated 8–1 on aggregate against Eintracht Frankfurt.[354] St Patrick's Athletic lost 9–3 on aggregate against Bordeaux in the first round of the 1967–8 season.[355]

The UEFA Cup trophy was introduced during the 1971–2 season, but the poor record of Irish clubs in European competitions did not change. Shelbourne were defeated by Vasas Budapest, 2–1 on aggregate.[356] In the 1972–3 season, FC Cologne defeated Bohemians 5–1 on aggregate in the first round.[357] Bohemians

343 Ibid.   **344** Interview with Alf Girvan, 27 Jan. 2020.   **345** Soar, Tyler & Widdows, *The Hamlyn encyclopaedia of football*, p. 110.   **346** Interview with Alf Girvan, 27 Jan. 2020.   **347** Ibid. **348** Football match – Drumcondra v. Munich, Complaint regarding overcharging of members of Drumcondra Football Club in a nightclub in Munich (1962), Letter from R. McHugh, Secretary of Irish Embassy in West Germany to the Secretary of the Irish Department of External Affairs, 20 Dec. 1962, NAI, Department of Foreign Affairs. 2001/43/367; *IT*, 11 Dec. 1962.   **349** Soar, Tyler & Widdows, *The Hamlyn encyclopaedia of football*, p. 110.   **350** Ibid.   **351** Ibid.; *IP*, 19 Nov. 1964.   **352** Soar, Tyler & Widdows, *The Hamlyn encyclopaedia of football*, p. 111. **353** Ibid.   **354** Ibid., p. 112.   **355** Ibid.   **356** Ibid., p. 116.   **357** Ibid., p. 117.

were defeated 4–0 on aggregate by S.V. Hamburg in the 1974–5 competition.[358]
They returned to the UEFA Cup in the 1977–8 season and were defeated 4–0 on
aggregate against Newcastle United.[359] In the 1979–80 season, they were beaten in
Portugal in the first round, losing 2–0 on aggregate against Sporting Lisbon and
drawing nil–nil at home.[360] In the 1982–3 competition, Shamrock Rovers beat Fram
of Iceland by 7–0 on aggregate but lost 4–2 over two legs against Universitatea
Craiova of Romania.[361] John Coady recalled that their Eastern European opponents
'were a fantastic side ... they just handed out a lesson'.[362]

In the 1984–5 competition, Bohemians defeated Glasgow Rangers 3–2 at
Dalymount Park but lost 2–0 at Ibrox.[363] The match in Dublin was tarnished by
rioting by Rangers supporters, with twelve supporters and five members of An
Garda Síochana injured.[364] In the 1985–86 season Bohemians again faced Scottish
opposition, losing to Dundee United by 7–2 on aggregate, and in the 1987–8 competition they were defeated 1–0 away to Aberdeen having drawn at home.[365] In
the 1988–9 UEFA Cup, St Patrick's Athletic were defeated 4–0 on aggregate by
Hearts.[366]

In the 1993–4 UEFA Cup first round Bohemians were defeated 6–0 by Bordeaux
on aggregate.[367] The following season, Shamrock Rovers lost to Polish opposition
Gornik Zabrze 8–0 on aggregate as the poor results in Europe continued.[368] In
1998, Shelbourne played Rangers in the UEFA Cup and almost produced a shock
in the first leg, which was played at Tranmere Rovers' Prenton Park (due to fears
of a repeat of the 1984 violence), when they went three–nil up before conceding
five goals.[369] Pat Fenlon recalled:

> We were 2–0 up at half-time. It was just incredible, because you could see
> the actual fear in their faces. I think it was Advocaat's first game. They'd
> spent absolutely gazillions on players and the fear on his face and the play-
> ers' faces – what was going on? Here was a part-time team and we were
> actually playing really well against them. And Dermot's team talk at half-
> time was brilliant because he basically said, 'What am I supposed to do?
> You're not supposed to be winning 2–0! Just keep going.' We went out and
> scored again, so we were 3–0 up and we just ran out of legs then, we ran
> out of legs. I mean, they had some really good players at that time, some
> fantastic players and in the end they beat us well [5–3]. And we gave a good
> account of ourselves at Ibrox in the second leg as well, we only lost 2–0,
> late goal. No, it was a good occasion. I was fortunate to play in a lot of good
> European games.[370]

358 Ibid., p. 119.   359 Ibid., p. 122.   360 Ibid., p. 124.   361 Ibid., p. 127.   362 Interview with John
Coady, 22 Jan. 2020.   363 Canny & Desmond, 'Irish clubs in European Cups'.   364 'Riots as
Bohemians beat Glasgow Rangers 3–2', rte.ie/archives/2014/0919/644723-football-hooligans-at-
dalymount-park–1984, accessed 5 Apr. 2021.   365 Canny & Desmond, 'Irish clubs in European
Cups'.   366 Ibid.   367 Ibid.   368 Ibid.   369 *II*, 23 July 1998.   370 Interview with Pat Fenlon,
30 Jan. 2020.

However, two years later a Dublin club did manage to knock out Scottish opposition. Having lost preliminary round matches in the 1996–7 and 1997–8 competitions, in August 2000 Bohemians defeated Aberdeen 2–1 away and despite losing the home leg 1–0, went through to the UEFA Cup first round on away goals.[371] The following month, the Dalymount Park club were narrowly defeated 3–2 on aggregate against German club Kaiserslautern having lost the home leg 3–1 and winning the away match 1–0. The *Irish Independent* described the away game, the first time a League of Ireland club had won in fourteen attempts against German opposition in European competition, as 'one of the finest performances by an Irish side in Europe in recent years'.[372] A number of Dublin clubs also took part in the UEFA Intertoto Cup, including Shamrock Rovers.[373] However, this yielded little success.

CONCLUSION

As shown in this chapter, English clubs have travelled to Dublin for friendly matches since the late nineteenth century. In turn, Dublin clubs have also visited England for similar purposes. The relatively close proximity of Dublin's east coast location to English cities has allowed for the development of trading and sporting ties, while workplace teams have strengthened connections through occasional matches, such as Findlater's friendly against employees of the MV *Leinster* of Liverpool at Santry in August 1949.[374] The visit of leading English clubs became more common in the early twentieth century and the appearance of local stars such as Jimmy Dunne on English teams in Dublin helped attract supporters. Naturally, Irish clubs have also been aided by Irish-born players returning from spells at cross-Channel clubs. Scouting networks were fundamental to attracting Irish players away as for most of the twentieth century Ireland supplied the greatest number of non-British players to the English Football League, while by the late twentieth century clubs such as Arsenal and Manchester United had specialized scouts in Dublin.[375] English clubs of less prominence also utilized contacts in Ireland for the purpose of recruiting players, with Richard McFetridge, Bohemians' secretary in the late 1970s, taking on this role for Notts County.[376] It was Everton who first developed a supporters' club in the city in the 1950s and the growth of this following was linked to their recruitment of Irish players. While Liam Whelan's position in the Manchester United team increased support for the club in that decade, in the late 1960s domestic and European success strengthened this.

By the 1970s Liverpool's success in Europe, and the presence of Steve Heighway in the team, were significant factors in the growth of support for the

---

371 *II*, 11 Aug. 2000; Canny & Desmond, 'Irish clubs in European cups'. 372 *II*, 22 Sept. 2000. 373 Canny & Desmond, 'Irish clubs in European cups'. 374 *EH*, 6 Aug. 1949. 375 See, for example, *IE*, 23 July 2015. Manchester United's scout in Dublin was Joe Corcoran, a postman in the Ballsbridge area who had experience of youth soccer with Bolton Athletic and Cambridge Boys and was chairman of the Schoolboys FAI and Dublin and District Schoolboys' League. 376 Reid, *Bohemian AFC official club history, 1890–1976*, p. 2.

club in Dublin. Specialized sailings provided by shipping companies eased transport access for supporters. The visit of Liverpool to Dublin for friendly matches
attracted much interest and by the early 1990s support for Everton was much less
noticeable, despite links with Home Farm. Some Dublin clubs continued to travel
to Britain for friendly matches, with Shelbourne undertaking their pre-season tour
there in 1989, while a number of Dublin clubs also organized summer tournaments
or 'football festivals' which at times attracted big names in Britain and others from
around the world.[377] Some clubs ran into problems on the pitch, with Wayside
Celtic banned by the Leinster FA from competing in overseas tournaments for a
year after some players were ill-disciplined in an Easter competition in the Isle of
Man in 1988.[378] These events also provided the opportunities for players to socialize and relax, with Shelbourne's players apparently arriving back in Dublin 'the
worse for wear' after a trip to the Isle of Man in 1991, only to discover, in the pre-
internet days, that they were almost immediately due to play Aston Villa, with the
match apparently arranged at short notice.[379] By the late 1990s, top English clubs
still visited Dublin for friendlies, with Manchester United, Liverpool and Leeds
United taking part in matches as part of Shelbourne's centenary celebrations, but
in the early twenty-first century these appearances were less common, as Premier
League clubs attempted to further extend their global fanbases.[380] In 1999, the Old
Trafford club agreed to invest in Shelbourne's Soccer Academy.[381]

Dublin clubs had met European clubs in competitions prior to the inauguration
of major European competitions from the late 1950s onwards, but the implementation of the European Cup, European Cup Winners' Cup and Fairs Cup by the
early 1960s allowed teams to meet annually as representatives of their respective
nations. However, Irish clubs have generally struggled to progress past the opening
rounds. This is not to say that these matches have not provided much entertainment as well as the opportunity for players and supporters to travel to continental
Europe for competitive matches. Chapter six examines the role of schoolboy and
colleges' soccer in strengthening the game's growth in Dublin.

---

377 Sands, *Shels*, pp 122–3.   378 Senior Council Meeting Minutes, 14 July 1988, Leinster Football
Association Archives, P239/35.   379 Fitzpatrick, *Shelbourne cult heroes*, p. 101.   380 Sands, *Shels*,
p. 128.   381 *IE*, 22 July 1999.

6

Soccer at schools and higher-education level

ASSOCIATION FOOTBALL IN IRISH SCHOOLS IN THE EARLY TWENTIETH CENTURY

At primary school level, physical drill was formally introduced through the Revised Programme for Schools in 1900, following the report of the Belmore Commission of 1898.[1] By the early 1900s, physical exercise, through the inclusion of forms of drill and games, was becoming commonplace in Ireland's Intermediate schools. It was in the Intermediate schools that codes such as association football and rugby were more commonly found. Drill was not universal in all these schools, and the choice of sport available often depended on the patronage of the school, its ethos, the playing space available and the interest of headmasters and teachers.[2] Structures for school soccer in Ireland were a lot slower to gain permanency than in England, where, as Matthew Taylor has noted, competitions were in place in London, Sheffield, Manchester and Birmingham by the last decade of the nineteenth century, with individuals often most prominent in their organization.[3] Taylor states that 'London seems to have been the epicentre of the emerging schoolboy game', with 'the first schools body in Britain', the South London Schools FA, established in 1885, followed by the London Schools' FA in 1892.[4] As Gary James has shown, 'the first organized fixture list' was in place for Manchester schools in 1890, with 'three leagues of six clubs' structured for a shield competition in the early part of that decade.[5] While another competition for older pupils was added in 1894, an enthusiasm for developing schools soccer was a lot slower to take hold across the Irish Sea, with rugby more prominent in Irish schools at that time.[6] In 1889, twenty-one Intermediate schools were registered with the Irish Rugby Football Union.[7]

In line with more general developments in soccer's growth in Ireland, it was in Belfast where attempts to develop the first schools' structures for association football were evident. A schools' soccer cup had been established by the Irish Football Association in Belfast in 1883, but distance from the northern city hindered any schools in the island's capital from entering.[8] Attracting interest from schools nearby was also difficult, and in 1887 the competition was said to have

1 Curran, *Physical education in Irish schools*, p. 26. 2 Ibid., pp 72–85. 3 Taylor, *The association game*, pp 79–82. 4 Ibid., pp 80–1. 5 Gary James, *The emergence of footballing cultures: Manchester, 1840–1919* (Manchester, 2019), p. 241. 6 Ibid. 7 *Sport*, 28 Sept. 1889. 8 *BN*, 10 Nov. 1883.

fallen through as a result of 'the paucity of entries'.[9] Teams made up of schoolboys were engaged in matches in Munster as early as 1877, but soccer there lacked a competitive structure at the time.[10] Some schools such as Belvedere College and Clongowes Wood played their own version of football in the nineteenth century.[11] Neal Garnham has noted that soccer was being played at St Vincent's College, Castleknock, by 1885 although a difficulty in procuring opponents meant that games in this code remained internal there.[12] The standard of play there was said to have been improved by the attendance of students from Belfast, and the recruitment of coaches including a soldier and two professional footballers, Bob Holmes, in 1901, and Archie Goodall, in 1905.[13] Garnham also notes that 'Castleknock thus provided a nursery for football in Dublin, from which, it was alleged, many pupils graduated to the Bohemian club in the city'.[14] In 1895 the Catholic University Association Football Club was established, and drew its players mainly from Clongowes Wood in Kildare and St Vincent's in Castleknock.[15] As noted earlier, St Helen's School was a founder member of the Leinster FA in 1892 and at least three other schools had soccer teams at that time.[16] While connections with Scotland and its migrant workers were highly significant in soccer's early development in Belfast, Garnham has stated that 'in Dublin, the sport's other main stronghold in Ireland, the role of the public schoolboy, who developed into the university student, was crucial'.[17] William Sanderson recalled in 1940 that some of Bohemians' early games were against school teams of Castleknock, Clongowes and Newbridge, and that 'the all-day trip to Clongowes was always a great outing'.[18] By 1900, Clongowes versus Bohemians was reported to be an 'annual match', with the home team winning by six goals to one against a 'rather weak' Bohemians team in March of that year.[19] Indeed, one reporter noted in 1895 that Clongowes was the *alma mater* of Bohemians, illustrating the close linkage between their members.[20]

Garnham has also noted that 'impromptu games with a rag ball took place' in Kildare Street National School, and it is highly likely that this school was not unique within the city in this regard.[21] The compulsory introduction of physical drill into Irish national schools in 1900 meant that formal physical training was finally inaugurated at that level, but sports and team games were not mandatory and in many schools, playground space was limited.[22] Despite initial enthusiasm regarding the provision of physical drill, the failure of the Board of Education to provide adequate facilities and resources towards its implementation, allied to the negative attitudes of many teachers towards the subject, meant that by the second decade of the twentieth century its provision was haphazard in numerous schools, although it remained compulsory subject in independent Ireland until 1925.[23]

9 *Sport*, 17 May 1887. 10 Toms, *Soccer in Munster*, p. 1. 11 Moore, 'Association football in Ireland', p. 507. 12 Garnham, *Association football and society*, p. 25. 13 Ibid. 14 Ibid. 15 Ibid., p. 26. 16 *IT*, 27 Oct. 1892; Dodd, *100 years*, pp 33–58. 17 Garnham, *Association football and society*, p. 27. 18 *SI*, 15 Dec. 1940. 19 *II*, 30 Mar. 1900. 20 Garnham, *Association football and society*, p. 26. 21 Ibid., p. 22. 22 Ibid. 23 Curran, *Physical education in Irish schools*, p. 105.

There are numerous references to 'football' being played in boys' schools in Dublin in the 1909–10 intermediate education inspectors' reports, but the difficulty lies in establishing which code – rugby, association or Gaelic – it was, as not every inspector clarified this. It is clear that it was soccer in some cases. At the Avoca School in Blackrock, 'cricket, hockey and association football' were 'occasionally organized by the staff'.[24] At St Vincent's Orphanage School, Glasnevin, a soccer league was organized for the pupils, who had 'an open airy field at the back of the school' that was 'full size for football'.[25] Soccer was also played, along with rugby, cricket and handball, at Glasthule Presentation College, which was home to a 'football field, 89 yards by 57 yards'.[26] Another intra-school competition took place in a school with a strong military background. The Hibernian School Shield was held in December 1904, with F Company defeating G Company.[27]

THE LEINSTER FA MINOR CHALLENGE CUP

A Juvenile Association had been established for under-16s in Belfast in 1895, but this was restricted to local teams.[28] The Leinster FA inaugurated a competition for under-18 players in 1898, and public school teams were eligible, but initially they were slow to enter.[29] The Leinster FA Minor Challenge Cup was established at a meeting of the Leinster FA in Wynn's Hotel at the end of August 1898, with the rules signifying that the competition would be an annual one 'and open to teams composed of eighteen years of age on the 1st October each season, and who are bona fide members of a senior 3rd XI, a junior 2nd, a Boys' Brigade company team or a public school team'.[30] Players' birth details had to be registered with the association's honorary secretary, William Sheffield, and in the case of a protest being lodged against a player regarding his age, the young footballer needed to produce his birth certificate or a copy of it to prove he was eligible to play.[31] The draw for the first round of the Leinster FA Minor Cup took place at a meeting held in December 1898 in the Royal Exchange Hotel, Parliament Street, with Mr Walsh of the Catholic University presiding.[32] Eight teams entered, with Dundalk Educational meeting Morgan's School, who were allowed to push back the fixture until the middle of January as they were on vacation. In the other fixtures, Belleville were drawn against Wilton; Myra faced St Patrick's and Richmond Rovers 3rd team were paired with Glasnevin Reserves. Tritonville, Shelbourne 3rd team and Drumcondra received byes.[33]

In the final, which took place at the Catholic University ground in Sandymount before the Leinster FA's Senior Cup final between Bohemians and Richmond Rovers in April 1899, St Patrick's won 2–0 against Tritonville, with H.E. Thornton, the president of the Leinster FA, presenting the cup and medals afterwards.[34] It

24 Intermediate Education Board for Ireland, *Reports of inspectors, 1909–10*, i: *From No. 1 to No. 81* (Dublin, 1910), report 23. **25** Ibid., report 73. **26** Ibid., report 93. **27** *EH*, 3 Dec. 1904. **28** *UFCN*, 16 Aug. 1895. **29** *II*, 2 Sept. 1898; Clenet, 'Association football in Dublin'. **30** *II*, 2 Sept. 1898. **31** Ibid. **32** *DDN*, 16 Dec. 1898. **33** Ibid. **34** *II*, 1 May 1899.

appears that the competition attracted little interest from school teams or Boys' Brigade selections in its opening season. However, some clubs were founded with the sole purpose of playing underage matches, including the Carmelite AFC, who had their rooms at 53 Aungier Street, and announced they were happy to play against 'junior teams, colleges and clubs under 16' in September 1898.[35] That same month, Claremont FC were open to 'receive challenge from all junior teams under 16' and stated their intention to enter the Leinster Minor Cup, although they then failed to do this in the competition's opening season.[36]

While the GAA had organized a schools' league in Dublin by 1904 with eighty teams participating in hurling and Gaelic football, as shown above, soccer competitions for school teams were less prominent and rugby was also a direct opponent in terms of codes favoured by schools, particularly at second level.[37] Following the organization of the Leinster FA Minor Challenge Cup in 1898, a minor league was also operational in the early 1900s.[38] In November 1904, the Leinster FA's minor league was up and running with St George's Second XI, Swifts' Thirds, St Catherine's Reserves and Nomads' Reserves all fulfilling fixtures in the Phoenix Park.[39] The draw for the first round of the Leinster Minor Cup in November 1904 included twelve teams.[40] By January 1912 there were also twelve clubs in the league.[41] There is some indication that the monitoring of the ages of those playing in the Leinster FA's minor competitions was difficult, with some players tampering with birth certificates to ensure selection.[42] In February 1913, one Frankfort FC official noted how his club had undertaken much work 'in purifying the Minor Cup competition by means of appeals, against the dishonest practices that had made the competition a farce'.[43] Despite these issues, the competition took place throughout the war and beyond, with Annally FC winning the trophy four years in a row, from 1916 to 1919.[44] The Phibsboro club was said to be 'defunct' by 1923, but was revived later in the decade, and it was important in the development of 1927 FA Cup-winning goalkeeper Tom Farquharson, who played for them in the 1915–16 season and was described by one reporter as 'the penalty king' who was 'as agile as a panther'.[45]

The organization of the Leinster Minor League after the First World War was due in no small measure to its honorary secretary, J.F. Harrison of Annally FC, who was one of a number of organizers of the game in Dublin who gave 'their time and labour freely without fee or reward'.[46] He became FAI chairman in 1923.[47] Some individual clubs and their personnel did try to initiate other

35 Ibid., 24 Sept. 1898. 36 Ibid. 37 Richard McElligott, '"Boys indifferent to the manly sports of their race": nationalism and children's sport in Ireland, 1880–1920' in Brian Griffin & John Strachan (eds), 'Sport in Ireland from the 1880s to the 1920s', Special edition of *Irish Studies Review*, 27:3 (2019), pp 344–61, p. 347. 38 *II*, 2 Sept. 1898. 39 *EH*, 19 Nov. 1904. 40 *IDI*, 19 Nov. 1904. 41 *DDE*, 23 Jan. 1912. 42 Senior League Council Minutes, Council Meeting, 27 Apr. 1904, Leinster Football Association Archives, P239/23. 43 *EH*, 5 Feb. 1913. See also *DDE*, 12 Mar. 1903. 44 *Sport*, 3 Feb. 1923. 45 Ibid., and 21 July 1923; *EH*, 14 Apr. and 15 Aug. 1927. 46 *Sport*, 12 Oct. 1918 and 3 Feb. 1923. 47 Ibid., 3 Feb. 1923.

underage competitions for young players. In 1904 St Mary's United offered a Challenge Cup for competition between 'any Altar Society team under 16 years of age'.[48] A St Joseph's FC were noted as deciding to enter a team in this competition, but there is scarce evidence that it developed into anything more widespread.[49] The place of advertisements regarding meetings, usually by organizers and secretaries, was an initial step in attempting to organize these local competitions. E. McMahon of Kevin Street invited under-17 teams to compete in a city and county minor league, which was open to under-17s, in August 1906.[50] Not every organizer had clubrooms to avail of, with T. Byrne inviting clubs to send delegates to his house in New Street on the evening of 27 September 1906, with a view to organizing the Raymond Cup for under-17s.[51] In October 1906 Thomas Thornton of Finglas Road announced in the national press that a competition known as the Phibsboro Cup was to be played for by under-19 teams.[52] By January of the following year, ten clubs were involved in this competition, which was run on a league basis.[53] Similarly, Reginald United offered a cup and medals for their under-18 competition in January 1907.[54] That same month the Bohemian Boys' Cup competition, which was open to under-16s, included seven teams.[55] These competitions illustrate the ad hoc attempts to organize localized underage competitions outside of the Leinster FA's administration. Despite the presence of a boys' team at Shelbourne in 1904, there is no indication that they dominated the fledgling schoolboy game at that time, although a number of their players did go on to play for the club's first team.[56]

A few underage teams took on the names of English clubs, with Everton AFC, a club operating out of North Strand, who had secured a ground in Phoenix Park prior to Christmas 1905, seeking matches against under-14 teams, while Blackburn AFC, who were centred in Phibsboro, sought under-17 opposition at that time.[57] This naming policy is indicative of the growing appeal of English soccer for those in Dublin even at the beginning of the twentieth century, with newspapers coverage fundamental to this interest. Some clubs began initially in the Leinster FA Minor League, before continuing on to junior leagues, including Brunswick FC, who were described as one of Dublin's 'most successful junior teams' by early 1926 and who won the FAIFS Junior Cup later that year before temporarily going into decline.[58]

ATTEMPTS TO DEVELOP SCHOOLS' AND BOYS' BRIGADE COMPETITIONS

Matches continued to also take place between school selections in the opening decade of the twentieth century, including a friendly in December 1904 when the O'Brien

---

48 *EH*, 16 Dec. 1904. 49 Ibid. 50 *DDE*, 23 Aug. 1906. 51 Ibid., 22 Sept. 1906. 52 *FJ*, 9 Oct. 1906. 53 *EH*, 5 Jan. 1907. 54 Ibid. 55 Ibid. 56 *Shelbourne Football Club golden jubilee*, p. 18. 57 *FJ*, 21 Dec. 1905. 58 *FSW*, 26 Feb., 15 May 1926 and 27 Aug. 1927.

Institute defeated Howth Road Schools by ten goals to nil.[59] A few years later, there was enough interest for a Leinster schools' competition for soccer to be organized through the honorary secretary of the Leinster FA, J.A. Ryder.[60] In March 1907, the first Sunday Independent Cup, presented by the newspaper's proprietors to the Leinster FA in October of the previous year, was won by Meath Industrial School (Blackrock) when they beat Hibernian Marine School by three goals to two in the final at Dalymount Park 'before a very good gathering of spectators'.[61] The number of entries was low, reflecting the strength of rugby and Gaelic football in many schools, and perhaps a lack of interest on the part of teachers. Only six teams initially entered, with Meath Industrial School beating Dundalk Educational to reach the final, while the Hibernian Marine Schools defeated both the O'Brien Institute and Rathmines College. Morgan's School withdrew without playing any matches.[62]

In April 1908, the O'Brien Institute won the competition, having beaten Pembroke Institute by two goals to one in the final match at Dalymount Park before a 'moderately big crowd'.[63] The newspaper itself reported that Pembroke had only been in the final as a result 'of the withdrawal, through dissatisfaction with the governing of the competition, of St Vincent's Orphanage, a team of miniature marvels', who were apparently 'as popular as either of the Metropolitan cracks, Bohemians and Shelbourne'.[64] Pembroke had won a protest against St Vincent's Orphanage, who had beaten them with an extra-time winner in the replayed semi-final.[65] The competition, which was run by the Leinster Junior Council, was not done so satisfactorily, according to the cup donors, who were unhappy with the number of protests and objections in that season's matches.[66] They hoped to see the Leinster Junior Council alter the competition rules at their next meeting 'to obviate a recurrence of this season's unpleasant features'.[67] However, the cup final did offer the young players a chance for some glory. It was noted that 'there was great enthusiasm at the close of the game, Copeland, the centre forward of O'Brien's Institute, the winning team, being carried off on the shoulders of admirers'.[68] The low number of participants, and the lack of involvement from some of the more prestigious Dublin schools, was not helpful in developing interest. Pembroke Institute were temporarily suspended by the Leinster FA 'because of its playing in an unaffiliated competition' and although they were readmitted in March 1910, these matters did not help the sustenance of the Schools' Cup.[69] By December 1911 it appears that this trophy was no longer being contested by schools and instead had been offered for the Leinster Minor League by the Leinster FA Junior Council following instruction from the *Sunday Independent*'s editor.[70]

59 *FJ*, 5 Dec. 1904.   60 *DDE*, 23 Oct. 1906.   61 Senior League Council Minutes, Council Meeting, 31 Oct. 1906, Leinster Football Association Archives, P239/23; *SI*, 24 Mar. 1907.   62 *SI*, 24 Mar. 1907.   63 Ibid., 3 May 1908.   64 Ibid.   65 Ibid.   66 Ibid.; see also Senior League Council Minutes, Council Meeting, 11 Mar. 1908, Leinster Football Association Archives, P239/23.   67 *SI*, 3 May 1908.   68 Ibid.   69 Senior League Council Minutes, Council Meeting, 9 Mar. 1910, Leinster Football Association Archives, P239/24.   70 *II*, 9 Dec. 1911 and 19 Oct. 1912; Senior League Council Minutes, Council Meeting, 8 Nov. 1911, Leinster Football Association Archives, P239/23.

Boys' Brigade matches also offered some young players the opportunities to develop their skills. In November 1904, ten teams were involved in the Boys' Brigade League, which, as noted earlier, had been founded in 1894, and by 1905 this number had risen to twelve.[71] Brendan Power has written that 'football fulfilled a practical role for a religious organization such as the Boys' Brigade as the organization hoped that football would attract and retain members, not for its own sake, but as a means of developing spiritual ambitions'.[72] However, he also states that 'the facilities for sport were inadequate during the early development of the Brigade and the values displayed on the pitch were sometimes at variance with the ideals espoused by the leadership'.[73]

In January 1921 there were fourteen teams in the Dublin Boys' Brigade League.[74] By September 1925 two competitions were operational for Boys' Brigade teams, with the McCrae Cup restricted to seniors while entry for the Duckett Cup was 'confined to teams, the ages of which should not exceed in the aggregate 154 years'.[75] The league was apparently 'one of the oldest leagues in the Irish Free State', with one reporter noting that 'it was in the Boys' Brigade teams that many of Ireland's best were found'.[76] One of these players was Frank Haine of Bohemians and the Irish amateur international team.[77] By the autumn of 1925 an Old Boys' Union BB League was operational, with a number of these also affiliating to the Leinster FA.[78] Boys' Brigade selections also had the opportunity to take on their Belfast counterparts. In April 1895 representative teams of the Dublin and Belfast Boys' Brigade battalions met on the ground of Leinster Nomads.[79] These matches continued into the twentieth century and post-partition, and were rotated between Dublin and Belfast.[80] On Easter Monday 1927 an excursion was run from Dublin for the match between Dublin Old Boys and Belfast Old Boys in Belfast, with the home team winning 3–0.[81] Matches also took place against those in England, with Boys' Brigade teams of Dublin and Liverpool meeting annually by 1908.[82]

THE DUBLIN SCHOOLBOYS' LEAGUE

For those not connected to the Boys' Brigade and not yet physically big enough for matches at minor level, competitions appear to have been scarce in the early twentieth century. Writing in September 1919, one newspaper correspondent queried the situation regarding the lack of development of schoolboy soccer in Dublin.[83] The following year some action had been taken. A Dublin schoolboys' league was operational by the autumn of 1920, with twelve teams invited to participate for the Fenlon Cup, a 'newly formed competition' for players who were of an average age of 14, through a newspaper advertisement placed by J. Maguire of

71 *IDI*, 19 Nov. 1904; Power, 'The functions of association football in the Boys' Brigade in Ireland', p. 46. 72 Power, 'The functions of association football in the Boys' Brigade in Ireland', p. 57. 73 Ibid. 74 *SI*, 16 Jan. 1921. 75 *Sport*, 12 Sept. 1925. 76 Ibid. 77 Ibid. 78 *FSW*, 17 Oct. 1925. 79 *BN*, 11 Apr. 1895. 80 *FSW*, 3 Apr. 1926. 81 *Sport*, 16 Apr. 1927. 82 *IWT*, 2 May 1908. 83 *DET*, 26 Sept. 1919.

2 Lennox Street.[84] It appears that these schoolboy matches generally took place at Phoenix Park.[85] By the end of December, twelve teams were involved in the Dublin Schoolboys' League.[86] By the end of the following year most of these teams appears to have dropped out and had been replaced by others, and the overall total had risen to twenty-two.[87] The competition continued throughout the 1920s, although newspaper reports are patchy.[88] Schoolboys' leagues for soccer initially proved difficult to establish, despite the efforts of Bohemians to organize a league and cup in 1925.[89] A Leinster Juvenile Cup was operational by the latter part of that decade, with Queen's Park, who, like many other schoolboy clubs, acted as a nursery for senior clubs, winning this competition in 1926–7.[90]

Travel difficulties affected some schools' participation in competition, including the Hibernian Marine School, who were anxious to join a juvenile league in 1925 but wanted to play all matches at home 'owing to the school's regulations'.[91] Monitoring of players' eligibility continued to be an issue. In February 1927, one correspondent writing in *Sport* complained that St Peter's had used overage players in a Schools Cup semi-final match against Emorville in Ballymun, although it is not clear how many teams were involved in this competition.[92] While Dublin clubs did not participate in competitions against schools in Northern Ireland, in December 1927 'the first inter-City game' between Belfast and Dublin schools selections took place at Flush Park, Belfast, resulting in a two-all draw.[93]

Religious organizations at times initiated leagues for young players, with St Dominick's Boys' Sodality Football League, which was confined to their members, operational by the mid-1920s for under-18s, under-16s and under-14s.[94] In April 1926, A.J. Fitzpatrick and P.V. Smith, administrators of the St Joseph's Altar Boys FC, who were attached to Whitefriar Street, purchased a cup for competition between 'the different altar football (soccer clubs) of the city and suburbs'.[95] In September 1926 the Rev. Fr Gleeson, who had been the local curate in Our Lady of Lourdes Church in Dublin before moving to Bray, also presented a challenge cup for sodality teams in Dublin.[96] Some underage clubs grew out of religious organizations connected with youths at this time, with Ozanam United, a team with an average age of 17 years, developing from Our Lady of Lourdes Boys' Club, Ozanam House, Mountjoy Square in October 1926.[97] In May 1927 plans were

84 *EH*, 3 Sept. 1920. 85 *SI*, 10 Oct. 1920 and 12 Dec. 1920; *FJ*, 24 Dec. 1920. 86 *EH*, 11 Oct. 1920 and 31 Dec. 1920; *SI*, 12 Dec. 1920. These were Dundrum Boys, Vernon, Shamrock Boys, Munster Athletic, Fairmount, St Kevin's, Leinster Boys, Ormonde Athletic, Frankfort, St Patrick's and Norfolk. 87 *SI*, 6 Nov. 1921, 18 Dec. 1921 and 29 Jan. 1922. By Dec. 1921 Alton, CDFC, Palmerstown United, Corinthian United, YMCA Boys, Munster Athletic, Munster Athletic 'B', Harding Boys, Kapp and Peterson's, Ardnilaun, Chapelizod Boys, Pembroke, Ellesmere, Glasnevin Boys, Hibernians, Hibernians 'B', Hibernian Military School, CDAS, Brookfield, Ozanam United, and the 7th and 14th company teams of the Boys' Brigade were all involved in the Dublin Schoolboys' League. 88 *EH*, 14 Nov. and 25 Dec. 1925 and 20 Apr. 1926. 89 Curran, *Irish soccer migrants*, p. 86. 90 *FSW*, 31 Mar. 1928. 91 *FSW*, 10 Oct. 1925. 92 *Sport*, 12 Feb. 1927. 93 *FSW*, 31 Dec. 1927. 94 *FSW*, 12 Sept. 1925. 95 *FSW*, 3 Apr. 1926. 96 *FSW*, 4 Sept. 1926. 97 *FSW*, 29 Oct. 1926.

underway in Dublin to establish a new altar boys' league, with one reporter of the view that 'an eleven from every church in Dublin will likely compete'.[98] The aims of the league were reported to be 'to promote clean, healthy sport and unity amongst the Altar Boys of Dublin', with players required to be 16 years old on 1 September 1927.[99] This appears to have been an attempt to amalgamate all altar boys' teams in the city.

At times local businessmen acted as patrons, with Shamrock Rovers' owner and president, Joe Cunningham, presenting a cup for football competition to the captain of St Joseph's Deaf Mutes team in Cabra in April 1928.[100] Apparently, they had earlier switched from Gaelic football to soccer and Brother D'Alton insisted they adhere to the latter code as damage to their hands could have impacted on their ability to use sign language.[101] Cunningham also presented a cup bearing his name for the winners of the Altar Boys' Sodality League First Division that spring.[102] A former Dublin billiards champion, he had 'always taken a great interest' in junior soccer and could 'be often seen in both Phoenix and Ringsend parks' in his capacity as vice president of the Leinster Junior Football Association.[103]

With the foundation of the Altar Societies Football League, new clubs were organized in order to participate, including St Mary's Altar FC, who were based at the Pro-cathedral in Marlborough Street, and held their inaugural meeting in August 1927.[104] Home Farm FC was established in 1928 by a number of schoolboys for this league and quickly became one of Dublin's leading schoolboy clubs.[105] They were an amalgamation of street teams (Home Farm and Richmond Road) with founding members Brendan Menton and Don Seery the club's first officers.[106] They won the Leinster Minor Cup in 1931, 1932 and 1933, and in April 1934 met Botanic Minors, the league leaders, in the semi-final second replay at Dalymount Park with a special bus service provided from Home Farm Road.[107] Writing afterwards in the *Evening Herald*, 'J.C.' noted that:

> In a death or glory struggle that was splendidly featured by sound teamwork, an abundance of individual skill, and thrills in plenty, Botanic and Home Farm played a draw of 2–2 after extra-time in their third meeting … The extra period brought no change, although the teams fought desperately to the call of time.[108]

The third replay was held at Tolka Park on a Friday night, with Botanic defeating the holders 2–1 thanks to two late goals before 'a large crowd'.[109] The following month, Botanic beat Drogheda 2–0 in the final in Drogheda.[110]

98 *Sport*, 28 May 1927. 99 *FSW*, 9 July 1927. 100 *FSW*, 7 Apr. 1928. 101 Con Lynch, 'Football/GAA in St Joseph's' in *St Joseph's School for Deaf Boys Cabra, 1857–2007* (Dublin, 2007), pp 37–8. 102 *FSW*, 10 Mar. 1928. 103 *FSW*, 19 Dec. 1925. 104 *FSW*, 13 Aug. 1927. 105 Curran, *Irish soccer migrants*, p. 35. 106 Menton, *Home Farm*, p. 3. 107 *EH*, 20 Apr. 1934. 108 *EH*, 25 Apr. 1934. 109 *II*, 28 Apr. 1934. 110 *II*, 14 May 1934.

Munster Victoria were founded by Tom Tunney of Drumcondra in 1932 after Munster Boys and Victoria Boys, who played in the former Dublin Schoolboys' League, were amalgamated.[111] He had formed the St Peter's team, which played in the Altar Boys' League, in 1932.[112] In 1942, Munster Victoria won their third Leinster Minor Cup in five seasons.[113] Seán Ryan has written that they were 'the great rivals of Home Farm in those days', and by 1946 the former club had pro-duced a combined total of seven players who appeared in the FAI Cup final for Drumcondra or Shamrock Rovers that year.[114]

In September 1933 a new league, for under-14s, began when Parkview Boys and Hammond Celtic Boys met in Phoenix Park.[115] This had been organized by Leinster Junior FA following pressure from senior clubs about the lack of a structure for younger players.[116] By May 1934 a Schoolboys' Cup was also in operation, but there were still difficulties in getting all schools to take part.[117] In November 1934, one reporter noted a lack of enthusiasm among Dublin schools for the promotion of soccer, but stated that Mount St Joseph's of Clondalkin had recently played St Joseph's Terenure, while St Mary's Rathmines and a school in Cabra were also said to be interested in matches.[118] Teams from O'Connell Schools in Richmond Street were also reported to have played and trained at Dalymount Park during the previous season. The revival of a schoolboys' league that winter was said to be the responsibility of Tom Tunney and by the end of November twelve teams had indicated they would participate, although they did not use school names and instead local clubs were involved.[119]

The Leinster FA sought to clarify their stance on schoolboy soccer in Dublin later that year. In December 1934 Leinster FA-backed Leinster Minor and Juvenile League officials indicated that they intended to hold a meeting of the Leinster Schoolboys' League at Parnell Square in relation to the organization of a league.[120] Clubs were asked to note that this league was 'the only one of its kind officially rec-ognized by the Football Association of the Irish Free State'.[121] Prior to Christmas 1934, the schoolboys' league began, to add to the minor and juvenile leagues the Leinster FA had in operation at that time.[122]

Connections had earlier been formed between organizers of underage soccer in Dublin and those in regional Irish areas, with Mr Craigmyle, R.F. Murphy and J. Christian arranging the visit of Waterford Juveniles to play Dublin Boys in April 1928.[123] However, it was not until the middle of the 1930s that national competitions

111 *SI*, 27 Jan. 1957.   112 Ibid.   113 Briggs & Dodd, *100 years of the LFA*, p. 53.   114 Ryan, *The official book of the FAI Cup*, p. 113. These were Peter Keogh, Con Martin, Joseph 'Robin' Lawler, Jimmy Lawler (Drumcondra) and Noel Kelly, Charlie Byrne and Tommy Eglington (Shamrock Rovers).   115 *SI*, 1 Oct. 1933.   116 Ibid.   117 *EH*, 24 May 1934.   118 *EH*, 21 Nov. 1934.   119 Ibid. The teams involved included Seapark Boys (Skerries), Corinthians (Blackrock), Inchicore Boys, Star United, Cabra Boys, Young Elms (Ashtown), Munster Boys, Red United Boys, Fairview, Cabra, Dundrum and Sandymount.   120 *EH*, 1 Dec. 1934.   121 Ibid.   122 *EH*, 24 Dec. 1934. Corinthians, Inchicore, Grange Boys, Munster Boys, Boro Boys, Stars United, Corinthians, Reds United Boys, Seaforth Rangers, Dolphin Celtic, Young Elms, Ballinteer Boys, Dundrum and Celtic were involved.   123 *FSW*, 14 Apr. 1928.

for these players were underway. In 1935, the first FAI Minor Cup competition was held.[124] This followed a proposal at a meeting of the FAI's Junior Committee, which was welcomed by its chairman, J. Younger.[125] The draw was made in January of that year and featured twenty-two teams in the Dublin district, with provincial club Longford given a bye.[126] Sixteen teams entered from the Cork district with Limerick United granted a bye. There were ties listed in the Drogheda, Galway, Sligo and Waterford districts, with one club in the Galway area, Crusaders, also being given a bye.[127] Naturally, the competition was clustered geographically initially, with, for example, Westport of Mayo beating Donegal side Killybegs 2–1 in the first round.[128] Perhaps surprisingly, a Dublin club were not the winners of the first competition. In the semi-finals, Home Farm were defeated 3–2 by Cork team Greenmount Rangers at Tolka Park, while Drogheda beat Sligo United by the same score in Sligo.[129] The final, played at Tolka Park at the beginning of June 1935, ended in a 1–1 draw.[130] The replay, at the same venue the following week, was won by the Greenmount side by two goals to one.[131]

The 1935–6 season saw the number of Dublin-area teams included in the FAI's Minor Cup increase to thirty-four, with work teams such as Eason's and the Gas Company fielding selections. This growth was not reflected in the provincial areas however.[132] Home Farm gained a place in the 1936 final after they protested that a Rockwell player was ineligible following their semi-final loss to the Cork club.[133] In the final, played against Drogheda United at Tolka Park, Home Farm became the first Dublin club to win the trophy but were then subjected to a protest by the Louth club.[134] However, this was dismissed and they received their winners' medals at a presentation at the club's AGM in July 1936.[135]

This victory followed Home Farm establishing their own venue at Whitehall, which was officially opened at the start of the 1935–6 season by the lord mayor, Alderman Alfie Byrne TD.[136] A match was also played between Home Farm and Bohemians minors in connection with the occasion.[137] Their success attracted new players. In the latter half of the 1930s Home Farm were holding trials, with interested players advised in the press to contact the honorary secretary at his residence at Upper Drumcondra Road.[138]

Although a Schools' Challenge Cup was operational in Munster by 1937, Dublin was the centre of schoolboy soccer in independent Ireland and the selection of players for the first national schoolboys' teams reflected this throughout the remainder of

---

124 *II*, 12 June 1953. **125** *II*, 26 June 1934. **126** *EH*, 23 Jan. 1935. Dublin district clubs in the draw included St Mary's Pembroke, Cross Park Boys, Avon Boys, Blues Celtic, Russelglen Minors, Oakview, Inchicore United, Juverna, Queen's Celtic, Botanic Minors, Kimmage Rovers, St Thomas Aquinas, Ashbourne, Swifts United, Aldboro Rovers, Arcadians, Munster Boys, St Michael's United, Eustace Wanderers, Keogh Rangers, Home Farm Minors, Inchicore St Mary's, Longford (bye). **127** Ibid. **128** *EH*, 4 Feb. 1935. **129** *II*, 27 May 1935; *IE*, 27 May 1935. **130** *II*, 3 June 1935. **131** *IP*, 6 June 1935. **132** *EH*, 1 Nov. 1935; *IP*, 21 Nov. 1935. **133** *II*, 28 May 1936. **134** *EH*, 8 June 1936. **135** Ibid., 23 July 1936; Menton, *Home Farm*, p. 5. **136** *EH*, 1 Feb. 1933, 23 July 1936; *II*, 26 Sept. 1935. **137** *II*, 26 Sept. 1935 **138** *EH*, 7 Aug. 1936.

the twentieth century.[139] A schoolboys' team representing the Irish Free State played a Northern Ireland schoolboys' selection in Dublin for the first time in June 1937, with five of the Free State players coming from Dublin club Munster Victoria.[140] The Free State Schoolboys' selection was mainly made up of players from Dublin schools. These were Westland Row (3), O'Connell Schools (2), Synge Street, Milltown, Central Model Schools, Haddington Road and Dundalk (Louth), while the reserve was from St Mary's of Booterstown.[141] The match ended in a 2–2 draw.[142] In March 1939 they played Wales at Pontypridd in what appears to be their first match abroad, but, like the senior team, did not meet England until after the war.[143]

This was predated by more regional representative matches, with a Dublin schoolboys' selection taking on a Merseyside Catholic Schools XI in April 1935 in Liverpool.[144] In January 1937, Munster Victoria prepared for their 'annual Eastertide visit to Liverpool' by organizing a friendly against 'a selection of the Dublin Schoolboys' League'.[145] It was noted that 'the hon. sec. of the latter competition, Mr Luger, in order to get together the strongest side, invited each of the 14 clubs to forward to him the names of their best players' as the selection was to be made from those.[146] In August 1937 Munster Victoria, then Dublin Schoolboy League champions, defeated Liverpool Schoolboy League winners St Silvester's by three goals to one at Harold's Cross, with both teams said to be composed of players under 14 years of age.[147]

Schoolboy matches continued during the Emergency. In April 1940 Munster Victoria, Distillery Rovers, Dublin City, Haroldville, Leinster, Wasps, Reds United and Johnville were all registered with the Leinster Schoolboy League.[148] According to Brendan Menton, the Dublin and District Schoolboy League was established in 1944.[149] The FAI's Junior Committee had decided to concentrate on developing schoolboy football for the 1943–4 season, and took control of the Dublin Schoolboy League.[150] They reported that they had enjoyed 'a very successful season' with twenty teams participating in two divisions.[151] At the end of the following year, they stated that the Dublin Schoolboy League 'had a satisfactory and progressive season'.[152] The Harry Cannon Cup final, for under-15s, had been played before the FAI Cup final and was named after the former Ireland and Bohemians goalkeeper and army commandant who had died in March 1944.[153] As Taylor has stated of schoolboy soccer in England, prestigious schoolboy matches 'often took place at major grounds and drew crowds comparable with the professional game'.[154] Those key to the development of the Dublin and District Schoolboys' League included Jim Troy, Paddy Reilly, Joe O'Leary, Jim 'Jem' Kennedy, Jack Blakely and Bob Hennessy.[155]

139 Toms, *Soccer in Munster*, p. 152. 140 *II*, 9 June 1937; *EH*, 10 July 1937. 141 *IP*, 9 June 1937. 142 *SI*, 13 June 1937. 143 *II*, 4 Mar. 1939. 144 Curran, *Irish soccer migrants*, p. 63. 145 *EH*, 6 Jan. 1937. 146 Ibid. 147 *IP*, 31 Aug. 1937. 148 *SI*, 28 Apr. 1940. 149 Menton, *Home Farm*, p. 19. 150 Junior Committee 22nd Annual Report, 1943–4, FAI Archives, P137/29. 151 Ibid. 152 Junior Committee 23rd Annual Report, 1944–5, FAI Archives, P137/29. 153 Ibid.; *II*, 16 Mar. 1944. 154 Taylor, *The association game*, p. 82. 155 Briggs & Dodd, *100 years of the LFA*, p. 55.

The FAI's junior committee highlighted in their report at the end of the war that a number of schoolboy leagues had been formed throughout Ireland, but noted 'the difficulties confronting these leagues, in view of official school prejudices' and promised 'to surmount these obstacles'.[156] The FAI and the Football League of Ireland's *Official handbook and fixture list* stated in 1946 that since schoolboys' leagues had been 'taken under the direct control of the FAI three seasons ago' they had 'achieved much success'.[157] There were three leagues in operation for boys under the ages of 14, 15 and 16, while the schoolboys' league also had a knock-out competition for each division.[158] It appears that the Leinster Junior FA continued to administer minor and juvenile leagues but by the early 1950s the Leinster FA had donated the Jack Blakely Memorial Cup, for under-17s, and the Leinster Juvenile Cup to the Dublin Schoolboys' League.[159]

Certain Dublin clubs led the way in schoolboy soccer in the capital. By late 1949 Home Farm were running a total of eight teams, with five of these schoolboy selections, two juniors and one minor team.[160] However, it was noted that 'still they cannot meet the demand from players, as every position in some of the schoolboy sides can be filled twice over'.[161] The club had also nurtured numerous players who went on to English football clubs, including Johnny Carey, Tommy Godwin, Theo Dunne and Robin Lawler, while rugby players included Jack Belton and Karl Mullen, the latter going on to captain Ireland to Triple Crown victory.[162] Home Farm raised money through annual dances, exhibition matches and club draws and by 1954 had built a pavilion and floodlit training facility at Whitehall at the cost at around £12,600, although it appears the pitch retained a slight slope into the following decade.[163] Some schoolboy managers such as Home Farm's Joe Fitzpatrick developed networks with foreign clubs. Paddy Mulligan recalled how his Home Farm schoolboy manager used to make trips abroad to watch games and coaching, and Fitzpatrick's initiative led to a number of West German regional teams visiting Dublin in the 1950s and 1960s.[164] In turn, the Whitehall club travelled abroad to meet European clubs in underage competitions, and were voted the most sporting team at a tournament in West Germany in 1958.[165] In 1963, they met a Duisburg selection at Tolka Park, with three of their Leinster Senior League team, including schoolboy footballer of the year Mulligan, in the home team.[166] Preparation and appearance on the pitch were taken very seriously at the club, with players expected to turn up with their kit in pristine condition; as Mulligan noted, 'no way would you go down to Home Farm with your boots dirty, to play – under no circumstances'.[167]

156 Junior Committee 23rd Annual Report, 1944–5, FAI Archives, P137/31. 157 *Association football official handbook and fixture list 1945–46 and '47 authorized by the FAI and Football League of Ireland* (Dublin, 1946), p. 71. 158 Ibid. 159 Briggs & Dodd, *100 years of the LFA*, p. 55. 160 *EH*, 14 Dec. 1949. 161 Ibid. 162 Ibid. 163 *II*, 23 Apr. 1949; *EH*, 13 May 1949; *Drumcondra Football Club Limited official programme versus Shelbourne, 24 Dec. 1961* (Dublin, 1961), p. 2; Curran, *Irish soccer migrants*, p. 35. 164 Interview with Paddy Mulligan, 4 Oct. 2019; *IP*, 3 Sept. 1959; *EH*, 8 Oct. 1963. 165 *EH*, 3 July 1958. 166 *EH*, 8 Oct. 1963. 167 Interview with Paddy Mulligan, 4 Oct. 2019.

Stella Maris Boys' Club was said to have been established in a stable in 1940.[168] In September 1944 the club's 'spacious new premises' were opened at 40 Great Charles Street by Rev. James McNamee of Arran Quay, 'spiritual director', who blessed the venue.[169] The club was 'run by the Legion of Mary' and had nearly 150 members at that stage. It was noted that the club's activities 'ranged from woodwork, boot repairing and arts and crafts to drama and debating classes'.[170] In addition, boxing, swimming and physical culture were encouraged, while they had 'five football teams'.[171] Rev. McNamee founded the soccer team in 1943 along with Dermot O'Kelly and Percy Mulligan.[172] The club were helped greatly by Joe Grennell, 'who footed the £450 bill which enabled Fr McNamee and his boys, then playing in the Phoenix Park, to buy their ground at Richmond Road, with a 99 years' lease, and so gave the club permanence'.[173]

Another club that was fundamental to the growth of schoolboy soccer in Dublin was Johnville, based at Milltown, who were founded by John Joe McCarthy, Jim 'Jem' Kennedy and Richie Leonard.[174] In August 1945 they held their annual dinner at Clery's, following what was their most successful season at that point.[175] They had won the Leinster FA's Juvenile Cup, the AUL Juvenile Cup, the Under-15 Schoolboys' League for the third year in a row, the Harry Cannon Memorial Cup, the Under-14 Schoolboys' League, and had been runners-up in the AUL Juvenile League and the Paddy Thunder Memorial Cup.[176] By the early 1950s they were 'a noted football "nursery"' as 'many of the top-ranked players in Dublin League of Ireland teams learned their football' with the club.[177]

THE SCHOOLBOYS' FOOTBALL ASSOCIATION OF IRELAND

In May 1946 the FAI schoolboys' selection that took on the IFA schoolboys at Dalymount Park consisted of players from St Joseph's, Stella Maris, Johnville, Home Farm, Dublin City and Seaview Rangers, indicating the strength of these clubs at this time.[178] In 1947, the Dublin Schoolboys' League sponsored the first Irish schoolboys' team to play England, after an initial agreement between FA secretary Stanley Rous and Irish officials P.J. Reilly and Jim Troy at the 1946 senior match between the two countries.[179] On 29 May 1947 Ireland Schoolboys beat England 8–3 at Dalymount Park, with George Cummins of St Patrick's Athletic scoring four goals.[180] The return game was held in London on 8 May 1948, with Ireland winning by a goal to nil, illustrating the strength of the game in Dublin.[181] The Schoolboys' Football Association of Ireland was established in October 1948

---

168 *II*, 27 Sept. 1944. 169 Ibid., and *II*, 3 Nov. 1959. 170 *II*, 27 Sept. 1944. 171 Ibid. 172 Briggs & Dodd, *100 years of the LFA*, p. 106. 173 *II*, 3 Nov. 1959. 174 Briggs & Dodd, *100 years of the LFA*, p. 106. 175 *EH*, 28 Aug. 1945. 176 Ibid.; 36th Annual Report, July 1928, Leinster Football Association Archives, P239/27. The Paddy Thunder Memorial Cup was named after PJ Thunder, who was accountant and auditor to the Leinster FA. 177 *LL*, 5 Dec. 1953. 178 *IP*, 31 May 1946. 179 *SI*, 6 Jan. 1957; *Charles Buchan's football monthly*, 95 (July 1959), p. 21. 180 *SI*, 6 Jan. 1957. 181 Ibid.

following work by the council of the Junior Football Association of Ireland.[182] Myles Murphy was appointed as secretary and Matt Kenny was named treasurer, both of them having previous experience of these administrative roles within the FAI.[183] Fixtures between representative schoolboy associations were a lot slower to take hold in the Republic of Ireland than in England where matches between inter-regional selections were underway by the early 1900s, with Glasgow Schoolboys beating their London counterparts 4–2 at Hampden Park before 10,000 spectators in 1905.[184] The English Schools' FA was established in 1904 while the Welsh Schools' FA was set up in 1912.[185] It was not until September 1950 that the Mardyke in Cork hosted the first inter-provincial schoolboys' soccer match in the Republic of Ireland, when Leinster faced Munster.[186]

As noted above, Tom Tunney had helped to re-establish the Dublin Schoolboys' League in the 1930s and had brought Munster Victoria on trips to England since 1932, although this ceased temporarily during the Second World War between 1939 and 1945.[187] However, it continued after the war, with players such as John Giles gaining some early experience of the game in England through their own matches and trips to those in the First Division, having travelled over on the boat from the North Wall, an eight-hour trip across the Irish Sea to Liverpool.[188] Tunney had also been involved with Dublin City, a club formed in the late 1930s that merged with Munster Victoria in 1951.[189] He later noted the presence of Irish priests in English schoolboy soccer clubs as being helpful to fostering these cross-Channel links.[190] These included a Father Kieran and Father O'Keeffe, who assisted in the organization of Strandvilla 'C''s trip to Liverpool at Easter 1927.[191] In June 1946, with travel restrictions lessened after the Second World War, a Liverpool team from a Catholic School League there were noted as being 'the first cross-Channel schoolboys' representative team to play in Dublin'.[192] The Liverpool team had won the Lancashire Schools' Cup and the Merseyside Shield and had reached the quarter-finals of the English Schools' Shield.[193]

By the late 1940s the popularity of soccer was well established among young players in Dublin. One reporter was of the opinion in 1949 that 'never before … was the game so popular and widespread among schoolboys. Lads from 14 years old are flocking to soccer at such a rate in all the principle centres that some clubs have to run two teams to cater for the needs of the budding footballers at their most impressionable age.'[194] In addition, he noted that 'in Dublin alone there are over 100 teams competing in the schoolboys' league, and further extension is becoming necessary to provide facilities for the growing number of young recruits coming into the game'.[195]

The growth of organized competitions for schoolboys was much slower throughout Ireland despite the interest in the game in many areas, but the lead

---

182 *EE*, 20 Feb. 1958.   183 Ibid.   184 Taylor, *The association game*, p. 82.   185 Ibid.   186 *EE*, 7 Sept. 1950.   187 *SI*, 27 Jan. 1957.   188 Giles, *A football man*, pp 31–2.   189 *SI*, 27 Jan. 1957.   190 Ibid.   191 *FSW*, 5 Mar. 1927.   192 Curran, *Irish soccer migrants*, p. 63.   193 *IP*, 28 June 1946.   194 *EH*, 14 Dec. 1949   195 Ibid.

taken by Dublin organizers and clubs was fundamental to strengthening confidence and providing a model structure. Early in 1944, the FAI's Junior Committee agreed to resume the Minor Cup after a year's break, and while noting 'that relatively few provincial clubs would participate', they felt that it was better for the game's development if the competition continued.[196] However, this national competition was not enough to sustain regional clubs, and in November 1948, the Cork Schoolboys' League was established.[197] Outside of Dublin, it was in Cork and Waterford where schoolboy leagues also flourished by the middle of the twentieth century, with the Cork schoolboy league having twelve teams involved in 1958, while another was said to be in formation.[198] In Waterford, the Waterford and District Association were said to be in the process of organizing a twelve-team league. It was hoped by one journalist that leagues would also be formed in provincial centres including Athlone, Galway, Limerick, Sligo and Mullingar and promoters and organizers were advised to affiliate with the Schoolboys' Football Association of Ireland.[199]

The 1950s also saw the initiation of a number of competitions that benefited schoolboy soccer in Dublin. In 1951 there were 'approximately 200' schoolboy teams registered with the FAI, with this figure said to have risen to 300 by 1955.[200] By 1952 the inaugural Evans Cup competition, the first national schoolboy competition under the Schoolboys' Football Association of Ireland, was up and running, with Dublin clubs heavily represented in the draw, which also included clubs from Limerick, Galway, Cork, Tipperary and Waterford.[201] The final was played in June 1953, with Glasheen of Cork taking on Rathfarnham at Richmond Park, Inchicore, with the trophy donated by Dublin businessman R.J. Evans. The competition, for under-15 players, was said to be 'an important milestone in progress of soccer' in Ireland.[202] The Dublin team won the match by three goals to two, despite the Cork side fighting back from a two goal deficit before succumbing to a late winner on a pitch that had become saturated from a thunderstorm at half-time.[203] The following year, Johnville defeated Hibernians of Waterford in the final at Ozier Park.[204] Like Home Farm and Munster Victoria, Johnville also produced players who went on to senior level, with four of Shamrock Rovers' 1955 FAI Cup final winning team coming from the club.[205]

By the mid-1950s, the Crusade League was reported to be an important 'nursery' for players in the Harold's Cross-Mount Argus area of south Dublin, with Manchester City's Fionan Fagan, Albie Murphy (Clyde), Eamon Darcy (Oldham), George Cummins (Luton Town) and Terry Murray (Bournemouth) having

---

196 Junior Emergency Committee Minutes, 6 Jan. 1944, FAI Archives, P137/29. 197 Ibid. 198 *Evening Echo*, 20 Feb. 1958. 199 Ibid. 200 Junior Committee 29th Annual Report, 1950–1 and 23rd Annual Report, 1954–5, FAI Archives, P137/31. 201 *EH*, 23 Sept. 1952 and 12 June 1953. 202 Ibid., 12 June 1953; *II*, 12 June 1953. 203 *II*, 15 June 1953. 204 *IE*, 21 July 1954. 205 Ryan, *The official book of the FAI Cup*, p. 200. These were Ronnie Nolan, Hughie Gannon, Mickey Burke and Gerry Mackey.

experience of this competition before moving on to senior clubs.[206] This league had been established by Fr Paul Mary in 1950, 'with the object of providing a sound spiritual and civic training and for the promotion of cultural and sporting activities for the youths of the confraternity attached to Mount Argus'.[207] He was later succeeded in his organizational role by Fr Anselm, who was assisted by Willie Norton of Rathfarnham FC, a club said to be the south-side rivals of north-side club Home Farm.[208] In 1958 the Catholic church's soccer committee estimated that there were 'about 115 teams' in the Dublin and District Schoolboys' League, which had 'over 1500 boys' involved. There were also 'two main leagues for boys between the ages of 12 and 17 years' run by the Catholic Youth Council League, with up to 600 members of Catholic boys' clubs taking part, and 'various' leagues 'attached to Youth Sodalities'.[209] The Schoolboys' Football Association of Ireland's honorary secretary in 1957 was Jim Troy, who had been involved in soccer administration since 1932.[210] He was also the secretary of the Leinster Junior FA and was their representative on the FAI's Junior Committee. In addition, he was the secretary of the Dublin Minor League and the Dublin Schoolboys' League, as well as being the chairman of St Paul's AFC.[211] Financially, the Schoolboys' Football Association of Ireland, which catered for underage groups from 13 to 17, were said to be struggling and relied on volunteers and support from the FAI and the Leinster FA, who provided 'free accommodation for the Dublin Schoolboys' League'.[212]

A number of clubs that became well-known for their schoolboy teams were founded in the 1950s, with Cherry Orchard of Ballyfermot established in 1957, although they did not take part in schoolboy football until 1970.[213] St Joseph's of Sallynoggin were founded in 1953 by Fr Frank McCabe, who was instrumental in organizing local activities for youths.[214] By 1958 they had nine teams and these ranged from under-13 to under-17, although securing a home ground was initially difficult until a suitable facility was secured through the assistance of local man Michael Scott.[215] They later opened their own headquarters in 1964.[216] St Kevin's Boys', based in Santry, were founded in 1959 by Fr Des Williams, who later became a bishop of Dublin.[217] Although less well known for its underage playing success, St Francis, a club rooted in the Liberties, were founded by John Hyland in 1958, and later came to prominence as a Leinster Senior League club, and briefly, a League of Ireland club, at the turn of the millennium.[218]

206 *IP*, 5 July 1955. 207 *Irish Soccer*, 1:1 (1955), p. 14. 208 Ibid. 209 Diocesan Soccer Committee's General Report, Sept. 1958, Trade Unions XXII 48/22/2, Archbishop McQuaid Papers, Dublin Diocesan Archives. 210 *SI*, 6 Jan. 1957. 211 Ibid. 212 Ibid. 213 Briggs & Dodd, *100 years of the LFA*, p. 106. 214 Survey of Youth Organizations Touching on Sallynoggin. 1958, Youth Affairs XXVIII 1464/4/1 (2), Archbishop McQuaid Papers, Dublin Diocesan Archives; and 'Soccer in the "Boro"' – St Joseph's Boys', soccerintheboro.com/st-josephs-boys–1.php, accessed 25 Nov. 2021. 215 Survey of Youth Organizations Touching on Sallynoggin. 1958, Youth Affairs XXVIII, 1464/4/1 (2), Archbishop McQuaid Papers, Dublin Diocesan Archives. 216 *Soccer Reporter* (Apr. 1979), p. 12. 217 'St Kevin's Boys Club: club history – our history', skbfc.yourclub.ie/history, accessed 2 July 2020. 218 *ST*, 22 Sept. 1996.

Another famous Dublin schoolboy club was developed much later. Although a Belvedere Boys' team was in existence in the 1920s, Belvedere FC began in 1971 'with four teams in the "G" and "H" leagues of the DDSL [Dublin and District Schoolboys' League]'.[219] By the late 1980s they had teams in every division of the DDSL, ranging from under-9s to under-18s.[220] By 1989 they had twenty-four players registered with League of Ireland clubs, while the club had also had been strongly represented at underage international level since 1976. Fifteen Belvedere players were on US soccer scholarships and one reporter noted that for a team 'based in the inner city where unemployment is high the influence of the club cannot be underestimated'.[221]

Home Farm, Cherry Orchard and Belvedere were the three leading schoolboy club suppliers of Irish-born English league players in the 1945–2010 period.[222] These leading Dublin schoolboy clubs have therefore attracted many young players keen to play at the highest levels of schoolboy soccer and to gain the attention of British scouts.[223] By the early part of the 1970s players were moving to Cherry Orchard in search of a better level of schoolboy football, including Ringsend native David Langan, who moved from 15E football at Bath Rangers to 15A at Cherry Orchard.[224] Some other teams also emerged, with Cambridge Boys, based at Ringsend Park, reported to be 'one of the strongest schoolboy soccer clubs on the south side of Dublin' by the summer of 1972.[225]

Dublin schoolboy players remained the backbone of Irish underage selections. For those who were chosen, schoolboy internationals could offer a taste of what was to come in professional football if they could break into the highest levels. Paddy Mulligan recalled that he had his first encounter with Ron 'Chopper' Harris in an under-15 schoolboy international against England at Tolka Park on a wet night in May 1960.[226] He noted that

> we drew with them two each. Ronnie Harris was marking me – again, I was playing inside-forward, we had a right kicking match. We drew with them two each, and I remember, because the Schoolboy League and 'Jem' Kennedy, in particular, they were so excited by the fact that we had played very well, and drew two each with an excellent England team, that they brought us down to the Clarence Hotel, down on the quays, for lunch the following day. And we were walking up Capel Street after that, and 'Jem' Kennedy gave us all two and six pence in the old, the real old money – I don't know what it would equate to today, maybe 40 cents or 50 cents. They told us, 'That was great last night, thanks very much indeed.'[227]

219 *FSW,* 4 Dec. 1926; *EH,* 16 Jan. 1989.   220 *EH,* 16 Jan. 1989.   221 Ibid.   222 Curran, *Irish soccer migrants,* pp 34–8.   223 Ibid., p. 36.   224 David Langan (with Trevor Keane & Alan Conway), *Running through walls* (Derby, 2012), pp 22–5.   225 *EH,* 27 July 1972.   226 Interview with Paddy Mulligan, 4 Oct. 2019; *II,* 14 May 1960.   227 Interview with Paddy Mulligan, 4 Oct. 2019.

15. An aerial view of Dalymount Park and the surrounding Phibsboro area (1956). Courtesy of the National Library of Ireland.

The Irish team that night, denied victory only by a late English equalizer, included Eamon Dunphy of Stella Maris, and two other players from that club; three from Home Farm; and one apiece from Dublin clubs St Joseph's and Bluebell United; while Munster was represented through players from Ringmahon Rangers (Cork), Southend United (Waterford) and Tramore Athletic (Waterford).[228] Along with Harris of Hackney, a future Chelsea teammate of Mulligan's, England fielded two others who would go on to make their names in professional football, mainly as managers, David Pleat of Nottingham and Barry Fry of Bedford.[229]

The opportunity to play in the Harry Cannon Cup final before the FAI Cup final at Dalymount Park remained a motivating factor for young players. Mulligan recalled that the venue was

> the home of Irish soccer – a magnificent stadium, the crowd in on top of you, wonderful. The opposition could see the whites of their eyes. That's what you want – you wanted to put the frighteners on them. But it was a wonderful, wonderful stadium. The atmosphere was always great. The first time I played there was in 1960 for Home Farm against Southend United. We

228 *II*, 14 May 1960.   229 Ibid.

were playing them in a cup final – before the FAI Cup final between Shels
and Cork Hibs – and we beat them 4–2, and I fell in love with Dalymount
… You were sharing a dressing room with Shels, and you met the likes of
Freddie Strahan and so on playing, and Joey Wilson playing for Shels. They
won the cup that year – they had Tony Dunne, it was his last year before
he went to Man. United, and they won it 2–0 – I think it was against Cork
Hibs. So again, I had the best of times.[230]

In December 1975 the Republic of Ireland youth team, said to be 'composed mostly
of Home Farm and Stella Maris players', took on a Connacht panel at Terryland
Park.[231] One reporter felt that the two Dublin clubs had 'been proven to be the
nursery of Irish soccer down through the years'.[232]

Family involvement in the game was important to the development of many
players. Dave Henderson got involved in football through his father Paddy, a well-
established League of Ireland goalkeeper. He moved from Cabra to Coolock as a
child and recalled joining Stella Maris, where he trained twice a week, in the early
1970s:

Initially my da would have brought me down for trials down there, from
Coolock. From Coolock to Drumcondra at the time, at ten years of age you
would get a bus to Fairview, and Fairview Strand at the time was huge to a
kid, that would be like the M50. You had to make your way across that, walk
all the way up Richmond Road, up into Stella Maris, do a bit of training, go
back down to Fairview, and run. The back of the bus used to be open at the
time – you could run and hop on to the step, and get back out to Coolock.
But you were doing that at eleven and twelve. I don't think you'd see many
kids doing that now … it was an adventure all the time.[233]

He also noted that 'schoolboy football at that time started under 12s, from when I
was about nine or ten, the nearest club to Coolock at the time was Stella Maris, so
I would have joined then at nine or ten and played at two years below the under 12
age'.[234] Similarly, Brian O'Shea, who started with Home Farm, was introduced to
the game by his father, Frank, who was also a goalkeeper:

He didn't play professionally and it was funny, we only found out after he'd
passed away that he'd turned down a trial with Hibernians in Scotland. He
was quite private in that respect. But he played for the Match Factory and
he played for a team called Bendigo, which was a very old Dublin team from
north inner-city. He worked for Dublin Corporation so he played some
games for the Corporation as well.[235]

230 Interview with Paddy Mulligan, 4 Oct. 2019. 231 *CT*, 12 Dec. 1975. 232 Ibid. 233 Interview
with Dave Henderson, 22 Nov. 2019. 234 Ibid. 235 Interview with Brian O'Shea, 21 Nov. 2019.

O'Shea recalled why he had chosen Home Farm as his schoolboy club:

> There were a couple of schoolboy clubs around the area but I think my dad
> wanted me to go to Home Farm because of the reputation the club had,
> and it proved right because I got a lot of opportunity when I went to Home
> Farm. Obviously it exposed me to international selectors and Leinster rep-
> resentative selectors, so that kind of convinced you to play in goal because I
> didn't always want to play [there]. As I got older I wanted to play out, and it
> was probably only when I hit around thirteen, fourteen that I decided that
> that was my best position and it was going to offer up my best opportunity
> to go further in the game.[236]

He had come through the club's mini-league system at St Mobhi Road, which
'really were trials for Home Farm'.[237] Home Farm had inaugurated these in 1962
following the acquisition of grounds at St Mobhi Road in Glasnevin.[238] They were
run annually from late May to mid-July at under-8, under-10 and under-12 levels,
and despite losing part of the ground when it was put up for sale by its owners in
1969, in the 1970s there were over forty teams involved.[239] A member of a number
of highly successful underage teams at the club, O'Shea recalled that they had

> won every trophy. Now, in the early years, because I played in the 'B' team
> and couldn't quite get in – so I was probably playing under-11s 'B' – couldn't
> get into the 'A' team until I was probably under-12s and the goalkeeper got
> injured, and that's when I ended up going in goal, then the rest is history.
> So, [I] would have won two FAI youth cups, two leagues, All-Ireland league
> medals with them, under-16, -17, -18 All-Irelands, and I'd say, probably my
> most successful time in football was actually at Home Farm.[240]

The strength of schoolboy soccer in Dublin was evident in international schoolboy
selection policies throughout the latter half of the twentieth century, while Dublin
sides also dominated the Kennedy Cup, an under-14 competition for representative schoolboy areas, by the early 1980s.[241] In the 1983–4 season, two new national
cups, the Troy Cup for under-13s and the Goodson Cup for under-14s, were introduced in addition to the under-15s Evans Cup and the Barry Cup for under-16s.[242]

By the late twentieth century, Home Farm had an international reputation as
the Republic of Ireland's leading schoolboy club, having developed a number of
highly successful underage teams, with Liam Tuohy central to this. He had become
director of football to the club's schoolboy teams in 1989.[243] Two teams featured in

236 Ibid.   237 Ibid.   238 Menton, *Home Farm*, pp 26, 236.   239 Ibid., pp 26–7, 236.
240 Interview with Brian O'Shea, 21 Nov. 2019,   241 Minute Book of the Senior Council, FAI
Annual Report 1982–3, June 1983, FAI Archives, P137/24.   242 Minute Book of the Senior Council,
FAI Annual Report 1983–4, June 1984, ibid.   243 Menton, *Home Farm*, p. 238.

the *Guinness book of records*, with the first winning seventy-nine successive matches between 1968 and 1970 and the second achieving recognition for an unbeaten run from 1983 until 1990, which amounted to 203 matches undefeated from the under-10 level to the under-18 level.[244] As well as winning domestic honours, they collected trophies in international competitions in Northern Ireland, Scotland and Belgium, while team members Graham Kavanagh and Gary Kelly went on to represent the Republic of Ireland at senior international level.[245]

Kelly had moved from Drogheda Boys to play for Home Farm.[246] He was later signed by Leeds United in 1991, and by the beginning of 2000 there were nine former Home Farm players at Elland Road. At that point, Home Farm and Leeds United had established a formal five-year alliance with Leeds United, who were then managed by David O'Leary, offering technical support and Home Farm wearing the Yorkshire club's crest on their jerseys.[247] In the previous decade, the Whitehall club had been formally connected to Everton through sponsorship from the Merseyside club.[248]

Movement to more developed clubs in Ireland from less prominent schoolboy teams continued late into the late twentieth century. Robbie Keane, for example, moved from his initial club, Fettercairn, to Crumlin United as a 12-year-old in 1992 as he felt he would have a better chance of getting spotted.[249] Other players continued to come through the mini-league system at other clubs, with Shane Supple, who grew up in Castleknock, beginning with local club Verona. He recalled that these were usually held 'in the summer … like a World Cup kind of thing'.[250] He went on to play in the Brenfer League before moving on to Home Farm and playing in the Dublin and District Schoolboy League and then joining Ipswich Town in 2002.[251]

The best Dublin clubs have also attracted players from the Irish countryside.[252] Players such as 1980s Home Farm starlet Tony Lawlor from Laois regularly travelled to Dublin for training and matches.[253] Lawlor was part of a highly successful Home Farm youth team that won provincial and national honours. He was also an Irish youth international who had trials in England before moving to Boston University to take up a soccer scholarship.[254] Other players have utilized Dublin clubs as stepping stones to British clubs and have migrated within Ireland to play schoolboys soccer in Dublin, including Diarmuid O'Carroll and Alan Smith.[255] Longford-based Seán Prunty travelled to Dublin every weekend to play for Belvedere prior to his move to Middlesbrough, such was his determination to make a career in professional football.[256] Like Tony Lawlor and others, he benefited from highly supportive parents. He recalled that in the late 1990s

---

244 Ibid., p. 236; *EH*, 1 and 8 Dec. 2008. **245** *EH*, 1 and 8 Dec. 2008. **246** *IT*, 9 Oct. 1999. **247** *II*, 6 Jan. 2000. **248** *IE*, 10 Nov. 1995. **249** Andrew Sleigh, *Robbie Keane: the biography* (London, 2007), p. 8. **250** Interview with Shane Supple, 24 Sept. 2019. **251** Ibid. **252** Curran, *Irish soccer migrants*, pp 36–7. **253** *EH*, 13 Apr. 1984. **254** Ibid. **255** Curran, *Irish soccer migrants*, p. 36. **256** Interview with Seán Prunty, 23 Oct. 2019.

16. The entrance to Home Farm FC in the early twenty-first century (2022). Author's own collection.

17. Home Farm's ground at Whitehall (2022). Author's own collection.

my dad would drive me up on a Saturday, I'd stay overnight on a Saturday and play the games then on the Sunday. So that's how that came about and it was great because the standard within the Dublin leagues was definitely sort of a level, two levels above what I was playing. That's no disrespect to the guys I was playing with, but in order for me to progress as a footballer I had to play in Dublin, and that's the way it was at the time. There was different types of coaching, [and] you were playing obviously against, you know, top teams every single week, and it was a challenge. It was difficult coming up, it was difficult for my parents, my family, I'm sure, driving up from Longford every single week, every weekend, to drop me up to training. Dad would go home, and he'd come up again on the Sunday to watch me play. There was no motorways back then, you know, so you're looking at a two-hour-plus journey.[257]

THE GROWTH OF SCHOOLS' SOCCER IN DUBLIN

Despite the development of schoolboy soccer leagues in Dublin, there was resistance to the game in many schools where authorities saw it as their national duty to promote what they saw as Irish culture. Some Christian Brothers clearly encouraged soccer, such as Brother McGurk, who was instrumental in encouraging the establishment of Tramore Celtic of Waterford during the First World War.[258] However, after partition, Gaelic games were clearly favoured, as noted by numerous soccer players, including John Giles, who attended Brunswick Street CBS in

257 Ibid.   258 Toms, *Soccer in Munster*, p. 33.

the 1940s and early 1950s.[259] Growing up in Dublin in the 1960s, Eoin Hand has written of the physical and psychological abuse he was forced to endure as a result of his connection with Stella Maris from one Christian Brother known as 'the Bull'.[260] Mick Lawlor similarly witnessed the disdain with which soccer was held in some Christian Brothers schools:

> Well, I played with Sheriff United, so some of our players went to the Laurence O'Toole School, and the Christian Brothers were quite firm about students playing for the Gaelic team, particularly if you were good, they would obviously want you. But unfortunately, there were a couple of instances where the players preferred to play with my team in Sheriff United and when they got back to school on the Monday morning, they were very harshly treated – that's the only way I'll put it – very harshly treated, to the point where one or two parents went up and there was all sorts of physicalities between Christian Brothers and parents because of the ill-treatment, which was terrible, but that was the culture at the time and that's the way it was. But not pleasant.[261]

This discrimination against soccer players continued into the 1970s, the most notorious case being then 15-year-old Liam Brady's temporary expulsion from St Aidan's CBS in Whitehall in April 1971 for captaining the Republic of Ireland's schoolboys team in a match in Wales instead of playing a Gaelic football challenge match.[262] Given the prohibition of soccer in many Dublin schools, an important part of learning the game for young players was the street and neighbourhood in which they lived as well as in clubs. John Giles recalled life in Ormond Square in Dublin's inner-city, where, as a child, he played with a 'bouncer' with his friends.[263] Mick Meagan learned the game informally in Churchtown, near Shamrock Rovers' ground in Milltown, by playing a game known locally as 'combo', where a 'shammy' ball, which was an old tennis ball, had to be kept off the ground.[264] Theo Dunne has stated that 'we'd play with a tennis ball. You went from a rag ball to a tennis ball to a "bouncer" and then onto a football.'[265] Without school teams, some pupils set up their own clubs, with Joe Carolan, who joined Manchester United from Home Farm in 1956, recalling how a number of his former schoolmates founded their own team, St Peter's.[266] Street football remained an important outlet for many children growing up in Dublin in the later twentieth century, with some areas gaining a reputation for their local leagues.

By the late 1950s, the Easter Vacation League for school and college players was established by the Universities' and Colleges' Football Union.[267] Annual organizing meetings were usually held at Home Farm's pavilion.[268] The Leinster Secondary

259 Giles, *A football man*, pp 41–5. 260 Hand, *First hand*, p. 7 261 Interview with Mick Lawlor, 29 Feb. 2020. 262 Brady, *So far so good*, pp 11–13 and *II*, 29 Apr. 1971. 263 Giles, *A football man*, p. 15. 264 Interview with Mick Meagan, 11 Nov. 2013. 265 Rice, *We are Rovers*, p. 63. 266 *Charles Buchan's football monthly*, 98 (Oct. 1959), p. 21. 267 *EH*, 12 May 1958. 268 Ibid.; *II*, 16 Mar. 1960; *EH*, 1 Apr. 1963 and 11 Mar. 1965.

18. Pearse Square Play Centre with children playing soccer (1970s). Courtesy of Dublin City Council Photographic Collection, Dublin City Library and Archives.

Schools' selection also annually met the Ulster Grammar Schools team by that time.[269] By Easter 1963 twenty-three teams made up six sections of the Easter Vacation League, with matches to be played over a week at a variety of venues in Dublin, such as Whitehall and Belfield.[270] The 1965 final between Castletown and Academia was played at Dalymount Park, illustrating how the competition was growing in stature.[271] Following the success of the Easter Vacation League and the under-15 cup competition, in May 1968, the Irish Universities' and Colleges' Football Union issued a circular to all secondary schools in Leinster inviting them to attend a meeting on 7 June at Newman House, St Stephen's Green, to finalize plans for the following season.[272] It was intended to set up a Secondary Schools' branch of the IUCFU and to arrange a coaching course for schoolteachers, with a view to them completing the FA Coaching Certificate examination.[273] Previously, the Easter Vacation League had included teams who were not officially representing their schools, but this new venture would see schools having to have the sanction of their authorities.[274] Schools including Blackrock College, who won the league in successive years as Castletown, had competed under informal names initially.[275] Blackrock's 1965 victory in the Easter Vacation League 'was altogether unexpected

269 *BN*, 2 Apr. 1959. **270** *EH*, 9 Apr. 1963. Teams included Boro United, St Patrick's United, Newtown Park, Ranelagh United, St Kevin's, Leeson Rovers 'A' and 'B', Sparta 'A' and 'B', Berwick Rangers, Hibernians, Corinthians, Kostka Dynamo, Magpies, Jacobites, DC Dynamo, Rathmines Rangers, Albion, St Paul's, Spurs, Rockwell, North End and Golden Eagles. **271** *EH*, 17 May 1965. **272** *EH*, 31 May 1968. **273** Ibid. **274** Ibid. **275** *EH*, 17 Mar. 1971.

and not entirely welcome, especially as it was seen by some school authorities to conflict with training for athletics during the final term' and 'soccer had not yet been accorded official recognition by the college authorities for inter-schools competitions', although it had been played there previously.[276]

The first national Secondary Schools' final took place in May 1968 when Chanel College Dublin, who had come through the Easter Vacation League successfully, met Connacht champions Summerhill College of Sligo at St Mel's Park Athlone.[277] The cup was donated by Alec McCabe, a League of Ireland patron and former pupil at Summerhill.[278] By the spring of 1971 the first Leinster Schools' soccer competitions were underway, with 'a huge entry' noted for the senior, under-14 and junior competitions.[279] By that point, a number of schools traditionally associated with rugby – such as St Mary's, Clongowes, Castleknock, Blackrock and Terenure – were fielding soccer teams, while similarly, schools with a Gaelic football ethos such as St Vincent's Glasnevin, O'Connell Schools, Chanel and De La Salle Ballyfermot were also taking up the game.[280]

By 1971 there were estimated to be over 10,000 players in the Dublin Schoolboys' League, yet only £400 was given to the game by the government.[281] One reporter noted that 'although soccer is one of the most popular games in this country, especially in the cities, facilities have never been on a par with several of the lesser sports'.[282] He felt that the game had been ignored in schools and that 'virtually every schoolboy club in Dublin, with regard to both membership and location, can be termed as "working class", for want of a better phrase, and so with little finance many Dublin Schoolboy League teams have had to play, dress and train in rather primitive conditions'.[283] Coaching of young players had improved, however, with the Dublin Schoolboys' League having 'a very extensive programme for coaching' in operation by the early 1970s.[284] By the middle of that decade, the Football Association of Irish Schools (FAIS) was operational.[285] In 1976, the FAIS Leinster branch was encouraging the involvement of teams from outside Dublin in counties such as Meath and Louth, 'which had been "shy" in official soccer competitions for schools'.[286] The Department of Education had also become more involved in assisting the improvement of soccer, with the FAI's coaching committee noting the receipt of a grant of £8,000 from the department in July 1976.[287] By the summer of 1977 a quarter of all boys' post-primary schools had affiliated to the FAI, while there were thirty primary schools involved in Leinster competitions.[288] In 1977, Dublin hosted the World Schools' Football Tournament, with schools from sixteen nations across three continents involved.[289]

276 Farragher & Wyer, *Blackrock College, 1860–1995*, p. 336. **277** *EH*, 17 May 1968. **278** Ibid. **279** *EH*, 17 Mar. 1971. **280** Ibid. **281** *EH*, 14 Apr. 1971. **282** Ibid. **283** Ibid. **284** Coaching Committee Meeting 19 Mar. 1971, FAI Archives, P137/16. **285** Minute Book of the Senior Council, FAI Annual Report 1978–9, FAI Archives, P137/24. **286** *DI*, 27 Feb. 1976. **287** Coaching and Development Committee Meeting, 30 July 1976, FAI Archives, P137/17. **288** Minute Book of the Senior Council, FAI Annual Report, 1976–7, FAI Archives, P137/24. **289** Schoolboys' Football Association of Ireland, 2007/125/62 (1975–7), NAI.

Naturally, players with aspirations of a career in professional football have been drawn to schools which encouraged the game. Stephen McGuinness noted of his time at primary school in Finglas in the 1980s:

> First of all, I went to St Canice's Boys' in Finglas, I went to that school first. [I was] bitterly disappointed they didn't play football – soccer. It actually still sticks in my gut to this day if I'm honest with you. I was desperate to play soccer and I went to the school and quickly realized that they only played Gaelic football. I played it, obviously, because I'd do anything to play sport and I wasn't into hurling – they were trying to get me to play hurling, I didn't fancy playing that – and we played soccer every single day in the yard and it was Man. United v Liverpool, actually Man. United and Arsenal v Liverpool … I ran from my home to school every day to get in for about ten past eight or a quarter past eight to play football, and all we did was play football, every single day. School then, we had a little game between us, which was the biggest deal ever between two classes, of a soccer game. But I always held that against the school that we didn't have soccer.[290]

By 1980, sixty-one schools in Leinster were affiliated to the Football Association of Irish Schools, and Beneavin College and Patrician College had established themselves as the best two senior schools' teams in Dublin.[291] Beneavin's victory over their rivals after a replay at Dalymount Park that year was their third consecutive win against them in the Leinster Senior Schools' final.[292] Beneavin went on to represent Ireland in the Schools' World Cup in Sweden in July 1981, along with fifteen other international teams, although this required fundraising throughout the year for the travel required.[293] The early 1980s saw the emergence of Greenhills College (Walkinstown), who won the Leinster Schools' Senior League and Cup in 1981, along with the under-14 cup.[294] In 1983, Patrician College of Finglas reached six out of eight schools' finals at national level, winning five.[295] For those who did not make the schools' panels, internal school leagues helped their development, while by the early 1980s they also had 'a squad of teachers all young and still playing football themselves who not only manage and coach the teams, but develop self-esteem, self-confidence, respect and teamwork in the boys'.[296] McGuinness felt that his decision to attend secondary school there was based mainly on the school's reputation for producing professional footballers:

> With all due respect to Patrician College, which I went to – this isn't having a go at anybody – it wasn't the best. If I was making the decision about

290 Interview with Stephen McGuinness, 22 Oct. 2019.   291 Minute Book of the Senior Council, FAI Annual Report, 1979–80, FAI Archives, P137/24.   292 Ibid.   293 Minute Book of the Senior Council, FAI Annual Report, 1980–1, June 1981, FAI Archives, P137/24.   294 Ibid.   295 *Soccer Reporter* (Aug. 1983), p. 14.   296 Ibid.

education, I would never have gone to Patrician College ... Beneavin and Kevin's would have been the best two. But I made the decision based on Martin Russell, Pat Fenlon, Ronnie Whelan, Derek Brazil had come from Patrician College – I knew that – I didn't know their families but I knew guys who knocked about with them and the general feeling was that if you wanted to be a footballer, Patrician College was the place to go to. My decision was 100 per cent around football. Going to Patrician College, it was nothing about education, and it was the right decision, because football-wise it was a very, very good school.[297]

However, despite the growth in schools' soccer in Dublin and more regional areas such as Sligo and North Donegal, it was not until the late twentieth century that schoolboy leagues with club teams began to get a foothold in some peripheral areas such as south Donegal, where a local schoolboys' league was first established in 1988, as the organization of Gaelic football provided stiff opposition.[298]

At the end of the 1988–9 season the FAIFS noted 'a large increase in affiliated schools, especially in Leinster'.[299] With the success of the Republic of Ireland's international soccer team under Jack Charlton in the period from 1986 to 1995, it was then that sponsorship for soccer competitions began to increase and attempts to develop infrastructures for underage soccer in rural areas gained more support.[300] Success at underage and schoolboy international level had largely eluded the Republic of Ireland until the late 1990s, although victory in the 1982 European Schoolboys' Championship was notable.[301] Victory was secured through a penalty shoot-out against Italy, with Belvedere players Martin Russell and Tommy McDermott and St Kevin's Derek Ryan to the fore in the competition.[302] In 1998, Brian Kerr, along with his assistant, Noel O'Reilly, led the Republic of Ireland to victory in the European under-18 championship following success in the European under-16 championship earlier that year.[303] The under-19 team had previously finished in third place at the World Championships under Kerr.[304] Kerr, who had attended St Michael's CBS, Inchicore, and was a graduate of Kevin Street College of Technology (TU Dublin), nurtured the early development of players such as Richard Dunne, Robbie Keane, Stephen McPhail and Damien Duff, who went on to become senior internationals.[305] Kerr had been involved in athletics and boxing, with his father Frank a noted amateur boxer, and he himself had been managing soccer teams since he was 15. Having initially taken charge of Crumlin United under-12s, he was Shamrock Rovers' B manager at 19 and took over the St Patrick's Athletic job in 1986.[306] He won two league championships there despite the club's financial problems, and was appointed as manager of the Republic of

297 Interview with Stephen McGuinness, 22 Oct. 2019. 298 Curran, *Irish soccer migrants*, p. 95. 299 Football Association of Ireland Annual Report, 1987–8, June 1988, p. 8, FAI Archives, P137/24. 300 Curran, *Irish soccer migrants*, pp 95–8. 301 *Soccer Reporter* (May 1982), p. 1. 302 Ibid. 303 *SI*, 10 May 1998; *EH*, 27 July 1998. 304 *ST*, 26 July 1998. 305 Ibid. 306 Ibid.

Ireland's youth teams late in 1996, before taking over the senior team in 2003.[307] He was awarded an honorary doctorate from DIT in November 2005 'for his out-standing contribution to sport', shortly after his term as senior international team manager ended.[308]

THE COLLINGWOOD CUP AND OTHER THIRD-LEVEL COMPETITIONS

The Collingwood Cup, the premier soccer competition for Irish universities, unsur-prisingly had its origins in Dublin. Although it has generally failed to attract the media publicity and television coverage offered to the GAA's annual Sigerson Cup and Fitzgibbon Cup competitions, the Collingwood Cup competition has also been in existence since the early twentieth century. The trophy was donated for compe-tition by Professor Bertram J. Collingwood of UCD in 1914, with UCD beating Queen's University, Belfast by 2–1 in the final at Dalymount Park that year.[309] Professor Collingwood had been appointed as chair of physiology at UCD in 1912, having previously been at Oxford University, where he played for the New College team.[310] He also appeared for the amateur side Corinthians and was a nephew of the mathematician Charles Dodgson, otherwise known as Lewis Carroll.[311]

With the partition of Ireland, soccer became less prominent in some educa-tional establishments, including St Patrick's College, Drumcondra, which had a club officer registered with the Leinster FA in 1916 but not by 1922.[312] In the early 1920s Queen's, UCD and TCD participated in the Collingwood Cup, but it was not until February 1954 that the five Irish universities in operation at that time – UCC, UCD, UCG, TCD and QUB – all entered the competition.[313] At that point, UCD had won it twenty-two times while Queen's had won it eight times and they had shared it on two occasions.[314] The competition has been played on an all-Ireland basis, although Queen's did not participate for a few years in the early 1950s due to the conflict between the IFA and FAI.[315] In 1933 University College Dublin purchased the site that would eventually become their permanent location in Belfield.[316] While UCD's soccer club were the only university team affiliated to the FAI by the 1930s, by the latter part of that decade, TCD, the Royal College of Surgeons and the Veterinary College had also registered.[317] West has noted that at Trinity, 'between the wars the [soccer] club had a somewhat hap-hazard existence'.[318] Writing in 1925, one journalist noted that while they usually entered the Collingwood Cup annually, they no longer took part in any Leinster competitions.[319] He described the Collingwood Cup competition that year as 'a dismal failure owing to the last minute defection of Trinity FC who failed to raise

307 Ibid.   308 *SI*, 13 Nov. 2005.   309 *II*, 5 Feb. 1914; *IE*, 6 Feb. 1990.   310 Ibid.   311 Ibid.   312 Officers and Council Book, 1916–17 and 1921–2, Leinster Football Association Archives, P239/77.   313 *BN*, 10 Feb. 1923; *II*, 11 Feb. 1954.   314 *II*, 3 Feb. 1954.   315 Ibid., 11 Feb. 1954.   316 Donal McCartney, *The history of University College, Dublin* (Dublin, 1999), p. 115.   317 *SI*, 9 Dec. 1956.   318 West, *The bold collegians*, pp 91–2.   319 *FSW*, 5 Dec. 1925.

a team'.[320] As a result, only one game took place, with UCD defeating Queen's University at Cherryvale in Belfast.[321] The following year, only UCD and Queen's took part again.[322] It appears that the Trinity club were forced to play outside the College Park until they re-affiliated with Dublin University Central Athletics Club in 1940, although they did appear intermittently in the Leinster League.[323]

In 1939 the Irish Universities and Colleges Football Union was established, with Dr S. Barry Hopper of UCD said to be the driving force behind this move.[324] A new trophy was also presented that year by members of the new organization, as the initial Collingwood Cup had been lost in the 1920s.[325] The competition continued during the war, with Queen's winning their first since the 1920s in 1940 as UCD had dominated the event.[326] Queen's, UCD and Dublin University took part in 1941, with UCD the winners that year.[327] They won again in 1943, 1944, 1945 and 1946, illustrating their strength in the competition.[328] In 1947, Dublin University were beaten by Queen's in the final after a replay.[329] UCD's success continued late into the decade as they again won the trophy in 1948.[330]

The organization of soccer in universities was at times a struggle, as shown in the case of Trinity College Dublin. By the middle of the twentieth century soccer there was in a reasonable state, although rugby remained the most important football code, and the soccer first team lagged behind that of UCD, who won the Collingwood Cup again in 1952.[331] Dublin University Association Football Club's captain, George B. Wheeler, noted in his report of the 1951–2 season that it had been one of 'mixed fortune' as the first XI had played sixteen matches, winning eight, losing five and drawing three.[332] This was the thirteenth season since they had been revived, and they also travelled to Bangor University' in North Wales along with playing Glasgow University in Dublin.[333] The TCD Second XI fared much better, winning the Second Division of the Universities' and Colleges' League, although the Third XI finished bottom of their league.[334] The team did have some talented players, but ultimately they lacked sufficient strength all over the pitch. Dublin University AFC had sixty-seven members that year and most notable among these was K.B. Shiells, a Cliftonville player who was chosen for the IFA's amateur international team against England at Portadown and Scotland at Ibrox. He narrowly missed out on the Great Britain squad for the 1952 Helsinki Olympic Games.[335] There was also some representation for TCD on the Irish Universities' and Colleges' League team, with G.B. Wheeler, D.R. Robson and J.D. Tate playing in their 5–1 victory against the Eastern Army Command at Glenmalure Park.[336] The following season, Dublin University AFC were narrowly

---

320 Ibid. **321** Ibid. and *BN*, 2 Dec. 1925. **322** *EH*, 23 Nov. 1926. **323** 'Dublin University AFC', duafc.ucoz.com/index/history/0–10, accessed 12 Aug. 2021. **324** *II*, 3 Dec. 1934; *SI*, 9 Dec. 1956. **325** *SI*, 9 Dec. 1956. **326** *BT*, 25 Jan. 1940. **327** *BN*, 17 Feb. 1941. **328** Ibid., 1 Mar. 1943, 14 Feb. 1944 and 4 Mar. 1946. **329** Ibid., 17 Feb. and 27 Mar. 1947. **330** Ibid., 10 Feb. 1948. **331** Dublin University Association Football Club Report on 1951–2 Season, Trinity College Dublin Archives, MUN/CLUB/DUCAC/59/1. **332** Ibid. **333** Ibid. **334** Ibid. **335** Ibid. **336** Ibid.

beaten 2–1 by UCD in the Collingwood Cup final in Cork, having played for two hours and fifteen minutes against UCC in the semi-final the previous day.[337] They also toured North Wales, playing the RAF station at Valley and Bangor University and non-competitive matches against the Eastern Command of the army and Christ Church Cardinals, an Oxford College team on tour in Dublin.[338]

Issues with facilities were also evident. Trinity College Dublin hosted the 1954 Collingwood Cup, but the first round and final had to be played at Bird Avenue (Milltown), then home to the College of Surgeons, as the College Park was 'a virtual quagmire'.[339] The Dublin University AFC also availed of Grangegorman AFC's pitch during the season, with the lack of a home pitch throughout the week said to be their 'annual grouse', and to have prevented them from entering the Leinster League, 'the best training' for the Collingwood Cup.[340] As in previous years, a scarcity of fit players appears to have impeded the team's development, as only eleven were available for their trip to North Wales and Liverpool, with the secretary J. Hyland describing this as 'a disgraceful state of affairs'.[341] There was a drop in membership to forty-five, the lowest since 1939, with a number of players having graduated and 'no compensatory influx of new members'.[342] They appear to have relied mainly on the administrative drive of their president, Dr Arthur A. Luce, to whom the club owed a 'tremendous debt' since their reorganization in the late 1930s.[343] Injuries were again an issue for the Dublin University AFC in the 1954–5 season, and as a result they had to cancel their tour of North Wales. Injuries were also 'a decisive factor' in their defeat in the Collingwood Cup semi-final to the hosts, University College Galway.[344] In winning the competition, UCG broke 'the monopoly of UCD who had won the cup for the previous five years'.[345]

UCG did not win their second Collingwood Cup until 1967–8 when a number of their star players, including goalkeeper Ciaran Keyes, were awarded international recognition through Irish universities' representative matches.[346] By the spring of 1973, twelve teams were involved in the Collingwood Cup, with the National College of Physical Education and the Ulster Polytechnic in Belfast among the new entrants that year.[347] Although the competition was switched from February to December later that year to allow for better preparation, it has generally remained within the shade of competitions organized by the GAA.[348] The Harding Cup, a competition for under-19s, named in memory of Bert Harding, the chairman of the UCD club, was inaugurated in 1970.[349] The UCD graduates' team, Pegasus, won the FAI Intermediate Cup in 1977.[350] Dublin University AFC's victory in the

337 Dublin University Association Football Club Report on 1952–3 Season, Trinity College Dublin Archives, MUN/CLUB/DUCAC/60/1.　338 Ibid.　339 Dublin University Association Football Club Report on 1953–4 Season, Trinity College Dublin Archives, MUN/CLUB/DUCA C/61/2.　340 Ibid.　341 Ibid.　342 Ibid.　343 Ibid.　344 Dublin University Association Football Club Report on 1954–5 Season, Trinity College Dublin Archives, MUN/CLUB/ DUCAC/62/2.　345 Ibid.　346 *CS*, 31 Dec. 1968.　347 *SI*, 4 Mar. 1973.　348 Ibid.　349 *IP*, 11 Mar. 1970; *Soccer Reporter* (Feb. 1977), p. 13.　350 Minute Book of the Senior Council, FAI Annual Report 1976–7, Football Association of Ireland Archives, P137/24.

1979 Collingwood Cup final was assisted by future Irish international rugby star Hugo MacNeill, who scored two goals in a 2–0 win over Maynooth in the final, and the acquisition of Liam Tuohy as manager.[351] In the 1982–3 season, the number of teams competing in the Irish universities' competition increased to fifteen, with the inclusion of NIHE of Dublin.[352] By the early 1980s a ladies' inter-varsity soccer competition was also being held.[353] In 1985 the All-Ireland Universities League was inaugurated, with League of Ireland side UCD winning this, having not lost a match.[354] It was in the 1984–5 season that the Dave Faiers Memorial Trophy, named after the *Evening Herald* soccer journalist, was introduced for the winners of the annual TCD versus UCD colours match.[355]

Remarkably, like the Sigerson trophy in the early twenty-first century, the Collingwood Cup again went missing in the 1990s.[356] Having been stolen on a night out after the 1990 final between UCC and TCD at the Mardyke, the soccer trophy was 'drop-kicked' into the river Lee at O'Donovan Rossa Road by a member of the Queen's team, but later recovered by sub-aqua expert David Woosnam of Carrigaline.[357] After the 1990 incident, the Irish Universities Football Union pondered retaining the Collingwood trophy themselves after its presentation.[358]

SCHOLARSHIPS

Those seeking to combine education with a career in professional sport in Ireland were ignored by Irish governments for much of the twentieth century and anyone hoping to take up a full-time professional soccer or athletics career has generally had to look to structures in place abroad. The majority of those with league experience of English football have not gone on to university, although some have managed to undertake undergraduate and post-graduate education after retiring from full-time professional soccer.[359] In 1979, the first soccer scholarship scheme in Ireland was introduced by Dr Tony O'Neill at UCD.[360] This allowed players to combine third-level education with professional football in Ireland, with places offered on the basis of Leaving Certificate examination points and football trials. UCD had been accepted as a member of the League of Ireland's 'B' Division in 1970 and were elected to the League of Ireland in 1979 after Cork Celtic had been ejected.[361] Seán Ryan has written that 'an arrangement with Vancouver Whitecaps helped the club get over a tricky patch for a couple of years, while the soccer scholarship scheme was gradually producing players of League of Ireland ability'.[362] They began signing professionals after their fourth season and, strengthened by the initial appointment of Dermot Keely as player-manager (although he left

351 *IP*, 21 Feb. 1979. 352 Minute Book of the Senior Council, FAI Annual Report 1982–3, June 1983, FAI Archives, P137/24. 353 *IP*, 29 Jan. 1983. 354 Minute Book of the Senior Council, FAI Annual Report 1985–6, June 1986, FAI Archives, P137/24. 355 Minute Book of the Senior Council, FAI Annual Report, 1984–5, June 1985, FAI Archives, P137/24; *II*, 21 Feb. 1986. 356 *IE*, 6 Feb. 1990. 357 Ibid. 358 Ibid. 359 Curran, *Irish soccer migrants*, p. 294. 360 Ibid., p. 339. 361 Ryan, *The official book of the FAI Cup*, p. 278. 362 Ibid., p. 279.

mid-season), and the acquisition of a number of players from other League of Ireland clubs, they won the FAI Cup in 1984.[363]

One former soccer scholarship awardee, Seamus Kelly, remains the only Irish-born player with English League experience to have obtained a doctorate. He had represented Offaly's Gaelic football team at underage and senior levels as a teen-ager and had played for Tullamore Town in the Leinster Senior League in the early 1990s.[364] He joined the UCD soccer scholarship scheme in 1993, having heard about it from a teammate, John Tierney.[365] Having repeated his Leaving Certificate examinations, he was called for trials at UCD and, having impressed Dr Tony O'Neill, was drafted into their 'B' team. He attained the results required to gain university entry and began a commerce degree. Kelly helped UCD gain promo-tion to the Premier Division, and he recalled that the standard there was much higher, as there was a 'huge gap – the pace of the game, it was just much quicker and faster, you'd get absolutely destroyed if you're out of position, you're gone. So it was quicker and faster, and players were obviously a bit technically better as well, you know.'[366] In 1998 he joined Cardiff City, and noted that

> You're going from UCD, which is kind of sheltered, there's not a huge amount of fans, not a huge amount of pressure … And then you're going into an environment where you're taking someone's job, potentially. So, while you're all very friendly and there's a good bit of banter and craic, it's tougher, it's a lot more ruthless. So like if I'm playing in a game, and I mess up and lose the game, the other ten players lose their win bonuses, or their appearance money, so they will [be upset] – and I got hammered, slaugh-tered, verbally. It's tough, and that's the environment, back then, Division Four. Some great people there though.[367]

Although he was later offered another contract, he decided to return to Dublin and joined St Patrick's Athletic and undertook a master's and later a doctorate. Kelly enjoyed his time with full-time professional football in English League football but was always interested in a return to education and had completed a number of night courses in Cardiff as he found he had a lot of spare time there.[368] While he was able to help his teammates in the dressing room with their accounts, at times his educational background was frowned upon by other players. Since returning to Dublin, he has been heavily involved in higher education as a lecturer at UCD.[369]

A few other UCD soccer scholars have also completed undergraduate degrees before moving to England, including Ken O'Doherty and Joe Hanrahan, but tradi-tionally, players looking to develop a full-time professional career in British football will move before completing their Leaving Certificate.[370] While there have been other exceptions, such as Kevin Moran, who graduated with a degree in commerce

363 Ibid.   364 Interview with Seamus Kelly, 2 Oct. 2019.   365 Ibid.   366 Ibid.   367 Ibid.
368 Ibid.   369 Ibid.   370 Curran, *Irish soccer migrants*, p. 294.

before joining Manchester United, due to the competitive nature of sport at that level clubs are eager to recruit players as young as possible in order to mould them.[371] Education within British clubs has improved with the establishment of the youth training scheme (YTS) system, which had evolved into the academy structure by the early 2000s, but a number of academy players have admitted that the education expectations have been low within their clubs, with performance on the field of paramount importance. A number of professional footballers have also cited the prioritization of recovery off the field and a lack of flexibility around schedules as hindering academic interests.[372]

Some Irish soccer clubs have attempted to foster links with educational institutions. In the late 1970s, having taken over at Shamrock Rovers, manager Johnny Giles attempted to establish a system whereby young players could stay in Ireland rather than move to England.[373] Despite setting up the aforementioned scheme allowing for some players to undertake second-level courses, these efforts failed to develop due to a lack of interest from other clubs.[374] Irish athletes seeking a professional career have benefited from scholarship schemes in the USA, with Tom Hunt's work illustrating how these links were in operation since the late 1940s.[375] Soccer scholarships were slower to be developed, with the first Irish-born soccer scholar, Greg McElroy, availing of a move engineered by a Sligo priest with links at the University of South Florida to complete a degree there in the early 1970s.[376] Since then, structures for recruitment to US colleges for soccer scholarship purposes have become more formal, with Finglas-based Coláiste Íde providing SAT examinations (held at St Patrick's College, Drumcondra by the mid-1990s) along with trials for those aspiring to move to a US college team.[377] Few, however, have made it big in Europe's 'big five' professional soccer leagues having completed their time in the USA, although one scholarship awardee, Dublin-born Paul Keegan, played in the League of Ireland, Major League Soccer and in Scotland.[378] One Dublin man who initially began as a soccer scholar, Neil O'Donoghue, later became a field-goal kicker with a number of professional American football teams in the 1980s, but this type of transition was not a common one for Irish players there.[379]

Other Dublin-born players to move to the US included Fergus Hopper, who later became a Hall of Fame awardee at the University of South Florida, while Mickey Whelan received the same award from three colleges he attended in the 1970s although he was not initially recruited as a soccer scholarship recipient.[380] US universities guaranteed education along with the opportunity to play soccer, with movement continuing throughout the rest of the century for talented players

371 *IP*, 20 Oct 1976.   372 Conor Curran, 'Republic of Ireland-born football migrants and university access, 1945–2010', *Irish Educational Studies*, 39:1 (2020), pp 65–82, pp 69–76.   373 *IP*, 12 Mar. 1980.   374 Interview with Dave Henderson, 22 Oct. 2019.   375 Tom Hunt, *The little book of Irish athletics* (Dublin, 2018), p. 139.   376 Curran, 'Republic of Ireland born-football migrants', p. 74.   377 Ibid., p. 76.   378 *TBG*, 20 May 1996; *II*, 20 Nov. 1999; *EH*, 17 Jan. 2007.   379 *EH*, 17 Feb. 1978; *IE*, 6 Aug. 1983.   380 *Irish Times*, 22 Apr. 2009.

including Mick Riordan of Stoneybatter, Finglas native Brian Ainscough and Kempes Corbally of Glasnevin.[381] By the mid-1990s a more formal recruitment structure had been established through Coláiste Íde in Finglas, although players continued to migrate through word of mouth, family and scouting connections.[382] Some Dublin-born players who undertook scholarships at US universities have also played professionally in the USA, including the aforementioned Paul Keegan of Boston University, who was recruited by New England Revolution manager Frank Stapleton for the Major League Soccer inaugural season in 1996. Dublin-born soccer scholarship awardees have generally failed to break into this level of competition in the USA, but many have had successful coaching careers at US universities.[383]

Talented Irish women have also been able to further their education and playing career interests through soccer scholarships in the USA. In August 1985, North Circular Road native Anne Beirne won a four-year soccer scholarship at Villanova, 'the university which had propelled Ronnie Delany and Eamon Coughlan to athletics stardom'.[384] In doing so, the 19-year-old, the daughter of a 1940s Roscommon inter-county footballer, became the first Irish woman to obtain a soccer scholarship in the USA.[385] She had been spotted by two Villanova representatives while appearing as a guest player for Belvedere in a number of friendly matches against a Philadelphia youth selection the previous year.[386] Dublin clubs dominated the girls' competitions run by the Leinster branch of the FAI in 1985, with, following the success of the Leinster Schools' Cup the previous year, a Senior League and Junior Cup also inaugurated.[387] The Senior Cup was won by Rosary College Crumlin, while Scoil Íde of Finglas won the Junior Cup. The Leinster Senior League was won by Ballymun Comprehensive School.[388]

While a ladies' inter-varsity soccer league was operational in the 1982–3 season, with six teams involved, it was not until November 1987 that the Ladies' Soccer University Association of Ireland was established, in order to improve the standard of ladies' soccer at third level.[389] By the end of the spring of the following year, league and plate competitions had been founded, and a combined universities panel had been selected from the Intervarsity Championships.[390] In March 1998, eleven female Irish footballers were offered soccer scholarships in the USA.[391] This came after contact between the Ladies' Football Association of Ireland and Gareth O'Sullivan, who was Memphis University's head soccer coach. The girls had been chosen from eighteen players who were completing a FÁS soccer skills course and included Irish internationals Emma Byrne, Carol Conlon, Ciara Grant, Susan Kelleher, Grainne Kearns and Gillian Bennett. They were offered four-year scholarships at universities in Boston, Memphis, Mississippi and Pennsylvania.[392]

381 Curran, 'The migration of Irish-born players to undertake US soccer scholarships', pp 101–31. 382 Ibid. 383 Ibid. 384 *EH*, 14 Aug. 1985. 385 Ibid. 386 Ibid. 387 Football Association of Ireland Annual Report 1982–5, June 1985, FAI Archives, P137/24. 388 Ibid. 389 *II*, 25 Jan. 1983; *EE*, 22 Apr. 1988. 390 Ibid. 391 *EH*, 2 Mar. 1998. 392 Ibid.

It was noted that 'the tremendous success of the men's senior team during the Charlton era has spawned a dramatic increase in interest in the ladies' game in the Republic of Ireland'.[393] The soccer course itself was run at Leixlip Amenities Centre in Kildare and also included instruction in communications, computers, life-saving, swimming and first-aid.[394] However, it appears that only two players, Susan Kelleher and Gillian Bennett, took up the US soccer scholarships at that time.[395] In 2000, three St Catherine's players – Sonya Hughes, Emma Merrigan and Elaine O'Connor – left the club to take up US soccer scholarships.[396]

Irish international Olivia O'Toole noted when interviewed that she regretted not going to America to undertake a soccer scholarship, stating that 'to go to America to do a scholarship and do college was daunting because I'd no education', having left school at 13.[397] One fellow Irish international from Dublin who did avail of the opportunity was Claire Scanlan, a native of Rush who moved to Mercyhurst College in Pennsylvania in 1992.[398] By April 1996 she had been named NCAA National Division Two Player of the Year, majoring in business while on her scholarship.[399] She had begun her career with Rush Celtic and Swords Athletic and returned to Ireland after playing in the J League for OKI FC Winds in Japan.[400] Following two years at Shelbourne, she returned to the USA to undertake a master's at Troy University in Alabama, and then went to England, where she played for Leeds and Bristol Rovers.[401] While in Bristol in 2008 she became involved in coaching in the club's academy and later returned to Troy University to take up a coaching post. She has also worked at Oakland University in Michigan, SUNY Albany and Temple University.[402] Scanlan's career path has illustrated how the scholarship system in the USA can benefit a player by helping her stay in the game.

With the success of the UCD scheme, a number of other Irish universities were offering soccer scholarships by the 1990s, and in addition, scholarships in other sports became more common.[403] In January 1990, the Football Association of Ireland announced that it would be beginning a soccer scholarship scheme at Irish universities in the 1990–1 season.[404] It was to include the five Irish universities with teams who played competitively at that time: University College Galway, University College Dublin, Trinity College Dublin, University College Cork and Dublin City University.[405] It was stated that 'the FAI's decision to launch a scholarship programme is totally in keeping with the association's attempt to ensure that players won't have to sacrifice their careers while they further their football ambitions'.[406] The national governing body for soccer had been slow to assist young players who had aspirations of combining education with a career in soccer, and although they had introduced a FÁS football apprentice scheme the previous year, the academic side of this focused mainly on computers and English, with classes

---

393 Ibid. **394** *EH*, 15 June 1998. **395** Ibid. **396** *EH*, 7 Aug. 2000. **397** Ibid. **398** *IT*, 13 Apr. 1996. **399** Ibid. **400** *FI*, 17 Apr. 2021. **401** Ibid. **402** Ibid. **403** Curran, 'Republic of Ireland-born football migrants and university access', p. 76. **404** *IP*, 5 Jan. 1990. **405** Ibid. **406** Ibid.

held on three afternoons a week after training had finished.[407] Currently the education training board system provides aspiring players with some education along
with developing their playing skills. The FAI's scholarship move marked a new
development in their support for aspiring players' educational needs, but Irish soccer migrants returning from Britain still await the provision of a comprehensive
system for developing their post-professional football career options, and without proper guidance from their clubs, retirement from a full-time soccer career
remains a tough challenge for many. Attempts to establish a system at DCU, known
as REAP (Reinvention, Education, Appraisal, Preparation), lasted only briefly in
the early 2000s, while the FAI have been slow to establish a player welfare officer to
assist young Irish soccer migrants.[408]

CONCLUSION

This chapter has illustrated that the development of schoolboy leagues in Dublin
was a much slower process than in a number of British cities in the late nineteenth
and early twentieth century. However, there were similarities with Belfast, where
attempts to establish leagues for schoolboys struggled until the 1920s, with rugby
more prominent in many schools there.[409] In addition, the strength of the GAA in
numerous Catholic schools in Northern Ireland hindered the growth of schools'
soccer there.[410] While schoolboy leagues in Dublin were well established by the
1950s, competitive structures for schools' soccer were still in their infancy there
and throughout the Republic of Ireland at that stage. Along with the Ban culture,
which persisted in Irish society, a lack of government support was detrimental to
soccer's development in schools. The formation of the Easter Vacation League was
helpful in overcoming this, although opposition to the playing of soccer remained
in many schools.

By the late twentieth century some schools had developed a reputation for
assisting in young players' soccer careers, and in some cases this influenced the
decision to attend a particular school. Their soccer careers were also greatly helped
by a concentration of well-established schoolboy clubs within Dublin. Home Farm
was the most prominent of these, breaking numerous records and gaining a reputation with English clubs as a nursery for Irish soccer talent. Many of these clubs
relied on fundraising, with Stella Maris by 1981 said to be run 'on a purely voluntary basis by a group of hard-working people who give their time and energy to
the maintenance of the ground, the clubhouse and, of course, the teams'.[411] They
raised funds mainly through a monthly draw and an annual walk with club president Fred Bulley associated with the club since their foundation.[412] Some clubs have
been eager to maintain the memories evoked by previous successes, with Donore

407 Curran, 'Republic of Ireland-born football migrants and university access', p. 76.   408 Curran,
Irish soccer migrants, p. 341.   409 Ibid., pp 74–8.   410 Ibid., p. 84.   411 *Soccer Reporter* (Jan.
1981), p. 10.   412 Ibid.

United's Leinster Minor Cup-winning team of 1954–5 deciding in 1997 to form 'an Old Boys Club in memory of their late mentor and coach Barney Farrell'.[413] The development of players was also assisted by third level competitions and the awarding of scholarships (firstly in the USA), with a number of Dublin institutions heavily involved in this by the late 1990s. International underage success also came in that decade, although this was mainly due to the input of Dublin-raised players and the craft of Brian Kerr and his assistant, Noel O'Reilly, as they ignored the long-ball style of play that had become prominent at senior international level in favour of a fluent passing game they had grown up with.[414] Chapter seven examines the careers of a number of players at Dublin clubs in what has generally been a part-time professional soccer environment.

413 *EH*, 15 Sept. 1997.   414 *SI*, 10 May 1998.

7

Dublin players in domestic soccer

DUBLIN'S EARLIEST PLAYERS

As shown earlier, university students played a key role in the development of Dublin's first soccer clubs, with Neal Garnham stating that 'the result was, to some extent, an initial perception of association football in the capital as an elitist concern'.[1] In addition, he states that 'in 1900 it was still apparently the case that the majority of players in Dublin were students of one kind or another'.[2] More recently, the work of Julien Clenet has challenged this view, noting that 'the university-educated gentlemen who belonged to the Dublin AFC or Dublin University AFC in the mid-1880s had largely given way to skilled workers and clerks by 1901'.[3] Dublin's earliest players were generally based with the city's teams, and in particular the Dublin University Association Football Club and the Dublin Association Football club. Some of these men had experience of the game in England, including Irish international Manliffe Francis Goodbody, who also played for the Corinthians and Dublin University AFC.[4] According to Garnham, he 'typified the gentleman player of the game's early heydays in Dublin'.[5] Some of the late nineteenth-century players lined out for a number of clubs, including Gonzalo Canilla, a Gibraltar-born student at the Royal College of Surgeons who played for Bohemians and Freebooters as well as the Phoenix Cricket Club.[6] At times, they moved between sporting codes. Clenet has noted that the Hamilton brothers of the Dublin Association FC were renowned sportsmen of their day, while William Drummond was a top cricket player and Willoughby James was Wimbledon Men's Champion in 1890.[7] Both represented Ireland at international level in association football, while Goodbody, who was a US tennis championship finalist in 1894, was also capped by Ireland.[8]

Some information on the socio-economic background of the inaugural Leinster FA Cup-winning Leinster Nomads team of 1893 can be gleaned through newspaper reports and census records. By 1911, the aforementioned Dublin-born James

1 Garnham, *Association football and society*, p. 27.   2 Ibid., p. 26.   3 Clenet, 'Association football in Dublin', p. 811.   4 Garnham, *Association football and society*, p. 21; *IT*, 7 Feb. 1889.   5 Garnham, *Association football and society*, p. 197.   6 Gerry Farrell & Michael Kielty, 'Freebooting around the Rock of Gibraltar', abohemiansportinglife.wordpress.com/2019/06, accessed 30 July 2021.   7 Clenet, 'Association football in Dublin'.   8 Ibid.; 'NIFG-Manliffe Goodbody', nifootball.blogspot.com/2006/12/manliffe-goodbody.html, accessed 6 Aug. 2021; 'NIFG-Willoughby and Drummond Hamilton', nifootball.blogspot.com/2006/12/willoughby-william-hamilton.html, accessed 6 Aug. 2021.

H. Webb, an architect who later become an assistant commissioner of the St John Ambulance Brigade, was married with two sons and a daughter and had two servants and lived in Glenageary Road near Kingstown (Dún Laoghaire).[9] Webb later noted that his team-mate, W. St George Perrott, who still lived in Simmonscourt, Donnybrook in 1901 and was a land agent,[10] was by 1940 the honorary secretary of the Irish Lawn Tennis Association, while Dr E. Louis Farrell had a practice 'for many years' in Westland Row.[11] Another player, Hugh Morshead, was a brewer with Guinness, while G. Groves was a watchmaker in a jeweller's on the corner of Wicklow Street. Claude Bennett, who was injured in the final, later emigrated to America, but his occupation is not clear.[12]

Clenet states that by the early 1900s, 'many teams' consisting mainly of skilled workers and clerks appeared around the city and its suburbs.[13] He has identified 160 players and administrators from the 1896 to 1902 period and notes that the average age of players from his selection was 18.8 years old and 75 per cent were aged 20 or under.[14] Seventy-six per cent of the players analysed were born in Dublin, while over 9 per cent were born in Britain, illustrating that they were attracted to a game with which they were familiar and more culturally connected – as opposed to Gaelic football.[15] Clerks and skilled workers made up over 60 per cent of his sample while just over 14 per cent were unskilled workers. Almost 11 per cent were employees and senior clerks, while more than 9 per cent were semi-skilled workers. Only 5 per cent were professionals.[16] As shown elsewhere, the earliest GAA players in Dublin were often 'rural migrants, who left the land to find employment in the city' and were concentrated 'around institutions, trades and associations'.[17] These included the 1891 Young Ireland team, who won the All-Ireland Gaelic football championship for Dublin that year, and were formed by a number of Wexford employees of Guinness brewery, with GAA matches more common on Sundays.[18]

Clenet also notes that 'soccer was the game of the city and its immediate suburban belt', with almost 97 per cent of his sample living within three miles of the GPO, while 'the near total absence of soccer clubs, and footballers, outside the city' and its nearest parishes can be explained by the strength of the GAA in those areas.[19] Almost 68 per cent of players identified by Clenet were Roman Catholic. He states that 'the Dublin footballer of the early 1900s was likely to be a young Catholic man born and living in the city or its immediate suburbs and engaged in skilled manual work or a clerkship. He was also most likely politically nationalist.'[20] A previous study

9 'Residents of a House 20 in Glenageary Road, Upper (Kingstown No. 4, Dublin)', census. nationalarchives.ie/pages/1911/Dublin/Kingstown_No__4/Glenageary_Road__Upper/98137, accessed 7 Apr. 2020; *Sunday Independent*, 22 Dec. 1940. 10 'Residents of a house 11 in Simmonscourt, (Donnybrook, Dublin)', census.nationalarchives.ie/pages/1901/Dublin/ Donnybrook/Simmonscourt/1284375, accessed 7 Apr. 2020. 11 *SI*, 22 Dec. 1940. 12 *SI*, 22 Dec. 1940. 13 Clenet, 'Association football in Dublin', p. 811. 14 Ibid., pp 810–11. 15 Ibid., p. 810. 16 Ibid. 17 Mike Cronin, Mark Duncan & Paul Rouse, *The GAA: county by county* (Cork, 2011), p. 134. 18 Ibid., p. 135. 19 Clenet, 'Association football in Dublin', p. 812. 20 Ibid., pp 812–13.

of soccer players in the Ulster counties of Fermanagh, Tyrone, Cavan and Monaghan from the years 1887 to 1914 undertaken by this book's author highlighted that the largest employment category was 'un/semi-skilled', with just over 33 per cent of the 215 players recorded in this group.[21] The majority (60 per cent) were noted as being Roman Catholics, and had an average age of 26.6 years old.[22] An assessment of a sample of 286 of Donegal's first soccer players from the period 1891 to 1915 revealed that the largest share, almost 45 per cent, came from the industrial category, they had an average age of 23 years old and they were mainly Roman Catholic (85 per cent).[23] Tom Hunt's work on seventy-five soccer players in Athlone and Mullingar in 1900–4 demonstrated that the majority, 67 per cent, were skilled employees, all were Roman Catholic and they had an average age of 22.2 years old.[24]

Garnham has illustrated in his study of fifty-five early professional footballers in Belfast that the majority were skilled employees (38 per cent) while 36 per cent were labourers and unskilled workers.[25] Almost 44 per cent were Presbyterians and the average age of these players was 22.7 years old.[26] Therefore, the average soccer player in Ireland in the pre-First World War era was generally involved in industrial work and in his early twenties, although religious backgrounds differed depending on the area, with Garnham noting only a quarter of his Belfast sample were Roman Catholics.[27] A sample of primary employment of fifty Irish-born soccer migrants to Britain, mainly drawn from the early twentieth century, illustrated that the majority, 48 per cent of players, had a parent who was a labourer or unskilled.[28] The occupational backgrounds of three Dublin-born players were positively identified. These were Val Harris, a gas worker; Patrick O'Connell, who was a glass fitter; and Jack C. Slemin, who was recorded as an unspecified fitter.[29]

Aside from transfers to British clubs, performances of note for local soccer teams could naturally lead to an increase in the esteem in which a player was held among his teammates. The departure of a respected player or administrative member of a club could at times lead to an event to mark the occasion. In February 1898, Tritonville AFC chose to mark the departure of W. Worlidge by presenting him with a medal for 'brilliant goalkeeping' at a special event at their headquarters at London Bridge Road, Sandymount.[30] In May 1907, Reginald FC marked the emigration to the USA of Mr J. Lightholder, 'one of their prominent members', by presenting him with, 'as a souvenir of their esteem … a valuable pipe and case and a handsome scarfpin'.[31] He was a member of a family who were mainly bricklayers and resided in Merchant's Quay.[32]

21 Conor Curran, 'The social background of Ireland's pre-World War I association football clubs, players and administrators: the case of South and West Ulster', *International Journal of the History of Sport*, 33:16 (2016), pp 1982–2005, pp 1995–7. 22 Ibid. 23 Curran, *The development of sport in Donegal*, pp 192–4. 24 Hunt, *Sport and society in Victorian Ireland*, pp 186–8. 25 Garnham, *Association football and society*, p. 97. 26 Ibid. 27 Ibid. 28 Curran, *Irish soccer migrants*, p. 115. 29 Ibid., p. 114. 30 *II*, 1 Mar. 1898. 31 *EH*, 11 May 1907. 32 'Residents of a house 18.1 in High Street (Part) (Merchants Quay, Dublin)', census.nationalarchives.ie/pages/1901/Dublin/Merchants_Quay/High_Street__Part_/1303664, accessed 2 Jan. 2022.

MILITARY INVOLVEMENT OF DUBLIN SOCCER PLAYERS

Given the military presence in Ireland by the turn of the century and the coming and going of military teams, it was natural that some of these rose to prominence via their exploits on the playing fields. Military men who were notable players within Dublin soccer at the turn of the century included Irish international John Mansfield of Freebooters, the club that contested the 1901 Irish Cup final against Cliftonville.[33] However, he missed the match as a result of army involvement as 2nd Lieutenant in the Royal Engineers.[34] Similarly, Philip Meldon, another Freebooters player who was capped by Ireland, was commissioned as a 2nd Lieutenant in the Royal Field Artillery in 1900 and did not participate in the 1901 Irish Cup final.[35] He was wounded in the Second Boer War (1899–1902) and returned home in 1902, although he continued his military career, and later became a lieutenant colonel.[36] Another Dublin footballer to serve in the Second Boer War was William Eames, who was born in India, where his father was a senior chaplin with the East India Company.[37] He attended Trinity College Dublin between 1882 and 1886 and captained Dublin University AFC and Ireland. He had a medical practice at Leeson Street before he moved to Australia and he also participated in the First World War, reaching the position of major general in the Royal Army Medical Corps.[38] Fellow Irish international and Dublin University player Lionel Bennett later became a captain in the British Army.[39]

Medical and military men were notable in the early Bohemians club, with George Sheehan, a founder member and the only Dublin-based player in the Ireland team that lost 2–0 to England at Lansdowne Road on St Patrick's Day 1900, serving in the Second Boer War and later the First World War, reaching the rank of lieutenant colonel in the Royal Army Medical Corps.[40] John Fitzpatrick, the first Bohemians player to be capped by Ireland, was a boxing champion in the British Army, a competent rugby player and a soldier with the 15th King's Hussars.[41]

Dublin soccer players also participated in military service during the years from 1914 until 1918, and unfortunately some had their careers, and lives, ended abroad in the conflict. Some 4,884 men from Dublin were killed in the First World War, which was more than 19 per cent of the overall total of Dublin recruits.[42] Dublin's death rate was 'by far the highest for any city or county in Ireland, comprising 16 per cent of the total'.[43] Soccer in Dublin continued although some clubs were at least temporarily affected by the loss of manpower.[44] In November 1915 the

33 'NIFG-John Mansfield', nifootball.blogspot.com/2007/12/john-mansfield.html, accessed 6 Feb. 2021. 34 Ibid. 35 'NIFG-Philip Meldon', nifootball.blogspot.com/2007/12/james-meldon.html, accessed 6 Aug. 2021. 36 Ibid. 37 'NIFG-William Eames', nifootball.blogspot.com/2006/11/william-eames.html, accessed 6 Aug. 2021. 38 Ibid. 39 'NIFG-Lionel Bennett', nifootball.blogspot.com/2006/10/lionel-bennett.html, accessed 6 Aug. 2021. 40 'NIFG-Dr George Sheehan', nifootball.blogspot.com/2008/07/dr-george-sheehan.html, accessed 6 Aug. 2021. 41 'NIFG-John Fitzpatrick', nifootball.blogspot.com/2006/11/james-fitzpatrick.html, accessed 6 Aug. 2021. 42 Yeates, *A city in wartime*, p. 75. 43 Ibid. 44 Curran, *Irish soccer migrants*, p. 106.

19. A soldiers' team in Ireland in the early twentieth century (1908). Courtesy of the National Library of Ireland.

Evening Herald reported on the 'meteoric' rise of Olympia FC, who had been affiliated to the Leinster FA in 1911.[45] In the 1913–14 season, they narrowly failed to win the Central League. They did win the Leinster Minor Cup final against Seaview II, captained by R.F. Kinninmont, who was the son of an artist in the Royal and Gaiety theatres.[46] In the 1914–15 season they 'broke all records' and won four competitions. By the winter of 1915 twenty-two members of the club had served in the war effort. The club had four ex-captains serving in the war: Sergeant M. Nolan, Corporal R.F. Kinninmont, Gunner J. Cashin and Private J. Downes.[47] The newspaper published a letter from their former minor team captain, who had become Corporal Kinninmont of the South Irish Horse in France, in which he gave details of the situation he was involved in, in an area that was not revealed:

> I am anxious to know how 'the old team is going on.' How are all the play-
> ers who won the Minor Cup with me? I hope they are all well and sticking
> in the club. Our squadron was in the big fighting around ___. I often think,
> especially on Saturday afternoon – how the football is going on in Dublin. We

45 *EH*, 27 Nov. 1915; Senior League Council Minutes, Council Meeting, 13 Sept. 1911, Leinster Football Association Archives, P239/24.   46 *FJ*, 1 May 1914; *EH*, 27 Nov. 1915.   47 *EH*, 27 Nov. 1915.

captured some prisoners the other day, they had been tied to machine guns by their officers and could not escape. Good luck to all the boys and Olympia.[48]

Despite the loss of players, Olympia persevered, and the remaining members of their team, having matured sufficiently, defeated Shelbourne in the 1918 Leinster Senior Cup final.[49] Olympia later played in the first Free State League, but were not elected in 1923, having finished near the bottom.[50] Other clubs similarly lost former players or members in the conflict, with the aforementioned M.F. Goodbody of Dublin University AFC drowning in the English Channel near Dieppe in March 1916 when the SS *Sussex* was torpedoed.[51] He was brought up in Blackrock but had moved to England, where he was an Inspector of the 'C' Division, Metropolitan Special Constabulary, as well as a partner in the Harris Brothers' grain brokers firm. He was noted as 'an all-round sportsman, being in the front rank of amateur tennis players, a great lover of horses, and was well-known in the show ring'.[52]

Like rugby and GAA players, soccer players throughout Ireland enlisted in the war, including Irish League footballers such as Annesley (Glentoran), Willkin (Cliftonville) and Cowell (Belfast Celtic), who joined the North Irish Horse in May 1915.[53] David Fitzpatrick has written that 'recruiting strategists were well aware of the power of the sporting motif, and their stories of football in no-man's land lent glamour, and the illusion of fair play, to trench warfare'.[54] The IRFU initiated a 'Pals' Company of the 7th Royal Dublin Fusiliers, but the IFA did not take a similar step for its soccer players.[55] While two footballers' battalions connected to the Middlesex Regiment were established in England with some players signing up, such as Tommy Barber, a former Aston Villa player who scored the winning goal in the 1913 FA Cup final, there was no similar arrangement made for Irish soccer players within Ireland.[56] Although it is difficult to

---

48 Ibid.; *Sport*, 24 Aug. 1918. Other Olympia members to serve in the war included Pipe-Major Hogge, who was also a Clontarf rugby player; Private P. Watters, who was killed in the Dardenelles landing; Private H. Tisdall, who fought at Suvla Bay; Private E. Thompson, who served at Gallipoli; Corporal D. McLoughlin, who was wounded at the Battle of the Marne; driver Stephen Hopper, who was based in France and had brothers in the Bohemians' team; Lance Corporal Michael Gorman, who also served at the Dardanelles; Private S. Hall, who was stationed in France; Private T. Walker, who was based in Drumeres; Trooper J. Coates and Private J. Neary, who were serving in France; Signaller Sam Hope was in the Royal Navy, as was Michael Orr; Sergeant George Harding was based in France; Private A. Stewart was wounded and was based in Egypt and Private J. Downes, driver W. McDermott and Private J. Caprani were also members of the Olympia club. 49 *FJ*, 19 Mar. 1919. 50 Kennedy, *Just follow the floodlights!*, p. 307. 51 *Leinster Reporter*, 22 Apr. 1916. 52 Ibid.; *Wicklow Newsletter*, 1 Apr. 1916. 53 *II*, 25 May 1915. See also Curran, *Irish soccer migrants*, pp 105–6. Others included Bernard Donaghey, Jack Doran, Jack McCandless, Jack Wright, Joe Enright, Harry Hampton, Johnny Houston, Billy O'Hagan and Charlie O'Hagan. For an overview of some players who died in the war, see Stephen Walker, *Ireland's call: Irish sporting heroes who fell in the Great War* (Newbridge, 2015) and for an assessment of GAA involvement, see Ross O'Carroll, 'The GAA and the First World War, 1914–18' in Gearóid Ó Tuathaigh, *The GAA & Revolution in Ireland, 1913–1923* (Cork, 2015), pp 85–104. 54 Fitzpatrick, 'Militarism in Ireland, 1900–1922', p. 390. 55 Ibid. 56 *Sport*, 26 Aug. 1916; 'Tommy Barber', footballandthefirstworldwar.org/tom-barber, accessed 26 July 2021.

estimate how many Irish players served, Dublin clubs were well represented in the war. Those wishing to join these battalions usually moved back to England first, with English-born Oscar Linkson leaving Shelbourne to sign up.[57] He was killed in action in December 1916.[58] He had played for the Dublin club in the 1914–15 season and 'was considered one of the best backs in the kingdom'.[59] Belfast-born Jack Doran also joined a footballers' battalion and having survived the war, he returned to English football to play for a number of English clubs and later joined Shelbourne.[60] Lieutenant Harrie Barron of Portobello had played for Dublin University and Shelbourne as well as in England for Queen's Park Rangers and Sheffield Wednesday before being wounded in 1916 on the Western Front at Ypres as a member of the Royal Garrison Artillery.[61] Lieutenant Fred Chestnutt, a goalkeeper, 'first came into prominence with the Dublin University AFC' before starring for Bohemians.[62] West has stated that 'athletic activities ground to a halt in Trinity during the First World War', and numbers dropped by over a third as students and staff joined the war effort.[63] Some facilities there were utilized for military training as clubs' activities were suspended, and sheep were allowed to graze on the College Park.[64]

Another Shelbourne player who enlisted was Victor Pollock, who survived and married a French woman; they settled in Kimmage after the war.[65] Ned Brierley, who was given three awards for bravery for his actions while serving with the 16th Irish Division, returned to Dublin and played for Shelbourne in the 1923 Irish Free State Cup final, and later joined St Mary's AFC.[66] Less fortunate was Corporal Freddie Morrow, who had spells at Tritonville, Shelbourne and Bohemians before being killed in action at the age of 21 in October 1917.[67] One correspondent noted that Shelbourne, whose 'greatest capture ever secured … was in all probability, Walter Scott of the Sunderland club' was 'forced back on its original lines' as a result of the war and again recruited locally.[68] It was noted that 'as a custodian in this country he was truly a giant … and but for the war' would have stayed with the Dublin club.[69] Scott had initially left England after losing his form and being dismissed by his club, with Taylor noting how English League regulations at that time encouraged this type of treatment.[70] He returned to England and later played for Grimsby Town after the war.[71]

57 'Oscar Horace Stanley Linkson', footballandthefirstworldwar.org/oscar-linkson-footballer, accessed 29 July 2021. 58 Ibid.; *II*, 19 Dec. 1916. 59 *II*, 19 Dec. 1916. 60 Curran, *Irish soccer migrants*, pp 105–6; 'John Francis Doran', footballandthefirstworldwar.org/jack-doran-footballer, accessed 29 July 2021. 61 Richard Grayson, *Dublin's great wars: the First World War, the Easter Rising and the Irish Revolution* (Cambridge, 2018), p. 118. It appears he did not play in the English Football League but had spells at these clubs as he does not appear in Joyce's *Football League players' records*. 62 *EH*, 25 Sept. 1915. 63 West, *The bold collegians*, pp 59–60. 64 Ibid. 65 Sands, *Shels*, pp 27–9. 66 Ibid., p. 40 and 'Stories / Private Ned Brierley, 1896 – 1955 8th Battalion, Royal Dublin Fusiliers', greatwar.ie/stories/edward-brierley, accessed 20 Aug. 2021. 67 *EH*, 9 Oct. 1917. 68 *Sport*, 17 Nov. 1917. 69 Ibid. 70 Matthew Taylor, *The leaguers: the making of professional football in England, 1900–1939* (Liverpool, 2005), pp 95–6. 71 Joyce, *Football League players' records*, p. 259.

Shamrock Rovers players also served in the war, including James Keogh and the Skinner brothers, William and James, although of these three, only James, the younger Skinner brother, survived.[72] One of those who was wounded early in the war was Private Templeman, of the King's Own Scottish Borderers, who had 'played many fine games for the Tritonville club' in the Irish League along with Sergeant Quick.[73] A number of those involved in Dublin soccer had joined the 4th and 5th Battalions of the Royal Dublin Fusiliers by September 1915, including Lance Corporal Shelley and Private Masterson, 'prominent members of the Richmond and Roseville clubs', respectively.[74] Corporal McQuill, 'one of the most dashing of Frankfort players' and 'one of Dublin's best amateur boxers', also enlisted in the Royal Dublin Fusiliers, while Sergeant Staines of Clarence FC and Quartermaster Sergeant Payne, 'a well-known referee in Dublin football circles and a member of the Leinster Referees' Association', also served.[75] Private Joseph Kane of St James's Gate AFC died from wounds sustained early in the war at the Battle of Mons.[76] Another player from his club, Frank Heaney, an Irish amateur international, fought at Flanders.[77] One reporter described the 1914–15 season as 'disastrous' for the club.[78]

Bohemians' goalkeeper J.C. Hehir, an Irish international, left to join the War Office in February 1915, and it was reported that he would be 'a big loss to Bohemians', who had 'lost nearly all their best players through the war'.[79] Players' withdrawal from soccer clubs in order to enlist was often staggered rather than all at once. Trojans FC lost Sergeant Paisley to the Royal Irish Fusiliers in September 1915, and two months later, two of their 'popular members', Frank Flynn and Jack Fox, to the Irish Guards.[80] Both were employed by the Irish United Assurance Company, and 'a large crowd of the old friends and clubmates' gave them 'a rousing send off' at the London and North-Western Railway Company's premises as they headed for the boat at North Wall.[81] Prior to his departure, Fox was selected to play for the Guards Depot team at Caterham.[82] As shown earlier, in 1917 the Trojans club dropped out of soccer due to having an insufficient number of players.[83] In October 1918, it was reported that a former player of theirs, Lieutenant Sam Moran of the Royal Irish Fusiliers, had been killed.[84]

In December 1915 Frankfort FC player Alec McLaughlin enlisted with a group of friends in a 'pals' battalion. He was said to be 'well known in racing and boxing circles'.[85] J. Rowe of the East Surrey Regiment, a former Bohemians player, returned to the war in March 1916, and was said to have been wounded eighty-three times prior to that.[86] In January 1917 Bohemians and Ireland player Harold

72 Gerard Farrell, 'Rovers of the Sea', abohemiansportinglife.wordpress.com/2018/01, accessed 30 July 2021. 73 *FJ*, 5 Sept. 1914. 74 *EH*, 28 Sept. 1915. 75 Ibid. 76 Ibid.; *Sport*, 27 Oct. 1917. 77 *Sport*, 27 Oct. 1917. 78 Ibid. In addition to Heaney and Kane, St James's Gate players P. Coleman, F. Dunne, A. Keeble, A. Nolan, H. Gaston and J. Thornton also joined the war effort. 79 *II*, 12 Feb. 1915. 80 *EH*, 28 Sept. 1915; *DDE*, 27 Nov. 1915. 81 *DDE*, 27 Nov. 1915. 82 Ibid. 83 *II*, 12 Jan. 1917. 84 *II*, 7 Oct. 1918. 85 *II*, 7 Dec. 1915. 86 *II*, 30 Mar. 1916.

Sloan was killed less than three months after going to the Western Front.[87] He had initially joined the war effort through the Cadet School and later entered the Royal Garrison Artillery. Having become a member of the 198th Siege Battery in Bristol, he became a 2nd lieutenant in Combles with a heavy artillery group.[88] Other Bohemians players to serve included Harry Willets, Frank Larkin, Thomas Johnston and Ernie and Charlie Crawford, both of whom later fought for the Irish Republican Army in the War of Independence.[89] Herbert Charles Crozier, who was awarded a Military Cross for bravery shown serving with the Royal Dublin Fusiliers at Sedd-el-Bahr on the Dardenelles, had also previously captained his regimental football team in Egypt. He was also awarded the Medal of the Royal Humane Society for trying to save an officer who had fallen into the Nile.[90] Players from other clubs around Ireland also served, including Sergeant George Gray of the 5th Inniskilling Fusiliers, who was a member of Drogheda United.[91] Naturally, some players who became administrators were also involved, including later IFA president James Wilton, a footballer with a number of northern clubs, who joined the 36th Ulster Division and was later awarded the Military Cross for bravery at the Battle of the Somme in July 1916, where he was wounded.[92] Dublin's lower league clubs were also affected, including St Mark's Athletic, with 'almost the entire team' joining the British forces. While the club did not field any teams during the war, they remained active and recommenced playing again in 1919.[93] Regional teams also experienced losses, with five members of the Cahir Park club from Tipperary killed.[94] The decision to enlist was often based on economic considerations, family traditions, a sense of adventure and friendships. 'Those belonging to militias, fraternities or sporting clubs were particularly susceptible to collective pressure' and religious or political preferences were not always the deciding factors.[95] Enlistment was highest in Ulster, particularly in the north-east, and was greater in the Belfast district than in Dublin.[96]

As unearthed elsewhere by Aaron Ó Maonaigh, according to Lieutenant John Shouldice, of 'F' Company, 1st Battalion, Dublin Brigade, a member of the Irish Republican Army during the Irish Revolution (1913–23), although the GAA had been 'a great recruiting ground' for the nationalist movement, 'other sporting and non-sporting bodies, or members of them, contributed their quota to the Volunteers and IRA'. He recalled that 'soccer, rugby, Gaelic League, National University, Literary and Press organizations were represented, especially in Dublin where

87 Walker, *Ireland's call*, p. 232. 88 Ibid. 89 Gerry Farrell, 'Bohemians of World War I', abohemiansportinglife.wordpress.com/2016/06/29/bohemians-of-world-war-i, accessed 29 July 2021. For a list of Bohemians players in the First World War, see, in particular, *EH*, 25 Sept. 1915. 90 *EH*, 25 Sept. 1915 and 'Our Heroes/Ár Laochra: Captain HC Crozier', our-heroes.southdublin.ie/Serviceman/Show/16056, accessed 4 Dec 2021. 91 *EH*, 28 Sept. 1915. 92 *Sport*, 21 Oct. 1916; Brodie, *100 years of Irish football*, p. 12. 93 *Soccer Reporter* (Apr. 1976), p. 11. 94 Toms, *Soccer in Munster*, p. 40. 95 Fitzpatrick, 'Militarism in Ireland, 1900–1922', pp 389–91. 96 Ibid., p. 389.

these bodies were strong'.[97] Gerry Farrell and Brian Trench have written that although there is no record of any Bohemians players being involved in the 1916 Rising on the side of the rebels, some of those linked to the club were part of the British administration at the time, including founder member Andrew P. Magill, the private secretary to Chief Secretary Augustine Birrell, who later resigned.[98] Joe Irons, an army reserve, was sent to the Viceregal Lodge in Phoenix Park on defensive duties when fighting began.[99] Wren, de Búrca and Gorry have stated that 302 players from 52 GAA clubs in Dublin took part on the rebels' side, and although it is difficult to identify how many soccer players were involved, some can be positively identified.[100] Frank Robbins, a member of St Vincent's FC of North William Street, was active in the Easter Rising and became a sergeant in the Irish Citizen Army.[101] Another member of St Vincent's FC, Michael 'Tiger' Smith, also took part in the fighting and, much later, 'was the man who made the shears that cut the bolts on the gates of Kilmainham Jail', which assisted the escape of Frank Teeling, Simon Donnelly and Ernest O'Malley in February 1921.[102]

At least one soccer player was publicly identified in the press as being involved in the 1916 Rising. On 5 May 1916 some of the men captured were tried by court martial, with Patrick McNeary noted in the press as being an association footballer as well as a silversmith, although his club was not given.[103] Denis O'Callaghan, a GPO employee, was 'a well-known Gaelic footballer'. Both received sentences of ten years.[104] One sportsman who had his career cut short during the Rising was W.J. O'Gara, a cricketer and footballer with Merrion, who lost his leg as a result of a bullet coming through his window as he lay in bed.[105] He was unable to get to a hospital, and 'lost a lot of blood', with amputation deemed necessary when he did finally receive medical treatment.[106] As Ó Maonaigh has shown, both Oscar Traynor and Robert Holland attested to the presence of former soccer players at prison camps in Frongoch (Wales) and Knutsford (England), respectively, with Holland noting Strandville, Distillery and St James's Gate footballers.[107] Traynor recalled that he (temporarily) 'broke with football' when he saw 'that there was something serious pending', joining 'F' Company, 2nd Battalion Dublin Brigade in 1914.[108]

The Spanish flu epidemic of 1918–19 claimed the lives of some footballers, including former Irish international James Connor of Belfast Celtic, who died in

97 Aaron Ó Maonaigh, '"Who were the shoneens?" Irish militant nationalists and association football, 1913–1923' in Conor Curran & David Toms, *New perspectives on association football in Irish history* (Abingdon, 2018), pp 33–49, p. 35; John Shouldice, Witness Statement 679, Bureau of Military History, militaryarchives.ie, accessed 2 Feb. 2022. 98 Gerry Farrell & Brian Trench, 'Bohemians during Easter 1916', abohemiansportinglife.wordpress.com/2016/03, accessed 29 July 2021. 99 Ibid. 100 Wren, de Búrca & Gorry, *The Gaelic Athletic Association in Dublin*, i: *1884–1959*, pp 149–61. 101 Frank Robbins, Witness Statement 586, Bureau of Military History, militaryarchives.ie, accessed 2 Apr. 2022. 102 Ibid. 103 *II*, 6 May 1916. 104 Ibid. 105 *Sport*, 12 June 1916. 106 Ibid. 107 Ó Maonaigh, 'Who were the shoneens?', pp 35–6; Robert Holland, Witness Statement 371, Bureau of Military History, militaryarchives.ie, accessed 2 Apr. 2022. 108 Ó Maonaigh, 'Who were the shoneens?', p. 40; Oscar Traynor, Witness Statement 340, Bureau of Military History, militaryarchives.ie, accessed 2 Apr. 2022.

November 1918.[109] It was also noted that 'several clubs in Dublin and throughout Ireland' were 'seriously affected'.[110] Victims included P. Boyne of CYMS, who died in February 1919, while his clubmates F. Murphy and L. Doyle (who later died) had also been hospitalized by then.[111] W.R. Morrison, the captain of Christian Brothers' Past Pupils Union (CBPPU) FC, who had formerly been with Clarence and Shelbourne, also died.[112] W. Lee, who had 'played many brilliant games for Bohemians' before joining Richmond Asylum AFC, died in March 1919.[113] Naturally, players in other codes were also affected, including Dublin Gaelic footballer Patrick Lynch of St Laurence O'Tooles.[114]

Some of those who were killed or injured (on both sides) in the War of Independence and subsequent conflict were also soccer players. Some clubs fielded soldiers, with Olympia player and IRA man Michael Chadwick suspended by the Leinster FA in 1920 for taunting a number of Jacob's players in a match between the clubs as the factory team were said to be fielding former British military men.[115] Two Jacob's players were also suspended after being found guilty of entering the Olympia dressing room after the match.[116] Later that year, a Jacob's player was killed. In October 1920 the funeral of William Robinson took place at Halston Street Church.[117] Robinson, of Stafford Street, 'was an ex-soldier and a popular member of the Jacob's football team'.[118] He had been 'shot under mysterious circumstances in Little May Street' on 15 October. The funeral cortege was reported as being 'very large' and included those from Dublin soccer circles such as other Jacob's FC members, their secretary, Mr McEvoy, and members of North End FC, Belmont FC and the Leinster team.[119] Michael Foley has stated that Robinson was shot by the IRA after having been asked to show some identification while out with three friends.[120] Despite being taken to Jervis Street Hospital, he died the night he was shot in Dublin and was buried at Glasnevin Cemetery.[121] Footballers in other areas were not unaffected by the conflict. In November 1922, Special Constable Ernest Storey, who was wounded at Garrison, County Fermanagh, in April 1922 and later discharged, sought compensation for his injuries in the Fermanagh County Court.[122] Born in England, he had been a professional goalkeeper at a number of clubs, including Hull City, Bradford City and Distillery.[123] As Toms has shown, Cahir Park were listed by the IRA as one of their 'enemy institutions' due to their close connection to their patron, Lieutenant Colonel Richard Butler Charteris, who owned their playing field.[124]

109 *BN*, 29 Nov. 1918.   110 *EH*, 1 Mar. 1919.   111 Ibid. and 7 Mar. 1919.   112 Ibid.   113 Ibid. 114 *II*, 4 Nov. 1918.   115 Byrne, *Green is the colour*, p. 60; Gerry Farrell, 'The lost clubs – Jacob's FC', abohemiansportinglife.wordpress.com/2018/06, accessed 30 July 2021; Emergency Committee Meeting Minutes, 16 Apr. 1920, Leinster Football Association, P239/36.   116 Byrne, *Green is the colour*, p. 60; Gerry Farrell, 'The lost clubs – Jacob's FC', abohemiansportinglife.wordpress. com/2018/06, accessed 30 July 2021.   117 *EH*, 21 Oct. 1920.   118 Ibid.   119 Ibid.   120 Foley, *The bloodied field*, pp 224–5.   121 Ibid., p. 225.   122 *FH*, 11 Nov. 1922.   123 Ibid.; Joyce, *Football League players' records*, p. 278.   124 Toms, *Soccer in Munster*, p. 37.

Gerry Farrell has noted that a number of those connected to Bohemians were involved in the events surrounding Bloody Sunday of 21 November 1920, when a total of thirty-two people were killed.[125] Following the assassination of a number of British intelligence operatives by the IRA that morning, the British forces opened fire on the crowd at the Dublin versus Tipperary Gaelic football match at Croke Park in the afternoon.[126] Charlie Dalton, a Bohemians player, was involved in an attack on a house in Pembroke Street, while Jeremiah 'Sam' Robinson acted as a lookout during his fellow IRA members' strike on a house in Mount Street.[127] Dublin's trainer that day, Charlie Harris, was also involved in that capacity with Bohemians, while future player Joe Stynes acted as a steward at the match and apparently helped to dispose of Volunteers' guns.[128] Michael Carroll of A Company, 3rd Battalion, Dublin Brigade, recalled when interviewed that he and four other players in an unnamed team who had trained with Windsor AFC at Usher's Quay were arrested in the aftermath of Bloody Sunday.[129]

The Civil War fought between the pro-Treaty Free State Army and the anti-Treaty Irish Republican Army between June 1922 and May 1923 also saw soccer players involved. With the fall in attendances and disruption of sporting events, some players moved abroad. On entering the new Free State League in 1921, Shelbourne had maintained the same squad from the previous season, with the exception of the small but stocky W. Hamilton, 'who was really an old player, and a champion weight-lifter, wrestler, gymnast' and 'as a footballer he was very good anywhere'.[130] However, one reporter noted in October 1922 that with the disturbed state of the country, and the resultant low attendances, 'Shelbourne went practically en bloc' as wages decreased and players sought opportunities in Britain.[131] Similarly, some Irish League clubs were also badly affected, with Distillery releasing all their professional players by November.[132]

The aftermath of the 1922 Irish Free State Cup final between St James' Gate and Shamrock Rovers earlier that year saw IRA member Jack Dowdall, the brother of a St James' Gate player, firing a gun into the team's dressing room ceiling to disperse the Shamrock Rovers players and supporters who had gained an unwelcomed entry.[133] Ó Maonaigh has illustrated that 'despite their commitment to the cause of Irish political independence, Irish revolutionary soccer players experienced sustained criticism from their advanced cultural nationalist peers who deemed their sporting choice as irreconcilable with their political values'.[134] In particular, he has identified a number of Dublin-based men who were active in the Irish Revolution and were also involved in soccer teams. Along with the aforementioned Jimmy Dunne and Joe Stynes, these included Christopher 'Todd' Andrews

125 *IT*, 21 Nov. 2021; Gerry Farrell, 'Bohs and Bloody Sunday'; abohemiansportinglife.wordpress.com/2020/11/21/bohs-and-bloody-Sunday, accessed 11 Aug. 2021. **126** *IT*, 21 Nov. 1921. **127** Ibid. **128** Ibid. **129** Michael Carroll, Witness Statement 1210, Bureau of Military History, militaryarchives.ie, accessed 2 Apr. 2022. **130** *Shelbourne Football Club golden jubilee*, p. 27. **131** Curran, *Irish soccer migrants*, p. 110. **132** Ibid. **133** Keogh, *Twentieth-century Ireland*, p. 35; Ó Maonaigh, 'Who were the shoneens?', p. 41. **134** Ó Maonaigh, 'Who were the shoneens?', p. 42.

of UCD, John 'Kruger' Fagan, who played for Shamrock Rovers and the Free State League's XI; Frank Henderson, who had played soccer while at CBS Fairview, and the aforementioned Michael Smith of St Vincent's FC.[135] Oscar Traynor, who later defended the right to play soccer in a number of articles in *Football Sports Weekly*, had played for Frankfort, Strandville and Belfast Celtic.[136] As noted, Frank Robbins played with St Vincent's FC, and while Thomas Pugh, who was the secretary of an unnamed soccer club, and Gerald Boland did not appear for soccer clubs, they were also involved in the game.[137] Pugh recalled that although he used to read the nationalist newspapers such as the *United Irishman* while he was growing up, and had worn badges during the Boer War, he was 'more interested in the soccer crowd'.[138] As Ó Maonaigh states of his sample, 'almost all of the revolutionary soccer players were young males (20–9 years old), educated by the Christian Brothers, and came predominantly from the working and lower middle classes'.[139] He adds that 'what differentiated them from their revolutionary brethren was a simple love of the "Garrison Game"'.[140] The aforementioned 'Sam' Robinson of Bohemians played for the Irish Free State and won an FAIFS Cup medal in 1928 against Drumcondra, while Emmet Dalton of Bohemians was also active.[141] Robinson's brother Christy also fought in the Irish Republican Army.[142] He later played for Ormond Celtic, Brooklyn, Bohemians and Bendigo.[143]

While much has been made of the claim by Oscar Traynor that 1923 Irish Free State Cup winners Alton United of Belfast were IRA volunteers, Ó Maonaigh has shown that only two of these actually were, despite the team being given an armed guard by the IRA on their way from Amiens Street station to Dalymount Park for the final against Shelbourne.[144] Some clubs' progress was affected by the Civil War, including Rutland, who apparently became inactive 'for a few years … owing to the war in Ireland', having won the Junior Metropolitan League in 1922.[145] Doctor, author and footballer Oliver St John Gogarty, who, as a Free State senator was kidnapped by anti-Treaty forces during the Civil War, escaped his captors by swimming the river Liffey.[146] A strong swimmer and cyclist, he had played for Clongowes and Bohemians, where he won the Leinster Senior Cup in 1897, before enjoying a spell with Preston North End reserves.[147]

There is little indication that British players at Dublin clubs were deliberately targeted during the Irish Revolution. English players lined out for Dublin clubs in the early 1920s, with, for example, Prentice, formerly of Coventry, playing for Shelbourne in November 1921.[148] This freedom of movement appears to have still

---

135 Ibid., pp 48–9. 136 Ibid., p. 49. 137 Ibid. 138 Thomas Pugh, Witness Statement 397, Bureau of Military History, militaryarchives.ie, accessed 2 Apr. 2022. 139 Ó Maonaigh, 'Who were the shoneens?', p. 40. 140 Ibid. 141 Ibid.; Foley, *The bloodied field*, p. 225. 142 Gerry Farrell & Brian Trench, 'Harry Willets: the Darling of Dalymount', abohemiansportinglife.wordpress.com/2016/05/19/harry-willits-the-darling-of-dalymount, accessed 29 July 2021. 143 *FSW*, 21 Nov. 1925. 144 Ó Maonaigh, 'Who were the shoneens?', p. 41. 145 *FSW*, 28 Aug. 1926. 146 West, *The bold collegians*, p. 47. 147 Ibid.; Garnham, *Association football and society*, pp 26, 85. 148 *Sport*, 5 Nov. 1921.

been the case in the early years of the Irish Free State. In September 1925 the Free State League was reported to be 'the open door for Irish League and English players'.[149] Dublin clubs continued to recruit those with experience of the game in Britain, with Shelbourne bringing in James 'Jock' McMillan, Hugh Meek, William Burns and Billy Lacey in the 1926–7 season.[150] Meek and Burns had also played in the Irish League while Sam Russell and Mick Foley had also played in England.[151] Corinthians, who had access to Brideville's ground every second Saturday, were described as a 'new club' in August 1926, and consisted mainly of 'army personnel', although they were 'run entirely on civilian lines'.[152] In January 1927, an attempt was made by J.J. Clarke of North Great George's Street to form a team made up of 'British ex-service men', to be known as Dublin Rangers.[153] Two months later they were still trying to secure a ground, which, as shown earlier, remained a concern for many Dublin clubs by the late 1920s.[154] British military involvement in Dublin soccer naturally declined after partition and the handover of power in January 1922.[155] Despite four military teams being registered with the Leinster FA in 1916, by beginning of the 1921–2 season there were none.[156]

Some civilian clubs did, however, include former British soldiers in their teams, including Bohemians. A member of their 1928 FAIFS Cup-winning team, Billy Dennis, had played for Port Vale as an amateur. Having joined the North Staffordshire Regiment in 1918, and being stationed at the Curragh in 1919, he met an Irish girl, married her following military service in India and decided to remain in Ireland.[157] However, in December 1930, two English players at 'two prominent Dublin clubs' were instructed, via letters, to leave Ireland along with 'all other cross-channel players', before Christmas 'and not to return or else'.[158] It was not clear if the threat was a prank or one which needed to be taken seriously. Alex Hair, a Scot, continued to play for Shelbourne that season, and scored twenty-two goals in twenty-nine games as they won the Free State League.[159]

Some foreign-born players did make their way into the Free State League, but generally not by transfer between clubs. Dickson has noted that 'in the late 1870s, Ashkenazi Jews from Tsarist Lithuania, the "Litzaks"', started arriving in Dublin and they soon became 'the largest new ethnic ingredient in the city since the Huguenot migration two centuries earlier'.[160] By 1911, there were almost 3,000 Jews living in Dublin.[161] A member of a Lithuanian family who had initially arrived in Cork, Louis Bookman had previously played for Adelaide, Frankfort and Belfast Celtic before joining Bradford City that year.[162] He moved to West

149 Ibid., 5 Sept. 1925. 150 Sands, *Shels*, p. 45. 151 *FSW*, 21 Aug. and 16 Oct. 1926. 152 *FSW*, 14 Aug. 1926. 153 *FSW*, 22 Jan. 1927. 154 *FSW*, 26 Mar. 1927. 155 *IT*, 17 Jan. 1922. 156 Officers and Council Book, 1916–17 and 1921–2, Leinster Football Association Archives, P239/77. 157 Ryan, *The official book of the FAI Cup*, pp 35–6. 158 *II*, 8 Dec. 1930. 159 Sands, *Shels*, p. 51; Joyce, *Football League players' records*, p. 121. 160 Dickson, *Dublin*, p. 439. 161 Ibid. 162 Eoin O'Callaghan, 'Louis Bookman: solving the mystery of a revolutionary and pioneering sportsman', the42.ie/louis-bookman-jewish-irish–1960912-Feb2015, accessed 1 Sept. 2021; Joyce, *Football League players' records*, p. 32

Bromwich Albion in 1914 and, following spells with Glentoran and Shelbourne, continued his career in England after the war with Luton Town and Port Vale before rejoining Shelbourne in 1923.[163] Born as Louis Buchalter before taking up the English version, he was capped internationally by Ireland at cricket and football, and had played for the Dublin Jewish CC and Railway CC before later joining Leinster CC.[164] By the summer of 1930, Bookman was running a watch and jewellery repairs shop at 14 Parliament Street, but by 1941 had moved his business to 31 Pearse Street.[165] Upon his death in June 1943, he was living at Scion Hill Avenue on Casimir Road.[166]

Another player of note from that era also initially came to Ireland for non-football related purposes. In November 1927, the 'well-known and popular' Billy Otto returned to his native South Africa following six seasons with Bohemians.[167] As Gerry Farrell has stated, he had come to Ireland via England having been injured in the First World War, where he fought for the 1st South African Infantry, and began work in the Civil Service.[168] He was born on Robben Island, where his father was a pharmacist, in 1898, and went on to play for Bohemians between 1920 and 1927.[169]

Seán Ryan has written that Shamrock Rovers had 'gradually lost its Ringsend look' by the early 1930s, having built up a 'cross-Channel colony' by recruiting players such as the Scots Jimmy Buchanan and Jimmy Smith, and the Englishman Vincent Matthews.[170] Similarly, Shelbourne 'accelerated' their recruitment of cross-Channel players in the 1930–1 season.[171] However, local talent was not completely neglected and by the mid-1930s the club had developed 'one of the finest teams in junior ranks'.[172] Less famous British players also came to play for Dublin clubs, particularly during the Great Depression, when, for example, in August 1930, there was 'an unusually large influx of cross-channel talent', although this later led to tensions with English Football League authorities.[173] They refused to recognize registrations or arrange representative matches until, as it turned out, after the Second World War.[174] Some other British-born players also turned out for Dublin clubs, often near the end of their careers, including the Scot Alex James, who appeared twice for Drumcondra in September 1939 but failed to agree terms with them.[175]

163 Joyce, *Football League players' records*, p. 32; *Sport,* 13 Jan. 1917 and 19 Feb. 1919; *NW,* 8 Mar. 1919. 164 *DDE,* 3 Aug. 1906; *BT,* 9 June 1943. 165 *EH,* 23 May 1930; Walsh, *Twenty years of Irish soccer,* p. 40. 166 *BT,* 9 June 1943. 167 *FSW,* 19 Nov. 1927. 168 Gerard Farrell, 'The remarkable life of Bohs captain William H. Otto', bohemianfc.com/?p=11512, accessed 1 Sept. 2021; 'One-way traffic? – 100 years of soldiers, mercenaries, refugees and other footballing migrants in the League of Ireland, 1920–2020' in Curran (ed.), 'The growth and development of soccer in Dublin', Special edition of *Soccer & Society,* 22:8 (2021), pp 873–86. 169 Ibid. 170 Ryan, *The official book of the FAI Cup,* p. 55. 171 *Shelbourne Football Club golden jubilee 1895–1945,* p. 28. 172 Ibid. 173 Curran, *Irish soccer migrants,* p. 111; *EH,* 15 Aug. 1930. 174 Ibid. 175 *II,* 24 Feb. 1968.

THE SECOND WORLD WAR AND POST-WAR YEARS

Around 70,000 citizens from neutral Ireland are thought to have served in the British Armed Forces in the Second World War (1939–45).[176] Two of the most notable Dublin-born footballers who did so were Alex Stevenson and Johnny Carey. Former Seaview United player Stevenson's career at Everton stretched from the 1933–4 season until the 1948–9 season.[177] He won the league with the Merseyside club in 1938–9 having won all the major club honours available in Scotland.[178] During the war, he joined the RAF, although he was still able to line out for Everton in local matches at various times.[179] By September 1945 Stevenson was in India, where he generally worked as part of the ground crew.[180] He also appeared as a guest player for Blackpool and Tranmere Rovers during the war and continued his career with Everton when it ended.[181] Some Irish players in Britain instead returned home to play in Ireland during the war. The *Belfast Newsletter* reported in August 1941 that 'nearly all the [Irish] international players of a season ago who were with cross-Channel clubs are in the Army or are with League of Ireland clubs'.[182]

Johnny Carey, who captained Manchester United to FA Cup victory in 1948 having joined the club from St James's Gate for £250 in 1937, served in the British Army in Italy and the Middle East during Second World War.[183] He also played as a guest for a number of clubs in England, as well as Shamrock Rovers, before returning to league football with Manchester United in the 1946–7 season after the war ended in 1945.[184] He was a pivotal player as Matt Busby led the club to the 1952 First Division championship and later became the manager of a number of English clubs.[185] As Gerry Farrell has shown, Bohemians' Paddy Ratcliffe also served in the war, joining the RAF and later spending time in the prisoner of war camp Stalag 357 in Germany.[186] He returned to play for Bohemians and was later signed by Notts County, before joining Wolverhampton Wanderers and later Plymouth Argyle.[187] Another Bohemians player who joined the RAF was Paddy Farrell, who was instrumental in their 1935 FAIFS Cup win.[188] Having joined Hibernian, he also went to university in Edinburgh and qualified as a dentist, a rarity among professional footballers in any era.[189] John Burke, who was part of the Shamrock Rovers team that won five consecutive FAIFS Cups from 1929 to 1933, was evacuated from Dunkirk in 1940, and had also fought in the First World War.[190]

176 Geoffrey Roberts, 'Neutrality, identity and the challenge of the Irish Volunteers' in Dermot Keogh & Mervyn O'Driscoll (eds), *Ireland in World War Two: neutrality and survival* (Cork, 2004), pp 274–84, p. 274. 177 *Soccer Reporter* (Jan. 1983), p. 10; Steve Emms & Richard Wells, *Scottish League players' records: Division One, 1890–91 to 1938–39* (Nottingham, 2007), p. 217. 178 *EH*, 18 Apr. 1988. 179 *LLE*, 23 May 1942. 180 *LS*, 15 Sept. 1945; James Quinn & Tom Feeney, 'Stevenson, Alexander Ernest', *Dictionary of Irish biography*, dib.ie, accessed 26 July 2021. 181 Quinn & Feeney, 'Stevenson, Alexander Ernest'. 182 *BN*, 11 Aug. 1941. 183 Curran, *Irish soccer migrants*, p. 118; *Soccer Reporter* (Oct. 1982), p. 3. 184 Ibid. 185 *EH*, 18 Apr. 1988. 186 Gerard Farrell, 'The tail-gunner at full-back', abohemiansportinglife.wordpress.com/2018/08, accessed 30 July 2021. 187 Ibid. 188 Ryan, *The official book of the FAI Cup*, p. 36. 189 Ibid. 190 Ibid., p. 39.

In the post-war years, Dublin clubs also continued to recruit British-based players, with Scot Jock Dodds said to be an attraction for Dublin soccer followers in 1946 having joined Shamrock Rovers.[191] Others made greater use of cross-Channel players, with Dundalk having five Scots in the team at the beginning of the 1948–9 season.[192] However, local recruitment seems to have been more common. One reporter noted that 'with so many of our best players gone across the Channel, the juniors must fill the gaps', and that 'there is very little to report in the way of captures by the senior clubs; indeed, it has been mainly a question of looking for juniors'.[193]

Some notable signings were made, however. Raich Carter, the ex-England international, was reported to be receiving £50 per match to fly over in 1953 to play for Cork Athletic at the weekends.[194] He had fallen out with Hull City's chairman and went on to win the FAI Cup that year to add to his FA Cup medals won with Sunderland in 1939 and Derby County in 1946, earning much more weekly in Ireland than the £20 available in England with the maximum wage set there until the early 1960s.[195] In 1955, Frank Broome, who had played for England versus Germany in 1938, signed for Shelbourne, and similarly chose to fly over from Birmingham Airport at the weekend rather than move from his home in Derby to Dublin.[196] He was put up at the Gresham Hotel but played only six matches due to the expense incurred.[197]

Some players from other countries living in Dublin also signed for teams in the post-war years, although admittedly these were much rarer than those born in Britain. Shelbourne were said to have acquired the services of Italian Wilson Fornica, who was involved in the Radio Éireann Orchestra in 1948.[198] However, most Dublin clubs maintained a preference for local talent. This included Shelbourne, who were said 'to have come to a crossroads' late in 1957, as 'after a trial with cross-Channel players' the team were noted as 'trying to build a local side'.[199] One foreign footballer who played briefly for Shelbourne in 1965 was the Spaniard Alvaro Rodriguez Ros, who had come to Ireland to study English.[200] He had played for Atletico Madrid against Drumcondra in the European Cup in the previous decade. However, his appearances for Shelbourne were cut short by injury.[201]

Although numerous lesser-known players came to Ireland from Britain to play, some more famous British players continued to appear near the end of their careers in the later twentieth century, including Gordon Banks, once, for St Patrick's Athletic in 1977.[202] Jimmy Johnstone's four-month spell at Shelbourne later also illustrates the lack of interest of many aging former stars in remaining at Dublin clubs for very long.[203] Much later, former Scottish international and ex-Tottenham Hotspur and Barcelona striker Steve Archibald joined a struggling Home Farm team in 1996

191 *II*, 6 Sept. 1946. 192 *IP*, 20 Aug. 1948. 193 *II*, 12 Aug. 1948. 194 *SS*, 14 Feb. 1953. 195 Ryan, *The official history of the FAI Cup*, p. 141. 196 Fitzpatrick, *Shelbourne cult heroes*, pp 22–3. 197 Ibid. 198 Ibid. 199 *II*, 21 Dec. 1957. 200 Fitzpatrick, *Shelbourne cult heroes*, p. 155. 201 Ibid. 202 *IE*, 12 Feb. 2019. 203 Fitzpatrick, *Shelbourne cult heroes*, pp 107–10.

at the age of 40 along with fellow countryman, Alan Sneddon, who was aged 38, but remained only temporarily.[204] Lesser-established non-Irish-born players who have come to Dublin from abroad have been more interested, at least temporarily, in a career in the League of Ireland, with more youthful players such as Brendan Murphy, Mark Rutherford, Brian Gray, Henry McKop, William de Graaf, Joey Ndo, Avery John and Brad Jones (prior to his time at Liverpool) all having spells at Dublin clubs.[205] Some players have been drafted in as emergency cover for injuries, including Robbie Raeside, who had a chance meeting with Shelbourne physio Larry Byrne at a coaching session in Glasgow in 2000.[206] The presence of British managers at Irish clubs has also eased movement of players from Britain into Ireland, with Willie McStay of Sligo Rovers using connections in his native country in recruiting three Scottish players in the early 1990s.[207] Occasionally, some British players did run into difficulty on account of their nationality, with Steve Lynex forced to leave Sligo Rovers, where he was on trial in 1978, having apparently been threatened with a gun and told to depart.[208] He moved to Home Farm, where he enjoyed FAI Cup success that year.[209] Some Irish managers at English clubs have been instrumental in the movement of English players to Dublin clubs, with Huddersfield Town's Eoin Hand loaning Gary Haylock to Shelbourne in the early 1990s.[210]

DUBLIN PLAYERS AND THE 'BAN' IN THE POST-WAR YEARS AND BEYOND

In 1945 Oscar Traynor reiterated that a number of those involved in the Irish Revolution, including Kevin Barry and Cathal Brugha, had, like himself, also played the so-called 'foreign' games and that this did not affect their nationality.[211] His comments received criticism from some GAA officials, including Antrim county board chairman Seamus MacFerran.[212] Gaelic football players continued to join soccer teams despite the Ban. In 1947, Bohemians signed Daly, 'a recruit from GAA ranks', as goalkeeper.[213] Other more well-known Gaelic footballers also joined Dublin's leading soccer clubs. In September 1947, Shelbourne were said to have acquired Antrim Gaelic football player Harry O'Neill, who had helped his county to win the 1946 Ulster Senior Gaelic football championship.[214] O'Neill was reported to be 'the second big "transfer" from GAA to soccer' that year, following Cork hurler Derry Beckett's move to Cork United.[215] Other notable dual players included Con Martin, Peter Corr and Johnny Carey.[216] Martin had played for St Maur's of Rush and St Mary's of Saggart as well as the Dublin inter-county team, where he won the Leinster Gaelic football championship before being suspended

204 *IT*, 2 Dec. 1996. 205 Ryan, *The official book of the FAI Cup*, p. 294; Fitzpatrick, *Shelbourne cult heroes*, pp 154, 157–60. 206 Fitzpatrick, *Shelbourne cult heroes*, pp 148–50. 207 Ryan, *The official book of the FAI Cup*, p. 332. 208 Ibid., pp 250–1. 209 Ibid. 210 Ibid., p. 327. 211 *SC*, 20 Jan. 1945. 212 Ibid. 213 *II*, 26 Aug. 1947. 214 *II*, 3 Sept. 1947. 215 Ibid. 216 Ibid.

for playing soccer for Drumcondra 'B'.[217] While they faced a clash of commitments and the physical difficulties of playing both codes, rugby players were not
subjected to any formal ruling forbidding them to play soccer in Dublin. In May
1946, a rugby selection chosen by Con Martin met a soccer XI at Harold's Cross
to raise funds for the Rosary Fete.[218]

While soccer struggled to match Gaelic football's image and identity as
Ireland's national footballing code, some attempts were made to illustrate that the
former game also had its place within the revolutionary movement, through com-
memorations. In the spring of 1966, the FAI decided to commemorate the fiftieth
anniversary of the 1916 Rising by inviting around 200 survivors to the FAI Cup
final between Shamrock Rovers and Limerick at Dalymount Park, and by com-
missioning a painting of Oscar Traynor.[219] A special ceremony was held before the
match.[220] However, national broadcaster Raidio Éireann decided not to offer live
coverage of the match, illustrating that soccer was still not fully accepted in some
sections of the media by the late 1960s.[221]

The advent of televised soccer matches by the late 1950s made a mockery of
the GAA's Ban, as it rendered monitoring of would-be offenders impossible if, for
example, they chose to watch soccer in their own homes.[222] In addition, the system
of appointing vigilance committees to monitor players' movements was becoming
more publicly frowned upon, with one reporter stating at that time that

> whatever can be said for the ever-controversial BAN nothing at all can be
> said by any sporting organization for the method of enforcing it … to have a
> system of spying (only a hard word for the 'vigilance' idea) on fellow mem-
> bers surely must undermine the very roots of a sporting body.[223]

One writer has suggested that Limerick hurling legend Mick Mackey took a place
on his local vigilance committee so that he could attend rugby and soccer to watch
these games himself, illustrating the farcical nature of this structure.[224] Even the
Mayo-based Ballina Stephanites club, from a town said to be 'the stronghold of
Gaelicism in the west', were having doubts about the Ban as players and committee
members had 'turned away and entered into rugby and soccer circles' by the late
1940s.[225] Many of those playing Gaelic games were clearly against it, with eighteen
of the St Eunan's Gaelic football team, which won the Donegal county championship in 1967, voicing their opposition to it when interviewed on the subject the
following year.[226]

217 *II*, 11 Dec. 1945. 218 *II*, 25 May 1946. 219 Curran & Toms, 'Introduction' in Curran
& Toms (eds), *New perspectives on association football in Irish history*, p. 5; Emergency Committee
Meeting, 19 Apr. 1966, FAI Archives, P137/16. 220 Curran & Toms, 'Introduction' in Curran &
Toms (eds), *New perspectives on association football in Irish history*, p. 5 221 Ibid., pp 5–6. 222 *DN*,
20 June 1959; *AC*, 2 May 1964. 223 *DN*, 20 June 1959. 224 *Irish Farmers Journal*, 24 Aug.
1991. 225 *Ballina Herald*, 24 Mar. 1947. 226 *DN*, 13 Jan. 1968.

Some GAA players took to using false names or abstained from team photographs while participating in the so-called 'foreign games', with Brian McEniff, who managed Donegal to their first All-Ireland Gaelic football championship in 1992, playing soccer under an 'alias' in the League of Ireland with Cork Hibernians and Drumcondra in the 1960s.[227] Some professional soccer players in Dublin continued to also play Gaelic football, but not all were rewarded for their efforts. Eoin Hand recalled in his second autobiography that, as a professional footballer with Swindon Town in 1964, he was an instrumental part of the Scoil Uí Chonaill under-21 team that won the Dublin under-21 county championship that summer.[228] However, he was later refused a medal by the GAA club's president at the awards ceremony.[229] Some clubs maintained cordial relations despite the GAA's Ban, with Home Farm's young footballers also playing for St Vincent's GAA club.[230] The Whitehall club was also connected to Clontarf GAA club through Fr Tom Menton, a brother of Home Farm co-founder Brendan, with the former becoming Clontarf GAA club president in 1971.[231]

The removal of the Ban was partly the result of campaigning by Tom Woulfe of the Civil Service club in Dublin in the 1960s.[232] By the beginning of the following decade there was continued opposition towards its presence, and some even voiced their opinions outside GAA grounds on match days. In July 1970, a protest against the Ban, led by disc jockey Frank Godfrey, took place before the Leinster Senior Gaelic football final.[233] In April 1971, at the GAA's national congress, held in the Whitla Hall of Queen's University in Belfast, it was agreed that the Ban should be ended, with GAA president Pat Fanning announcing that a new charter was required to replace the former rules.[234] Only two counties, Antrim and Sligo, had voted to retain what one newspaper columnist described as 'the most ridiculous posture that any Irish association has ever adopted' at their county conventions.[235]

After the Ban was officially removed, open participation in soccer allowed some Gaelic football players to more publicly play in the rival code, with Dublin players Kevin Heffernan and Des Foley taking part in a match in aid of the Multiple Sclerosis Society of Ireland at Dalymount Park in June 1971.[236] Some soccer players continued to be regarded with scepticism by the GAA, however, with England World Cup winner Nobby Stiles' visit to Dublin as part of charity work for Gorta in 1972 indicative of this.[237] Initially it had been advertised that he would sign autographs in Croke Park, but following a discussion between organizer Gerry Connaughton and GAA general secretary Seán Ó Siofra it was agreed that he would be allowed to enter the stadium but not to sign autographs in it. Following the charity walk, however, he signed autographs inside the ground.[238] Some other fundraising matches took place between teams of both codes. In May 1974, a

227 *EH*, 9 Feb. 1993. **228** Hand, *First hand*, p. 14. **229** Ibid. **230** Menton, *Home Farm*, p. 161. **231** Ibid. **232** Diarmaid Ferriter, *Ambiguous republic: Ireland in the 1970s* (London, 2013), p. 318. **233** *II*, 20 July 1970. **234** Ibid., 12 Apr. 1971. **235** *DD*, 16 Apr. 1971; *SI*, 11 Jan. 1976. **236** *II*, 2 June 1971. **237** *IP*, 1 May 1972. **238** Ibid.

selection of Irish players including Dubliners Paddy Mulligan, who initiated the event, Eamon Dunphy, John Giles, Paddy Mulligan, Gerry Daly, Mick Lawlor and Eoin Hand met Galway in a charity match played under Gaelic football rules in Tuam, with the former winning by 3–11 to 2–13.[239]

Commitment by players to both codes was difficult in any case, and those who switched to English professional soccer generally stayed with that code with insurance restricting other sporting activities away from their clubs. Dublin Gaelic footballer Kevin Moran joined Manchester United in 1977, having been monitored by Billy Behan while playing for Pegasus, a team composed of UCD graduates, in the FAI Cup that year.[240] Moran had been centre-half along with Tommy Drum of Trinity College Dublin in the Irish Universities team in 1976, with both defenders winning All-Ireland Gaelic football medals with Dublin.[241] Moran played in three All-Ireland finals, winning in 1976 and 1977, and was allowed by Manchester United to play in the 1978 decider, before focusing fully on soccer, while Drum captained Dublin to All-Ireland victory in 1983.[242]

Despite the odd charity match, the legacy of the Ban lingered in Irish society. While it is unclear how strict all GAA inter-county managers were in removing players who took part in what had been known as 'foreign games' after the removal of the Ban, some, including Donegal manager Tom Conaghan in the late 1980s, took a hard-line approach to players who wanted to keep their sporting choices open.[243] Tyrone manager Art McRory, when he was asked to comment on the difficulties the previous manager had encountered in dealing with soccer players, made it clear on his appointment in 1980 that he would be selecting those who were mainly interested in playing Gaelic football.[244] In 1986, the Wicklow GAA county board lifted a two-year ban, instigated by their Gaelic football manager, on Noel Keohane, who had opted to play soccer instead of Gaelic football for his county.[245] Numerous players from inter-county teams also played soccer with, for example, two Longford Town players, Jude Quigley and Dessie Barry, part of Westmeath and Longford Gaelic football teams, respectively, in the late 1980s.[246]

In addition, Dublin players Kieran Duff and Brian Mullins played soccer and rugby, respectively, in that decade.[247] Dave Barry, who played for Cork City FC and Cork Gaelic football teams in the 1980s and 1990, was dropped from the latter team in 1987 after the Cork county board had decided to implement a 'code of conduct', to prevent their inter-county players from participating in other non-GAA sports.[248] Commitment issues therefore remained for some players at inter-county level into the next decade. In 1995, Gaelic football player Brian Nolan was temporarily dropped from the Kildare team for playing rugby with Naas and 'for defying the Kildare selectors' instructions'.[249] He was reinstated by manager Dermot Earley, having confirmed he would commit to Gaelic football.[250]

239 *CT*, 24 and 31 May 1974. 240 Ryan, *The official book of the FAI Cup*, p. 245. 241 West, *The bold collegians*, p. 104. 242 Ibid.; *IP*, 21 July 1979. 243 *DN*, 7 Feb. 1987. 244 *II*, 1 Mar. 1980. 245 *IP*, 16 May 1986. 246 *DD*, 30 Oct. 1987. 247 *EH*, 7 Feb. 1984. 248 *IE*, 27 Aug. 1987. 249 *Connacht Tribune*, 10 Mar. 1995. 250 Ibid.

The following year, two Clare hurlers were removed from the inter-county hurling team for playing soccer on the day of a hurling inter-county match.[251] Loss of inter-county players to other codes and clashes of fixtures remained a problem, with two Wexford Minor team Gaelic footballers opting to take part in a soccer trial for Leinster Youths rather than play in an all-Ireland Minor quarter-final against Laois the same day, with the latter match resulting in defeat for their county.[252]

In the late twentieth century, some footballers continued to play both Gaelic football and soccer at a high level in Dublin, perhaps most notably Jason Sherlock, who won an All-Ireland Gaelic football senior championship medal with Dublin in 1995 and also played for a number of League of Ireland clubs.[253] Sherlock later noted in his autobiography that Damien Richardson was not as tolerant of his switching of codes as some of his other managers had been.[254] The former Gillingham manager had allowed Dublin Gaelic football player Keith Barr to play for the English club in a number of friendly matches in Ireland in 1991, although the Erin's Isle player remained committed to his GAA club.[255] Irish junior international goalkeeper Gary Kelly, who won a number of Leinster GAA medals with Parnells, noted the physical demands of playing both codes:

> They [schedules] always clashed and so the Gaelic [manager] wanted you there three nights a week and a match the weekend, and the soccer [manager] wanted you there twice a week training and a match the weekend. So you could be training twice a week, and you could be doing five sessions a week, and it was really difficult. And you had to work as well, and you had to balance all that … So, yeah, trying to keep everybody happy was very, very difficult.[256]

PART-TIME PROFESSIONAL FOOTBALL IN DUBLIN AND WORK IN OTHER INDUSTRIES

As shown earlier, professional football was formally accepted by the Leinster FA in Dublin by 1905, although it had been legalized by the IFA in 1894.[257] Garnham has written that 'professionalism had become necessary in Dublin to advance the popularity and quality of the game, to ensure the provision of a properly fitted-out stadium, and to rid the game of its existing system of covert payments to players'.[258] Part-time professional football remained the only option for many Dublin clubs, however, throughout the twentieth century, as the vast majority lacked the capital and support to develop full-time structures for their employees. While full-time professional football seems enticing, not every Dublin-based player has

251 *City Tribune*, 24 May 1996. **252** Ibid. **253** 'Jason Sherlock on his soccer crossover: from West Ham trials to Liverpool's interest', offtheball.com/sport/jason-sherlock-team–33–153054, accessed 5 Jan. 2019. **254** Jason Sherlock, *Jayo: my autobiography* (London, 2018), p. 160. **255** *II*, 3 Aug. 1991. **256** Interview with Gary Kelly, 12 Dec. 2019. **257** Garnham, *Association football and society*, p. 73. **258** Ibid.

been interested in moving to England. At times, players have even rejected the opportunity to play abroad as they could earn more playing on a part-time basis in Ireland and working in other businesses than in lower-league English football. By September 1925, Jack Simpson had returned again to Shelbourne after a spell at Drumcondra and it was noted that 'but for business reasons [he] might have gone to several cross-Channel clubs'.[259] Some players, such as Joe Grace, who had spells at St Agatha's Boys, Leinster, Bohemians, Belfast Celtic, Olympia, Barrackton (Cork) and Drumcondra by the late 1920s, had apparently 'refused many offers to cross the water'.[260] Prior to the removal of the maximum wage in 1961, whereby players in English league football were not supposed to earn more than £20 per week, some Irish players, such as Paddy Coad, felt that it was better to remain in Ireland and play at a semi-professional level there while working in another job.[261] For some, such as Johnny Matthews, who turned down a move to West Ham in 1949, family commitments and stability took preference.[262] There was also the opportunity to coach or manage at Irish clubs in a part-time capacity. In 1942, Shamrock Rovers signed Coad from Waterford and he would go on to become player-coach at the Dublin club.[263] He recalled that the 1944 FAI Cup-winning team's bonuses increased as they progressed to the final, where an additional £5 was available in winning the match.[264] However, most players struggled to make any real money in the game in Dublin, and payment during the summer was not viable for many clubs, with Drumcondra player Tommy O'Rourke having to sell his 1943 FAI Cup medal in order to pay for a deposit on his house as he was getting married.[265]

Despite the Cunninghams' role within the club, Shamrock Rovers remained a part-time club in terms of training and playing schedules and professional contracts, although one player temporarily broke the mould in the early 1950s. Waterford man Richard 'Dixie' Hale, who came from a famous Irish footballing family – his brother Alfie signed for Aston Villa in 1960 and their father, Alfie Senior, had enjoyed a distinguished career in the League of Ireland and also played in the American Soccer League in the 1920s – was signed as a full-time professional by Shamrock Rovers as a 17-year-old in 1952.[266] However, as the only full-time professional at the club, he became bored with life in Dublin in the late 1950s. He later decided to return to his home-town club, and was told by Shamrock Rovers that he would never play for Ireland.[267] Seán Ryan has written that 'with Joe Cunningham the power-broker in Irish football, they had the person in place to see that he didn't', illustrating the influence in national selection that some Dublin clubs could hold at that time.[268]

259 *FSW*, 26 Sept. 1925.   **260** *FSW*, 17 Mar. 1928.   **261** Curran, *Irish soccer migrants*, p. 126.   **262** Ryan, *The official book of the FAI Cup*, p. 125.   **263** *SI*, 21 Oct. 1956.   **264** Ryan, *The official book of the FAI Cup*, p. 105.   **265** Ibid., p. 100; Tynan, 'Association football and Irish society during the inter-war period, 1918–1939', p. 148.   **266** Curran, *Irish soccer migrants*, pp 161–2, 251–2; *Waterford News and Star*, 21 May 2021. I am grateful to Alfie Hale for this information.   **267** Ryan, *The official book of the FAI Cup*, pp 166–7; *II*, 6 June 2021.   **268** *II*, 6 June 1921.

Some others have had full-time contracts at Dublin clubs, particularly in the late twentieth century, although this has been reliant on the rare spells in the Irish economy when it has been possible to sustain full-time professional footballers. Unfortunately, as shown in the early 2000s when Shelbourne overcame some of Europe's bigger names in European competition only to later go into decline with the downturn in the global economy in 2007, these periods have not lasted for very long.[269] Some players were also ultimately happier to develop a career in Dublin rather than at a cross-Channel club. Mick Lawlor, who had a number of trials with Manchester United and Leeds United in the 1960s and 1970s, felt relieved to come back and play in Dublin, having struggled with homesickness while in England.[270] He wasn't interested in playing at a lower level in English league football, and went on to have a successful career in the League of Ireland while also working for a number of mail-equipment companies.[271]

Much later, Professional Footballers' Association of Ireland chairman Stephen McGuinness, who had trials with Arsenal and Leeds United in the early 1990s, realized it was a different physical level to what he was used to at Dublin club Home Farm.[272] He also admitted that he was affected by homesickness while in England, stating that it was 'horrific' and he 'struggled with it massively'.[273] He noted that therefore returning to Ireland was not an issue, and he was able to continue with his club, Home Farm:

> I could handle that easily. Some of the other kids coming back can't handle it and they think, 'I can't make it now and England's the only place to be.' But I had, because, obviously being at Home Farm – I wasn't then having to go to St Pat's or Shamrock Rovers trying to break in there, I was breaking into a level I was at. The club I loved, the club who looked after me, were going to give me an opportunity, so I was more than comfortable. I knew exactly what I was doing and I was in an environment that I had been in since I was seven.[274]

For those that remain in Dublin, or have returned from British clubs, balancing a career in part-time professional football with other employment can be a challenge.[275] Having played in the League of Ireland and in the NASL, Dave Henderson took the decision to become a fireman while continuing to play League of Ireland football in the early 1980s. He noted that in playing full-time he had reached a certain level, and was once described by Republic of Ireland international Paul McGrath as equal to any goalkeeper he had played with, while the pair were at St

269 Paul Keane, *Gods vs mortals: Irish clubs in Europe ... a front row seat at ten of the greatest games* (Kells, 2010), pp 214–49. **270** Interview with Mick Lawlor, 29 Feb. 2019. **271** Ibid. **272** Interview with Stephen McGuinness, 22 Oct. 2019. **273** Ibid. **274** Ibid. **275** See, in particular, Conor Curran & Seamus Kelly, 'Returning home: the return of Irish born football migrants to Ireland's football leagues and their cultural re-adaption, 1945–2010', *Irish Studies Review*, 26:2 (2018), pp 181–98.

Patrick's Athletic.[276] But taking up a more mainstream job along with playing in the League of Ireland then impacted on his high standards:

> I was really, really, really on top of my game … I would have been really, really fit, really at it. After coming back from everywhere, just about a year and a half after that I went for the fire brigade … When I went for the interview the man says, 'You're gonna have to give up the football, you know that.' I said, 'Yeah no problem.' [laughs] … That was '83, so I played another fifteen years after telling the man that lie … You sort of felt like you weren't going to get to the heights that you thought you were going go to. So, a sort of part-time mentality then kicked in.[277]

Henderson felt that balancing a playing career with working hours was difficult:

> I remember finishing at ten o'clock … from Blanchardstown, driving to Sligo, playing a match, coming back, going in and doing the ambulance another fifteen hours … And then, the one night I said before, I delivered a baby just down the road here as well, about four or five in the morning. We had to go to Kilkenny [for a match], I wasn't – I don't know why I wasn't driving at the time, but me da brought me down, and just, all you could think every five minutes, was the vision of the night before, every time the ball was up the other end of the pitch, because it was the first baby I ever delivered. Jesus, that was hard.[278]

However, because of his reputation as a goalkeeper within Irish football, he was able to miss some games during the season and had understanding managers such as Brian Kerr who took his work situation into account.[279]

An Irish junior international goalkeeper across three decades, Gary Kelly played for a number of League of Ireland and Leinster Senior League clubs in his career, and was working as a storeman during Ashtown Villa's FAI Cup run in 1991. He noted the difficulties this brought:

> That's the difference between being a pro, obviously, and being an amateur. You've got to get up and go to work in the morning, whatever your job may be. I was a storeman. I had to go to work, I wasn't off until half five, you had to get home as quick as you could, Tuesday and Thursday, and get to training for seven o'clock, quarter past seven, so it was tough, yeah. You wouldn't be home then until ten, half-ten at night, you know. Then it was the same thing again: bed, and back to work the next day. So it was hard, yeah, definitely hard, definitely hard to balance it, with, maybe you've a

276 McGrath, *Back from the brink*, p. 110.   277 Interview with Dave Henderson, 22 Nov. 2019.   278 Ibid.   279 Ibid.

family as well, you have to balance that around the football. So it was difficult, yeah 100 per cent it was difficult, yeah.[280]

He had been a member of the Cherry Orchard team that won the FAI Junior Cup in 1990.[281] He was then signed by Tony O'Connell at Ashtown Villa, and the club reached the quarter-finals of the FAI Senior Cup in 1991, earning a reputation as giant killers along the way.[282] Having come through a number of intermediate matches, they faced a trip to League of Ireland Champions-elect Dundalk, winning by a goal to nil.[283] In the next round, they beat Derry City one–nil at the Brandywell, with Kelly named as man of the match. He stated that 'there wasn't any work for about three or four days after that, I can tell ya! It was fantastic, ah yeah, great memories, you know.'[284] However, they succumbed to another League of Ireland team, Kilkenny City, in the quarter finals, which Kelly described as

> devastating, absolutely. It was like if the ground opened up, you would have jumped into it. It was just an anti-climax. After beating the two big teams, we were actually favourites to beat them, and they were a League of Ireland team, and just on the day, things just didn't go our way. They beat us 1–0, they scored a goal in the first half, it was just – we didn't get any luck on the day, just no luck, and that's the way it goes, that's part of football isn't it? You have your ups and downs but that was a big downer, a big downer.[285]

Kelly also enjoyed success in the Metropolitan Cup with Ashtown Villa, and saved a penalty in the final against Parkvilla at Dalymount Park in May 1993.[286] He also enjoyed a spell with the Garda Club, who were allowed to field a number of civilians, and recalled that

> player for player, they wouldn't have been as good as Ashtown Villa, but the facilities were fantastic. The home ground, Westmanstown, up the back of Lucan there, it was a fantastic place, there was everything in it – club house, lovely pitches, training facilities – it was really top notch now, and they had a fantastic team as well. There was a mixture of Guards and non-Gardaí as well, so it was a really good team.[287]

He then earned a move to Waterford United of the League of Ireland. Like many Dublin-based players, he continued to train locally but travelled to his club at the weekend, which he found tough.[288] He noted that

280 Interview with Gary Kelly, 12 Dec. 2019. 281 Ibid. 282 *II*, 8 Apr. 1991. 283 Interview with Gary Kelly, 12 Dec. 2019. 284 Ibid.; *IP*, 25 Mar. 1991. 285 Interview with Gary Kelly, 12 Dec. 2019. 286 Ibid.; *II*, 13 May 1993. 287 Interview with Gary Kelly, 12 Dec. 2019. 288 Ibid. 289 Ibid.

it impedes your time. So, if you're playing Sunday in Waterford at three o'clock, what was happening was, the match was over, and I had to sprint into the dressing room, have a quick shower, get a lift up to the train station for a six o'clock train back to Dublin, and if I missed that, I'd be staying overnight! So you were always in a hurry to get somewhere, and didn't get home then until nearly ten o'clock at night, and then you're up for work … There wasn't much recovery.[289]

Having settled for Dublin soccer, he later won another FAI Junior Cup medal with Ballymun United and also enjoyed more success at the end of his career, playing with Cherry Orchard again until the age of 42.[290]

Similarly, fellow goalkeeper Brian O'Shea felt that 'working and playing is difficult'.[291] Before becoming a football coach, he had taken up employment as a panel beater, having returned from trials with Liverpool as a teenager. He stated that while playing professionally on a part-time basis with St Patrick's Athletic in the early 1980s,

I was serving my time as a panel beater for a company called Keogh Motors, and it wasn't by choice, it wasn't something that I wanted to do, but again, you have your parents saying, 'You gotta do this, you gotta do that', so taking that on, that was a huge burden. It felt like a weight around my neck because it interfered with my training schedule. I just found that I hadn't the energy to do the schedule that I'd put in place. It did interfere with me a little bit, but not a whole lot … I just would have liked the opportunity to stay with an English club for a year, just to prove a point of what I could do and what I would have done, you know.[292]

O'Shea later moved to Northern Ireland club Newry Town in 1986, with the prospect of higher wages a motivating factor as he could earn more through travelling expenses and bonuses in the Irish League than in the League of Ireland at the time. This meant that he could focus on football on a more full-time basis.[293] He later returned to the League of Ireland and, until he had to retire from the game prematurely in the early 2000s, was able to combine playing with Home Farm and coaching on their FÁS football trainee course with a job at Dublin Airport.[294]

Other players have alluded to the fact that they have only taken up non-football related jobs to make ends meet and to assist their playing careers. Stephen McGuinness noted that, as a player, he was also content to take up other jobs away from professional football but remained focused fully on his League of Ireland soccer career, which stretched from 1992 until 2005.[295] He stated that, having got an

290 Ibid.   291 Interview with Brian O'Shea, 21 Nov. 2019.   292 Ibid.   293 Ibid.   294 Ibid. 295 Interview with Stephen McGuinness, 22 Oct. 2019.

interview with a courier company through his father, he was adamant that his new job could not distract from football and told his recruiters that,

> 'If this job, in any way interferes with me being a professional footballer, it's not gonna be for me.' And luckily enough the guy, he was called Jimmy Savage, and was the HR manager, was a massive Bohs fan. He had a Bohs picture on the wall. And he said to me, 'Look, we're looking, from a job point of view, for a bit of profiling people with a sport background,' and he said, 'Okay, we'll work with you on your football and there's no problem.' So, I worked there for twelve years maybe, bit longer, and was able to manage professional football with the job.[296]

While he was well-treated by his employers, he was less concerned about moving up the career ladder and noted that:

> They were brilliant to me [but] I couldn't really move. The commitment levels at the football, as my career moved on, just went through the roof. So the opportunities to move within, and to educate myself to get better within that job – it was never really gonna happen … The work I was doing on the job was a supplement to football – I never saw it the other way around. I always saw it as a supplement. But in my head I also knew that there's not enough money here to go full-time, professionally in Ireland, so I needed to run that professional football career in parallel – to have a dual career as such.[297]

Similarly, Seán Prunty, who returned to Ireland and enjoyed success with Longford Town, having been released from Middlesbrough in 2000, noted that he remained fully focused on football although no longer a full-time professional, despite the demands this brought:

> Nothing would get in the way of football training and I think that's just the mind-set you get into in that period of time. You're dedicated. From that conversation I had with my mam and dad in Ballybrack, saying, 'I want to be a footballer', you know, I still had that in my head at twenty-four, twenty-five years of age, that football was going to be the number one. But everything revolved around it and it was difficult to do the jobs, to do work, but people understood, and they were great, my bosses at the time, they were fantastic, they'd give me time off in order to go and train and play matches.[298]

John Coady, who combined being a postman with playing in the League of Ireland with Shamrock Rovers before his move to Chelsea in 1986, felt that his An Post employees were 'fantastic' and 'couldn't have been more helpful' in regards to

296 Ibid.   297 Ibid.   298 Interview with Seán Prunty, 23 Oct. 2019.

rescheduling his work hours around matches, and he returned to the job after leaving Chelsea in 1988 and also signing for Derry City.[299] He felt that balancing playing and working got harder as he got older 'because your recovery isn't as quick. It was hard, when you used to play games on a Sunday, if you had a particularly hard game, to get up at like half-five on the Monday morning, then that was a bit tough.'[300] Not every player received support for their football careers within the workplace, and some League of Ireland players, including Paddy Mulligan, Seamus Kelly, Mick Lawlor and Alf Girvan, have lost their jobs when they had the opportunity to go abroad for trials or when matches clashed with work commitments.[301]

By the late 1990s, full-time professional football had become more viable for a number of League of Ireland clubs. Former Glasgow Celtic player Paul Byrne, who, at times, struggled to maintain his discipline off the pitch, stated that his focus needed to be fully on football after his return to the League of Ireland from Southend United at that time, if clubs were to get the best out of him:

> I always stated that when I came back to League of Ireland I wanted to be full-time. Because I was the sort of person that needed to train, I had to train. Like, Tuesday night, Thursday night was no good to me – I had to be kept busy every morning … But I felt I had to be full-time or nothing at all. And I think managers – Roddy Collins, Pat Dolan, Dermot Keely – realized that, and they put me full-time.[302]

Some other players returning from English league clubs have signed full-time contracts with League of Ireland clubs at a time when full-time professional football in the Republic of Ireland was an option. An increase in accessibility to university courses in Ireland in the early twenty-first century has also meant that some players can avail of this career path. Former UCD soccer scholar Seamus Kelly joined St Patrick's Athletic from Cardiff City in 2001 and was able to continue his studies on return to Dublin as a postgraduate student, while training with his new club in the morning.[303] For Kelly, who had become bored with the non-academic culture of English professional football, the transition was relatively smooth, but returning home from Ireland after being released from Derby County was initially tough for Chris Deans. He had captained their reserve team and the Republic of Ireland at underage level.[304] He was released following a bad knee injury in 2003 and recalled that:

> Yeah it was difficult. For the first while, I mean when I first came back, I didn't do anything. And I kind of did what any kind of late teenage/ twenty-year-old

299 Interview with John Coady, 22 Jan. 2020. **300** Ibid. **301** Interview with Paddy Mulligan, 4 Oct. 2019; interview with Seamus Kelly, 2 Oct. 2019; interview with Alf Girvan, 27 Jan. 2020; interview with Mick Lawlor, 29 Feb. 2020. **302** Interview with Paul Byrne, 26 Feb. 2020. **303** Interview with Seamus Kelly, 2 Oct. 2019. **304** Interview with Chris Deans, 15 Nov. 2019.

would do – I'd go out with my mates and drink a lot. And then I signed for Dublin City but that was part-time football – it was training in the evenings. I wasn't used to that, sitting around all day. I'd go training in the evenings, twice a week or three times a week. There weren't many gyms readily available as there are now [and] I wasn't driving. So it was it all those things and it was really difficult. It was difficult to adapt back to part-time again.[305]

Having been encouraged by his mother to look for a day job, he took up a sales role with UPS, and began to develop a career outside football. He was able to utilize his football discipline to develop in a new role. He felt that this had helped him in gaining educational qualifications to strengthen his career prospects:

When I was with UPS, I kind of got a couple of promotions in that job, and they had a corporate education programme, and I went back and done a degree. In Anglia Ruskin University in Cambridge – so I did a three-year B.A. honours in business strategy, business and leadership, business management. And I did that while I was playing, and working full-time as well. It was a bit of a juggle, but I mean, even when I was doing that – like, I struggled through it, when I was doing it, but when I graduated … I was on a career path then. I realized that in the work environment, I had a lot of good discipline from football that would get me very far, because I felt I was likeable, I got stuff done, I was a bit of a doer, so I said, 'Well there's a gap in me, that I need some education, and if I don't get education I'm going to get to a certain stage in my career and I'm gonna block it.' So I managed to get in on this corporate programme, and it was a degree that was paid for by the company, and I got it, and I got an honours degree. And then, it gave me the platform to continue to grow.[306]

He added that players returning to Ireland need something to fall back on, even if they have been in England's lower leagues for a lengthy time:

I think you've got to invest in yourself and you've got to be a little bit selfish because there's only a very, very small, small percentage that make it, and when I say 'make it', I mean, if you can play in England for the next ten years at a low level. But when you finish in your thirties, you're going to be some-what bereft, because the money that you earn in the lower, lower leagues is not going to get you to where you need to be for the rest of your life … when you finish at thirty or thirty-five, you've still got a long way left in your life.[307]

While still relatively young, as his career in business developed, he became less interested in a full-time professional football career in Ireland, and found he could

305 Ibid. 306 Ibid. 307 Ibid.

earn more with his day job and part-time football than by simply playing football with a full-time contract with Sporting Fingal.[308] Seán Prunty, who was forced to retire from League of Ireland football in 2007 with a heart complaint, similarly later completed a degree in business studies as he felt it would help his job prospects.[309]

RETIREMENT FROM PART-TIME FOOTBALL AND RELATED INJURIES

For some players, managing a full-time job away from football and organizing their semi-professional football career can lead to the decision to retire from playing, particularly if a player is in the latter stages of their career. In 1936, Dolphin player Ray Rogers, 'though not severing his connection with the club', signalled that he would be 'unable to turn out owing to pressure of business'.[310] Much later, in the mid-1980s, Mick Lawlor retired from playing in the League of Ireland as he had gone on to a business partnership and wanted to concentrate more fully on this.[311] Dave Henderson retired from football while at Bohemians in 1998, and stated he was glad to step away as the pressure had become too much:

> I actually remember the feeling of walking the first week [after retiring from football] – walking – I was actually home from work – leaving the fire station. I didn't have to go training, and I was thinking, 'This is fantastic!' I really did. And I remember that to this day – that day. My God. You just sort of feel the weight of having to not look six months ahead to be organizing shifts to get off work. Organizing – like, my wife would be working – babysitters, the kids were young. Trying to get around, 'How am I going to get to training? How am I not gonna miss training?' Injuries, at that time, my back had been in bits since before. So, everything, it was just the relief, you could feel the weight coming off, that you didn't have to do this anymore. No, I never missed it from that day.[312]

Although both Lawlor and Henderson were in any case coming to the end of lengthy careers in football, the demands of maintaining part-time careers in the game and other occupations were evident. Previous research by this author has illustrated that almost 90 per cent of 146 Republic of Ireland-born players with English Football League playing experience who moved back to Ireland in 1945–2000 returned to play in the League of Ireland.[313] Many players have attempted to stay involved in football after retiring from playing, but this can also be tough if coaching on a part-time basis. The lack of finance, and in turn the opportunity to develop most League of

308 Ibid. 309 Interview with Seán Prunty, 23 Oct. 2019. 310 *IP*, 5 Aug. 1936. 311 Interview with Mick Lawlor, 29 Feb. 2020. 312 Interview with Dave Henderson, 22 Nov. 2019. 313 Curran, *Irish soccer migrants*, p. 303.

Ireland clubs has also discouraged players from taking up positions, and many, including Paddy Mulligan, who have taken up posts, have been frustrated by this.[314] Having finished playing, Harry McCue took up management with Drogheda United in 2001, but found this difficult while working in Dublin city during the day:

> Managing and coaching in Ireland is very difficult on a part-time basis. So I was still working, I was in an agency in Baggot Street. My typical Friday morning would be: up at six, in work at half-six, get all my work done by two o'clock, and get on [the road]. [There was] no Drogheda by-pass then and all that, all that type of stuff – getting home at midnight, and then just flaked Saturday and Sunday. It was difficult, you know, trying to combine the two. I'd never do it again and it's not good for you, it certainly isn't and I just don't understand how a part-time manager can do it, you know. And I advise, if anyone asks me the question, I say, 'Just be very careful.' I did it for seven years and that was a long time, I just don't know how, and I'd say to everyone, just be careful, mind your health, because either you do one or the other.[315]

He now concentrates on the full-time coaching of young players.[316] John Coady also felt that a post-playing role in coaching or management could be difficult on a part-time basis given the level of commitment needed, and, having completed a UEFA 'B' licence and successfully managed a local junior team, he decided to step away from the game after a brief spell as assistant coach to Alan Matthews at Longford Town in the early 2000s.[317]

Few professional footballers can expect to come through a career without injury, although some have been luckier than others. Stephen McGuinness recalled when interviewed that he had had no serious injuries despite a highly successful career in League of Ireland football.[318] He finished playing in the early 2000s when the treatment of sports injuries in Ireland was much better developed than it had been in the 1960s, when Frank O'Neill, who noted the lack of physiotherapy within Irish soccer at that time, was a player with Shamrock Rovers. He felt that he had lost a yard of pace as a result of cortisone injections he received for leg injuries.[319] He added that he might have recovered quicker if it had been earlier in his career, but stated that 'it's the wrong time to get injuries in your early thirties, as a footballer'.[320] Alf Girvan, who played for Drumcondra in that decade, recalled that, 'I had my nose broken at least six times, from heading the ball, fellas coming back with their head – nose broke. That was the worst injury for me playing football.'[321] Playing through injuries was commonplace, and players were often ordered to do

314 Interview with Paddy Mulligan, 4 Oct. 2019. 315 Interview with Harry McCue, 10 Dec. 2019. 316 Ibid. 317 Interview with John Coady, 20 Jan. 2020. 318 Interview with Stephen McGuinness, 22 Oct. 2019. 319 Interview with Frank O'Neill, 30 Jan. 2020. 320 Ibid. 321 Interview with Alf Girvan, 27 Jan. 2020.

so by management, with Mick Meagan told by Everton manager Harry Catterick
that he had to continue despite suffering from issues with his achilles tendons in
the early 1960s.[322] When asked about his worst time in football, Meagan responded
that it was

> When you're injured. There's nothing as bad as injury. Because the train-
> ers, they want you out on the pitch, [they'd say,] 'Come on, there's nothing
> wrong with you, get up there and do it – have a run around, there's nothing
> wrong with you!' No, that was the worst time. And then, you'd play, and
> you wouldn't be fit, and you'd be going through a lot of pain. You'd be sort
> of suffering, but you'd keep motoring on. Because it was either that or get
> stick, [such as] 'There's nothing wrong with you, go on, get up and run!'[323]

Similarly, Turlough O'Connor felt that 'the worst time in anybody's football
[career] is injuries and not being able to play, and missing out on matches'.[324]

Some players sought alternative treatment specialists away from their clubs.
Paddy Mulligan, who began his career at Shamrock Rovers before moving to
England to join Chelsea in 1969, was increasingly troubled by an earlier knee
injury by the latter half of the 1970s while playing for West Bromwich Albion.[325]
Prior to Ireland's match with England at Wembley Stadium in 1976, he attended
an acupuncturist in London, who had a number of clients including Danny Kaye,
the American actor, to assist his recovery. Mulligan also persuaded teammate John
Giles, who had a slight hamstring injury, to attend, and both came through the
game without any complaints.[326] Similarly, Mick Lawlor, who played for a number
of League of Ireland clubs between 1965 and 1986, regularly travelled to Belfast
to receive treatment from a man frequented by numerous players in Ireland and
Britain, Bobby McGregor.[327]

> Apparently he didn't have a diploma or qualification but what a genius. He
> was so talented, in terms of getting to the root of the problem. As a con-
> sequence, most of the Northern Ireland international squad, in England,
> if they got an injury over there that wasn't kind of [getting better], they'd
> jump on a plane and come over to Bobby. The top orthopaedic surgeons in
> hospitals in Belfast, when they were stymied a little bit, they'd say to Bobby,
> 'Bobby, I'm going to send this person in to you and I want you to come back
> to me and tell me what you feel about it.'[328]

McGregor believed his talent was God-given, according to Lawlor.[329] He had
helped Finn Harps' Tony O'Doherty – a Derry man who was smuggled to his home

322 Interview with Mick Meagan, 30 Sept. 2019.   323 Ibid.   324 Interview with Turlough
O'Connor, 10 Oct. 2019.   325 Interview with Paddy Mulligan, 4 Oct. 2019.   326 Ibid.
327 Interview with Mick Lawlor, 29 Feb. 2020.   328 Ibid.   329 Ibid.

in Belfast in the boot of his car before the 1974 FAI Cup final at the height of the Troubles – to overcome a groin injury using his own intuition. He diagnosed that the injury was actually connected to a displaced bone in his back, which he then manipulated into place.[330] He had also treated Dundalk's Mick Fairclough, whose career in English football had been ended by a knee ligament injury in the early 1970s, but made a comeback to win the FAI Cup in 1981 having attended him for treatment.[331] Not every player was convinced of these methods, however, with Northern Ireland international Norman Whiteside writing in his autobiography that one hip-related treatment he had received as a teenager from the same practitioner had damaged his career forever.[332] At least one Dublin-born player resorted to his faith to help him recover. Maurice Swan, who had spells at Cardiff City, Hull City, Dundalk, Drumcondra and Finn Harps before a back injury kept him out for two years, returned to play, albeit at Leinster League level, with Aer Lingus in January 1975.[333] He had visited a priest in County Donegal, who had advised him to 'have faith'.[334]

By the late twentieth century full-time professional players could expect more professional treatment, with John Coady noting that he received physiotherapy twice a day at Chelsea when recovering from an Achilles-tendon injury that kept him out for six weeks in the late 1980s.[335] Some injuries were obviously worse than others, with Harry McCue, who played mainly in the League of Ireland as well as the Irish League and the North American Soccer League, noting that he never fully recovered from rupturing his ankle ligaments, although he had learned how to treat the injury and play with it.[336]

While in January 1982 the PFAI and the League of Ireland agreed that an insurance scheme for League of Ireland players would be made available, in line with measures undertaken by the IRFU and GAA, treatment of injuries in Ireland remained basic in that decade.[337] In February 1985, Dr Moira O'Brien, medical officer of the Irish Olympic Council, presented a report to the government in which she highlighted that the system of sports-injury treatment was 'inadequate due to lack of resources and training both at voluntary and statutory level'.[338] This naturally had an impact on some of the players interviewed for this book. Liam Buckley was forced to retire after a cruciate-ligament operation in 1989 as at that time, the procedure was in its infancy and affected the movement of his hamstring.[339] A back injury forced Dave Henderson to retire, and he felt that the treatment he received was insufficient. He recalled

> being put on a traction machine and I'm going, 'This is stupid.' They knew themselves they weren't doing any good and then they'd leave you there, and then, you know, for sciatica, and then they'd go off, and then the half an

330 Ibid.   **331** Ryan, *The official book of the FAI Cup*, p. 263   **332** Norman Whiteside, *Determined: Norman Whiteside* (London, 2007), pp 60–1.   **333** *IP*, 14 Jan. 1975.   **334** Ibid.   **335** Interview with John Coady, 22 Jan. 2020.   **336** Interview with Harry McCue, 10 Dec. 2019.   **337** *Soccer Reporter* (Jan. 1982), p. 7   **338** *II*, 7 Feb. 1985.   **339** Interview with Liam Buckley, 24 Mar. 2020.

hour's up, there was nothing, nothing, nothing – no scans, like – to see if it was getting any better. And then, as a legacy of that now I have a limp – you see me there limping around. That's all the strength of that, the bad treat-ment, over the years.[340]

On the eve of the twenty-first century a much better level of treatment was availa-ble, although, as shown in Henderson's case, some injuries were harder to diagnose and recover from than others. Getting the correct treatment in the first place was very important, as Pat Fenlon recalled of a triple fracture of his shin he suffered while playing for Shelbourne in 1999:

> I got taken off in an ambulance. Greg Costello, who was playing for Shels at the time, was out, he wasn't playing that night – he came with me and, in fairness to the chairman of Shels, Gary Brown, at the time, he made sure that I was looked after at the hospital, I got the proper surgeon. Thankfully I did because if I didn't, I probably wouldn't have played again. When I woke up the next day, and he explained to me what had happened, I sort of said [will I be able to play again] and the doctor said to me, 'This is going to be tough. You will, if you put your mind to it, you can play again. What level [I'm not sure] ...' And I did. Thankfully, I got myself back.[341]

Despite this, injuries took their toll. Some players resorted to painkillers to get through matches following surgery and injuries. Chris Bennion recalled that after a back operation he had in 2000,

> they removed some of the disc. It was a long, long six, seven months [of] rehab and building everything back up. I think when you get on in your career and you've felt niggles it's just Difene or soluble Solpadeine, Nurofen, just to take the edge off the pain to play. It would be scary what you put your body through sometimes, you know.[342]

One player felt that the higher level of intensity of full-time professional training in England than in Ireland had impacted on the progress of his career there, with double training sessions common. Seán Prunty stated that while at Middlesbrough in the late 1990s,

> It was definitely tough. It took its toll on the body because I ended up pick-ing up a lot of injuries while I was over there that – they definitely held me back. I think the second season I was there, I started off fantastic, and even coaches were coming up to me saying, 'Look, keep going the way you're

340 Interview with Dave Henderson, 22 Oct. 2019.   341 Interview with Pat Fenlon, 7 Feb. 2020.   342 Interview with Chris Bennion, 21 Oct. 2019.

going, you know, there's opportunities for you to break into the first team.'
But then, just an injury, and then I came back and another injury, so, you
know, at the end of the day it's a business for them, you know, and there was
younger lads coming through – they were saying I was probably a bit injury-
prone, as a result of that then.[343]

A failure to manage one's lifestyle properly as a professional footballer could
spell the end of a full-time career in football, with Paul Byrne returning to the
Irish League in the late 1990s following a broken ankle received as a Southend
United player.[344] He admitted when interviewed that he 'felt there was no way back
between the gambling and the drinking and not performing on the field after my
injury, I felt it was time to come home'.[345]

Retirement from the game can come prematurely as a result of injuries received
as a player. One recent study by Paul Ian Campbell on black players in England has
shown how some have physically struggled with adapting to life in offices due to
their injuries and an inability to sit at a desk for a full day because of the resulting
stiffness.[346] Following careers in professional football, a number of Irish-born players have alluded to daily management of injuries received as players. Both Seamus
Kelly and Shane Supple noted that they undertook yoga regularly to alleviate stiffness that had developed as a result of back and hip injuries, respectively.[347] Supple
recalled of the hip injury that had forced him to retire from League of Ireland
football in 2018 that 'it was ongoing for a couple of years I think and then it just
kind of came to a head, I had to make a call really for quality of life after football as
well, so that was the reason [I retired]'.[348] For Kelly, who had been stretchered off
unconscious with prolapsed discs in his lower back following a collision in a match,
which left him temporarily unable to feel his feet, the risk of further damage was
too great and he decided to retire having come back and played a few games following rehab.[349] He noted that, 'I still have problems if I don't do the yoga – like
two years ago I was very bad. I couldn't get out of bed, I was in bed for a week.'[350]
Chris Deans, who retired from the game in the early 2000s, recalled that he had
'really bad back trouble, even now, I can't drive for long, my back's in bits [if I do].
I've got a couple of cortisone injections over the years. It's later now that I'm feeling the effects.'[351]

While most players interviewed have successfully transitioned from careers in
professional football to other occupations, for some who had to retire prematurely
because of injuries or health issues, the transition has been traumatic.[352] Brian

343 Interview with Seán Prunty, 23 Oct. 2019. 344 Interview with Paul Byrne, 26 Feb.
2020. 345 Ibid. 346 Paul Ian Campbell, *Education, retirement and career transition for 'black' ex-
professional footballers: from being idolized to stacking shelves* (Bingley, 2020), pp 66–7. 347 Interviews
with Shane Supple, 24 Sept. 2019 and Seamus Kelly, 2 Oct. 2019. 348 Interview with Shane
Supple, 24 Sept. 2019. 349 Interview with Seamus Kelly, 2 Oct. 2019. 350 Ibid. 351 Interview
with Chris Deans, 15 Nov. 2019. 352 Interviews with Seán Prunty, 23 Oct. 2019 and Brian O'Shea,
21 Nov. 2019.

O'Shea recalled that he 'would have loved to retire as a player, playing and to say, "this is my last game now"', but following a car accident, he was forced to retire earlier than expected with a back injury.[353]

Some players, such as Mick Meagan and Mick Lawlor, continued to play at an amateur level for local teams following retirement from professional football.[354] Others, such as Stephen McGuinness and Dave Henderson, have said they are happy to move away from playing.[355] Gary Kelly noted that he would have continued playing as long as he could, but injuries had taken their toll by the time he stopped playing in his early forties:

> Yeah, yeah, like I had a cruciate injury that held me back a bit – just the training end of things, I was mad for training. I'd train every day of the week if I could, and that's what kept me going up to forty-two. I was fit and I really worked hard on my game. So that's what got me to that stage, but the injuries were telling, were taking their toll, so it was time to go, yeah. It was time to retire, officially and forever.[356]

CONCLUSION

Dublin's initial players were mainly of a middle- or upper-class background and generally saw the game as a recreational and social activity. However, the late 1890s and early 1900s saw the emergence of more serious workplace teams and the game in Dublin took on a more popular appeal, as in numerous cities and towns around the world. As shown above, in the first half of the twentieth century many Dublin players participated in military activity. Some survived and returned to their playing careers but there were many who did not. Professional soccer in England was not for every player and this chapter has also illustrated the tough demands faced by semi-professional players in balancing their football careers with other more mainstream jobs. In examining the lives of a number of players in the League of Ireland, it has shown that some players have preferred to play at that level rather than in the lower professional leagues in England, and can do so in more familiar and homely surroundings. A number of players affected by these factors have therefore been glad to come home to Ireland, and to play in an environment to which they are more accustomed. Some have fully embraced their careers on their home soil. Stephen McGuinness spoke with tremendous pride of his achievements within domestic soccer in Ireland, winning every title that he could.[357] While maintaining a career in professional football in any of England's professional football

353 Interview with Brian O'Shea, 21 Nov. 2019.   354 Interviews with Mick Meagan, 30 Sept. 2019 and Mick Lawlor, 29 Feb. 2020.   355 Interviews with Stephen McGuinness, 22 Oct. 2019 and Dave Henderson, 22 Oct. 2019.   356 Interview with Gary Kelly, 12 Dec. 2019.   357 Interview with Stephen McGuinness, 22 Oct. 2019.

leagues is a major sporting challenge and is an accomplishment in itself, there has been less public focus on those who have had successful careers playing League of Ireland football.

Some part-time League of Ireland players have benefited from having employers with a fondness for football, and have deliberately maintained their focus on football even if this has meant remaining in jobs with no career progression. A few others have seen education as a vehicle to further their careers, as is evident from the cases of Seamus Kelly and Chris Deans, both of whom saw their futures as being outside football even while they had full-time contracts. A few, such as Paul Byrne, have been able to command full-time contracts with League of Ireland clubs, although this has not been a consistent state of affairs due to the chronically weak infrastructures for professional football in Ireland. Although less publicly recognized, a covert system of part-time professionalism has also existed within regional soccer leagues in Ireland, including the Leinster Senior League. More research needs to be undertaken on the working conditions of part-time professional footballers at a historical and contemporary level in other national leagues so that an accurate comparison can be made with this study. However, this chapter has offered some insights into a level of player who has generally not received the attention of those at the higher echelons of international football. In doing so, it has shed some light on some of the pressures faced by part-time professional footballers in furthering their playing careers and how they have coped with the lack of full-time employment within the game in Dublin. The final chapter examines the careers of a number of players who have moved to professional leagues outside of Dublin in search of what they view as a more fulfilling playing and work experience.

8

Dublin players in other professional leagues

THE EMERGENCE OF DUBLIN-BORN PLAYERS WITHIN ENGLISH LEAGUE FOOTBALL

Irish-born footballers have played in English League football since the opening 1888–9 season, with Belfast-born Archie Goodall, a son of a soldier, the first of these.[1] In the period from 1888 until 1939, at least 16 per cent of Irish-born football migrants to England whose places of birth could be positively identified were from Dublin (43 of 262).[2] As the overall figure was 286 and a number of birthplaces could not be identified, this figure is probably slightly higher.[3] Although no Dublin native appears to have transferred from a Dublin club to one in England in the nineteenth century, in 1894 Dublin-born Robert Brown joined Burton Wanderers; it is not clear if he played soccer in Ireland.[4] He later had spells at Southampton, Bristol Rovers, Queen's Park Rangers and Swindon Town.[5] In 1905, Matt Reilly, a military man born in Donnybrook in 1874, joined Notts County from Dundee, having played for Glasgow Benburb and the Royal Artillery in Portsmouth and having had loan spells in the Southern League at Southampton St Mary's and Freemantle.[6] Reilly was described in one Scottish newspaper as 'undoubtedly a custodian of the highest class'.[7] It was also noted that 'indeed, it is a moot question whether he had a superior in Scotland … he is fit for any team'.[8]

By the early 1900s Dublin players had begun to move to English clubs directly through those in Ireland. Val Harris, who signed for Everton on the train between Aberdare and Crewe after an international match, had won the Irish Cup with Shelbourne (in 1906) as well as the All-Ireland Gaelic football championship by the time he moved to Everton from Shelbourne in 1908.[9] He returned to Shelbourne after six years having 'been the recipient of a magnificent benefit' at the Goodison Park club and by the mid-1920s was still at the Dublin club.[10] His early career path illustrates a rise from lower-level soccer to one of Dublin's top clubs. *Football Sports Weekly* noted in 1926 that he had initially played soccer for Liffeys in the Saturday Alliance League for three seasons before joining Pembroke in 1900, which dispels the notion that he was playing Leinster League soccer aged 13.[11] It was at

1 Curran, *Irish soccer migrants*, pp 25–6. 2 Ibid., p. 27. 3 Ibid. 4 Joyce, *Football League players' records*, p. 42. 5 Ibid. 6 Ibid., p. 242; Emms & Wells, *Scottish League players' records*, p. 195. 7 *DC*, 7 June 1905. 8 Ibid. 9 *INBMN*, 13 Apr. 1908; *Sport*, 7 Nov. 1925; *FSW*, 25 Dec. 1926; *Shelbourne Football Club golden jubilee*, p. 39. 10 Ibid.; Joyce, *Football League players' records*, p. 128. 11 *FSW*, 25 Dec. 1925.

that club that he lost a Leinster Junior Cup final versus Tritonville. He later joined Emeralds, where he won the County Dublin League. That club then advanced to the Leinster Junior League before he joined Shelbourne.[12]

As will be discussed in more detail later, some Dublin-born players moved to England through Irish League clubs. One of the most successful was Patrick O'Connell, who moved to Sheffield Wednesday in 1908 from Belfast Celtic, having had spells at Frankfort and Strandville.[13] He later played for Hull City, Manchester United, Dumbarton and Ashington before becoming a manager.[14] His move to Sheffield Wednesday came along with that of fellow Dubliner Peter Warren, with the two players reported to have moved for a combined total of £50.[15] Although English club Glossop were accused of poaching Belfast-based players by local clubs there in 1904, some clubs were happy to accommodate the sale of their players to specific clubs in England, providing they were approached properly.[16] By the start of the second decade of the twentieth century some Dublin clubs were orchestrating moves with individual clubs for a number of their players, with Shelbourne the first to see the value of this. In 1910, the start of 'the first big exodus' from the club, then located at Sandymount Road, took place when three of their players, Joe Enright, George Cunningham and Mick 'Boxer' Foley, joined Leeds City, while, the following year, both Joe Moran and Jimmy Fortune also made this switch.[17] The Yorkshire club had recruited five other Irish players between 1909 and 1911, with Leeds City historian Gary Edwards stating that 'financial restraints on the club' were evident at that time and they were trying to save money by buying these players.[18] Dave Tomlinson has noted that they even changed their jerseys to green to make the Irish players feel more at home, a rarity for English clubs.[19]

On the eve of the war, Shelbourne's Joe Cassidy played in one league match, said to be a trial, for Grimsby in 1912 and Andrew Byrne appeared in three league matches for Hull City in 1913, having moved from the same Dublin club, but neither played regularly.[20] Naturally, player movement between Britain and Ireland was not a one-way system, but was restricted during the years from 1914 to 1918. As shown earlier in this book, some players who had played in England and Ireland served in the war. Despite the disruption of the Irish War of Independence (1919–21), players in Dublin continued to attract the interest of English clubs. Following the revival of the English Football League it was not until 1920 that another Dublin-born player moved to England for professional football purposes when Ned Brooks joined Stockport County from Bohemians.[21] Some Dublin natives moved to England through Welsh clubs, with former Shelbourne player Dermot Doyle joining Hull City in 1921 via Pontypridd.[22] Similarly, Frank McGloughlin joined Bradford Park Avenue from Pontypridd having had spells

12 Ibid.   13 Joyce, *Football League players' records*, p. 220.   14 Ibid.   15 Ibid., p. 220 and p. 302; 'Peter Warren–NIFG', nifootball.blogspot.com/2008/11/peter-warren.html, accessed 6 Aug. 2021.   16 *Manchester Courier*, 26 May 1904.   17 Joyce, *Football League players' records*, pp 72, 93, 101, 102, 209; *Sport*, 7 Nov. 1925.   18 Edwards, *Every cloud*, pp 109–16.   19 Ibid., pp 112–13.   20 Joyce, *Football League players' records*, pp 48, 54.   21 Ibid., p. 39.   22 Ibid., p. 85.

at Olympia and Shelbourne.[23] He had also been watched by Liverpool and Aston Villa in July 1921, indicating that British scouts were active in Ireland as the conflict drew to a close.[24]

Many of the Dublin-born players who moved to England continued to return home afterwards and the vast majority in the pre-Second World War period did not enjoy lengthy careers in English football. An exception was Mick 'Boxer' Foley, who was at Leeds City from 1910 to 1919 (although this included the First World War years, when English League football temporarily ceased), playing 127 league matches.[25] The career path of John Joe Flood, who joined Leeds United from Shamrock Rovers in 1924, illustrates the haphazard nature of life as a migratory Irish professional footballer at that time. Flood had played for a number of lesser-known Dublin clubs, including Windsor Rangers and St Patrick's (Ringsend), before moving to Shamrock Rovers.[26] He then joined Shelbourne before returning to Shamrock Rovers and later joining Leeds United in 1924, where he made no league appearances before returning to Shamrock Rovers. He then decided to return to England, moving to Crystal Palace in the 1926–7 season, before again moving back to Dublin to see out his career at Shamrock Rovers and Reds United.[27] Flood remarked that he found the game in England 'much faster ... than in the Free State' but it was not 'played much cleverer'.[28] Some, such as Jimmy Dunne, had more successful careers than others. Dunne, known as 'Snowy' because of his blonde hair, joined English Division Three North club New Brighton from Shamrock Rovers in 1925 and went on to break a number of goal-scoring records at Sheffield United. He was reported in 1927 to be 'a steady, well conducted lad' who was 'most unassuming ... the type that "makes good"'.[29]

One player who remained in England was Harry Duggan, who joined Leeds United from Richmond United, without playing senior soccer in Dublin, in 1925.[30] He made his first-team debut for Leeds United in January 1927 and scored the winner in an FA Cup victory against Sunderland.[31] Later that year he made his debut for the Irish Free State team against Italy in their 'first international proper', but he also later played for the IFA's international team.[32] He played 187 games and scored 45 goals for Leeds United before joining Newport County in 1936. He married a Leeds woman and remained in England, where he became a school games' master after retiring from football.[33] Numerous Dublin players who migrated throughout the twentieth century have taken on the life of a 'settler' who finds 'a home and a wife, along with a stable job, in their host country,' as described by Pierre Lanfranchi and Matthew Taylor.[34]

23 Ibid., p. 187. See also the case of Alex Kirkland, who joined Bradford Park Avenue via Pontypridd in 1923 having moved to the Welsh club from Shelbourne in Joyce, *Football League players' records*, p. 185. 24 *Sport*, 23 July 1921. 25 Joyce, *Football League players' records*, p. 101. 26 Ibid., p. 100. 27 Ibid. 28 *FSW*, 15 Jan. 1927. 29 *Sport*, 5 Feb. 1927; *EH*, 18 Apr. 1988. 30 *SI*, 28 Oct. 1956; Joyce, *Football League players' records*, p. 56. 31 *SI*, 28 Oct. 1956. 32 Ibid. 33 Ibid. 34 Pierre Lanfranchi & Matthew Taylor, *Moving with the ball: the migration of professional footballers* (Oxford, 2001), p. 6.

However, Dublin-born players' spells at English clubs in the 1920s were generally short and league football was not always guaranteed, as the case of Samuel George Wilson shows. In 1925, following spells at Tritonville, Wilton YMCA and Shelbourne, he joined New Brighton after an unsuccessful spell at Liverpool. After leaving New Brighton, where he played twelve league games, he joined Clapham Orient, where he did not play a league match, before returning to Ireland to play for Bray Unknowns and St James's.[35]

Arguably the greatest Dublin-born player of the interwar years, Ballybough native Paddy Moore, who scored all four goals for the Irish Free State against Belgium in a World Cup qualifier in February 1934, had spells with Cardiff City, Merthyr Town and Tranmere between 1929 and 1930.[36] He then returned to Shamrock Rovers, where he scored the winning goal in the 1931 FAIFS Cup final.[37] In 1932 the club won the league, cup and shield. Following a move to Brideville, he also had a spell at Aberdeen before returning home in 1935 to play for Shamrock Rovers, Shelbourne and Brideville.[38] In 1936, he starred for Ireland as they beat Germany 5–2 in what was reported to be his greatest performance, which, according to some sources, took place when he was still drunk.[39] However, he finished his career at Shamrock Rovers before the war as he suffered from alcoholism. He retired short of his thirtieth birthday and died aged 42.[40] He had sustained 'a bad leg injury', reported in at least one newspaper as a broken leg, against Hungary in December 1934, which helps explain his decline.[41]

The 1920s also saw the temporary migration of a number of Dublin's best players to the American Soccer League, which began in 1921 and lasted until the early 1930s. This movement was at its height in 1927 when Philadelphia Celtic, under Belfast native Fred Magennis, put together a team largely made up of Irish League and Free State League players for professional purposes.[42] However, the majority of these, including Shamrock Rovers star and Ringsend native Bob Fullam, eventually returned to Ireland after the team folded early in the season as Magennis walked out on the Philadelphia Celtic club over financial difficulties.[43] An exception was Dinny Doyle, who remained there and mixed playing and business interests, eventually settling near Niagara Falls.[44] Fullam had also played in England with Leeds United in 1923, scoring two goals in seven games, but it was at Shamrock Rovers that he enjoyed his greatest successes, winning four FAI cups from 1929 until 1932.[45] A report of his return from the USA in May 1928 illustrates the

35 Joyce, *Football League players' records*, p. 316.   36 Ibid., p. 208; *PN*, 10 Mar. 1934; *EH*, 18 Apr. 1988.   37 Joyce, *Football League players' records*, p. 208; *EH*, 18 Apr. 1988.   38 Ibid.   39 Rice, *We are Rovers*, p. 50.   40 Joyce, *Football League players' records*, p. 208; *EH*, 18 Apr. 1988.   41 Emms & Wells, *Scottish League players' records*, p. 137; *BT*, 17 Dec. 1934; *NW*, 17 Dec. 1934.   42 Curran, *Irish soccer migrants*, pp 244–58.   43 Ibid., p. 256. See also Conor Curran, 'Unscrupulous adventurers who are domiciled in "the land of the Almighty Dollar"'? The migration of Irish born soccer players to the American Soccer League, 1921–31', *Journal of Sports History*, 45:3 (Fall 2018), pp 313–33.   44 Ibid.; see also *FSW*, 7 Jan. 1928; Doolan & Goggins, *The Hoops*, p. 20.   45 Joyce, *Football League players' records*, p. 105; *II*, 20 Nov. 1987.

esteem in which he was held among supporters of them game, with the *Evening Herald* reporting that

> The popularity of Bob Fullam, the Shamrock Rovers player, was convinc-ingly evidenced by the large crowd that awaited his arrival last night at Kingsbridge on his return from America. His admirers thronged the station premises and precincts, and loudly and enthusiastically greeted Fullam, whose arms ached with handshakes before he could gain access to the taxi in which he eventually reached home.[46]

His talents were less appreciated in England, it seems, and in 1955 he sued a newspaper over comments about having to wear a carpet slipper on his left foot to improve his right foot while in training at Leeds United.[47]

The work of Michael Kielty has highlighted the role of Dublin-born Peter J. Peel in the early twentieth-century development of soccer in the USA.[48] In 1917, he became president of the United States Football Association and was involved in the visit of the US Olympic team to Dublin in June 1924.[49] Some players who moved from Dublin to seek non-football-related employment also joined soccer clubs there, including John O'Brien of Brooklyn and Bohemians and Jack O'Farrell of Bohemians, who joined Boston Celtic, 'the only Irish team in the State of Massachusetts', who played in the Boston league and were run by William J. O'Brien.[50] By the beginning of 1928, the Dublin Bohemians team, based in New York, was active.[51] This had been formed by four former members of Bohemians and Christopher Mullery, 'an early pioneer of Sunday football in the Phoenix Park'.[52] The club attracted a number of players with Free State, Irish and Scottish League experience, and were based at the Oval in New York. They also had a ladies' committee who were in charge of the social side, and took on the black and red colours of the Dublin club.[53] Much later, a group of Irish emigrants established a London Irish soccer team in the English city in the 1960s, although the formation of this soccer club was probably not a unique develop-ment among Irish migrants in England.[54]

In any case, the majority of players' movement was generally to England from Dublin rather than vice versa, although some Dublin-born players such as Alex Stevenson, who moved from Rangers to Everton in 1932, joined English clubs through Scottish teams.[55] Stevenson was awarded only seven caps for the Free State, and despite his own suspicion that this was because he was a Protestant, it appears that the Goodison Park club's reluctance to release him for international duty was the determining factor in this low number.[56] This issue of gaining release

46 *EH*, 15 May 1928.   47 *BT*, 6 Dec. 1955.   48 Michael Kielty, 'Peter J. Peel: the soccer king' in Curran (ed.), 'The growth and development of soccer in Dublin', Special Issue of *Soccer and soci-ety*, 22:8 (2021), pp 901–18.   49 Ibid., pp 910–12.   50 *FSW*, 14 Nov. 1925.   51 *FSW*, 7 Jan. 1928.   52 *FSW*, 14 Jan. 1928.   53 *FSW*, 7 and 14 Jan. 1928.   54 *Soccer Reporter* (Mar. 1977), p. 16.   55 *DJ*, 2 Feb. 1934.   56 *EH*, 18 Apr. 1988.

was also a problem for players such as Harry Duggan and continued into the late twentieth century.[57]

Movement by Dublin players to Continental clubs was rare in the early decades of the twentieth century. An exception was Arthur Johnson, who was born in Dublin in 1879 and later played for Real Madrid, having joined the club in 1902.[58] He scored the club's first official goal in a 3–1 loss to Barcelona that year and later became their first coach, serving from 1910 until 1920.[59] In 1934, Dubliner Tommy Davis moved from New Brighton to FC de Metz of the French League, which took on a professional structure in 1932.[60] In 1931, the much-travelled Davis joined Torquay United, having had spells at Beaumont, Frankfort, Shelbourne, Midland Athletic, Cork FC, Exeter City (on trial) and Boston Town.[61] He later played for New Brighton, FC de Metz (1934), Oldham Athletic, Tranmere Rovers, Cork City, Dundalk, Workington, Drumcondra, Shelbourne and Distillery.[62] In 1935 he was suspended by the FA for breaking his contract at FC de Metz to join Oldham Athletic.[63]

MOVEMENT TO SCOTLAND IN THE PRE-SECOND WORLD WAR YEARS

In the years from 1890 until 1939 at least seventy-two players who were born in Ireland, including Alex Stevenson, participated in the Scottish First Division.[64] Naturally, a number of Dublin-born players also joined Scottish clubs, with seven identified, although the majority (forty-nine) were born in Northern Ireland, with strong cultural, religious and industrial links between the north-east and Scotland, and in turn club connections, present by the early twentieth century.[65] These moves were less common than those by Dublin natives to English clubs, but they did occur. Initial movement to Scottish clubs by Dublin-born players included that of the aforementioned Matt Reilly, who played three games for Dundee in the 1904–5 season having already played in the Southern League.[66] In 1913 Dublin-born William Crone joined Glasgow Celtic from Belfast Celtic. He spent four years there before returning to play for Distillery, Glentoran and Linfield.[67]

Some players were able to continue their cross-Channel careers after the war. In 1914 Harry Leddy moved from Shelbourne to Clyde, where he spent one year before returning to Shelbourne.[68] He then relocated to Belfast. Described as 'a

57 *SI*, 28 Oct. 1956.   58 Kristofer McCormack, 'The Irishman who taught Real Madrid how to play football', thesefootballtimes.co/2019/02/21/arthur-johnson-the-irishman-who-taught-real-madrid-how-to-play-football, accessed 12 Aug. 2021.   59 Ibid.; 'Arthur Johnson, a pioneer at the helm of the team', https://www.realmadrid.com/en/about-real-madrid/history/football/1900-1910-juan-padros-and-julian-palacios-found-madrid, accessed 12 Aug. 2021.   60 Curran, *Irish soccer migrants*, p. 231.   61 Joyce, *Football League players' records*, p. 77.   62 Ibid.   63 Curran, *Irish soccer migrants*, p. 231.   64 Ibid., p. 221.   65 Ibid., pp 221, 48–50; and see, for example, Jonathan Bardon, *A narrow sea: the Irish-Scottish connection in 120 episodes* (Dublin, 2018), pp 257–60.   66 Emms & Wells, *Scottish League players' records*, p. 195.   67 Ibid., p. 48.   68 Ibid., p. 118.

popular chap', he became manager of the United Bar, 'a great football house in the centre of the city' of Belfast.[69] Having played for a number of Irish League clubs, he moved to England to join Tranmere Rovers, and also had spells at Everton, whom he joined in 1921, Chesterfield and Grimsby Town before returning to Dublin to play for Shamrock Rovers and Frankfort.[70]

Peter Joseph Kavanagh, who began at Melrose Celtic of Fairview, Drumcondra and Bohemians before joining Glasgow Celtic in 1929, also had spells with Hibernian and Stranraer and a number of English clubs.[71] As noted earlier, Patrick O'Connell joined Dumbarton, playing thirty-two league games in the 1919–20 season, while the aforementioned Alex Stevenson joined Glasgow Rangers from Dolphin in 1932 before later signing for Everton.[72] In 1932 Aberdeen signed three players from Dublin clubs: James Daly, Joe O'Reilly and Paddy Moore.[73] Moore's spell at Aberdeen, where he scored forty-four goals in sixty-four league appearances between 1932 and 1935, was more successful on the playing field than his time in England until his major injury.[74] He died in 1951 at the age of 41, and although Aberdeen gave his family £100, surprisingly they received no financial assistance from Shamrock Rovers, where he had spent so much of his career.[75]

MIGRATION TO ENGLISH LEAGUE FOOTBALL, 1945–2000

In the post-war years moves from Dublin to English clubs became more common, and by the end of the twentieth century, the numbers had more than doubled in comparison with those in the late 1940s. A total of 239 Dublin-born footballers played English League football between 1945 and 2000.[76]Although structures for competitive football in England had been amended to ensure some continuation of domestic matches and home internationals during the Second World War, the English Football League recommenced fully in 1946 and Dublin-born players again began to move to English clubs.[77] In the remainder of this decade, thirty-seven Dublin natives signed and played league football for English clubs and nineteen were capped at senior international level, with Con Martin appearing for both the FAI and IFA international selections.[78] While in the army he played for the Eastern Command, before joining Glentoran in 1946 after the Belfast club bought him out of the Air Corps that summer.[79] He moved to Leeds United in 1947 and also played for Aston Villa and spent eight seasons in England before returning to the League

69 *Sport*, 21 Oct. 1916.   **70** Joyce, *Football League players' records*, p. 171.   **71** Emms & Wells, *Scottish League players' records*, p. 109.   **72** Ibid., pp 181, 217.   **73** Ibid., pp 51, 137, 183; *EH*, 30 Sept. 1988.   **74** Emms & Wells, *Scottish League players' records*, p. 137.   **75** Rice, *We are Rovers*, pp 51–2.   **76** Hugman (ed.), *The PFA Premier and Football League players' records, 1946– 2005*.   **77** Curran, *Irish soccer migrants*, pp 117–18.   **78** Hugman (ed.), *The PFA Premier and Football League players' records, 1946–2005*, p. 416. Curran, *Irish soccer migrants*, p. 7. Players born in Ireland could play for both the IFA and the FAI's national teams until 1950, when FIFA ruled against this.   **79** *II*, 28 Mar. 1946 and 19 Dec. 1999.

of Ireland. Martin played as a goalkeeper and centre-half in England and stated in a 1999 interview with Seán Ryan that he might have had a longer career had he stuck to the former position.[80] Martin also played in goal for the FAI international selection against Portugal and Spain in 1946, having stood in for the injured Ned Courtney.[81] Although he appeared six times for the IFA's selection, he ceased to play for them in 1950 after pressure from Aston Villa chairman Fred Normansell, who felt it would damage the club's reputation in Dublin if he continued to play for the IFA's team. Following the announcement that he would no longer play, other players from the FAI's jurisdiction also stopped making themselves available to the IFA selectors.[82]

In the 1950s, thirty-eight Dublin-born players joined English clubs and played league football there and twenty-eight were awarded senior international caps.[83] Among the best of these was John Giles, who, in joining Manchester United as an apprentice from Stella Maris in 1955, followed in the footsteps of his cousin, Christy, who had signed for Doncaster Rovers from Drumcondra along with Kit Lawlor in 1950.[84] His uncle Matt had managed Transport, while another uncle, Jim Redmond, played for Leinster League club Distillery, and Bohemians.[85] At Stella Maris, he won the Evans Cup, the Harry Cannon Cup and the Under-15 Schoolboys' League, and was capped by Ireland Schoolboys in a draw with England at Tolka Park in 1955.[86] Manchester United assistant manager Jimmy Murphy stated afterwards that he was the best player on the pitch. Having moved to Manchester, he was unlucky not to win the FA Youth Cup in 1958, missing out on their semi-final defeat to a Blackburn Rovers team, which included fellow Dubliner Paddy Mulvey, through injury.[87] The Munich Air Disaster also impacted on the Manchester United youth team that season, as Mark Pearson and Alec Dawson were brought into the first team.[88]

Giles was only 4 feet 6 inches when he joined Manchester United, but apparently Matt Busby said that 'he was the most accurate kicker of a ball he ever saw'.[89] He made his senior international debut against Sweden at Dalymount Park in 1959, having grown in height and strength, and scored the first goal in a 3–2 victory.[90] Although he won the FA Cup with Manchester United, along with Tony Dunne, in 1963, he left the club after a falling out with Busby and it was at Leeds United that he really shone, particularly in the 1970s under Don Revie.[91] Liam Whelan had initially been helped in settling in at Manchester United, before his untimely death, by Irish players Paddy Kennedy and Noel McFarlane, with all three part of their FA Youth Cup win in 1953.[92] Other Irish players to move to Manchester early in that decade included Fionan Fagan, who was spotted by Hull City's chief

80 Ibid., 19 Dec. 1999. 81 Ibid. 82 Ibid. 83 Hugman (ed.), *The PFA Premier and Football League players' records, 1946–2005*. 84 Giles, *A football man*, pp 37–49; Hugman (ed.), *The PFA Premier and Football League players' records, 1946–2005*, pp 235–6; *II*, 2 June 1950. 85 *II*, 3 Nov. 1959. 86 Ibid. 87 Ibid. 88 Ibid. 89 Ibid. 90 Ibid. 91 Giles, *A football man*, pp 123–4, 238–9. 92 *IE*, 12 Feb. 1958; *Charles Buchan's Football Monthly*, 70 (June 1957), p. 10.

20. Liam Whelan memorial plaque at Home Farm FC (2022). Author's own collection.

scout, Jack Hill, while playing for Transport in 1951, and later played in the 1955 FA Cup final for Manchester City in their defeat to Newcastle United.[93] One other Dublin native who did not have as much impact in English football was Jackie Hennessy, who returned from Manchester United to Shelbourne and helped them win the 1958 FAI Minor Cup.[94] Some players undertook apprenticeships in other trades while at English clubs, including Joe Haverty, who joined Arsenal from St Patrick's Athletic in 1954 and worked as a wireworker during the summer months, finishing his training in July 1962 prior to leaving Blackburn Rovers before joining Millwall.[95]

Without agents, young players often relied on their own club officials for advice in moving, with George Cummins receiving this from St Patrick's Athletic secretary William McCormack prior to moving to Everton in 1950.[96] Cummins had been recommended to the club by goalkeeper Jimmy O'Neill.[97] Another one of the seven Dublin-born players recruited by Everton in 1945–55, Mick Meagan, grew up in Churchtown, near Shamrock Rovers' ground at Milltown, and his move to Everton from Johnville in 1952 came after the English club had spoken to his father.[98] He recalled going on trial for a month before being asked to sign, and then making friends with the younger Everton players, who helped him to settle in at the club.[99] He also noted that

> My first rented digs was a place called Norris Green, it was a great football area, just up the East Lancs Road from Everton at Goodison. It was between Liverpool and Manchester, but it was a great place. ... You'd go up to the church hall for a game of snooker and things like that. There was always something to do. And the people of Liverpool were great, great people.[100]

Frank O'Neill joined Arsenal in 1959, despite being approached while playing in the Leinster Senior League for Home Farm by Con Martin and Aston Villa's chief scout with a view to signing for the Birmingham club, while Everton also contacted him with a view to him attending pre-season training in 1959.[101] He was instead signed by Arsenal manager George Swindin following trials at the club at Christmas 1958 and Easter 1959 after he was spotted playing for Home Farm.[102] He grew up in Summerhill Parade, and made his debut for Arsenal on New Year's Eve 1960 in a 5–3 win against Nottingham Forest. He recalled that:

> The club were excellent, they looked after their players very well. You couldn't fault them for anything, you had your passes for the underground,

93 *Charles Buchan's Football Monthly*, 43 (Sept. 1956), p. 43. **94** *II*, 3 Nov. 1959. **95** *Charles Buchan's Football Monthly*, 131 (July 1962), pp 44–5. **96** Ibid., 95 (July 1959), p. 21. **97** Ibid. **98** Interview with Mick Meagan, 30 Sept. 2019. **99** Ibid. **100** Ibid. **101** Interview with Frank O'Neill, 30 Jan. 2020. **102** Ibid.

they kitted us out with blazers and flannels and things like that, you know. They were probably in the top six in the league at that time. United and Burnley and Spurs were the main contenders.[103]

Despite a promising start, the 19-year-old found breaking into the first team difficult as there were no substitutes in those days, and he returned to Dublin to join Shamrock Rovers having played two league matches.[104]

Twenty-five Dublin-born footballers joined English clubs and played English league football in the 1960s.[105] Sixteen of these played senior international football for the Republic of Ireland.[106] Some achieved success in Europe as well as in England, with Tony Dunne part of Manchester United's European Cup-winning team of 1968. Paddy Mulligan, who joined Chelsea in 1969, was part of their squad that won the 1971 European Cup Winners' Cup.[107] Some others, such as Liam Tuohy, who joined Newcastle United in 1960 but left two years later after thirty-eight league appearances, had shorter spells in English football.[108] For those who left part-time football in Dublin, the transition could be hard. Athlone-born Turlough O'Connor had got a printing job through Bohemians after he signed for them in 1965, and was happy living in Dublin with his aunt and uncle, but became a full-time player on moving to Craven Cottage along with Jimmy Conway.[109] Although he never settled in London, and returned to Ireland after two seasons, he recalled that it was 'a great experience':[110]

> Well, the difference was having so much time to yourself because as a professional you trained in the mornings mostly so it meant for a lot of time, you were off, so it's [a question of] what did you actually do with that time? And you spent a lot of time walking around Oxford Street and Regent Street to fill in different hours so it was very, very difficult to settle. I had my family back in Athlone, I found it difficult.[111]

Although he had moved with Conway, he lived on the other side of London to his fellow Irishman and this made it harder to settle, while a number of injuries also hindered his progress.[112] Despite moving in with his cousins in Ealing during the second year of his contract, which helped, he decided to move back to Ireland as he had become engaged to an Irish woman. He joined Dundalk in 1968 and also took up a role with Jodi Manufacturing Company.[113] Those who did migrate from what was essentially part-time football in Dublin to the English Football League could expect a higher standard, particularly in terms of fitness. Paddy Mulligan noted that the biggest difference was

---

103 Ibid.   **104** Ibid.   **105** Hugman (ed.), *The PFA Premier and Football League players' records, 1946–2005.*   **106** Ibid.   **107** Curran, *Irish soccer migrants*, pp 51, 198.   **108** Hugman (ed.), *The PFA Premier and Football League players' records, 1946–2005*, p. 620.   **109** Interview with Turlough O'Connor, 10 Oct. 2019.   **110** Ibid.   **111** Ibid.   **112** Ibid.   **113** Ibid.

the training. I thought I was fit. I would have classed myself as being really fit. I missed out on a pre-season, you need a pre-season, as I discovered the following season. But no, I got myself up to speed and I played about eight or nine games for Chelsea from October till the end of the season. But I knew that I wasn't as fit as other lads because I hadn't gone through the pre-season regime, shall we say. But I decided the next season that I would be [ready], and I did [it].[114]

Having settled in during his first season – his room-mate on away trips was fellow Irish international John Dempsey – his first experience of pre-season training at a top English club was an eye opener:

> We went to Austria, we went to Sweden, we went to Germany – not all in the one go. We went to Holland and played a few games, ran through the forests at seven in the morning – do a three-mile run. I don't think they do that anymore, any club, I don't think they go for runs like that. We did that, and you'd be timed. And you'd normally get it done. You'd stroll it in about sixteen, seventeen minutes, approximately. And then you'd have ball work, and then in the afternoon, you might very well have sprints, you might do an 800 metres, or 800 yards it was then, or you would do 400. You would do 200. You would do 100. And then the following day you'd be doing the short, sharp stuff. You'd be doing all the long heavy work. And nearly every Monday, when the season started, we'd end up over Epsom Downs, running over hill and dale and running in sand.[115]

The number of Dublin-born players who signed for and played league football with English clubs rose slightly to twenty-seven in the 1970s, with nineteen of these representing the Republic of Ireland at senior level.[116] These included talents such as Liam Brady, Frank Stapleton and Steve Heighway.[117] Future Irish international Ronnie Whelan joined Liverpool in 1979 and went on to enjoy success in the 1980s and early 1990s.[118] Whelan was the son of Ronnie Whelan (Senior), a former League of Ireland player, mainly with St Patrick's Athletic, who scored 109 goals in a career that spanned from 1956 to 1973, while his brother Paul also played at that level, captaining Bohemians to the FAI Cup in 1992.[119]

Moving to England from Dublin took on a different dimension for many players with the beginning of the Troubles in 1968. After the Irish Republican Army's bombing campaign escalated in England in the early 1970s, Irish players increasingly were subjected to anti-Irish abuse. Eoin Hand has written that he received

114 Interview with Paddy Mulligan, 4 Oct. 2020.   115 Ibid.   116 Hugman (ed.), *The PFA Premier and Football League players' records, 1946–2005*.   117 Ibid., pp 76, 280, 583.   118 Ibid., p. 651.   119 *FI*, 1 Sept. 2000.

death threats in the aftermath of the Birmingham pub bombings in 1974, while one Hull City opponent spat in his face and racially abused him in a match.[120] Paddy Mulligan recalled the difficulties at that time:

> It was a nightmare. It was very tough being an Irish person, full stop. In London or in Birmingham it was of nightmare proportions. I'm not exaggerating when I say you'd be afraid to open your mouth, because they knew – of course they knew – the Irish accent straight away. But you'd get looks. And I got them. Even walking up Knightsbridge you got them. And the same in Birmingham. I remember going back after we played France in '77 here [in Dublin] – we beat them 1–0, it was a great performance that day, because they were a very good French team – and the lads at the checkpoint in Birmingham knew me, we were talking about the football, [but] they still kept me there for two hours.[121]

During his time at Chelsea, Mulligan was poorly treated by his manager, Dave Sexton, whom he felt was too heavily influenced by coach Dario Gradi in his team selection. He then went on to sign for Crystal Palace in 1972 and West Bromwich Albion in 1975, although he regretted moving to Selhurst Park as the standard was lower than that at Stamford Bridge.[122] He enjoyed his time at West Bromwich Albion under manager Johnny Giles, and was one of a number of Irish internationals recruited by him in 1979 after he took over as Shamrock Rovers manager the previous year.[123]

Giles was hoping to blend youth with experience and to stem the movement of Dublin's best talent to England. One player who remained was Dave Henderson, who decided to stick with League of Ireland football after spells on trial at Coventry City and Leeds United, where he had been offered contracts.[124] He recalled 'getting into a few scrapes' in Birmingham 'over the Irish thing' and this discouraged him from moving to England.

> So Johnny came to the house and gave me an offer to go there which at the time, in England, you might have been offered £10 a week and digs, and [Shamrock Rovers were] giving you £30 a week to stay so, at that time, for about three or four years, none of the younger, better Irish kids went to England. They all went to Shamrock Rovers, so that's how I ended up there.[125]

Despite these attempts, Irish football migrants continued to move to Britain, with, as noted in chapter five, the development of scouting networks at clubs such as Arsenal fundamental to this.

120 Hand, *First hand*, pp 26–8.   121 Interview with Paddy Mulligan, 2 Oct. 2019.   122 Ibid.
123 Ibid.   124 Interview with Dave Henderson, 22 Oct. 2019.   125 Ibid.

In the 1980s, thirty-five Dublin-born players signed with and played league football for English league clubs.[126] Nine of these were also capped internationally at senior level.[127] These included Niall Quinn and Kenny Cunningham, while some others such as Roddy Collins and Martin Bayly, who both struggled badly with injuries while in England, returned to Dublin after short stints and enjoyed spells in domestic soccer at playing and managerial level.[128] Along with homesickness, many Irish players continued to endure anti-Irish abuse, including Gary Kelly at Grimsby Town while on trial there.[129] There were numerous complaints in the *Irish Post* newspaper about anti-Irish jokes on television and elsewhere in that decade.[130] However, the success of Dublin-born players such as Ronnie Whelan at Liverpool, and Kevin Moran and Frank Stapleton at Manchester United, along with that of London-born Irish internationals who grew up in Dublin, Paul McGrath and David O'Leary, at Manchester United and Arsenal, respectively, meant that they were feted on television and in the media.[131] Despite this, the vast majority of young Irish football migrants, from Dublin and elsewhere in the country, failed to attain those heights, but the financial state of League of Ireland clubs did little to encourage players to stay. Some were glad to get home, however, after their time at English clubs turned sour. While culturally, there are many similarities between the two countries, being away from home can be demoralizing, particularly if there is tension with a manager or if they are injured. John Coady spoke of his relief on leaving Chelsea to return to Dublin after being frozen out by manager Bobby Campbell in 1988, stating that it had been 'mental torture'.[132] His experience was not unique, with Ken DeMange encountering a similar situation with manager Terry Dolan at Hull City early in the following decade.[133] Having contacted over fifty clubs he 'only received minimal interest', and the former Home Farm, Liverpool, Scunthorpe United and Leeds United player returned to Ireland where he joined Limerick.[134]

The 1990s saw the number of Dublin football migrants in English League football more than double as seventy-seven played in league matches after joining clubs there.[135] This illustrates that club links and scouting networks had become intensified by this time and that players were more enthusiastic about joining lower-league clubs in England in that decade. By that time, the reputation of Irish players had increased sufficiently through the success of the aforementioned players at clubs such as Liverpool, Manchester United and Arsenal in the previous decades. Only twenty-five of the 1990s signings were capped internationally, including current record cap holder, Robbie Keane, as breaking into top-flight football was becoming tougher.[136] With the increased internationalization of the Premier League in the

126 Hugman (ed.), *The PFA Premier and Football League players' records 1946–2005.* **127** Ibid. **128** Ibid., pp 48, 131, 150, 507; Curran, *Irish soccer migrants*, pp 205, 213–14. **129** Interview with Gary Kelly, 12 Dec. 2019. **130** See, for example, *IPT*, 14 June 1986. **131** Curran, *Irish soccer migrants*, p. 3. **132** Ibid. **133** *Soccer Magazine*, 77 (Feb. 1993), p. 15. **134** Ibid. **135** Hugman (ed.), *The PFA Premier and Football League players' records, 1946–2005.* **136** Ibid., p. 339.

21. Gary Kelly and Robbie Keane and other teammates with Dublin Lord Mayor Michael
Mulcahy prior to the Leeds United vs Dublin City FC match at Tolka Park (2001). Courtesy
of Dublin City Council Photographic Collection, Dublin City Library and Archives.

1990s, opportunities for Dublin players, and Irish footballers in general, to establish themselves at that level were becoming scarcer.[137] For those who had gained
contracts, breaking into the first team remained tough, with injuries curtailing the
careers of Dubliners Seán Prunty and Chris Deans at Middlesbrough and Derby
County, respectively, where both players had played for reserve teams.[138]

    One of those who managed to develop their career at the highest levels was
Richard Dunne, who joined Everton as a schoolboy from Home Farm and in 1997
made his first-team debut.[139] He came from a family with a long line of Dublin footballers. In the 1920s, both Bob and John Thomas were members of the Bohemians
team and John Thomas appeared for Ireland after the 1924 Paris Olympics.[140] In
the 1960s Shelbourne were captained to FAI Cup success (in 1960) and league
victory (in 1962) by their nephew, Theo Dunne, who also played for Drogheda
United, Shamrock Rovers and Athlone Town before becoming a coach. By the
early 2000s Richard, Theo's nephew, was an Ireland international and English
Premiership player.[141] Other playing members of the Dunne clan included Tommy
Dunne (son of Theo) and Tony Cousins, who both played for Shamrock Rovers but
did not play for English clubs.[142]

137 Curran, *Irish soccer migrants*, p. 325. 138 Interviews with Seán Prunty, 23 Oct. 2019 and Chris
Deans, 15 Nov. 2019. 139 *II*, 10 Oct. 2018. 140 *EH*, 17 Oct. 2000. 141 Ibid. 142 Ibid.

By the late twentieth century, the issue of anti-Irish abuse had not gone away, despite the IRA's ceasefire, the Good Friday Agreement and popular notions that the Irish were more accepted within English society.[143] Seán Prunty recalled being subjected to abuse from one player within his club, Middlesbrough, in the aftermath of the Omagh bombing in August 1998, and felt that 'I don't think even to this day they can fully understand those comments, they're not well received, definitely not, but they didn't have the education, they didn't understand the history of it either.'[144] This issue still remains rather hidden within English football, as the majority of debates about racism have focused on skin colour, despite efforts by Irish international James McLean to draw more public attention to the matter.[145]

MOVEMENT TO SCOTLAND, 1945–2000

Dublin-born players migrating to Scotland in the 1945 to 2000 period was a lot less common than to clubs in England. However, Scottish First Division (and later Premier League, then Premiership) clubs did attract a number of Dublin natives, with eighteen signing with them and playing top-flight league football there. In the late 1940s, Dublin-born Albert Murphy, who began his career with Rathfarnham schoolboy club St Joseph's, joined Clyde from Transport, while in the same decade Louis Ross signed for Hibernian, although he does not appear to have moved from a Dublin club.[146] Home Farm player Vincent Ryan joined Celtic in 1953 before moving to St Mirren.[147] He spent six seasons in Scotland before returning to Dublin to join Drumcondra.[148] Another ex-Home Farm player to join Celtic was Joe Haverty, who spent one season on loan from Millwall in the 1964–5 season before returning to England.[149] Others to join Celtic included Paddy Turner, a former Shelbourne player who had initially joined Morton in 1961.[150] Much later, in 1981, Pat Byrne joined Hearts from Leicester and played there for two seasons while commuting from Dublin at the weekend having trained with Shamrock Rovers during the week.[151] In 1984 Shamrock Rovers player Pierce O'Leary joined Celtic following a spell with Vancouver Whitecaps.[152] The 1990s saw more Dublin-born footballers play league football in Scotland than in previous decades, with Vinny Arkins having spells at Dundee United and St Johnstone.[153] Paul Byrne joined Celtic in 1993 following a successful spell in the Irish League.[154] However, he struggled at the Glasgow club, despite scoring

143 See also Curran, *Irish soccer migrants*, pp 202–4. 144 Interview with Seán Prunty, 23 Oct. 2019. 145 Curran, *Irish soccer migrants*, pp 195–6 and pp 227–8. 146 Richard Beal & Steve Emms, *Scottish League players' records: Division One, 1946/47 to 1974/75* (Nottingham, 2004), pp 97, 136; *Irish Soccer*, 1:14 (1955), p. 5. 147 Beal & Emms, *Scottish League players' records*, p. 138. 148 Ibid. 149 Ibid., p. 63. 150 Ibid., p. 156. 151 Aaron Gallagher, 'You were against Pele and Beckenbauer. It was like going to play in Hollywood', the42.ie/pat-byrne-shamrock-rovers-league-of-ireland-legend-shelbourne-premier-division–3437647-Jul2017, accessed 17 May 2021. 152 Derek Gray & Steve Emms, *Scottish League players' records: Premier Division and Premier League, 1975/76 to 1999/2000* (Nottingham, 2002), p. 74. 153 Ibid., p. 6. 154 Ibid., p. 14.

twice against Rangers in 1995, with off-the-field problems a factor in this, and he returned to Ireland, where he rebuilt his career.[155]

DUBLIN PLAYERS AT EUROPEAN CLUBS

In the years after the end of the Second World War, Dublin-born players' moves to clubs in Western Europe were relatively uncommon. However, later exceptions include Liam Brady, who joined Juventus in 1980 from Arsenal before going on to play for Sampdoria, Inter Milan and Ascoli before returning to England in 1987, and Robbie Keane, who played for Inter Milan in the 2000–1 season (on loan).[156] Moves to Central Europe were also rare, although Eric Barber had a short stint at Weiner Sportclub having moved there in 1970, while the following year Noel Campbell transferred from St Patrick's Athletic to SC Fortuna Köln.[157] In 1975, John Conway joined Swiss club FC Winterthur.[158] A small number of Dublin-born players migrated to Spain in the late twentieth century, including Martin Bayly (Figueras), Ashley Grimes (Osasuna) and Kevin Moran (Sporting Gijon).[159] Some others also sought a different cultural experience as professional footballers. Frank Stapleton joined Ajax in 1986 but injury curtailed his development there and he returned to English football at Blackburn Rovers, via Le Havre of France, in 1989.[160] Moves to Scandinavian clubs were also rare among Dublin-born players, although former Home Farm player Maurice Daly joined Swedish club IFK Vasteras in 1979.[161]

Liam Buckley enjoyed spells in Belgium, Spain and Switzerland between 1984 and 1989. In 1984, he moved from Shamrock Rovers to KSV Waregem, a club based in Flanders.[162] When interviewed, he stated that he migrated as he wanted to play full-time and Shamrock Rovers had become a part-time club at that point (he had been on a full-time contract since 1978).[163] He recalled that he enjoyed travelling and that he and his wife settled well in Belgium, as they had English television channels and they 'really enjoyed the people and the country as well'.[164] The club reached the semi-final of the UEFA Cup in 1986, losing to FC Cologne, although Buckley missed most of that campaign due to injury.[165]

In 1986, he joined Racing Santander, following news of the offer from his agent. He made his debut against Barcelona at the Nou Camp before 90,000 spectators and noted that it was

155 Interview with Paul Byrne, 26 Feb. 2020. See also Gray & Emms, *Scottish League players' records*, pp 15–98. Other Dublin-born footballers to join teams in the Scottish top division in that decade included Alan Campbell (Dundee), Liam Dunne (St Johnstone), Declan Roche (Celtic, Partick Thistle), David Byrne (Dundee United), Graham Coughlan (Livingston), Keith O'Halloran (St Johnstone), David Worrell (Dundee United), David Van Zenten, who had two spells at St Mirren as well as playing for Celtic, St Mirren, Hibernian, Morton and Hamilton, and Barry Prenderville, who had a loan spell at Hibernian while at Coventry. 156 Curran, *Irish soccer migrants*, pp 235–6. 157 Ibid., pp 234, 238. 158 Ibid., p. 238. 159 Ibid., pp 236–7. 160 Ibid., p. 240. 161 Ibid., p. 238. 162 Interview with Liam Buckley, 24 Mar. 2020. 163 Ibid. 164 Ibid. 165 Ibid.

a fantastic experience, bearing in mind where I'm coming from. Now don't get me wrong, the crowds were good in Belgium as well, when we were playing the likes of Anderlecht, Club Brugge, and KV Mechelen [who] had won the Cup Winners' Cup in 1988. There were some big teams at the time. But to go down there, and obviously play at the Nou Camp, it was fantastic, another great experience. I had a couple of chances which I do remember. We lost two–nil. Lineker got the two of them. But, again, it was a really, really top experience from where we were at.[166]

In 1987 he joined FC Montreaux Sports of Switzerland, and reflected that 'it wasn't as tough a league because it wasn't the Premier Division there, it was down a division, and it wouldn't have been anywhere near as tough as Spain or Belgium or anything like that, but we enjoyed our stay there'.[167] He returned to Ireland, but his second spell at Shamrock Rovers was hindered by injuries, and he turned to management.[168] As will be seen, he had also enjoyed a spell playing soccer in North America. Finance, historic migratory connections and the lack of a language barrier encouraged Irish players to move to clubs there at various stages in the twentieth century.

COMPETITIVE PROFESSIONAL SOCCER IN NORTH AMERICA, 1945–2000

Dublin-born players were also attracted to competitive soccer in Canada and the United States of America at various times in the years from 1945 to 2000. Alf Girvan moved to Canada in 1961 to take up a position at Toronto Ukrainians of the Canadian National Soccer League.[169] He had been informed by a friend of his, Mickey Burke, who was a Toronto Ukrainians player, that they needed a centre-half. Girvan wrote to the club and sent them newspaper reports of his performances with Drumcondra as requested.[170] After migrating to Canada, he moved in with a local family and was also given a job as a mechanic while at the Canadian club. He recalled it as being a great experience:

The conditions were good because they'd players from Italy, England, Germany – you know, the talent was definitely good, the crowds were good, and it was very enjoyable playing. So it would have been similar to League of Ireland, maybe a slight bit above it … They paid for my digs and food and all that carry-on. It cost me nothing to live there, other than if I wanted to go for a few drinks or that, that's the only money I spent. So I came home with a good few quid.[171]

---

166 Ibid.   167 Ibid.   168 Ibid.   169 Interview with Alf Girvan, 27 Jan. 2020.   170 Ibid.
171 Ibid.

He was also chosen for a league selection which played a Russian team, but later decided to return to the League of Ireland and rejoined Drumcondra.[172]

Some Dublin-born players such as Joe Haverty also took part in the National Professional Soccer League in 1967 with Chicago Spurs.[173] The majority of Republic of Ireland-born footballers who played in the North American Soccer League, which began in 1968 and folded in 1984, were born in Dublin. Haverty was among the first of these, having transferred to Kansas City Spurs, while others included Paddy Mulligan, who had one season with Boston Beacons.[174] The Beacons' team was managed by Jack Mansell, who had played for a number of English clubs and was an England 'B' international.[175] Mulligan moved to Boston in March 1968 and the presence of fellow Dubliners David Pugh and Tom Kelly at the club helped him settle in. The club had mixed results, including a heavy defeat against a Kansas City Spurs team that featured Haverty and Eric Barber.[176] Mulligan returned to Shamrock Rovers in September 1968 as the Beacons club folded. While he enjoyed his time in the USA, he had been carrying a knee injury. Having played well in the USA, he became more determined to play at a higher level and set his sights on English football, moving to Chelsea in 1969.[177] Mulligan, who retained an interest in Gaelic games throughout his career, having spent a lot of his childhood in Galway, would practice Gaelic football with his Irish teammates before training. He recalled eagerly awaiting the GAA results as he rang home to Dublin from the USA every Sunday evening.[178]

In the 1970s, the NASL continued to be an alternative pathway to a career in professional football in England for some players. Damian Ferguson joined Dallas Tornado in 1972 following a spell at Manchester United.[179] Ed Kelly, who later became one of the most successful US soccer college coaches, left Crumlin to move to the USA with his family in the 1960s, and later joined Hartford Bicentennials in 1975, having served in the US Army.[180] He was joined at that club that year by Tom O'Dea.[181] Loan spells during the summer months remained an option for England-based players at that point. Tony Macken played for Washington Diplomats in 1976 and 1977 on loan and also played for Dallas Tornado in 1977.[182] He had spells in the League of Ireland, the Irish League as well as in England with Derby County, Portsmouth and Walsall.[183] Don O'Riordan played for Tulsa Roughnecks in 1978 and 1979, while Gerry Daly also spent two loan spells in the NASL, with New England Tea Men.[184] Some others such as Terry Daly, who joined St Louis Stars in 1977, were not attached to English clubs.[185] Eddie and Pat Byrne joined Philadelphia Fury in 1978 along with Fran O'Brien, who also played for Montreal

172 Ibid.   173 Colin Jose, *North American Soccer League encyclopaedia* (Haworth, 2003), p. 121.   174 Interview with Paddy Mulligan, 4 Oct. 2019.   175 Hugman (ed.), *The PFA Premier and Football League players' records, 1946–2005*, p. 412.   176 Interview with Paddy Mulligan, 4 Oct. 2019.   177 Ibid.   178 Ibid.; see also Curran, *Irish soccer migrants*, pp 262–3.   179 Jose, *North American Soccer League encyclopaedia*, p. 90.   180 Ibid., p. 148.   181 Ibid., p. 221.   182 Ibid., p. 175.   183 Ibid.   184 Ibid., pp 66, 225.   185 Ibid., p. 66.

Manic (1981–2) and Vancouver Whitecaps (1983–4).[186] Tommy Lang joined Colorado Caribou in 1978 and played for Atlanta Chiefs the following year.[187] Some players moved to the NASL at the end of their careers in England, including Ray Treacy, who joined Toronto Mets in 1978 and Tony Dunne, who joined Detroit Express in 1979.[188] In 1979, British clubs discontinued the practice of loaning players to NASL clubs after a dispute surrounding George Best's positions at Derby County and the LA Aztecs.[189]

Having joined Philadelphia Fury in 1978, Johnny Giles later managed Vancouver Whitecaps from 1981–3.[190] He recruited a number of Dublin-born players, including Dave Henderson and Jimmy Holmes in 1981.[191] Henderson had previously played for Toronto Blizzard in 1979.[192] He stated when interviewed that the move had come through Johhny Giles' agent, and while he enjoyed the experience and it made him a better goalkeeper, the playing conditions were difficult as 'some of the times you would be playing, the goal would be in a baseball diamond, and then the other ones were old astroturf, which was like carpet, like concrete'.[193] Henderson also noted that the ball travelled faster and could also take on a 'ridiculous' bounce because of the hard surface.[194] He recalled that home matches at both of his NASL clubs in Toronto and Vancouver were well attended.[195] Liam Buckley also joined Vancouver Whitecaps in 1981, having been asked to do so by Johnny Giles for a few months during the League of Ireland close-season in the summer, and lived with Henderson initially.[196] Buckley, who was not homesick as he had the company of his girlfriend (who later became his wife), recalled that

> Well, the significant difference was the pitches. They were all-weather pitches mainly over there … We didn't play on all-weather pitches in the League of Ireland at that stage. The standard would have been a little better, obviously, because they're bringing in players from around the planet and better ones from different leagues and whatever, so, but it was a reasonable standard at the time.[197]

The 1980s saw some veteran Dublin-born players such as Steve Heighway take up playing positions at NASL clubs. He joined Minnesota Kicks in 1981 from Liverpool.[198] Most others were not at that stage and some saw it as an opportunity to further develop their professional careers. In 1983, Harry McCue joined San Diego Sockers.[199] Having almost been signed by Glasgow Celtic, he was put in touch with

186 Curran, *Irish soccer migrants*, pp 265–7. 187 Jose, *North American Soccer League encyclopaedia*, p. 159. 188 Ibid., pp 82, 298. 189 Curran, *Irish soccer migrants*, p. 164. 190 Ibid., p. 267. 191 Interview with Dave Henderson, 22 Oct. 2019; Jose, *North American Soccer League encyclopaedia*, p. 128. 192 Jose, *North American Soccer League encyclopaedia*, p. 343. 193 Interview with Dave Henderson, 22 Oct. 2019. 194 Ibid. 195 Ibid. 196 Interview with Liam Buckley, 24 Mar. 2020. 197 Ibid. 198 Curran, *Irish soccer migrants*, p, 268. 199 Interview with Harry McCue, 10 Dec. 2019.

the NASL club through a friend who knew an agent in the USA.[200] He stated when interviewed that all the travelling was tough, but he enjoyed the experience and would have stayed on longer but the outdoor league went into decline.[201] He roomed with Polish international Kazimierz Deyna, who attracted support from the Polish community when the team were travelling, and Polish fans would visit Deyna in the hotel. The club had a strong Mexican support base for their home games:

> We used to go down to Mexico then every Sunday – we played Saturday night – and we used to go out to Tijuana every Sunday, for lunch and it was just cheap as chips, yeah, fantastic, beautiful food, and we socialized down there most Sundays. But the Mexicans got to know us, and they used to get to the games, as I said, and we signed Hugo Perez, that was the start of the huge Mexican support.[202]

McCue later returned to Dublin and was signed by Glentoran in the autumn of 1983.[203] Another player who returned to Europe as the NASL drew to a close was Pierce O'Leary, who had two spells in the NASL, at Philadelphia Fury in 1978 and at Vancouver Whitecaps from 1981 to 1984, before joining Glasgow Celtic.[204] Mick Martin, who was nearer the end of his career, joined Vancouver Whitecaps in 1984, but played only two matches.[205] With the disbandment of the NASL that year, the option of migration to that league disappeared.[206] The initiation of Major League Soccer in 1996 has afforded some Dublin-born players the opportunity to move there. The aforementioned soccer scholarship awardee, Paul Keegan, returned to Ireland after a four-year spell with New England Revolution in the early 2000s, while Robbie Keane joined LA Galaxy at the end of his professional career in 2011, remaining there for five years.[207]

THE MIGRATION OF FEMALE PLAYERS

The migration of women for professional football purposes began tentatively in the early 1970s. In September 1972, an Irish ladies' selection travelled to France to play Stade de Reims in a friendly match at Stade Auguste Delaune.[208] The following year, the French club visited Ireland for a series of friendly matches.[209] Described as 'the world club champions', they were shocked by a physically stronger Irish XI, made up of players from Dublin, Kilkenny, Galway, Limerick and Dundalk in the first of these matches at St James's Park in Kilkenny, with the home team winning

200 Ibid.   **201** Ibid.   **202** Ibid.   **203** *II*, 16 Sept. 1983.   **204** Jose, *North American Soccer League encyclopaedia*, p. 222.   **205** Ibid., p. 180.   **206** Curran, *Irish soccer migrants*, pp 261–9.   **207** Curran, 'The migration of Irish-born players to undertake US soccer scholarships, 1969–2000', pp 101–31; *BG*, 20 May 1996; *II*, 20 Nov. 1999; *EH*, 17 Jan. 2007.   **208** I am thankful to Helena Byrne for sharing this information with me.   **209** *KP*, 28 Nov. 1975; 'RTÉ Archives, 21 Jan. 1974: Inchicore girl bound for Reims', https://www.rte.ie/archives/2019/0118/1024047-french-soccer-club-sign-irish-girl, accessed 27 Jan. 2022.

by two goals to one.[210] In the second match, against Club Kilkenny, the French club won by three goals to nil at Tennypark.[211] Although Kathleen Ramsbottom of Club Kilkenny was offered a position there following her part in defeating the visitors in the first of those matches, she turned it down and it was a Dublin woman who later joined the French club.[212] In 1973, Inchicore native Anne O'Brien signed for them, having been invited to spend some time there that Christmas and to play for the club against a number of boys' teams.[213] The 17-year-old joined the club, 'who were technically amateurs', shortly afterwards, leaving her All-Stars team 'based around Inchicore and Ballyfermot', and a £15 a week job 'packing frozen chickens'.[214] She was offered employment in another factory, on a salary of £75 a week, by the French club's patron, along with the time off to train three nights a week and play matches.[215] One reporter noted in March 1974 that Stade de Reims had been North-West champions five years running but left their league 'to play only teams of young men to toughen themselves up'.[216]

A cousin of both John Giles and Jimmy Conway, it was O'Brien who was to emerge as the most successful Irish female footballer of the twentieth century. Having been signed by Pierre Geoffroy at Stade de Reims, she won three French League titles between 1974 and 1976.[217] She moved to Italy from France in 1976, joining Lazio and winning the league championship in 1979 and 1980.[218] In 1981 she transferred to Trani, winning the league again in 1984, before rejoining Lazio that year.[219] By the start of the 1983–4 season, she was the only Irish woman who was a full-time professional footballer.[220] She was one of only twelve 'foreigners' in the Italian League in 1985, with the others from Denmark, Iceland, France, Spain, Sweden and Scotland.[221] In 1986 she joined Modena, and also had spells at Napoli, Prato (where she won two more league titles, in 1990 and 1991) and finished her career in 1994 at Milan at the age of 38, having won the league there in 1992. She also won two Italian cups with Lazio, in 1977 and 1985, and one with Trani in 1983.[222]

Despite playing in the Italian League, she continued to be overlooked by the Irish selectors, winning only four caps.[223] It appears that the FAI were generally unwilling to invest in bringing her back to Ireland to represent her country.[224] The financial state of Italian ladies' football and its related structures allowed O'Brien to display her talents and earn a decent living from it, something she could not have done at that time in Ireland or Britain.[225] By 1990, she had won the European Player of the Year three times and was earning almost £40,000 a year at Reggiana.[226] O'Brien stated at the time that in Italy, 'they take the game very seriously as the

210 *KP*, 31 Aug. 1973. 211 Ibid. 212 Ibid., 28 Nov. 1975. 213 *IP*, 14 Jan. 1975; 'RTÉ Archives, 21 Jan. 1974: Inchicore girl bound for Reims', rte.ie/archives/2019/0118/1024047-french-soccer-club-sign-irish-girl, accessed 27 Jan. 2022. 214 *IP*, 8 Mar. 1974. 215 *EH*, 25 Jan. 1974. 216 *IP*, 8 Mar. 1974. 217 *IE*, 30 Aug. 2016; *II*, 4 Sept. 2016 218 *EH*, 1 May 1990; *II*, 4 Sept. 2016. 219 I am grateful to Helena Byrne for this information. 220 *EP*, 12 Oct. 1983. 221 *SI*, 17 Feb. 1985. 222 I am grateful to Helena Byrne for this information. 223 *II*, 4 Sept. 2016. 224 *IE*, 2 Sept. 2016. 225 Ibid. 226 *EH*, 27 Apr. 1990.

ladies' teams are part of the men's clubs'.[227] She had retired from playing by the mid-1990s, and became involved in coaching, before passing away in 2016, after a struggle with cancer.[228]

A few other Irish players also moved abroad in the latter decades of the twentieth century, but one case in particular illustrates that this was not always straightforward and highlights the precarious nature of football migration, particularly when little is known of the conditions on offer. In January 1975 Carol Carr, a native of Bray and initially a member of the local Pete's Angels club, was reported to have signed for European Ladies' Champions Standard Liege following negotiations between her Irish team manager, Pat Noone, and club president Albert Tilken.[229] She had been national captain, played as a striker for the Avengers in the Ladies' League of Ireland and had scored a hat-trick against France for Ireland.[230] A sales assistant in Stillorgan, she thought she had signed for £150 a week and 'a free university education', which was reported to be a place on a physical education degree and a French language course in Liege.[231] However, shortly afterwards, she discovered, having arrived in Brussels, that she would not actually be signing for Standard Liege as promised, and instead it was Standard Femina, 'a small ladies' club in Liege'.[232] In addition, the sum available was only around £35 a month.[233] She was forced to confront the club president to sort out the matter.[234] Tilken, a millionaire industrialist, later clarified the story to state that she would get 'free board, free lessons, two return trips home a year and £6 or £7 a week pocket money'.[235] She scored four goals on her debut in the Belgian women's league, which included fourteen other teams, but her club were eager to stress that it was 'strictly amateur'.[236] Three months later, Carr was back in Ireland, and announced she did not intend to return to Belgium.[237] Although she played fourteen games and scored, on average, two goals per match, she disliked 'the quietness of the Belgian town' while 'her lack of French made life difficult for her'.[238] She hoped to open a boutique in Dublin with the money she had earned in Belgium.[239]

Despite the promise of some European clubs, and the successful movement of Anne O'Brien, Irish women's migration to the Continent for professional football purposes failed to develop into a regular trend at that time. In November 1975, Dublin Castle ladies travelled to Reims to face the local club, but Irish player movement to the Continent was limited.[240] An exception was Limerick native and Irish international Grainne Cross, who had joined Italian club Fiamma Ambroziana of Monza by August 1986, and stated that in Ireland, 'the standard is terribly low, the referees are worse and the players are all wearing different jerseys'.[241] In contrast, sponsorship was much more forthcoming in Italy, and Roman club Trani were known to attract attendances of 10,000 spectators.[242]

---

227 *EH*, 1 May 1990. **228** *IE*, 2 Sept. 2016. **229** *II*, 18 Aug. 1970; *IP*, 14 Jan. 1975. **230** *IP*, 14 Jan. 1975. **231** Ibid. **232** Ibid., 18 Jan. 1975. **233** Ibid. **234** *EE*, 18 Jan. 1975. **235** Ibid., 29 Jan. 1975. **236** Ibid. **237** *SI*, 13 Apr. 1975. **238** Ibid. **239** Ibid. **240** *IP*, 21 Nov. 1975. **241** *EP*, 1 Aug. 1986. **242** Ibid.

In 1991, the English Women's Football Association founded a national league, with twenty-four clubs involved.[243] The FA took over the administration of the Women's National Cup competition in 1993 and the National League and League Cup the following year, with the league becoming known as the FA Women's Premier League.[244] The FA announced their plans to develop women's football in 1997, and in 1998 twenty centres of excellence were established, with league and cup sponsorship secured.[245]

By the late 1990s, migration to professional clubs with ladies' teams in England was becoming more common for female players from Dublin. Liberties native Susan Heapes, who joined Arsenal as an 18-year-old in 2000, recalled:

> Yeah I was playing for Ireland, Republic of Ireland under-18s, and I was just gone eighteen, and Vic Akers, the Arsenal ladies' manager, came over to watch the game, and he liked the three of us – myself, Caroline Thorpe and Yvonne Treacy – so he approached the three of us after the game and said, 'Look, would you like to come over for a trial?' So, within a couple of weeks, we went over for a trial for a weekend. He showed us around, we obviously played a bit of football, and then when we were going back home on the Sunday he offered us a year contract, the three of us, so, we took it straight away. So then, I'd say within the month, we were over pre-season training with the reserves, so I had to pack in everything here – I was only eighteen years of age – and moved over there. He got us an apartment, somewhere to live, so we were living together, which helped a lot, and we lived in Highbury Stadium because it was the old Highbury at that time, it wasn't the Emirates.[246]

She had started her career with a local church team, St Catherines's, having been invited to join the club's under-12 team as a 9-year-old through their manager, Brother Bernard Twomey, who contacted her mother initially.[247] Having moved to London, they trained only on Tuesdays and Thursdays and played a match on a Sunday, as it was not professional at that time. Instead, she was set up with a job by the club:

> It was for Nike, it was for postal, people ordered online and we sent out the deliveries. Yeah, we did that for a while, a few months, and then he got us a job in the laundrette, in Arsenal's training ground, so we were washing the men's kit. So when we were over there we were obviously playing football and training and working, and trying to keep our heads down. Like, where we were washing the kit, all the men's team were training, so we got to eat our lunch on the break with the likes of Patrick Viera and Freddie

243 'The History of Women's Football in England', thefa.com/womens-girls-football/history, accessed 23 Jan. 2021. 244 Ibid. 245 Ibid. 246 Interview with Susan Heapes, 28 Feb. 2020; *EH*, 7 Aug. 2000. 247 Interview with Susan Heapes, 28 Feb. 2020.

Ljungberg. Thierry Henry was there. Like you'd be taking your lunch on your plate and he's next behind you, so it was a brilliant experience, I'm delighted I did it and I've no regrets whatsoever.[248]

Heapes was one of six Irish players in the team along with Caroline Thorpe, Yvonne Treacy, Grainne Kearns, Ciara Grant and Emma Byrne. The rest were English, including Alex Scott and Fay White.[249] Having found it difficult to break into the first team, and because her sister had just had a baby, she decided to return to Dublin and rejoined St Catherine's.[250] Heapes noted that Olivia O'Toole was her toughest opponent.[251] O'Toole was also asked to join Arsenal but recalled that she did not want to work in a laundrette washing and printing jerseys for £150 a week, and added that she was 'a bit of homebird'.[252]

By the opening decades of the twenty-first century there was increased interest in a career in women's football in England as it became more professional and sponsorship grew, with the eight-team FA Women's Super League founded in 2011.[253] Irish international Jamie Finn, who worked as a personal trainer while playing for Shelbourne, joined Birmingham City of the Women's Super League in 2021.[254] A native of Swords, she began at the age of 5 by playing in a boys' team, before moving on to ladies' teams Raheny United and Shelbourne.[255] Irish under-19 player Chloe Darby also got involved in soccer through her family, with her father, Frank Darby having played for Athlone Town and Longford Town.[256] The Coolock local had a spell with Athlone Town before she joined Bohemians.[257] Like men's soccer in Dublin, the part-time nature of the women's game will ensure that aspiring players will have to continue to look abroad in the hope of securing a full-time career in professional football.

DUBLIN-BORN PLAYERS IN THE IRISH LEAGUE

Dublin-born players have also been attracted to the Irish League for much of the period since the late nineteenth century, when a professional structure was put in place there.[258] Some non-Ulster-born players did move to Belfast clubs in the early 1900s. Among these was Billy Synnott, an amateur Shelbourne player who moved to Belfast Celtic in 1901 and initially travelled to Belfast at weekends for matches for £2 a game. He later moved there permanently, earning £4 a week, before joining English club Glossop.[259] Billy Halligan, who played for Old St Mary's in Dublin prior to moving to Cliftonville, Belfast Celtic and Distillery, joined Leeds City in 1909.[260] However, the presence of two Dublin clubs – Shelbourne (who

248 Ibid. 249 Ibid. 250 Ibid. 251 Ibid. 252 Interview with Olivia O'Toole, 16 Apr. 2020. 253 'The History of Women's Football in England', thefa.com/womens-girls-football/history, accessed 23 Jan. 2021. 254 Interview with Jamie Finn, 9 May 2020. 255 Ibid. 256 Interview with Chloe Darby, 7 Apr. 2020. 257 Ibid. 258 Garnham, *Association football and society*, pp 72–3. 259 *SI*, 9 Sept. 1956. See also Joyce, *Football League players' records*, p. 281. Apparently Synott was born in Widnes. 260 Joyce, *Football League players' records*, p. 123.

became professional in the 1905–6 season) and Bohemians – in the Irish League and Cup until the early 1920s, meant that footballers there could play at a decent level against their Ulster counterparts.[261] In general, the best Dublin-based players in the early twentieth century, such as Billy Lacey and Val Harris, looked to English clubs rather than those in Belfast as a means to fully develop their professional careers.[262]

Following the fall-out between a number of Dublin clubs and the Irish Football Association over what those in the capital perceived to be unfair treatment, a professional soccer league was established there in 1921 with the foundation of the Football Association of Ireland.[263] With the partition of Ireland into the Irish Free State and Northern Ireland in 1921, players from both areas now faced the prospect of crossing a border if they were to participate for clubs outside their own jurisdictions, although, as Cormac Moore has shown, customs barriers were not introduced until 1923.[264] This 'resulted in numerous psychological and physical divisions, including some which had never existed before', while in 1925, the Boundary Commission decided not to make any changes to the agreed territory despite the hopes of Sinn Féin that more of the northern area would be given to the Free State.[265]

POST-PARTITION MOVEMENT FROM DUBLIN TO NORTHERN IRELAND

Attempts to end the dispute between the FAI and the IFA at conferences in 1924 and 1932 were unsuccessful.[266] Some players based in the Irish Free State continued to play for Irish League clubs, however, as the standard of play there remained higher.[267] In October 1929 Newry Town fielded two former Drumcondra players, Coyle and Moore, in a defeat away to Bangor.[268] Naturally, it was not just Dublin-based players who were recruited from the Irish Free State by Irish League clubs. Donegal-born Jimmy Kelly had spells for a number of Northern Ireland clubs, including Newry Town, Coleraine, Derry City, Ballymena United and Ballymoney, as well as making guest appearances for Irish Free State clubs Shamrock Rovers and Dundalk.[269] League of Ireland clubs' financial difficulties could, at times, also mean a transfer north was necessary to sustain a realistic professional football career. Tom Arrigan won the IFA Cup with Glentoran, an East Belfast club with a strong unionist following, and also the FAI Cup with Waterford during his playing career.[270] He had moved to the Belfast club in the early 1930s, 'when financial

261 Garnham, *Association football and society*, pp 177–8. **262** Curran, *Irish soccer migrants*, p. 26. **263** Garnham, *Association football and society*, pp 177–8. **264** Cormac Moore, *Birth of the border: the impact of partition in Ireland* (Kildare, 2019), p. 5. **265** Ibid., pp 4–5. **266** Moore, *The Irish soccer split*, pp 163–7, 200–2. **267** *FSW*, 12 Sept. and 14 Nov. 1925. **268** *II*, 14 Oct. 1929. **269** 'NIFG-Jimmy Kelly', nifootball.blogspot.com/2007/01/jimmy-kelly.html, accessed 24 Feb. 2020. **270** *II*, 14 Feb. 1957.

difficulties caused Waterford temporarily to lose hope', but rejoined the Munster club in the 1936–7 season after four and a half seasons with Glentoran when the southern team regained their senior status.[271]

In 1940, the Irish League became the Northern Wartime Regional League until it was restored in the 1947–8 season.[272] In the post-Second World War period, this movement to Northern Ireland continued, with a number of Irish League clubs having the financial clout to maintain it. One reporter stated in April 1946 that 'Northern money is making a big bid for Southern craft'.[273] Thomas 'Bud' Aherne joined Belfast Celtic from Limerick United in 1946, although as the northern club folded in 1949 he joined Luton Town.[274] Other players from the Free State to join Belfast Celtic in that decade included Joseph 'Robin' Lawlor, who had played for Drumcondra in their 1946 FAI Cup final win, and Cork-born Billy O'Neill, who played for Burnley and Walsall after a spell at Belfast Celtic prior to their disbandment.[275]

By August 1946 three other League of Ireland players had joined Glentoran: Con Martin, Noel Kelly and a footballer referred to only in the press as McCormack.[276] A number of players seem to have used moves to clubs in Northern Ireland as a stepping stone to a transfer to those in Britain, which would indicate that signing-on fees were attractive while the standard in Northern Ireland meant that scouting and networks with those in England were better developed that those in Dublin at this time. Glentoran had recruited Kelly from Shamrock Rovers before his move to Arsenal in 1947.[277] Others to move north at that time included Dublin-born Paddy Watters, who joined Glentoran from Bohemians before moving to Preston North End the following year.[278] Dublin-born players continued to play for Irish League clubs in the following decade, although there is less evidence that they were as sought after as they had been in the late 1940s following the aforementioned Glasgow meeting in 1946 in relation to retained lists and transfers (see p. 154).[279] This partially explains the volume of signings by northern clubs of League of Ireland players. The closing of this loophole may also explain a decrease in players moving north immediately after 1946.

There were a few Dublin players who joined League of Ireland clubs in the 1950s, including Kit Lawlor, who left Doncaster Rovers for Ballymena United in a swap in December 1954 that saw Liam Coll sign for the English club.[280] By the start of the following season Lawlor was back at one of his former clubs, Drumcondra, after he expressed a desire to be nearer home.[281] Some players, such as Liam Munroe, who joined Bristol City from Ards in 1957, and Paddy Mulvey, who moved to Stockport County from Glentoran the same year, continued to

271 *II*, 16 Apr. 1959. 272 *The Malcolm Brodie Northern Ireland soccer yearbook, '14–15* (Belfast, 2014), pp 56–7. 273 *II*, 23 Apr. 1946. 274 *IE*, 15 Mar. 1949. 275 Hugman, *The PFA Premier and Football League players' records*, pp 362, 470. 276 *IP*, 22 Aug. 1946. 277 Hugman, *The PFA Premier and Football League players' records*, p. 344. 278 Ibid., p. 642. 279 *EH*, 27 Nov. and 11 Dec. 1946. 280 *IE*, 11 Dec. 1954. 281 *II*, 30 July 1955 and 23 Aug. 1955.

aspire towards a higher standard of football.[282] Munroe refused an offer from Drumcondra in November 1957 and was reported to travel north each week to play for Ards.[283] The following year, Drumcondra's Dermot Cross joined Distillery, but other transfers north from Dublin appear to have been scarce.[284] By the 1960s, League of Ireland football had reached its peak as a popular public attraction, with the success and rivalry of clubs such as Shamrock Rovers and Waterford in that decade a notable factor.[285] This improved standard of play might have been a reason in the lessening of numbers moving north for professional football purposes. It is unclear what impact the IRA's Operation Harvest, which took place from 1956 until 1963, had on player movement.[286]

In any case, players did continue to move from Dublin to clubs in Northern Ireland. On the eve of the Troubles in 1965, Dublin-born Terry Conroy joined Glentoran from Home Farm before moving to Stoke City in 1967.[287] Glentoran's recruitment of Conroy, Con Martin, Paddy Turner and Tony Macken, who joined the club in 1969, was said to have been down to chairman Tom McNeice, who was based in Dublin for business reasons until the 1970s.[288] In the early 1970s, some Republic of Ireland-born players such as Tony Cavanagh continued to join Belfast clubs from those in the League of Ireland, despite the rise in violence in the city.[289] However, at this point the numbers had lessened substantially from those moving in the immediate post-war years, indicating that players were less inclined to move there with the escalation in social disorder. As Dickson has stated, 'the collateral effects of the Northern Ireland Troubles were indeed felt in Dublin in many ways during the 1970s, not least in the huge growth in indictable crime, falling detection rates and the proliferation of illegal firearms'.[290] In particular, a number of bombings in Dublin in 1973 and 1974, the last of which saw the deaths of twenty-six people, brought the violence to the city.[291] The deaths of three members of the Miami Showband in July 1975 in a UVF attack that was allegedly assisted by UDR soldiers while the musicians were on their way back to Dublin after a performance in Northern Ireland highlighted the dangers of making the journey there.[292] The meeting of Linfield and Dundalk in the European Cup in 1979 also illustrated the tension within Irish society at this time, with IRA bombings at Mullaghmore and Warrenpoint heightening this further prior to the match. Dubliner Mick Lawlor, who captained Dundalk that night, recalled that

> The game just wouldn't go ahead now. Like I'm going up for the toss-up, and the stones are coming into the centre circle. Stones thrown, I mean, I

282 Hugman, *The PFA Premier and Football League players' records*, pp 445–6. 283 *IT*, 22 Nov. 1957. 284 Ibid., 21 Nov. 1958. 285 Whelan, *Who stole our game?*, pp 71–2. 286 Jonathan Bardon, *A history of Ulster* (Belfast, 2005), pp 605–8. 287 *II*, 28 Sept. 1966; Hugman, *The PFA Premier and Football League players' records*, p. 134. 288 *BT*, 3 June 1997. 289 *IP*, 13 Apr. 1972. 290 Dickson, *Dublin*, p. 544. 291 Ibid. 292 David McKittrick & David McVea, *Making sense of the Troubles: a history of the Northern Ireland conflict* (London, 2012), p. 317.

saw some of the weirdest things. You're on the pitch, and there's mayhem going on, all-around mayhem. And you're kind of cocooned, and you can't help but be drawn to different things that were happening. Linfield had a big lad, he was known as 'the bald eagle', Rafferty was his name – big, big man, 6 feet 4 inches, tough, hard as nails – but a ball came to me in the air, and I'm kind of backing on to him and somehow, I controlled the ball and got around him, but when I got around him, and I looked up, to either have a shot, or pass it, there was three policemen running straight at me. And the reason for that was, when I was facing that way, I didn't see this Linfield supporter running behind me, from one side of the pitch to the other, and three policemen – it was like Keystone Cops or whatever, but – and there was the three policemen running at me – what have I done wrong? – but they just ran straight past me and after this lad.[293]

Both clubs were fined by UEFA after the first leg at Oriel Park – Linfield for supporter misconduct, Dundalk for inadequate security – and Linfield was forced to play their home leg a minimum of 300 miles away from Windsor Park.[294] They chose to play the match in Holland, with Dundalk winning by two goals to nil. Despite the hooliganism, relations between the two clubs remained stable.[295]

THE 1980s

The early 1980s saw no let-up in the conflict, with the IRA's hunger-strike campaign in 1981 leading to the restoration of their prisoner-of-war status, while the deaths of ten of the hunger strikers 'elicited massive sympathy throughout Ireland'.[296] Players moving to Northern Ireland from Dublin to join Irish League clubs in this decade were again few, but some did make the decision to travel north for professional football purposes. In May 1981 Dermot Keely completed a transfer from Dundalk to Glentoran in what was said to be 'a record signing-on fee between a North and South club'.[297] Keely's move, he stated in a newspaper interview, was partially motivated by a six-game League of Ireland suspension he had received, which he felt was 'too severe', and which was due to begin at Dundalk at the start of the 1981–2 season.[298] The prospect of playing in European competition was also an important factor. He added that while he would miss playing for Dundalk, he would not miss playing in the League of Ireland. Keely had been banned for six matches for being sent off four times that season, but the ban was lifted in September 1981 by the FAI and he was allowed to play in Europe for Glentoran against Progress Niedercorn of Luxembourg.[299] He added that it was

---

293 Interview with Mick Lawlor, 29 Feb. 2020. 294 Ibid. 295 '1979 European Cup-Linfield', dundalkfc.com/history/dundalk-fc-in-europe/1979–european-cup-linfield, accessed 23 May 2020. Dundalk won 3–1 on aggregate. 296 Bartlett, *Ireland: a history*, p. 525. 297 *IP*, 30 May 1981. 298 Ibid. 299 *IP*, 12 Sept. 1981.

'an offer too good to refuse' and that Glentoran were 'a very professional outfit'.[300] He also admired the Irish League's more effective organization of their fixture list and their disciplinary system.[301]

Keely spent two years at Glentoran before moving to UCD to take up a player-manager role.[302] By the early 1980s, the system of 'retain and transfer' was still operational in the Irish League, meaning that clubs there could keep a player until they got a 'reasonable' fee, with one reporter stating that 'transfer fees in the North are much higher than in the South, so most League of Ireland clubs could not afford the North's interpretation of "a reasonable fee"'.[303] It appears that he continued to maintain his secondary-school teaching job in Dublin while playing for Glentoran.[304]

Keely, who travelled to Belfast on the train each Saturday for matches, later recalled in a newspaper interview that he 'thoroughly enjoyed' his time at the Oval.[305] His move had, according to Harry McCue, 'broken the ice' in terms of League of Ireland players joining Irish League clubs in that decade.[306] By the autumn of 1983, Dublin-born McCue was back in the League of Ireland at Athlone Town following his spell in the North American Soccer League with San Diego Sockers. With the NASL's imminent decline, he had decided to move home.[307] McCue was contacted by Glentoran manager Ronnie McFall and was offered a three-year contract with the East Belfast club. This offer was reportedly better than any made by a League of Ireland club, illustrating the more affluent state of some Irish League clubs.[308] One reporter noted at that time that 'Irish League clubs can heavily outbid their Southern counterparts these days'.[309] There were only two other Dublin-born Catholics playing in the Irish League, Leo Flanagan and Damien Byrne, who were both based at Crusaders, and as McCue recalled, other League of Ireland players generally did not travel to play with clubs in Northern Ireland at that time. He noted that Glentoran fielded four Catholic players in their team: Gerry Mullen, Jim Cleary, Tony Connell and himself. He added that, 'If you were good enough, I think, Glentoran signed you, you played for the shirt as they often say, you know, but [they are a] great club.'[310] He noted that his teammates quickly accepted him, stating that 'they were superb'. The club had also signed former Northern Ireland international Billy Caskey from NASL team Tulsa Roughnecks and there were a number of other international players involved. McCue did not become resident in Belfast but instead travelled up on Thursdays to train, and then stayed in the Park Avenue Hotel near the club's Oval ground until after the match on Saturday before returning home. He added that he 'was more or less full-time … the money was that good'.[311]

Despite the positive welcome from the club, there were a number of occasions when manager McFall rang him to tell him not to come up as the political situation

300 *II*, 30 May 1981.   **301** *Soccer Reporter* (Oct. 1981), p. 7; (Nov. 1981), p. 3.   **302** *EH*, 25 Oct. 1983.   **303** *IP*, 5 May 1982.   **304** *IP*, 17 June 1983.   **305** *II*, 16 Sept. 1983.   **306** Ibid. **307** Interview with Harry McCue, 10 Dec. 2019. **308** *II*, 16 Sept. 1983. **309** Ibid. **310** Interview with Harry McCue, 10 Dec. 2019.   **311** Ibid.

was 'too tense'.[312] He also recalled that he was once told by McFall to refrain from entering Coleraine FC's social club after a win against the Derry club, as a number of those with links with the UVF were involved in running the bar there and the atmosphere was not good. However, Glentoran captain Jim Cleary was unhappy with this and ordered his players to leave the social club.[313] Enniskillen-born Cleary had been signed by manager Ronnie McFall in 1980.[314] McFall later stated in a club website interview that

> It was a big statement by the club ... Glentoran had always had a good cross community support and a lot of great players from across the community. But because of the Troubles in the seventies that had stopped. I knew if we were going to kick on, we had to get back to Glentoran's traditional way of doing things. The Troubles were still at their height then, but Jim was very keen to come to the club and there was very little resistance to it, then when everyone saw how good he was everyone idolized him. Rightly so because he was a great player for Glentoran from the minute he came in and he broke down any reluctance other players had to coming to Glentoran.[315]

McCue recalled that while he was also welcomed by the Glentoran fans, away supporters were different:

> The away supporters were the usual, you'd get the whole nine yards – Fenian this and Fenian that, you know. My own supporters – just fantastic, they were really good to me, so ... I could go down to the social club, I could stay overnight, and I never had a problem whatsoever really, you know.[316]

Sectarian sledging from opposition players was also an issue at times but McCue never let it affect him. Travelling to Northern Ireland during the Troubles could be difficult with border crossings and checkpoints to be negotiated and these regularly slowed the flow of traffic between Northern Ireland and the Republic of Ireland and led to lengthy delays at times. However, one particular trip north for a match turned into a nerve-wracking experience for the defender after he ran out of petrol near the border while on the way to a home European match against Monaco. He stopped off for help at a house in the South Armagh area but the owner did not answer the door. He recalled that instead,

> A Volkswagen pulled up, and a fella got out with a gun and wanted to know what I was doing, what I was at. I explained everything, showed him my

312 Ibid.   313 Ibid.   314 'Glentoran FC: the Managers: Ronnie McFall (part two)', glentoran. com/news/managers-ronnie-mcfall-part-two, accessed 21 Sept. 2020.   315 Ibid.   316 Interview with Harry McCue, 10 Dec. 2019.

bag, Glentoran, the whole lot. So they drove up, got my petrol, came down and asked me for my autograph – and I gave him my autograph. I was so nervous. They [Glentoran] rang home and they said where was I. They said, 'He left hours ago', so there was a big worry about where I was, the whole lot. When I arrived at Park Avenue, I said it to them [what happened], [and] they said, 'Ah yeah Harry, South Armagh IRA.' They told me they were vigilantes. There was a lot of sectarian stuff going on here, so they were looking after the whole area. But it was scary. And funny enough I went into the hotel, Paisley was in the reception, so I met the Reverend Ian. All in the one day, the both sides of the one thing. The owner of the hotel introduced me to him.[317]

Another Dublin-born player who moved to a club in Northern Ireland in that decade was goalkeeper Brian O'Shea, who joined Newry Town, a club located in what could generally be described as a nationalist area, in 1986, following spells at Home Farm, St Patrick's Athletic and Shelbourne.[318] Newry Town had been re-admitted to the Irish League in 1983 and began to look to the Republic of Ireland for players, with Dundalk-born Ollie Ralph signing that year.[319] O'Shea joined Newry Town as a 20-year-old, but had previously been on trial at Liverpool FC as a 16-year-old. It was while in digs that he was first exposed to the reality of the situation in Northern Ireland when he shared a house with a number of other trialists, some of whom were Protestants from Belfast:

My father wasn't one to pass remarks on anybody, he was a live-and-let live guy. And his saying to me was, 'Son, listen, if you can't do somebody a good turn don't do them a bad turn.' Never spoke about politics in the house … even during the Troubles, you know. He wouldn't be shouting and screaming at the television about this, that and the other. So I was brought up very protected, in regard to the Troubles in Ireland. So when I met these guys from Belfast, the only thing different for me then was the accents were a little bit different. Unfortunately for them, they were living with what was going on and I was obviously seen as the enemy and as the weeks went on that became more prevalent, you know.[320]

However, he was able to deal with the situation in his own way:

It was just kind of bullying stuff, but look, I'm a north inner-city boy from Dublin 7. You learn quickly to fight your corner, otherwise you literally become housebound. So it was no problem to me to stand up for

317 Ibid. **318** *Soccer Magazine* (Feb. 1989), p. 5. **319** 'Dundalk F.C. Who's Who: Ollie Ralph', dundalkfcwhoswho.com/player.php?id=365, accessed 22 May 2020. **320** Interview with Brian O'Shea, 21 Nov. 2019.

myself, which I did, and it came to an abrupt end! ... Yeah, I think that
was the only sour note, my whole time at Liverpool – from Mrs Pike, to
the training sessions, to the staff at Liverpool, to the players – was just
unbelievable.[321]

O'Shea's motivation to play for Newry Town stemmed from a desire to gain first-
team football experience, as he had been unable to cement a place in the first team
at Shelbourne, his third League of Ireland club. He recalled that initially, it was a
bit daunting, but he soon adjusted:

> I went to Newry and I went straight into the first team. I think one of
> their first games was against Crusaders, which was kind of a little bit of an
> eye-opener, because everyone talks about the two big teams, Glentoran and
> Linfield, but when you go into Crusaders' ground it's a different part of the
> world, it's Union Jack city, and it's a very staunchly Protestant neighbour-
> hood and there was a big crowd. Again, I played very, very well – I think we
> drew the game – and I knew there was something special, I knew this was
> going to be different, and I spent five great years up there.[322]

Like Keely and McCue before him, O'Shea did not move to Northern Ireland but
would commute up and down for matches, and recalled that his father would drive
him up so that he would have a rest, and he himself would then drive home after
the game. For away matches, they would travel to Newry and then be collected and
taken by car to their match-day destination. With the geography of Irish League
clubs, he usually did not have to go too far from Newry, with Belfast about an hour
away, and stated that 'most of the away matches were in Belfast or County Down
– we had a couple of long haul, Larne would have been the longest and Coleraine –
they were the two longest ones'.[323] While O'Shea quickly established himself with
teammates and supporters with a number of fine performances, he noted that as
a goalkeeper he was an easy target, and away fans would routinely throw objects
at him while also giving him verbal abuse.[324] He also stated that 'it was tough – it
was tough travelling up, going through the checkpoints and obviously the longer
trips, it was even harder when you'd be stopped on the backroads by the UDA –
they weren't my favourite parts, the memories – you know, it was a tough time up
there'.[325]

Despite having full-time professional status with the club, he trained with
St James' Gate in Dublin on Tuesdays and Thursdays with another goalkeeper,
and trained on his own every other day except Friday, the day before matches.[326]
He also noted that financially, the pay was better in the Irish League than the
League of Ireland, but 'it depended on what club you were with'.[327] He added
that

321 Ibid.   322 Ibid.   323 Ibid.   324 Ibid.   325 Ibid.   326 Ibid.   327 Ibid.

Obviously you were getting paid sterling at the time, you were getting the change-over, you were getting travelling expenses as well. You were also involved in win bonuses and things like that. So, yeah, it was, I was doing quite well at the time, you know. I was happy with what I was getting.[328]

He left Newry Town in 1991, having been disillusioned that the club turned down an offer for him from Glasgow Celtic, and joined St Patrick's Athletic for £10,000, which made him the most expensive goalkeeper in the League of Ireland.[329]

Commuting from the Republic of Ireland for matches appears to have been common among players there who signed for Irish League clubs during the Troubles, with Paul McGee travelling from Sligo to play for Ballymena United at weekends after signing from Shamrock Rovers in 1984.[330] A number of Dublin-born players also moved to nationalist-leaning Derry City, who had been elected to the League of Ireland in 1985, in this decade. They were the only Northern Ireland-based club in the Republic of Ireland's professional national league, having withdrawn from the Irish League in 1972 after a number of clubs in that competition voted against them returning to their home ground, the Brandywell. They had temporarily played their home matches in Coleraine after security issues.[331] Following a spell at Chelsea, former Shamrock Rovers player John Coady joined Derry City in 1988. He recalled that he had signed for them as they were the only Irish club who had made an offer to Chelsea at that time, and his former club Shamrock Rovers could not afford him.[332] He added that 'Derry were on the up, they had 11,000 people in the Brandywell every week. So, it was a fantastic move as it turns out', because the club won the League of Ireland, FAI Cup and League Cup in the 1988–9 season.[333] Despite this, he continued to train every Tuesday and Thursday in Dublin, with Shelbourne, who trained at Three Rock Rovers in Rathfarnham. Derry City manager Jim McLaughlin organized this with Shelbourne manager Pat Byrne.[334] He was joined by Derry City's other Dublin-based players, Mick Neville, Kevin Brady and Paul Doolin.

The four players would leave Dublin on Saturday morning for pre-match training in Derry, as League of Ireland matches were played on Sundays at that time. They would stay overnight at the Everglades Hotel on the Saturday night. Naturally, the geographic spread of the League of Ireland's clubs meant that they did not always have to travel to Derry.[335] Playing for a nationalist-leaning club in a majority Catholic city, the Dublin-based players were 'welcomed with open arms' by supporters.[336] However, travel to Derry meant that the four players had a long journey up from Dublin, and this was made more difficult by delays at the border checkpoints. Coady recalled that the players were generally treated well by the squaddies, but the mood changed when the paras were on duty and harassment increased.[337]

328 Ibid.   329 Ibid.; *IP*, 2 Jan. 1989.   330 *EH*, 19 Dec. 1984.   331 Curran, *Irish soccer migrants*, p. 51; *BT*, 30 July 2015.   332 Interview with John Coady, 22 Jan. 2020.   333 Ibid.   334 Ibid. 335 Ibid.   336 Ibid.   337 Ibid.

THE 1990s

Irish League clubs remained capable of attracting Republic of Ireland-born players in the early 1990s, despite the continuation of atrocities. It was in this decade that the movement of League of Ireland players based in Dublin to the Irish League reached its peak during the Troubles and the level of finance was clearly a strong attraction for the players despite the dangers to life there at that time. In August 1990, Paul Doolin of Derry City joined Portadown for £20,000, which was then a record fee for an Irish League club.[338] In an interview in December 1990, Doolin stated he felt that 'the vast majority' of home supporters had accepted him.[339] In January 1991, manager Ronnie McFall commented that 'the stick that Paul gets from some of our supporters is unbelievable, yet he never hides like some lesser players. He's a tremendous pro.'[340] Doolin returned to the League of Ireland in November 1991, joining Shamrock Rovers. He stated that he had 'been on the road for four years now and it's a long time', as he had joined Derry City in 1987.[341] While at Portadown, he had commuted to Shamrock Park from Dublin to training and matches, having, as noted above, also remained based in Dublin while a Derry City player.[342] By the time of his return to the League of Ireland from Portadown, he had won league and cup doubles with Shamrock Rovers, Derry City and Portadown.[343] In February 1994 he rejoined Portadown from Shelbourne.[344] McFall had taken over at Portadown in 1986, having been Glentoran manager from 1979 until 1984.[345] He stayed at Portadown until 2016 before returning to Glentoran in 2018 for a short spell, and, as shown in the signing of Paul Doolin in 1990, he had continued his policy of recruiting Catholic players as well as those from other religious backgrounds during the Troubles.[346]

Republic of Ireland-born players returning from English clubs were also attracted to Irish League sides and Martin Russell joined Portadown from Middlesbrough in 1991.[347] He was signed by McFall with finance and the prospect of European Cup football motivating factors. Russell continued to live in Dublin while playing with the Irish League club.[348] He later recalled that

> I was probably able to just get by in terms of week-to-week stuff, able to pay towards the mortgage with the money that was in the Irish League at the time. That was, I think, the attraction of going there, at the time. [In] the League of Ireland, down south, there wasn't the sort of investment going into the clubs – it was the north. That sort of has changed, and changed again in the time I've been back, where some of the clubs down here ended up paying a lot of money to players and then went bust. But I was able to get by on a few quid coming through Portadown.[349]

---

338 *BT*, 2 Aug. 1990. 339 *BT*, 12 Dec. 1990. 340 *BT*, 14 Jan. 1991. 341 *BT*, 13 Nov. 1991. 342 *BT*, 23 Oct. and 12 Dec. 1990. 343 *BT*, 13 Nov. 1991. 344 *BT*, 16 Feb. 1994. 345 'Glentoran FC: the Managers: Ronnie McFall (part two)', glentoran.com/news/managers-ronnie-mcfall-part-two, accessed 21 Sept. 2020. 346 *BT*, 10 Mar. 2016 and 3 Jan. 2019. 347 Ibid., 14 Aug. 1991. 348 Ibid., 18 Nov. 1991. 349 Curran, *Irish soccer migrants*, p. 304.

Another player who chose an Irish League club on returning home in the early part of that decade was Paul Byrne, who had been at Oxford United and Arsenal and joined Bangor in November 1991 with League of Ireland clubs reluctant to take him on because of his off-the- field reputation.[350] When discussing the security risks of playing in Northern Ireland in the early 1990s, he stated that 'it was always a chance you were going to take'. However, he was highly motivated to succeed and stated that 'you know, you stepped on that train on a Saturday morning, but when you've got that drive and passion in you for football and all you want to do is play football … nothing else was going to stand in my way'.[351] He saw it as an opportunity to prove himself and get back to playing at a higher level in England or Scotland again, eventually gaining a transfer to Glasgow Celtic in 1993.[352] He looked back fondly on his first spell in Irish League football and stated that

> I actually burned the Irish League up. I won the Young Player of the Year and the Players' Senior Player of the Year, the Writers' Junior and the Writers' Senior. I scored the winning goal in the Bass Irish Cup final and Georgie Best gave me the trophies, and to cream it all off, I signed a three-year contract at Celtic.[353]

He also continued to train in Dublin while signed with Bangor, and travelled up and down every Saturday for the Irish League matches.[354] He added that if a player was talented enough, fans would appreciate it: 'I think a lot of people put a lot of negativity and bad-minded things to the back of their mind to enjoy obviously, a decent footballer coming to play for their football club.'[355]

However, having been a Glasgow Celtic player from 1993 until 1995, and having scored against Glasgow Rangers, his return to the Irish League in 1998 with Glenavon, following spells with Brighton (on loan) and Southend United, was different. He noted that he 'never had any one bit of trouble at Bangor', but he when he later joined Glenavon 'it all changed, because it's [also] a Protestant area, and I was playing for – what did they say – "Linfield's second team", basically, and yeah, I used to get serious abuse – no death threats, but serious abuse'.[356] At Glenavon, he shared a car which the club hired, with three other Dublin based players, Steve McCaffrey, Dermot O'Neill and Tony Grant, for travel purposes to Northern Ireland.[357]

The early 1990s also saw Linfield begin to again recruit players from the League of Ireland, with Dessie Gorman the first of this new batch in December 1992.[358] This had followed the signing of Catholic Chris Cullen from Irish League club

350 *BT*, 15 Nov. 1991; *Soccer Magazine*, 80 (May/ June 1993), p. 14.   **351** Interview with Paul Byrne, 26 Feb. 2020.   **352** *BT*, 2 Apr. 1993.   **353** Interview with Paul Byrne, 26 Feb. 2020.   **354** Ibid. **355** Ibid.   **356** Ibid.   **357** Ibid.   **358** Daniel Browne, 'Linfield's "Hawk of Peace": pre-ceasefires reconciliation in Irish League football' in Curran & Toms (eds), *New perspectives on association football in Irish history*, pp 81–94, p. 90.

Cliftonville that summer. As Daniel Browne has shown, by this time, the Belfast club had come under increased pressure for what many perceived to be a policy of not recruiting Catholics, although, as noted earlier, Davy Walsh had enjoyed a spell there in the post-war years. Browne points out that there had been other Catholic involvement within the club, most famously player and trainer Gerry Morgan, and that the situation had been more complex than had been portrayed. During the Troubles, Catholic player recruitment by Linfield had been affected by the club's overtly British and Protestant image, but there was no bar on signing Catholics.[359] In February 1993, Martin Bayly scored his first goal for Linfield, having joined the club the previous month and was the first Dublin-born Catholic to be recruited by them in that decade.[360] Browne believes that 'the political changes, hailed later in the decade, were apparent in the social fibres of local football long before'.[361]

By the latter stages of the following year the number of players from the Republic of Ireland who had joined Irish League clubs appears to have grown significantly. In the months following the IRA's ceasefire in August 1994, some of the League of Ireland's best players were regulars within the Smirnoff Irish League. One reporter noted that 'there are more Southern-born players in the Smirnoff Irish League than the Carling Premiership – or any other foreign division'.[362] With the higher wages available in Northern Ireland's top league, he estimated that 'up to thirty players' made the journey north each weekend to play for Northern Ireland's professional clubs, and noted that Pat Fenlon, 'the Republic's best non-English based midfielder', was 'running the show at Linfield' and had earned the nickname 'Billy Fenian'.[363] It was stated that 'Linfield freely admit they can match, and in some cases beat, top southern wages', with chairman David Campbell stating that 'we have a more stream-lined operation with bigger attendances'.[364] He added that they were more selective than the League of Ireland clubs in regards to the quality of the players they recruited.

Dessie Gorman had also made his mark at the Windsor Park club, with his jersey said to be 'the biggest selling shirt in the Supporters Club shop'.[365] Linfield had also bought English-born Gary Haylock from Dublin club Shelbourne and Campbell claimed they were the best team in Ireland.[366] Haylock later stated he was highly influenced by the money available at the Belfast club.[367] Fenlon's own move was eased by the presence of Gorman, while Stephen Beattie, whom he knew from a three-year spell at Chelsea, was also at Linfield.[368] Linfield also had another Catholic, Raymond 'Soupy' Campbell from County Down, in their midfield, and club secretary Derek Bowen said they signed Catholics 'all the time now'. He added that they had 'a lot of Catholics in the youth teams as well. If they come through [then that's] fine. It's all about wanting the best and wanting to win.' Campbell stated that Linfield 'did not buy Fenlon, Gorman or Haylock thinking about where they came from. Those three were quality and were available. They are virtually our three best players.'[369]

359 Ibid., p. 87.   360 *BT*, 10 Feb. 1993.   361 Browne, 'Linfield's "Hawk of Peace"', p. 81. 362 *EH*, 7 Oct. 1994.   363 Ibid.   364 Ibid.   365 Ibid.   366 Ibid.   367 Fitzpatrick, *Shelbourne cult heroes*, p. 95.   368 *EH*, 7 Oct. 1994.   369 Ibid.

As well as the financial incentive, the style of play was also said to be a motivating factor. Former Newcastle winger Mark Gill was playing at Cliftonville at that time, along with Dubliner Gary Sliney. Gill noted that 'it's so much better up here … they don't adhere so much to systems and only one club … uses the offside trap all the time'.[370] Dublin-born Roddy Collins of Bangor was said to have 'helped set up a lot of trials and loans' and was 'regarded as the senior advisor in the party'.[371] Collins felt that in the Irish League, 'the pitches, stadiums, crowds and the standard' were all higher than in the League of Ireland.[372] Despite the tense atmosphere of Windsor Park during the Republic of Ireland and Northern Ireland's World Cup qualifying decider in November 1993, the reporter noted that the same venue 'bore no resemblance' during the Irish League match he had seen there in October 1994, as 'neither Fenlon nor Gorman were barracked' and two Dublin players at Ballymena Comrades 'were not singled out'.[373] He felt that 'southern Irish fans' perception of Windsor is completely misleading because of last November'. It was also noted that with two divisions of eight teams in operation, 'failure to make the top eight will spell financial disaster for the bottom eight, hence the increased activity in cross-channel transfers'.[374] Both Mark Kenny and Gary Sliney had moved to the Irish League after having failed to establish themselves in English football, while other Republic of Ireland-born players in the Irish League at that time included Padraig Dully (Cliftonville), Ricky McEvoy (Bangor), and, as noted above, Paul Byrne (Bangor) and Paul Doolin (Portadown). A number of comments from Linfield supporters published at that time allude to the fact that some were happy with having the Republic of Ireland-born players in their clubs if it meant success. One fan felt that 'I don't care if Pat Fenlon is green, white or purple with yellow dots. Once in a Linfield shirt he's blue. He is our hardest grafting midfielder. That's what counts.'[375]

When interviewed, Fenlon stated that the move 'came out of the blue' and that he had been unhappy with his career at Bohemians at that time.[376] He had been approached by Ards manager Roy Coyle, but did not want to move there. He was later contacted by Linfield scout Jim Emery and met with him and Linfield manager Trevor Anderson at Dublin Airport, 'and they just convinced me that it was the right move for me and thankfully it worked out really, really well'.[377] Fenlon, a Catholic and Glasgow Celtic fan, when asked did the fact that he would be joining a traditionally Protestant club concern him, stated that

> Yeah it played on your mind, of course. Listen, as you say, I signed in '94 and the Troubles were still on. Belfast was a difficult place for everybody at the time, but I was only interested in playing football. I am a Celtic fan, that's just what I am. I signed and, you know, I was apprehensive about it, but I have to say, and I've been on record as saying, it is the best club I've

370 Ibid. 371 Ibid. 372 Ibid. 373 Ibid. 374 Ibid. 375 Ibid. 376 Interview with Pat Fenlon, 7 Feb. 2020. 377 Ibid.

ever played for, from a football point of view and from how they looked after me, from everything. And it was a great move.[378]

The move certainly worked out. In his first season he won the Irish League and scored against Bangor in the IFA Cup final, which they won, while they also won the League Cup. He also scored in the last game of the season, the game that clinched the league against Glentoran. An ankle injury had hampered his early progress but he recalled that later in the season:

> I remember Trevor Anderson, who was the manager, taking me off in a game against Cliftonville, and the supporters had booed him for taking me off, and in fairness he said to me, 'Well that's you, sort of won over the support now'. So then I was just fortunate I went on a great run, league cup final, we won the cup, we beat the Glens on the last day, major turnaround.[379]

Like most other Dublin-born players assessed here who joined Irish League clubs, he continued to live in Dublin, but he did attend training in Belfast during the week on Tuesday and Thursday nights. For training, Fenlon would travel up to the Fairways Hotel in Dundalk to be collected by the Linfield kit man, Gary Eccles, along with his teammates Dessie Gorman and Gary Haylock. He also noted that Crusaders and Cliftonville had some players who trained in Dublin, but he preferred to train with Linfield in Belfast during the week. He added that Linfield had always ensured that they 'got up and down very easily'.[380]

For matches, the Dublin-based players at Linfield would take the train up, and get out at Newry 'because there was always the potential of a bomb scare or something from there on, so again, we'd get picked up whether we were home or away'.[381] He also recalled that 'sometimes you ended going all the way to Belfast but – it was a bit different at the time but it was really enjoyable'.[382] He noted that Linfield offered him what was a 'fantastic deal at the time, it was very difficult to turn down, so, yeah, at that time there seemed to be a bit more money around the Irish League than there was in the League of Ireland'.[383] In terms of the standard of play in both the Irish League and the League of Ireland alluded to by other players earlier, Fenlon felt that

> it would have been very close. Both leagues would have been really tight at that time in relation to the standard, because, like you said, there was a lot of players in the North going in from the south, and there was a lot of players from Scotland playing in the North at the time as well, good players. So the standard was quite good – [there were] four or five teams that were capable of winning the league. The standard in the south was strong as well, so they were two good leagues.[384]

378 Ibid.   379 Ibid.   380 Ibid.   381 Ibid.   382 Ibid.   383 Ibid.   384 Ibid.

In 1996, Fenlon returned to the League of Ireland to join Shamrock Rovers, as he had been running his own business and found it hard to keep this going while playing in Belfast.[385] Most of these players did not seek lengthy careers in the Irish League in this decade, often moving on after three or four seasons, a few notable exceptions being Robbie Lawlor and Martin Murray, who played for Crusaders from 1991 until 1998.[386] Martin Russell also played for Portadown over the same time span.[387]

In 1998, the Good Friday Agreement was signed between what were then the majority political parties in Northern Ireland, the SDLP and the Ulster Unionist Party.[388] Relations between clubs north and south of the border continue to be cordial, and the idea of an all-Ireland League has been circulated. Movement of players between the two leagues continues, although recent recessions have impacted on club finances, particularly in the Republic of Ireland in the aftermath of the Celtic Tiger, with the global recession affecting the fortunes of clubs such as Bohemians, Cork City, Shelbourne and Monaghan United.[389] Most young aspiring footballers in Ireland continue to look to England, but movement to the Irish League, and from the Irish League to the League of Ireland, is also an option. It remains to be seen if the League of Ireland and the Irish League will be able to develop a proper system of professional football that supports full-time players, but there is now much greater freedom of movement than during the dark days of the Troubles.

CONCLUSION

Since the early 1900s, players at Dublin clubs have been attracted to the prospect of a career in professional football in England and Scotland. Cross-Channel movement and the loss of players was a concern for some journalists, but deteriorating Anglo-Irish relations in the second decade of the twentieth century generally did not deter movement between Irish and British clubs.[390] As the centre of professional player production in the Republic of Ireland, some of the best Dublin footballers have reached the highest levels of the game in Britain, while a few have become successful managers abroad. A small number of Dublin-born players, including Phil Kelly and Joe Kinnear, moved to England as children before later joining English clubs.[391] For much of the twentieth century, Irish-born players were able to command places within First Division teams, although naturally there were spells of inactivity during the First and Second World Wars. However, by the 1990s, the globalization of the Premier League meant that opportunities for Dublin-born players to break into that level of soccer had lessened. Some Dublin players have looked further afield to continental Europe, with Liam Brady the most successful of these. North America has also been an option, particularly in the 1920s and

---

385 Ibid.   386 'Dundalk F.C. Who's Who: Martin Murray', dundalkfcwhoswho.com/player. php?id=373 and 'Dundalk F.C. Who's Who: Robbie Lawlor', dundalkfcwhoswho.com/player. php?id=345, both accessed 22 May 2020.   387 *BT*, 14 Aug. 1991; *DD*, 3 Sept. 1998.   388 Bartlett, *Ireland: a history*, p. 566.   389 Ibid., p. 552.   390 *Sport*, 26 Nov. 1921.   391 *Charles Buchan's Football Monthly*, 136 (Dec. 1962), p. 15; *Charles Buchan's Football Monthly*, 185 (Jan. 1967), pp 26–7.

again in the late twentieth century. Women's football migration from Ireland initially began in the 1970s, although Anne O'Brien was the exception rather than the rule in terms of those who made a career in professional soccer at the highest levels in Italy. By the latter years of the twentieth century, movement to English clubs was becoming more common, and professional football there has only become even more financially worthwhile for players in recent years.

While Dublin's League of Ireland clubs have generally failed to offer satisfactory working conditions for Irish professional footballers, with the part-time nature of the game ensuring that migration continues to be a popular career choice, settling in at English clubs for those who have negotiated the initial movement process remains difficult. Despite this, Dublin has produced many great players who have truly lit up the English game. Returning to Ireland after a full-time professional career in Britain can be a culture shock, and it takes a high level of motivation to stay in the game at a part-time level on returning home. Support has generally been informal. Seán Prunty recalled that he was encouraged by Stephen Kenny to return to playing football, for Longford Town, on leaving Middlesbrough.[392] He noted that 'it was never about money, for me, to be honest with you, it was like you know, trying to enjoy the game again, and see how I got on'.[393] Despite the insecure nature of a playing career within the professional football industry – a number of players interviewed here further confirmed this in highlighting issues with the trial process on entering British clubs and in seeking other opportunities on leaving them – England remains the dream destination for many young Dublin players.[394]

This chapter has also examined one aspect of the labour-related movement of Dublin-born players to what was effectively a war zone in the late twentieth century. It would appear that the players assessed were not overly concerned about security issues, and their talent as professional footballers generally meant that they were accepted into teams by players and supporters of their new clubs in Northern Ireland, despite varying religious backgrounds. While opposing supporters, and players, felt that they were legitimate targets for sectarian abuse, there is little evidence to suggest that any of the players interviewed were viewed as targets by paramilitary organizations. As Catholics from the Republic of Ireland who were signed by clubs in Northern Ireland, they were generally left to get on with their sporting careers. Once they had proved themselves to supporters, players and administrators, settling in at their clubs was then relatively straightforward, and as professionals, they generally focused on playing the game and did not get involved in political matters. Travelling was a burden, but the relatively concentrated spread of Irish League clubs, with Belfast the central hub, meant that a trip there from Dublin was no further, distance-wise, than going to Waterford, Limerick or Cork with a Dublin-based League of Ireland club. The main difference was that they were entering a completely different political and social environment, and this,

392 Interview with Seán Prunty, 23 Oct. 2019. **393** Ibid. **394** Ibid.; interviews with Dave Henderson, 22 Oct. 2019 and Gary Kelly, 12 Dec. 2019; and see Curran, *Irish soccer migrants*.

allied to the more overt religious background of clubs there, must have been to some extent stressful. At times, this movement was aided by the open-mindedness of Irish League managers, with Ronnie McFall a key figure in this in the late twentieth century at both Glentoran and Portadown.

While Catholic players moving from Dublin to Irish League clubs differed to Catholic players in Belfast in their religious and cultural outlook to some degree, and had not been living in a conflict zone, they were of course aware of club histories and the sectarian nature of Northern Irish society at that time. However, they probably did not have the same nationalist and religious identity as someone who had lived in that environment and had to deal with the Troubles on a daily basis. Naturally, the financial incentive was there, particularly in the early 1990s when movement to Irish League clubs increased dramatically. More research needs to be undertaken on the historical movement of players from the Irish League into the League of Ireland, but, as shown in this chapter, the financial situation of the former was stronger for much of the twentieth century. It would be interesting to know the views of Protestant players from Northern Ireland who joined League of Ireland clubs further south in the late twentieth century. In addition, the movement of players in other conflict zones in the late twentieth century still awaits a major publication. This would help put transfer developments in Northern Ireland addressed above into a wider context, and would add greatly to the historiography of sports migration and soccer in times of civil unrest.

Conclusion

This book has attempted to trace the development of soccer in Dublin from the late nineteenth century until the early twenty-first century. The game was slow to take hold in comparison with parts of Ulster, where, after the foundation of the IFA in 1880, affiliated regional bodies grew, with, for example, the County Derry Football Association being established in 1886.[1] This had grown into the North-West Football Association by the early part of the following decade, at a time when Dublin did not even have its own county association for soccer.[2] Differing growth rates were also experienced in some areas of Britain. In discussing the reasons why association football was slower to take off in Liverpool than in East Lancashire, the Midlands and South Yorkshire, John Williams has noted that 'the Liverpool area lacked the folk forms of football that had been common in East Lancashire and around Sheffield'.[3] In addition, 'because of the stark divisions between rich and poor in the city, sport could not be so easily passed down from local social elites, as had happened elsewhere'.[4] Factory Acts had less impact than in some cities such as Birmingham, 'where most men' had Saturday afternoons off from the 1870s onwards; in Liverpool this did not occur until 1890 as working conditions differed.[5] Finally, rugby was 'a powerful force in the city' and was 'jealously guarded by its local elites'. However, as soccer became popular in areas such as Burnley and Preston, which had been 'staunch rugby towns', it also began to increase in popularity in Liverpool, with a former rugby man, John McKenna, prominent in the early development of Liverpool Football Club, founded in 1892, as soccer took off there between 1878 and 1892.[6]

Some similarities can therefore be drawn with soccer's delayed development in Dublin and that of Liverpool, although it was migrants from Belfast who were more significant than rugby men in spreading the game there in the early 1890s. As shown at the beginning of this book, there is evidence that forms of folk football were played in Dublin, but not on the scale of some areas of England where this tradition was more pronounced and where it is still commemorated, albeit to a much lesser extent, through annual matches in areas such as Ashbourne.[7] The Factory Acts, which had been influential in the game's development in Belfast, had less impact in Dublin, which, like in Liverpool, slowed down the ability of many workers to engage with it.[8] Dickson has stated that 'Dublin has also had

---

1 Conor Curran, *Sport in Donegal: a history* (Dublin, 2010), p. 46. 2 Ibid. 3 Williams, *Reds: Liverpool Football Club*, p. 19. 4 Ibid. 5 Ibid., p. 21. 6 Ibid., p. 22. 7 See, for example, Hugh Hornby, *Uppies and downies: the extraordinary football games of Britain* (Swindon, 2008). 8 Garnham, *Association football and society*, p. 11.

the reputation of being a city divided to an extreme degree by class and material wealth' and while noting that 'the story is more complex', he adds that 'the
city has been the centre of social and economic innovation within Ireland, but at
times of change it has also been an economic battlefield, suffering as a result of its
metropolitan strength of vested interests working within it'.[9] Therefore there was
initially less opportunity for sport to be passed down from social elites, and this
appears to have been the case in Dublin in the 1880s as Dublin Association FC and
Dublin University AFC generally failed to do this. Rugby authorities were also
initially eager to discourage soccer from invading their sporting space, as shown in
the opening years of that decade.

As Ireland's largest urban centre, and a major Irish port, Dublin was similar in
many ways to Liverpool, and has differed in many ways to rural Ireland. However,
Gaelic football was already popular there by the late 1880s, with the result that
Dublin's soccer organizers faced an additional football code in their attempts to
secure a foothold within the city's ball games. The Parnell Split, and its effect on
GAA clubs, meant that some GAA clubs switched to soccer, although many did
not and the organization was revived later in the 1890s. The GAA's 'Ban' on its
members' involvement in 'foreign games' was detrimental to the growth of soccer in many Irish towns and villages, but there were numerous players who defied
it. Some were punished and others got away with indiscretions, but there is no
doubt soccer's development in many Irish counties was hindered by perceptions
of it as 'the garrison game'. Crossover to other sports was not uncommon, and
some have also left soccer to try their luck elsewhere, with, more recently, Marlon
Billy of Shelbourne switching to rugby league and joining Rochdale Hornets in
the mid-1990s.[10]

The GAA's grip on society was less noticeable in Dublin than in some rural
areas as a result of a bigger and more diverse mix of people, which arguably led to
more cosmopolitan and less conservative attitudes, and greater numbers to organize
a wider selection of sports. A wider choice of sporting codes was often more freely
available in cities, and societal pressure from GAA organizers – as seen in the case
of that brought on soccer-playing members of the Balla GAA club of Mayo and St
Kevin's GAA club of Castlerea (Roscommon) in the 1980s – was not as restrictive
in bigger urban areas.[11] Elements of British culture, such as association football,
and somewhat later, English pop music and anglicized television, were often more
evident in Dublin than in many regional areas, with transport and trading relations
between Ireland's capital and British ports well established by the late nineteenth
century. The visit of British clubs to Dublin, and at times international superstars
such as Kevin Keegan and Bryan Robson on promotional work, also helped whet
the appetite of Irish soccer fans for cross-Channel teams.[12] However, despite its
urban nature, Dublin has managed to retain a close-knit community atmosphere in

9 Dickson, *Dublin*, p. x.   10 Fitzpatrick, *Shelbourne cult heroes*, p. 16.   11 *Soccer Reporter* (Mar.
1984), p. 1.   12 *Soccer Reporter* (Mar. 1981), p. 7; (Jan./Feb. 1984), p. 9.

many areas, and the development of street, club and workplace teams has allowed its soccer clubs to develop despite its lack of a 'parish' feel more notable in the countryside. Liam Brady has stated that in contrast to the more heavily populated London, which a number of Irish footballers have remarked is quite an unfriendly city, 'living in Dublin means living in a community. People know you. They want to know you. In many ways you are all the same type of people.'[13] Despite this, numerous Dublin clubs have had to maintain a nomadic existence owing to issues securing playing fields, often shifting from ground to ground, with Tolka Rovers, founded in Finglas in 1922, moving around various locations until they finally officially opened their own ground and sports complex at Griffith Avenue Extension sixty years later, marking this with a match against Bohemians.[14]

As shown in Brady's case and many others, family connections and traditions have been notable among the Dublin football community, including goalkeepers Frank and Jimmy Collins.[15] Frank kept goal in the Free State's first international versus Italy at Lansdowne Road in 1926, while his nephew Jimmy had established himself as St Patrick's Athletic's first choice goalkeeper by the early 1950s having previously played for St Paul's, Bohemians and Shamrock Rovers, with whom he won the FAI Cup in 1946.[16] Much later, Mick Meagan appeared in the same team as his son Mark, as both played for Shamrock Rovers in the 1976 FAI Cup.[17] It is evident that many players have aspired to emulate the achievements of their older family members, with stories passed down from generation to generation and pride and even sibling rivalry factors in this, not to mention natural talent.

As Gary James has stated, cup success, in particular Manchester City's FA Cup win in 1904, was important in developing 'a footballing identity' within the north-western English city.[18] National cup success in the early twentieth century also assisted the popularity of the game in Dublin. Soccer there remained in a relatively stable condition after the First World War, like in Belfast, despite the movement of numerous players to participate in the war effort. Toms has noted that in Munster, 'soccer all but came to a halt' due to recruitment, with the game there having suffered a precarious start in the cities of Waterford, Cork and Limerick.[19] In Dublin, as its clubs became more proletarian in the late nineteenth and early twentieth century, the game had a broad enough social structure to survive the social dislocation of a global war, and, unlike cricket in many areas, the Irish Revolution, although the number of clubs affiliated to the Leinster Football Association at times decreased and adaptions to structures were necessary. Domestic conflicts including the Easter Rising, War of Independence and Civil War did not severely impact on soccer's progress in Dublin. Numerous soccer players were involved in Ireland's struggle for independence, but, as has been

---

13 Brady, *So far so good*, p. 19; Curran, *Irish soccer migrants*, pp 142, 157–8. 14 *Soccer Reporter* (May 1983), p. 11. 15 *II*, 21 Aug. 1953. 16 Ibid. 17 Ryan, *The official book of the FAI Cup*, p. 282. 18 James, *The emergence of footballing cultures*, p. 256. 19 Toms, *Soccer in Munster*, pp 15–16, 30–40.

shown, support among soccer players for enlistment in the British army was also notable, particularly in the First World War. After the 'split' with the IFA in 1921, Dublin's soccer authorities grew in strength through their own competitions, although governmental support was not usually forthcoming as Gaelic games were generally favoured due to their nationalist links. Despite members of the clergy becoming involved in soccer clubs, by the middle of the twentieth century the hierarchy of the Catholic church remained distant from Ireland's national soccer authorities, and their awkward attempts to influence the FAI in the latter part of that decade were not a success.

Matthew L. McDowell has noted that Scottish soccer clubs' trips to Denmark in the pre-First World War period were motivated by the exchange of technical knowledge of the game from the professional Scottish clubs to the amateur Danes, finance and the opportunity to relax.[20] Dublin clubs also benefited from the visit of British teams, and in turn their trips across the Irish Sea allowed them to experience a different football setting. This was particularly the case for many young schoolboy players, who gained experience of English football through seasonal trips and the possibility of seeing full-time professional footballers in the flesh during their stays in areas such as Liverpool added to perceptions of a career in the game. Schoolboy football in Dublin grew in strength throughout the twentieth century, despite the struggle to have soccer formally played in schools themselves. The Dublin and District Schoolboys' League claims to be the biggest in Europe and in 2010 had over 2,000 affiliated clubs and more than 16,000 registered players.[21] Since the 1880s, with the development of a special sporting press, the media have been important in the popularization of sport in Ireland, as readers were kept up to date with results, developments and the profiles of personalities such as players and administrators. In the late twentieth century, British football magazines such as *Shoot!*, *Match* and *Roy of the Rovers* were eagerly awaited each weekend by Irish youngsters in many areas.

With the attractiveness of the former First Division and English Premier League, many young footballers growing up in Dublin have dreamt of a full-time career in English professional football. Damien Duff, for example, stated in a school form that 'footballer' was his 'desired profession'.[22] Some of the Republic of Ireland's greatest players grew up in Dublin, with Johnny Giles, Liam Brady and Paul McGrath becoming household names by the late twentieth century.[23] Most Irish soccer migrants who have broken into English league football grew up in Dublin, and the League of Ireland's most successful clubs have historically been centred there.[24] Many have been willing to sacrifice other career choices for the opportunity to become a full-time player, although the rates of rejection are

---

20 Matthew L. McDowell, '"To cross the Skager Rack": discourses, images, and tourism in early "European" football: Scotland, the United Kingdom, Denmark, and Scandinavia, 1898–1914', *Soccer and Society*, 18:2–3 (2017), pp 245–69, 245. 21 *EH*, June 21, 2010. 22 Joe Miller, *Damien Duff: the biography* (London, 2007), p. 10. 23 Curran, *Irish soccer migrants*, pp 27–38. 24 Ibid.

high. Damien Richardson has stated that he was earning more money in his job at a motor company and with semi-professional club Shamrock Rovers in Dublin but chose to move to Gillingham for a smaller income in 1972.[25]

Professional soccer in Dublin has generally been undertaken on a part-time basis, and the game in the city has been dominated by a small number of clubs in that regard. At times the domestic transfer market has looked like a merry-go-round of movement between these teams. However, according to Seán Fitzpatrick, only a few footballers have played for Dublin's 'big four' of Shelbourne, Shamrock Rovers, St Patrick's Athletic and Bohemians, these being Mark Rutherford, Trevor Molloy, Pat Fenlon and Dave Campbell.[26] Some players have sought higher wages in Belfast, with this trend occurring intermittently since the early 1900s and continuing after partition. In general, however, those seeking full-time careers in professional football have travelled to Britain, with Dublin's close proximity and tradition of semi-professional soccer, coaching and schoolboy structures ensuring that most migrants who do break into English league football have been native to the east-coast city. In the late twentieth century, the movement of female players to clubs such as Arsenal began, although a few talented players such as Anne O'Brien had secured contracts at clubs in France and Italy. Women's soccer has finally begun to receive the support of the FAI, although this was not always the case, as shown earlier. Post-playing careers have not been adequately catered for within the game. While much has been written about mental health in sport in the early twenty-first century, studies of female players' retirement have been particularly scarce. Olivia O'Toole recalled that a number of her teammates had struggled with this, while she also suffered:

> The camaraderie with your teammates, the laughs, the banter, everything is gone, just like that. And it's hard. It is hard because, like, I sat down and I looked at it and I went, 'Jesus, did people just like me because I played for Ireland?' You know what I mean? And I know exactly where Gary Speed is coming from.[27] I know it's like nobody knows what happened, but a footballer does goes through depression. Well, I did. I missed everything. I missed training, and I was depressed for a long time when I retired. I didn't know what to do. You either have it in coaching or you haven't got it in coaching. I'm coaching now at the moment so it works, but you don't know.[28]

A failure to deal with racism within soccer in Ireland also remains an issue. A number of Dublin clubs have begun to take on a more international look, fielding players with African and Eastern European backgrounds, reflecting the changing demography of Dublin society. By 2002, Dublin's population had risen to just over

---

25 Ibid., pp 285–6.   **26** Fitzpatrick, *Shelbourne cult heroes*, p. 35.   **27** This is a reference to the former Welsh international who died, apparently by suicide, in 2011.   **28** Interview with Olivia O'Toole, 16 Apr. 2020.

1 million, a growth of over 5 per cent from the 1996 total of slightly over 950,000, with the city the centre of the Celtic Tiger economy.[29]

As demonstrated in this book, soccer has played a highly significant role in the lives of many Dubliners, whether as players, managers, coaches, club organizers or supporters. Dublin will again host the Europa League final in 2024, having previously hosted the event in 2011, with FAI CEO Jonathan Hill noting the economic benefit this would bring to the city.[30] With the Aviva Stadium, opened in 2010 in Ballsbridge, replacing the demolished Lansdowne Road as the primary venue for international soccer and rugby matches in the early twenty-first century, Dublin now has a modern venue for the hosting of matches in both these codes at the highest levels.[31] Relations between the GAA and the FAI still remain tentative, despite the former's opening of Croke Park to international soccer and rugby matches for a brief spell in the opening decade of the twenty-first century when the Aviva Stadium was being constructed.[32] It was the rugby team's victory there over England in 2007 that has become etched into recent popular memory, given the historic links with Bloody Sunday, and to a lesser degree, as the Republic of Ireland were enduring an uninspiring time under manager Steve Staunton. Their first match at the GAA venue, a one–nil win over Wales, was an unremarkable event for many fans and at least one player.[33] More recently, the future of two of Dublin's historic soccer landmarks, Dalymount Park and Tolka Park, looks to have been put on a more secure footing.[34] It remains to be seen whether either will ever again draw the interest of supporters as witnessed in the 1950s – it appears highly unlikely – but the maintenance of both as venues of soccer will at least help to ensure two of Dublin's spiritual homes of association football are preserved in some physical form for future generations of Dublin's soccer people and the communities in which they are located.

29 *IE*, 4 July 2003. 30 *IT*, 16 July 2021. 31 *IT*, 13 May 2010. 32 *IE*, 23 Mar. 2017. 33 Ibid. 34 *II*, 18 Feb. 2022.

Bibliography

PRIMARY SOURCES

Archbishop McQuaid Papers (Dublin Diocesan Archives, Drumcondra)
Communists – XXIII.
Government – XVIII.
Parishes – LIV.
Trade Unions – XXII.
Youth Affairs – XXVIII.

English Football League Archives, Preston
Charles Buchan's Football Monthly (1951–74)
Shoot! (1969–72)

Football Association of Ireland Archives (University College Dublin)
P/137/16, Minute Book of the Emergency Committee, Senior Clubs Disciplinary Committee,
    Phoenix Park and Sundry Committees, 1962–76.
P/137/17, Minute Book of the Coaching and Development, Appeals, Referees and Disciplinary
    Committees, 1976–82.
P137/24, Minute Book of the Senior Council, 1976–89.
P137/29, Junior Emergency Committee Minute Book, 1940–5.
P137/31, Junior Committee Minutes, 1949–54.

Gaelic Athletic Association Archives (Croke Park)
GAA/CC/01/02 1911–25, Central Council Minute Books 1899–1981.

Irish Football Association Archives (Public Record Office of Northern Ireland)
D/4196, Irish Football Association Papers.
D/4196/A1, Minute Book of the IFA, 1898–1902.
D/4196/A3, Minute book of the IFA, 1909–28.
D/4/196/5/1, Cash Book of the IFA, 1880–97.
D/4511, Irish Football League Papers.

Leinster Football Association Archives (University College Dublin)
P239/21–35, Senior League Council Minutes.
P239/36–41, Emergency Committee Meeting Minutes.
P239/60–70, LFA Committee Meetings Minutes
P239/77, Officers and Council Book, 1916–17 to 1921–2.

National Archives of Ireland, Bishop Street
Department of Foreign Affairs

2/35/123, Invitation to football match between Bohemians and Continental team Sports Club Saaz (1934).

5/305/298, Visit of Yugoslavia soccer team to Ireland. October 1955.

5/305/345, Visit of Romanian football team to Ireland. October 1957.

6/410/260, Enquiry re tickets for football cup final at Wembley (1957).

2001/43/366, Football match in Lisbon between Shelbourne and Lisbon Sporting Club (1962).

2001/43/367, Football match – Drumcondra v. Munich. Complaint regarding overcharging of members of Drumcondra Football Club in a nightclub in Munich (1962).

Department of Justice

90/5/42, An Garda Síochána claim against Brideville Association Club for services rendered (1934–5).

90/5/45, An Garda Síochána: Gardaí services requisitioned. Dolphin AFC Limited (1937).

90/71/16, Football and sports fields. Suggestion that legislation should be introduced providing for public safety precautions.

Schoolboys' Football Association of Ireland.

2007/125/62 (1975–7).

National Library of Ireland – Directories and contemporary works of reference
Association football official handbook and fixture list 1945–46 and '47 authorized by the FAI and Football League of Ireland (Dublin, 1946).

Drumcondra Football Club Limited official programme versus Shelbourne, 24 Dec. 1961 (Dublin, 1961).

Intermediate Education Board for Ireland: reports of inspectors 1909–10, i: *From No. 1 to No. 81* (Dublin, 1910).

Irish Soccer, 1:1–16 (1955).

Soccer Magazine (1984–96).

Soccer Reporter (1975–84).

Thom's Official Directory of the United Kingdom of Great Britain and Ireland for the Year 1883 (Dublin, 1883).

Newspapers

Anglo-Celt
Athletic News
Ballina Herald
Ballymena Observer
Belfast Evening Telegraph
Belfast Newsletter
Berkshire Chronicle
Boston Globe
Bray People
City Tribune
Connacht Sentinel
Connacht Tribune
Daily Express

Daily News
Derry Journal
Donegal Democrat
Donegal News
Drogheda Conservative
Drogheda Independent
Dublin Daily Express
Dublin Daily Nation
Dublin Evening Mail
Dublin Evening Telegraph
Dundalk Democrat
Dundee Courier
Empire News

Evening Echo
Evening Herald
Evening Press
Fermanagh Herald
Fermanagh Mail
Fingal Independent
Football Sports Weekly
Freeman's Journal
Ireland's Saturday Night
Irish Daily Independent
Irish Examiner
Irish Farmers Journal
Irish Independent
Irish News and Belfast Morning News
Irish Post
Irish Press
Irish Times
Kilkenny People
Lancashire Evening Post
Leinster Reporter
Leitrim Observer
Limerick Chronicle
Liverpool Daily Post
Liverpool Evening Express
Londonderry Sentinel
Longford Journal

Longford Leader
Manchester Courier and Lancashire General Advertiser
Midland Counties Advertiser
Munster Express
New Ross Standard
Northern Whig
Northern Whig and Belfast Post
Scottish Referee
Sligo Champion
Sport
Strabane Chronicle
Sunday Independent
Sunday Times
Sunday Tribune
The Economist
The Field: The Country Gentleman's Newspaper
The Guardian
The Nationalist
The Sporting Life
The Sportsman
Ulster Football and Cycling News
Waterford Standard
Waterford News and Star
Wicklow Newsletter and County Advertiser

Player interviews

Bennion, Chris, 21 Oct. 2019.
Buckley, Liam, 24 Mar. 2020.
Byrne, Paul, 26 Feb. 2020.
Coady, John, 22 Jan. 2020.
Darby, Chloe, 7 Apr. 2020.
Deans, Chris, 15 Nov. 2019.
Fenlon, Pat, 7 Feb. 2020.
Finn, Jamie, 9 May 2020.
Girvan, Alf, 27 Jan. 2020.
Heapes, Susan, 28 Feb. 2020.
Henderson, Dave, 22 Oct. 2019.
Kelly, Gary, 12 Dec. 2019.

Kelly, Seamus, 2 Oct. 2019.
Lawlor, Mick, 29 Feb. 2020.
Meagan, Mick, 30 Sept. 2019.
McCue, Harry, 10 Dec. 2019.
McGuinness, Stephen, 22 Oct. 2019.
Mulligan, Paddy, 4 Oct. 2019.
O'Connor, Turlough, 10 Oct. 2019.
O'Neill, Frank, 30 Jan. 2020.
O'Shea, Brian, 21 Nov. 2019.
O'Toole, Olivia, 16 Apr. 2020.
Prunty, Seán, 23 Oct. 2019.
Supple, Shane, 24 Sept. 2019.

Supporter interviews

Clarke, Ryan, 6 May 2020.
Farrell, Gerry, 3 Apr. 2020.
Keane, Mark, 9 May 2020.

Looney, Dermot, 31 May 2020.
White, Gavin, 5 May 2020.

Trinity College Dublin Archives
MUN/CLUB/DUCAC/59–62, Dublin University Association Football Club Reports, 1951–5.

ONLINE PRIMARY SOURCES

British Pathé Historical Collection
(From britishpathe.com, accessed 2 Jan. 2022)

'French Footballers 1923'.
'Football–Dalymount'.
'One Goal Each'.

Census of Ireland 1901/11
(From census.nationalarchives.ie)

'Residents of a house 51 in Arranmore Terrace (Inns Quay, Dublin)', accessed 17 Mar. 2022.
'Residents of a house 13.1 in Bath Avenue Place (Pembroke West, Dublin)', accessed 17 Mar. 2022.
'Residents of a house 44 in Carlingford Rd. (40 to End.) (Glasnevin, Dublin)', accessed 17 Mar. 2022.
'Residents of a house 7.7 in Gardiner Street, Lower (Mountjoy, Dublin)', accessed 2 Jan. 2022.
'Residents of a house 20 in Glenageary Road, Upper (Kingstown No. 4, Dublin)', accessed 7 Apr. 2020.
'Residents of a house 37.4 in Lr. Gloucester St. (Mountjoy, Dublin)', accessed 17 Mar. 2022.
'Residents of a house 1 in Harcourt Lane (Fitzwilliam, Dublin)', accessed 17 Mar. 2022.
'Residents of a house 18.1 in High Street (Part) (Merchants Quay, Dublin)', accessed 2 Jan. 2022.
'Residents of a house 87 in Innisfallen Parade (Inns Quay, Dublin)', accessed 17 Mar. 2022.
'Residents of a house 176.2 in New Grove Avenue (Pembroke East & Donnybrook, Dublin)', accessed 17 Mar. 2022.
'Residents of a house 239 in Pembroke Cottages Ringsend (Pembroke East & Donnybrook, Dublin)', accessed 17 Mar. 2022.
'Residents of a house 74 in Seville Place (North Dock, Dublin)', accessed 17 Mar. 2022.
'Residents of a house 11 in Simmonscourt, (Donnybrook, Dublin)', accessed 7 Apr. 2020.
'Residents of a house 2 in Valleymount (Ushers Quay, Dublin)', accessed 17 Mar. 2022.

Dáil debates
(From oireachtas.ie, accessed 8 Apr. 2022)

'Ceisteanna – Questions. Oral Answers. – Phoenix Park Amenities', Tuesday 7 May 1974, vol. 272, no. 6.
'Ceisteanna – Questions. – Departmental Correspondence', Wednesday 25 Oct. 2000, vol. 524, no. 6.
'Finance Bill 1932–Committee (Resumed)', Thursday 7 July 1932, vol. 43, no. 3.
'Select Committee on Enterprise and Economic Strategy Debate', Tuesday, 17 Dec. 1996'.

Everton Football Club Online Archives
(From evertoncollection.org.uk, accessed 11 June 2018, unless noted otherwise)

Everton Football Club Minute Book, 6 Apr. 1891–27, June 1892, Everton Fixtures 1890–1, League Team.

Everton Football Club Minute Book, 14 Dec. 1909–28, Mar. 1911, Meeting of Directors Held at Goodison Park on 10 April 1910, p. 91.

Everton Football Club Minute Book, 4 Apr. 1911–26 Nov. 1912, Meeting of Directors Held at Goodison Park, 13 Feb. 1912, p. 162.

Everton Football Club Minute Book, 29 Nov. 1912–4 May 1914, Meeting of the Directors Held at Goodison Park, 15 Oct. 1913, pp 173–4.

Everton Football Club Minute Book, 4 Feb. 1919–15 Feb. 1921, Meeting of Directors Held at the Bradford Hotel, Liverpool, on 25 Feb. 1919, p. 9.

Everton Football Club Minute Book, 11 Dec. 1924–11 Jan. 1927, Meeting of Directors Held at Exchange Station Hotel on Tuesday 10 Nov. 1925, p. 137.

Everton Football Club Minute Book, 25 Jan. 1927–15 Mar. 1929, Meeting of Directors Held at Exchange Station Hotel on Tuesday 13 Mar. 1928, p. 80.

Everton Football Club Minute Book, 19 Mar. 1929–7 Apr. 1931, Meeting of Directors Held at Exchange Station Hotel, Tuesday 30 Sept. 1930, p. 231.

Everton Football Club Minute Book, 1 Apr. 1947–11 Oct. 1950, Meeting Held at Exchange Hotel, Liverpool, 26 May 1949.

Everton Football Club Minute Book, 17 Oct. 1950–19 Oct. 1953, Meeting Held in Exchange Hotel Liverpool, 4 Mar. 1952, p. 149.

Everton Football Club Minute Book, 17 Oct. 1950–19 Oct. 1953, Meeting Held at Exchange Hotel, 28 Apr. 1953, p. 257.

Everton Football Club Minute Book, 27 Oct. 1953–30 Oct. 1956, Meeting Held at Exchange Hotel, 4 May 1954, p. 55.

'Honours', evertonfc.com/honours, accessed 3 Jan. 2017.

Liverpool Football Club Online Archives
(From lfchistory.net, accessed 29 Dec. 2017)

'Games for the 1903–1904 Season'
'Games for the 1910–1911 Season'
'Games for the 1962–1963 Season'
'Games for the 1980–81 Season'
'Games for the 1981–82 Season'
'Games for the 1982–1983 Season'
'Games for the 1991–1992 Season'
'Games for the 1992–1993 Season'

'Games for the 1993–1994 Season'
'Games for the 1994–1995 Season'
'Games for the 1995–1996 Season'
'Games for the 1996–1997 Season'
'Games for the 1997–1998 Season'
'Games for the 1998–1999 Season'
'Games for the 1999–2000 Season'
'Games for the 2001–2002 Season'

Military Archives
Military Archives. Bureau of Military History 1913–21, militaryarchives.ie

National Folklore Collection
(From duchas.ie, accessed 2 Aug. 2020)

'School: Mulhuddart (roll number 16675)', Schools' Collection, vol. 0790, p. 102.
'School: Swords (roll number 7339)', Schools' Collection, vol. 0788, p. 125.

SECONDARY SOURCES

Bardon, Jonathan, *A history of Ulster* [updated edition] (Belfast, 2005).

——, *A narrow sea: the Irish-Scottish connection in 120 episodes* (Dublin, 2018).

Bartlett, Thomas, *Ireland: a history* (Cambridge, 2010).

Beal, Richard & Steve Emms, *Scottish League players' records: Division One, 1946/47 to 1974/75* (Nottingham, 2004).

Bolsmann, Chris & Dilwyn Porter, *English gentlemen and world soccer: Corinthians, amateurism and the global game* (Abingdon, 2018).

Boyce, D. George, *Nineteenth-century Ireland: the search for stability* [Revised edition] (Dublin, 2005).

Brady, Liam, *So far so good: a decade in football* (London, 1980).

Briggs, George & Joe Dodd, *100 years of the LFA Leinster Football Association: centenary year-book, 1892–1992* (Dublin, 1993).

Brodie, Malcolm, *100 years of Irish football* (Belfast, 1980).

Brown, Terence, *Ireland: a social and cultural history, 1922–2002* (London, 2004).

Browne, Daniel, 'Linfield's "Hawk of Peace": pre-ceasefires reconciliation in Irish League football' in Curran & Toms (eds), *New perspectives on association football in Irish history*, pp 81–94.

Byrne, Helena, 'How it all began: the story of women's soccer in sixties Drogheda' in Curran & Toms (eds), *New perspectives on association football in Irish history*, pp 110–31.

——, 'Women's soccer in the Republic of Ireland', unpublished PowerPoint presentation, 2021.

Byrne, Peter, *Green is the colour: the story of Irish football* (London, 2012).

Campbell, Paul Ian, *Education, retirement and career transition for 'black' ex-professional footballers: from being idolized to stacking shelves* (Bingley, 2020).

Caprani, Vincent (ed.), *Liffey Wanderers centenary year, 1885–1995* (Dublin, 1985).

Clenet, Julien, 'Association football in Dublin in the late nineteenth century: an overview' in Conor Curran (ed.), 'The growth and development of soccer in Dublin', Special edition of *Soccer & Society*, 22:8 (2021), pp 805–19.

Collins, Tony, *A social history of English rugby union* (Abingdon, 2009).

——, *How football began: a global history of how the world's football codes were born* (Abingdon, 2019).

Comerford, R.V., *Ireland: inventing the nation* (London, 2003).

Creedon, Seán, 'Previous meetings' in *Ireland Olympic XI versus Liverpool official programme* (Dublin, 1987), p. 14.

Cronin, Mike, 'The Lansdowne Road riot of 1995: Ireland, the English far right and the media' in Neil O'Boyle & Marcus Free (eds), *Sport, the media and Ireland: interdisciplinary perspectives* (Cork, 2020), pp 75–92.

Cronin, Mike, Mark Duncan & Paul Rouse, *The GAA: county by county* (Cork, 2011).

Cronin, Mike & Roisin Higgins, *Places we play: Ireland's sporting heritage* (Cork, 2011).

Curran, Conor, *Sport in Donegal: a history* (Dublin, 2010).

——, 'Networking structures and competitive association football in Ulster, 1880–1914', *Irish Economic and Social History*, 41 (2014), pp 74–92.

——, *The development of sport in Donegal, 1880–1935* (Cork, 2015).

——, 'The social background of Ireland's pre-World War I association football clubs, players and administrators: the case of South and West Ulster', *International Journal of the History of Sport*, 33:16 (2016), pp 1982–2005.

——, *Irish soccer migrants: a social and cultural history* (Cork, 2017).

—, '"Ireland's second capital"? Irish footballers' migration to Liverpool, the growth of supporters' clubs and the organization of Liverpool Football Club matches in Dublin: an
historical assessment', *Immigrants and Minorities*, 36:3 (2018), pp 258–86.

—, 'The role of the provincial press in the development of association football in pre-First
World War Ulster: the cases of Donegal, Fermanagh and Cavan' in Ian Kenneally & James T.
O'Donnell (eds), *The Irish regional press, 1892–2018: revival, revolution and republic* (Dublin,
2018), pp 53–64.

—, '"Unscrupulous adventurers who are domiciled in 'the land of the almighty dollar'"'?: the
migration of Irish born soccer players to the American Soccer League, 1921–31', *Journal of
Sports History*, 45:3 (Fall 2018), pp 313–33.

—, '"It has almost been an underground movement": the development of grassroots football in
regional Ireland: the case of County Donegal, 1971–1996' in Jürgen Mittag, Kristian Naglo &
Dilwyn Porter (eds), 'Small worlds: football at the grassroots in Europe', Special issue of *Moving
the Social: Journal of Social History and the History of Social Movements*, 61 (2019), pp 33–60.

—, 'From Ardara Emeralds to Ardara FC: soccer in Ardara, 1891–1995' in Gary James (ed.),
'International football history: selected submissions from the 2017 & 2018 conferences',
Special edition of *Soccer and Society*, 21:4 (2020), pp 433–47.

—, 'Republic of Ireland-born football migrants and university access, 1945–2010', *Irish
Educational Studies*, 39:1 (2020), pp 65–82.

—, 'The cross-border movement of Republic of Ireland-born footballers to Northern Ireland
clubs, 1922–2000' in Curran (ed.), 'The growth and development of soccer in Dublin',
Special edition of *Soccer and Society*, 22:8 (2021), pp 858–72.

— (ed.), 'The growth and development of soccer in Dublin', Special issue of *Soccer and Society*,
22:8 (2021), pp 799–804.

—, 'The migration of Irish-born players to undertake US soccer scholarships, 1969–2000' in
Conor Curran and Conor Heffernan (eds), 'Sport and Irish migration: new perspectives on its
history and development', Special edition of *Immigrants & Minorities* 39:1 (2021), pp 101–31.

—, 'The playing and working conditions of League of Ireland footballers in a part-time
Euro 2021 host nation: the Republic of Ireland's League of Ireland' in 'The EURO cup
and European football: some critical reflections', Special edition of *Soccer and Society*, 22:4
(2021), pp 343–54.

—, *Physical education in Irish schools, 1900–2000: a history* (Oxford, 2022).

— & David Toms, 'Introduction' in Curran & Toms (eds), *New perspectives on association football in Irish history*, pp 1–9.

— & David Toms, *New perspectives on association football in Irish history: going beyond the 'garrison game'* (Abingdon, 2018).

— & Seamus, Kelly, 'Returning home: the return of Irish-born football migrants to Ireland's
football leagues and their cultural re-adaption, 1945–2010' in *Irish Studies Review*, 26:2
(2018), pp 181–98.

Delaney, Enda, *Irish emigration since 1921* (Dundalk, 2002).

—, *The Irish in post-War Britain* [paperback edition] (Oxford, 2013).

Dickson, David, *Dublin: the making of a capital city* (London, 2014).

Dodd, Joe, *Soccer in the Boro' year book* (Blackrock, 1990).

—, *100 years: a history: Leinster Senior League centenary, 1896/7–1996/7* (Dublin, 1997).

Doolan, Paul & Robert Goggins, *The Hoops: a history of Shamrock Rovers* (Dublin, 1993).

Dunphy, Eamon, *The rocky road* (Dublin, 2013).

Edwards, Gary, *Every cloud: the story of how Leeds City became Leeds United* (Chichester, 2019).

Emms, Steve & Richard Wells, *Scottish League players' records: Division One, 1890–91 to 1938–39* (Nottingham, 2007).

Falkiner, Keith, *Emerald Anfield: the Irish and Liverpool FC* (Dublin, 2010).

Farragher, Seán P. & Annraoi Wyer, *Blackrock College, 1860–1995* (Dublin, 1995).

Farrell, Gerard, 'One-way traffic? – 100 years of soldiers, mercenaries, refugees and other footballing migrants in the League of Ireland, 1920–2020' in Curran (ed.), 'The growth and development of soccer in Dublin', Special edition of *Soccer and Society*, 22:8 (2021), pp 873–86.

Ferriter, Diarmaid, *Ambiguous republic: Ireland in the 1970s* [paperback edition] (London, 2013).

——, 'Social life and the GAA in a time of upheaval in Ireland: a retrospect' in Gearóid Ó Tuathaigh (ed.), *The GAA & revolution in Ireland, 1913–1923* (Cork, 2015), pp 251–60.

Fitzpatrick, David, 'Militarism in Ireland, 1900–1922' in Thomas Bartlett & Keith Jeffery (eds), *A military history of Ireland* (Cambridge, 1996), pp 379–406.

Fitzpatrick, Seán, *Shelbourne cult heroes* (Dublin, 2010).

Foley, Michael, *The bloodied field: Croke Park, Sunday 21 November 1921* (Dublin, 2014).

Friedman, Michael T. & Jacob J. Bustad, 'Sport and urbanization' in Robert Edelman & Wayne Wilson (eds), *The Oxford handbook of sports history* (Oxford, 2017), pp 145–58.

Garnham, Neal, *Association football and society in pre-partition Ireland* (Belfast, 2004).

——, 'Ein spiel in zwei nationen? fussball in Irland, 1918–1939' in Christian Koller & Fabian Brändle (eds), *Fussball zwischen den kriegen: Europa 1918–1939* (Zurich, 2010), pp 65–85.

Giles, John, *A football man: the autobiography* (Dublin, 2010).

Gillespie, Simon & Roddy Hegarty, 'Caman and crozier: the Catholic church and the GAA, 1884–1902' in Dónal McAnallen, David Hassan & Roddy Hegarty (eds), *The evolution of the GAA: Ulaidh, Éire agus eile* (Armagh, 2009), pp 112–22.

Goldblatt, David, *The ball is round: a global history of Football* (London, 2006).

Grayson, Richard, *Dublin's great wars: the First World War, the Easter Rising and the Irish Revolution* (Cambridge, 2018).

Griffin, Brian, *Cycling in Victorian Ireland* (Dublin, 2006).

Gunning, Paul, 'Association football in the Shamrock Shire's Hy Brasil: the "socker" code in Connacht, 1879–1906' in Curran & Toms (eds), *New perspectives on association football in Irish history*, pp 10–32.

Hand, Eoin, *First hand: my life and Irish football* (Cork, 2017).

Heffernan, Conor & Joseph Taylor, 'A league is born: the League of Ireland's inaugural season, 1921–1922' in Curran (ed.), 'The growth and development of soccer in Dublin', Special issue of *Soccer and Society*, pp 845–57.

Herbert, Ian, *Quiet genius: Bob Paisley, British football's greatest manager* (London, 2018).

Hornby, Hugh, *Uppies and downies: the extraordinary football games of Britain* (Swindon, 2008).

Hugman, Barry (ed.), *The PFA Premier and Football League players' records, 1946–2005* (Harpenden, 2005).

Hunt, Tom, *Sport and society in Victorian Ireland: the case of Westmeath* (Cork, 2007).

——, 'Harry Cannon: a unique Irish sportsman and administrator' in Curran & Toms (eds), *New perspectives on association football*, pp 95–109.

——, *The little book of Irish athletics* (Dublin, 2018).

——, 'Ireland's footballers at the 1924 and 1948 Olympic Games: compromised by the politics of sport' in Curran (ed.), 'The growth and development of soccer in Dublin', Special issue of *Soccer and Society*, 22:8 (2021), pp 887–900.

Jack, Max, 'On the terrace: ritual performance of identity and conflict by the Shamrock Rovers Football Club ultras in Dublin', *Ethnomusicology Review*, 18 (Los Angeles, 2013), pp 94–9.

James, Gary, *The emergence of footballing cultures: Manchester, 1840–1919* (Manchester, 2019).

Jose, Colin, *North American Soccer League encyclopaedia* (Haworth, 2003).

Joyce, Michael, *Football League players' records 1888 to 1939* (Nottingham, 2012).

Kavanagh, Barney, 'All these years ago' in Pauline Seymour (ed.), *Dalkey United AFC golden jubilee, 1953–2003* (Dublin, 2003), pp 17–19.

Keane, Paul, *Gods vs mortals: Irish clubs in Europe ... a front row seat at ten of the greatest games* (Kells, 2010).

Kearns, Kevin C., *The bombing of Dublin's North Strand: the untold story* [paperback edition] (Dublin, 2010).

Kelly, James, *Sport in Ireland, 1600–1840* (Dublin, 2014).

Kennedy, Brian, *Just follow the floodlights! The complete guide to League of Ireland football* (Dublin, 2011).

Kennedy, David, 'Red and blue and orange and green', *Soccer and Society*, 12:4 (2011), pp 552–64.

Keogh, Dermot, *Twentieth-century Ireland: revolution and state building* [revised edition] (Dublin, 2005).

Kermode, Jenny, Janet Hollinshead & Malcolm Gratton, 'Small beginnings: Liverpool, 1207–1680' in John Belchem (ed.), *Liverpool 800: culture, character and history* (Liverpool, 2006), pp 59–112.

Kielty, Michael, 'Peter J. Peel: the soccer king' in Curran (ed.), 'The growth and development of soccer in Dublin', Special issue of *Soccer and Society*, pp 901–18.

Killeen, Richard, *Historical atlas of Dublin* (Dublin, 2009).

Kinsella, Eoin, 'Football and hurling in early modern Ireland' in Mike Cronin, William Murphy & Paul Rouse (eds), *The Gaelic Athletic Association, 1884–2009* (Dublin, 2009), pp 15–31.

Lanfranchi, Pierre & Matthew Taylor, *Moving with the ball: the migration of professional footballers* (Oxford, 2001).

———, Christiane Eisenberg, Tony Mason & Alfred Wahl, *100 years of football: the FIFA centennial book* (London, 2004).

Langan, David (with Trevor Keane & Alan Conway), *Running through walls* (Derby, 2012).

'Liverpool clubs in the Republic' in *Ireland Olympic XI versus Liverpool, official programme*, 19 Aug. 1987 (Dublin, 1987), p. 22.

Lynch, Con, 'Football/GAA in St Joseph's' in *St Joseph's School for Deaf Boys Cabra, 1857–2007* (Dublin, 2007), pp 37–8.

Mason, Tony, *Association football and English society, 1863–1915* (Brighton, 1980).

Mauro, Max, *Youth sport, migration and culture: two football teams and the changing face of Ireland* (London & New York, 2018).

McCartney, Donal, *The history of University College, Dublin* (Dublin, 1999).

McCue, Ken, 'Who's SARI now: social enterprise and the use of the medium of sport to further human rights in society' in Curran (ed.), 'The growth and development of soccer in Dublin', Special issue of *Soccer and Society*, pp 919–33.

McDowell, Matthew L., '"To cross the Skager Rack": discourses, images, and tourism in early "European" football: Scotland, the United Kingdom, Denmark, and Scandinavia, 1898–1914', *Soccer and Society*, 18:2–3 (2017), pp 245–69.

McElligott, Richard, '"Boys indifferent to the manly sports of their race": nationalism and children's sport in Ireland, 1880–1920' in Brian Griffin & John Strachan (eds), 'Sport in Ireland from the 1880s to the 1920s', Special edition of *Irish Studies Review*, 27:3 (2019), pp 344–61.

McGauley, Patrick (ed.), *The New Link*, 93 (Dublin, 2011).

McGrath, Paul, *Back from the brink: the autobiography* (London, 2007).

McKittrick, David & David McVea, *Making sense of the Troubles: a history of the Northern Ireland conflict* (London, 2012).

McManus, Ruth, *Dublin, 1910–1940: shaping the city and suburbs* (Dublin, 2006).

_____ & Lisa Marie Griffith (eds), *Leaders of the city: Dublin's first citizens, 1500–1950* (Dublin, 2013).

McMillan, Norman & Douglas (eds), *A history of soccer in County Carlow* (Dublin, 1984).

Mellor, Gavin, 'The genesis of Manchester United as a national and international "super-club", 1958–68', *Soccer and Society*, 1:2 (2000), pp 151–66.

Menton, Brendan, *Home Farm: the story of a Dublin football club, 1928–1998* (Dublin, 1999).

Miller, Joe, *Damien Duff: the biography* (London, 2007).

Moore, Cormac, *The GAA v Douglas Hyde: the removal of Ireland's first president as GAA patron* (Cork, 2012).

_____, *The Irish soccer split* (Cork, 2015).

_____, *Birth of the border: the impact of partition in Ireland* (Kildare, 2019).

Moore, Martin, 'The origins of association football in Belfast: a reappraisal', *Sport in History*, 37:4 (2017), pp 505–28.

_____, 'Early association football in Ireland: embryonic diffusion outside Ulster, 1877–1882', *Sport in History* 42:1 (2022), pp 24–48.

Murden, Jon, 'City of change and challenge: Liverpool since 1945' in John Belchem (ed.), *Liverpool 800: culture, character and history* (Liverpool, 2006), pp 393–45.

O'Brien, Owen (ed.), *The Skerries soccer story: a celebration of soccer, 1932–2007* (Skerries, 2007).

Ó Caithnia, Liam P., *Báirí cos in Éirinn (roimh bhunú na ncumann eagraithe)* (Dublin, 1984).

O'Carroll, Aileen & Don Bennett, *The Dublin docker: working lives of Dublin's deep sea port* (Newbridge, 2017).

O'Carroll, Ross, 'The GAA and the First World War, 1914–18' in Gearóid Ó Tuathaigh, *The GAA & revolution in Ireland, 1913–1923* (Cork, 2015), pp 85–104.

O'Mahony, E.J. (ed.), *Bohemian Football Club golden jubilee souvenir* (Dublin, 1945).

Ó Maonaigh, Aaron, 'Who were the Shoneens?': Irish militant nationalists and association football, 1913–1923' in Curran & Toms, *New perspectives on association football in Irish history*, pp 33–49.

_____, '"In the Ráth Camp, rugby or soccer would not have been tolerated by the prisoners": Irish Civil War attitudes to sport, 1922–3' in Curran (ed.), 'The growth and development of soccer in Dublin', Special edition of *Soccer & Society*, 22:8 (2021), pp 834–44.

O'Neill, Eddie, *Broadstone United FC, 1947–1997* (Dublin, 1997).

Porter, Dilwyn, 'Whistling his way to Wembley: Percy Harper of Stourbridge, cup final referee', *Sport in History*, 35:2 (2015), pp 217–40.

Power, Brendan, 'The functions of association football in the Boys' Brigade in Ireland, 1888–1914' in Leann Lane & William Murphy (eds), *Leisure and the Irish in the nineteenth century* (Liverpool, 2016), pp 41–58.

Quinn, Niall, *The autobiography* [paperback edition] (London, 2003).

Rathbone, Keith, *Sport and physical culture in occupied France: authoritarianism, agency and everyday life* (Manchester, 2022).

Reid, Tony, *Bohemian AFC official club history, 1890–1976* (Dublin, 1977).

Rice, Eoghan, *We are Rovers: an oral history of Shamrock Rovers FC* (Gloucestershire, 2005).

Roberts, Geoffrey, 'Neutrality, identity and the challenge of the Irish Volunteers' in Dermot Keogh & Mervyn O'Driscoll (eds), *Ireland in World War Two: neutrality and survival* (Cork, 2004), pp 274–84.

Rouse, Paul, *Sport in Ireland: a history* (Oxford, 2015).

Russell, Dave, *Football and the English* (Preston, 1997).

Ryan, Seán, *The official book of the FAI Cup* (Dublin, 2011).

Sands, Christopher, *Shels: a grand old team to know* (Dublin, 2016).

Shelbourne Football Club golden jubilee, 1895–1945 (Dublin, 1945).

Sherlock, Jason, *Jayo: my autobiography* (London, 2018).

Soar, Phil, Martin Tyler & Richard Widdows, *The Hamlyn encyclopaedia of football* (London, 1980).

Sleigh, Andrew, *Robbie Keane: the biography* (London, 2007).

Stapleton, Frank, *Frankly speaking* (Dublin, 1991).

Taylor, Matthew, *The leaguers: the making of professional football in England, 1900–1939* (Liverpool, 2005).

———, *The association game: a history of British football* (Harlow, 2008).

———, 'The global spread of football' in Robert Edleman & Wayne Wilson (eds), *The Oxford handbook of sports history* (Oxford, 2017), pp 183–95.

The Malcolm Brodie Northern Ireland soccer yearbook, '14–15 (Belfast, 2014).

This is Anfield: official matchday programme: Liverpool FC v Athletic Club Bilbao (Liverpool, 2017).

Toms, David, '"Darling of the Gods": Tom Farquharson, Irish footballing migrant', *Soccer and Society*, 16:5 (2015), pp 508–20.

———, *Soccer in Munster: a social history* (Cork, 2015).

Tynan, Mark, '"Inciting the roughs of the crowd": soccer hooliganism in the south of Ireland during the inter-war period, 1919–1939' in Curran & Toms (eds), *New perspectives on association football in Irish history*, pp 50–64.

Vonnard, Philippe, 'A competition that shook European football: the origins of the European Champion Clubs' Cup, 1954–1955', *Sport in History*, 34:4 (2014), pp 595–619.

Walker, Stephen, *Ireland's call: Irish sporting heroes who fell in the Great War* (Newbridge, 2015).

Walsh, Thomas P., *Twenty years of Irish soccer: under the auspices of the Football Association of Ireland, 1921–1941* (Dublin, 1941).

Weir, Colin, *The history of Oxford University Association Football Club, 1872–1998* (Harefield, 1998).

Whelan, Daire, *Who stole our game?: the fall and fall of Irish soccer* (Dublin, 2006).

White, Colin, *Dalymount Park: the home of Irish football* (Dublin, 2015).

Williams, John, *Reds: Liverpool Football Club: the biography* (Edinburgh, 2010).

West, Trevor, *The bold collegians: the development of sport in Trinity College Dublin* (Dublin, 1991).

Wren, Jim, Marcus de Búrca & David Gorry, *The Gaelic Athletic Association in Dublin*, i: *1884–1959*, ed. William Nolan (Dublin, 2005).

Yeates, Padraig, *A city in wartime: Dublin, 1914–18* (Dublin, 2011).

———, *Lockout: Dublin 1913* [paperback edition] (Dublin, 2013).

Theses

Tynan, Mark, 'Association football and Irish society during the inter-war period, 1918–1939' (PhD, NUI Maynooth, 2013).

Other online sources

'1979 European Cup-Linfield', dundalkfc.com/history/dundalk-fc-in-europe/1979–european-cup-linfield, accessed 23 May 2020.

'1992/93 Season: French first in inaugural Champions League Season', uefa.com/uefachampionsleague/history/seasons/1992, accessed 5 Apr. 2021.

'Arthur Johnson, a pioneer at the helm of the team', realmadrid.com/en/about-real-madrid/history/football/1900–1910–juan-padros-and-julian-palacios-found-madrid, accessed 12 Aug. 2021.

'Baltic United FC', facebook.com/balticunitedfc, accessed 3 Aug. 2021.

Blake, Ben, 'Liverpool make light work of Athletic Bilbao in front of a full house at the Aviva Stadium', the42.ie/liverpool-athletic-bilbao-aviva-stadium-dublin-3532091–Aug2017, accessed 29 Dec. 2017.

'Brady pays tribute to Bill Darby', arsenal.com/news/brady-pays-tribute-bill-darby, accessed 13 May 2021.

Brannigan, Kevin, 'Ronnie Whelan's homecoming during the tumultuous summer of 1981', the42.ie/ronnie-whelan-liverpool-1981–ireland-5292252–Dec2020, accessed 25 Aug. 2021.

Canny, Julian & Fergus Desmond, 'Irish clubs in European Cups', rsssf.com/tablesi/ier-ec.html, accessed 5 April 2021.

'David O'Leary', arsenal.com/historic/players/david-oleary, accessed 5 May 2021.

'Dublin dazzles for UEFA Europa League final', fai.ie/domestic/news/dublin-dazzles-for-uefa-europa-league-final, accessed 28 Apr. 2020.

'Dublin University AFC', duafc.ucoz.com/index/history/0–10, accessed 12 Aug. 2021.

'Dundalk F.C. Who's Who: Martin Murray', dundalkfcwhoswho.com/player.php?id=373, accessed 22 May 2020.

'Dundalk F.C. Who's Who: Ollie Ralph', dundalkfcwhoswho.com/player.php?id=365, accessed 22 May 2020.

'Dundalk F.C. Who's Who: Robbie Lawlor', dundalkfcwhoswho.com/player.php?id=345, accessed 22 May 2020.

'Dynamo Dublin FC', soccer-ireland.com/dublin-football-clubs/dynamo-dublin.htm, accessed 3 Feb. 2021.

Farrell, Gerry, 'A tribute to Ray Keogh-by Gerry Farrell', sseairtricityleague.ie/news/a-true-trailblazer-for-the-irish-game-tribute-to-ray-keogh/id-2967, accessed 1 Sept. 2021.

Farrell, Gerry, 'Bohs and Bloody Sunday', abohemiansportinglife.wordpress.com/2020/11/21/bohs-and-bloody-sunday, accessed 11 Aug. 2021.

Farrell, Gerry, 'Bohs in Europe', abohemiansportinglife.wordpress.com/2020/09/08/bohs-in-europe, accessed 3 Mar. 2021.

Farrell, Gerry, 'Bohemians of World War I', abohemiansportinglife.wordpress.com/2016/06/29/bohemians-of-world-war-i, accessed 29 July 2021.

Farrell, Gerry, 'Rovers of the Sea', abohemiansportinglife.wordpress.com/2018/01, accessed 30 July 2021.

Farrell, Gerry, 'Taking a lax attitude: George and the magic magnetic board', abohemiansportinglife. wordpress.com/2017/12, accessed 30 July 2021.

Farrell, Gerry, 'The lost clubs – Jacob's FC', abohemiansportinglife.wordpress.com/2018/06, accessed 30 July 2021.

Farrell, Gerry, 'The lost clubs: Reds United', abohemiansportinglife.wordpress. com/2020/03/25/the-lost-clubs-reds-united, accessed 14 Oct. 2021.

Farrell, Gerry, 'The remarkable life of Bohs captain William H. Otto', bohemianfc. com/?p=11512, accessed 1 Sept. 2021.

Farrell, Gerry, 'The tail-gunner at full-back', abohemiansportinglife.wordpress.com/2018/08, accessed 30 July 2021.

Farrell, Gerry, 'Who you calling scab? Bohs, Shels and the 1913 Lockout', abohemiansportinglife. wordpress.com/2020/10/04/who-you-calling-scab-bohs-shels-and-the-1913–lockout, accessed 11 Aug. 2021.

Farrell, Gerry & Brian Trench, 'Bohemians during Easter 1916', abohemiansportinglife.wordpress. com/2016/03, accessed 29 July 2021.

Farrell, Gerry & Brian Trench, 'Harry Willets: the Darling of Dalymount', abohemiansport-inglife.wordpress.com/2016/05/19/harry-willits-the-darling-of-dalymount, accessed 29 July 2021.

Farrell, Gerry & Michael Kielty, 'Freebooting around the Rock of Gibraltar', abohemiansportinglife. wordpress.com/2019/06, accessed 30 July 2021.

'FC Ted EX', soccer-ireland.com/dublin-football-clubs/fc-tedex.htm, accessed 3 Aug. 2021.

Gallagher, Aaron, 'You were against Pele and Beckenbauer. It was like going to play in Hollywood', the42.ie/pat-byrne-shamrock-rovers-league-of-ireland-legend-shelbourne-premier-division-3437647–Jul2017, accessed 17 May 2021.

'Glentoran FC: the Managers: Ronnie McFall (part two)', glentoran.com/news/managers-ron-nie-mcfall-part-two, accessed 21 Sept. 2020.

'Irish clubs in European cups', rsssf.com/tablesi/ier-ec.html, accessed 5 Apr. 2021.

'Irish Football Fans at Hillsborough 1989', rte.ie/archives/2019/0403/1040446–irish-liverpool-fans-return-from-hillsborough, accessed 19 Jan. 2022.

'Jason Sherlock on his soccer crossover: from West Ham trials to Liverpool's interest', offtheball. com/sport/jason-sherlock-team-33–153054, accessed 5 Jan. 2019.

'John Francis Doran', footballandthefirstworldwar.org/jack-doran-footballer, accessed 29 July 2021.

'Linfield o Shamrock Rovers o', uefa.com/uefachampionsleague/match/63894—linfield-vs-shamrock-rovers/events, accessed 5 Apr. 2021.

McCormack, Kristofer, 'The Irishman who taught Real Madrid how to play football', thesefootballtimes.co/2019/02/21/arthur-johnson-the-irishman-who-taught-real-madrid-how-to-play-football, accessed 12 Aug. 2021.

'NIFG-Dr George Sheehan', nifootball.blogspot.com/2008/07/dr-george-sheehan.html, accessed 6 Aug. 2021.

'NIFG-Jimmy Kelly', nifootball.blogspot.com/2007/01/jimmy-kelly.html, accessed 24 Feb. 2020.

'NIFG-Joe Ledwidge', nifootball.blogspot.com/2007/04/joe-ledwidge.html, accessed 6 Aug. 2021.

'NIFG-John Fitzpatrick', nifootball.blogspot.com/2006/11/james-fitzpatrick.html, accessed 6 Aug. 2021.

'NIFG-John Mansfield', nifootball.blogspot.com/2007/12/john-mansfield.html, accessed 6 Feb. 2021.

'NIFG-Jim Nolan-Whelan', nifootball.blogspot.com/2007/12/jim-nolan-whelan.html, accessed 11 Aug. 2021.

'NIFG-Lionel Bennett', nifootball.blogspot.com/2006/10/lionel-bennett.html, accessed 6 Aug. 2021.

'NIFG' Manliffe Goodbody', nifootball.blogspot.com/2006/12/manliffe-goodbody.html, accessed 6 Aug. 2021.

'NIFG-Peter Warren', nifootball.blogspot.com/2008/11/peter-warren.html, accessed 6 Aug. 2021.

'NIFG-Philip Meldon', nifootball.blogspot.com/2007/12/james-meldon.html, accessed 6 Aug. 2021.

'NIFG-William Eames', nifootball.blogspot.com/2006/11/william-eames.html, accessed 6 Aug. 2021.

'NIFG-Willoughby and Drummond Hamilton', nifootball.blog spot.com/2006/12/willoughby-william-hamilton.html, accessed 6 Aug. 2021.

'Northern Ireland Women's Football Association', irishfa.com/ifa-domestic/leagues/northern-ireland-womens-football-association, accessed 9 Jan. 2022.

O'Brien, Shane, 'Liverpool stroll to Napoli win in Dublin', rte.ie/sport/soccer/2018/0804/983172–liverpool-stroll-to-napoli-win-in-dublin, accessed 12 June 2020.

O'Callaghan, Eoin, 'Louis Bookman: solving the mystery of a revolutionary and pioneering sportsman', the42.ie/louis-bookman-jewish-irish-1960912–Feb2015, accessed 1 Sept. 2021.

'Oscar Horace Stanley Linkson', footballandthefirstworldwar.org/oscar-linkson-footballer, accessed 29 July 2021.

'Our Heroes/Ár Laochra: Captain HC Crozier', ourheroes.southdublin.ie/Serviceman/Show/16056, accessed 4 Dec. 2021.

'Our History', stjamesgatefc.com/club-history, accessed 3 Jan. 2022.

'PFC White Eagles FC', soccer-ireland.com/dublin-football-clubs/pfc-white-eagles.htm, accessed 3 Aug. 2021.

Quinn, James & Tom Feeney, 'Stevenson, Alexander Ernest', *Dictionary of Irish biography*, dib.ie, accessed 26 July 2021.

'Real Transilvania FC', facebook.com/RealTransilvania, accessed 3 Aug. 2021.

'Relatives of Hillsborough Disaster victims at emotional park ceremony', echo.ie/relatives-of-hillsborough-disaster-victims-at-emotional-park-ceremony, accessed 19 Dec. 2021.

'Riots as Bohemians beat Glasgow Rangers 3–2. 1984', rte.ie/archives/2014/0919/644723–football-hooligans-at-dalymount-park-1984, accessed 5 Apr. 2021.

'RTÉ Archives, 21 Jan. 1974: Inchicore girl bound for Reims', rte.ie/archives/2019/0118/1024047–french-soccer-club-sign-irish-girl, accessed 27 Jan. 2022.

'St Kevin's Boys Club: Club History – Our History', skbfc.yourclub.ie/history, accessed 2 July 2020.

'Stories/Private Ned Brierley, 1896–1955 8th Battalion, Royal Dublin Fusiliers', greatwar.ie/stories/edward-brierley, accessed 20 Aug. 2021.

'Soccer in the "Boro" – St Joseph's Boys', soccerintheboro.com/st-josephs-boys-1.php, accessed 25 Nov. 2021.

'Tallaght Stadium – About Us', tallaghtstadium.ie, accessed 4 Aug. 2021.

'The History of Women's Football in England', thefa.com/womens–girls–football/history, accessed 23 Jan. 2021.

'The Irish Toffees', irish-toffees.com/about-us.html, accessed 13 May 2018.

'Tommy Barber', footballandthefirstworldwar.org/tom-barber, accessed 26 July 2021.

'UEFA.com History', www.uefa.com/uefaeuro/history/index.html, accessed 28 Apr. 2020.

Index

Soccer and society in Dublin